RAWLS

To the memory of John (Jack) Rawls

RAWLS

AN INTRODUCTION

Sebastiano Maffettone

polity

First published in 2010 by Polity Press

Polity Press
65 Bridge Street
Cambridge CB2 1UR, UK

Polity Press
350 Main Street
Malden, MA 02148, USA

ISBN-13: 978–0–7456–4650–3 (hardback)
ISBN-13: 978–0–7456–4651–0 (paperback)

A catalogue record for this book is available from the British Library.

Typeset in 10 on 12pt Sabon
by Servis Filmsetting Ltd, Stockport, Cheshire
Printed and bound in Great Britain by the MPG Books Group, Bodmin, Cornwall

The publisher has used its best endeavors to ensure that the URLs for external websites referred to in this book are correct and active at the time of going to press. However, the publisher has no responsibility for the websites and can make no guarantee that a site will remain live or that the content is or will remain appropriate.

Every effort has been made to trace all copyright holders, but if any have been inadvertently overlooked the publisher will be pleased to include any necessary credits in any subsequent reprint or edition.

For further information on Polity, visit our website: www.politybooks.com

CONTENTS

PREFACE

"Success never forgives you" is a common saying. But it never held for John Rawls. In a book of photographs of living philosophers, Rawls' short auto-biographical statement concludes with this astonishing sentence: "Around 1950 I started to write a book on justice, which eventually I completed." The "book on justice" concerned was *A Theory of Justice* of 1971, a work whose destiny has been to radically change political philosophy. It was even mentioned by the President of the United States Bill Clinton as an exemplary book on equality and freedom, and later quoted in similar tones by the Chinese leader Hu Chin Tao. It has sold more than 300,000 copies in English alone, extraordinary for such a complex theoretical work, and if one enters "Rawls" in the Google search engine more than 2,000,000 webpage addresses are returned. Rawls' ideas are discussed daily in academic contexts across the world, and the scholarly articles on his work now number around 6,000. This huge impact is even more surprising in the light of Rawls' modest, shy, and intellectually rigorous nature and the fact that, although there was much public response to his death in November 2002, aged 81, he was not a public intellectual.

I first met John, or "Jack," Rawls when preparing the Italian translation of *A Theory of Justice* in the late seventies. I then met him many times at Emerson Hall, home of the philosophy department at Harvard University, at his house in Lexington in the company of his wife Mard, at some conferences, and during his visit to Naples in Italy in 1988. I was, as were many, particularly touched by his gentle manner and his approachableness. He was undoubtedly not only a great philosopher, but also a wonderful person. These meetings were always mildly bizarre – one often had the feeling that this must have been what it was like to have lunch with Kant, or someone very like him.

The work and thought of Rawls changed my intellectual life – his ideas regarding social justice, political legitimacy, and international law led me to revise my initial liberalism. This revision began when I first read *A Theory of Justice* in England in the mid-seventies, and continued as I read his later works, including those which further contributed to his fame, like *Political Liberalism* in 1993 and *The Law of Peoples* in 1999. I have lectured on Rawls many times on undergraduate and postgraduate courses in Italy and abroad. I have also tried to convince Italian political leaders and Marxist, Catholic, and social-democratic students and scholars of the need to take his ideas seriously. I hope to have managed to introduce these ideas into the political vocabulary in some way and to have gained a broader cultural audience for them. Having engaged with Rawls' work for over 30 years, then, my first aim in this book is rather personal – namely, to submit my interpretation of his work to a broader scholarly public in the English-speaking world, so as to determine whether – and if so, to what extent – what I have said about Rawls over half a lifetime has been correct or reasonable.

From a more impersonal point of view, *Rawls: An Introduction* aims to be the most complete introduction to the work of the American philosopher John Rawls (1921–2002). This book is divided into three parts that correspond to Rawls' three major books. The first concentrates on *A Theory of Justice* (1971). In chapter 7, some of the most relevant critiques of Rawls are discussed. The second part of the book highlights *Political Liberalism* (1993–6). The third part includes a discussion of *The Law of Peoples* (1999). A biographical note and a selected bibliography complete the book. Each chapter is preceded by a short summary.

Between the mid-1970s and the present day, there have been three main waves or patterns of Rawlsian interpretations. The first one, for obvious reasons, made reference to *A Theory of Justice*. Within it, the most relevant topics were the deduction of the principles of justice (both from the formal and the substantive point of view) and the relationship within the theory between the good and the right. The second was influenced by the appearance of *Political Liberalism* and by the revisions internal to Rawls' thought. Here, the most relevant points concern the central role played by legitimacy in the perspective of stability. Important new concepts, introduced by Rawls in the 1980s and 1990s, such as "political conception," "comprehensive doctrine," "overlapping consensus," and "public reason" acquire their full significance from this point of view. The third, contemporary, interpretational attitude pivots around the notion of "basic structure." This notion surely highlights some problems related to *The Law of Peoples*, and in this sense comes with the new millennium. It is, however, more encompassing and claims to be the best perspective from which one can read the whole of Rawls' work. It must be considered that a great part of this book has been written during the years in which the second stream of interpretation was the prevalent one (to be more precise in the second part of the 1990s). For this reason, it reflects the hermeneutic mood of the time in which it was elaborated. Notwithstanding this proviso, I think the book takes into consideration, albeit with different emphasis, all three waves or patterns of interpretation just mentioned. This fact is due to two different orders of reasons. On the one hand, Rawls' waves or patterns of interpretation reciprocally overlap. Or rather, they work in a kind of Hegelian way, so that the later takes away the earlier and includes it within the new framework. On the other hand, I myself made a significant effort through all the book to be impartial to these rival interpretive trends.

In writing the book, I have benefited from the contributions and support of so many people that I cannot thank them all here. Among the most significant are the following. In the 1970s Marco Mondadori, Norberto Bobbio, and Salvatore Veca helped in different, but equally significant, ways to develop my initial understanding of Rawls and in my attempt to increase the awareness and improve the understanding of his ideas in Italy and in continental Europe. Jack and Mard Rawls constantly supported my theoretical efforts, and over the years my friends Ronald Dworkin, Tom Nagel, and Tim Scanlon have made me feel a welcome member of the best philosophical community one could desire, convincing me even that being a Rawlsian is a less solipsistic enterprise than one might imagine. Tim Scanlon, Erin Kelly, Sam Freeman, Thomas Pogge, Joshua Cohen, Stephen Macedo, David Rasmussen, Ian Carter, Will Kymlicka, Leif Wenar, and Kok-Chor Tan have explained various aspects of Rawls' thought to me in the best possible way, that is, by reading and commenting on parts of my manuscript.

I have also received suggestions and criticism from Bruce Ackerman, Dario Antiseri, Daniele Archibugi, Charles Beitz, Antonella Besussi, Cristina Bicchieri, Akeel Bilgrami, Luigi Caranti, Mario De Caro, Peter De Marneffe, Giampaolo Ferranti, Alessandro Ferrara, Elisabetta Galeotti, Vanna Gessa, Jonathan Glover, David Held, Eugenio Lecaldano, Lionel McPherson, Pietro Maffettone, Claudia Mancina, Michele Mangini, Raffaele Marchetti, Fiona Marshall, Frank Michelman, Stefano Micossi, Darrell Moellendorf, (the late) Robert Nozick, Antonino Palumbo, Gianfranco Pellegrino, Stefano Petrucciani, Philipp Pettit, Stefano Recchia, Ingrid Salvatore, Daniele Santoro, Fabrizio Sciacca, Amartya Sen, Giacomo Sillari, Aakash Singh, Carlos Thibaut, Dennis Thompson, Francesco Trincia, Nadia Urbinati, Philippe van Parjis, Stephen L. White, Andrew Williams, and many of the invited speakers at the Colloquium in Ethics, Politics, and Society at LUISS University in Rome. Doug Paletta, while a Ph.D. student at the University of Pennsylvania, read the whole manuscript, generously correcting both my English and many of my arguments. Tom Bailey did the same, equally generously, for a number of the chapters. My former Ph.D. students, Michele Bocchiola and Domenico Melidoro, also read the whole manuscript, helping me to identify errors and misinterpretations. I thank all of these people in the warmest way – without them my efforts would have been pointless.

I have also benefited from presenting chapters of the manuscript at universities across the world, including the following: in Italy, Roma ("La

Sapienza"), Palermo, Napoli, Milano, Cagliari (Statale), Torino, Pisa, Padova, Suor Orsola Benincasa in Napoli, and St. Anna in Pisa; Harvard, Columbia (and the Italian Academy at Columbia), Pennsylvania, Tufts, Boston College, Princeton, and Stanford in the United States; Thsing Hua, Beijing and Shanghai in China; Calcutta, Delhi, and Mumbai in India; LSE and Durham in the United Kingdom; Paris Sciences PO in France; and Humboldt Universität in Berlin, Germany. I thank those who invited me to speak at these meetings and the audiences for their questions and comments.

More than anyone, however, I thank my university, LUISS in Rome, my assistant Gaia di Martino, and all my current and past students, whose support has made my work possible. My final thanks go to Polity Press for their general editing and for the anonymous reader who provided many useful suggestions.

Lastly, a thought on my aims in this book. It is subtitled "An Introduction," and, like anyone undertaking to write an introductory book, I hope to have succeeded in being clear enough for beginners and sophisticated enough for experts. This is a difficult task. But at least I am not alone in this. Jack Rawls, when he sent me his last published article, accompanied it with a note that read, "Dear Sebastiano, finally I got public reason more or less right. Yet that's impossible?" Without wishing to compare my work with Rawls', it is comforting to know that all authors have such doubts, doubts that ultimately only their readers can resolve. So, "habeant sua fata libelli!"

Sebastiano Maffettone, Rome, Spring 2010

ABBREVIATIONS

BiMF   *A Brief Inquiry into the Meaning of Sin and Faith*, ed. Thomas Nagel, Cambridgge MA, Harvard University Press, 2009.

CP   *Collected Papers* (1999), ed. Samuel Freeman, Cambridge, MA: Harvard University Press.

IMT   "The Independence of Moral Theory," in CP 286–302.

IPRR   "The Idea of Public Reason Revisited" (1997), *Chicago Law Review* 64 (3): 765–807.

JFR   *Justice as Fairness: A Restatement* (2001), ed. Erin Kelly, Cambridge, MA: The Belknap Press of Harvard University Press.

HRE   Habermas–Rawls exchange.

KCMT   "Kantian Constructivism in Moral Theory" (1980), *Journal of Philosophy* 77 (9) (September): 515–72.

LHMP   *Lectures on the History of Moral Philosophy* (2000), ed. Barbara Herman, Cambridge, MA: Harvard University Press.

LHPP   *Lectures on the History of Political Philosophy* (2007), ed. Samuel Freeman, Cambridge, MA: Harvard University Press.

LoP   *The Law of Peoples* (1999), Cambridge, MA: Harvard University Press.

ODPE   "Outline of a Decision Procedure for Ethics," *Philosophical Review* 60 (1951), pp. 177–97.

Ph.D.   "A Study on the Grounds of Ethical Knowledge: Considered with Reference to Judgments on the Moral Worth of Character," Ph.D. dissertation, Princeton University, 1950.

PL   *Political Liberalism* by John Rawls (© 1993; paperback edn. 1996, with a new introduction), New York: Columbia University Press. Reprinted with permission.

PRIG   "The Priority of Right and Ideas of the Good," *Philosophy & Public Affairs* 17 (4) (Fall 1988): 251–76.

TJ   Reprinted with permission of the publisher from *A Theory of Justice* by John Rawls, Cambridge, MA: The Belknap Press of Harvard University Press, (Copyright © 1971, 1999) by the President and Fellows of Harvard College.

TKMP "Themes in Kant's Moral Philosophy" (1989) in *Kant's Transcendental Deductions*, ed. E. Forster, Stanford: Stanford University Press.

1

INTRODUCTION

John Rawls' *A Theory of Justice* (1971) transformed political philosophy, beginning with the English-speaking academia then spreading worldwide.[1] In the 1950s and 1960s, political philosophy seemed to have reached a dead end characterized by a loose predominance of utilitarian theses. Rawls' conception of liberalism gave political philosophy new energy and substance.[2] Civil liberties and social justice became the core of the theory and utilitarians were put on the defensive.[3] Rawls' influence is further confirmed by some of his most insightful critics who, although supporting conflicting theses, acknowledge his theory's extraordinary merits.[4]

This book aims to be an introduction to the entire body of Rawls' work.[5] Chapter 1, part 1 presents the life and works of John Rawls; Part 2 presents the conceptual scheme of the book, which begins in section 1.2.1 with some general remarks. Section 1.2.2 provides an overview of Rawls' vision of political philosophy. Section 1.2.3 outlines my interpretation. Section 1.2.4 puts forward three hermeneutical hypotheses: "interpretive," "methodological" and "theoretical." In sections 1.3., 1.3.1, and 1.3.2, I argue for these hermeneutical hypotheses. These arguments are rather abstract and require philosophical expertise. Readers not familiar with Rawls' work can either skip them or read them at the end. These hypotheses, however, influence the whole structure of the book. They are based on a particular reading of the continuity of Rawls' work (interpretive hypothesis); on the centrality of the priority of right (methodological hypothesis); and on the dichotomy of justification and legitimation (theoretical hypothesis).

The book is divided into three parts that correspond to Rawls' three major books. The first concentrates on *A Theory of Justice* (1971, 1999; hereafter TJ). It contains five chapters (2–6), including a chapter in which I try to reconstruct Rawls' general vision of social justice in TJ (chapter 2). In chapter 7, I will discuss some of the most relevant critiques of Rawls.

The second part of the book (chapters 8–11) highlights *Political Liberalism* (1993, 1996; hereafter PL), beginning with a chapter dedicated to the "passage" from TJ to PL. The third part (chapter 12) includes a discussion of *The Law of Peoples* (1999; hereafter LoP). A biographical note and a bibliography complete the book. Each chapter is preceded by a short summary.

1.1 A Beautiful Life

John Rawls was the most influential political philosopher of recent times.[6] Though he never aimed at this, he was, as remembered by Ronald Dworkin, one of the few intellectuals of the modern era whose work, like Freud's and Darwin's, crossed from his field into general culture. Personally, Rawls was witty, timid, gentle, and modest. In his life, he conscientiously avoided the role of a celebrity. His life was not particularly adventurous and knowledge of it is perhaps not necessary for understanding his thought, in contrast to the life histories of other great philosophers such as Spinoza or Nietzsche. Rawls had two lifelong heroes, Immanuel Kant and Abraham Lincoln, and his liberal political philosophy combined the interests of both the philosopher and the statesman. His compromise between utopia and reality is very sophisticated; one can say with Thomas Nagel that he was "the most unworldly of social and political philosophers." Rawls was aware of the threats, both internal and external, faced by constitutional liberal democracy, which he tried to defend through his own political philosophy.

John (Jack) Bordley Rawls was born on February 21, 1921 in Baltimore (Maryland, USA), and died in his house in Lexington (Massachusetts) in 2002. He was the second of five sons of William Lee Rawls (1883–1946) and Anna Abell Stump (1892–1954), upper-middle-class parents whose roots lay in the US South (John's later concept of black slavery as a paradigm of injustice perhaps developed as a reaction against the traditional racial bigotry of the South). The other sons were William Stove (Bill, 1915–2004), Robert Lee (Bobby, 1923–8), Thomas Hamilton (Tommy, 1927–9), and Richard Howland (Dick, 1933–67). Bobby and Tommy died in early childhood, in each case as a result of diseases contracted from Jack. The death of Bobby in particular was an enormous shock to Jack and may have provoked his stammer.

Notwithstanding poor health and early financial difficulties, William managed to become a successful tax lawyer, eventually joining the Marbury Law Firm, the best in Baltimore. Later, he also became President of the Baltimore Bar Association. Both William and Anna had significant political interests. William was drawn to the Democratic Party, even though he once voted Republican, due to an attempt by Franklin D. Roosevelt to break the Supreme Court's resistance to his legislation. Anna was a brilliant woman, an incipient feminist with a passion for portrait paintings. Rawls was later to observe both these traits in his own wife.

Rawls started his school years at the Calvert (1927–33), after which – from 1935 to 1939 – he attended the Kent School, a religious boys' school in the High Church Episcopal tradition. Intellectually successful there, he also enjoyed many sports, including baseball, on which he later wrote a famous letter (to Owen Fiss, "The Best of All Games") and tennis, a sport he played until a late age. He exercised throughout his life, which – together with a frugal diet – enabled him to retain his tall, slim, and athletic figure. I remember an occasion when – visiting me in Capri after a conference in Naples – he said he wanted to take a short walk. The result was a five-hour trek during which – despite being 27 years younger – I could barely speak for trying to catch my breath and keep up with him. During his youth Rawls also acquired his lifelong love of sailing.

After high school Jack followed his brother Bill to Princeton University, the start of his time there in 1939 coinciding with the beginning of the Second World War. Before choosing philosophy as his major, he experienced a period of indecision during which he tried his hand at mathematics, chemistry, and even music, but, by his own admission, he struggled with all of these. His first teachers in philosophy were Walter T. Stace, David Bowers, and Norman Malcolm. The most influential among these was probably Malcolm, a young teacher who had joined Princeton from Cambridge, England, where he had worked with Wittgenstein. Wittgenstein's influence on Rawls' thought was never limited to linguistic and meta-ethical analysis; it is evident in the idea of "basic structure" and, more generally, in the thesis according to which principles of justice cannot be practice independent. Rawls received a BA *Summa cum laude* in philosophy in 1943.

In the same year, he entered the US army and was sent as an infantryman to the Pacific. During this period he began to doubt the religious sentiments that, just a few years earlier, had led him to consider studying for the (Episcopal) priesthood in a divinity school. He wrote movingly of this in an essay entitled "On My Religion" (composed in the 1990s, published in the posthumous *A Brief Inquiry into The Meaning of Sin & Faith*), trying to explain why his religious sentiments changed. Three "incidents" proved decisive in this. The first was in 1944 when a Lutheran pastor urged US troops to slaughter Japanese civilians. The second was the death in May 1945 of a friend engaged in a military mission that, but for good fortune, Rawls himself might have undertaken. The third – and one that can hardly be defined as an "incident" – was the breaking news of the horrors of the Holocaust. This in particular seriously affected Rawls, for whom resulting doubts "took the form of questioning whether prayer was possible." Beyond these specific factors, one could also argue that Rawls' troubles with religion had a more profound Kantian motivation. He thought that "God's will must be in accord with the most basic ideas of justice as we know them. For what else can the most basic justice be? Thus, *I soon came to reject the idea of the supremacy of the divine will*" (from "On my Religion," emphasis mine). In other words, Rawls' problem with (Christian) religion was not simply that God permitted the Holocaust and the indiscriminate bombing of so many cities, but rather how one could possibly imagine a divine will behind human cruelty. It is for such a reason that morality does not need God to be justified. With Kant, Rawls realized that: "Reasoning in its most basic forms is invariant with respect to the various kinds of beings that exercise it. Hence God's being, however great the divine powers, does not determine the essential canons of reason" ("On my Religion"). Rawls, however, firmly believed in a "realistic utopia" (LoP), his fundamental idea being that, within this utopia, justice is mundane and can be realized on earth by reasonable people. The presence of God constitutes only the guarantee that human good and justice can be coherent.

There have been many discussions in recent years on "Rawls and religion" (see chapter 11 in this volume), and nobody should forget how deep his religious nature was and how respectful his considerations of this topic throughout his life. Moreover he was convinced that many religious people, foremost among them Abraham Lincoln and Martin Luther King, have made extraordinary contributions to the flourishing of liberal democracy. His main philosophical shift, the one between Rawls1 and Rawls2 (see section 1.2 in this volume) depends – as I was told many times by Rawls himself – on the fact that TJ could have been taken by some readers as insensitive to religious considerations.

After serving in New Guinea and the Philippines, Jack was stationed for a time with the US troops occupying Japan, where he saw firsthand the recently bombed city of Hiroshima. This experience was profound. Rawls later wrote – to mark the fiftieth anniversary of the American bombing of Hiroshima – an essay against the use of nuclear weapons (now in CP), his thoughts on this finding an echo in LoP. Despite being awarded a Bronze Star, Rawls judged his contribution to the war as being altogether irrelevant, describing it in a short autobiographical sketch composed for a reunion of Kent School 50 years after graduation as "singularly undistinguished."

After the war, Rawls withdrew from the military, having resolved also not to pursue a theological career. He began his postgraduate studies in philosophy at Princeton in 1946. His course included a year at Cornell University (working with Malcolm and Max Black), during which time he began to write his dissertation – on moral methodology – with Walter Stace, for which he was awarded a doctorate at Princeton in 1950. The topic of moral methodology occurs frequently in Rawls' later writings, and partially coincides with what is called "reflective equilibrium" in TJ, although germs of the idea were already apparent in Rawls' first significant publication, "Outline of a Decision Procedure for Ethics" (1951). Rawls was extremely consistent in his philosophical interests and never abandoned the idea. In the autumn of 1950, he started work on what later evolved into TJ, as Rawls later recalled in an interview for *The Harvard Review of Philosophy*.

During his time at Princeton, Rawls met his wife-to-be, Margaret (Mard) Warfield Fox, whom he married a few months later in June 1949, the couple going on to have four children (Ann, Robert, Alexander, Elisabeth). For more than 50 years of married life Margaret was to be an invaluable help meet, not only editing many of her husband's books and papers (in particular LoP), but also contributing to Rawls' thought, as reflected, for example, in the attention he devoted to the issue of women's rights. The warm traditional atmosphere of the nineteenth-century house in Lexington in which the family lived contrasted sharply with the novelty of Rawls' ideas.

During the academic year 1949–50, Rawls studied economics and constitutional law at Princeton – studies that reinforced his competence in these domains and contributed in no small part to the acclaim of his work among numerous economists and lawyers. From 1950 to 1952 Rawls taught in the Princeton philosophy department, after which he successfully applied for a Fulbright fellowship, spending the academic year 1952–3 at Oxford. That year was particularly important for his intellectual development. Oxford was then a vivid philosophical center, where – among others – philosophers like Austin, Ryle, Hart, Berlin, Hampshire, Grice, and Strawson were teaching. Their influence, and that of Oxford philosophy in general, is visible in many of Rawls' works. He also wrote a review of Toulmin's *The Place of Reason in Ethics*, a paper that curiously was not included in the edition of his *Collected Papers*. Around this time Rawls also began to develop one of his central ideas, namely that of justifying substantive ethical principles through procedural means; an idea which, according to Rawls, came to him after reading an essay by the economist Frank Knight. Just afterwards the idea was restructured, starting with a hypothetical choice situation, which became the celebrated "original position." This notion allows Kant's categorical imperative to be presented in a social form, which is more appropriate in dealing with theoretical political problems. In such a way, Rawls gradually reformulated the classic notion of social contract.

After his return from Oxford, Rawls became an assistant professor at Cornell, where he spent years of reflection and wrote some fundamental essays. He was invited to spend the academic year 1959–60 at Harvard, and, being in Cambridge, Massachusetts, was offered a tenured professorship at MIT. Rawls accepted the offer and over the next year worked to develop a new department of philosophy there. Then, in spring 1961, he received an offer to teach at Harvard University, where he was to spend the next 30 years, from the autumn of 1962 to his retirement in 1991, continuing afterwards as Professor Emeritus until his first stroke in 1995.

Rawls' first ten years at Harvard (1962–71) were devoted to the completion of his masterpiece, TJ. He taught parts of TJ during these years, alternating them with courses on the history of moral and political philosophy.

His theoretical courses were usually devoted to four issues: perfectionism, utilitarianism, intuitionism, and Kantian constructivism. In the mid-1970s he changed this order, concentrating on Kantian constructivism, with particular emphasis on Kant's *Groundwork for the Metaphysics of Morals*, to coincide with the preparation of his Dewey Lectures of 1980 (see chapter 8). Historical courses became fixtures in his academic teaching. He was convinced that the study of philosophical classics is much more important than many American philosophers think, and, contrary to mainstream analytical philosophy, he always believed that the history of philosophy and philosophy itself are reciprocally connected.[7] His lectures on moral philosophy (published when Rawls was severely ill) and political philosophy (published posthumously) show his love for key authors of the past, such as Hobbes, Locke, Rousseau, Kant, Hegel, Marx, Hume, Butler, Sidgwick, and Leibniz. In "Some Remarks about My Teaching" (1993), Rawls declared, speaking of such authors: "A doctrine is not judged at all until it is judged in its best form . . . The text has to be known and respected, and the doctrine presented in its best form." Later in the same article, he wrote: "I always assumed, for example, that the writers we were studying were always much smarter than I was. If they were not, why was I wasting my time and the students' time by studying them?" Substantially, Rawls rejected a purely detached study of the classics, but at the same time he rejected an ahistorical importation of modern concepts into the text. In the conclusion of his "My Teaching," he observed, speaking of Kant though the comment applies more generally:

> I never felt satisfied with the understanding I could gain of Kant's overall concep-
> tion. This leaves a certain unhappiness and I am reminded of a story about John
> Marin, a great America watercolorist . . . [for] eight years in the 1920s Marin
> went to Stonington, Maine, to paint; and Ruth Fine, who wrote a splendid book
> on Marin, tells us of going there to see if she could find anyone who had known
> him then. She finally found a lobsterman who said, "Eeah, eeah, we all knew him.
> He went out painting in his little boat day after day, week after week, summer
> after summer. And you know, poor fellah, he tried so hard, but he never did get
> it right." That always said it exactly for me, after all this time: "Never did get
> it right."

In the USA, the atmosphere of the mid- and late 1960s was dominated by the Vietnam War, and Rawls could not avoid reflecting upon it. He gave a course on "Problems of War" in 1969, in which he discussed possible justi-fications of the war. Rawls considered the war unjust, expressing the thesis in TJ that such a war might be precipitated by pressure exerted by corporate lobbies on government (a thesis commensurate with the Rawlsian emphasis on the protection of political liberties from the power of money). Echoing the mood of this period, famous sections of TJ and various paragraphs of LoP take up the theme of civil disobedience and conscientious refusal.

Rawls spent the academic year 1969–70 at The Center for Advanced

Studies at Stanford University, where he completed TJ (by a strange coincidence, Robert Nozick's book *Anarchy, State and Utopia* – one of the most cogent criticisms of Rawls – was later completed in the same place). TJ came out in late 1971, after Rawls himself had finished the index, which is one of the best analytical indexes ever compiled, made all the more admirable when we consider it was created without the aid of a computer. TJ's ambitious task was to present a political theory able to detect the main problems of utilitarianism and to provide an alternative based on justice. We can say now that Rawls' theory of justice as fairness succeeded, and the dictionary of political thought changed coherently with new expressions like "original position," "veil of ignorance," "difference principle," and "future generations" becoming popular in the philosophical jargon and beyond.

TJ was unexpectedly successful, obliging Rawls to modify his plans. Instead of writing a book on moral psychology, as he had intended, he was obliged to defend TJ against thousands of criticisms. Roughly, Rawls received sympathetic responses from liberals and social-democrats, and hostile responses from the radical left, libertarians, and the extreme right. Alongside these came postmodernist, relativist, religious, and feminist philosophical critiques. In 1979 Rawls was appointed to one of the highest-ranking academic positions at Harvard, that of University Professor (following Kenneth Arrow as Bryant Conant University Professor). University Professors have special academic freedom; for example, they can teach courses in other departments or skip terms to undertake research. Among his Harvard colleagues during this time were Dreben, Cavell, Quine, Goodman, Putnam, Scanlon, Nozick, Sen, and Korsgaard.

For many years TJ was Rawls' only published book, although in the 1980s he published a few articles reworking key parts of TJ. Then, in 1993, he published his second *magnum opus*, PL (second revised edition 1996). PL focuses on a different topic from TJ, namely political legitimacy rather than a liberal theory of justice. It depends also on a process of self-revision, because in the late 1970s Rawls began to have doubts about a central argument given in Part III of TJ, namely that concerning the stability of society coherent with the principles of justice. In PL, the centrality of political ethics characteristic of TJ is in part substituted by a more austere political view. PL, one might say, has more Lincoln, and TJ more Kant. The two books, however, have strong internal connections (see this volume, section 1.2). No doubt the first reactions to PL were critical, especially from the original Rawlsians. They felt a sense of loss, and many envisaged a surrender to Rawls' critics. Today, though, it is difficult to deny the originality and relevance of PL. Some ideas from the book – in particular the relationship between religion and liberal democracy – were later better represented in Rawls' last published essay "The Idea of Public Reason Revisited" (1997), now included in the *Collected Papers* (CP 1999). In 1997 Rawls also contributed as an "amicus curiae" to the so-called "Philosophical Brief" presented to the Supreme Court. The writing

– promoted by Ronald Dworkin and signed also by Thomas Nagel, Robert Nozick, Thomas Scanlon, and Judith Jarvis Thomson – was in support of physician-assisted suicide. The Supreme Court decided against the intentions of the six philosophers, and Rawls with a *super partes* attitude typical of his character said that the Court was not wrong.

Over the course of his academic career Rawls helped to train an impressive number of philosophers, among them Thomas Nagel, Thomas Scanlon, Alan Gibbard, Norman Daniels, Sissela Bok, Samuel Freeman, Barbara Herman, Joshua Cohen, Christine Korsgaard, Jean Hampton, Thomas Pogge, Paul Weithman, Sharon Loyd, Onora O'Neill, Erin Kelly, and Nancy Sherman. Many were women, Rawls never discriminating on the basis of gender or, indeed, of the status of his students. He treated all of them as fellow philosophers and in so doing drew numerous talented people into the field of moral and political philosophy.

In 1995 Rawls suffered a major stroke. It was the first of a series that made his professional career progressively impossible. After the stroke, Rawls published LoP (1999), finished with the help of his wife and of his colleague and friend Burton Dreben. LoP presents and defends the principles of justice that ought to guide the foreign policy of a liberal democracy. Rawls had published little concerning this aspect of justice until his 1993 essay "The Law of the People" presented at an Oxford Amnesty International series of lectures on human rights. Debate on LoP focused upon a supposed incoherence of Rawls' views: he would have permitted in foreign politics what he would have never conceded in domestic politics. He was accused in other words of maintaining a double standard, abandoning at the global level the ideals of liberty and equality for which TJ was celebrated. In recent years, however, a more sympathetic interpretation has emerged, according to which LoP exemplifies Rawls' institutional methodology at its best. All of Rawls' main works seem to have this characteristic in common: after a period of harsh criticism they tend to come back stronger than before.

Other published works of Rawls', such as JFR (2001, see chapter 8 in this volume), LHMP (2000), and LHPP (2007) were edited by former students of his. JFR is probably the best guide to Rawls' mature view of justice. LHMP and LHPP, collected by Rawls' former students, are fundamental sources for understanding the connection between Rawls' thought and modern political philosophy. Rawls died aged 81 at home, in Lexington, on November 24, 2002. After his death, the obituaries in major US newspapers were surprisingly numerous and extensive.

Despite his fame, Rawls refused to be a public figure, and usually rejected honors. He did, however, accept degrees from Princeton, Harvard, and Oxford (the main universities of his life). In 1999, he received the Rolf Schock Prize in Logic and Philosophy from the Swedish Academy of Sciences. In the same year, President Bill Clinton awarded Rawls the National Humanities Medal. Conferring the award to his wife, Clinton said:

John Rawls is perhaps the greatest political philosopher of the twentieth century. In 1971, when Hillary and I were in law school, we were among the millions moved by a remarkable book he wrote, *A Theory of Justice*, that placed our rights to liberty and justice upon a strong and brilliant new foundation of reason. Almost single-handedly, John Rawls revived the disciplines of political and ethical philosophy . . . he has helped a whole generation of learned Americans revive their faith in democracy.

Rawls pursued these goals with what he could have called a Kantian sense of equality. He cherished a world where we, in virtue of our common human-ity, could relate to each other as equals. He did so not only in his books but also in his everyday practice of philosophy. As I myself can testify, the philosophical world he created around himself was a world of equals. And, as noted by Christine Korsgaard, the very fact that Jack seemed to regard everyone as an equal made him seem superior to everyone else. This world he created remains the world in which many of us work, gratefully and with an enormous intellectual debt. Jack was not only a great philosopher; he was also a wonderful person with an incredible moral sense in his dealings with other human beings, as many of us had the fortune to experience. This conjunction of superb philosophical capacity and admirable humanity, both of which he so fully embodied, inspired me to call part of this introduction "A Beautiful Life."

1.2 The Book

1.2.1 Rawls' revolution

Most works in analytical philosophy are ignored by widely circulated media in the English language. The release of Rawls' TJ was an exception to this tendency. Considering just the Anglo-Saxon world, TJ received prestigious reviews from such widely circulated newspapers as the *New York Times*, the *Washington Post*, the *Observer*, *The Times Literary Supplement*, *The Economist*, and the *New York Review of Books*. Such elite magazines as the *Spectator*, the *New Republic*, the *Nation*, the *New Statesman*, and the *Listener* enthusiastically welcomed it. The academic spin-offs have been so numerous as to make a strict control of the literature on TJ practically impos-sible. Furthermore, countless single issues on TJ have been published in the major languages by philosophical magazines, as well as by magazines that specialize in different subjects ranging from economics to law.

It is not easy to explain this success, because TJ is a long (nearly 600 pages) and difficult book. As Rawls wrote in its Preface: "This is a long book, not only in pages." Besides, TJ is a book based on an extraordinary argumentative rigor, a praiseworthy thing in itself but certainly not the harbinger of any easy popularity. This success may lead one to believe that TJ expresses complex, original, and radical political theses like, for instance, those expressed by

Marx in *Capital*, another long, difficult yet widely read book. Rawls' type of liberalism is surely original and much more egalitarian than one is used to being confronted with, especially if compared with US rather than EU standards. Strictly speaking, however, the substance of Rawls' political and economic arguments in TJ is neither particularly new nor radical. They are rather common in the European and North American establishment. Rawls is a typical American "liberal," who could be defined as a "social-democrat" in continental Europe (as he affirms in the Preface to the French edition of TJ in 1987). What is really innovative, in summary, is more the way in which Rawls argues in favor of these theses than the content of them.

One might also believe that the impact of the book was due to the weariness that academics and cultured readers alike felt for that formalistic and purely semantic way of being involved in moral and political philosophy that prevailed for a number of years in the Anglo-Saxon tradition.[8] There is certainly some truth in this. Indeed, in TJ, Rawls initiated a return to the major classical substantive themes of ethics and politics that were typical of Hobbes, Locke, Rousseau, and John Stuart Mill. Nonetheless, even this explanation only holds up to a certain point. If you read TJ, you will find just a few pages on the topical subjects of public debate, while you will run into hundreds of sophisticated arguments that are unlikely to give rise to widespread enthusiasm. Moreover, Rawls' style in TJ may not be likened to that of those classical authors referred to above who were often pleasing writers. Rawls, instead, is rigidly academic and makes no allowance for non-professional readers.

We certainly need to acknowledge that the economic-political content of TJ moves beyond what may be derived from its direct use of the traditional terms and concepts of the social sciences. Rawls approaches the idea of distributive justice in a very different way from that of modern and contemporary liberals as well as socialists.[9] Rawls' basic idea is that the life of normal people is affected to a considerable extent by factors that are beyond their control (for instance, the family) and depends to a considerable extent on where they are born in an existing institutional system. Chance plays an important role in everybody's life in many respects, in an individual's starting point, which largely determines her economic–social fate. For instance, prior to the civil war in America little could be done for the children of slaves. However, while chance may be somehow irremediable, the same is not true for institutions. Institutions, at least in a liberal democracy, depend on the will of the citizens. Slavery is obviously a consequence of an unjust institutional system.

Rawls' conception of distributive justice is normative and institutionalist. It is founded on the thesis that citizens of a liberal-democratic state should never accept socio-economic inequalities resulting from a system of institutions that they are unable to morally justify. These inequalities may differ considerably: they may have a political nature; they may be due to differences in gender, caste, or race; they may depend on status and – in the present day – particularly on the existence of various levels of material wellbeing.

Such a thesis has egalitarian economic–social consequences, but they are less simple than we might expect. For instance, given the significance of equality, there could be an easy and immediate solution: it would be enough to endorse a pure egalitarianism. However, Rawls does not accept this simplistic solution. According to him, institutions are systems of rules that ought to secure mutual advantage through cooperation. Adopting a pure or radical egalitarianism would not be satisfactory since doing so would rule out institutional solutions able to benefit all. In fact, pure egalitarianism would be to the detriment of social and economic incentives and, therefore, would translate into less efficiency. Hence, the best justification is based on an equilibrium between efficiency and equality, for which we may use the Rawlsian term "fairness."

In any event, it is quite likely that TJ generated enthusiasm on account of its ethical-political significance. During the late 1960s and early 1970s, the United States and Europe went through a special time: the USA experienced marches for Civil Rights, the Black Liberation Movement, and the mobilization against the Vietnam War. In continental Europe, this period of cultural and social unrest is called "1968." Characterized by social protest, this called for a theoretical synthesis capable of proposing an institutional reconstruction that also accounted for the spirit of the preceding movements. TJ succeeded in taking such a position.

The rigor, the consistency, and the strength of Rawls' ethical and political-theoretical reasoning are unquestionably extraordinary. This explains TJ's pervasive cultural and philosophical influence. The way Rawls explored the foundations of his position, both in TJ and, later, in PL, has a profundity with few precedents in the history of political thought, with the exception of Aristotle and Kant.

Rawls is a liberal political philosopher, albeit of a special kind.[10] Traditional liberalism originated in and developed from the defense of individual rights against the state. Throughout his work, Rawls instead meant to promote trust in institutions by showing how their force can coincide with a defense of individual rights. For him, as we shall see, the first principle of justice, based on liberty, in some way implies the second principle, based on equality. Liberty, in TJ, means "fair value of political liberty," and this fair value requires a substantial amount of equality to be realized. Indeed, this is the reason why inequalities must not be accepted and imposed by the institutional system if they are not justifiable to all its citizens. In this way, all the differences of class and gender, as well as of caste, are automatically ruled out. Rawls' concern extends to material inequalities, which his theory of social justice opposes with all its strength.

The justification that Rawls is thinking of is a public justification, as he says in PL, and starts from the assumption that citizens share fundamental ideas about politics. Hence, the citizens' consent to the public culture of the liberal democracy ends up being the basis of the Rawlsian rationale. From this perspective, political obligation is based on the consent of all citizens. In Rawls' case, this is not a question of an effective consent, but of virtual consent based on reasons that depend on the social contract. This call for consent has unquestionably been a further appealing element in Rawls' work in general and TJ in particular.

1.2.2 Rawls' political philosophical vision

Rawls' political philosophical project is not particularly obscure and its general aims are almost always transparent. Rawls was never particularly interested either in designing the best political regime from the point of the view of the universe or in comparing different political regimes. Rather, he always started from the firm assumption that political philosophy strongly depends on the social structure and the institutional framework in which it is embedded.[11] These institutionalist presuppositions are relevant, for Rawls, only if they correspond with the ones that characterize liberal democracy. Rawls never questions liberal democracy in his texts and people uninterested in it find no alternative to liberal democracy in them. There is nothing mysterious, from this point of view, to discover in the realm of political philosophy. That is why Rawls states in one of his clearest passages on this topic: "Those who write about such a doctrine are not to be viewed as experts on a special subject, as may be the case with sciences. Political philosophy has no special access to fundamental truths."[12]

Here, Rawls emphasizes that political philosophy in itself has no authority, because in liberal democracy the authority lies exclusively in the hands of the citizens. Even if political philosophy had some claim to represent what we could call the role of human reason, for Rawls this claim is not independent from citizens' decisions. It is just another way to make an appeal to the collective judgments expressed across time by all citizens. In this sense, Rawlsian political philosophy is not Platonic. There are no philosopher-kings even in the minimal sense in which they try to figure out what is the real nature of justice or some common good to realize in public institutions. Rather, political philosophy starts from the shared culture of a liberal-democratic society, to which it can of course contribute in its peculiar way.

This apparent modesty has a much more sophisticated theoretical counterpart, which perhaps will become more understandable if we reflect on what Rawls calls "constructivism." With regards to the methodology of his ethical and political philosophy, Rawls claims to be a "Kantian" constructivist ("Kant," LHMP, pp. 237ff.). Rawlsian constructivism is a complex theoretical strategy and we shall properly investigate what Rawls means by it later (see in particular chapters 8 and 9). We can anticipate here that constructivism is an alternative to Platonism, naturalism and realism. Moral and political philosophy do not consist – for Rawls – in the discovery of truths that exist before and independently from the social context of human interaction.[13] They consist in deriving the appropriate arguments that can rely on moral assumptions already present within the intersubjective relations that characterize the public culture of liberal democracy. Also based on this stance is the deep structure of the "social contract," an old expression within political philosophy that, after Rawls, has taken on a new significance.[14]

Given these premises, the most significant function of political philosophy according to Rawls is to make citizens understand the importance of their own political role. Liberal democracy cannot survive apathy or skepticism. Citizens must enter politics with conceptions and ideals that reinforce their political institutions. Citizens can become ever more conscious of this fact through the writings of political philosophers. These writings reinforce the conversational apparatus of the civic society and emphasize in particular the prominence of its political values. By being part of the rich background culture of an open society, political philosophy invites people to reason and reflect critically upon their institutions, beginning the search for consensus even among the most disputed questions and hottest disagreements.

As we see in PL, public consent is the main idea behind Rawlsian liberalism. This liberalism derives historically from the wars of religion, and the search for peace that followed them, with the successive creation of constitutional regimes before and of majoritarian democracies afterwards. For Rawls, consent must be consent for the right reasons and liberalism should never be an instrument to defend social stability at the cost of an unjust status quo. The central thesis of Rawls' liberalism follows from this premise. Political legitimacy, which depends on consent, is connected with the possibility of justifying the basic structure of a liberal-democratic regime to all citizens.

According to Rawls, such unanimity would be possible if liberal-democratic regimes were able to ensure some fundamental elements, such as: a list of basic liberties, with their degrees of priority; the means to make possible an effective use of these liberties; a socio-economic system that guarantees equality of opportunities for all and a minimum standard for the worst-offs. These are indeed the essential constituent parts of Rawls' famous theory of justice as fairness (in TJ). All reasonable political doctrines, however, should share these general goals, according to Rawls, even if they diverge in the way they argue for them (in PL).

1.2.3 Outline of this book

More than 50 percent of this book is dedicated to TJ. TJ amounts quantitatively to significantly less than half of what Rawls wrote (even if we consider that the content of some of the articles from 1951 to 1971 has been represented in TJ) and it is chronologically situated around the two-fifths mark of

Rawls' whole intellectual career (beginning around 1950 and ending with his death in 2002).

This choice depends on several factors. On one hand, TJ is Rawls' most important book, inaugurating a formidably productive paradigm in moral, social and political philosophy. At the same time, outside the circles of the specialists of political philosophy, TJ is the only work by Rawls normally read. A similar point can be made if we move away from an American – and generally from an English-speaking – readership to a more international one. For many people and in many places, in other words, John Rawls is only known as the author of TJ. On the other hand, this choice has to do with the division of Rawls' work into two periods, which we can call Rawls1 and Rawls2. If we accept this division, then TJ can be considered the core of the first period. This makes it easier to justify dedicating over half of this book to TJ. I must also say that the quantitative priority given to TJ here is compensated by the particular relevance accorded to PL. In these chapters, PL is considered a necessary step to understanding – as we will see – the whole of Rawls' work, including TJ.

Let us assume that dividing Rawls' work into two periods is plausible. Given that we have to start around 1950 (after the end of his Ph.D. and before the first published paper), when is this first period supposed to end? Obviously, it must be after 1971 (the year in which TJ was published), but when? Rawls' writings immediately following TJ serve as a kind of appendix to the main work, even if there are in them also interesting hints for the future development of his thought. The real debate is whether to begin the second period in the mid-1970s or in 1980, the year in which Rawls published the highly innovative paper "Kantian Constructivism in Moral Theory" (hereafter KCMT). Eventually, I selected this second option, both because the links with TJ are more vivid in his work from the 1970s and because KCMT seems altogether like a substantive revision of TJ and more innovative in the direction of PL.

This means that I will go on assuming that the first period of Rawls' work, Rawls1, goes roughly from 1950 to 1980 and is dominated by TJ. The second period, Rawls2, begins with the basic new assumptions about the notions of person and society in KCMT (1980) and continues until the death of Rawls (2002). There are, however, in my reading, not just two periods but three parts. The first part coincides with the first period and concerns mainly TJ and other papers connected with it written before and after TJ. The second period has two parts: one dedicated mainly to PL (1993, 1996) and the other to LoP (1999), the book in which Rawls organically presents his thoughts on international political theory.

I hope that this three-part division is reasonable even if it has some costs. By accepting it, we lose some alternative interpretations, such as one that favors a Kantian path within the whole of his work, starting from TJ and going through the papers of the mid-1970s until KCMT. Another reasonable line of reading centers on the special relevance of "publicity" and "public reason," assuming that to pursue justice implies to do it in a visible way. This interpretation would begin with TJ, continue through KCMT and PL, and stretch to the end of his life (the paper entitled "The Idea of Public Reason Revisited" was the last one written by Rawls). I mention only these (alternative) possibilities here to avoid confusion. I will of course discuss both the Kantian side of Rawls' theory and the idea of public reason in some detail during the book. However, I feel the three-part division better captures Rawls' work than an interpretation that focuses only on Kant's thought or the idea of publicity.

This reconstruction partially obscures other significant books by Rawls: the *Lectures on the History of Moral Philosophy*, published in 2000, with Rawls' interpretations of – among others – Leibniz, Hume, Kant, and Hegel; the *Lectures on the History of Political Philosophy*, published in 2007 (LHPP), with Rawls' interpretations of – among others – Hobbes, Locke, Hume, Mill, and Marx; another book of lectures, this time dedicated to Rawls' self-interpretation after TJ, entitled *Justice as Fairness: A Restatement*, published in 2001 (hereafter JFR); and finally Rawls' undergraduate senior thesis together with a brief autobiographical essay "On Religion" from the 1990s, both devoted to religious beliefs, published posthumously under the title *A Brief Inquiry into the Meaning of Sin & Faith* (hereafter BIMSF). Rawls presented the lectures that comprise the first three books during the courses he taught at Harvard University from the mid-1960s until his retirement in 1995. None of these texts were properly finished by Rawls and they were published only after heavy editing, undertaken with the help of original notes and handouts. Most of the lectures were not written with the intention to publish them later. The same could be said for the writings behind BIMSF. Nevertheless, they deserve attention. Rawls himself, speaking now for what concerns LHMP and LHPP, thought that political philosophy could be properly practiced only after carefully reading the classics, or, as he said: "by studying the exemplars – those noted figures who have made cherished attempts – and we try to learn from them."[15]

These works will be used in the book as a support to my general reading of Rawls' work. Both LHMP and LHPP are used throughout, especially when I go through some passage in Rawls' political and moral theory inspired by the classics of political philosophy. JFR will be discussed separately – together with Rawls' revisions of TJ as they appear in the second edition and an interpretation of KCMT – in the chapter in which I treat the transition from TJ to PL (chapter 8). BIMSF is mentioned when discussing the relationship between Rawls, religion, and communitarian ethics. The other articles Rawls published during his long intellectual career – now available to the reader in the edition of Rawls' *Collected Papers* (hereafter CP) – are also used in support of the general interpretation; likewise with Rawls' Ph.D. dissertation on moral methodology.

1.3 Hermeneutical hypotheses

I lay down three hermeneutical hypotheses: the interpretive hypothesis, the methodological hypothesis and the theoretical hypothesis.[16] Their function is different. The interpretive hypothesis formulates an answer to the question of how we are supposed to read Rawls over time. The methodological and the theoretical hypotheses offer some reasons in favor of the answer formulated in the interpretive hypothesis and supply general tools for reading the author.

The interpretive hypothesis concerns the much-debated question of the continuity or discontinuity between the two main periods of Rawls' work (1950–80, 1980–2002). I defend the continuity option, but I admit that my argument is controversial.[17] The methodological hypothesis is designed to complement the interpretive hypothesis by presenting a unitary thread through which we can trigger the desired continuity in our reading of Rawls. This thread follows the basic device Rawls never abandoned, namely the famous – at least within the universe of Rawlsology – "priority of right":[18] in the whole of Rawls' work, the right precedes the good in the sense that all practical deliberations concerning justice, desires, and preferences (which define the good of persons) must be subordinated to the demands of the principles of right. Still, one cannot master Rawls' work without the support of a more theoretical hypothesis. To approach it, one is obliged to leave behind strict reading of the Rawlsian texts. My theoretical hypothesis is based on a distinction – which I will present later in this Introduction – between justification on the one side and legitimation on the other (for more, see chapter 11). By justification, I mean the normative force of a political-theoretical conception of justice based on freedom and equality. By legitimation, I mean both the evidence of a shared consensus on fundamental institutional matters among the citizens and the general acceptability of political power in a liberal-democratic regime. The theoretical hypothesis consists in affirming that justification and legitimation are complementary and indispensable theoretical tools in exploring the architecture of Rawls' thought. Both the methodological and the theoretical hypotheses confirm Rawls' institutional reading of political philosophy.

1.3.1 The Interpretive Hypothesis: Continuity versus Discontinuity

The interpretive hypothesis concerns the debated issue of continuity versus discontinuity between the two aforementioned periods of Rawls' work (Rawls1 and Rawls2). Prima facie, discontinuity seems to prevail, given that Rawls' main books discuss three different subjects: TJ deals with social justice; PL with the main flaws of TJ as well as with political legitimacy; LoP extends and modifies the previous model in the light of global justice. However, upon reflection one can detect a substantial continuity. According to both Rawls1 and Rawls2, the justification of a political conception cannot coincide with the content of a moral theory.[19] The validity of a political conception, on the contrary, depends heavily on the legitimacy of its institutional background (the main subject of PL). But, on the other side, legitimacy, as we shall see, is not independent from a specific liberal political theory such as justice as fairness (the content of TJ). Therefore, TJ relies on PL and vice versa, in a spirit of normative institutionalism, as one could call it. For normative institutionalism, the justification of some principles of justice is not with respect to the institutional practices it governs. LoP shows, perhaps better than TJ and PL, how principles of justice can vary across different institutional settings. In such a way, the three parts and two periods outlined above are in some way connected and continuity can hold.

The upshot of the continuity hypothesis is roughly this: one can conceive of Rawls' work as a continuous project from the beginning to the end. Within this project, internal changes – including those justifying my proposed division into two periods and three parts – are due more to the need to adjust his paradigm to new challenges brought in by the content matter of original problems than by an internal dramatic shift of theoretical nature.

On this interpretation, we can see Rawls' three main oeuvres, namely TJ, PL and LoP, in the form of three concentric circles. In the first, TJ, Rawls treats the problem of social justice from a liberal normative standpoint. The output of the exercise is the best theory of justice within a given institutional setting. This theory, however, can be taken as excluding too much, beginning with religious people. Religious persons, however, and more generally people inspired to "comprehensive" doctrines, as Rawls would later label them, are often "reasonable" and ready to put aside their deeper views in the name of their loyalty towards liberal-democratic institutions. Their exclusion from the *res publica* would thus represent a loss, at least if we have in mind the "stability" of the political system. The second circle widens the scope of political theory to explicitly include, through the creation of a political conception, non-strictly-speaking liberal citizens who are nevertheless morally faithful to the basic institutions of liberal democracy. The third circle broadens it more, to include in the "society of peoples" also non-liberal peoples, who (in a way to be better defined) can be considered "decent."

There is resistance to this continuity hypothesis. Some scholars maintain that it is not simply the main topics and the scope of problems that change from Rawls1 to Rawls2, but rather the substance of the theory. Under this assumption, critics see with disappointment Rawls2 as insulating political morality from its ethical background. Some of these critics believe in a more comprehensive liberalism, and are dissatisfied by the move from justice as fairness to the political conception.[20] Others even maintain that Rawls2 himself attributes to TJ errors that he did not in fact commit.[21]

If we accept interpretations of this kind, then the discontinuity hypothesis should prevail, the main breaking point being the gap in Rawls2 between ethics (and metaphysics or religion) on one hand and politics on the other. Now, there is no doubt that ethics and politics are more distant from each other in the second part of Rawls work. That granted, it still seems that the interpretive problem lies elsewhere: did the distance between ethics and politics, already present in Rawls1, become larger because Rawls2 had to expand and clarify his theory, or rather because Rawls changed his theoretical perspective passing over social justice in the name of political legitimacy? My answer is in favor of the first option. The idea of political legitimacy is central to a proper understanding of the concept of social justice also, along a path that is already present in TJ but that becomes more perspicuous in PL. Both in Rawls1 and in Rawls 2, the conception of justice basically depends on the institutional practice.

Even opting for continuity rather than discontinuity, one cannot think that there is a knock-out theoretical argument for either interpretation. The way in which you assign weights to the two options remains in part pragmatic. As a matter of fact, my further reasons for continuity are pragmatic reasons. First, this book aims to be a general introduction to a significant author, and the continuity hypothesis can contribute to reconstructing the whole thought and whole person behind it. This kind of argument can also have a deeper counterpart, making appeal to hermeneutical arguments in favor of integrity. The hermeneutical tradition always made a plea for an interpretation in terms of totality. So reformulated, the thesis says that any author must be read in terms of unitary perspective, so as to get a better understanding in the sense of the German traditional hermeneutic term "Besserverstehen" (better understanding). This option is also the one Rawls himself adopts in his reading of the classics of moral and political philosophy.

A second pragmatic reason for continuity depends on Rawls' self-interpretation. He himself was determined to defend what I have called the continuity thesis, as he explicitly said in a conference in Naples in 1988 (Rawls mentions the event in PL xxxiii). Of course, one cannot assume an authority principle in matters of interpretation: authors' intentions, however relevant they might be, are not and ought not to be the sole instruments of interpretation, because text and readers have their own autonomous and decisive weight. Notwithstanding this obvious proviso, Rawls' thesis on self-interpretation seems relevant.

A third pragmatic reason for continuity is reconstructive. It suggests that one should try to read Rawls1 knowing what Rawls2 wrote. Accepting the continuity thesis changes the attitude one should take towards Rawls' body of work. The traditional attitude saw Rawls1 as more foundational, in a way that many readers find implausible after reading PL. Within the traditional attitude, it was absolutely normal to think of Rawls1 as a philosopher like Plato, Kant, or Hobbes, trying to find the correct theoretical connection between rationality and justice. Starting from there, it was rather straightforward to conceive PL, and Rawls2 in general, as evidence of a kind of retreat from this epochal philosophical enterprise and maybe to feel a sense of philosophical loss (the negative reactions to PL mentioned before are typical offshoots of such reading).[22] If instead we begin, as suggested before, from PL, to reinterpret TJ, one may realize Rawls' focus to have been somehow different from the start. This means that we can suppose that he always wanted to produce a public justification rather than a pure demonstration. In particular, the relevance of the "basic structure" and the "reflective equilibrium" within his theory since the beginning is revealing. Rawls' justificatory apparatus is never independent from the institutional practices that it norms. Consequently, the main principles of justice can change according to the variations of the relevant institutional practices. Ultimately there would not be any discontinuity between the foundation of the basic liberal values in TJ and the defense of Western democracies in PL and LoP. In sum, one can conceive of a unitary project, in which there is no moral justice without institutional stability.

From now on, I will work under the assumption of the continuity thesis, but will move away from it when necessary. For this continuity must be taken as a relative continuity, as shown by our previous distinction between two periods and three parts. In other words, there are significant local discontinuities. Among these discontinuities, there are explicit repudiations, like the ones Rawls enjoins with regard to rational choice theory and, more relevantly, with regard to some passages within the third part of TJ concerning stability. Furthermore, among the local discontinuities there are also smoother progressive changes, like those Rawls effects with the method of "reflective equilibrium." The origin of his interest in the meta-ethical basis of political theory, from which the method of reflective equilibrium springs, lies in the beginning of Rawls' career. Throughout his works, he introduced progressive emendations – which we can note, for example, when reading the second edition of TJ in comparison with the first – that surely changed the meaning of reflective equilibrium. Finally, Rawls introduced several new concepts after TJ that became rather central to the general understanding of his work. Among these, I see the formulation of a "political conception" with the emphasis on a political interpretation of the person, the more explicit constructivist foundation of the theory, the notion of overlapping consensus, and the idea of public reason.

1.3.2 Methodological hypothesis: the priority of right

The second hermeneutical hypothesis is the methodological hypothesis, based on the priority of right.[23] Few people would deny the centrality of the priority of right within the Rawlsian paradigm.[24] Nevertheless we must admit that Rawls does not insist too much on it. In TJ, he presents the priority of right in two pages (30–2; rev. edn. 27–30), to return to it only at the end of the book (section 85). In PL, reformulating his previous article "The Priority of Right and Ideas of the Good" (1988), he proposes a more elaborate distinction between a general meaning and a particular meaning of the priority of right:

> The priority of the right means (in its general meaning) that the ideas of the good used must be political ideas, so that we need not rely on comprehensive conceptions of the good but only on ideas tailored to fit within the political conception. Second, the priority of right means (in its particular meaning) that the principles of justice set limits to permissible ways of life: the claims citizens make to pursue ends transgressing these limits have no weight. (PL 209)

The usual interpretation of the priority of right coincides with what Rawls calls its "particular meaning." That is, it coincides with the idea that the permissible choices of people, oriented towards the good, cannot exceed – if we take justice seriously – the limits posed by the right. This means that the principles of justice have an absolute priority over other kinds of considerations. They do not even figure in standard deliberations, because they precede and override them.

The priority of right has two implications that transform it into a general methodological device. The first is more intuitive and immediate, being connected with what Rawls calls in PL the "particular meaning" of the priority of right. Rawls denies here any idea of equal consideration of preferences. This denial contrasts sharply with the spirit of the utilitarian paradigm. Personal desires and claims – if we accept Rawls' priority of right – do not count if they conflict with the principles of the right. In such a reading, the priority of right – limiting the way in which persons can deliberate about the good – signals what is perhaps the most significant target in TJ, namely to find an alternative to the dominant utilitarian tradition in the area of theories of justice.

The priority of right, however, can be used, in a less intuitive way, as having what Rawls in PL calls the "general meaning" of the priority of right. In this sense, the priority of right implies a restriction of the comprehensive conceptions of the good to the "political conception," from which follows the formulation of what Rawls will call reasonable comprehensive views. Only reasonable comprehensive views can have a legitimate claim to participate in the most relevant among political procedures (concerning constitutional essentials and matters of basic justice). Other comprehensive conceptions fail to supply a basis coherent with the idea of political legitimacy, which – as we have said – is the core idea behind PL. The fundamental notions (in PL) of "overlapping consensus" and "public reason" depend on this restriction and do so in such a way that they also depend indirectly on the priority of the right over the good.

The fact that the priority of right helps to get at some of the main targets both in TJ and PL exhibits perhaps a necessary, but certainly not sufficient, condition to show that the priority of right itself could be considered a common thread that renders the continuist interpretation less vague. One can combine, however, the two readings of the priority of right in order to make them more coherent among themselves and able to capture the deep nature of Rawls' political philosophical project as a whole. We can proceed in this direction by taking into account the fact that Rawls – just because there exists something like the priority of right – never considers the disagreements about the right (and justice) as on the same level as disagreements about the good. Disagreements about the good are permissible insofar as they express the rich background culture of an open society. By contrast, disagreements about the right must be substantially limited in order to serve as shared and public side constraints able to select what desires and claims are permissible within a just society. Under this interpretation, the way in which the priority of right excludes the logic of utilitarianism (in TJ) and the way in which it limits the use of comprehensive doctrines in the most significant public debates (in PL) come together to form a permanent and fundamental Rawlsian vision of politics based on the asymmetry between the right and the good. This asymmetry depends on the institutionalist basis of the theory and cannot be properly accounted for, unless we introduce the distinction between legitimation and justification.

1.3.3 Theoretical hypothesis: justification and legitimation

The theoretical hypothesis is based on the idea that the asymmetry between the right and the good depends on a deeper dialectics between justification and legitimation. These terms usually overlap in the political-theoretical literature, but it is important to distinguish appropriately between them.[25] According to this distinction, justification looks for the best theoretical argument, is intrinsically substantive, goes top-down, and is rooted in the moral and metaphysical bases of a specific culture. Legitimation, on the other hand, is normally based on an institutional practice, concerns mainly the inputs of a political process, goes bottom-up, and does not directly appeal to the moral and metaphysical roots of a culture. My thesis is that justification and legitimation must be seen as complementary. Assuming the fact of pluralism in contemporary liberal-democratic societies, we can have different plausible justifications in reciprocal conflict, but we have to rely on the same institutional legitimation for the sake of stability (for the right reasons). One can also suppose that the concept of justification, so conceived, coincides with a successful normative argument. The concept of legitimation, in these terms, is more unusual. By legitimation, I mean a specific form of widespread legitimacy conferred on the main institutions, in a way that will become clearer later in the book, when I come back to it in the first of the three chapters devoted to PL (chapters 9–11). A divorce between these concepts cannot be durable. On the one hand, a country can legitimate a dictator through consent – such as, for example, in Italy during the era of Fascism – but after a while such unjustified legitimation proves unacceptable. On the other hand, an intellectual or religious group can justify a norm different from an established legitimated practice – for example, thinking that world poverty should be immediately eliminated – but has no right to use public institutions against the general will.

Jürgen Habermas has made an implicit use of this distinction between justification and legitimation. In *Between Facts and Norms*, he urges a structural compromise between "practical reason" and "social praxis."[26] He assumes that validity claims are not too different from the dictates of traditional practical reason without any contact with factual reality. To avoid this kind of abstraction, critical theory goes beyond what is considered the standard scope of philosophy to enter the domain of positive law. In such a way, according to Habermas, normativity tries to objectivate itself. The outcome should be the re-conjunction of ideal validity, which is normative and decontextualized, and social validity, which is on the contrary connected to factual criteria. According to Habermas, this re-conjunction requires the public recognition of the legal validity of a democratic law, guaranteed by the equilibrium between the evidence of general legal compliance and the possibility of justifying this compliance in the name of the dialogical nature of liberal democracy. This duplicity of functions is the standard counterpart of the integration necessities of a complex contemporary society. This kind of society cannot be integrated merely through some normative values, but rather requires the complement of factually operating institutions such as the market, the democracy and the judiciary power. In my view, this strategy can be better explained through the cooperative force of justification and legitimation, as previously defined. Justification would provide the meaning of the moral content on which any critical theory is based, while legitimation will be at the basis of the actual performance of a working legitimated system.

Albeit with greater philosophical prudence, a similar move is made also by John Rawls in PL. Rawls actually does not think in terms of a coherent integration between a normative-philosophical justification and a factual legitimation. Rather he continues to work within the horizon of a philosophical theory of justice. Nevertheless, in order to settle the central dilemma between stability and pluralism, he must concede that a pure philosophical justification of liberal democracy is itself insufficient to guarantee the equilibrium between these opposing claims. For just this reason he comes up with a social device, overlapping consensus, giving to it a more general normative validity. Within a well-ordered society, citizens with comprehensive but reasonable world-visions can peacefully coexist with other citizens analogously oriented. This providential equilibrium is permitted by a successful constitutional history, like the one that has characterized US public life since the founding fathers. Only this background permits the coexistence of doctrines and persons that make reference to worldviews that are deeply diversified from both the ethical and metaphysical points of view. The history of an empirical success, like the one of the American constitution across time, becomes in such a way coherent with the ethical-political normative premises of Rawlsian discourse. To translate into my terminology, here the philosophical justification offered by the principles of justice meets the factual legitimation given by the American public legal history.

The parallels in how Habermas and Rawls – each in his own way – combine justification and legitimation can be taken as a consequence of a larger project of the institutionalization of reason that they both independently share.[27] To adopt some familiar schemas from within the history of political ideas, it could be said that this common trend – between Habermas and Rawls – depends on their following certain basic Kantian ethical recommendations with the hindsight of Hegelian critical reflections on Kant. If one accepts this sketchy reconstruction, then some differences between Habermas and Rawls, emphasized by their debate – to which we will return in chapter 7 – are less relevant than might have been expected.

If we transfer the abstract argument about justification and legitimation into the problem concerning the foundations of justice, then this model corresponds to the solution to the problem posed by the asymmetry of the right and the good. Building on it, we can construct the thesis that the existence of a just basic structure cannot depend exclusively on a theoretical justification. It must depend also on a successful model of institutional interaction. Only this kind of legitimation permits the construction of a durable consent, even if the support of some theoretical justification was to be taken for granted. In practice, only a quasi-empirical notion of legitimation potentially unifies the structural pluralism of justifications under a coherent vision of justice. The priority of right is the methodological counterpart of this theoretical construction. Principles of the right trump desires and claims based on the good precisely because we can share not only a theoretical justification but also the empirical existence of liberal democracy.

The conjunction of legitimation and justification constitutes the unification of a legal entity and an ethical project from the point of view of what I have called "normative institutionalism." I claim that, for Rawls, it characterizes the deep nature of liberal democracy. Never, I think, does Rawls affirm this complementarity so strongly as in the last pages of his "Themes in Kant's Moral Philosophy" (hereafter TKMP), where he states: "We also know that under favourable conditions, a realm of ends is some form of constitutional democracy" (CP 526).

Justification is normative and comes from the ethical argument according to which we should find fair terms of cooperation among ourselves as citizens of a liberal-democratic state. Legitimation is institutional and comes from the fact that liberal democracy is, in our age, a (relatively) successful practice. From the point of view of Rawls' normative institutionalism, this capacity to join justification and legitimation is not present within any political regime except liberal democracy, and allows the adoption of an original normative perspective. Only this normative perspective allows limits on pluralism when we face disagreements about justice: constitutional essentials and basic matters of justice constrain the possibilities of political dissent just because they are the foundation upon which the building of liberal democracy is grounded. Discussing public reason – as we shall see, one of the main concepts within PL – Rawls goes as far as saying: "Those who reject constitutional democracy . . . will of course reject the very idea of public reason" (CP 574). Political philosophy, according to this thesis, is connected, through the priority of right, to the fact that liberal democracy must be selected a priori – given its legitimation – even if we have no independent intellectual strategy to overcome the natural pluralism of conflicting philosophical justifications.

I have tried to show how the three hermeneutical hypotheses contribute to providing a unified and coherent imaging of Rawls' whole work. If you accept the continuity hypothesis, with the priority of right and the complementarity of justification and legitimation, you have – in fact – a better idea of what Rawlsian contractualism is all about.[28] Liberal-democratic institutions, taken as a basis for legitimation, are a necessary premise of the contractual agreement – from which we derive normative implications. Otherwise different justifications, in a regime of pluralism, would never converge towards the potential unanimous consent that Rawls has in mind. Nevertheless, given that we want a social contract based on consent for the right reasons, justification originated by a reasonable comprehensive doctrine is necessary. Justifications, even if they vary, must all presume that free and equal citizens look for fair terms of cooperation among themselves under a regime of reciprocal respect. In such a way, we show how legitimation and justification complement one another in Rawls' general scheme of thought. Moreover, justification comes from the deep roots of a "reasonable" vision, and the idea of the reasonable, as a counterpart to the rational, is a direct consequence of the priority of right.[29] The priority of right could not be defended, however, if we did not accept the premise according to which liberal democracy has no valid alternative. This is why Rawlsian political philosophy is anti-Platonic from the start and why the political thinker must be content to make some shared ideas coherent and fruitful within the public culture of liberal democracy. As a consequence, every hypothetical contract we can imagine is rooted not just in a special content of the agreement but also in the interpersonal relations we can justify through it, providing in so doing a new reasoned consent.

2

THE THEORY

Chapter 2 provides a general presentation of TJ (1971). It goes through several key concepts: the centrality of justice (2.1); the distinction between deontology and teleology (2.1.2); the fundamental notion of basic structure as the primary subject of justice; the Rawlsian version of the social contract (2.1.1); and the distinction between Rawls' theory and other theories such as utilitarianism and intuitionism (2.1.3). My interpretation uses JFR, PL and Rawls' later writings as a guide for how these concepts should be interpreted in TJ.

TJ is divided into three parts: the first is entitled "Theory," the second "Institutions," and the third "Ends." Each part has three chapters. In TJ, even if there are many new issues, Rawls also reformulates ideas already present in articles published since 1958. In the first part, Rawls includes aspects of revised articles such as "Justice as Fairness" (1958) and "Distributive Justice: Some Addenda" (1968). In the second part, we find elements already discussed in "Constitutional Liberty and the Concept of Justice" (1963), "Distributive Justice" (1967), and "Civil Disobedience" (1966). The third part is comparatively the most original, because just one previous article – "The Sense of Justice" (1963) – concerns topics analogous to the ones of TJ. The debate on TJ has focused – at least in the 1970s – on the first part of the book. Only in recent years, due also to Rawls' revisionary attitude towards it, has the third part received the attention it deserves. The second part has almost always been neglected, which has provoked several interpretive mistakes. In particular, one might say that a careful reading of Part II undermines republican criticisms of Rawls, and a careful reading of Part III undermines communitarian criticisms of Rawls. We will come back in more detail to the third part, in chapter 9, analyzing Rawls' reformulation of it in PL.

Within the history of social justice, Rawls' main opponents are perfectionism and utilitarianism. Rawls aims to provide a deontological rather than teleological foundational ground for the principles of justice. In this sense, his inspiration is typically Kantian. Unlike Kant, Rawls centers his theory on institutions rather than individuals. The central idea of the social contract mediates between the deontological and the institutional side of the theory.[1]

2.1 First Part: Theory

The fundamental ideas of TJ are introduced in the first sections of the first chapter. Here, Rawls introduces the role of social justice, the centrality of the basic structure, reflective equilibrium, the importance of the justification in TJ and the contrast with other doctrines such as utilitarianism and intuitionism. The second chapter presents the two principles of justice. Finally, the third chapter – perhaps the most important in the book – introduces the notion of "original position," which underlies to a considerable extent the justification of the principles.

The project of TJ is to propose and defend a liberal and egalitarian conception of social justice. According to Rawls, social justice relates to what he refers to as "basic structure," and the way in which the major social institutions are governed within this context. Justice represents for Rawls the ultimate virtue of social systems, as he tells us at the beginning of the first section of the book in lines that have become famous: "Justice is the first virtue of social institutions as truth is of systems of thought. A theory however elegant and economical must be rejected or revised if it is untrue; likewise, laws and institutions no matter how efficient and well-arranged must be reformed or abolished if they are unjust" (TJ 3; rev. edn.).

Rawls conceives of society as a cooperative venture destined to benefit all its members. Within the context of the general visions of economics, in the major division between those who view labor merely as a production factor to be remunerated depending on its marginal contribution and those who view it as an aspect of a more extensive social cooperation, Rawls falls into the second group.[2] According to him, the remuneration of labor should usually exceed its marginal contribution. Those who are advantaged the most by the cooperative surplus are supposed to indemnify those who are the advantaged given the market results. But even the latter may not push their luck: their advantages depend on a share of the gains of those who are better situated and more endowed. Therefore, even the least advantaged are not interested in causing the gains of the most advantaged to decrease.

This distributive model brings about that type of problem that forms the main subject of a theory of social justice, beginning with that of "fairness." To design a system of institutions that succeeds. in making society "fair" means designing the public bases of a "well-ordered" society. A society is well ordered – according to Rawls –

when it is not only designed to advance the good of its members but when it is also effectively regulated by a public conception of justice. That is it is a society in which (1) everyone accepts and knows that the others accept the same principles of justice, and (2) the basic social institutions generally satisfy and are generally known to satisfy these principles. (TJ 4–5; rev. edn. 4)

If we look at this structure of rules from the perspective of individuals, each individual wants the greatest possible share of the benefits and the lowest share of the costs. A problem of justice originates from the conflict of such claims, a conflict that the members of society experience together with their will to cooperate, given the assumption that social cooperation ensures as a whole the greatest advantages to all. The priority of right – the general significance of which in Rawls' work has already been stressed in the introduction – ensures that all the Rawlsian individuals are willing to sacrifice their personal preferences in the name of respect for the principles of justice capable of justifying a given social order to all the citizens. There are choices that the priority of right does not allow, excluding them a priori from the individual deliberations of all the citizens. From this point of view, the rights that a conception of justice grants to the individuals are not "subject to political bargaining or to the calculus of social interests" (TJ 4; rev. edn.).

In game theory, a problem of distributive justice can take the form that characterizes some *n*-coalitions games. Each coalition prefers to cooperate because the civil society that originates from the social contract is better than the state of nature, but each is unwilling to give up a share of the social goods that it deems to correspond to what it is entitled to according to a criterion of justice. The equilibrium, often called the "core," is attained in this type of game when every coalition believes it has a payoff in terms of resources that is roughly equivalent to its contribution and threat capacity. The difference of this model with respect to Rawls' main thesis in TJ consists in the fact that, for Rawls, the equilibrium is not reached through negotiation but rather through the unanimous conviction that everyone must be able to justify to everybody else, starting from the worst-off, their own advantages in the social distribution of their resources. In a well-ordered society:

> while men may put forward excessive demands on one another, they nevertheless acknowledge a common point of view from which their claims can be adjudicated. If men's inclinations to self-interest makes their vigilance against one another necessary, their public sense of justice makes their secure association together possible. Among individuals with disparate aims and purposes, a shared conception of justice establishes the bonds of civic friendship; the general desire for justice limits the pursuit of other ends. (TJ 4–5; rev. edn.)

A society may aspire to say that it is just when the rights and duties that the major social institutions assign to the individuals are consistent with an idea of fair distribution. The group of the major institutions is the "basic structure," being the main subject of a theory of justice.[3] As Rawls writes in the initial pages of TJ: "For us the primary subject of justice is the basic structure of society, or more exactly, the way in which the major social institutions distribute fundamental rights and duties and determine the division of advantages from social cooperation" (TJ 7; rev. edn. 6).

The concept of basic structure is centrally important both within TJ and throughout Rawls' work.[4] The basic structure is conceived as the way in which the major social institutions work together in assigning rights and duties that arise from social cooperation. The political constitution, legal property, the organization of the economy, the nature of family, belong to the basic structure (PL 258; JFR 10). If the goal of TJ is to find first principles which can provide reasonable guidelines for dealing with the problem of social justice, then it is clear that these principles are not independent from the social practice which the basic structure frames, and in TJ: "There is no attempt to formulate first principles that apply equally to all subjects"[5] (PL 258).

This thesis implies that existing institutions are relevant in formulating a conception of justice. This relevance does not concern only the implementation of a conception of justice. It concerns, also, its fundamental justification. If we accept a basic structure argument *à la* Rawls, then the justification of the first principles of justice depends on the institutional practices it is meant to regulate. Principles of justice like Rawls' do not appeal to independent and primitive moral considerations, but rather to the specific kind of political setting they refer to. From this point of view, the basic structure establishes through its network of institutions – which represents, in the case of Rawls, an interpretation of liberal democracy – a set of political relationships that shape the reasons for and against specific principles of justice.

First of all, the basic structure proves fundamental from the point of view of the attainment of what Rawls calls "background procedural justice."[6] It assures, in other words, that the starting conditions on which a process of just distribution depends are reasonably fair. In addition, even if these conditions are initially fair, they could become not so as a consequence of people's standard relations. For example, the market system can create oligopolies and unjust accumulations. Therefore that basic structure must include special institutions to preserve the auspicated background justice. Here, Rawls grants an initial advantage to what he calls the "ideal historical process view" of Locke and Nozick with respect to the type of social justice supported by utilitarianism. The utilitarians only conceive of an allocative view of justice. Adding to or subtracting from people's holdings, on the allocative view, assumes that one does not need to know how the present situation came about. In so doing, utilitarians fail to understand that, to achieve a just distribution, one has to take into account everybody's contribution to social cooperation. Antecedents matter for distributive justice. At the same time, however, Rawls contrasts the "ideal historical process view" with his "ideal

social process view." The main difference between these two positions consists in the fact that, in evaluating the distributive processes, Rawls' view aims
to consider not only an initial state and the admissible transfers deriving from
it, but also the starting social conditions included among the requirements of
the basic structure that need to underlie any fair agreement.[7] From this point
of view, as he writes: "The kind of limits and provisos that in Locke's vision
apply directly to the separate transactions of individuals and associations in
the state of nature are not sufficient enough to ensure that fair background
conditions are maintained" (JFR 53). This is generally so because the libertarian framework of the "ideal historical process view" tends to systematically
confuse the state with any other private association (PL 264). As a consequence, in this vision there is no public law that applies to all citizens, but just
private interactions. Finally, if utilitarians do not understand the relevance
of the antecedents for distributive justice, libertarians do not understand the
relevance of fair background social conditions.

Justice in distribution is a moral property of states of affairs. Yet the question can be also treated in terms of pure procedural justice. A social system of
cooperation can be conceived of as one of pure procedural justice. The notion
of pure procedural justice is better understood – for Rawls – by comparison
with the notions of perfect and imperfect procedural justice:

- *Perfect procedural justice*: when there is a prior and independent criterion
  for a fair division and we know the procedure needed to get the desired
  outcome (e.g. sharing a cake);
- *Imperfect procedural justice*: when there is an independent criterion for the
  right outcome but the procedure needed to get it is not sure (a fair trial is
  a good example);
- *Pure procedural justice*: when there is not an independent criterion for the
  right outcome, but the procedure can be fair (like in a poker game). Justice
  here depends on actually carrying out the fair procedure.

For Rawls, principles of justice are principles for institutions and not principles for individual conduct. The basic structure of a just society consists of
the institutions to which we delegate the execution of justice's requirements.[8]
With institutions of that kind, people know that justice is sustained independently from how they choose from their spaces of decision. Given the inevitable
constraints of everyday life, the basic structure represents a case of imperfect
procedural justice. The separation of institutional and personal spaces of
decision affords a division of labor. Within this division, the basic structure
comprises the institutions that can provide a proper social background and
keep it immune from the natural tendencies to erode background fairness.
This division in its turn creates the problem of connecting personal lives and
public institutions (see chapter 4, sections 4.3.3 and 4.4.1). A general solution
can be found in a sort of permanent democratic education. More generally,

Rawls maintains that the basic structure will eventually affect individuals (PL 269ff.), because an institutional scheme fashions the sentiments and the desires of people.

Rawls' theory of justice as fairness only addresses those who belong to the same basic structure.[9] Therefore, membership and reciprocity are fundamental to being entitled to have a justification of inequality and, therefore, to be an outright subject within the context of the distributive paradigm in TJ. In other words, the theory of justice as fairness addresses normal persons capable of cooperating most of the time in the attainment of the collective wellbeing in a system of reciprocity. These are the persons who share, by and large throughout their life, a system of major institutions that succeeds in assigning burdens and benefits to them in terms of resources and liberties.[10]

The view has attracted a large body of criticism.[11] This is also the reason why the theory of justice as fairness – presupposing membership and reciprocity – does not apply easily to foreigners or the disabled. Foreigners and the disabled do not normally cooperate in the attainment of collective wellbeing in a regime of reciprocity throughout their life and, therefore, are borderline with respect to the basic structure.[12] No doubt, Rawls' constraint – according to which social justice concerns only the basic structure of a closed system and includes only people within a normal range – is strong. It is, however, mitigated by the general idea that if we succeed within this first constrained domain then we can extend the method to further situations.

More generally, Rawls' basic structure argument seems to be exposed to a fundamental ambiguity. The basic structure is – for Rawls – a necessary condition for attaining social justice. For claims of justice are dependent on a shared scheme of social cooperation in a situation of reciprocity. This presupposition, however, can be interpreted in two opposite ways.[13] Given that the scheme of cooperation I am referring to is assumed to be a "fair" scheme of social interaction, we can draw the conclusion that to have social justice one must confront a society in which we already have this background fairness. In this interpretation, the basic structure argument becomes a very rigid condition and (perversely, in my opinion) implies that demands of justice arise only when social interaction is already conducted on conditions of fairness. There is, however, a less rigid interpretation. This second interpretation maintains that the existence condition of the basic structure does not imply the fairness of social interactions as a pre-existing datum. In this second interpretation, any scheme of cooperation still requires a basic structure as a condition of justice, but we do not need to assume that social interaction is fair before demands of justice arise. I think this second interpretation is more plausible, making exclusions dictated by the basic structure argument less severe.

A different type of fault in the debate over the basic structure – a fault that has been extensively criticized[14] – is the lack of any treatment in TJ of issues related to gender difference. The family – as upheld by Rawls' critics – is unquestionably one of the most important social institutions and, therefore, the very idea of starting from the basic structure should really have made a discussion of justice inside the family easier. Besides, since Rawls was personally sensitive to the issue of women's rights, its exclusion from TJ appears even more strange. Afterwards, Rawls endeavored to answer these criticisms. His main attempts are in section 50 of JFR (162–8) and in section 5 of IPRR. In these two works, Rawls' thesis is almost the same, to the degree that we might claim one repeats the other, concept by concept. The most significant differences between the two works consist in two passages of IPRR (not present in JFR), passages devoted to the role of religion as a factor favoring the voluntary choice of a division of labor between sexes and to the role of parents as educators. The main thesis in both works is that: (i) the family is an important part of the basic structure; (ii) its main role consists in the raising of and caring for children, ensuring their moral development and education within a wider culture; (iii) in such a way, the family favors the formation of a sense of justice in its future citizens; (iv) being part of the basic structure implies that the family is limited by its constraints, beginning with the effort to achieve equality of opportunity; (v) principles of justice do not apply directly to the family (and to many other associations); (vi) it is a "misconception" to think that (v) implies there is no equal justice for women and children, given that lack of direct application corresponds to the imposition of essential constraints; (vii) there is a distinction between the point of view of people as citizens and as members of the family; (viii) however, the political and the non-political domain are not fully separated spheres; (ix) the traditional gender-based division of labor is felt by many as unjust, but political liberalism cannot say that such a division is forbidden because it is connected with freedom of choice; (x) democracy aims for equality of all citizens and must include arrangements to achieve it, but even what these arrangements are in particular historical situations is not for political philosophy to decide; and (xi) the problem then becomes whether and to what extent the constraints of the principles of justice can mitigate the unequal consequences of gendered structured institutions.

Indeed, this argument does not directly challenge the philosophical ground of the feminist criticism raised against Rawlsian liberalism. The philosophical targets of feminist criticism across the years have been mainly the following:

(i)   The methodological approach implicit in TJ – based on abstraction, universalism, and individualism – does not take into consideration the relational side implicit in the ethics of care. The original position, and in particular the veil of ignorance (see chapter 5), would be unable to represent real experiences of women, and thus would also render their way of reasoning incompetent.

(ii) The Rawlsian type of reasoning cannot challenge the traditional "sexist" system of power.[15]

I do not see the first of these two critical arguments as being particularly compelling. It implies two controversial consequences. The first is that the relational aspect of the ethics of care is correct from a moral-political point of view, which is intrinsically doubtful. As many critics of Gilligan have shown in recent years, not all women are care-takers or, more generally, contextual thinkers.[16] Moreover, this same criticism implies that one cannot derive a relational ethics of care from Rawls' apparatus. It is hard to draw this conclusion if one carefully reads TJ and in particular its Part III. The original position and the veil of ignorance are not meant to address the whole moral and political life of individuals but rather the part of it connected with a model for generating principles of justice. That is why one cannot say that the original position, as a device of representation, excludes people reasoning coherently within the model of the care. If something like this happens in practice, I suspect, it cannot be evaluated *in abstracto* independently from concrete practices.

The second feminist type of criticism is probably more compelling, namely that the Rawlsian vision is unable to challenge a traditional sexist system of power. In fact, Rawls' moderate approach to gender, as evident both in JFR and IPRR, never treats gender as part of a system of power but rather as a way towards an identity which people are supposed to leave behind when they begin to discuss topics of justice. The idea itself, often stated in TJ, according to which the parties in the original positions are "heads of families" (128, n. 4; rev. edn. 111 n.4), does not directly exclude women but it seems clear that the representative persons Rawls has in mind are typically "fathers" (TJ 289). This characterization is unacceptable to many feminist points of view for two complementary reasons: (i) male heads of households (TJ 289; rev. edn. 255–6) are not necessarily the most fair representatives of the community; and (ii) it becomes difficult, starting with Rawls' approach, to investigate family life from the point of view of justice.

On this matter, Rawls' defensive thesis, which partly takes up Susan Moller Okin's[17] arguments, is that the theory of justice as fairness does not address the problem directly but, in any event, its "conceptions and principles should be widely applicable to our own [namely gender] problem." In fact, heads of households could be both males and females, and it is plausible to maintain (with Okin) that Rawls' view of justice implicitly requires a genderless and not sexist society, helping in such a way also to sketch the bases of an egalitarian family life. In LoP, Rawls briefly tackles the question once again in an interesting manner, affirming that the status of women and their treatment should be a part of human rights.

This second feminist critique of Rawls can be also presented in another way. If one could look at Rawls' basic structure following a purely legal or coercive interpretation of it, then a sexist personal relationship could be perfectly consistent with a sex-neutral family law and institutional setting. In other words, the consequences of socially constructed expectations

– concerning gender – could be at odds with a decent idea of justice, notwithstanding an innocent basic structure. This sophisticated criticism, however, depends on a controversial reading of the notion of basic structure and on a difficult general argument against Rawls' theory of justice (we will go back to it in section 4.4.1).

2.1.1 Social justice and contractualism

In TJ, a problem of justice may only be dealt with seriously if the implicit conflict in the plurality of interests of the social parties could be overcome in the name of a collectively appealing agreement. Explaining the reasons that warrant this fundamental consensus is the main purpose of a Rawlsian conception of justice: "A conception of social justice, then, is to be regarded as providing in the first instance a standard whereby the distributive aspects of the basic structure of society are to be assessed" (rev. edn. 8, slightly different from TJ 9).

Such a conception of justice has a relatively modest domain. It does not concern all the virtues of living together, as a "social ideal" may, but only relates to a unanimous criterion of moral evaluation for the institutions. Even within these limits, it aims at a specific type of agreement. Rawls bases this agreement on the idea of social contract. In fact, in TJ, Rawls dusts off the traditional but also partly discredited analytical tool of the social contract in order to formulate his hypothesis on the universal justification of the basic structure.[18] As he writes in the third section of TJ, drawing a distinction between his specific position and the contractualist classical tradition: "the guiding idea is that the principles of justice for the basic structure of society are the object of the original agreement. They are the principles that free and rational persons concerned to further their own interests would accept in an initial position of equality as defining the fundamental terms of their association" (TJ 11; rev. edn. 10).

In the modern age, the concept of social contract was – for authors like Hobbes, Locke, Rousseau, and Kant – the innermost core of what political philosophers usually call a theory of political obligation. Substantially, a contractualist theory consists in a justification of political authority. Such a justification endeavors to explain why and within what limits the citizens are obliged to comply with given norms that, in their turn, depend on the system of institutions. The justificatory strategy, more or less explicit in classical contractualism (as in Hobbes and Locke), consists in assuming a "state of nature," highlighting the difficulties that human beings would find in living together in the absence of a political society. From this perspective, the contract marks the beginning of the political society, with the merits connected with it, and consequently the acceptance of the political obligation.

There is a remarkable difference between at least two distinct ways of conceiving the social contract.[19] According to the first, the central idea of which may be attributed to Hobbes, the social contract does not depend on moral rights. Rather, it must guarantee the fundamental objective of attaining lasting conditions of peace and reciprocal advantage among the parties. According to the second, which is upheld by Rawls (but also by Locke, Rousseau, and Kant), the social contract partially depends on pre-existent moral claims.[20] On this account, the second version must add to the political obligation theory, which explains why the authority of the state exists, a legitimation theory based on the consent of the citizens. The failure to distinguish between these two models of social contract can be deeply misleading.[21]

In a more primitive version of the contract theory, the state of nature and the social pact have a meaning that is not merely metaphorical but historical or, in any event, realistic. However, after Hume's criticism,[22] what is stressed is the hypothetical and virtual character of the contract itself, as a thought experiment. This is clear in the tradition that goes from Kant to Rawls. In this later version of contractualism, political obligations depend on imagining a merely hypothetical initial situation in order to set up against it the civil society and the origination of ethical-political constraints. The social contract is then a success if every citizen can recognize its underlying reasons and undertakes to accept its constraints.[23]

If a justice problem consists for the most part in finding an agreement on conflicting distributive claims, then any actual agreement that may be reached will be initially affected by the bargaining strength of the parties. In this regard, it is easy to believe that there is no previously conceivable point of equilibrium and, even if there were one, it would not necessarily correspond to a just agreement. In his article "Justice as Fairness" of 1958, which is usually identified as the beginning of the Rawlsian reasoning on social justice leading to TJ, Rawls confined himself to suggesting that the contracting parties to the social pact were "sufficiently equal in power and ability to guarantee that . . . none dominate the others" (JFR 138).

In TJ, this initial suggestion turns into a bold analytical construction that reaches its peak in the so-called "original position":

> In the theory of justice as fairness, the original position of equality corresponds to the state of nature in the traditional theory of the social contract . . . Among the essential features of this situation is that no one knows his place in society, his class position or social status, nor does any one know his fortune in the distribution of natural assets and abilities, his intelligence, strength, and the like. I shall even assume that the parties do not know their conceptions of the good or their special psychological propensities. The principles of justice are chosen behind a veil of ignorance. (TJ 12; rev. edn. 11)

According to Rawls, the original position is an indispensable tool to reach a "fair" agreement that, after all, is the only one capable of guaranteeing a "firm commitment in advance." It is a purely hypothetical construction with a specific analytical function. Therefore, from this point of view, the original position has little in common with the state of nature of the classical doctrines of the social contract from which, nonetheless, it draws its inspiration.

2.1.2 Contractualism as an alternative to utilitarianism

Contractualism represents – for Rawls – a feasible alternative to the political and moral theory of utilitarianism: "My aim is to work out a theory of justice that represents an alternative to utilitarian thought generally and so to all different versions of it." (TJ 22).

Rawls' intellectual relationship with utilitarianism is complicated.[24] Rawls knew the classical works of Hume, J. S. Mill, and Sidgwick, respecting them so much as to be also considerably affected by their work. Indeed, for some time, Rawls had even been considered an advocate of rule-utilitarianism.[25] He had written prior to TJ an article that, on the whole, defended it,[26] at least against the criticism he considered simplistic after the manner of W. D. Ross.[27] In TJ, Rawls turned into a systematic critic of utilitarianism. However, the contradiction between the two views on utilitarianism is merely apparent. According to Rawls, the greatest merit of utilitarianism is its ability to provide a complete arrangement of our choices in matters of social justice. Its worst fault is represented by the fact that utilitarianism selects a dominant end, for instance the attainment of pleasure in its hedonistic version, and aims to maximize the overall attainment of that end.[28] Rawls considers any dominant end theory irrationally illiberal: it basically deprives the person of her real interests putting her at the service of a previously given end and, for similar reasons, it sacrifices individuals' values for the sake of collective values.

Now, it should be noted that, prior to Rawls, similar objections to utilitarianism had already been raised. These criticisms range from Ross' intuitionism to those closer to Rawls, which might be called pluralist objections, raised by Brian Barry or Nicholas Rescher. Rawls himself in his thesis insisted on the separateness of the persons within the "I–thou" relation (BIMSF 116–17). Criticisms such as those voiced by Ross, Barry,[29] or Rescher[30] recognize that utilitarianism has several qualities, but add that it lacks certain required features, ranging from loyalty and sincerity to equality. Such criticisms also claim that, when these characteristics conflict with the utility principle, they usually ought to get the upper hand. Rawls often considers these objections sensible, but incapable of providing a systematic alternative to utilitarianism.[31] The intuitionist objections, for instance, lead to a pluralism without solutions, which tends to replace some faults of utilitarianism with a radical incapacity to make decisions. A similar thesis is confirmed, from the point of view of distributive shares, in TJ section 49, devoted to the "mixed conceptions" (which, for instance, accept the first principle of justice, but not the second one). According to Rawls, the fault of the mixed conceptions is not that they are actually wrong, but that they propose alternative solutions that are unable to replace utilitarianism in full.

These are the reasons why Rawls formulated in TJ – and subsequently refined (in the second half of the 1970s) – a Kantian hypothesis that systematically opposes the utilitarian foundation. In so doing, Rawls meant to avoid what he saw as the most evident defects of a deontological critique inspired by intuitionism or pluralism, meaning the provision of rules of conduct that are not consistent one with the other and that are often based merely on intuitions. According to Rawls, a theory of justice should be endorsed neither in order to ensure a given social result inspired by a dominant end, as might be the maximization of the collective utility, nor on a purely deontological intuition. Rather, one endorses it because there are "good reasons," on which the primacy of justification is based. In TJ, these good reasons explain why the parties in the original position reach a fair agreement to govern mutual relations. Rawls himself said, reconsidering the initial ideal formulations of his theory, that he was reminded of the philosophical climate of the beginning of the 1950s.[32]

Rawls' good reasons approach relies on a deontological concern, as opposed to a teleological concern. The interpretation of the teleological vision and its relation to Rawls' deontological vision is quite peculiar. For Rawls, a teleological theory of justice favors the thesis according to which the right consists merely in the maximization of the good. This is a standard definition, but Rawls adds that a teleological vision defines the good independently of the right (TJ 24; rev. edn. 21–2). A deontological theory is then defined specifically as one that is not teleological. Note that the difference from utilitarianism, as a teleological doctrine, does not lie in the first part of the definition of teleology, namely consequentialism, but in the second part. Rawls, in other words, is not a pure anti-consequentialist.[33] Even rejecting any kind of maximizing criterion, he believes that it is impossible to separate a theory of justice from the fact that positive consequences from the point of view of a conception of the good must derive from it.[34] The third part of TJ dwells for a few dozen pages on this point. Rawls' criticism addresses the idea of the possibility of a sensible conception of justice where the good is defined independently from the right. The concept of the good must not fail – according to Rawls – to be preceded and constrained by a public criterion of the right, for instance a "fairness" criterion.

Rawls' criticism of teleology reads: "It is essential to keep in mind that in a teleological theory the good is defined independently from the right . . . [so] the [teleological] theory enables one to judge the goodness of things without referring to what is right . . . The problem of distribution falls instead under the concept of right as one intuitively understands it" (rev. edn. 22, slightly different from TJ 25).

The criticism of teleology and the preference for a deontological position expressed by Rawls in TJ are related to the priority of right, but are not the same thing. The teleological–deontological distinction concerns the relationship between the concepts of the good and the right. Instead, the priority of right sets the constraints that – in the name of social justice – individuals need to comply with before deliberating in the light of their own preferences. Furthermore, accepting the priority of right requires a more sophisticated view of the motivational aspects of the theory.[35] After all, while it is easy to understand that one is motivated by the pursuit of what is good for oneself, it is harder to understand why one should be so motivated in the light of a social ideal of justice. This fact explains some of the complications that Rawls had to address initially in the last chapter of TJ and subsequently in PL.

In TJ, Rawls opposes both perfectionism and utilitarianism in the name of pluralism and individual rights. According to him, perfectionism intends "to arrange institutions and to define the duties and obligations of individuals so as to maximize the achievement of human excellence in art, science and culture" (TJ; rev. edn. 285–6).

Perfectionist theories have a teleological structure. From this point of view, social institutions are designed to obtain what is deemed a prevailing objective. This vision engenders, according to Rawls, problems for individual liberty, because there are different versions of what is good or excellent. Indeed, this is the reason why Rawls refuses perfectionism at the political level. A perfectionist state would not allow its citizens to choose their own conception of the good in agreement with the interests and the wishes of each one of them. Later on, Rawls will explicitly uphold that liberal-democratic political institutions are "freestanding," meaning independent, and, just on this account, they belong to all the citizens. Therefore, a liberal democracy cannot impose a specific vision of the good on its institutions.

Rawls' substantive criticism of utilitarianism is somewhat similar. For Rawls, utilitarianism unduly generalizes from the impersonal to the interpersonal case and therefore pays no heed to the "separateness" of the persons (TJ 27; rev. edn. 23). For this reason, utilitarianism cannot have, other than indirectly, a distributive view and, therefore, an actual theory of justice: "The striking feature of the utilitarian view of justice is that, it does not matter, except indirectly, how this sum of the satisfactions is distributed among the individuals" (rev. edn. 23, slightly different from TJ 26).

On the contrary, it is indeed this distributive and deontological aspect that matters for Rawls. As far as I am concerned, I could decide without problems to sacrifice my current wellbeing in the name of a long-term project, but it would be more difficult to require people to sacrifice their present happiness in the name of the future happiness of society as a whole or of some of its members. In the first case, the trade-off is internal to my person and I have every right to make it. In the second case, it instead affects the lives of different persons and we are not entitled to make it on their behalf. What is justified inside a life may be unacceptable across lives. In this case, the attack on teleology is a corollary of a principle of respect for the separateness of the persons. The utilitarians do not take this into account, because:

This [the utilitarian] view of social cooperation is the consequence of extending to society the principle of choice for one man and then, to make this extension work, conflating all persons into one through the imaginative acts of the impartial sympathetic spectator. *Utilitarianism does not take seriously the distinction between persons.* (rev. edn. 24, slightly different from TJ 27, emphasis mine)

Contrary to what Rawls says, Kymlicka[36] suggests utilitarianism is better interpreted as a doctrine that initially assumes a principle of equal consideration of interests – central from Bentham to Singer – and only later advocates a sort of maximization. This reading, however, would not pose a problem because – in view of Rawls' definition of teleology – this interpretation of utilitarianism would not be a teleological doctrine. It would be instead a deontological doctrine and being so could not accept improper sacrifices as utilitarianism does.

2.1.3 Fairness and principles of justice

After his article on "Distributive Justice" of 1967 and in a more clear-cut manner in TJ, Rawls asserted that the most important condition for constructing his original position consists in the so-called "veil of ignorance." It is a hypothesis according to which the contracting parties lack information concerning their specific lives and the actual condition of the society in which they live. The veil of ignorance aims to ensure impartiality. From this point of view, it constitutes a link between the deontological grounds of the theory and its institutional consequences, providing a fair basis for a neutral procedure.

While the veil of ignorance deprives the parties in the original position of some knowledge, it does not deprive them of all knowledge. Indeed, Rawls believes that they have sufficient information to succeed in formulating a hypothesis concerning the "basic structure" of society. It is important to consider that, in this type of decision, the parties must choose not general moral rules but institutional rules that exclusively concern the distribution of "primary goods." The possession of these primary social goods is necessary to obtain any end one wants in life. Hence, even behind the veil of ignorance, one may understand the importance of these goods and the need to divide them fairly, according to principles of justice. Just on this account, Rawls speaks of "justice as fairness": "These principles are to regulate all further agreements; they specify the kinds of social cooperation that can be entered into and the forms of government that can be established. This way of regarding the principles of justice I shall call justice as fairness" (TJ 11; rev. edn. 10).

According to this hypothesis, Rawls argues that the parties would choose a special conception of justice based on the two principles outlined below (which I quote here from a version subsequent to TJ):

[1] Each person has an equal claim to a fully adequate scheme of equal basic rights and liberties, which scheme is compatible with the same scheme for all; and in this scheme the equal political liberties, and only those liberties, are to be guaranteed their fair value. (PL 5)

[2] Social and economic inequalities are to satisfy two conditions: [a] first, they are to be attached to positions and offices open to all under conditions of fair equality of opportunity; and [b] second, they are to be to the greatest benefit of the least advantaged members of society. (PL 6; JFR 42–3)

Rawls claims that the first principle takes priority over the second, meaning that it is not possible to sacrifice freedom in the name of other primary social goods. Moreover, the first part of the second principle (2a) is given priority over the second part (2b). Equality of opportunity may not be traded-off for greater amounts of primary social goods for the least advantaged.

There is also a relationship in TJ between the special conception of justice, based on the two principles, and a "general" conception of justice, which Rawls defines as follows: "All social goods – liberty and opportunity, income and wealth, and the bases of self-respect – are to be distributed equally unless an unequal distribution of any or all of these goods is to the advantage of the least favored" (TJ 62; rev. edn. 54).

It is not clear in what specific manner the general conception relates to the thesis in favor of the two principles. Certainly, the general conception looks like the difference principle (the second part of the second principle) and, somehow, inspires it and depends on it. It can be considered, in this regard, as a generalization of a principle of equality. On the other hand, we know little about the relationship between the general conception and the first principle of justice. In any event – maybe even on account of this partial obscurity – the general conception is considerably toned down in the second revised edition of TJ (see chapter 8).

The general conception results from the original position by applying to such a position the rule of the decision under uncertainty called "maximin." Even the two principles of justice, in which the special conception consists, and the original position from which it derives, are comparable to a situation of choice solvable in terms of maximin (see later chapter 5). This hypothesis in terms of the theory of rational choice, which contributes to creating one of the innovative aspects of TJ with respect to the traditional versions of the social contract, was critically debated and finally withdrawn by Rawls (at least, in its more direct and explicit form).

A theory of justice needs a structure able to establish priorities between imperatives that may conflict with each other in order to single out its conception from any other conception that criticizes utilitarianism on typically intuitionist grounds. As some utilitarian positions on social distribution appear to be counterintuitive, a normal way of opposing them consists in appealing to moral intuitions. And Rawls recognizes that:

No doubt, any conception of justice will have to rely on intuition to some degree. Nevertheless, we should do what we can to reduce the direct appeal to our considered judgments. For if men balance final principles differently, as presumably they often do, find their conceptions of justice are different . . . An intuitionist conception of justice is, one might say, only a half conception. (rev. edn. 36–7, slightly different from TJ 41)

The need for priority among the principles of justice comes from this necessity of avoiding the most evident stalemates linked to an intuitionist conception.[37] The latter conception is interpreted and criticized in a peculiar manner by Rawls. Generally, the central problem of intuitionism is conceived as an epistemological difficulty. It is hard to believe that there is a list of intuitive values shared by all and there is no guarantee that an appeal to intuitions might offer a reliable tool of knowledge. Instead, Rawls believes that the chief difficulty for intuitionism concerns its decision-making, rather than its epistemic, nature. Hence, in an unusual manner, Rawls presents intuitionism as "a doctrine that there is an irreducible family of first principles, which have to be weighed against one another by asking ourselves which balance, in our considered judgment, is the most just" (rev. edn. 30, slightly different from TJ 34).

Given this presentation of intuitionism, it ensues that such a doctrine does not provide for constructive criteria that impose priorities among principles of justice with an alternative content (to utilitarianism). Intuitionism, in other words, fails to provide a decision-making procedure because it cannot reconcile either the case in which we consider the conflicting intuitions of different people, or when we have the same conflict within ourselves. Hence, Rawls is looking for a doctrine that is not utilitarianism and escapes the decision-making difficulty facing intuitionism. In his opinion, the two principles of justice, with their relative priorities, satisfy this demand.

2.2 Second Part: Institutions

In the second part of TJ, Rawls poses the problem of what laws and institutions support a plausible attainment of the principles of justice. By institutions we mean both the political ones, such as the constitution and parliament, and the economic ones. Rawls' prevailing interest in TJ is in an "ideal" theory characterized by what he calls "strict compliance," rather than in a theory coping with real (non-ideal) situations even from an institutional point of view. However, there are unquestionably important aspects of the work in the fourth chapter, devoted to "equal liberty" (we will debate this also in the next chapter), which emphasize the likely institutional applications of the theory, for instance when the so-called "four-stage sequence" is formulated. Then, the fifth chapter, entitled "Distributive Shares," presents the problem of justice between generations – which will become a standard topic of debate after Rawls – and the controversial thesis according to which individual merit substantially depends on the institutional system. Finally, the sixth chapter on "Duty and Obligation" includes, within the context of a treatment of individual duties, two extraordinary final sections on civil disobedience and conscientious objection. In them, Rawls interprets the protest, properly understood, as a contribution to the proper working of a liberal democracy. In these cases, one starts from the political obligation that requires compliance with the law in cases of relative justice. However, individual duties require individuals to do their part and, at times, these duties also suggest the possibility of infringing the law, giving rise to conflicting natural duties.

2.2.1 Institutionalization of the principles of justice

The difference from intuitionism explains why the theory of justice as fairness has greater possibilities for having institutional applications, such as those imagined in the second part of TJ. However, Rawls recognizes – given the vagueness of the theory – that the principles of justice cannot be realized in an actual state. As regards this subject, Rawls happens to say in an Olympian manner: "This indeterminacy in the theory of justice is not a defect. Indeed it is what we should expect" (TJ 201; rev. edn. 176).

The actual form of the institutions will be democratically decided by the people, and this is the reason why a few of Rawls' critics (among them Habermas and some republicans), had they read the second part of TJ more carefully, would have avoided saying that his model lacks space for deliberation. Ultimately, there is in TJ a sort of necessary mediation between the indicative capacity of the principles of justice and their actual implementation in a democratic regime through the people's will.

The four-stage sequence imagined by Rawls exemplifies this mediation. The first stage is the original position, which culminates with the declaration of the two principles of justice. However, three other stages are needed before the effects of the principles succeed in affecting the lives of the people directly. The second stage has as its object the formation and the working of a just constitution. The third stage relates to the ability of the legislative bodies to formulate plausibly just laws. The fourth stage relates to the judicial and legislative application of the laws to the citizens. It is only natural that this application hypothesis – presented in chapter 4 of TJ – is extremely vague. It is certainly hard to imagine that our rulers might make a real effort to apply to real cases such abstract and complicated rules as Rawls' principles of justice.

Having left the first stage behind, the veil of ignorance lifts gradually and this fact entails that the decision-makers, this time persons in the flesh rather than imaginary parties to the agreement, are exposed to greater information in the three subsequent stages. This change seems to imply a certain relativism in the application of the principles, in the sense that different cultures and institutional structures would probably apply them in a different manner. The vagueness that characterizes the entire four-stage sequence poses the problem of the relationship between the two principles and the four stages. There seems to be a certain affinity between the first principle and the constitutional stage, as well as between the second principle and the other two stages – the legislative and the judicial-administrative ones. In other words, in order to implement the difference principle, one would need greater information and political-institutional activity. The consequence of this would be that the second principle of justice is not a constitutional matter. As we shall see later on, in PL Rawls defends this thesis, which is not explicit in TJ.

The vagueness encountered in concrete application of the principles of justice sometimes reaches extraordinary levels. In TJ, Rawls claims that the theory of justice as fairness is unable even to choose between capitalism and socialism. In any event, socialism and the market are not incompatible for Rawls, given that by socialism he means only the public ownership of the means of production. In this case, Rawls follows J. S. Mill in accepting a clear-cut distinction between allocation and distribution of resources.[38] However, as was said at the beginning of this volume, there is nonetheless the impression that Rawls confines himself to thinking that the principles of justice are compatible with a market economy.

After TJ (roughly from the mid-1970s), its economic-political model became more complex and took the more specific form of what Rawls calls "property-owning democracy," in its turn preferred to a liberal-socialist regime (which acts as second optimum), gradually replacing the initial generic propensity for the welfare state.[39] As Rawls says in JFR and in the introduction to the revised edition of TJ written in 1975 (from which I am quoting): "To see the full force of the difference principle, it should be taken in the context of a property owning democracy (or of a liberal-socialist regime) and not a welfare state: it is a principle of reciprocity, of mutuality for society seen as a fair system of cooperation between free and equal citizens" (TJ; rev. edn. xv).

The impression is that property-owning democracy (and liberal socialism directly afterwards) is preferred to the welfare state for two reasons: (i) it puts economic power in the hands of the citizens rather than in those of the rulers, as the welfare state would instead do; (ii) it allows less inequality between the rich and the poor. According to Rawls, economic resources and their distribution are never ends in themselves. They are always at the service of a collective agreement that makes all citizens independent, from the ethical-political point of view.

Then, in the second part of the fifth chapter, Rawls analytically specifies the difference between his theory of justice, with its priorities listed in section 46, and any form of intuitionism or mixed conception. This difference is expressed in a particularly clear and convincing manner in sections 47 and 48, on "The Precepts of Justice" and "Legitimate Expectations and Moral

Desert," respectively. Here Rawls stresses the constantly subordinated and often contradictory character of the commonsense maxims of justice. This makes some higher-level principle indispensable (TJ 304; rev. edn. 268). Commonsense maxims, such as those that deem it right to assign goods to each individual in relation to the effort made, the risks run and even the contribution given to the total product, appear vague and dependent on circumstances.[40] Only a prior definition of principles of justice and priority rules, such as those upheld by Rawls, within the context of a given basic structure, explains how to understand their content. As specified in section 48, a distribution based on desert or virtue would be senseless if one fails to specify beforehand the sense of entitlements and legitimate expectations. In general, the concept of moral value has no direct distributive consequences (TJ 312; rev edn. 275). These assertions do not imply that the intuitionist theses on distribution have no content. They only imply that their value may be corrective at the most, should the outcome of the principles of justice lead to consequences that clearly prove counterintuitive.

Rawls' remarks about desert in section 48 are particularly interesting. His central thesis, which is counterintuitive from a liberal point of view, would seem to uphold that desert has no independent moral significance within the theory of justice as fairness. At the most, it would have a secondary or derivative value. It would be up to just institutions to determine the meaning and the value of legitimate expectations that, in the last analysis, would take the place usually attributed to desert. It would be senseless – from this point of view – to talk about desert in purely "pre-institutional" terms. Obviously, such a thesis would have a questionable impact on Rawls' conception of justice which would be considered anti-meritocratic. In fact, the moral concept of "desert" is usually believed to differ from the institutional concept of "entitlement," with the former having a positive critical meaning with respect to any institutional system.[41]

There is consequently the problem of getting desert and entitlement mixed up: a male worker may get higher wages than a female worker for the same amount of work. This, however, does not mean that the male deserves more even though, in a specific contract of employment, the male worker's expectation of getting higher wages may be considered legitimate. It is indeed the distinction between the two concepts that allows for criticizing an institutional system that permits a methodical cleavage between legitimate expectations and desert. This shows how relevant it is, from a critical point of view, to grant space to desert.[42] I believe that Rawls may be defended on this subject in two different manners.

First, Rawls does not support a purely institutionalist thesis on the nature of desert. This also applies to section 17 of TJ, when he defends the difference principle and the institutionalist approach. Here, Rawls basically says that he who obtains greater advantages may rightly claim to be entitled to these advantages, but not to have a special desert linked, for instance, to his natural talent which allows him to have the advantages under consideration. This is due to the fact that no one deserves having the talent that he has, since he is endowed with it by nature (see section 4.3.3). However, it does not mean that Rawls' thesis endorses an institutionalist view of desert in full.[43] On one hand, in section 48 of TJ, where Rawls debates the question at length, he admits that there is a desert from the point of view of retributive justice: an offender may deserve punishment. Therefore, there are cases where desert has a pre-institutional meaning. On the other hand, the relationship established by Rawls between desert and legitimate expectations does not fully rule out that the latter are in their turn connected with some form of desert conceived in a more traditional manner. It is, rather, possible to say that, for Rawls, desert cannot go against the sense of justice but this does not mean that it must be conceived entirely in an institutionalist manner.

Second, I believe that we must never forget the highly idealized nature of the Rawlsian proposal. We are within the context of an ideal theory in a regime of strict compliance. This implies that the institutions we are dealing with are fair. In consequence, the legitimate expectations that depend on them may not go against desert. The two different wages of the preceding example would instead presuppose an unfair institutional system where discrepancies are based on gender difference. Put differently, it is as if Rawls were to say, "a comparative desert evaluation would be meaningful if and only if everyone were to have real equal opportunities in a community where respect for all, under conditions of substantial fairness, prevailed."[44] In short, one might argue that, in the light of these assumptions by Rawls, there is no special need of the concept of desert in order to criticize institutions.

In the second part of TJ (chapter 5), Rawls considers how his theory responds to the problem of the future generations, a theme that after TJ has become a recurring subject in the international literature. The intergenerational justice issue concerns the way in which today's generations decide in the name and on behalf of those of tomorrow. Every generation, from this point of view, must take care not only to guarantee the benefits ensured by the difference principle for its current members, but also to ensure a similar treatment for future generations. They may do so, for example, by regularly putting aside real capital shares. Here, Rawls' theory faces a specific problem: while utilitarianism runs the risk of earmarking too much, so maximizing utility across many generations at the expense of the present generation, the parties in the original position run the opposite risk of favoring the generation they know they belong to. To avoid such an outcome, Rawls tries to find what he calls "a just savings principle." Rawls' contractualist theory looks at the problem from the perspective of the original position and requests the parties to decide based on an appropriate just savings principle. The problem arises when the parties know which generation they belong to, even if they ignore the type of society to which they belong (whether it is prevailingly agricultural or industrial, for instance). The solution proposed by Rawls –

under these constraints – is based on two assumptions: (i) that the parties represent family lines, which are at least concerned about their more direct descendants; (ii) that the parties would have liked the past generations to have decided in a way similar to the way they are about to decide. These assumptions, together with the veil of ignorance, should guarantee that each generation takes all the other generations into account. In any event, the limits of the just savings principle cannot be fixed with any accuracy, because much depends on the concrete circumstances in which the agreement takes place. Even so, it should guarantee a certain consistency between the principles of justice and intergenerational relations.

2.2.2 Principles for individuals

Rawls' two principles of justice apply to institutions. This is a consequence of the "purely procedural" nature of Rawlsian contractualism and the selection of the basic structure as the primary subject of the theory. This leaves unsolved the problem of how, in the original position, the principles that concern individuals should be shaped. It is worth remembering that Rawls has chosen an ideal theory with an assumption of "strict compliance." Generally speaking, Rawls assumes that the state endorses the principles of justice, the laws are all just, and everyone complies with them. It is a particularly demanding choice. In fact, it is clear that many of the most important problems that real people have to cope with usually fit within a situation of merely partial compliance. We are dealing, for instance, with problems that are often handled by criminal law and international justice. However, Rawls believes that without the premise of an ideal theory there is no consistent way to decide in real cases.

We are here in the presence of a robust idealization. It consistently presupposes natural duties and strict obligations from the point of view of the behavior of individuals: chiefly, the obligation to abide by the law. As Rawls says: "From the standpoint of the theory of justice, the most important natural duty is that to support and to further just institutions" (TJ 34; rev. edn. 293).

However, as shown by chapter VII in TJ, Rawls is willing to make exceptions to such a rigid moral and institutional geometry. Even if citizens have an initial duty to abide by an unjust law (TJ, section 53), there will be interesting cases where individuals will be able to suspend their strict compliance obligation.[45] Somehow, when dealing with the principles for individuals, we meet some of the uncertainty which Rawls identified in intuitionism. If the major problem of the intuitionists is the creation of controversial cases and the generation of uncertainty in the domain of pure theory, now something similar is happening to Rawls at a lower and applied level. At any rate, it is quite likely that this difference is not devoid of intellectual advantages given that Rawls – in so doing – guarantees greater theoretical rigor. At the same time, he may avoid adopting the extremist position in which all the citizens must abide by all the laws in all cases.[46]

The method for deriving principles for individuals is the same as that used to derive those for the institutions: by means of the original position. In the case of the principles for individuals we have, however, already opted for the two principles of justice and we are aware of this fact. The natural duties have a variety of sources, but the primary source of the obligations is the so-called "principle of fairness" (in chapter II, section 18), according to which any individual needs to: "do his part as defined by the rules of an institution when . . . first the institution is just (or fair), that is, it satisfies the two principles of justice; and second, one has voluntarily accepted the benefits of the arrangement or taken advantage of the opportunities it offers" (TJ 111; rev. edn. 96).

The obligations resulting from the principle of fairness are stricter than the general natural duty to comply with the law. What ensues is a political obligation consistent with a strict application of contractualism. But – as Rawls affirms in both chapters II and V – such obligations apply in a partial manner. They do not apply to those who do not enjoy in full the legal and practical advantages that should result from an accurate and comprehensive application of the principles. In these cases, the principle of fairness, with the obligations that result from it, comes to nothing and what remains is just the natural duty. This opens space within which the citizens are allowed a more elastic attitude and, therefore, are able to escape the absurdity previously referred to whereby everyone complies with everything.

The sections on civil disobedience and conscientious objection (TJ, sections 55, 56, 57, 58, 59) exemplify this space where individuals have the freedom to make decisions. Rawls claims that providing specific rules controlling the recourse to civil disobedience and conscientious objection would be impossible. Instead, he formulates some general conditions of admissibility. For civil disobedience, he lists a few that would make it at least reasonable. It must be limited to protest against "instances of substantial and clear injustice" or against "serious infringements . . . of the principle of equal liberty" (TJ 373; rev. edn. 326). Before resorting to it, the protestors should exhaust all avenues of legal recourse and, in any case, the recourse to such a protest must be rare. A similar argument applies to "conscientious refusal" which usually has a moral nature as against the political nature that characterizes civil disobedience. In this case, Rawls is clearly thinking about the resistance of the American youth to the Vietnam War, an example that allows him to outline a few general principles of a "law of nations," to which we shall return in chapter 12.

2.3 Third Part: Ends

In the third part of TJ, the seventh chapter focuses on Rawls' theory of the good, a theory that had already been partially used to specify the nature of the primary goods and the interests of the parties in the original position. The theory of the good is divided into two parts: a "thin" theory and a "full" theory. Rawls' theory of the good is founded on the idea that a person's good depends on his individual choices in full deliberative rationality. Then, the eighth chapter is devoted to moral and social psychology and deals with the origin and development of the sense of justice within a just social system. The ninth and final chapter presents a controversial argument about stability, later to become famous, based on the consistency between the individual good and the sense of justice.

2.3.1 A person's good

A person's good consists in the realization of a rational life plan in the light of reasonably favorable circumstances (TJ 395; rev. edn. 347). Given the deontological nature of the theory, the right is conceived independently of the good. However, without a thin theory of the good it would be impossible to get to the principles of justice because we would have no knowledge of what the parties in the original position want. Without the thin theory we would have no idea as to the rationality of the parties and the nature of the primary goods. Once we have at our disposal the principles of justice, we may have a more comprehensive vision of the good and, at this point, we may have recourse to the full version of the theory of the good. In the light of the principles of justice, the complete theory of the good allows us to examine in a more reliable manner the moral concepts in which goodness plays a role of its own. Finally, when we consider the good of social activities and the advantage that each person derives from acting in compliance with the principles of justice, then we may appeal once again to the full theory. However, as Rawls says at the end of section 60 (TJ 398; rev. edn. 350), as soon as we pose ourselves the question of stability, wondering whether it is good to adjust our behavior to the principles of justice, going back to the thin theory becomes unavoidable – even under pain of circularity. Goodness is viewed by Rawls as rationality. This implies that a person's life plan is rational, if: (i) it is consistent with a theory of rational choice; and (ii) it is applied with full deliberative rationality, meaning with full knowledge of the relevant facts and a careful consideration of the consequences (TJ 408–9; rev. edn. 358–9).

This definition of the good applied to life plans is merely formal, just as the concepts of deliberative rationality and the principles of rational choice are formal. Up to now, we have no criteria to evaluate the goals that we set ourselves when we adopt a life plan. To generate criteria, we need to start from a few assumptions on the general events that characterize human wishes and needs. Rawls starts by postulating a principle of motivation, which he calls the "Aristotelian Principle" (TJ, para. 65). According to this principle: "Human beings enjoy the exercise of their realized capacities . . . and this enjoyment increases the more the capacity is realized, or the greater its complexity" (TJ 414; rev. edn. 364).

It is a principle of motivation that expresses a psychological law, even though it obviously fails to say what capacity is actually more complex and, therefore, to be encouraged. Indeed, this is the reason why the Aristotelian Principle is compatible with the thin theory of the good. However, once the principles of justice have been selected in the original position, we can better evaluate the good of individuals and that of society in the light of the full theory.

In this more comprehensive perspective, a "good person" is the person who has at the highest level those moral qualities that we would like to see in others. Foremost among these virtues is the sense of justice. This attaches significance to the idea of moral value that, in turn, accounts more fully for the good of one's self-respect and of the various forms of human excellence. All this is attained without violating the liberal Rawlsian postulate according to which the visions of the good change from person to person even though the same is not true for the visions of the right (TJ 447; rev. edn. 393). This fact further emphasizes the difference between contractualism and utilitarianism. The theory of justice as fairness leaves less space for indeterminacy since the principles of justice do not depend on the wishes of the people. In Rawls' theory, the wishes of the people count for nothing if they conflict with the principles of justice. This safeguards a few fundamental values from the risks of populism.

The sense of justice, defined as a wish to respect just institutions and reciprocally give one another what is due (TJ 312; rev. edn. 274–5), is the most important virtue of a citizen and indispensable to ensuring the stability of a well-ordered society. In the eighth chapter of TJ, Rawls tries to discover the foundation of this sense. His answer is that it is founded on a general human bent for "reciprocity" (TJ, sections 75–6). This means that, owing to a sort of psychological law in conditions favoring a proper moral development, if a person benefits from the institutions that are just and publicly known to be just, this person will develop a sense of justice that, in turn, contributes to the stability of society.

The argument presupposes a rich philosophical and psychological background including aspects of the thought of Rousseau, Kant, Mill, Freud, Piaget, and Kohlberg. It passes through three psychological laws (TJ, section 75):

(i)   since the family is a just institution and parents usually love their children openly, the latter end up by loving them back;

(ii) given the first law, and assuming a just social system, people develop feelings of friendship and trust towards those with whom they are associated if the latter comply with their own duties and obligations;

(iii) given the first two laws, assuming that the institutions of a society are just, then people acquire and maintain over time a corresponding sense of justice.

This course leads every person from a morality based on authority through an associative morality and eventually to a morality consistent with the principles of justice. An important connection is therefore created between natural and moral attitudes. While, according to Kant, anyone who does not respect morality is irrational, according to Rawls the relevant thesis is less strong. He who lacks a sense of justice expresses a difficulty in realizing this link between nature and morality.[47] All this makes the sense of justice, connected with the theory of justice as fairness, more capable of producing stability than an analogous sense based on other theories. The rival is once again utilitarianism. Ultimately, Rawls argues that – from the point of view of stability – reciprocity connected with his vision represents a more definite and stronger guarantee than simple preferences connected instead with the utilitarian vision.

2.3.2 The good of justice

In the last chapter of TJ, Rawls proposes the final and most important thesis of his three-part argument on stability. The first part of this argument lies in the importance of publicity within the theory of justice as fairness (section 5.2.4), while the second part lies in the psychological–moral evolution that leads to the development of the sense of justice. The third part is founded on the so-called "congruence argument." According to this argument, individuals who are only motivated by a thin theory of the good will independently converge on the same sense of justice. As we have already seen, the latter depends on Rawls' theory. In the ninth chapter of TJ entitled "The Good of Justice," Rawls aims to show that "justice as fairness and goodness as rationality are congruent" (TJ 513; rev. edn. 450). Rawls' thesis rests on a "cumulative" rather than a demonstrative argument. It covers nearly 50 pages in sections 78–86 of TJ. The latter deal with difficult themes that, besides, are not always mutually related (autonomy and objectivity, the idea of social union, envy, equality, the priority of liberty, the theory of the dominant end, hedonism). The thesis reaches its climax in the decisive 86th section, entitled "The Good of the Sense of Justice."

It is not easy to reconstruct the argument in favor of congruence in TJ. First of all, we need to assume that Rawls' congruence problem does not correspond to the classical problem, which is that of showing the need for morality to the skeptic (TJ 568; rev. edn. 497–8). In fact, the argument assumes a unanimous agreement on the principles of justice. On this basis, we may try to reconstruct Rawls' reasoning as specified below:

(i)   there is a fundamental connection between acting fairly and the natural attitudes of the human being (TJ, section 74);

(ii)   the Aristotelian Principle calls upon us to consider participation in the complex life of a just society as being good (TJ, section 79);

(iii) the Kantian interpretation shows that acting fairly is something we want as free and rational agents (TJ, section 40);
(iv) human beings need to express their deep nature as moral beings;
(v) the principles of justice chosen in the original position by parties who are free and equal correspond to what is required in i–iv;
(vi) in particular, action based on them gives rise to a fundamental rational wish called "sense of justice";
(vii) the good is actually the satisfaction of a rational wish;
(viii) in particular, this wish succeeds. in contributing to the formulation of a harmonious life plan since – given the condition of finality (see chapter III of TJ) – it is a regulative and overriding wish with respect to others (TJ 574–5; rev. edn. 503);
(ix) given what was specified in i–viii, it is good for every person to act in conformity with the sense of justice that depends on the principles of the theory of justice as fairness;
(x) the conclusion is that congruence is possible and that the theory of justice as fairness is able to make society stable.

There are two main points where this conclusion faces conceptual difficulties, and, over time, both of them have been noted by Rawls.[48] A first problem consists in the strong idealization implicit in his vision of a well-ordered society. This vision, in TJ, presupposes a strict compliance with the dictates of the theory of justice as fairness, an assumption already shown to be out of touch with reality. The reformulation, in this case, consists in thinking in terms of partial compliance and, then, of greater realism. A second problem, which concerns the internal consistency of the conclusion, is more important. An integration of goodness and justice of the type proposed by the congruence argument faces the obvious problem of giving the upper hand to a substantially liberal conception of the good inspired by Rawls' theory, compared with other conceptions of the good. This gives rise to an obvious problem of compatibility with that hypothesis of neutrality cherished by the liberal tradition and by the pluralism that is so important for Rawls.[49]

Over time, Rawls' answer was bound to pivot around the attempt to make the congruence between the good and the right independent of his own theory of justice as fairness, to anchor it to the public culture shared in a liberal democracy. In PL, it will be the citizens – free and equal, committed to a liberal-democratic regime and to social cooperation – who will have from the very beginning two fundamental moral powers: the sense of justice and the capacity to have a conception of the good. Therefore, they will try to act on the basis of these powers, with no need to have recourse to a direct congruence with Rawls' theory of justice.

In general, in connection with the revision of an important formal aspect of TJ, in the second part of his work, Rawls insisted – from 1980 onwards – in formulating two new hypotheses: the political conception of the person, viewed as a free and equal citizen, and of the well-ordered society, which could help to make the model of the original position less abstract. Even if it is admissible to attribute – as I have just done – the centrality of these concepts to the period subsequent to TJ, it is worth noting that already in TJ Rawls had written that "embedded in the principles of justice there is an ideal of the person that provides an Archimedean Point for judging the basic structure of society" (TJ 584; rev. edn. 511).

Actually, the centrality of the concept of person depends on the priority of right. It is not even true that such a vision of the person is conceived outside the social and political context in TJ. It may only be affirmed that, with the passing of time, those deciding what is the right institutional structure are no longer noumenal individuals, as the right institutional structure depends instead on what free and equal citizens are likely to choose under given constraints. This revision strengthens the role of reflective equilibrium and promotes a more realistic vision of social decision-making processes.

3

THE FIRST PRINCIPLE OF JUSTICE

This chapter covers the arguments for and against the first principle of justice. This principle defends liberty and its priority within the theory of justice as fairness. The main argument for it consists in Rawls' anti-perfectionist, anti-teleological and liberal orientations (section 3.1.). On the one hand, many readers consider this principle too rigid, because the idea that freedom can never be restricted except for the sake of freedom itself appears extreme. On the other hand, Rawls does conceive liberty as a list of singular liberties (3.1.1) and this leads to two problems: the first concerns the relative arbitrariness of such a list, and the second concerns the question of the trade-offs between different, and possibly, conflicting liberties (section 3.1.2). Rawls changed his mind about the best formulation of this principle during his career, and one can argue about the reasons behind this decision (sections 3.1.1 and 3.1.3). Contrary to what many readers of TJ appear to think, the first principle of justice is more egalitarian than the second principle. Liberty must always be "equal liberty," and this raises the question of the effectiveness of this equality. Rawls, from this point of view, distinguishes liberty in itself from what he calls the "worth of liberty" (3.2). This distinction leads to the argument for the "fair value of political liberty," which implies a severe restriction of permitted economic inequalities when they threaten equal liberties. The chapter ends by presenting the institutionalization of the first principle through the so-called "four-stage sequence," and considers the difficulties raised by the relation between the ideal priority of the principles of justice and the necessity of popular democratic participation in order to ensure their realization (3.3).

3.1 A Liberalism of Liberties

The first principle of justice requires that "[e]ach person has an equal claim to a fully adequate scheme of equal basic rights and liberties, which scheme is compatible with the same scheme for all; and in this scheme, the equal political liberties and only those liberties are to be guaranteed their fair value" (PL 5).

This version of the first principle is the final one, presented in PL. The course leading to this definition is tortuous, and the different ways Rawls describes this principle reflect the development of his thought about liberties. In TJ (see TJ 60, 250, and 302; rev. edn. 52–3, 220, and 266), he formulates the first principle in the following terms: "each person is to have an equal right to the most extensive total system of equal basic liberties compatible with a similar system of liberty for all" (TJ 250; rev. edn. 220).

An intermediate version is proposed in JFR, where Rawls says that every person is entitled to "the same indefeasible claim to a fully adequate scheme of equal basic liberties" (JFR 42). The PL version had been preceded, in its turn, by an identical one in the essay on "The Basic Liberties and Their Priority" (Lecture VIII in PL). The most noteworthy change between the first and the final version lays in the difference between the "most extensive system of equal basic liberties" (TJ) and the "fully adequate scheme" (PL). The idea of maximizing the liberties, as dealt with in TJ, disappears, turning into the project of a rich and consistent scheme of basic liberties. As regards the term "basic liberties," there are times when Rawls uses instead the expression "basic rights," but they are synonymous and, therefore, I will only use "basic liberties."

In order to understand the nature and meaning of Rawls' first principle of justice – a principle that deals with the scheme of basic liberties – one needs to start from the ideal implicit in the notion of a well-ordered society. This is a pluralist and anti-perfectionist ideal. Rawls believes in a liberalism "of freedom" as opposed to a liberalism "of happiness."[1] The liberalism of happiness addresses the attainment of aggregate wellbeing, while the liberalism of freedom aspires to the liberty of the citizens. The agreement on the principles of justice does not presuppose any agreement on life goals and plans. It assumes that citizens have a wide and differentiated range of ends, all of them equally worthy. Referring to Isaiah Berlin,[2] Rawls deems it impossible to avoid such a basic pluralism. Therefore, he criticizes perfectionism, the ethical-political doctrine that aims "to arrange institutions and to define the duties and obligations of individuals so as to maximize the achievement of human excellence in art, science and culture" (TJ 325; rev. edn. 285–6).

For Rawls, perfectionist theories are characterized by a teleological argumentative structure. These theories assume that there is a prevailing common end and the institutions should be designed in such a way as to attain it.

Given the fact of pluralism, such a common end would pass over the head of the individuals and their legitimate aspirations. For Rawls, a similar problem also applies to utilitarianism. The protection of individual rights – connected with the basic liberties – causes him to view as improper any global calculation of happiness for society as a whole. Because of this, Rawls opposes Bentham's act utilitarianism while being more open to compromise with respect to John Stuart Mill's indirect utilitarianism.[3] Pluralism denies the possibility of any teleological vision that causes a common end to precede those of the individuals. Indeed, Rawls turns such an impossibility into a matter of interpretation of the nature of the good with respect to individuals, given that "human good is heterogeneous because the aims of the self are heterogeneous" (TJ 554; rev. edn. 486).

According to Rawls, political theory is entrusted with the task of translating this pluralist ideal into an institutional design. Unlike perfectionism and utilitarianism, the theory of justice as fairness can perform this task because of the way it conceives of liberty. Such a vision depends on the general conception and the special conception of justice as fairness. According to the general conception, social primary goods are to be distributed equally unless an unequal distribution is to the advantage of the least favored (TJ 62; rev. edn. 54).

The special conception of justice is expressed in the two principles, with the proviso that the first principle based on liberty must take priority with respect to the second.[4] Liberty-related considerations trump welfare-related considerations. Indeed, this is the sense of the priority of liberty. The major difference between the general and the special conception lies in the choice of liberty as a special good and in the priority connected with it. From this point of view, Rawls' argument – which is unquestionably normative – has also a positive side, since the constitutions of the liberal-democratic world – beginning with the American constitution – would somehow reflect the lexicographical ordering of Rawls' two principles.

The two principles of justice are subject to a priority rule that takes the first principle to be lexicographically prior to the second principle (or more simply lexically prior, as Rawls prefers to say) – that is, placed in an order of priority like the words in a dictionary: "*The principles of justice are to be ranked in lexical order and therefore liberty can be restricted only for the sake of liberty. There are two cases: (a) a less extensive liberty must strengthen the total system of liberty shared by all; (b) a less than equal liberty must be acceptable to those with the lesser liberty*" (TJ 250; rev. edn. 220, emphasis mine).

To understand what priority means, one should consider this definition of lexical or lexicographical order: "This is an order which requires us to satisfy the first principle in the ordering before we can move on to the second, the second before we consider the third, and so on" (TJ 43; rev. edn. 38).

These definitions lead Rawls to conclude in an unambiguous manner that "liberty can be restricted only for the sake of liberty itself." The priority of liberty, conceived in such a manner, may be upheld as the centerpiece of the theory of justice as fairness, together with the defense of the least advantaged offered by the second principle of justice. Besides, since Rawls became increasingly doubtful about the possibility of making the second principle compatible with liberal constitutions, the priority of liberty comes to have a more crucial place in the theory of justice as fairness. It differentiates the theory of justice as fairness from both utilitarianism and intuitionism. More specifically, the fact that justice as fairness does not consider all goods interchangeable distinguishes it from utilitarianism, and the system of priorities distinguishes it from intuitionism.

3.1.1 The meaning of the priority of liberty

The first principle has given rise to extensive debate. The main resistance comes from the fact that a liberty may only be limited for the sake of another liberty and not, for instance, on socio-economic grounds. This problem is compounded by the lexicographical (or "lexical") nature of such a priority: the slightest breach of the first principle would be disallowed even where the consequence would be a great advantage in terms of the second principle. This has been seen as excessive rigidity on Rawls' part in at least two different ways. On the one hand, there are those[5] who consider the lexicographical priority of the principle of liberty too radical ("outlandishly extreme") and those[6] who view it as the fruit of a certain liberal dogmatism. On the other hand, often it becomes difficult to determine to what extent a principle of justice, such as that based on the priority of liberty, rules out real democratic decisions.[7]

It is not fully clear which argument Rawls uses in TJ to defend the priority of liberty. The central argument in favor of the first principle should also be the one in favor of the priority of liberty. This is in part the same liberal and anti-perfectionist argument, which leads the parties in the original position to exclude any government authority with respect to religious, moral, or philosophical matters:

> The government has no authority to render associations either legitimate or illegitimate any more that it has this authority in regard to art and science. These matters are simply not within its competence . . . It does not concern itself with philosophical and religious doctrine but regulates individuals pursuit of their moral and spiritual interests in accordance with principles to which they themselves would agree in an initial situation of equality. (TJ 212; rev. edn 186)

Alternatively,[8] Rawls may take the priority of liberty partly for granted, relying more on the sum of a series of different considerations than on an actual conclusive theoretical argument. Three of them deserve to be mentioned. The first links the priority of liberty to the primary good represented by "self-respect."[9] This links the priority of liberty and political equality. If, as Rawls says, a citizen were to have a smaller package of basic liberties than another citizen, his self-respect would end up being impaired. However, this argument would seem to dwell more on the fact that the basic liberties must be equal for all than on the fact that it is necessary to have a priority of liberty. A second consideration relates to the significance of the freedom of conscience, particularly if religious and moral choices are at stake. This argument appears too limited to mandate a general priority of liberty. What is, instead, more persuasive is the third consideration, the one that views the priority of liberty as at the service of the formation of "higher order interests." This argument is also consistent with the centrality of the concept of the person in Rawls from 1980 onwards (see chapter 8). Finally, somehow convinced that he had not wrapped up the case for the priority of liberty in TJ, Rawls has added an argument in PL according to which the priority of liberty contributes to the stability of a just society (PL 74–6).

The debate on the first principle and its priority after TJ relies on an essay by Herbert Hart. In this essay, Hart states that one should question such rigid ideals as that of the primacy of liberty, given that the entire experience of law teaches us to measure one person's liberty against the liberty of others. Besides, Hart pointed out two weaknesses in the Rawlsian version of the first principle.[10] First, Hart expressed skepticism about how purely rational actors in the original position could agree to Rawls' first principle and its priority. Second, Hart denied that we have any way of saying how possible conflicts among different liberties could be solved by Rawls' generic criterion.

In fact, the Rawlsian principle of liberty has appeared too generic to many interpreters, so much so as to cause them to be unable to account for the way in which the various liberties mutually balance out.[11] It was not at all clear how the restrictions on some liberties in the name of others should be justified. It may be stated that some limitations of the liberties are fundamentally unjust, as in the case when a regime meeting with political difficulties, for instance today's case of Burma, limits freedom of expression. However, the case when a similar limitation may seem justifiable even in the light of the theory of justice as fairness is unclear. Which limitations of the basic liberties are compatible with the priority of liberty and for what reasons? Rawls does not express himself with accuracy on such an issue.[12] We may uphold that a general and vague constraint is represented by the "common interest." Talking about the first principle, Rawls says: "According to this principle institutions are ranked by how effectively they guarantee the conditions necessary for all equally to further their aims . . . Thus reasonable regulations to maintain public order and security, or efficient measures for public health and safety, promote the common interest in this sense. So do collective efforts for national defense in a just war" (TJ 97; rev. edn. 83).

In any event, Rawls never systematically worked out a principle of limitation of liberties based on the common interest. Any attempt in this direction threatens to contradict the general anti-teleological formulation of the argument. Subsequently, he has also tried to answer these objections through a partial review of the initial vision of his first principle. The weight of the priority of liberty and the argument in favor of the first principle have shifted increasingly from the deduction of the parties in the original position to a more comprehensive vision. The latter unquestionably starts off from the Rawlsian conception of the person as endowed with "highest order interests," such as the capacity to have and revise a conception of the good and the sense of justice, essential to her development (and he draws for the most part on the third argument referred to above in relation to the priority of liberty).

Rawls modifies – in the way we have seen – the formulation of the first principle. As a first consequence, one should avoid conceiving of the first principle and the priority of liberty with reference to a sort of general and abstract concept of liberty.[13] Rawls has in mind a set of specific and concrete liberties, which he believes to be more important than others.[14] Therefore, these liberties must be limited in number, and the list needs to be characterized by a certain level of vagueness.[15] Hence, the basic liberties may be presented in the form of a list made up as follows:

- liberty of religion and conscience;
- political liberties, including freedom of expression, of the press, of assembly, of vote, and of association;
- freedom of the person, starting from the inadmissibility of slavery and enslavement and the freedom from physical and psychological oppression, and including also the freedom to hold personal properties and the liberties of movement and of choice of one's occupation;
- rights and liberties laid down by the "rule of law," like the right to personal freedom, habeas corpus and the right to a proper administration of justice.

One must not neglect, in the formulation of the above list, the historical experience of the constitutional state. It goes without saying that this origin, although significant, is not enough to cause us to accept the peculiar list of liberties that Rawls has in mind. Indeed, it is strange, given the relevance of the first principle in TJ, that Rawls does not provide a more detailed argument in favor of this specific list of liberties. Perhaps such reasoning, not being strictly philosophical, may not be made independently of socio-historical conditions. Moreover, some exclusions from the list are not justified. This becomes clear when one considers that Rawls does not mention among the basic liberties property rights, or the freedoms of commerce and contract.

> It is essential to observe these basic liberties are given by a list of liberties . . . Of course, liberties not on the list, for example, the right to own certain kinds of property (e.g. means of production) and freedom of contract as understood by the doctrine of laissez-faire are not basic: and so they are not protected by the priority of the first principle. (rev. edn. 53–4)

This choice is certainly connected with Rawls' fundamental egalitarianism. At the same time, he does not include in the list the freedom to choose an independent lifestyle, including the sexual liberties. These exclusions are not explicitly justified. One may certainly argue that caution about private ownership of the means of production leaves open the choice between capitalism and socialism within the limits of a theory of justice as fairness.[16] However, it is quite baffling that – in working out his list of basic liberties – Rawls fails to deal with this as well as with other fundamental liberties. This does not mean that we must censure Rawls' list of liberties or merely consider it superficial. It just means that this list has a prevailingly general or exemplary value in the theory of justice as fairness. It must be assumed that a significant list of basic liberties may not set aside the historical reality and the political debates among the citizens. In the revised edition of TJ, Rawls added this sentence: "It is difficult, and perhaps impossible, to give a complete specification of these liberties independently from the particular circumstances-social, economic, and technological of a given society" (TJ 61; rev. edn. 54).

3.1.2 Liberty and the conception of the person

Some flexibility in the list of basic liberties would seem unavoidable. Even in TJ, paragraph 8 decidedly laid down the priority of liberty, while paragraph 82 – quite significantly entitled "The Grounds for the Priority of the Liberty" – considers several trade-offs between liberties and other goods. Indeed, there would seem to be a concession to the idea that there is decreasing marginal significance of material wellbeing, matched by a greater significance of the basic liberties.[17] Such a conception would automatically introduce a less radical and more pluralistic vision of the priority of liberty that we could associate with a typically lexicographical ordering. The very idea that, under a given threshold of wellbeing, we should not worry too much about liberty is quite strange (is liberty in Darfur irrelevant?). Perhaps we have simply to think that in such cases what Rawls calls the "circumstances of justice" are not realized (see chapter 5), so that principles of justice cannot apply.

The priority given by the theory of justice as fairness to these liberties implies that they have a special status (PL 294ff.). First of all, they have greater weight when compared with alternative goods. Second, such liberties cannot be bartered or assigned for any reason that is not internal to the system of the basic liberties. At the same time, however, they are not absolute. Otherwise, those compensations within the system that make it a "fully adequate scheme" would not be possible and a working system of associated life would prove impossible. Again in the revised edition of TJ, Rawls added: "Since they may be limited when they clash with one another, none of these liberties is absolute; but however they are adjusted to form one system, the system is to be the same for all" (rev. edn. 54).

The idea of an adequate and comprehensive scheme of basic liberties presupposes that they be somehow compatible. The compatibility may not be derived merely from the fact that the Rawlsian persons are conceived as equal persons endowed with the essential moral powers to have a conception of the good and a sense of justice. Indeed, it depends also on the historical situation that creates specific constraints and opportunities regarding the determination of the liberties, as well as on the constitutional and legislative arrangements that succeed in actually implementing the scheme of liberties. This means that a reliable representation of the scheme of liberties may not be obtained exclusively from the original position, but presupposes the gradual political implementation of the principles of justice (in what Rawls calls the four-stage sequence).

The case of freedom of religion is emblematic and reflects that mixed formation of the list of basic liberties. On the one hand, freedom of religion has something to do with the main causes that, historically, have generated liberalism and the political interest in the liberties. On the other, freedom of religion represents an occasion for the exercise of such fundamental prerogatives of the person as those protected by freedom of conscience and that of association. Besides, it allows for the exercise of the moral powers. As Rawls explicitly says in PL, the basic liberties constitute "an essential social condition for the adequate development and full exercise of the two powers of moral personality over a complete life" (PL 293).

Hence, the basic liberties are necessary for effective assertion of citizens' moral powers. Let us consider the capacity to form a conception of the good. We know that the parties in the original position are endowed with it, but we do not know what makes up the conception of the good of each party. Freedom of conscience guarantees the capacity to develop and revise such different conceptions of the good in an autonomous manner. Freedom of conscience protects the possibility for each person to cultivate her religious beliefs without any interference from the state. At the same time, a political liberty such as that of association gives substance to freedom of conscience. It would be hard to form any independent philosophical, moral and religious visions without the possibility of having contacts with other equally interested persons. The Rawlsian ideal of a person who chooses – in full "deliberative rationality" – her plan of life and, therefore, her long-term goals depends on the guarantees offered by the basic liberties. This is the reason why the basic liberties not only are primary goods but also take priority with respect to all other primary goods.

Little can be said about the liberties of the person – as conceived by Rawls – under the aegis of the rule of law. Beyond the liberties connected with the habeas corpus, Rawls fails to propose a specific list. As regards, instead, the freedoms of speech, assembly, conscience and thought, what applies is what concerns the interest of the parties in the original position in defending them, subjecting the public authority to constraints. The parties themselves attribute special value to the unhindered pursuit of their own cultural and spiritual interests. Obviously, all this gives rise to a problem of compatibilities of and conflicts among liberties. It is not hard to imagine how these liberties may be subjected to constraints. For instance, one may assume that a liberal government has the right to forbid a neo-Nazi demonstration in a neighborhood inhabited for the most part by Jews. Additionally, a government may enact rules that impose order in a debate and may sometimes limit freedom of expression in cases where no rules would lead to chaos and so would undermine the very freedom at issue. However, when cases are more complex, the relative priorities are hardly comprehensible, and one needs. to reflect on the sense of the expression "adequate scheme."

3.1.3 The adequate scheme of basic liberties

The citizens of a liberal-democratic state have a sense of justice. To have a sense of justice does not mean to support a particular conception of justice. The assumption is in part formal: whatever the principles chosen by the parties in the original position, provided that these principles are compatible with a well-ordered society, citizens will have a corresponding sense of justice (PL 315). The sense of justice makes the moral sentiments of the people coherent with the institutional framework of a well-ordered society, thus providing the basis for stability. The basic liberties ensure the sense of justice, and through it stability, for three sets of reasons:

(i)   because the stability based on liberty allows the flourishing of individual conceptions of the good, and, in their turn, the principles of justice ensure a stability that would not be guaranteed by other conceptions (because they correspond to the moral powers of the person);
(ii) because there is a relationship between principles of justice and self-respect (again based on the correspondence with the moral powers);
(iii) because the idea of reciprocity and implicit cooperation in the vision of the well-ordered society as "a social union of social unions" (TJ) ultimately promotes the conceptions of the good of the individuals.

We are now in a position to get a clear picture of the second problem raised by Hart – that is, the compatibility problem within the scheme of basic liberties. Should conflicts crop up among the different liberties, how would they be solved? Hart[18] wondered explicitly what it means to say that liberties could only be restricted in the name of a greater system of liberty "as a whole" (TJ 203; rev. edn. 178), or that the restriction of a liberty was allowed ultimately only in favor of "a greater equal liberty" (TJ 229; rev. edn. 201). The very idea of restrictions of liberty only in the name of liberty seemed obscure to him. What he requested was a strong qualitative-type criterion that clarified this balancing.[19]

Rawls, in his revision of the first principle, declared that he too was convinced that the eminently quantitative criterion of the greater extension of the liberties proposed in TJ was not satisfactory and proved unable to cope with conflicts among liberties. Rawls proposed that the criterion of agreement with the interests of the citizen go alongside the quantitative criterion already present in TJ. In other words, the idea that the basic liberties presuppose free and equal persons acquired a more substantive basis in the justification of the first principle from 1980 onwards. Retrospectively, Rawls thought also that this twofold criterion could be confusing and that greater clarity was required (PL 331–2).

In general, the entire argument in favor of the priority of liberty leaves – perhaps intentionally – grounds for doubt. In the original position, there is a general interest in limiting the authority of the government on matters that have cultural and spiritual significance. Indeed, we are aware of the fact that such an interest increases with the improvement of living conditions. However, we also know out of expediency that restrictions of the basic liberties may be proposed in the name of the common interest. What we do not know is on what type of theoretical grounds these three interests may be balanced. Perhaps the answer is that the balancing cannot be done beforehand since it requires a knowledge of the facts that is still lacking in the original position.

The liberties and their priorities instead always need to be viewed from the perspective of granting each individual an adequate development of his main moral powers. From this point of view, we may assume a sort of division of labor. Essentially, political liberties are based on the sense of justice. The civil liberties (such as freedom of conscience) are related first and foremost to the capacity critically to form a conception of the good that might serve as a guide for the formulation of a plan of life.

The "fully adequate" scheme of liberty envisaged by Rawls when he reviewed the first principle derives from these two "fundamental cases" (PL 332). This reintroduces the criterion of TJ that takes into account the rational interests of the citizen, although it does so in a more convincing manner by referring to the two moral powers.

Once an adequate scheme of liberties has been provided, one needs to see how it works in the subsequent stages that determine the institutional set-up of a society. Political liberties, such as freedom of the press and freedom of expression, help to make a just society stable by ensuring the development and strengthening of a sense of justice. Liberties of conscience and association guarantee the real possibility of critically choosing a conception of the good and making it capable of controlling a rational plan of life. The remaining liberties, such as that of the integrity of the person and those connected with the "rule of the law," contribute instead to making the system of liberties more balanced and consistent. This indicative taxonomy of liberties causes a criterion to emerge: a liberty is more essential the greater its usefulness in the actual exercise of the moral powers. So, different modes of the freedoms of expression and of the press need to be protected based on a similar criterion. A given form of freedom of speech may be sacrosanct, while another may be restricted and a third even considered harmful or offensive.

There are two standard trade-offs among basic liberties: (i) "a less extensive liberty must strengthen the total system of liberty shared by all" (TJ 302) – we may also say that, under special circumstances, the suspension of a basic liberty may strengthen the total system of liberty; (ii) "a less than equal liberty must be acceptable to those with the lesser liberty." Should there be a group that experiences the loss of part of its basic liberties, it will be necessary to justify the loss to this very group. A case in which these two conditions occur jointly is when an intolerant group endangers the general security and the freedom of all. In this case, it stands to reason to decrease its prerogatives of liberty in the light of both criteria referred to above. Another similar eventuality is that of requiring national military service, particularly in the context of a just war, such as that against Hitler (JFR 47).

This way of accounting for the theoretical fault identified by Hart helps to order liberties at a constitutional level, even if in a general and approximate manner. The actual organization of the liberties in the public sphere is left to the legislative stage. All this still proves to be very abstract, and Rawls debates a few relevant modes of basic liberties in relation to the freedom of speech in politics and freedom of the press. According to Rawls, we should not ask too much of a philosophical conception and, therefore, the idea of the adequate scheme of basic liberties may serve as a general guide even if it does not solve or best cope with problems in constitutional law.

Hart's contribution closed with the claim that, in TJ, Rawls affirmed that the first principle was inferred on the basis of the rational interests of the parties in the original position but that such an intent would be distorted by the surreptitious inclusion of ideals in the reasoning that favor the first principle. Rawls basically answered Hart by breaking the subject into two parts. What counts in the original position is the nature of the rational interests of the parties. But, in addition to the argument of the original position, one needs to consider the notion of the person, as free and equal, in a political context. This notion is certainly not independent of ideals. Indeed, it is inspired by the ideals of political liberalism, just as political liberalism is based on it. Splitting the argument for liberty in two parts can also imply that we take seriously the distinction between rights on one hand and values on the other. Rights are institutionally protected values and cannot be properly balanced, whereas values can.[20] When we have to balance rights, because their constraints or prerogatives clash, we can however adopt values as a "guiding framework" to solve the conflict of rights. The basic liberties are rights insofar as they are institutionally protected values.

3.2 Equal Liberty and Worth of Liberty

The correspondence between the notion of the person and liberalism becomes clearer when one considers the Rawlsian notion of "political justice" in TJ, where it means primarily constitutional justice and the related concept of "participation" (TJ sections 36 and 37, pp. 221ff.; rev. edn. 194ff.). The latter are important sections, strangely neglected by interpreters. As we can see from the significance of participation, it is not true that the priority of liberty entails an a priori exclusion of political debate. Indeed, the principle of equal liberty (the first principle), in its application to the procedure defined by the constitution, itself implies a principle of equal participation: "It requires that all citizens are to have an equal right to take part in and to determine the outcome of the constitutional process that establishes the laws with which they are to comply" (TJ 221; rev. edn. 194).

Such a principle preserves equal participation, which is typical of the most abstract level of the original position, in the legislative and constitutional practice.

Participation, viewed in the way specified above, is explicitly connected by Rawls with Constant's so-called "liberty of the ancients." Participation has an essentially political nature which consists in allowing citizens the actual governance of the common good (TJ 222; rev. edn. 195). It takes place in the traditional constitutional context through the democratic election of a representative body with extensive legislative powers – powers that are usually subject to constraints in the forms laid down in the constitution itself.

Equal liberty is defined by the participation principle according to three criteria, which relate to its meaning, extent, and real worth (usually "worth" according to Rawls, but sometimes also "value"). The meaning must reflect the idea that attributes a vote to each elector, in other words, a criterion according to which every citizen has more or less the same power in determining the electoral result. The extent of the principle relates to the use of the majority rule that, generally, presides over the most important events of the national politics (even though a few restrictions are compatible with the principle of participation). Finally, the worth of participation consists in the actual possibility for each citizen – regardless of class, gender, and status – to have access to public office and to have an effect on political life. This last point introduces an important restriction on the possibility for persons to own material goods. Wealth as such is not evil for Rawls if it can be justified by the difference principle. However, it may unbalance political results and, therefore, it must be limited to allow fairness in the political process. Later on, when we debate the difference principle, we shall see that some economic inequalities are ruled out not directly by the difference principle but by this political constraint that implies the desirability of a society without too many inequalities in status and wealth.

This point also has a more general import when we look at the question of the priority of liberty as a whole. We have seen that, for many interpreters, the priority of liberty expresses a point of view that is too rigid. What is the sense in defending it when people are unable to satisfy a few basic needs? According to Rawls, part of the answer to this question is given a priori, by the argument from the circumstances of justice (see chapter 5). The priority of liberty simply does not exist when a few minimal necessary conditions of wealth and stability are lacking. As always, for Rawls, liberty and equality are connected.

Political liberties represent a remarkable exception to Rawls' general thesis that forbids trade-offs between basic liberties and socio-economic resources. In fact, in the case of political liberties, the indifference of the material conditions ceases. Given that wealth brings with it political advantages, and given that the political liberties need to be equal, liberties may be sacrificed with a view to preventing the undue influence of money in politics. According to Rawls, this goal may be attained in two ways: (i) taxing wealth and reducing the inequality (in the name of liberty, and not of equality); (ii) vigorously limiting the impact of money in the realm of politics. In these terms, the defense of the fair value of the political liberties is already present in TJ (section 14), even though it has a more accurate formulation in terms of campaign financing regulations only in PL (356–63).

Traditional civil and political liberties, such as the freedoms of speech, association, and conscience, are considered as the presuppositions of a democratic regime. In fact, the principle of participation requires that each citizen be adequately informed, and be allowed to form her own opinion on the controversial issues of the public agenda and, should she wish, to present her own proposals. The redistribution of income through taxes, and the political parties, are among the traditional tools that ensure the fair value of participation. In fact, it should not be overlooked that, historically, one of the major faults of constitutional and democratic regimes has been their failure to ensure opportunity for participation, and thus a fair value of equal liberty (TJ 226; rev. edn. 198–9). This outcome is also due to the fact that economic and social disparity has all too often ended up affecting the results of politics.

Rawls never considers liberty solely in abstract terms. For him, what counts is not only liberty in itself, but also the fact that citizens succeed in actually taking advantage of it, for instance through having a minimum material wellbeing. In this case, we are dealing with Rawls' famous insistence on the worth of liberty that must never be merely formal. Persons must have powers, resources and opportunities that allow them a use of the liberties. In his words: "The basic liberties are a framework of legally protected paths and opportunities. Of course, ignorance and poverty, and the lack of material means generally prevent people from exercising their rights and from taking advantage of these openings" (PL 325, 326).

Just on this account, Rawls makes a distinction between liberty and worth of liberty: "Freedom as equal liberty is the same for all; the question of compensating for a lesser than equal liberty does not arise. But the worth of liberty is not the same for everyone. Some have greater authority and wealth and therefore greater means to achieve their aims" (TJ 204; rev. edn. 179).

The difference in terms of worth of liberty depends on the fact that, even if all have the same rights, some will derive from them greater benefit than others during their lifetime. The liberties, in other words, must be the same for all but – within the limits of the second principle – inequalities in the worth of liberty are allowed. The worth of liberty is protected by the second principle of justice, while equal liberty is protected by the first. This is the reason why differences related to the worth of liberty are admitted within certain limits. The egalitarian trend of the theory as a whole, including the principle of fair equality of opportunity and the difference principle, makes the attainment of a minimum material wellbeing for all more plausible, allowing therefore a real fruition of the basic liberties.

Notwithstanding Rawls' specific interest in the worth of liberty, he fails to show the same interest in the fair value of liberty beyond the strictly political field. It could be remarked that Rawls remains a liberal and not a socialist, but assuring an equal worth of liberty for all would probably prove an impossible task and would require in all probability the presence of an excessively intrusive or even authoritarian state.

In fact,[21] the problem depends, in the final analysis, on the fact that liberty on the one hand and worth of liberty on the other may easily come apart. However, is such a distinction still possible when the difference principle allows considerable discrepancies in terms of income and wellbeing? It is not at all easy to provide an answer. The question, after all, draws on the traditional leftist criticism of liberalism. According to this criticism, liberals worry to a considerable extent about civil and political liberties, but too little about the effect that economic inequalities have on those civil and political liberties. From this point of view, Rawls is a liberal swimming against the tide. The second principle of justice witnesses his aspiration towards equality of resources. However, in the case at hand, we need to admit that we cannot take for granted the possibility of singling out the worth of liberty as something independent of liberty. The inequalities that are allowed by the second principle in the name of a general economic efficiency may actually affect liberty.

With the passing of time, Rawls seems constantly aware of such a problem, so much so that, in PL, he appears to be more willing to consider certain basic needs as being on the same level as the basic liberties (PL 227–30), creating the possibility of trade-offs between the former and the latter. In these pages, there is also a timid attempt to turn certain basic needs into aspects of the constitutional essentials.

3.3 The Four-stage Sequence

The institutional plausibility of justice as fairness – that is to say, the fact that real institutions could actually follow Rawls' principles – is assessed in the so-called "four-stage sequence" that Rawls formulated in the second part of TJ. The four-stage sequence aims to make it easier for a democratic society to apply the principles of justice. The sequence consists in: the original position, the constitutional stage, the legislative stage and the stage in which one applies rules to cases decided by judges, administrators and single citizens. Of course, they must not be taken as historical events in time. They are rather supposed to be deliberation models, defined by non-specific informational constraints.[22]

The first of the four stages is represented by the original position. Here, questions concerning the justice of the basic structure are considered. After having chosen, in the original position, a specific conception of justice based on the two principles, the contracting parties move on to a further stage – the "constitutional convention," as Rawls calls it. Such a stage is subject to the constraints of the principles of justice that have already been chosen in the original position.

In this second stage, the contracting parties must declare themselves in favor of a scheme of constitutional prerogatives of the major political institutions and of basic rights of the citizens. In this stage, the veil of ignorance is less thick so the contracting parties suitably know "the relevant general facts about their society, that is, its natural circumstances and resources, its level of economic advance and political culture, and so on" (TJ 197; rev. edn. 172–3).

Any specification of the basic rights is incomplete. That is why we need to go further. The third stage is the legislative one and, here, the veil of ignorance is lifted almost entirely so that the legislators are informed about everything except for the peculiar facts that relate to them.

Finally, the fourth stage is represented by actual compliance with the rules on the part of judges, managers and citizens. In this case, each knows all the facts. The criterion is that, at each stage, the veil of ignorance keeps people in the dark about those events that are not necessary for solving justice-related issues that concern the level of that stage. The conclusions of the preceding stage are binding on each new stage.

The latter point is what creates the greatest problems for Rawls' interpretation. If everything that is decided in the preceding stage is binding, then the principles of justice seem to assume all the ethical-political contents of justice, leaving to the three subsequent stages merely application-related matters. In other words, is disagreement about justice even possible after the original position?[23] In one of the final paragraphs of TJ, Rawls claims that:

> The reasoning leading up to the initial agreement is to be accessible to public understanding. Of course, in working out what the requisite principles are, we must rely upon current knowledge as recognized by common sense and the existing scientific consensus . . . We have to concede that as established beliefs change, *it is possible that the principles of justice which it seems rational to choose may likewise change.* (TJ 548, emphasis mine; rev. edn. 480)

Notwithstanding this possibility of revision, many interpreters have felt that the principles chosen in the original position, just on account of the fact that they are rational and reasonable, end up blocking any genuine procedure of change related to justice on the part of the citizens.[24] In other words, in the Rawlsian model, the will of the people would be overwhelmed by the impossibility of expressing any substantial disagreement about the subject of the principles, and everything would be decided in advance in the original position. The paragraphs on participation, as well as the end of section 82, seem to point to a less rigid attitude on this subject on Rawls' part.

One could argue that this more flexible attitude is not adequately supported in TJ terms. If we consider the participation principle, we may note that it applies to institutions and, therefore, does not represent the realization of an ideal of citizenship. This premise makes it even simpler to accept the limits that may be set, as it were, a priori on the participation principle. The first and most obvious of these limits consists in the set of constitutional constraints to which the application of democratic procedures may be subjected. From this point of view, it is unquestionable that one of the dogmas of liberalism is that the liberties of conscience and of the person are more relevant than the political liberties, and it may be assumed that some of these restrictions depend on this dogma. The extent to which these restrictions are supposed to count is not a question that, in the name of the priority of liberty, may be decided once and for all. As a rule, the relevance of the democratic procedures depends on the probability that they produce better political results than the alternatives. In any event, it should not be forgotten that "the grounds for self-government are not solely instrumental. Equal political liberty when assured its fair value is bound to have a profound effect on the moral quality of civic life" (TJ 233; rev. edn. 205).

In order to consider this point, one may look at the first stage, the one that leads from the original position to the constitutional convention. Were it impossible to modify the principles with the support of the principles of justice of TJ at this level, it would be so even later.

We are not dealing with the usual problem, questioning the two principles for their capacity to express the citizens' sense of justice. It is rather the problem of seeing how their constitutional application is independent. From this point of view, Rawls must face a difficult compromise: on the one hand, it must be assumed that the two principles determine an institutional order but, on the other, the debate subsequent to the selection of the principles and a reasonable disagreement might actually count in attaining an institutional equilibrium. It is a question of balancing conflicting needs: if the principles of justice were to exercise a sort of monopoly-type power, then the political debate would be excessively sacrificed; if the debate were to be entirely free to change the content of the principles, then the centrifugal effect would go beyond the expectations of the theory of justice as fairness.

It is important to bear in mind that, while bearing some similarities with the historical–institutional reality, the set-up of the four-stage sequence is completely abstract and hypothetical. As Rawls writes:

The idea of the four-stage sequence is part of a moral theory, and does not belong to an account of the working of actual constitutions, except insofar as political agents are influenced by the conceptions of justice in question . . . The aim is to characterize a just constitution and not to ascertain which sort of constitution would be adopted or acquiesced in, under more or less realistic (though simplified) assumptions about political life . . . (TJ 197; rev. edn. 173 n.2)

Rawls does not say that the choices in stage 1 (original position) determine those in stage 2 (constitutional convention), other than through the influence they have on the actors. Furthermore, as we have already seen, changing the stage also causes a change in the information available to the parties. In these terms, the problem becomes: up to what point is Rawls' theoretical construction to affect the choices in a subsequent stage where there is further information, and to what extent is such information able to cause people to change their mind in the constitutional convention? Naturally, this applies all the more to the subsequent legislative and juridical–administrative stages, where there is even more information. The problem is compounded by the fact that the construction of the original position presupposes a number of simplifying background assumptions, from the idea of "basic structure" to that of "primary goods," which subject the parties to considerable constraints on the possibility of making choices that might differ from Rawls' choice. It is normal to want to question a theoretical construction[25] where the assumptions carry so much weight.

The event of the formation of the historical constitutions, starting from the American constitution from which Rawls draws his inspiration, shows that the universalistic aspiration underlying them is strongly mediated by compromise and political pluralism. After all, Rawls himself explicitly recognizes that modern constitutionalism depends on the idea that "the sovereign people . . . have final authority and the institutionalizing of this authority by means of elections and parliaments . . ." (TJ 385; rev. edn. 338). In any event, it is also clear that he does not wish the delegates to the constitutional convention, in their most important decisions, to steer too far away from the ideal point, represented by the principles of justice. Hence, for instance, Rawls fully recognizes the significance of a principle of "loyal opposition," but does not explain at all how far such loyal opposition may or must go. In the original position, the agreement among the parties is unanimous and, later on, the additional information is the same for all, so that it is not easy to understand from where a likely disagreement may originate. There is no certainty that a change in information may revise important aspects of a conception of justice, given that the latter seems to be linked to the rationality of the parties more than to the information package. A compromise solution consists in saying that the principles of justice are compatible with different constitutional assets. The constitutional stage is needed just for this.[26]

In conclusion, it is not clear what type of disagreement would be acceptable – at the various stages – in Rawls' construction. For instance, some have objected that a religious conception of life would not find an adequate expression in the model of the original position.[27] Rawls would back a liberal and skeptical stance from a religious point of view. Are the opinions of the religious individual supposed to find a political compromise in the constitutional convention or are they supposed to stop ahead of it, remaining on the threshold of the original position? Perhaps a third solution may be found in the recourse to reflective equilibrium, which would allow greater flexibility at the very stage of the original position, with no need to get to the actual political level. Naturally, however, in so doing one would rule out disagreement from the second stage.

A similar problem crops up once again if our preoccupation is stability, which acquires increasingly greater significance in Rawls' theory as the years go by. As the stages advance, and as the veil of ignorance is being lifted, empirical, ethical, and conceptual mistakes become more probable (see TJ 354; rev. edn. 311), beginning with the errors that are implicit in the majority rule typical of the third stage – the legislative one – as compared with the rational unanimity of the original position. Rawls, however, always insists on the fact that, over time, a real participation in the legislative procedures produces in the citizens "an effective desire to act in accordance with the rules for reasons of justice" (TJ 261; rev. edn. 230).

All this may produce an excessive exclusion of alternative political values. As we shall see, much of the fault found with Rawls and many of the changes that he introduced in the model of TJ were based on this exclusion. One should not forget that the very same principles of justice are deemed to be compatible with different constitutional, legislative and administrative frameworks.

4

THE SECOND PRINCIPLE OF JUSTICE

This chapter discusses the second principle of justice. The second principle is divided into two sub-parts: the principle of fair equality of opportunities and the so-called "difference principle" (4.2). Social and economic inequalities are evaluated by Rawls in terms of social primary goods, such as basic rights and liberties, freedom of movement and free choice of occupation, powers and prerogatives of offices and positions of responsibility in the political and economic institutions of the basic structure, income and wealth, and the social bases of self-respect. Analogously, the least advantaged members of society are those people who have least in terms of an index of these social primary goods (4.2). Social primary goods are considered by Rawls to be more relevant than natural primary goods, because they are distributed by the institutional system. The difference principle is an egalitarian principle. However, it permits substantial social and economic inequalities in order to favor economic efficiency. These inequalities are permitted only under the proviso that they will also work to the advantage of the worst-off (4.3). Furthermore, they can be limited both by the fair value of political liberty (3.3.1), and by the fair equality of opportunity principle (4.4). There is a disputed analogy between the choice of the difference principle in the original position and the maximin rule of choice in decision theory. Some ambiguity here depends on the fact that in TJ Rawls presents the maximin argument for the principles of justice within the same section 26 in which he opts for the difference principle (4.3).

According to the fair equality of opportunity principle, no one can be discriminated against with respect to the possibility of having access to the most significant social positions. The ban on discrimination is meant not just formally, but also substantively, so that, for example, all citizens are supposed to be offered roughly equal educational opportunities. This principle is considered difficult to apply in a capitalist society (4.3). In the second part of this chapter (4.4, 4.5, 4.6), we shall discuss a general moral argument for the second principle. The substance of this argument is that liberal-democratic citizens should never accept social and economic inequalities that are arbitrary from a moral point of view. It must be distinguished from the argument of "luck egalitarianism" (4.6). The fair equality of opportunity principle – unlike luck egalitarianism – requires membership in the basic structure. Both the fair equality of opportunity and the difference principle apply just to the basic structure. This institutional side of Rawls' theory of justice has been criticized because it causes too neat a separation between personal and institutional morality (4.7).

4.1 The Second Principle as a Socio-Economic Criterion of Equality

The second principle of justice, in one of its various expositions in TJ, maintains that: "Social and economic inequalities are to be arranged so that they are: (a) to be to the greatest benefit of the least advantaged, consistent with the just savings principle and (b) attached to offices and positions open to all under conditions of fair equality of opportunity" (TJ 302; rev. edn. 266).

In a slightly different form, the principle is repeated in PL and JFR as follows: "Social and economic inequalities are to satisfy two conditions: first, they are to be attached to positions and offices open to all under conditions of fair equality of opportunity; and second, they are to be to the greatest benefit of the least advantaged members of society" (PL 6; JFR 42–3).

Unlike the first principle, there are no significant differences among the first, the second and the later formulation of the second principle, except for a reversal of the two parts, and the lack of the just savings principle (that, in any event, may be considered as being merely put off to another place in the second version). This does not mean that Rawls' attitude with respect to the second principle remained unchanged. As time went by, Rawls nourished many doubts about the second part of the second principle, that is, the difference principle. In particular, the idea that the difference principle may be derived in the original position from a peculiar interpretation of a rational choice theory, present in the first version of TJ, was initially scaled down (in the revised version of TJ) and subsequently given up for good (JFR 95 in an unequivocal manner; JFR 132–3 in a vaguer manner).

There have been plenty of objections to the first principle of justice. However, the second principle of justice has been far more criticized. Rawls divides it into two parts. In the first part, he affirms the "fair equality of opportunity" criterion, while in the second he affirms the "difference principle." The principle of fair equality of opportunity must already be satisfied in order to proceed in the direction of the difference principle (TJ 77, 264–7; rev. edn. 66–7, 233–6). It should be recalled that there is already a lexicographical priority of the first principle over the second, heightened by a further priority of a part of the second principle over the other. As we shall see, the fact that we cannot move directly to the actual difference principle other than through two preventive constraints is not devoid of consequences.

The principles of justice serve a dual purpose. On the one hand, they aim at the best possible set-up of the political institutions while, on the other, they relate to the socio-economic structure of distributive justice. It is quite easy to suggest that the first principle – based on liberty – concerns for the most part political institutions, while the second – focusing on equality – concerns socio-economic relations among citizens. Rawls has added to the revised edition of TJ the following claim:

> Their formulation presupposes that, for the purposes of a theory of justice, the social structure may be viewed as having two more or less distinct parts, the first principle applying to the one, the second principle to the other. Thus we distinguish between the aspects of the social system that define and secure the equal basic liberties and the aspects that specify and establish social and economic inequalities. (TJ; rev. edn. 53)

The ordering of Rawls' principles is however highly relevant. The two principles of justice need to be considered together, and only their combination is coherent with the theory of justice as fairness. This means that the so-called "difference principle" should not be considered independently from the liberty principle and the principle of fair equality of opportunity. In addition, there are some fundamental moral reasons for favoring the difference principle. Prevalent among these reasons is a general "tendency to equality."

This way of presenting and defending the second principle is also adopted in this chapter. At first, I will take for granted a few difficulties connected with a purely analytical and deductive inference of the difference principle (to which we shall return in chapter 5 and its appendix). Then, I will explain the sense of the difference principle from the perspective of distributive justice. Afterwards, the analysis of the fair equality of opportunity principle and the introduction of a more general moral argument will show that Rawls' thesis may also be defended in a more plausible way.

Therefore, even if an expository logic would cause the fair equality of opportunity principle to be preceded by the difference principle, I prefer to begin by debating the more controversial part of the argument: that is, the difference principle.[1]

4.2 The Difference Principle and Primary Goods

The difference principle asserts that social and economic inequalities are to be to the greatest benefit of the least advantaged members of society. The relevant socio-economic positions are defined in terms of "social primary goods." It may not be possible to lay down a sensible list of primary goods in a neutral manner.[2] The problem concerns a difficulty that relates to the foundations of economics. Interpersonal comparisons, on which the usefulness of a list of primary goods depends, are not restricted to income but relate to welfare. Welfare may not be viewed as a linear function of income. There are two standard alternatives in considering welfare functions: either we propose a limitation to a merely ordinal measure of welfare; or we make room for a cardinal measure of welfare. In both cases, the problem of interpersonal comparisons arises.[3] Rawls' thesis considers an ordinal measure of welfare and limits the comparison to a set of previously selected goods. While Rawls overcomes the most obvious difficulties of utilitarianism, his solution does give rise to new ones, linked to the criterion used to select such goods (see Appendix to chapter 5).[4]

The primary goods are the *distribuendum*, that is, the main object to be distributed within a theory of distributive justice. They are initially defined by Rawls as "things that every rational man is presumed to want" (TJ 62; rev. edn. 54). After the first version of TJ, they are referred to as "what persons need in their status of free and equal citizens" (rev. edn. xiii). The primary goods that Rawls has in mind include the power attached to one's position or office, income and wealth and the social bases of self-respect (when not already included in the first two goods) (TJ 62; rev. edn. 54). In PL (181), Rawls provides a slightly different list that includes among the social primary goods:

(i)   basic rights and liberties;
(ii) freedom of movement and free choice of occupation;
(iii) powers and prerogatives of offices and positions of responsibility in the political and economic institutions of the basic structure;
(iv) income and wealth;
(v)   the social bases of self-respect.

These goods taken together make up an "index," meaning a unit of measurement of different goods. Obviously, it is quite arbitrary to group only these goods in an index. Later, Rawls, perhaps following Musgrave's suggestion,[5] has included leisure time (CP 455), and Pogge has suggested including the quality of the work being carried out.[6] In any event, even if additional goods are included, Rawls' index remains vague because he does not even try to work out some sort of unit of measurement corresponding to it.

The least advantaged are considered to be those that occupy the lowest positions in the light of an index conceived as specified above. The term "least advantaged" does not represent for Rawls a rigid designator; that is, it does not correspond to any specific person but it refers to an indeterminate group. Therefore, the principle works under a condition of anonymity: Rawls talks about a "least advantaged representative man" and, therefore, he clearly does not have in mind persons viewed as individuals. The idea is not to choose the individual who is worse off according to any criterion whatsoever – for instance, taking a disabled person with no resources and modeling the difference principle on her. Instead, the idea is to show representative social positions. The latter are defined, as previously pointed out, in terms of primary goods.

A distinction must be drawn between two types of primary goods, natural goods and social goods. The natural primary goods are qualities and talents such as health, beauty, intelligence and so on, and, while they are affected by the social structure, they do not depend directly on it. Rawls does not consider these goods insignificant from the point of view of distributive justice but he does maintain that, with reference to these goods, their natural distribution is neither just nor unjust. What is just or unjust is rather how the "institutions deal with these facts" (TJ 102; rev. edn. 87).

Social primary goods, on the other hand – such as income, wealth, liberty, and opportunity – are distributed by social institutions. In formulating his argument in favor of the difference principle, Rawls considers only the social primary goods. This may engender apparent injustices in the sense that, at times, we may think of the least advantaged as those who are placed very badly in terms of the distribution of natural goods, starting with – but not limited to – health, even if they do not rank lowest in terms of the distribution of social primary goods.

Thus, the difference principle seems to neglect the destinies of those who contingently find themselves suffering from natural deficits, including disabilities.[7] This is the reason why quite a few critiques have been voiced on the subject, beginning with those of Amartya Sen and Martha Nussbaum.[8] According to Sen's capability approach, what counts is not only the resources being distributed but also the relation between goods and persons. This relation has to function adequately, and this is why the Rawlsian division of the primary goods could prove inadequate, particularly in the case of serious deficits like the want of food and health.[9] In this case, Rawls may be defended by bearing in mind that the principles of justice apply to the basic structure and address the "normal" relations among persons who cooperate with one another under conditions of reciprocity. As Rawls says: "the first problem of justice concerns the relations among those who in the normal course of things are full and active participants in society and directly or indirectly associated together over the whole range of life" (CP 258–9).

This fact rules out the possibility that the difference principle might take into account special situations, even though these may be so tragic and morally relevant as to arouse, as Rawls says, our "pity and anxiety" (CP 259). In any event, the latter will not be excluded from within the context of justice, as there is a "remedial justice" context where it may be conceived that special situations are considered in their specificity.[10] Furthermore, in PL, Rawls explains that, given the complexity of the matter, it would be better to put off the solution of this type of problem to the legislative stage rather than approaching it in the original position, with a view to making the most of the higher level of information available to citizens.

The difference principle proposes to enhance the expectations of the least advantaged in terms of social primary goods, such as income, welfare, opportunities, power and self-respect. The following definition of a general conception of justice is supposed to be coherent with the difference principle: "All social values – liberty and opportunity, income and wealth, and the bases of self-respect – are to be distributed equally unless an unequal distribution of any or all of these values is to everyone's advantage" (TJ 62; rev. edn. 59).

All this does not automatically tell us who are the least advantaged. As Rawls happens to say, there are two ways to identify the "class" of the least advantaged. First, one may select a specific social position, for instance that of the unskilled unemployed worker, and proceed with modeling the category on it. In so doing, the least advantaged would be considered unskilled unemployed workers and all those taking advantage of the social primary goods at their level or below it. Second, one may resort to a statistical definition that does not take into account a special status, for instance the definition of "least advantaged" would apply to all those who have an income and a wealth that is, say, less than a half of the average per capita income. It goes without saying that the creation of such an index is complex, as witnessed by the fact that there is a tendency to confine the interpersonal comparison to income and wealth. This has the consequence that other primary goods would be excluded in this case from the determination of the class of the least advantaged.

In "A Kantian Conception of Equality" (p. 96), Rawls presents a mixed and more general criterion that seems to identify the least advantaged according to three parameters (it is not clear whether they must all be present or whether at least two are enough, given that Rawls talks also about an "overlap" of the parameters). According to this subsequent definition, the least advantaged would include all the members of the class of persons who prove worse off in terms of historical, natural and social contingencies.

4.2.1 Inequalities Compatible with Social Justice

Various considerations call upon us to consider the difference principle as being unlike a formal principle of social choice.[11] The principle seems more general. First, it applies to the whole socio-economic system – that is to say, independently from comparing local states of affairs. Second, contrary to what is often believed with respect to the difference principle, the problem is not merely to protect the worst-off, guarding him/her from unacceptable inequalities. It is also, and perhaps mostly, to allow inequalities that are considered useful in the perspective of the general interest, protecting at the same time those who do not benefit from them. If, for instance, it is assumed that a system of incentives makes those endowed with talent more productive and that, in general, transfers of economic resources may occur from the laziest and least able persons to those who are more eager and able, then the difference principle should not prevent this.[12] In fact, in this way, the socio-economic system as a whole would benefit from it and, just on this account, it would be meaningless, according to Rawls, to rule out the consequent inequalities altogether. Rather, it is a question of making them compatible – if we want to stick to the logic of the difference principle – with a fair treatment of those who benefit least.

The difference principle is not an extremely prudential or radically egalitarian principle. Indeed, through the adoption of a system of transfers and incentives, its logic promotes inequalities that reward the most endowed. However, the difference principle subjects to a constraint the inequalities admissible within the context of the theory of justice as fairness: they must be justified to everyone. And, obviously, the only way in which such a justification may occur is by proving that the incentives for the most endowed contribute to creating an improved situation for all, starting from the worst-off. Rawls reasons on the assumption that social cooperation does not normally result in a zero-sum game. Were it a zero-sum game, the difference principle could have perverse distributive outcomes. But if that is not the case, as assumed by Rawls, it becomes possible to reward the most endowed, benefiting at the same time the worst-off consistently with the difference principle.

In order to make the aforementioned argument less obscure, suffice it to consider a simple case such as the following. Let us imagine a social system featuring an egalitarian distribution – calling this distribution D1 – where everyone has the same bundle of primary goods. Such a distribution is compatible with the difference principle. Nevertheless, according to Rawls, it is meaningful to defend it if and only if, by creating certain differences in terms of distribution that reward the most productive persons, it is not possible to increase the total amount of the set of primary goods to be distributed. Given that such a situation of impossibility is not very plausible, then we can think that there is another distribution – let us call it D2 – that, by stimulating the most productive persons and by moving their resources, succeeds in distributing among the members of society a total amount of primary goods that is greater than the total amount in D1. Let us say that, in D2, goods move from the hands of the least productive to those of the most productive individuals. Is D2 compatible with the difference principle? The answer to a question put in such a manner is that, under these terms, we may not know. In fact, the answer depends on what share of the product is distributed to the most advantaged members and what share to the least advantaged members. In substance, we have to believe that there are at least two possible alternatives – let us call them D2A and D2B. Let us suppose that D2A distributes a higher-than-average preferential share to the members that are more advantaged, leaving however to the least advantaged a definitely higher share than they would have had in D1. In addition, let us suppose that, under D2B, the greater benefit for the more advantaged does not turn into a condition for the least advantaged that is better than in D1. Based on these assumptions, we can then say that D2A is compatible with the difference principle, and preferable to D1, while D2B is not.[13]

In this regard, far from being too egalitarian and paralyzing, the difference principle may in practice allow inequalities. This fact is strengthened by Rawls' assumption that there is a "chain connection" so as to allow that socio-economic advantages get distributed more or less uniformly within the system, and a "close-knitness" (TJ 81–2; rev. edn. 70–1) according to which the expectations of the least advantaged are linked to those of the more advantaged. In other words, it is impossible for an advantage for the first and the last in a class not to be accompanied by some advantage for the person who is halfway between them. Actually, the difference principle is compatible with capitalism, but just in the egalitarian form of a property-owning democracy. Restrictions on the permissible inequalities may also come from other parts of the Rawlsian system, for instance from the fair value of political liberty that we have analyzed when dealing with the first principle. In this case, some socio-economic inequalities are not deemed acceptable as they could give rise to harmful political consequences. The Rawlsian system, which is in itself definitely egalitarian, needs to be analyzed as a whole, as does the fact that some differences in terms of socio-economic advantages as such are considered tolerable only if they do not entail differences with significant political weight. This thesis gets strengthened when we consider the theory of justice as fairness in its entirety, as this is an egalitarian theory in all its main features. Ultimately, egalitarianism is not linked solely to the second principle of justice, and even less so is it linked solely to the difference principle.

Rawls formulates the idea that the difference principle tolerates even considerable inequalities, but not all of them. The foremost difficulty with this reasoning, as previously pointed out, is to successfully identify the least advantaged. But there could be another difficulty, which is usually overlooked. General advances in terms of gross product, compatible also with the difference principle, could come about at the cost, for instance, of serious damage to the natural environment or cuts to the rate of public education for society as a whole. Given the socio-economic limits of the difference principle, a distribution like D2A above could not be blocked by resorting merely to the difference principle, even if its consequences were to damage the environment or reduce the rate of public education. However, within a Rawlsian framework, it could be blocked by resorting to the just savings principle or to the fair equality of opportunity principle. The former provides for certain obligations of the present generations in favor of future ones, and some protection of the natural environment could also be included. As we shall see shortly, the latter principle sticks in particular to the purpose of enhancing and protecting educational opportunities for all, including those who are endowed with talent but lack resources.

Another difficulty due to the difference principle may depend upon the fact that – as recognized by Pogge[14] – it addresses exclusively the absolute levels of advantage and disadvantage among the members of a society. In so doing, it neglects in full the relative levels. Thus, a society – compatibly with the difference principle – could prevent the enjoyment of certain goods, in particular the so-called "positional goods," by the least advantaged who, however, in absolute terms would be better off than before. This would occur because the more advantaged would secure the most desirable goods thanks to their surplus tolerated by the difference principle. Furthermore, in such a case, I believe that little else could be done other than appealing – should it be plausible – to the protection of such principles as the fair value of liberty and the fair equality of opportunity. Perhaps such a general theoretical hypothesis as Rawls' cannot be evaluated in so much detail, and we have to be content with a general plausibility, which it surely has.

4.3 The Fair Equality of Opportunity

A principle of equality of opportunity is part of many liberal theories, even though Rawls' interpretation of it is by no means standard. The difference principle deals only with the socio-economic effects of a distribution of primary goods and, from this perspective, what counts is only that the size of the social pie be maximized, consistent with a distribution that privileges the worst-off. But something similar may unquestionably occur even if some members of society are excluded a priori from the possibility of competing for the most important and profitable social positions. Let us imagine a society where the important social positions are linked to the level of education, and let us suppose that the system of education in that society is both private and expensive. In such a society, those who are born into the poorer families will not have the possibility of securing access to the most important social positions, or, in any event, it will be very hard for them to do so. Despite this discrimination, it is possible for the current distribution to pass the test of the difference principle.

The fact that a distribution of primary goods may succeed in passing the test of the difference principle while excluding some members of society from competition is more common than usually thought. Historically, for instance, it has affected blacks, women and poor people. It is also natural for a person endowed with a liberal mentality to find this type of situation despicable. The principle of equality of opportunity does away with this type of discrimination and, indeed, this is the reason why Rawls ultimately considers it to take priority over the difference principle. We are in the presence of a sort of filter that is applied to the various likely distributions of primary goods before choosing which of them is to be preferred.

According to the principle of equality of opportunity, careers and important positions must be open to all. This thesis entails an a-priori exclusion of discrimination. In the standard interpretation, it is a formal provision according to which "all have at least the same legal rights of access to all advantaged social positions" (TJ 72; rev. edn. 62). No one, if we take the principle seriously, may be excluded from competing for access to educational institutions or to advantaged offices or positions of responsibility.

Such a clause potentially prevents the possibility of having recourse to forms of affirmative action or reverse discrimination. They violate the condition of equality of opportunity. This attitude, which is normal among those who might be called right-wing liberals, is more unusual for such an egalitarian liberal as Rawls.[15] If we adopt such an attitude, women and blacks cannot regularly be given preferential treatment with respect to other competitors for important social positions. At the most, if at times we deem it advisable to defend certain type of quotas for minorities that have been subject to past discriminations, the move will only be remedial and temporary.

Rawls recovers his liberal egalitarianism when he affirms that the principle of equality of opportunity must not be merely formal. Rawls calls this more substantive principle the principle of "fair equality of opportunity." The formal principle of equality of opportunity allows everyone to compete on an equal basis for all the most important positions and careers, but makes no reference at all to the starting conditions of this competition. With a view to making up for this type of injustice, Rawls proposes the principle of fair equality of opportunity:

> those who are at the same level of talent and ability, and have the same willingness to use them, should have the same prospects of success regardless of their initial place in the social system . . . Chances to acquire cultural knowledge and skills should not depend upon one's class position, and so the school system, whether public or private, should be designed to even out class barriers. (TJ 73; rev. edn. 63, cf. also JFR 44)

The principle of fair equality of opportunity appears very demanding, as it affirms that all those who have equal natural endowments – regardless of their initial place in society – should be similarly rewarded by the institutional system. There are numerous factors that give rise to different "prospects of success," beginning with the greater stimuli that a well-off and knowledgeable family offers its children. Is it possible to step in to deal with this variety of facts without perverting the nature of social life? More generally, if we were to create an institutional system out of nothing, this type of principle would perhaps seem difficult but plausible. However, working from historical contingencies – as we must in every real society – the matter becomes much more complicated.

Rawls supplies a moderate interpretation of the principle. Ultimately, he is interested in the elimination of the main "class positions" that determine different life prospects. A direct consequence of the principle, in this moderate interpretation, would be a system of public education that allows all the members of society to attain an adequate level of knowledge. In this respect, Rawls is inspired by the Deweyan tradition of American liberalism.

From this point of view, other forms of discrimination, including sexual and racial discrimination, seem to have less importance for Rawls. This is probably due to the fact that natural distinctions depend less directly on the basic structure. Various reasons may be found for this reductionist approach (according to which class differences count more), starting from the fact that Rawls presents an ideal theory where factors such as sex and race should have no significance. However, I feel that the limitation to class differences is insufficient in relation to the principle of fair equality of opportunity (see also chapter 5).

A separate problem stems from the possible effects of the priority of the principle of fair equality of opportunity over the difference principle. In the case of conflict between the two principles, not all societies would be willing to sacrifice a better distribution of primary goods for the sake of access to public education. Opposition to such a sacrifice has been upheld and generalized by the theses of some market liberals, such as Friedman and Nozick. They argue that the principle of equality of opportunity is not acceptable, since it places unjustified restrictions on the choices of consenting adults. Moreover, in so doing, it would not only limit individual liberty but would also create problems of efficiency. In view of what has been said above, I believe that we may reject the second part of this critique on the ground that the rationale of the fair equality of opportunity principle is not itself economic. That rationale does not consist in efficiency; rather it is based on the attainment of the equal status of free and equal citizens. Even if a given distribution were acceptable in terms of the difference principle – we might suggest – it would not pass through the filter of the fair equality of opportunity principle should the type of inequality caused by this distribution jeopardize the equal intellectual and moral growth of citizens.

A further answer to this type of dilemma may come from the centrality of education and training in the formulation of the principle of fair equality of opportunity. Culture and professional training, linked perhaps to the so-called "Aristotelian Principle" (see chapter 2), could be goods of a special nature. This is, after all, less strange than might at first appear if we consider that Rawls is an academic and, therefore, particularly sensitive to this type of good. Something of this kind is suggested, for instance, by statements of the following kind:

> the value of education should not be assessed solely in terms of economic efficiency and social welfare. Equally if not more important is the role of education

in enabling a person to enjoy the culture of his society and to take part in its affairs, and in this way to provide for each individual a secure sense of his own worth. (TJ 101; rev. edn. 87)

Personally, I feel sympathetic towards Rawls' proposal but, as worded, it seems somehow inconsistent with the general vision of distributive justice in terms of primary goods. A special place for education would mean, to maintain the consistency of the theory, that education is a special primary good. But such a thesis is not laid down anywhere in TJ, and, to be accepted, it would most probably require changes in the general structure of the theory of justice as fairness. Besides, it is quite likely that such a proposal would create difficulties in the delicate balance of incentives and guarantees on which the difference principle is based. In fact, it is unquestionable that one of the incentives that the most productive members might want in order to cooperate better in relation to the general welfare could be to provide their children with a more stimulating intellectual environment. This is something that the principle of fair equality of opportunity would make more difficult or even impossible. The only way to defend the principle is to confirm its political meaning. The formation of the higher interests of the citizens depends on their intellectual education. Rawls says in TJ: "resources for education are not to be allotted solely or necessarily mainly according to their return as estimated in productive trained abilities, but also according to their worth in enriching the personal and social life of citizens" (TJ 107; rev. edn. 92).

4.4 A General Moral Argument in Favor of the Second Principle

There is a more general moral argument in favor of the second principle of justice. This argument, inspired by the Kantian notion of equality, covers the difference principle and the principle of fair equality of opportunity, the necessary relationship between the first and the second principle, and, in addition, the correctives imposed by the just savings principle. In the light of this comprehensive reading, one can succeed in gaining an understanding of the second principle. If we follow this reading, it turns out that perhaps the original position is not the only or even the best way to opt in favor of the second principle. Some insight in this respect may be gained in sections 12–17 of TJ's second chapter ("Interpretations of the Second Principle," "Democratic Equality and the Difference Principle," "Fair Equality of Opportunity and Pure Procedural Justice," "Primary Social Goods as the Basis of Expectations," "Relevant Social Positions," and "The Tendency to Equality"). I believe that the reading based on a general moral argument in favor of the second principle is supported by the following considerations:

(i)   Rawls' self-interpretations after TJ move in this direction. Rawls stresses the Kantian meaning of the theory, tones down the centrality of rational choice theory in TJ, and places emphasis on the significance of the moral interests of the person (see KCMT).

(ii)   Some influential readers of TJ have stressed this approach. Worth mentioning, *inter alia*, are Brian Barry, Thomas Nagel and Will Kymlicka.[16] For all of them, this choice has a special meaning, because it helps to defend a particular reading of TJ.

(iii)   An actual defense of the maximin in terms of rational choice may hardly be proposed at present in light of reasonable criticism expressed by many commentators and perhaps Rawls doubted it from the beginning.

(iv)   The interpretation of the second principle as being based on premises of a moral and political nature that precede the original position protects the theory of justice as fairness from other important criticisms. For instance, it defends it against the critique according to which Rawls conceals an implicit theory of the good in the formulation of the theory of the right, because in this case the theory of the good would be partially explicit.

(v)   Finally, this approach is consistent with emphasis on the notion of reflective equilibrium conceived as the central methodological tool of the theory of justice as fairness, a vision that has been gaining more and more credit in recent years.

The moral interpretation of the second principle rules out a possible outcome of the purely deductive interpretation: not every distribution of burdens and benefits that may be derived from such a hypothetical situation of choice as that of the original position is right. Instead, a Kantian axiom of equality has to be respected: "All social values – liberty and opportunity, income and wealth, and the bases of self-respect – are to be distributed equally unless an unequal distribution of any or all of these values is to everyone's advantage" (TJ 62; rev. edn. 54).

If you like, the notion of equality can be taken as given and, subsequently, it may be maintained that any departure from this default position has to be justified. Hence, justifying inequality becomes the main task of a theory of social justice when it deals with the distribution of primary goods. Let us keep in mind that Rawls' theory of justice confines itself to treating matters related to the distribution of primary goods that depend on the institutional basic structure (not all resources are relevant in the light of this distribution). A similar distinction is required to understand Rawls' thesis and may be appreciated in light of the difference between "legitimate expectations" and "moral desert." The theory of justice addresses merely the former:

> Moreover, the notion of distribution according to virtue fails to distinguish between moral desert and legitimate expectations. Thus, it is true that as persons

and groups take part in just arrangements, they acquire claims on one another defined by the publicly recognized rules . . . A just scheme, then, answers to what men are entitled to; it satisfies their legitimate expectations as founded upon social institutions. But what they are entitled to is not proportional to nor dependent upon their intrinsic moral worth. (TJ 311; rev. edn. 273)

Given the initial significance of equality, there would be an easy and imme-diate solution to the problem of social distribution. It would be enough to endorse a pure egalitarianism and no one would have anything to complain about. However, this solution is not accepted by Rawls. To understand the reason, one must consider the way in which he conceives the fundamental institutions of a society and the prospect of cooperation. For him, the institu-tions are structures that ought to secure mutual advantage. It ensues that a pure or radical egalitarianism would not be satisfactory, as it would rule out institutional solutions able to benefit all. In fact, pure egalitarianism would nullify social and economic incentives and, therefore, would translate into a lower total amount of primary goods to be distributed among the people. The second principle – and the general conception of justice as fairness – is based on this equilibrium between equality and inequality, or rather fairness and efficiency. This is how Rawls reasons in a sentence that summarizes his moral justification of the difference principle and privileges equality as the default position with respect to the demonstration through the original position:

Because we start from equal shares, those who benefit least have, so to speak, a veto; and thus we arrive at the difference principle. Taking equality as the basis of comparison, those who have gained more must do it on terms that are justifiable to those who have gained the least . . .
The conception of equality contained in the principles of justice is Kantian. ("A Kantian Conception of Equality," pp. 97–9)

The moral argument chooses an equilibrium between economic efficiency and political equality. What follows from this is that the least advantaged have a veto with respect to distribution. There is no need to interpret such a veto literally. The right of veto of the least advantaged translates, in the Rawlsian vocabulary, into the need to view the moral justification of any non-egalitarian distribution of primary goods in the light of the situation of those who are worst off. What cannot be justified, using Rawls' words, is any distributive outcome that is "arbitrary from the moral point of view."

4.4.1 Arbitrary from the Moral Point of View? Luck Egalitarianism versus Rawls

Arbitrariness from the moral point of view relates to what we are fated with by society and nature, where we are born, and, ultimately, who we are. No one deserves in a strict sense to be born into a given family or to be endowed with a few natural qualities. On this subject, Rawls famously states in TJ:

> It seems to be one of the fixed points of our considered judgments that no one deserves his place in the distribution of native endowments, any more than one deserves one's initial starting place in society. The assertion that a man deserves the superior character that enables him to make the effort to cultivate his abilities is equally problematic, for his character depends in large part upon family and social circumstances for which he can claim no credit. The notion of desert seems not to apply to these cases. (TJ 104; rev. edn. slightly different 89 and 274)

According to many interpreters, Rawls here commits himself to a "luck egalitarian view" according to which justice presupposes the elimination of the influence of the arbitrary factors on distribution. If this view is correct, then there is a blatant contradiction between such an approach and many other parts of Rawls' work, beginning with his treatment of disabled persons and foreigners. In my opinion, Rawls does not intend, however, to discuss the general problem of justice and luck in these terms.[17] Rather he confines himself to supporting his thesis in relation to the distribution of primary goods through the basic structure. In so doing, the arbitrariness of native and social endowment is not itself under attack, but only its arbitrariness insofar as it relates to the "basic structure." As Rawls affirms: "The natural distribution is neither just nor unjust; nor is it unjust that persons are born into society at some particular position. These are simply natural facts. What is just and unjust is the way that institutions deal with these facts" (TJ 102; rev. edn. 87).[18]

In other words, the fact of being born into a good family or of being endowed with significant natural talent is irrelevant from the point of view of the theory of justice. However, if this contingent fact affects the "basic structure" and becomes the main basis for distributing primary goods, then it gives rise to a problem of justification and, therefore, of justice.

The need to justify a distribution of primary goods, showing that it is not morally arbitrary, should not be mistaken for the viewpoint of the so-called "luck egalitarians." Luck egalitarianism is a thesis shared at least in part by important philosophers such as Dworkin, G. A. Cohen, Arneson, Kymlicka, and Roemer. The thesis maintains that a just distribution should try to compensate for the effects of "brute luck." Effects of misfortune, according to luck egalitarianism, should be as far as possible neutralized in the distribution of benefits and burdens.

According to this thesis, the main moral task of a vision of distributive justice is to compensate individuals for social and natural disadvantages that do not depend on their choices and for which they may not be blamed. The case of the disabled we have previously referred to represents an emblematic test of the thesis of luck egalitarians.[19] Rawls is criticized for having failed to consider this moral requirement to redress certain fundamental injustices, among which disabilities are paradigmatic. According to this accusation,

Rawls would in effect be inconsistent, because such unlucky fates are indeed those that are typically more arbitrary from a moral point of view.

In general terms, luck egalitarianism links luck, responsibility and distribution. Responsibility must be insulated from bad luck, and no one – from the perspective of distribution – is entitled to have more social benefits or burdens unless this separation is realized.[20] Luck egalitarianism, under these premises, may be built around four consistent parts:

(i)   distributions depend upon a mix of voluntary choices and random circumstances that every individual needs to confront in life;
(ii) inequalities in distribution may be broken down into inequalities that depend upon voluntary choices and inequalities that depend upon random circumstances;
(iii) there is a principle of responsibility that lays down that each may be blamed for the outcome of his voluntary choices, but not for the outcome of random circumstances. For example, there is a difference between my losing all that I own in a game of poker and my losing all that I own in an earthquake;
(iv) whoever is concerned about equality should take into account (i), (ii) and (iii) to conclude that inequalities due to random circumstances are particularly unjust and that their victims should be protected in a special manner.

From this general thesis, luck egalitarians derive both an attack on Rawls and an (egalitarian) principle of justice. The attack on Rawls is based on what is considered an ambiguous status in his position. According to luck egalitarianism, Rawls – for the difference principle to be consistent with the rest of the theory – should allow for the provision of compensation for victims of the natural lottery. To put it in the words of Will Kymlicka (speaking of Rawls): "He endorses: 2) Social inequalities should be compensated and natural inequalities should not influence distribution . . . But if natural and social inequalities really are equally undeserved, we should instead endorse 3): Natural and social inequalities should be compensated."[21] Put in these terms, the luck egalitarian position raises two evident problems:

(i)   Is Rawls inconsistent about the compensation of natural inequalities?
(ii) Can luck egalitarianism offer a sound vision of distributive justice alternative to Rawls'?

In my opinion, the answers to both questions must be negative.

(a) The answer to the first question is negative because: (ia) Rawls never said in TJ that the natural lottery must be directly compensated for; and (iia) the spirit of Rawls' theory of justice, beginning from the difference principle, is more institutional than his luck egalitarian critics admit.

(ia) The first point – defended by Samuel Freeman[22] – is arguable through two complementary Rawlsian theses. First, Rawls never says that people do not deserve their natural assets. He just says that nobody deserves the relative position in the distribution of these natural assets. This kind of arbitrariness is in some ways trivial, bearing in mind the obvious fact that nobody deserves for example to be born with a special talent (TJ 311–12; rev. edn. 274; cf. also JFR 74). The implication of this arbitrariness is not, however, that we should neutralize special talents. On the contrary, we should try to socialize them, making them collectively advantageous. This conclusion has nothing to do with the remedies one can derive from a luck egalitarian thesis, and is instead coherent with the difference principle via the selection of the incentives it permits. Gifted persons – within Rawls' vision – are actually entitled to larger social benefits, the reason being not so much that they deserve them for being naturally lucky, but that they must be encouraged to give the best possible contributions to the life of society. That is why compensations for misfortune deriving from brute luck are not allowed by the difference principle and by Rawls' theory of justice. This does not mean that there are no guarantees for people who are particularly unlucky. If inequalities connected with natural endowments are some way undeserved, then these inequalities must be compensated for. For Rawls, the first kind of compensation comes from what he calls "the principle of redress." Now, the difference principle is not of course the principle of redress (TJ 101; rev. edn. 86). The principle of redress instead is a subordinate part of the theory of justice as fairness and it cannot be taken as the sole criterion of justice.

Inequalities are instead more generally mitigated by the second principle, both as difference principle and as fair equality of opportunity principle. The first part gives a more egalitarian flavor to the theory, whereas the second part says that people with special misfortunes (e.g. disabilities) must be put in conditions that enable them to compete with others.

(iia) Second, Rawls assumes an institutional point of view. According to a simplified version of the luck egalitarian argument, morally arbitrary features of life should not influence people's entitlements. Our place of birth typically represents one of these arbitrary features. As a consequence, fair principles of justice should neutralize the distributional effects depending on the place of birth. If we think of global justice, such a view implies that principles of global justice should neutralize the difference between, for example, being born in the Congo and in the USA. Note that this kind of argument does not rely at all for its justification on the existing system of institutions. That is why it has nothing to do with a Rawlsian argument. According to a Rawlsian argument, political institutions that people share, for example within the state, create special relations among citizens and therefore give sound reasons to reject the thesis that the place of birth is completely arbitrary from a moral point of view. Applied to global justice, such a form of reasoning implies that sound principles of justice cannot directly neutralize the difference between being born in the Congo and in the USA. As always with Rawls, there is no argument for justice independently from the institutional system and outside the basic structure.

To this a luck egalitarian could object that Rawls gives different accounts of his own "institutional" view. At times, he sees the relevant institutional basis as a political order, in which people are bound by common laws (synonymous of citizenship). But at other times, he sees the relevant institutional basis as a regime of standard cooperation among individuals capable of contributing. These two interpretations are different and imply different consequences. Not all citizens of a political order are capable of contributing to a regime of standard cooperation. Yet such non-contributing members are citizens. For example, the disabled are citizens. And so, to say that Rawls' theory of justice is "institutional" could not yet explain why we don't have duties of justice to remedy the undeserved disadvantages arising from natural disabilities for our co-citizens. And it could seem from this point of view that a revised difference principle that incorporates natural primary goods is a plausible answer to that question.

Meeting such an objection requires a deeper insight into Rawls' moral arguments for distributive justice. From the start, Rawls considers parties in the original position as normally capable of contributing. Justice is conceived as a way to distribute the surplus of cooperation among contributors when these contributors are members of the same political community. That is why this objection fails: Rawlsian justice has in mind an overlap between normal contributors and co-citizens, and one cannot easily disentangle these two aspects of any social community. The institutional side of a Rawlsian theory of justice cannot separate the political community encompassing contributors and non-contributors from the effective participants to a scheme of cooperation. Willing such separation, luck egalitarians pretend a radical change within the very structure of a Rawlsian theory of justice, and not simply a revision including some natural goods among the goods to be distributed. And Rawls would be really inconsistent if he had accepted such a radical change. Instead, his view, in which co-citizens who are not able to contribute normally to the collective wellbeing are protected by other parts of the system is much more consistent with the whole. Rawlsian society is neither a political community encompassing contributors and non-contributors, nor a scheme of cooperation including only contributors. It is rather a bridge between these two options.

(b) My answer to the second question is negative, for the following four reasons. First, the idea of neutralizing fate is impracticable. The very possibility of clearly distinguishing between choices and circumstances is questionable (as those who have read Freud and Marx know). Samuel Scheffler, among others, says that this distinction is philosophically dubious and "morally implausible."[23] People's personalities and capacities are often a consequence of unchosen facts: where you were born, to whom, charm, sympathy, wittiness, etc. And there are of course apparently rational choices that turn out quite badly. That is why basing distributive justice on the choice–circumstance distinction, which is so indeterminate, is unworkable.

Second, in considering all inequalities that depend upon circumstances rather than choices to be unjust,[24] luck egalitarianism risks treating inequality as a fault or weakness of those who enjoy fewer goods. This potentially undermines the self-esteem of the least advantaged.[25] It looks at the problem more in terms of pity than justice. By contrast, for Rawls, moral equality and respect for others take priority and are not challenged by the fact that someone has fewer goods.

Third, there is no need to be radical in order to admit that voluntary choices in a capitalist market regime may give rise to unjust inequalities. Structural situations of strength and weakness can put individuals in the position to make wrong choices. It seems that luck egalitarians, relying on the market in order to determine distributive shares, should be obliged to admit that market outcomes are often a matter of chance, more or less like the natural lottery. Also, this fact seems to obscure the central distinction between choice and consequence. In addition, we know that individual preferences may often be "adaptive" and, therefore, are only partly authentic and evidence of responsible intentions. Indeed, this is more a weakness of luck egalitarianism as such than an argument in Rawls' defense.

Fourth, according to Rawls, the principles of justice apply to the "basic structure." The latter must address, through the second principle, the way in which economic institutions usually work. Moreover, the theory of justice as fairness applies to an ideal situation. All the movements of goods and resources, for Rawls, presuppose a regime of standard cooperation among individuals capable of contributing. It is just within this pre-formed ambit that redistribution applies.[26] As we shall see later on when dealing with international justice, a direct application of the second principle to foreigners is not plausible – if we go by the Rawlsian logic – owing to precisely the same reason for which we cannot begin from special cases, such as those of the disabled. In other words, the nature of the theory is not directly allocative, as it is first of all associative, and distribution of resources presupposes membership. From this point of view, equality is not so much a compensation for bad luck as a condition to keep a liberal-democratic society firmly and fairly together.[27] Therefore, it is only the normality of a fruitful cooperation under a system of institutions that justifies the application of the second principle. What needs to be redistributed is not manna from heaven, since the *distribuendum* depends upon the story of how it has been produced. There are facts that go beyond the mere distinction between choice and consequence, which have to form the basis of an account of distributive justice.

The combination of Rawls' arguments seems more effective than the luck egalitarian principle for several reasons, such as those in the following section.

4.5 The Origins of Inequality and the Interpretations of the Second Principle

In order to understand Rawls' position on equality, one can analyze the origin and nature of the possible inequalities and see the way they can be reconciled with a distribution that is not arbitrary from the moral point of view.

Thomas Nagel, in chapter 7 of his *Equality and Partiality*,[28] schematically mentions four different sources of inequality, as outlined below:

(i)   discrimination;
(ii) class;
(iii) talent;
(iv) personal commitment.

These four causes are all significant, but only if we consider them in a comparative perspective can we understand the Rawlsian interpretation of the second principle.[29] They move progressively from outside the conception of the person to within, from the involuntary to the voluntary, from the most institutional to the least institutional. This allows us to see how much harder it becomes, as we move progressively from the first to the fourth cause of inequality, to justify any political economic measure from a moral viewpoint. The democratic interpretation of the second principle stops at the inclusion of the third of these four levels within the distribution context. One of the main problems of the theory of justice probably consists in including this third level, which many would intuitively exclude.

Discrimination can hardly be defended as a cause of justifiable inequality. As a rule, we consider it wrong and – to use Rawls' expression – typically arbitrary from the moral point of view to exclude a priori some people from the opportunities that democracy and the market offer.

As far as class differences are concerned, it is easy to understand that there is no special desert in being born into one family rather than another. We know that this is an important and common cause of inequality. The taxation of inheritances, uniform public education, anti-nepotism rules in public offices, and a proper working of the market may decrease the relevance of what Rawls calls the "social lottery," that is, intergenerational class difference, but cannot fully do away with it. Perhaps only a powerful totalitarian government could try to obtain an equality of this type. This, however, is not a desirable solution. Human beings appear particularly attached to the product of their labor and to their offspring (as Aristotle objects to Plato in the *Politics*), so much so that recognizing incentives synchronically, so to speak, means partly admitting them diachronically; that is to say, it means agreeing to long-lasting consequences. However, we perceive such allowances as a source of injustice. If Sarah has been born to rich and knowledgeable parents, and Dick has been raised amid ignorance and violence, then we perceive that their life prospects are dramatically affected by this in a manner that is arbitrary from a moral point of view. We should also keep in mind that Rawls is not concerned about just any inequality: he is only concerned about those inequalities that may be related to institutions and that are connected with primary goods. Based on this proviso, we may posit the thesis that one of the ends of a liberal-democratic society is to promote and defend those institutions that ensure the maximum equality of opportunity compatible with the natural attachment of parents to their children and, generally, with a reasonable social trend.

Rawls argues for such a thesis both when he defends the second principle from the point of view of the fair equality of opportunity and when he criticizes an interpretation of the second principle of justice linked to what he calls the "system of natural liberty." The latter refers to a social system in which efficiency plays an extensive role of its own and is applied as a criterion to the major institutions and, furthermore, as a system in which careers are usually "open to talents." In this interpretation of the second principle, the priority of the principle of equal liberty is subsequently taken for granted. The system of natural liberty contends that, in a world so open to competition, every social distribution is morally justifiable. In this case, the distribution is governed by the outcomes over time of the competitive market. Rawls' critique of the system of natural liberty is based on the thesis according to which, in this regime, success is affected to an excessive extent by the luck and chance that determine one's birth into a favorable or an unfavorable context:

> But since there is no effort to preserve all equality, or similarity, of social conditions, except insofar as this is necessary to preserve the requisite background institutions, the initial distribution of assets for any period of time is strongly influenced by natural and social contingencies. . . . Intuitively, the most obvious injustice of the system of natural liberty is that it permits distributive shares to be improperly influenced by these factors so arbitrary from a moral point of view. (TJ 72; rev. edn. 62–3)

A classical liberal interpretation of the second principle of justice tends to rectify the intrinsic injustice of the system of natural liberty, adding to the procedural justice inherent in it the further condition of equality of opportunity. Persons with similar abilities and talents should have the same chances of success in life. In a just society, according to the liberal interpretation, each similarly motivated and endowed individual should have equal prospects, regardless of the social class he comes from. In this way, the liberal interpretation of the second principle tries to limit the scope of the social contingencies and chance in determining the citizens' distributive shares. As a result, the working of the free market must be subjected to legal constraints aiming at the preservation of the fundamental social conditions needed to ensure equality of opportunity. Suitable prohibitions or support measures that are likely to attain these ends may be devised, such as barring the transfer of property rights across generations and the provision of a public education for all.

According to Rawls, even the liberal interpretation still remains unsatisfactory (TJ 73–4; rev. edn. 62–3). Although it does away with part of the effects of the social lottery, the liberal interpretation allows ability and native talents to excessively determine distributive shares. The latter are practically dependent on the outcome of a sort of "natural lottery" and even this outcome may be viewed as being arbitrary from the moral point of view. As Rawls himself claims: "there is no more reason to permit the distribution of income and wealth to be settled by the distribution of natural assets than by historical and social fortune" (TJ 74; rev. edn. 64).

The failure of the liberal interpretation depends, for Rawls, on the inability to mitigate the effects of the natural lottery. This conclusion calls for another interpretation of the second principle. Rawls refers to the latter as the democratic interpretation.[30] Both the system of natural liberty and the one based on liberal interpretation fail to pass the test of moral arbitrariness.

The democratic interpretation of the second principle suitably combines the principle of fair equality of opportunity with the difference principle. As we have seen, the latter identifies a particular perspective – that of the least advantaged – from which the inequalities dependent upon the basic structure need to be examined. The fundamental intuitive idea is that the prospects of the more advantaged may not improve unless they provide improvement for the least advantaged as well. Taking up an example given by Rawls, the expectations of a representative member of an advantaged group – say, a member of the entrepreneurial class – cannot be improved without having first granted the same chance to a representative member, say, of the class of unskilled laborers (TJ 78; rev. edn. 67).

This option is not alternative to efficiency, but compatible with it. Considering all efficient distributions, Rawls intends to favor the one that appears the least arbitrary from a moral point of view. Efficiency only comes into play after the general objectives of the two principles have been met. An analogy with the first principle makes this conclusion less strange: most of us would not accept an increase in efficiency at the cost of basic liberties and Rawls' reading of the second principle adds that such a trade-off is inadmissible even for an interpretation of equality.

The theoretical difficulty regarding the democratic interpretation of the second principle occurs in passing from the critique of inequality based on discrimination and class, which many can accept, to the critique of the results of the natural lottery. This thesis can be criticized from two opposite points of view:

(i)   Rawls leaves some important inequalities unchanged;
(ii) the fruits of talents are not morally arbitrary.

In the first case, one wonders whether the inequalities allowed by the difference principle are really justifiable. From this point of view, one might agree with Dworkin and extend the protection of the least advantaged also to deficits of natural primary goods.[31] Consequently, one might suggest a reparatory tool, such as a generalized prenatal insurance, insuring all future citizens against the consequences of bad luck in the distribution of natural primary goods.[32] This solution, which draws inspiration from luck egalitarianism, does not follow from Rawls' perspective (as shown in the previous section).

In any event, it is the second critique – the one related to the social nature of individual talents – that has had a major impact. This critique was formulated by Robert Nozick in a particularly effective manner (see chapter 7). In this case, one wonders whether it is indeed possible to affirm that being endowed with talent and having the will to develop it is not sufficient from the point of view of justification. To answer such a critique one may try to draw a distinction between two different things: on the one hand, whether one deserves a moral reward for being endowed with talent and is entitled to recognition for the decision to make the most of it; on the other hand, the claim that such premises entail a specific reward in terms of primary goods distributed through main institutions.

From this point of view, one may object to Nozick's criticism that we may and must draw a distinction between: (i) the recognition of a talent and the character needed to develop it and (ii) one's personal entitlement to be endowed with a given distributive share connected with it. Rawls is steadfast with respect to this distinction, since: it seems to be "one of the fixed points of our moral judgments that no one deserves his place in the distribution of native endowments any more than he deserves his initial place in society" (TJ 104; slightly different rev. edn. 274 and 104).

It may be recognized that the notion of desert does not apply to the fact of being endowed with talent and a corresponding character. It should also be noted that the democratic interpretation of the second principle does not rule out meritocracy, because Rawls even allows the fact that the most talented should be rewarded institutionally. However he limits such rewards to ensure that their advantage also facilitates that of others, beginning with those who are worse off.[33]

Rawls' final thesis is that inequalities in terms of primary goods may not be justified merely by the difference in initial talent. This derives from the principle that no one deserves to be born with a given genetic endowment or with a special set of talents. We need to admit the existence of an "institutionally defined desert" that, in the end, is the means through which desert turns into primary goods. From this point of view, there is no innocent or neutral institutional system, in the sense that each system either transforms or does not transform a series of talents into goods. Above all, talent and the temperament to develop it are a suitable title for moral reward, but not necessarily for an economic reward or, otherwise, a reward in terms of primary goods (TJ

311; rev. edn. 273–4). In the end, it is not wrong to believe that intelligent, capable, and eager persons are more worthy of esteem and appreciation, but this does not mean that this implies an immediate translation of such recognitions into primary goods.

Criticisms such as Nozick's call for reflection on a more general theoretical question raised by the second principle. It is undeniable that the asymmetry between the worst-off and others, and the greater protection given to the former, is central to the difference principle. According to Rawls, this asymmetry is one of the distinctive features of his position with respect to utilitarianism. Utilitarianism imposes improper sacrifices on some to the benefit of others. However, sticking to Nozick's objection, could we not say that the Rawlsian asymmetry gives rise to the possibility of an analogous sacrifice for the most talented? Nozick raises the point with extreme clarity in *Anarchy, State and Utopia*: "No doubt, the difference principle presents terms on the basis of which those less well endowed would be willing to cooperate . . . But is this a fair agreement on the basis of which those worse endowed should expect the willing cooperation of others?"[34]

All things considered, those more endowed with talent could maintain that the primacy of the worst-offs required by Rawls would force them into making undue sacrifices.[35] From a Rawlsian perspective it is not easy to avoid such an objection, which would make the theory of justice as fairness much more similar to utilitarianism than its author would ever have wanted.[36] A way out is by taking social cooperation to be the source of every economic surplus and maintain that reciprocity is the very basis of cooperation.[37] On this basis, the most talented would have no reason to complain about the implicit asymmetry in the difference principle, as only the difference principle can succeed in creating fair terms of cooperation and, thus, the source of their advantages.

4.6 Anti-monism

A fundamental consideration in interpreting Rawls' second principle is that of the centrality of the basic structure for distributive justice. In TJ, Rawls is not interested in a correct distribution in general, as he is only interested in the one that depends on a given institutional system. He writes: "the principles of justice, in particular the difference principle, apply to the main public principles that regulate social and economic inequalities . . . It applies to the announced system of pubic law and statutes and not to particular transactions or distributions, *nor to the decisions of individuals and associations, but rather to the institutional background*" (PL 282–3, emphasis mine). This is the reason why Rawls' theory is associative (or institutional) rather than allocative, as pointed out when responding to the objection by luck egalitarians. This means that it presupposes that individuals do their share within the basic structure of the socio-economic system. A sophisticated way to state this criterion is to say that Rawls is an anti-monist. By anti-monism we mean the pluralist output of two distinctions: (i) the principles of justice vary across different practices and social settings; and (ii) the principles for individuals differ from the principles for institutions. It seems worthwhile to mention at this point how Rawls defines an institution as a "public system of rules which defines offices and positions with their rights and duties, powers and immunities, and the like. These rules specify certain forms of actions as permissible, others as forbidden" (TJ 55; rev. edn. 47–8).

The second principle, within Rawls' anti-monist perspective, depends on the institutional practice in which a specific society is embedded. This is so because it directly addresses the basic structure and only indirectly addresses individuals. Rawls separates principles for individuals from principles for institutions. In contrast, utilitarianism is typically monist. When debating the first principle, we have already drawn a distinction between a liberalism of liberty and a liberalism of happiness, saying that Rawls believes in the former but not in the latter. This very fact, translated in terms of basic structure, entails a general anti-monist attitude that is also a form of pluralist anti-perfectionism. From a liberal anti-monist point of view, this anti-monist attitude in turn implies a moral division of labor: what is required is that the institutions, which are not inspired by a dominant end-purpose, are free-standing, creating general rules capable of guiding the lives of citizens who normally have ideas that differ from each other's.

On the whole, Rawls tells us a very simple thing: there is no need to standardize the mentality of individuals in order to have a reasonably egalitarian theory of justice. We are dealing here with a typically liberal assumption. Every individual thinks of himself and his socio-economic success but, at the same time, there are social institutions that ensure a certain level of equality.

A left-oriented criticism of this thesis maintains that it rests on a great inconsistency. In its best-known form, this objection comes from the (late) Oxford philosopher G. A. Cohen.[38] According to Cohen, the inconsistency of Rawls' thesis lies in the fact that it is impossible to conceive of a social system where people think one way and the institutions behave in another.[39] Monists claim that interpersonal justice cannot significantly deviate from institutional justice.[40] Cohen believes that self-interested individuals with a capitalistic mentality are unable to appreciate the proper working of an egalitarian social system founded on the protection of the least advantaged. The objection, however, is more generally directed against anti-monism: for Cohen substantive injustice is absolutely compatible with a just basic structure in the Rawlsian sense. This can happen everywhere, not only in the domain of distributive justice, because one cannot disentangle the personal nature of justice from the institutional one. Our social constructions of life guide our daily behavior, which in turn affects justice. For example, a sexist traditional ethos can make the life of a couple unjust even if the basic structure of the society in which the couple lives is reasonably just.

It is not easy to do justice to Cohen's objection.[41] In its powerful reformulation in *Rescuing Justice and Equality*, this criticism concerns both the substantive (political-theoretical) and the meta-ethical sides of Rawls' argument. From the substantive side, the attack is directed against one of the most significant devices of the theory of justice as fairness, that is, the tendency to equality. From the meta-ethical side, the attack is directed against one of the most significant methodological devices of the theory, that is, constructivism. Cohen made a robust attempt to coordinate these two sides, making the criticism of equality strictly connected with the supposed failures of Rawls' constructivism.[42] If proven, his thesis would be highly destructive of the whole apparatus of Rawls' account of justice.

Cohen deems Rawls' combination of equality and constructivism substantially inconsistent. The difference principle, in particular, is based on an incentives argument which in his view wrongly presumes that justice should not severely limit market behavior from a moral point of view. Cohen instead prefers a more rigid perspective which is supposed to imply that citizens assume an "egalitarian ethos," the main consequence of which would be the adoption of a stricter difference principle in which incentives are considered incompatible with equality. Cohen's anti-anti-monistic stance is based relies on a distinction between "rules of regulation" and "fundamental principles of justice," the first being more superficial than the second.[43] From this point of view, Rawls is supposed to provide mere rules of regulation whereas his more ambitious intention would be to provide principles of justice. This is because – within Rawls' constructivism – the justification of the principles of justice is dependent on empirical assumptions, which in Cohen's intuitionist perspective should never affect principles of justice (whereas they are compatible with rules of regulation).

The outcome of Cohen's argument is that inegalitarian incentives, permitted by the difference principle, cannot satisfy "true" principles of justice, but only rules of regulation. This impossibility is, for Cohen, related – from a meta-ethical point of view – to Rawls' constructivism, because his construction procedure – culminating in the original position (see next chapter) – incorporates factual assumptions. But principles of justice must be pure and fact-free. Substantially, the requirements of justice are not related to the embedding of persons within the basic structure, which provides other requirements such as publicity and market rationality.

Here, I put to one side Cohen's meta-ethical argument to address his substantive and political-theoretical argument. From this point of view, if distributive justice is to work properly, it is necessary for the persons belonging to it to share in an *egalitarian ethos* from the beginning. Therefore, if we take seriously Cohen's thesis on the justice ethos, then the system of incentives, connected with the second principle, proves to be in contradiction with the

Rawlsian view. If we were really to believe in the principles of justice – according to Cohen – we would have no need of incentives and, even individually, we would behave like persons who believe in equality.

Cohen's criticism of the incentives arguments – implicit in Rawls' difference principle – runs like this:

(i)   Citizens in a just society are supposed to accept its principles of justice;
(ii) But they cannot accept the difference principle in a proper way if they have an acquisitive mentality. This thesis is based in its turn on an argument according to which an egalitarian society does not need material incentives, given that the better-off would in any case do their part for purely ethical reasons.

Consequently, Rawlsians are in trouble: to take the difference principle seriously, they have to abandon part of the theory of justice as fairness.

Replies to this criticism emphasized the so-called "basic structure argument," according to which – given the moral division of labor between the political and the personal implied by anti-monism – citizens in a just society can accept the difference principle independently from their individual choices (which can also be acquisitive).

That is why – to oppose the objection to his own criticism – Cohen attacks the basic structure argument and its anti-monist presupposition. Cohen presents a dilemma which a conscientious Rawlsian should resolve. Depending on his interpretation of the basic structure, the serious Rawlsian should:

> either admit application of the principles of justice to (legally optional) social practices, and, indeed to patterns of personal choices that are not legally prescribed . . . in which case the restriction of justice to [basic] structure collapses; or, if he restricts his concern to the coercive structure only, then he saddles himself with a purely arbitrary definition of his subject matter. (Cohen, *Rescuing Justice and Equality*, 137)

In the first, wide, interpretation of the basic structure the anti-monist side of Rawlsianism collapses with the division of labor between the personal and the political it presupposes. In the second, narrow, legalistic interpretation, instead, the anti-monistic perspective is saved, but at the cost of being implausible from the point of view of its effects on people's normal lives (here I follow Andrew Williams).

Cohen frames his critique of Rawls as a critique of liberal interpretations of capitalism. An immediate reply to him would be to claim that a socialist system or something similar to it, in the context of which individuals were endowed with an egalitarian ethos, would not be as efficient as a capitalist system. Rawls wants to connect efficiency and equity within justice. His protection of the worst-off presupposes a fair division of a maximal social product and, somehow, the latter seems to be connected with a competitive and, therefore, a capitalist market.

This reply faces two obstacles. First, that the assumption that a liberal socialist market system is less efficient than a capitalist market system should not be taken for granted. Above all, the question hardly seems to be decidable on the basis of the analytic tools of a theory of justice such as that of Rawls. This entails that we cannot use the argument of the superiority of capitalism within a theory of justice, such as Rawls', in order to criticize such an objection. From a second point of view, Cohen could claim that he is not petitioning in favor of socialism, but that he would be satisfied with any liberal (in the American sense) or social-democratic (in the European sense) regime where individuals' motivations were more consistent with the second principle of justice.[44]

In the light of this, Cohen may be seen as criticizing the nature of Rawls' sense of justice. The problem is serious and it is not easy to answer the objection without taking for granted a shared interest in a liberal society. Accepting something like this, an attempt can be made to answer the objection in two different ways. The first and more direct one is that, collectively, we are somewhat interested in maintaining a vigorous pluralism. This thesis is strengthened by the fact that, in TJ, Rawls perceived a connection between his principles of justice and an ideal of "fraternity" (TJ 105; rev. edn. 90) as one of the presuppositions for stability; such a link disappears and is implicitly considered unrealistic in PL, simply in the name of pluralism.

In other words, many of us do not like a society where everyone needs to think alike in order to achieve a form of distributive justice, even if this is inspired to a considerable extent by an ethos of justice that we could share. More substantially, it seems that – for Rawls – the most important duties for individuals rising after an egalitarian basic structure, inspired by the difference principle, already exist. In this case, Rawlsian individuals develop a "sense of justice," which mainly consists in a moral obligation to comply with the rules of a just society. This fact has profound implications for individual behavior in contexts of local justice. For instance, if I am able to benefit the least advantaged through an intensive recourse to a few rare gifts of mine, this does not mean that I am required to do so and it has nothing to do with my sense of justice. If we bear in mind the priority of the first principle over the second, a pluralist thesis such as this one follows. Once again, the second principle may not be interpreted on its own; it needs to be connected with the first one and with our fundamental interest in liberty.

The second answer depends to a considerable extent upon what we have already mentioned with respect to the need to combine in a single apparatus the first principle and the two parts of the second principle. Through the need to protect equal political liberties, the effort to guarantee that all have access to important social positions, and having recourse to the difference principle,

Rawls creates an egalitarian system of distributive justice. Over time, if this type of system is deemed just, it will also become stable for the right reasons, and citizens will accordingly develop their sense of justice. As Rawls says, it is a well-ordered society where "everyone accepts and knows that the others accept the same principles of justice, and the basic institutions satisfy and are known to satisfy these principles" (TJ 453–4; rev. edn. 397–8).

This means that, somehow, an egalitarian sense of justice (ethos) will be absorbed by Rawlsian individuals. Hence, in such a well-ordered society, all the citizens will "have a strong and normally effective desire to act as the principles of justice require" (TJ 454; rev. edn. 398). And this will gradually become a part of their sense of justice. Thus, the outward inconsistency denounced by Cohen would disappear.

Over the years, Rawls insisted on the fact that the basic structure of society exercises over time "a profound and pervasive influence on the persons who live under its institutions" (JFR 55). Thus, it stands to reason to believe that, notwithstanding the clear-cut division between basic structure and maxims for individuals, in TJ the motivations of individuals may not be greatly in conflict with the fundamental directives of the basic structure.

The last part of my argument shows a related failure of Cohen's thesis. Cohen's interpretation of the basic structure argument is either exceedingly formalistic or vaguely sociological. In the first option, Cohen interprets the basic structure argument in a legalistic way, separating it from the social practices it is supposed to cover. In the second option, he reads it as a mere social practice among others. It is not difficult to see that Rawls' basic structure does not correspond to either of these interpretations. Being institutional, the basic structure is instead deemed to cover social practices but from the standpoint of a "public system of rules." And a public system of rules coincides neither with a legal standard nor with a set of social facts. It corresponds rather to the way in which a set of social facts is regulated by a public system of rules. From a meta-theoretical point of view, these rules in their turn are not the last word of a Rawlsian theory of justice, because they presuppose the normative function of higher principles of justice.

One could say – to conclude – that part of the flavor of Cohen's argument evaporates if we consider that it is not an argument internal to the Rawlsian way of reasoning. Prima facie, it seems that Cohen is able to combine an internal criticism of Rawls, based on the incompatibility between the difference principle and anti-monism, with an external argument, based on his socialist option for equality. All considered, however, it is not so. In fact, his attack on anti-monism rests on a controversial reading of the basic structure and on a substantially non-liberal conception of justice. And both are clearly outside the Rawlsian framing of justice.

It would also be interesting to see whether part of Cohen's criticism can be taken without accepting the whole argument. For example, one could maintain that Cohen's original critique of incentives is independent of his later argument against anti-monism. In other words, one could accept that the principles applying to individual behavior differ from those applying to institutions (the substance of anti-monism), while still insisting that people in a just society would not threaten to withhold their scarce talents unless they are paid more than others. Recall that Cohen himself allows people to seek extra remuneration where it compensates for extra burdens. So the case is one where people actually enjoy exercising their talents, but nonetheless threaten to withhold those talents because they realize they can earn more by doing so. Cohen argues that anyone with an egalitarian sense of justice would not think this way. This is the core of Cohen's original argument. The question is whether the behavior of the most talented, in cases where they ask for more, is consistent with the Rawlsian sense of justice. There are, however, two problems implicit in this argument: (i) whether we can accept its force without accepting Cohen's argument against anti-monism; (ii) whether a broader reading of Rawls, like the one we suggested before, does not make the behavior of the most talented progressively consistent with the sense of justice.

These replies to Cohen are simply reactions to his criticism. However, a more analytical consideration of Cohen's thesis exceeds the limits of this book.

5

THE ORIGINAL POSITION

The original position is presented in the third chapter of TJ as the core of Rawls' contractualist argument (5.1) and then re-proposed by Rawls2 in a weaker form as a "device of representation." The main idea underlying the original position consists in separating real individuals in this world from the noumenal selves taking part in the foundational agreement concerning the justification of the basic structure (5.1.1). If this kind of justification presupposes an idea of fairness, then the conditions determining the original position should be able to make this choice purely procedural (5.1.2). In section 5.1.2, I deconstruct Rawls' procedural argument into three steps: (i) a *distribuendum*; (ii) a reliable procedure; and (iii) the possibility of universal agreement. In section 5.2, I examine the main components of the original position, like the "veil of ignorance," the rationality of the parties, and so on.

In section 5.3.1, I present two criticisms to such a constructivist contractual argument. The first, formulated by Ronald Dworkin, maintains that a hypothetical contract cannot be binding at all. I try to defend Rawls by pointing to the way in which his contract represents a procedural choice in which conflicting interests are at stake. The second criticism, formulated by Thomas Nagel, implies some form of circularity within Rawls' theory of justice. According to this thesis, the original position cannot exempt pure procedural justice from contamination by elements coming from Rawls' favorite theory of the good. I try to reply to this objection by saying that some kind of circularity between the right and the good can be an advantage rather then a dis-advantage within a theory of justice.

Many criticisms to the original position come from the axiomatic claim linked to it (5.4; see also appendix). It has never been clear whether initially Rawls thought that one could have a deduction of the principles of justice from the original position in analogy with decision theory. After sustained criticism by great economists like Arrow, Harsanyi, and Sen, combined with a personal process of maturation, Rawls decided to abandon this axiomatic claim. The original position becomes part of a larger argument for the principles of justice, an argument that includes a general moral tension towards equality and the practice of reflective equilibrium. In section 5.5, I examine the comparison between utilitarianism and the theory of justice as fairness. The conclusion is that justice as fairness cannot win the competition with utilitarianism on purely axiomatic grounds, which are here assessed in the appendix, but can be successful if it stresses the interpersonal side of the contractual argument.

5.1 The Leading Argument in Favor of the Principles of Justice

The central thesis within the theory of justice as fairness is that, under ideal conditions, free and equal persons would adhere to the two principles of justice. Rawls, in TJ, offers a variety of arguments for such a thesis. The centrality of the basic structure, the noumenal nature of the decision-makers, the balance between rationality and reasonableness, the four-stage sequence, the stability resulting from justice as fairness, and the method of reflective equilibrium are all part of this formidable and complex demonstrative strategy. It is unquestionable, however, that the primary argument in favor of the two principles is the argument of the original position. In TJ, Rawls attaches more significance to the argument based on the social contract, and the original position which serves as the basis of the contract, than to any other in the process of justification. Indeed, he explicitly declares that "none of the preceding remarks are an argument for this conception, since in a contract theory all arguments, strictly speaking, are to me made in terms of what would be rational to choose in the original position" (TJ 77; rev. edn. 65).

The original position represents an innovative version of the "state of nature." This version was initially introduced by Rawls in 1958 in an article called "Justice as Fairness" and subsequently reformulated in TJ.[1] It should be noted that, notwithstanding a few changes, the structure of the original position does not change even in Rawls' subsequent works. The idea underlying the original position is that, in this special situation of impartiality (see Ph.D.), the two principles of justice would be chosen by rational representatives of free and equal persons who mean to realize a well-ordered society.

5.1.1 A mental experiment

All the social contract theories – including classical versions formulated by Hobbes,[2] Locke, Rousseau, and Kant – substantially depend on how the initial situation is constructed.[3] The original position is the specific way Rawls constructs an initial situation for his theory of justice. Rawls' initial situation is not a realistic one.[4] Indeed, it is a hypothetical contract, a mental experiment. Here, Rawls explicitly follows Kant who contends that the social contract

> is in fact merely an *idea* of reason . . . This is the test of the rightfulness of every public law . . . if it is at least possible that a people could agree to it, it is our duty to consider the law as just, even if the people is at the present in such a position or attitude of mind that it would probably refuse to consent were it consulted.[5]

Rawls quotes Kant in an effort to solve a problem that had been left open by the *Rechtslehre* (in particular, sections 46–7) – that is the passage from autonomy as the primary principle of morality to the collective consent under contract.[6] Rawls' fundamental idea is that, if the mental experiment of the original position is well constructed, it should capture at best the moral intuitions of free and equal persons on the theme of social justice (the idea is central to Ph.D. part I). From this point of view, the original position is a model, a "device of representation."[7] Rawls endeavors to de-transcendentalize the Kantian model of subject and of contract in order to lower it into the historical reality of a modern liberal-democratic society.[8] This intent is already present in TJ, but it becomes fully clear only in KCMT in 1980.[9] As Rawls soberly says in the first chapter of TJ: "The idea here is simply to make vivid to ourselves the restrictions that it seems reasonable to impose on arguments for principles of justice, and therefore on these principles themselves" (TJ 18; rev. edn. 16).

All the peculiar conditions that Rawls is going to enter into the contract gradually derive from this premise. The preceding passage continues as follows:

> Thus it seems reasonable and generally acceptable that no one should be advantaged or disadvantaged by natural fortune or social circumstances in the choice of the principles . . . We should insure further that particular inclinations and aspirations and persons' conceptions of their own good do not affect the principles adopted . . . One excludes the knowledge of those contingencies which sets men at odds and allows them to be guided by their prejudices. In this manner the veil of ignorance is arrived at in a natural way. (TJ 18–19; rev. edn. 16–17)[10]

5.1.2 A reasonable construction procedure

The original position is the heart of an argument based on the idea of the social contract. We may wonder where the special demonstrative claim associated with the contractualist argument comes from, and what its specific strength is. In order to answer this question, we may point to a meta-theoretical aspect connected with what Rawls calls a "reasonable procedure of construction."[11] This aspect relates to the pure structure of the contractualist argument from the point of view of justification.[12] Let us assume, as Rawls does, that a "justification is argument addressed to those who disagree with us, or to ourselves when we are of two minds" (TJ 580; rev. edn. 508).

A contractualist argument may only justify a principle or some principles of justice if the underlying moral thesis can do so. In turn, the moral thesis may be justified if:

(i) all persons subject to this principle have a good reason to endorse (1) the *distribuendum* or what the theory of justice intends to distribute (for instance: general utility, the respect of the fundamental principles, the enjoyment of a few primary goods, etc.) and (2) the way in which it is to be distributed;
(ii) all the persons subject to this criterion have a good reason to respect it, supposing that the others do as well, in a regime of reciprocity and publicity (what Rawls calls "well-ordered society").

Conditions (i) and (ii) are quite general and relate to the constructivist idea of just distribution. In Rawls' case, they turn a comprehensive situation of choice into a case of pure procedural justice. They may be right for contractualism, but also for a form of institutionalist utilitarianism.[13] And yet, they still do not capture the sense of the actual contractualist argument, as the latter is only explained when the following condition is added:

(iii) the good reason to endorse a criterion – as laid down in (i) and (ii) above – is not merely the way in which the *distribuendum* is distributed or the form of the institutional structure it applies to. It is rather the fact that this specific way could be the subject of a hypothetical and unanimous agreement by the parties in the original position;[14] an agreement capable of satisfying the higher moral interests of free and equal citizens in a democratic society.[15]

Conditions (i), (ii) and (iii) define a contractualist justification.

Two different theoretical interpretations of this model can be made. First, a contractualist argument is purely procedural and constructivist if the morality of the selected criterion depends merely on conditions (i), (ii), and (iii). In this case, the procedure of construction alone determines the nature of the agreement in the original position. In short, this "hard" constructivism implies that, if the outcome of the agreement corresponds to the normative vision, then whatever principles of justice would be chosen are by virtue of this fact valid principles of justice. If, instead, one assumes independent moral premises and the procedure of construction has an ancillary value, then the constructivist proceduralism is only part of the story and we can speak of "soft" constructivism. I interpret the original position in terms of soft constructivism.[16] This ultimately means that the three-stage meta-theoretical construction, although worked out in detail as the original position, is not enough by itself to prove the acceptability of the principles of justice.[17]

On my interpretation, the acceptability of the principles depends on the relationship between the original position and the nature of the persons as free and equal citizens as well as on the relationship between these two ideas and the idea of a well-ordered society. If, as Rawls thinks, free and equal persons believe that equality is the fundamental virtue of a liberal-democratic society, then we are going to be more willing to accept his construction of the original position. Otherwise, the model of Rawls' original position will be less plausible.[18] In this sense, the simple procedural construction of the model of the original position is insufficient to show the theoretical need to opt for the principles of justice. My thesis rests on explicit statements by Rawls on the matter, such as the following: "the original position is not an axiomatic (or deductive) basis from which principles are derived but a procedure for singling out principles most fitting to the conception of the person most likely to be held, at least implicitly, in a modern democratic society" (KCMT; CP 358).

5.2 The Construction of the Original Position

The central characteristic of the original position is that special type of impartiality that Rawls calls fairness. Rawls explicitly introduces the notion of fairness in TJ through the concept of the "veil of ignorance." However, the original position includes additional constitutive elements such as the list of alternatives, circumstances of justice, the formal constraints of the concept of right, and the rationality of the parties. According to Rawls, in "Remarks on Political Philosophy,"[19] any social contract theory requires a version of its own of the initial situation. The situation must be founded on at least two general characteristics: (i) how the parties are situated in the bargaining position; and (ii) what the parties know, and in what way what they know as contracting parties differs from what normal people know in real life.

5.2.1 The list of alternatives

The list of alternatives from which the principles of justice are chosen represents the first element in the original position. The principles are chosen through a comparison with other theoretical distributive justice alternatives existing in the marketplace of ideas. With a certain degree of arbitrariness, Rawls excludes from his list some important alternatives, such as Marxism and libertarianism. However, he does include in his list significant alternatives, such as utilitarianism, the theory of justice as fairness, perfectionism, intuitionism, and rational egoism (TJ 124; rev. edn. 107). The comparison among these alternatives is very limited. Perfectionism is excluded a priori from the first principle (see chapter 3). Intuitionism is excluded owing to its incapacity to decide within the context of a pluralism of concurrent reasons (an argument introduced in the first chapter of TJ and confirmed by the formal constraints of the concept of right, but already present in Ph.D.). Rational egoism is done away with by one of the formal constraints of the concept of right (see 5.2.3). All this causes the real debate in the original position to be confined to a comparison between the theory of justice as fairness and utilitarianism.

5.2.2 The circumstances of justice

The second element of the original position is represented by the circumstances of justice. This is an idea that Rawls takes up from David Hume, but with a substantial difference: Hume characterizes these circumstances in terms of persons while Rawls refers to them in terms of institutions (LHMP 2ff.).[20] Hume considers that, in the absence of a few general conditions, the virtue of justice would not make sense. The thesis, in his words, is as follows: "from the selfishness and confined generosity of men, along with the scanty provision nature has made for his wants, that justice derives its origin."[21]

We are dealing with two different conditions. The first condition has an objective nature and relates to the scarcity of goods with respect to the demand for them. It is a necessary condition to have a distribution problem. The problem would not exist if the supply of goods were in excess of need (in this case we would be in a social situation "beyond justice").[22] The second is a subjective attitude and relates to the moderate egoism of human beings, with respect to whom Hume upholds that "if men pursued the public interest naturally, and with a hearty affection, they would have never have dreamed of restraining each other by these rules; and if they pursued their own interest, without any precaution, they would run headlong into every kind of injustice and violence" (*Treatise* 525).

A third and less significant Humean condition, which explicitly appears later in the *Enquiry*[23] (and not in the *Treatise*), is represented by an approximate equality of men's strengths (even Hobbes insists on this final condition in *Leviathan*; see LHPP).

Rawls captures the first condition by recognizing "conditions of moderate scarcity" and the subjective attitude in terms of the "mutual disinterestedness" of the parties. In the former case, he assumes that matters of justice presuppose a division of goods. In this case we are dealing with primary goods, and if each person could have as much of them as she desires there would be no problem at all. However, if the scarcity exceeds certain limits, then – for Rawls just as for Hume – there is no space for rules of justice. Below a minimum level of wellbeing, there is no space for freedom-and-justice concerns. An interesting corollary of this thesis may be found when

Rawls defends the "priority of liberty," but only in a context of relative prosperity. Only with relative prosperity does it make sense to think that there are no trade-offs between liberty and wellbeing.

On the other hand, the subjective attitude assumes that individuals have standard answers to objective circumstances. Rawlsian individuals in the original position are substantially interested in pursuing their ends, and the emphasis laid on their disinterestedness in others helps to show the connection between the circumstances of justice and a theoretical problem posed in terms of rational choice theory. In fact, the pure nature of the context – moderate scarcity – would not guarantee a conflict of interests. Therefore, it could lead to a spontaneous agreement in favor of principles of distribution that would make the problem of the rational choice superfluous. The condition of mutual disinterestedness proposed by Rawls is stronger than Hume's condition of moderate egoism because it assumes not only that individuals press their claims, but also that they take no heed of those of any other. It is also a condition that is more than necessary in order to pose the distributive problem in terms of rational choice, given that a distributive conflict may arise with no need to assume mutual disinterestedness.

5.2.3 The formal constraints of the concept of right

For Rawls, "formal constraints of the concept of right" exist in every moral theory that deals with justice. At the same time, they must not be made absolute but must be functional to the theory they belong to. In Rawls' words: "I do not claim that these conditions follow from the concept of right, much less from the meaning of morality . . . The merit of any definition depends upon the soundness of the theory that results; by itself, a definition cannot settle any fundamental question" (TJ 130; rev. edn. 112–13).

Rawls identifies five formal constraints of the concept of right:

- *Generality.* The justice principles should be general: "it must be possible to formulate them without the use of what would be intuitively recognized as proper names, or rigged definite descriptions" (TJ 131; rev. edn. 113).

  Moral judgments do not apply to specific individuals; they apply to categories of people under a constraint of anonymity. Moreover, Rawls connects the generality requirement to the public nature of the principles since such principles ought to be perpetual. This request should not surprise us, given that the moral imperatives are usually considered in terms of such a generality.
- *Universality.* The justice principles are to be universal in application: "They must hold for everyone in virtue of their being moral persons" (TJ 132; rev. edn. 114).

  Rawls also presents universality in terms of the hypothetical consequences of everyone following a principle. The principle should be done away with if its universal acceptance leads to undesirable consequences. Generality and universality are not the same thing. For instance, universalized egoism in the form of the imperative "everyone should follow Maffettone's desires" satisfies the condition of universality but not generality.

- *Publicity.* This constraint, according to which the pursuit of justice must be visible, emerges directly from Rawls' Kantian perspective. The central idea is to insist on a public conception of morality. For Rawls, it is not enough for a principle to meet a universalizability test, as provided for the preceding formal constraint. In addition, a principle of justice needs to be publicly recognizable as one of the fundamental rules of society. It is not clear whether this requirement applies to all the ethical principles or only to those that depend on a theory of the social contract. The question is not insignificant, given that an application to all the moral principles would exclude a priori a few utilitarian theories from the group of candidates for principles of justice, something Rawls does not seem willing to do. For he intends to show the superiority of his theory over utilitarianism on the basis of the argument from the original position and not merely on the basis of the formal requirements.

  The parties assume that everyone knows about the principles of justice and that they are the result of an agreement. This awareness will support the "stability of social cooperation." The publicity condition is considered by Rawls implicit in Kant's categorical imperative insofar as it requires us to act in accordance with principles that a rational agent would be willing to enact as law for a kingdom of ends.

- *Ordering.* The principles of justice must impose an ordering among conflicting claims. Even this, however, gives rise to a problem similar to the preceding one. This constraint excludes intuitionism. Intuitionism, according to Rawls, provides a set of principles that are not governed by mutual priorities. This leads to a permanent cause of indecidability (already referred to in Ph.D. part I). In this case, however, intuitionism would a priori not be considered a moral theory. This result appears too far-fetched. Rawls actually maintains that the intuitionist theories feature this kind of a problem, but there is a big difference between acknowledging that a theory has a problem and denying, formally, that it is a moral theory.

- *Finality.* The principles of justice must be viewed by the parties as a final court of appeal in disputes having a moral nature that relate to the institutional structure. In case of conflict between a moral obligation, represented by the principles of justice, and other considerations, for instance based on personal interest or tradition, the moral obligation must prevail. This principle has a peculiar significance of its own in defending the meaning of the contract according to Rawls. In his reply to Alexander, who had attacked the need for the contract, Rawls insists on the capacity of the contract to create such an obligation for the parties as to cause the latter to consider it substantially final.[24]

Taken as a whole, the five constraints of the concept of right introduced by Rawls exclude from the alternatives various forms of commonsense egoism (see Sidgwick).[25] It is not clear whether egoism is a moral theory, but Rawls' thesis seems plausible. Instead, the problem may arise from the way in which Rawls excludes it. It is hard to understand whether it is possible to do so starting from the idea of formal constraints of the concept of right or whether one needs to resort to the nature of every moral theory (rather than that of justice).

5.2.4 The veil of ignorance

The main function of the original position is to create an initial situation characterized by procedural fairness. As Rawls explicitly says, "the aim is to use the notion of pure procedural justice as a basis of theory" (TJ 136; rev. edn. 118). For this reason, the social choices take place behind a veil of ignorance so that the parties "do not know how the various alternatives will affect their own particular case, and are obliged to evaluate principles solely on the basis of general considerations" (ibid.).

This pretense, which makes Rawlsian contractualism different from the classical theories, tries to nullify as far as possible "the effects of specific contingencies which put men at odds and tempt them to exploit social and natural circumstances to their own advantage" (ibid.).

Hence, the main purpose of the veil of ignorance is to exclude partisan decisions by denying the parties any knowledge of the specific facts of a certain concrete situation. In other words, the knowledge of specific information that concerns the situation of some person – his intelligence, race, sex, religion, etc. – is not a sound reason to defend a principle of justice. This need for impartiality gives rise to the idea that no one should know his personal characteristics or even the historical context in which he lives (for instance the average income of the population to which he belongs). Decision-makers behind the veil still know principles of psychology, laws of physics, social sciences and other relevant general considerations. These do not threaten to undermine the impartiality of the principles. The connection between ignorance of one's own fate and choice in the original position makes Rawlsian contractualism different from bargaining theories, because the parties, given the veil of ignorance, are unable to mutually negotiate the terms of the agreement in the light of their particular interests.[26]

Insofar as the parties are concerned, Rawls maintains that, in the original position, no one knows:

> his place in society, his class position or social status; nor does he know his fortune in the distribution of natural assets and abilities, his intelligence and

strength, and the like. Nor again, does anyone know his conception of the good, the particulars of his rational plan of life, or even the special features of his psychology, such as his aversion to risk or liability to optimism or pessimism. (TJ 137; rev. edn. 118)

In fact, any such knowledge could drive the decision-makers to choose principles that favor themselves and those endowed with the same qualities. We may refer to the general moral argument in favor of the second principle and find, in the exclusions provided for by the veil of ignorance, arbitrary elements from the moral point of view that are unable to justify a just distribution. By placing each decision-maker in the condition of not knowing who he is going to be in the after-choice situation, the veil of ignorance introduces elements of morality within a rationality framework. From this point of view, it is clear that the fiction of the veil of ignorance tends to minimize the weight of the moral arbitrariness as the outcome of the voluntary choices of the parties.

The veil of ignorance invoked by Rawls is thick rather than thin. A thin veil of ignorance would allow some knowledge about society that would affect the choices of the parties in the original position. In KCMT (CP 335–6), Rawls asserts that the distinction between thin and thick reproduces the distinction between the disinterested and benevolent spectator found in Hume and utilitarianism (thin veil) and Rawls' Kantian position (thick veil).[27] Indeed, for Rawls the Kantian veil of ignorance needs to be "the thickest possible" (CP 335), because the autonomy of the parties and the nature of free and equal persons proves strengthened by it. Ultimately, this would enhance the noumenal nature of the parties in the original position, all of which would be placed in a prospect of mutual symmetry.[28] Can a fair choice indeed be considered autonomous in a Kantian sense, even behind the thickest veil of ignorance, given that the motivation of the parties underlying the veil remains always to obtain the greatest quantity of primary goods? In KCMT, Rawls explicitly denies the significance of this question, claiming that Kant's autonomy does not deny the existence of desires. Rather, what really counts is the way in which reason mediates the desires ordering the choices in a given way.[29] This final thesis reappears in a more complex manner in "Themes in Kant's Moral Philosophy" (1989), where Rawls deals with the theme of the categorical imperative procedure – which he calls the CI-procedure – starting from its applications in a "perturbed world" (CP 502ff.).

For similar reasons, the veil even excludes the knowledge of one's own conception of the good. Were we to know it, we would be tempted to favor partial principles that promote its realization. This becomes particularly significant when dealing with religions: a situation of fair choice may not allow for being inclined towards one religious vision rather than another. As we are going to see, such an idea is quite embarrassing to believers.[30]

Furthermore, the parties do not know their aversion to risk or their liability to optimism or pessimism (TJ 136; rev. edn. 118). This limit has an extraordinary impact on the deduction of the second principle of justice from the original position and, more generally, on the decision-making maximin rule (as we are going to see in the section below). This rule, when dealing with alternative solutions, calls for avoiding those connected with the worst outcomes at the risk of losing, perhaps, extremely promising intermediate outcomes. For Rawls, decision-makers should not risk too much in such a crucial choice as that of the original position. But such a strategy cannot be excessively affected in advance by the psychological attitudes of the decision-makers. This is the reason why we assume the parties are ignorant of their attitude towards risk as well as of their optimism or pessimism.

The veil of ignorance also conceals information that concerns special circumstances of the particular society we refer to. Therefore, we have no knowledge of the level of wellbeing of our society, or of our placement within generations that follow one another over time. Should we know this type of information, we would be tempted to opt for principles of justice that promote a given generation or a type of society with a certain economic level. The principles Rawls endorses should be fair among different generations and levels of development. Finally, the veil of ignorance excludes information that relates to one's socio-economic placement within society. Otherwise, the decision-makers could be prone to choosing principles of justice that further their socio-economic class.

The philosophical problem implicit in the concept of the veil of ignorance is indeed its capacity to select information according to criteria of fairness. As pointed out by Thomas Nagel, it is easy to accept ignorance of personal facts in the name of impartiality, so that one should ignore race, class, sex, and generation, as well as natural talent. But the parties in the original position are also deprived of information concerning their conception of the good. Hence, Nagel suggests, "it seems odd to regard that as morally irrelevant from the standpoint of justice."[31] After all, if one were to aspire to a set of principles of justice deeming them more consistent with one's vision of the world and conception of the good, one would not violate any rule of impartiality. Notwithstanding this, Rawls seems to argue that it would be just as unfair to be aware of one's conception of the good as it is to be aware of one's class or race.

Such a relevant omission of information is usually justified through the pluralism of the conceptions of the good and the aim of ensuring unanimity as the basis of the social contract. However, should the lack of information be too extensive, it may deprive the choice of the principles of the necessary ethical support. In TJ, Rawls' solution of the dilemma involves the selection of a series of primary goods, within the context of a thin conception of the good, on which it is assumed that there is general agreement. In Rawls' vision, there is no need for a complete conception of the good in order to accept that the parties are interested in the primary goods. Within this context, the notion of good is neutral with respect to the person's complete conceptions of the good, which, instead, remain mutually incompatible. What ensues, as Nagel affirms, is a "minimal conception of the good."[32] However, such a minimal conception requires a strong assumption according to which the minimal conception of the good is sufficient for the moral purposes of justice. This fundamental assumption gives rise in turn to the priority of the right over the good since the theory of the good does not affect the choice of the principles of justice other than at the minimal level referred to above.

There is no explicit special concern given to race and sexual gender in the argument from the original position and the veil of ignorance. However, we could say that such concern exists implicitly by depriving the parties of the contingencies that make up their specific identity. Given that the parties do not know their racial and sexual identities, they have no rational basis to choose principles that could favor a race or a gender over others. To quote Rawls: "racial and sexual discrimination presupposes that some hold a favored place in the social system . . . *From the standpoint of persons similarly situated in an initial situation which is fair, the principles of explicit racist doctrines are not only unjust. They are irrational*" (TJ 149; rev. edn. 129, emphasis mine).

A similar thesis could apply to sexual gender . Needless to say, it is difficult to believe that gender theorists or anti-racists will be fully persuaded by such an argument.[33] One could say – to defend Rawls – that he presents what perhaps is a necessary condition but surely not a sufficient one to maintain an argument in favor of any minority.

5.2.5 The rationality of the parties

The choice in the original position presupposes the rationality of the parties and must be consistent with their reasonableness. This is how Rawls defines the rationality of the parties: "A rational person is thought to have a coherent set of preferences between the options open to him. He ranks these options according to how well they further his purposes; he follows the plan which will satisfy more his desires rather than less, and which has the geater chance of being successfully executed" (TJ 143; rev. edn. 129).

It is a standard definition that, for the most part, attempts to make the decision in the original position formally consistent with rational choice theory. However, Rawls adds an unusual qualification, according to which "a rational individual does not suffer from envy" (ibid.). The assumption is controversial since envy is not always irrational. Indeed, it is rationally admissible whenever it depends on injustice or when there is an excessive inequality or when social and economic results depend too much on chance.

Such a concept of rationality cooperates with the subjective circumstance of mutual disinterestedness in order to provide a comprehensive picture of the attitude of the parties. If everyone looks at how the choice of an alternative in the original position may accomplish their purposes, then they do not consider the effects of that choice on any third party and, therefore, as a party, act according to a criterion of mutual disinterestedness. By bringing together self-interest and the veil of ignorance, one gets an impartial situation of choice.

5.3 Procedural Fairness: Two Critiques

The original position has a dual theoretical purpose: as an analytical tool capable of proceduralizing an extremely complex problem of social justice and as a justificatory apparatus.[34] Choosing principles of justice in the original position illustrates how those principles are better than others from a normative point of view. The central idea is that the original position represents a model of procedural fairness and, for this reason, the resulting conclusions should be accepted by free and equal persons able to reflect on the matter.

It is a substantial theoretical claim worth assessing. I will do so by taking into consideration some significant reactions to TJ, analyzing two specific critiques of the deductive model of the original position, and reviewing the developments of this concept by its author after 1971.

5.3.1 The critique according to which the contract is superfluous

This is a typical objection to the contractualist theories. The original position means to transform a complex social justice question into a neutral procedure that everyone may accept. This is the purpose of the simplified and constructivist procedural scheme presented in section 5.1.2. However, as this objection charges, the transformation fails because the subject of agreement is normatively significant regardless of the argument about the contract.[35] Thus, element (iii) in the previous scheme seems to become redundant. Were this true, then the entire mechanism of the original position would be superfluous, little more than a rhetorical expedient to stress an independent ethical-political substance. The latter is more or less Dworkin's position on the matter.[36]

Ronald Dworkin has pointed out how strange Rawls' emphasis on the contract is, given that the contractualist arguments are dated and notoriously weak.[37] However, Rawls clearly refers to a hypothetical rather than a real or historical contract and – for Dworkin – this highlights how the original position is a rhetorical, though enlightening, expedient rather than a decisive argument. Given that the contract is rhetorical, why should we worry about it? After all, as Dworkin states, "a hypothetical contract is not simply a pale form of an actual contract: it is no contract at all."[38] The reference to a hypothetical agreement does not provide the argument with special authority since "hypothetical contracts do not supply an independent argument for the fairness of enforcing their terms."[39] More broadly, it seems controversial that a hypothetical choice – especially under conditions of peculiar ignorance – might provide an independent moral justification of social arrangements on which there would be no unanimous agreement had they been actually known.[40]

There are two ways to get round this difficulty. Dworkin suggests one way that Rawls seems to affirm later in his career. This maintains that the original position may be interpreted in another manner. It may represent a powerful conceptual tool to lay down a few fundamental moral ideas implied in the very concept of justice; for instance, the ideas of freedom, equality, and a well-ordered society. This solution tends to bring together the general moral argument present in TJ and the original position within a wide conception of reflective equilibrium. In other words, the original position does not justify the two principles of justice so much as confirm their plausibility from a broader perspective.

This does not mean that the original position is superfluous. It helps to consolidate and test the considered intuitions of those free and equal persons who are the citizens as final addressees of the argument (see Ph.D. part I). At the same time, the original position carries on the function that is typical of every model in a theory. A theoretical model cannot start from nothing. It must always assume a few initial premises. Hence, the confirmation that the theoretical outcomes of the model are consistent with the premises strengthens the general structure of the theory. In this sense, we may answer Dworkin by pointing out that the original position and subsequent social contract are not supposed to create *ex nihilo* new obligations.

A second way of answering Dworkin is more sophisticated and controversial. The contractualist argument introduces a dialogic element of interpersonality into the theory of justice as fairness that is not present in other concurrent theories, including utilitarianism. Utilitarianism presents itself as a consequentialist, welfarist and impersonalist theory.[41] While criticizing these elements of utilitarianism, Rawls, in part, adopts and transforms each element. His theory is partly consequentialist, even though he introduces a significant deontological aspect that is not present in utilitarianism.[42] Additionally, welfarism is modified by the Rawlsian argument about the primary goods, which we have discussed in the preceding chapter. In any event, I believe that the decisive point is the third, where Rawls rejects utilitarian impersonality in the name of contractualist interpersonality. The idea that the principles depend on an initial agreement makes the relationship among persons more important in contractualism than it would be to a sympathetic and impartial spectator in utilitarianism.[43] Thus, a relationship among things in utilitarianism changes into relationship among persons for contractarians. The contract, though hypothetical, forces the interactive element of the Rawlsian theory.[44] The distinction between impersonality and interpersonality provides the fundamental basis for distinguishing the principles of justice from classical utilitarianism.

This attempt to interpret contractualism through impersonality can defend Rawls' view from one of the most radical criticisms. According to Jean Hampton, through the introduction of the veil of ignorance and the priority of right, Rawls makes all the decision-makers in the original positions identical. Indeed, it would ultimately reduce them to a single person. From this point of view, the choice of the principles of justice in the original position is all pretense. Instead, the different conditions laid down for the choice would determine the actual final decision. From this point of view, the theory of justice as fairness would be identical to utilitarianism, making the choices of the community identical to those of a single person with suitably defined characteristics. Hampton neglects the deliberative spaces, which open up in the Rawlsian scheme and which an interpretation in terms of interpersonality emphasizes.[45]

5.3.2 The critique according to which the conception of the right comprises Rawls' vision of the good

The justificatory value of the original position depends on a few substantive and not merely procedural assumptions. If this is the case, then the original position risks being meaningful, but only at the cost of causing the theory to lose the advantages of neutrality. Using the Rawlsian vocabulary, in this event the theory of the good would end up affecting, to a considerable extent, the theory of the right. Or, as Nagel puts it:

> It is a fundamental feature of Rawls' conception of the fairness in the original position that it should not permit the choice of principles of justice to depend on a particular conception of the good over which the parties may differ.
>
> The construction does not, I think, accomplish this and there are reasons to believe that it cannot be successfully carried out. Any hypothetical choice situation which requires agreement among the parties will have to impose strong restrictions on the grounds of choice, and these restrictions can be justified only in terms of a conception of the good. It is one of those cases in which there is no neutrality to be had, because neutrality requires as much justification as any other position.[46]

Similar reasoning asserts that the theory of justice as fairness cannot avoid imposing some conception of the good over the concept of the right, being somehow circular.[47]

This objection may be called into question in two different manners. Both grant that the purely proceduralist and constructivist argument – as set out in section 5.1.2 – is not enough to prove the principles of justice. However, the responses show how superimposing the theory of the right onto the theory of the good turns out to be an advantage. This point is important because the most widespread intuitive objection to the theory of justice as fairness relies on this charge of circularity between good and right.[48]

The first response begins with Rawls' "thin theory of the good" (TJ, section 25, 60). The thin theory of the good includes a few formal aspects that make it consistent with a rational choice theory. These aspects range from the principles of rationality (such as inclusivity, consistency between means and ends, and taking probabilities into account) to the very idea of deliberative rationality through which one chooses a plan of life. The thin theory of the good also contains substantive aspects, including the preference for the primary goods (for which see the preceding chapter),[49] the Aristotelian Principle,[50] and the idea that the parties have highest-order interests.

Based on this background rationality, the parties endeavor to realize in the original position to the greatest degree possible the thin conception of the good. Every party in the original position tries to pursue her ends as dictated by the thin conception of the good. This is the reason why the parties are mutually disinterested. The parties in the original position do not necessarily represent egoist individuals or lack affections and feelings. Rather, as contracting parties they merely endeavor to realize their ends as dictated by the thin theory of the good. Without a thin theory of the good, there could be no choice in the original position.

Over time, the role of the theory of the good expands and contracts at the same time within the Rawlsian model (see PL). On the one hand, the theory of the good becomes less thin and, on the other, its ambit is confined to the political interests of the citizens of a free democratic society. Rawls2 proposes three such interests. The first two consist in the origination and development of two fundamental moral powers: a sense of justice and a conception of the good. The first interest corresponds to the desire of a citizen of a well-ordered society to make her behavior conform to a public conception of justice. The second interest corresponds to the ability to develop a conception of the good having at the same time the capacity to review it critically. Both these interests presuppose autonomous individuals and, for this reason, Rawls' conception cannot help but be linked to a construction procedure. Otherwise, if the parties in the original position confine themselves to recognizing a pre-existent vision of justice, their choice would be heteronymous.[51] The third interest consists in realizing the two former interests to the greatest possible extent. In this second and more pretentious theory of the good, these interests – defined as "highest-order interests" – are substantially included in the conception of justice. Thus, the conception of justice will be unacceptable unless one first accepts the conception of the good.

This change of perspective permits an alternative reading. For, not only should we accept the supposed circularity between the good and the right, but this circularity is further made explicit and strengthened. A theory of justice compatible with the nature of political liberalism cannot leave aside a few fundamental political ideas shared by the citizens of a liberal-democratic republic. In other words, a theory of justice cannot rest merely on a normative and deductive justification. It needs to rely on a few factual elements that, historically, are essential to ensure given standards of justice that we now consider indispensable. As we are going to see, the political conception of justice in PL presupposes a liberal legitimacy (chapters 10 and 11 of this volume), the origins of which cannot but be partly historical. In other words, the most we can say with respect to Rawls' three fundamental interests is that they correspond to the American constitutional history and its success over time (and to those of liberal democracy in general). If such an interpretation is correct, then these interests are legitimated by a success story that proves that they are consistent with a few political virtues that we do not want to relinquish.

A second way to answer this circularity objection consists in showing how, from Rawls' perspective, the right – which corresponds for Rawls2 to the "reasonable" – and the good – which corresponds to the "rational" – are not opposed. Indeed, it is necessary for them to come together. After all, rationality and goodness are not confined to the formal interpretation borrowed from a rational choice theory, and reasonableness and rightness, which provide the basis of the sense of justice, are also elements of a rational choice of the parties in the original position.

In this regard, Brian Barry proposes a distinction between two different ways of conceiving of a theory of justice.[52] The first centers on the concept of mutual advantage, while the second is based on the concept of impartiality. If we imagine both of them within the paradigm of the social contract, we can say that the mutual advantage model causes the agreement to depend on the contractual power of the parties. This has the consequence that any hypothesis of justice that does not correspond to such power, the parties' rational self-interest, would be implausible. Within the impartialist model, the notion of justice proves instead to be "less parsimonious" (Barry's expression), because the choice in favor of the rationality of justice does not go back exclusively to the interest of the parties and their contractual power.[53] Starting from this general distinction, Barry divides all theories of justice into two separate categories. Indeed, in his opinion, many theories of justice fail to be sufficiently rigorous: appeals to mutual advantage are used to surreptitiously introduce impartialist assumptions and, vice versa, the impartialist theorists often endorse assumptions based on the mutual advantage.

If we follow this interpretation, Hume would be a mutual-advantage theorist, while Rawls would be an impartialist theorist. And yet, Barry argues, both would fall into the temptation of granting too much to the opposite model. Were we to interpret Rawls' original position in a narrow sense, it would be an example of betrayal of an impartialist approach in the name of a decision supported by the rationality of the parties conceived in terms of mutual advantage. Were we to accept a wider interpretation of the original position, such as the one I am suggesting, we would cause it to depend in part also on the general moral argument and reflective equilibrium. As a result, we might say that the consistency of impartialism is not adequately defended. My thesis is that Barry's interpretation is misleading if we take the complementarity of the good and the right, and the reasonable and the rational, in earnest.

Let us consider this final point. I believe that the fault in Barry's interpretation lies in the fact that by directly opposing mutual advantage to impartiality, he further indirectly opposes rationality to reasonableness. According to Rawls, instead, rational people are also reasonable, which means rational political choices take into account other people's claims. If we were to put this thesis in simple terms, we might say that Barry is wrong because being impartial is part of the mutual advantage. Both rationality and reasonableness are – for Rawls – aspects of practical political reason. Furthermore, even if the reasonable is connected with the right and the rational with the good, their complementarity is an indispensable element of a theory of distributive justice. It causes the choices of the persons steered towards their own conception of the good to coincide with the desire to comply with the requirements provided for by the preferred theory of justice.

5.4 The deduction

The mechanism of the original position causes the parties to decide in favor of the two principles consistent with rational choice under uncertainty. In TJ, Rawls introduces this type of argument in the final sections (26–30) of chapter III, entitled "The Original Position." This is an intrinsically complex argument where both formal and informal elements come into play in a way that is not easily decoded. It is a theme that Rawls has (self-)critically taken up again, reviewing it to a considerable extent. The revised edition of TJ is full of emendations in these pages (see chapter 8), some of which are carried over into JFR and PL.

Rawls starts by outlining his reasoning that leads from the original position to the principles of justice. This rather generic reasoning grants an initial plausibility to the two principles. The problem is one of giving this plausibility an independent deductive strength. In order to do so:

> it is useful as a heuristic device to think of the two principles as the maximin solution to the problem of the social justice. *There is a relation between the two principles and the maximin rule for choice under uncertainty.* This is evident from the fact that the two principles are those a person would choose for the design of a society in which his enemy is to assign him his place. (TJ 152; rev. edn. 132–3, emphasis mine)

On these grounds, the parties in the original position opt for the maximin rule, a rule that requires them to choose the alternative that will not lead to the worst possible result. The (numerous) objections made to this type of solution concern Rawls' capacity to appeal rationally to maximin reasoning in the original position. In particular, many authors have criticized the specific way that the derivation is proposed in terms of a rational choice theory.[54] Rawls uses the model of a theory of rational choice under uncertainty to opt for the maximin rule that . . . leads to the principles of justice. From this point of view, there seem to be two types of standard objections. First, can the model of the original position actually select the maximin principle as opposed to potential rivals, such as the principle of average utility or mixed criteria?[55] Second, can the two principles actually be derived from the maximin reasoning, given that the principles seem to depend on a number of assumptions independent of the theory of rational choice?[56] Although these types of objections may be formally answered through a few axiomatizations of the Rawlsian derivation of the difference principle,[57] the problem persists (see appendix to this chapter). It should be noted that, in the years subsequent to the formulation of the theory, Rawls considerably weakened the relationship between the maximin and the difference principle, until he nearly rejects it in full.

In the revised text of TJ, Rawls writes:

> Economists may wish to refer to the difference principle as the maximin criterion, but I have carefully avoided this name for several reasons. *The maximin criterion is generally understood as a rule for choice under great uncertainty (§ 26), whereas the difference principle is a principle of justice. It is undesirable to use the same name for two things that are so distinct* . . . In addition, calling the difference principle the maximin criterion might wrongly suggest that the main argument for this principle from the original position derives from an assumption of high risk aversion. There is indeed a relation between the difference principle and such an assumption, but extreme attitudes to risk are not postulated (§ 28); and in any case there are many considerations in favor of the difference principle in which the aversion to risk plays no role at all. (TJ rev. edn. 83, emphasis mine)

Nonetheless, the argument focusing on the maximin is explicitly a central argument of the deductive scheme in terms of rational choice in TJ. The maximin-related argument is built in two stages. First, Rawls tries to show that, given the model of the original position, the parties would choose the maximin rule. The formal structure of the maximin is simple. Let us imagine three possible results in a distributive choice (where the numbers stand for amounts of primary goods) that involves three parties: a, b and c:

	a	b	c
(i)	10	15	−1
(ii)	8	11	1
(iii)	5	7	4

The maximin rule invites us to choose, first, solution (iii) and, second, solution (ii), even if the sum of the numbers that stand for the primary goods would impose a different choice.

Second, it is necessary to show that the parties in the original position would really choose the maximin. The first stage is crucial: Rawls argues that the specific construction of the original position entails the choice of the maximin.

Rawls admits that the maximin is not usually a plausible rule for choices under uncertainty, but he affirms that there are three special features of the original position "that give plausibility" (TJ 154; rev. edn. 134) to the choice of the maximin. First, behind the veil of ignorance, there is no possibility of thinking in a probabilistic manner, in the sense that there is not sufficient information to have comparative probabilistic estimates of the outcomes of one's choice (ibid.). Second, each party in the original position is satisfied with the minimum guaranteed by the maximin. Finally, the worst outcomes of alternative solutions are outcomes that "one can hardly accept" (ibid.).

The first special feature of the original position, the impossibility of relying on probabilistic estimates, does not necessarily lead to maximin. In fact, the entire theory of rational choice under uncertainty starts from a similar assumption with respect to probabilities, and this makes the theory of choice under uncertainty different from that of risk (where the outcome is not known while the probabilities are known). But, even ignoring the probabilities, maximin is not the only acceptable decision rule. In this regard, different decision rules have been proposed in the relevant literature. In view of the above, this condition by itself is not enough to cause the selection of the maximin (after all, this seems clear to Rawls who mentions Baumol as a source for the treatment of rules of choice under uncertainty, and Baumol provides for five different ones, including the maximin).

The second special feature says that, moving away from the maximin, there is little to be gained and much to be lost. However, taken by itself, it is quite implausible, since it starts from the assumption that there is either a formidable decreasing marginal utility of the goods from the empirical point of view or an intransigent case in favor of equality from the moral point of view. Furthermore, when in the preceding chapter we considered the general argument in favor of the second principle, we were able to appreciate the balance between propensity to equality and the need for incentives shown by Rawls' thesis. However, if we take this assumption of a drastic decrease of the marginal utility of the primary goods in earnest, any option in favor of the incentives runs the risk of disappearing. This weakens the plausibility of Rawls' approach to justice from the standpoint of economic theory. Instead, the same condition seems more plausible if we cause the basic liberties and their priorities to fall within the maximin context. It is likely to protect these liberties better with a strict principle rather than relying upon complex actuarial calculations. More generally, Rawls' proposal may be viewed as more plausible when we reject the idea that the criteria of social choice may rest merely on subjective decisions. Indeed, the decisions are to start from objective criteria, perhaps centered on the relative urgency that a few needs have with respect to other needs.[58]

Thus, the weight of the argument should fall largely on the third special feature, whereby: "Other conceptions of justice may lead to institutions that the parties would find intolerable" (TJ 156; rev. edn. 134). Here, the assumption corresponds quite explicitly to the criticism Rawls levels against utilitarianism; namely, utilitarianism could accept outcomes that sacrifice a few minorities in the name of total utility. The intolerability of the conclusions of a utilitarian argument depends for Rawls mostly on the fact that such an argument would not guarantee the defense of the "basic liberties." However, there are two problems with Rawls' thesis: (i) all theories of justice tend to conflate different goods and desires in the same ordering and justice as fairness makes no exception; (ii) taking for granted that such an assumption does away with utilitarianism in its radical or simple forms, it remains to be seen whether it also does away with mixed forms. Mixed forms of utilitarianism accept constraints, rules or restrictions that prevent such unacceptable outcomes.[59] It would seem that Rawls' feature (iii) is actually unable to do away with moderate conceptions, such as a mixed conception including the principle of average utility in addition to the basic liberties and a form of guaranteed minimum.[60]

5.4.1 Maximin and two critiques

The choice of the maximin criterion has often been criticized for its conceptual and normative implausibility in the light of common intuitions concerning a just distribution from both a substantive point of view (Nagel, Dworkin, and Barry) and a formal point of view (Gauthier, Hampton, and Harsanyi). Quite a few believe that to attach relevance only to a few persons – the least advantaged – when distributing primary goods is likely to lead to absurd results. This thesis is authoritatively upheld by J. J. C. Harsanyi with a simple diagram such as the one below:

	Outcome A	Outcome B
Bet 1	$1	$2
Bet 2	10 cents	$1,000,000

This invites us to reflect on the fact that the maximin strategy would require us to choose Bet 1, with clearly "absurd implications" (see the Appendix).

It may be noted that Rawls is fully aware of this type of problem, so much so that in TJ he proposes a matrix quite similar to the one later proposed by Harsanyi to show the difficulty implicit in the choice of the maximin (TJ, rev. edn. 136). In Rawls' example the numbers stand for utility, income, or other goods:

	Event 1	Event 2
Choice 1	0	n
Choice 2	$1/n$	1

The maximin criterion always calls for Choice 2, while it is obvious that with a sufficiently big n (i.e., $n = 1,000,000$) it is advisable to opt for Choice 1. It is much better to take part in a lottery that offers 0 or 1,000,000 as prizes than in a lottery that offers a millionth or one as prizes, even though the second satisfies the maximin criterion. Rawls seems to consider the problem irrelevant because he deems it unlikely that such a situation of choice might occur in real life (TJ 157; rev. edn. 136). Furthermore, the very description of the original position would remove for Rawls "such abstract possibilities" (TJ 157; rev. edn. 136) from among the real possibilities. It would seem that, in this case, Rawls considers that no ethical-political vision may leave aside a certain realism of the assumptions, in order to avoid what he calls an "ethics of creation" addressing a purely utopian world.

A final critique is based on the epistemological difficulties connected with the maximin. Kenneth Arrow, from an ordinalist point of view in welfare economics, maintains that individual utilities are not measurable (this is what draws ordinalism apart from cardinalism)[61] and that interpersonal comparisons of utility are inconceivable. The classical utilitarian criterion, however, entails both cardinal measure and interpersonal comparisons of utility. Having accepted interpersonal comparisons, utilitarians are forced to admit that distributing the same amount of resources leads to different amounts of utility from one individual to another. Hence, it would become necessary to shift resources to the advantage of individuals who are most sensitive to satisfactions. This criterion entails paradoxical results, such as the one that those who are depressed or unhappy should be deprived of resources. This absurd consequence does not concern Rawls. However, according to Arrow, Rawls is affected by another absurd consequence of the maximin. The absurd consequence in this case would be represented by a sort of dictatorship of those who, being unable to experience pleasure, are the worst-off in Rawls' model. This problem is partly solved by Rawls' recourse to a list of primary goods that limits interpersonal comparisons. However, this solution, in turn, gives rise to another difficulty. In order to follow this criterion, we need a primary goods index and there is the risk that working out such an index might prove just as complicated as working out a sensible interpersonal comparison for the utilitarians.

5.5 The Comparison with the Principle of Utility

After considering the merits and faults of the maximin rule, Rawls considers what, in his view, is the most substantial rival to his principles: the principle of average utility. For Rawls, the principle of average utility is superior to the classical principle of utility. If Rawls can successfully prove parties in the original position would choose the maximin over the principle of average utility, then he further succeeds in proving that the principles of justice are superior to classical utilitarianism.[62]

When applied to the basic structure, the classical principle of utility tells us that institutions need to maximize the total sum of utilities expected by the representative individuals. This sum is obtained by adding the expected utilities of all the individuals. The result is that, if there is a twofold increase in the number of persons who belong to a given society, assuming that the utilities of each one of them remain the same, then there is also a twofold increase in the total utility. The principle of the average utility requires us to consider the average (per capita) utility rather than the total utility. Rawls affirms that this principle is more plausible than the classical one. However, why should it be preferred? It is easy to see that, keeping the population constant, there is no difference in the results called for by the application of either principle. Nonetheless, as the population increases, the classical principle may lead us to "repugnant" conclusions, including that one according to which – assuming that every living person experiences at least a few satisfactions – the more the population increases, the more the total utility increases. It is easy to conclude that recommending an indefinite increase in the population is not reasonable and, at least from this point of view, the principle of average utility prevails over the classical principle.[63]

Rawls' idea is that the principle of average utility works like a single rational individual who chooses which society he belongs to from among several models. Such an individual assumes that he may be any one of the individuals, and – under this assumption of symmetry – he chooses the principle that maximizes the average utility. Putting aside the question of the interpersonal comparison of utility and assuming persons with an average propensity to risk, we need to take into account the question of the ignorance of probabilities that, as we have seen, characterizes the original position. According to Rawls, in order to adopt the average utility principle, the utilitarian needs to play on the principle of insufficient reason.[64] This principle is used to compute the likelihood of outcomes in the absence of information (there are no objective bases to calculate likelihood and frequencies). Following the so-called "Rule of Laplace," in cases of insufficient information a rational actor should treat all outcomes as equiprobable.

With a view to settling the competition between the principle of average utility and the two principles of justice, from an analytic point of view Rawls' argument shifts to the comparison between the principle of insufficient reason and the maximin. According to Rawls, the weakness of the principle of insufficient reason consists in exposing the parties to risks that would instead be avoidable if they had endorsed the maximin principle. It is hard to say whether he succeeds in fully proving this thesis in TJ. For instance, the negative utility from the threat of such risks should already be incorporated into the individuals' utility functions. Regardless, it is strange that a probability problem might become so important within a theory of justice, but this is a consequence of relying on a theory of rational choice (that, later on, as previously pointed out, Rawls will finally reject).

For Rawls, the reasoning in favor of the principle of average utility features another substantial flaw. The principle views the utility expectations of all the individuals from the perspective of only one of them. The principle of average utility presupposes unified expectations. This fact seems to depend on a very general idea, which lies at the base of Rawls' distinction: utilitarianism has as its objective the global general interest but it is opaque with respect to individuals.[65] On the other hand, the theory of justice as fairness starts from the presupposition that each individual person must benefit. This is another reason why the contractualist theory adopts the assumption that all the individuals choose in a situation of mutual disinterestedness. According to Rawls, this difference leads to substantive consequences since, as regards the principle of average utility:

> It is crucial to note that this reasoning presupposes a particular conception of the person. The parties are conceived as having no highest order interests or fundamental ends by reference to which they decide what kind of persons they care to be. *They have, as it were, no determinate character or will. They are, we might say, bare-persons.* (TJ, rev. edn. 152, emphasis mine)

In the light of Rawls' theory, instead: "we have assumed that the parties do have a determinate character and will, even though the specific nature of their system of ends is unknown to them. *They are, so to speak, determinate persons*: they have certain highest-order interests and fundamental ends" (ibid., emphasis mine). This analysis exposes both flaws in the principle of average utility: the appeal to the principle of insufficient reason and the inability to grasp the difference between persons. From this point of view, Rawls believes that classical utilitarianism also "fails to take seriously the distinction between persons" (TJ 187; rev. edn. 163, as he had already said in section 5 of TJ). This occurs because, through the idea of a rational and disinterested spectator, the principle of choice for a person is extended to all. The most serious consequence of this is that utilitarianism allows improper sacrifices by a few to the benefit of others, because the utilitarian model does not account for the real conflict of interests among the parties. The theory of justice as fairness takes the conflict into account through the assumption of the mutual disinterestedness in the original position. The impartiality in TJ is preserved by taking as decision-makers the very persons having conflicts of interest, rather than by identifying different persons: "The fault of the utilitarian doctrine is that it mistakes impersonality for impartiality" (TJ 190; rev. edn. 166).

Now, we need to see whether the principles of justice can do any better.

With this view in mind, Rawls can appeal to his construction of the original position, the veil of ignorance and the finality and publicity constraints. That granted, it is hard to defend the choice of the maximin from a merely formal point of view. Settling in the abstract the controversy between supporters of the principle of insufficient reason and of the maximin is definitely challenging. Love for freedom and aversion to the most serious risks are, after all, normal elements of the utility function of any individual and, therefore, should turn up in the consequent aggregations. Quite likely, defending the choice of the maximin is advisable, in the light of a more complex consistency of the theory of justice as fairness, by taking up a few of Rawls' arguments subsequent to TJ ("Some Reasons for the Maximin Criterion," "Reply to Alexander and Musgrave").

Hence, if we want to take Rawls seriously with respect to the derivation of the maximin, we need to resort to a sort of mixed argument. According to this argument, the maximin is chosen not only because it is a rule of rational choice theory, but also because there are substantial reasons that encourage opting in its favor. These further reasons include appeals to the strains of commitment, the need to protect one's self-respect, and the will to defend stability.[66] The argument based on the strains of commitment, which is the foremost, claims that parties should refrain from accepting commitments in the original position that, once the veil of ignorance is lifted, would prove too straining. The maximin, unlike utilitarianism, would help individuals accept commitments laid out in the social contract because it rules out intolerable outcomes.[67]

All these arguments start from the common premise that the a-priori defense of equal liberties and the greater equality, guaranteed by the maximin, correspond to a better solution. The maximin does not force the parties to adopt commitments that are too taxing; it promotes self-respect and, on this basis, guarantees stability over time. The choice of the maximin rule would be required in the light of these three informal arguments or, rather, would be the product of the conjunction of the formal argument and the substantive arguments. However, it also depends on more general basic assumptions, such as the tendency to equality.

In the final analysis, Rawls considers the principle of utility psychologically unacceptable because of the tendency to equality. Needless to say, such an interpretation, though reasonable, defies any easy evaluation in analytical terms. In fact, the moral appeal to equality, which underlies the substantive arguments that censure utilitarianism, does not formally derive from the original position, as it is a substantive ethical presupposition.[68]

Rawls adds another argument that draws on the preceding distinction between "bare persons" and "determinate persons." The distinction in favor of the determinate persons, linked to the two principles, rather than the bare persons, does not relate merely to average utilitarianism but – in the last section of chapter III – applies also to classical utilitarianism (even though in a slightly different form). In the case of classical utilitarianism, the idea of the rational and impartial spectator is set up against the idea of the Rawlsian parties in the original position. The utilitarian spectator has no interests in the choice at hand and, under these conditions, takes equal interest in all the individuals who will be affected by her decision. This is why she imagines herself in everyone else's place. In this sense, she is fully informed and provided with powers of imaginative identification. In contrast to this, the parties in the original position are ignorant and mutually disinterested.

5.6 Summary

Apparently, from these arguments, one should infer that the parties in the original position should choose the maximin and the principles of justice. This argument is open to criticism for at least two reasons. First, those more endowed with talents could object that the maximin, and the difference principle, require from them sacrifices that are not adequately justified with respect to the worst-off. Second, Rawls' argument is no longer valid if one endorses mixed principles rather than the simple average utility principle.[69] These mixed conceptions can be constructed simply with a view to avoiding a few intolerable consequences by including clauses on the priority of liberty, the minimum guaranteed, and the like. Unlike the maximin and the principle of utility, the characteristic features of these principles are relatively flexible, which means they do not sacrifice a few institutional options by being overly rigid (which happens if we follow the maximin literally).

The attack on the maximin by both the utilitarians and the likely supporters of the mixed criteria consists in censuring its implicit rigidity (see the appendix to this chapter). Rawls cannot object to mixed-principle critics in the same way he does to utilitarians. Mixed-principle theories are not bound to meet with intolerable consequences, such as not protecting in an adequate manner a few liberties or allowing too much inequality. In the light of this second objection, Rawls needs to find a way out to show how the rigidity of the maximin relates to the general equilibrium of the theory of justice as fairness. Such a defense may be given in terms of publicity of the principles and stability of the socio-institutional system.[70]

There is both a formal and a substantive argument in favor of the maximin. Formally, the maximin solution differs from the maximization of the expected utility, which plays on the principle of insufficient reason. The set-up of the original position would make the choice of the principle of insufficient reason more difficult. However, it does not seem that this difficulty depends on this formal argument in terms of social choice theory so much as on Rawls' additional moral theses (which derive from the description of the original position). According to the most significant among these, we need to differentiate impersonality from interpersonality. In the case of impersonality, which pertains to the utilitarians, it is easier to choose the maximization of the expected utility. Things would not be the same in the case of interpersonality, which requires the consent of all the parties. The necessity of general consent leads to the choice of a prudential solution. According to the second thesis, given that Rawls' veil of ignorance is thicker than the thin veil of the utilitarian's impartial spectator, it is perhaps reasonable to risk less and prudentially opt for the maximin. This applies above all when the basic liberties are at stake.

One of the difficulties inherent in Rawls' theory is the close relationship between the formal and substantive aspects of his account. Perhaps this is one of the reasons why, with the passing of time, Rawls abandoned grounding the theory of justice as fairness in rational choice theory. From a merely formal point of view, there are various rules for choice under uncertainty and the choice of the maximin is usually criticized for a very simple reason. When using the maximin, only the worst solution is taken into consideration and the others are neglected. A similar decision, however, is often counterintuitive. Generally, granting a dictatorship or a power of veto solely to avoid a negative, and perhaps improbable, outcome is unreasonable. Elsewhere, I proposed a rule of choice with less perverse consequences than the maximin, although preserving in part its spirit. It should be noted that the other rules for choice under uncertainty have their faults and, thus, that the choice always depends on an overall vision. This is the reason why the choice of the maximin is defendable only in an extended vision of the theory of justice, where the aspects of the theory of rational choice are proportionate to the other assumptions of the theory.

Appendix

In this appendix, I show how the maximin criterion, related to Rawls' difference principle, can be deduced in two standard formal rational choice frameworks: Arrow–Sen collective choice and game theory. The exercise is useful in order to appreciate the originality of the Rawlsian solution. Rawls' originality begins with the refutation of the previously often undisputed link between utilitarianism and the ethical and psychological foundations of economics. The utilitarian solution suggests that society should maximize the sum total of utility, which, if averaged, means that society should strive to maximize $\Sigma u_i \, 1/n$ for each individual i having utility u_i. Instead, Rawls says that society should maximize min u_i. At the same time, the exercise highlights some of the difficulties related to the maximin proposal emphasized by prominent economists like Arrow, Sen, and Harsanyi. Rawls' decision, after TJ, to dispense with the maximin criterion follows at least in part from such difficulties. Since then, it is intrinsically controversial whether, and how, the difference principle and the maximin are connected. The Rawlsian attempt to separate the difference principle from the maximin principle notwithstanding, critical interest in the basic axiomatic framework in TJ and in the theorems that can be deduced from it remains lively from the vantage point of justice as fairness.

Collective choice

In Arrow's classic work *Social Choice and Individual Values* (1951),[71] he tries to establish what a social preference ordering should be as a function of individual orderings. Let us imagine a society containing two individuals 1 and 2, each having a preference ordering over two alternatives x and y. Each individual can prefer x to y, or y to x, or be indifferent between x and y.

We can represent a preference ordering on a set of alternatives S as a binary relation R defined over $S \times S$, that is the subset of ordered pairs $(x,y) \in S \times S$. With xRy, we mean that the relation R holds between x and y, i.e. that x is *at least as good as* y. The relation R enjoys the following properties:

Transitivity: $x, y, z \in S$: $(xRy \ \& \ yRz) \rightarrow xRz$
Reflexivity: $x \in S$: xRx
Completeness: $x,y \in S$: $(x{\neq}y) \rightarrow (xRy \ v \ yRx)$

Starting from the relation R (at least as good as), we can define its asymmetric and symmetric factors, P and I respectively, which stand for "strict preference" and "indifference":

Strict Preference: $xPy \rightarrow (xRy \ \& \ \neg(yRx))$
Indifference: $xIy \rightarrow (xRy \ \& \ yRx)$

We can then define a *maximal element* in a set as an element that is not preferred by any other element in the set:

Maximal Element: An element $x \in S$ is a maximal element in S with respect to a binary relation R iff

$(\neg \exists y : (y \in S \ \& \ yPx))$

For Arrow, a *function of social welfare* (FSW) is a functional relation f specifying a social ordering R for each given n-tuple of individual orderings R_i with $i = 1,...,n$:

$R = f(R_1,...,R_n)$

In *Social Choice and Individual Values*, Arrow proves his famous impossibility theorem starting from the idea that there be reasonableness conditions imposed on any viable FSW. One of these conditions is "independence of irrelevant alternatives." In order to define it, Arrow defines the *choice function* C(.) on the relation R as satisfying the so-called "Condorcet's condition," i.e. such that for all subsets S of X:

Condorcet: $C(S) = (x: x \in S \,\&\, \forall y \in S: xRy)$

From this condition:
Condition I (independence of irrelevant alternatives): for any two n-tuples R_i and R'_i in the domain of f, and for all $S \subseteq X$ with choice functions C(.) and C'(.) corresponding to $f(R_i)$ and $f(R'_i)$ respectively:

$(\forall i: (\forall x,y \in S: xR_iy \Leftrightarrow xR'_iy)) \Rightarrow C(S) = C'(S)$

This condition, intuitively, says that as long as individual preferences on a subset S of X are the same, then social choice on that subset is the same as well.

Arrow's proof hinges on certain mild ethical conditions imposed over the FSW as defined above. We shall refer to the presentation from Arrow's 1963 book, and will adopt Sen's formalism. The ethical conditions comprise the just-introduced condition I (independence of irrelevant alternatives). There are three more conditions:

Condition P (Pareto principle)
$\forall i: (xR_iy \rightarrow xRy)$

Condition U (unrestricted domain): The domain of the FSW comprehends all the n-tuples of individual orderings combinatorially possible.
Condition D (non-dictatorship): There is no individual i such that her individual ordering always dictates the social ordering:

$\neg \exists i, \forall x,y \in X : xP_iy \Rightarrow xPy$

If we denote by H the set of all individuals in society, and by #X the cardinality of the set of social states X, Arrow's Theorem can be stated as follows:

General Possibility Theorem: If H is finite and $\#X \geq 3$, there is no FSW that satisfies I, P, U, and D.

We sketch here the proof, based on a contraction and an expansion lemma. The first lemma, using Pareto principle and transitivity of the preference relation, shows that if a group of individuals is such that the preferences of its members are sufficient to determine the social preference with regard to some pair of alternatives x and y (let us say that, in this case, the group is *decisive* about *x* and *y*), then the group is decisive about *any* pair of alternatives in *S*. The second lemma shows that if a group has at least three members and is decisive about *x* and *y*, then any proper subset of it is decisive about *x* and *y*. But from the Pareto principle it follows that the group made of any member of society is decisive about some pair of alternatives and hence, by the first lemma, it is decisive about any pair of alternatives. The cardinality of such group is then reduced via the second lemma until we reach the point in which only one individual (the dictator) dominates the preferences of the entire society. That is to say: any FSW cannot avoid being dictatorial.

The political significance of Arrow's Theorem is evident: what is shown by it is that a procedure that is *latu sensu* democratic does not guarantee a rational outcome. On the contrary, any FSW will be either dictatorial or indefinite.

In the vast literature on collective choice many have attempted to avoid Arrow's impossibility result. One kind of attempt looks at the definition of FSW and at its formal aspects, trying to modify it to prevent the Arrovian result. Another kind looks at the ethical conditions instead. From the point of view of a theory of justice, attempts of the second kind are more interesting, analyzing the implications of the weakening of ethical conditions. Usually conditions *P* and *D* are not disturbed, since their ethical implications are deemed indispensable. Let us consider then the possibility of weakening the other two conditions. Condition *I* (irrelevance) has to do with the issue of the informational enrichment of the Arrovian paradigm, and for this reason it has been widely discussed in the literature.

The ethical rationale behind condition I is that the introduction of non-relevant alternatives in the choice process could pave the way to objectionable "threats" and "logrolling" among the parties. The irrelevant alternatives, in other words, could function as disincentives or as incentives to better play the alternatives actually available, which is undesirable.

In the combinatorics of possible individual measures of utility and inter-personal comparisons, Arrow adopts a model in which there is no cardinal measure of utility, nor are interpersonal comparisons possible. The two restrictions on such information are – for Arrow – linked in that if one ignores the intensity of the preferences of individuals, *a fortiori* it is impossible to meaningfully compare levels of utility interpersonally. The issue of the link between informational basis and impossibility thus originates relatedly with condition I.

Sen confronted this problem.[72] In his perspective, the informational basis of collective choice can be enriched by treating the relation *R* or the choice function *C(.)* *not* as a function of *n*-tuples of individual orderings R_j, but rather as a *functional*, that is a function of *n*-tuples of utility functions $U_i(.)$. In such a way, Sen can effectively measure the relevance of the restriction to ordinal utility without interpersonal comparison typical of the Arrovian framework. Sen demonstrates that using a cardinal function (i.e., being able to measure not just the ordering but also the intensity of individual preferences) does not eliminate Arrow's impossibility result, while the introduction of interpersonal comparison, even if combined with mere ordinal utility, is sufficient to enable non-dictatorial collective choice.

The result is relevant to understanding the Rawlsian choice function, since he uses an ordinal utility function with (limited) interpersonal comparison. Interpersonal comparison takes place in the context of the second principle as it is stated that social and economic inequalities ought to be for the greater benefit of the worst-off. The adoption of the maximin decision principle, requiring the maximization of the expectations of the least advantaged individual, presupposes that we can, by means of an interpersonal comparison of utility, establish who are the least advantaged. In a sense, the second principle establishes a "dictatorship of the worst-off."

It is, however, important to stress that the Rawlsian solution to the problem of interpersonal comparisons remains unusual. Rawls only allows comparisons with respect to a bundle of *primary goods*, which are supposed to be desired by everyone as means to satisfy different ends. Even in such a brilliant resolution of the Arrovian dilemma, we can easily spot two demanding assumptions. On the one hand, we presuppose a uniform interest for everyone in the same goods. On the other, we presuppose that such a bundle of primary goods is actually definable. More generally, even if we want to make a few primary goods compatible in an index that puts them together, we ought to solve the problem of their mutual incommensurability, which is not, after all, very different from the problem of interpersonal comparisons of utility (Arrow, *Social Choice and Individual Values*, p. 154). These assumptions presuppose that a given situation can be sufficiently known and interpreted.

The clearest intersection of Rawls' theory of justice and Arrow's formalism is yielded by the weakening of condition *U*. S. Strasnick[73] put forth an important axiomatization of the Rawlsian notion of justice based within the Arrovian paradigm assumption of unlimited (or unrestricted) domain.

Strasnick wants to show that accepting the original position as a valid procedure for identifying principles of justice entails the acceptance of the maximin criterion and hence of Rawls' difference principle. He adopts Arrow's framework and, in order to avoid the impossibility result, chooses a characterization of individual preferences that takes into account the relative weights of different preferences over the set of primary goods.

Intuitively, Strasnick's construction goes as follows: He considers a *priority principle* establishing the neutrality of original individual preferences. Strasnick then uses three assumptions to formally characterize the Rawlsian veil of ignorance in the context of collective choice *à la* Arrow. Finally, he demonstrates, by induction from the number of individuals in society, that, given the assumptions and an appropriate formal definition of the maximin in the Arrovian context, the priority principle implies the difference principle.

Formally, consider a society with n individuals $1,...,n$ and a set of social states S. States are described in terms of attributions of primary goods to individuals, that is, a state x consists of an ordered set of attributions $x_1,...,x_n$ for each individual $1,...n$. The expression $xP_iy \sim xP_jy$ means that individuals i and j have the same priority in their preference of x over y. Assume now the

Principle of Priority: $\forall i,j,x,z,u$: If $y_i = z_j$, then $xP_iy \sim uP_jz$.

The principle implies that there can be no legitimate claim to a larger share of primary goods prior to the application of the difference principle. To see that, suppose that individual i receives in x more than j receives in u: this must not entail that i's preference of x over y be stronger that j's preference of u over z (as, for instance, would be the case for utilitarians).

Rawls' veil of ignorance can be characterized through the following assumptions – where $R_i(x,y)$ and $R(x,y)$ represent the ordering of the preference over x and y of individual i and of society, respectively, while $\mathbf{R}(x,y)$ represents the set of individual preferences $R_1(x,y),...,R_n(x,y)$ with priorities attached:

(1) *Binariety*: If $[R_i(x,y) \leftrightarrow R'_i(x,y)$ & $R_i(x,y) \sim R'_i(x,y)]$, then $R(x,y) \leftrightarrow R'(x,y)$

(2) *Anonymity*: If $\mathbf{R}'(x,y)$ is the result of permutations in $\mathbf{R}(x,y)$, then $R(x,y) \leftrightarrow R'(x,y)$

(3) *Neutrality*: If $[R_i(x,y) \leftrightarrow R'_i(u,z)$ & $R_i(x,y) \sim R'_i(u,z)]$, then $R(x,y) \leftrightarrow R'(u,z)$.

The three conditions say that (1) social preference is independent from any factor other than statements of individual preference; (2) social preference is invariant under permutations of statements of individual preference; (3) social preference is invariant with respect to operations that change name to the alternatives. The fourth condition imposed by Strasnick is a consistency condition: let $Q = (Q_1,...Q_m)$ be a partition of $\mathbf{R}(x,y)$ and R_{Qk} the social preference in the k-th subset of Q, then the following holds:

(4) *Unanimity*: For each x, y and for each partition Q:
   a. If, for each i in Q_k, $R_i(x,y)$, then $R_{Qk}(x,y)$;
   b. If, for each $Q_k \in Q$, $R_{Qk}(x,y)$, then $R(x,y)$.

To be able to connect this formalism with Rawls' principle of justice, Strasnick needs to identify the "least advantaged" individual in society. He does so through the following three definitions:

(a) y_i is a *dominated minimal element* of (x,y) if and only if $x_i > y_i$ and, for each $j \neq i$, $xj > y_i$ & $y_j \geq y_i$. Denote that with: $y_i \in$ MinDom(x,y).

(b) The social preference P is *Rawlsian* if and only if, for each x and y, there exists an i such that $y_i \in \mathrm{MinDom}(x,y)$, then xPy.

(c) If $y_i \in \mathrm{MinDom}(x,y)$, then i is the *least advantaged individual* for states x, y.

This machinery of definitions and conditions allows Strasnick to prove his theorem showing that, if one agrees with the formalization of Rawls' original position, then one has to accept the second principle of justice:

Strasnick's Theorem: The Principle of Priority, along with conditions (1), (2), (3), and (4), entails that the social preference satisfies definition (b) above, i.e. it is Rawlsian.

Game theory

Game theory is based on the theory of utility formulated by von Neumann and Morgenstern.[74] They showed how certain coherence assumptions about the preferences of decision-makers imply that such preferences can be represented by a cardinal utility function and that, moreover, such coherence assumptions imply that decision-makers maximize the expected value of such a function. If we say that an individual is *rational* if and only if her preferences satisfy the coherence conditions informally listed below, it follows that rational individuals thus defined always maximize their expected utility.

To see von Neumann and Morgenstern's construction, let us begin by assuming that there is a choice between three alternatives A, B and C. Let us assume, moreover, that the decision-maker has an ordering $A > B > C$. This ordinal preference can be represented by three decreasing numerical indexes a, b, and c. Let us imagine that the decision-maker has to choose between two alternatives: (i) to obtain B for sure; or (ii) to enter a lottery that yields A with probability p and C with probability $1 - p$. If p is sufficiently close to 1, we should pick alternative (ii) since it almost offers A for certain and A, by assumption, is preferred to B. On the other hand, if p is close to 0 one should, for the same reason, prefer alternative (i), i.e. B. We can assume that there is one and only one point such that the decision-maker will be indifferent between (i) and (ii). The location of that point reveals the intensity of the agent's preference for B.

In game theory, individuals who are rational in the aforementioned sense pursue their aims in competition with other rational individuals who also are pursuing their own aims. The behavior of such individuals is strategic, in that the outcome obtained by an individual will depend not only on the choices made by that individual, but, crucially, also on the choices made by other individuals. The *extensive form* of a game is a description of the successive moves of a strategic interaction in the form of a tree. Games are often described in *normal form* rather than extensive form. The mathematical description of a normal form game contains these elements:

$$G = (N, \{S\}_i, \{M\}_i), \text{ with } i = \{1,\ldots,n\}$$

Where N represents the set of n players, S_i represents the set of strategies available to player i and M_i represents the payoff function relative to player i, associating to each strategy profile $(s_1,\ldots,s_n)$ a payoff for each player. Among different kinds of games, two-player *zero-sum games* are purely competitive games in that the positive payoff m of player A always corresponds to the negative payoff $-m$ of player B. In the following matrix a two-person zero-sum game is represented in its normal form, where each row represents a pure strategy for A and each column a pure strategy for B. The cells of the matrix indicate A's payoff:

	B1	B2	B3	Row Min.
A1	8	−3	−10	−10
A2	0	−2	6	−2
A3	4	−1	5	−2
Col. Max.	8	−1	−6	

Of course, A aims to maximize her payoff (which means that she aims to minimize B's payoff) and similarly B strives to minimize A's payoff (which means that he is trying to maximize his own payoff). In this matrix, the best outcome for A is 8, while the best outcome for B is −10. If A picks A1, she can obtain 8, or −3, or −10, depending on B's choice. Clearly, if A plays A1, B will pick B3, with the consequence that A's payoff will be −10. Thus, A will avoid A1, choosing the row in which the minimum is more advantageous to her, i.e. the row where the minimum is largest (maximin). In the example above, the largest row minimum is −1, linked to strategy A3. By the same reasoning, B will try to minimize the column maxima, looking for a minimax outcome. In this case, it is again −1, linked to strategy B2. Both players prefer to minimize possible loss, and hence they choose a strategy that serves such a purpose. Any deviation from (A3, B2) will bring about the risk of larger losses, that is risks that are disadvantageous for the players. The point in which maximin and minimax coincide is the saddle point of the payoff function. In this way, players pursue a strategy maximizing the security level of their choices. In the saddle point, both players maximize their security level and we say that the outcome is an equilibrium, as for instance is the case for (A3, B2) in the game above. Von Neumann and Morgenstern demonstrate the following, fully general, theorum:

Theorem: In any two-player zero-sum game with a pure strategy equilibrium, there exists a number v representing a maximin strategy for the first player that maximizes her security level and at the same time representing a minimax strategy for the second player that maximizes his security level. These strategies are in equilibrium. Conversely, if two strategies are in equilibrium, they yield a maximin solution for the first player and a minimax solution for the second player.

We can interpret the difference principle as induced by the game-theoretic result just mentioned, in that, in the original position, the decision-maker behaves as if she was playing a zero-sum game against a mysterious and opaque, malevolent Nature. The decision-maker will therefore try to minimize her possible loss by using a maximin strategy, prudentially obtaining an optimal security level.

A criterion of social justice

In Rawls' system, the selection of the principles of justice takes place in an original position constructed for that very purpose. The characteristic element of the original position is the veil of ignorance. Because of the veil of ignorance, decision-makers have a general yet not specific or personal knowledge of the options on which they are called to choose. For Rawls, the veil of ignorance imposes extremely prudent choices since individuals, ignoring their identity at the moment they make their decisions, end up preferring an insurance agreement. Given that the parties decide as if they were risk-averse, they prefer the maximin criterion, which allows them to avoid the worst-case scenarios they could end up finding themselves in. For these reasons, in the original position, the two principles are preferred to the utility principle. However Rawls also says that the maximin rule of choice cannot be used in every case; for example, it cannot be used to argue in favor of the difference principle when it is compared with mixed conceptions which include a social minimum.

According to Rawls, in the situation of lack of information experienced by decision-makers in the original position, the *maximin* criterion is preferred to the utility principle (in the form of the equiprobability rule, as we have seen in chapter 5) for various reasons. First, because in such a peculiar decision-making context, parties will be highly risk-averse. If we assume, says Rawls, the crucial nature of choice in the original position, then the principle of utility, if considered independently from risk, will be problematic. And if, on the other hand, risk will be included in the computation of utility, then the utilitarian decision should not differ much from the maximin choice. From this point of view, utilitarian choice approximates the maximin solution as risk-aversion increases indefinitely. Second, as decision-makers are under the veil of ignorance, Rawls argues that maximin is more apt in situations in which information is sparse. Comparatively, it would be much more difficult to identify the solution proposed by expected utility maximization, as more information would be required to do that. The maximin solution only requires that we be able to identify the least-advantaged group in society. This last motive can add further weight in favor of maximin, in that its relative roughness makes it more apt for the public and general knowledge of principles governing public choice. The same reason leads us to think that the maximin criterion is appealing also from the point of view of the "strains of commitment," as Rawls puts it. The parties in the original position should not favor the selection of principles that force moral rules too difficult to uphold, and maximin then fits the bill because of the aforementioned clarity and because of the same notion of agreement, which implies unanimity which, in turn, is more plausible given a principle that gives priority to the interests of the worst-off. Lastly, for Rawls, the fundamental rationale behind the maximin lies in its capturing the aspiration to liberty and equality that characterize the Rawlsian individual.

The maximin is preferred by Rawls to the utility principle in a series of binary comparisons. This aspect is quite interesting, as the idea of decision-making under a veil of ignorance had already been presented, in a somewhat different form, by utilitarian scholars.

In the utilitarian perspective, one ought to take seriously the so-called "Laplace rule," according to which ignorance is equivalent to equiprobability. We can therefore say that in the original position, each individual is to be thought of as having the same probability of being any member in society. Hence, if there are n members in society, and the ith member will have utility u_i after some allocative decision, then the value of that allocation for each individual in society will be $1/n \ u_i$, since $1/n$ is the probability that any individual will turn out to actually be individual i. It follows that – in Harsanyi's perspective – each individual in the original position will want to maximize the sum total of utility $\Sigma \ u_i$. In the end, collective utility is a linear aggregation of all individual utilities.

Rawls, starting from similar premises, argues that society should prioritize the maximization of min u_i (albeit, for Rawls, it is not properly utility but the share of primary goods that is to be maximized). This way, we introduce a "preference priority" for the least advantaged, which remains one of the fundamental characteristics of the Rawlsian principle. This realizes a kind of tyranny of the worst-off, yet eludes the circularity of the Arrovian mechanism. The consequences of the tyranny of the worse-off are both positive and negative: they are positive in that they reproduce in the formalism a clear need for justice; they are negative in that they make such a need too rigid and automatic.

However, the main problem related to the choice of maximin as a decision criterion is a different one. The problem is that maximin seems to imply that any benefit for the worst-off, no matter how small, should outweigh any loss for the better-off, no matter how large. This appears bizarre. Rawls himself is aware of this difficulty, so much so that one can say maximin should not be applied literally. Moreover, Rawls counts heavily on the principle of close-knittedness, which says that, insofar as we let the expectations of the better-off increase, the situation of the least advantaged also becomes better.

Rawls' difference principle, and the maximin, compete with the principle of maximizing expected utility. In the axiomatization of decisions under uncertainty, when comparing alternatives, the maximin criterion is characterized by disregarding the intermediate outcomes. Both the utility and maximin principles are used under uncertainty by an arbitrary participant in a hypothetical society who does not know her role and her personal characteristics. The alternatives are in this case competing directions for the hypothetical society. The most relevant difference between the two criteria, from a theoretical point of view, lies in the available information.

The Rawlsian decision-maker is characterized by a thick veil of ignorance, and it is the veil that compels her to use the maximin criterion. Indeed, the utilitarian criterion must accept the possibility of an a-priori knowledge of the probability distribution regarding the states of the world about which the decision is made. Rawls' thick veil of ignorance prevents the possibility of such knowledge. For this reason the maximin criterion neglects intermediate possibilities and only selects extreme solutions. For various reasons the informational prudence of the maximin is praiseworthy, but it is important to notice how this also translates into an extremely detrimental lack of intuitive plausibility for the maximin.

The Rawlsian maximin, as we have seen, selects the best alternative for the representative man who is worst-off. If $A_1,...,A_n$ is a set of alternatives for individuals $I_1,...,I_n$ representative of classes of individuals that stand for social groups, the Rawlsian decision-maker will choose the best alternative from the point of view of the worst-off individual. Once more, the choice of the principle is motivated, for Rawls, by the refusal to admit that a distribution of probability over the universe of alternatives can be known. But, as said above, this methodological option has an undesirable consequence. This can be easily seen by looking at a matrix in which columns represent the utility of alternatives and rows the distinction by representative individuals (or social classes). Maximin only compares the column minima. This, of course, excludes the utility principle, but makes the original position choice based on the maximin implausible:

	I1	I2	I3	I4
A1	10	10	10	10
A2	9	100	100	100

For instance, in the matrix above, maximin implies that A1 will be chosen over A2, as its minimum (10) is larger than the minimum of A2 (9). But, clearly, the gains of 90 for I2, I3, and I4 exceed the loss of 1 for A2, making the selection implied by the maximin unsatisfactory.

The maximin criterion implies such counterintuitive choices because it forces us to neglect the information relative to intermediate outcomes, concentrating our attention on maxima and minima only. This exclusion appears to be entirely unreasonable in the example considered here. Note that Rawls maintains that such extreme cases will not happen in the real world, in which there always must be a situation A3 in which the least advantaged fare better than in A2 and the more advantaged fare better than in A1.

Since both maximin and expected utility maximization present some defects, we are tempted to introduce a criterion that combines their qualities, at the same time limiting their defects. A principle calibrated on negative outcomes could represent the desired criterion. Our desideratum appears to be a principle less paralyzing and egalitarian than the Rawlsian maximin, and more sensitive than the principle of utility to the differences in the choice context and to the different positions of individuals. Individuals do not behave in the prudential way described by Rawls, nor do they maximize expected utility as utilitarians *à la* Harsanyi require. With respect to the latter, we also would like a principle more egalitarian than the principle of utility.

There is no doubt that the maximin is appealing because it is egalitarian. But let us go back to the paradoxes it implies, such as the one considered above. Our intention is that of preserving the maximin tendency to privilege equality – which makes it preferable to the utility principle – without incurring similar paradoxes. Let us then imagine a further choice of this kind:

	I1	I2	I3	I4	I5	I6	I7
A1	10	14	10	10	11	10	11
A2	95	95	8	95	95	95	95

Of course, we could say with Rawls that these extreme cases will never happen in the real world. But if, for the sake of the argument, we concede this possibility, then the maximin would induce the (perverse) choice of A1.

Let us consider now a different rule that could be of the following kind:

- Consider the minimum for A1 (10) and the minimum for A2 (8); consider their difference (10–8=2);
- Pick A2 over the maximin choice A1 iff the sum total of utility of A2 once subtracted the sum total utility of A1 is n times greater than 2.

Of course the first issue with such a rule is to fix the meaning of n. We could say that, for utilitarians, $n = 1$, so that A2 is preferred every time the sum total of utility is greater in A2, even if there are large distributive differences; for supporters of maximin, on the other hand, $n =$ infinite, and A1 is necessarily preferred to A2. Our intention, clearly, is to have n different from both 1 and infinity, and in fact to have n between those extreme values. However, we do not know what the value of n might be. The meaning of n is contextual and interpretative. It depends on the historical circumstances in which the choice that we want to understand, based on a principle of justice, takes place. It seems interesting to highlight that this kind of conclusion occurred in various issues that we have explored in this appendix. Considering collective choice, we have seen how the Rawlsian structure, using a limited interpersonal comparison by levels, is able to escape the Arrovian impossibility results. We cannot forget, however, that this way out clearly depends on recognizing, hermeneutically, a set of common values that serve as a horizon of meaning on which we base the selection of "primary goods." Speaking of decisions under uncertainty, we have noticed how the pros and contras of solutions based on maximin or on expected utility depend essentially on the quantity of knowledge that we are willing to attribute to the parties. However, that does not depend on an empirical inquiry, but rather on a philosophical hermeneutical analysis.

6

REFLECTIVE EQUILIBRIUM

Chapter 6 discusses the notion of reflective equilibrium. Reflective equilibrium is one of three different justification strategies within Rawls' theory of justice as fairness, which also justifies principles by appealing to the original position and the theory of stability (6.1). It seems interesting to see whether these three different strategies fit with one another. Reflective equilibrium and the original position present a kind of asymmetry: the first is inductive and bottom-up, whereas the second is deductive and top-down. We can also suppose, however, that this dual mechanism reinforces the general apparatus of justification. The same conclusion appears more complicated to reach if we consider the relationship between reflective equilibrium and the theory of stability. Reflective equilibrium starts with the idea that we are supposed to make our considered pre-theoretical moral judgments and our principles of justice reciprocally coherent (6.2). However, the very notion of stability, especially in Rawls2, assumes pluralism of reasonable comprehensive doctrines. Under these premises, we can suspect – given that different people's considered judgments in turn depend on their own background comprehensive doctrines – that we may obtain a potentially infinite number of equilibria (6.5). Rawls distinguishes between two different types of reflective equilibrium, calling them respectively "narrow" and "wide" (6.3). The main difference is that the wide reflective equilibrium does not consider just an ordered couple of judgments and principles. Wide reflective equilibrium also includes a third element, arising from the possibility of relying on different theoretical backgrounds. Rawls himself prefers wide reflective equilibrium, even if this more ambitious perspective makes it difficult to see how we can solve the aforementioned problem connected with the fact of pluralism. In (6.4) I consider critically three typical objections to the strategy of reflective equilibrium.

6.1 Justification in *A Theory of Justice*

As mentioned at the outset, the theory of justice as fairness includes three justification strategies: reflective equilibrium, the original position, and the theory of stability. These three different strategies may be viewed as an attempt to provide the requirements that, according to Rawls, a good theory of justice should have: (i) it must rely on the "shared convictions" of the citizens it addresses; (ii) it must guarantee a better demonstrative argument than that offered by competing theories; (iii) it must succeed in creating inside it the moral conditions for its support over time.

The use of reflective equilibrium is the most general and obscure of these three strategies. The concept of reflective equilibrium belongs to an extensive vision of the moral methodology on which Rawls has concentrated his attention throughout his academic and intellectual career (see Ph.D. part III). Its centrality within the context of Rawls' interests is definitely unquestionable: "Justification proceeds from what all parties to the discussion hold in common. Ideally, to justify a conception of justice to someone is to give him a proof of his principles from premises that we both accept, these principles having in turn consequences that match our considered judgments" (TJ 580–81; rev. edn. 508).

Justification begins from shared premises. It should be noted that Rawls had already devoted his long and complex doctoral dissertation at Princeton to a similar thesis of moral methodology, and the first article he published way back in 1951, "Outline of a Decision Procedure for Ethics," hinged on this subject. Besides, the same theme is unquestionably central to both TJ and PL. The general purpose of the method of reflective equilibrium is to find a criterion of acceptability for an ethical-political theory. While most scholars play directly on the normative strength of intuitions, with his reflective equilibrium Rawls "invents" a coherentist thesis that establishes a relation between the two aspects of the acceptance theory.

The coherence of this method with the other two justification strategies referred to above is problematic, though to a different extent, depending on whether we are talking about the original position or the theory of stability. On the one hand, with the original position, we may detect a strange asymmetry of the argumentative form. This asymmetry could also depend on contingent factors. For instance, at the time of ODPE it is unlikely that Rawls had in mind a justification strategy like the original position. Thomas Scanlon has observed that the original position offers a theoretical and deductive methodology,[1] whereas the structure of reflective equilibrium is instead based on intuitions in a substantially inductive manner. In any event, this asymmetry may be viewed as a support to the theory, meaning that the argument in favor of the principles of justice comes out strengthened by this possibility of working both deductively and inductively. On the other hand, dealing with the problem of stability, I believe that there is a risk that recourse to the method of reflective equilibrium might complicate matters. In fact, as we are going to see in the conclusion to this chapter, it is quite likely that, given the basic pluralism, a citizen's reflective equilibrium will not coincide with that of another, and this is bound to give rise to special stability-related problems.

6.1.1 The concept of reflective equilibrium

In TJ, Rawls introduces the notion of reflective equilibrium in the first chapter, more specifically in section 4, devoted to "original position and justification" (TJ 20–1; rev. edn. 189). Then, he goes back to it in the last section of the book (TJ 580; rev. edn. 508) when dealing with the sense of justification. This second time, Rawls stresses the difference between practical justification and logical demonstration – a difference that consists mostly in the fact that the former presupposes an initial consent. Such consent is primarily related to the constraints the original position is subject to, which must be considered reasonable. The introduction of reflective equilibrium helps to clarify the reasonableness of these constraints. Viewed from this point of view, reflective equilibrium presupposes a balancing between principles of justice and our "considered judgments":

> We can either modify the account of the initial situation or we can revise our existing judgments, for even the judgments we take provisionally as fixed points are liable to revision. By going back and forth, sometimes altering the conditions of the contractual circumstances, at others withdrawing our judgments and conforming them to principle, I assume that eventually we shall find a description of the initial situation that both expresses reasonable conditions and yields principles which match our considered judgments duly pruned and adjusted. This state of affairs I refer to as reflective equilibrium. (TJ 20; rev. edn. 18)

On the one hand, there are our pre-theoretical moral judgments that are only taken into consideration if opportunely "considered." To say it in Rawls' words: "Considered judgments are simply those rendered under conditions favorable to the exercise of the sense of justice, and therefore in circumstances where the more common excuses and explanations for making a mistake do not obtain" (TJ 47–8; rev. edn. 42).

In short, the considered judgments are the safest and most controlled. In addition, they are those we trust the most, and the examples given by Rawls on this point – such as the injustice of slavery or racial discrimination – are scarcely bold, to say the least. At the beginning, Rawls' vision of the considered judgments seems to be confined to a few fundamental ideas but, over time, it extends to comprise in PL the public culture of the liberal democracy as a whole:

> We start, then, by looking into the public culture itself as the shared fund of implicitly recognized basic ideas and principles . . . We express this by saying that

> a political conception of justice, to be acceptable, must accord with our consid-
> ered convictions, at all levels of generality, on due reflection, or in what I have
> called elsewhere "reflective equilibrium." (PL 8)

These elements of the public liberal-democratic culture act as starting points of any conception of justice. In fact, without these shared starting convictions we would lack that minimum of agreement that allows us to say that the political philosophy always answers the same questions, even if put from different points of view. The conceptions of justice, including the theory of justice as fairness, must endeavor to be in harmony with these considered judgments.

The method of reflective equilibrium is a coherentist method.[2] The central idea is that we look for coherence between our system of moral convictions and the rest of our beliefs. We are dealing with an equilibrium because, over time, principles and judgments should converge. The equilibrium is reflective because it aims to understand which principles are better suited to judgments and vice versa. At this point, we are in the presence of an orderly couple of (i) a set of considered moral judgments that seem acceptable to a given person at a specific time and that meet certain requirements: they are backed up by sufficient information and are not subject to special distortions; the person has had sufficient time to think them over, and so on; and (ii) a set of ethical-political principles that should account for the judgments.

We are not dealing with a necessarily stable equilibrium since, over periods of time that may be more or less extensive, revisions of the principles or judgments may prove indispensable. Therefore, there is necessarily a third stage where persons decide how and where to propend for judgments or principles. Are we required to modify the considered judgments because they are in conflict with the principles or, vice versa, are we required to modify the principles because they fail to account adequately for the judgments? There is no univocal answer to this question. Indeed, we work back and forth between judgments and principles, until we get to a conjunction characterized by a certain harmony. This final stage is the stage of reflective equilibrium.

6.2 A Coherentist and Inductive Argument

Any justification has an epistemological background and, from this viewpoint, the one based on reflective equilibrium is not too different from a mathematical demonstration or a scientific test. In all these cases, we are looking for sound reasons that might suitably back up our favorite thesis. However, it is from the epistemological viewpoint that reflective equilibrium has a peculiarity of its own. It is not a top-down or deductive justification, and this is by no means trivial in the history of ethics. In fact, quite a few moral theories have endeavored to justify their theses in the name of fundamental intuitions or on premises based on divine appeal. Even while allowing room for intuitions, reflective equilibrium unquestionably moves in a different direction with respect to these types of doctrines. As Rawls says: "A conception of justice cannot be deduced from self-evident premises or conditions on principles" (TJ 21; rev. edn. 19).

Quite the opposite, justification should rest on "the entire conception and how it fits in with and organizes our considered judgments in reflective equilibrium" (TJ 579; rev. edn. 507). From this point of view, the inductive aspect of reflective equilibrium is undeniable. The usual theoretical reference is represented in this case by Nelson Goodman's philosophy of induction[3] (referred to by Rawls, TJ 20; rev. edn. 18, note 7), which provides for a similar mutual adjustment between principles and judgments. We are facing a justification that proposes coherence between theories and beliefs. For Goodman, the problem is to choose from among theories that are inherently coherent but mutually incompatible. The solution is to prefer the one that maximizes the level of initial credibility.[4] Rawls, however, is not interested in the epistemological-metaphysical coherentist thesis as such.[5] Rather, he is interested in the plausibility of the moral methodology based on reflective equilibrium and, through it, in the possibility of successfully countering rival doctrines, particularly those having a naturalistic and intuitionist nature. Ultimately, Rawls is not interested in the philosophical method of the justification as such but in its application to ethics and political theory.

What has been said may be repeated with respect to an illustrious philosophical antecedent. The practice of reflective equilibrium may lead to a revision of existing moral opinions and, from that, we may infer that Rawls proposes a substantially globalist and anti-foundationalist method (there are no fixed points, as he happens to say).[6] Then, it would seem natural to talk about "holism" as regards this method,[7] even on account of such extrinsic elements as the long contemporary presence of Rawls and Quine in the same Harvard philosophy department. This methodological likeness is confirmed by note 33 (rev. edn. note 34) to the last chapter of TJ (TJ 579; rev. edn. 507), which states that the general justification idea owes much to Quine's thought. However, in the Preface to TJ, Rawls explicitly denies any relation of his method to that of Quine (TJ xi; rev. edn. xx). It is a merely intellectual curiosity but, nonetheless, it may be speculated that this negation depends (i) on what has been previously specified with respect to Rawls' prevailing interest in ethics and the political theory; and (ii) on the fact that he had started working on that problem from the end of the 1940s (see Ph.D.) – that is, even before Quine had.[8]

6.2.1 Persons' moral capacity and the theory of justice

In the article ODPE, dating back to 1951, the general conception of the method on which reflective equilibrium is based is broken down into three phases: first, isolate the moral facts; second, account for them; thirdly, rationally evaluate the preceding stages. Rawls intends to implement this comprehensive procedure by having recourse to a class of competent judges and a set of considered judgments. The final outcome is based on the considered judgments of the competent judges. The result of the meeting between competent judges and considered judgments offers a plausible and controlled version of moral facts, which are those that emerge from concrete, rather than theoretical, moral judgments under ideal conditions of decidability.

On these grounds, a further consideration may be made in order to gain an insight into the nature of reflective equilibrium. In fact, through it, Rawls tries to join together two unusual types of justification. The first type draws a distinction between a justification of the principles and a justification of the people, while the second type draws a distinction between a justification within the theory and a justification outside the theory.

In the first case, one considers both a person under special conditions, like the competent judge referred to above, and a theoretical thesis that leads to the justification of a principle. The second requirement is more stringent than the first. In other words, a person may be justified in having a moral belief even if the latter is not adequately justified in the light of the theory.[9] This very fact, however, seems to point to the existence of a "moral capacity" of the persons that precedes and is independent of the principles of justice. Indeed, reflective equilibrium is meaningful because something like that actually exists.

The second consideration is partly related to the first, but exposes an even more daring justificatory claim on the part of Rawls. To clear things up, let us take into consideration the most typical type of justification in the TJ model, the original position. Such justification is clearly part of Rawls' theoretical apparatus. It is a substantial part of the theory of justice as fairness. Now, from this point of view, the claim of reflective equilibrium is threatening because it seeks a justificational complement that – although obviously present in TJ – is fundamentally outside the theory of justice as fairness. As Rawls says in PL: "It is important to distinguish three points of view: that of the parties in the original position, that of citizens in a well-ordered society, and finally, that of ourselves – of you and me who are elaborating justice as fairness and examining it as a political conception of justice" (PL 28). This type of justification comes from outside the theory. It addresses those free and equal citizens for whom, in the last analysis, the theory is intended. That is, Rawls addresses his theory to us, his readers, and even to himself. This gives rise to a formidable problem. If these outside estimators, including us, agree on the whole with the principles of justice and the latter seem to confirm their considered judgments, then there is no problem at all. But what if it was not so and different people affirm different visions of justice? I will get back to this problem at the end of this chapter but, straight away, I have the impression that its solution, if there is one, is rather problematic.

The method is re-proposed in TJ in section 9 of the first chapter, devoted to the general theme "Some Remarks about Moral Theory" (TJ 49ff.; rev. edn. 40ff.). In this case, reflective equilibrium is presented on the background of our sense of justice. The latter does not correspond – for Rawls – to the set of considered judgments viewed in an independent manner that takes priority over the theory. Rather, the sense of justice of each of us is more conveniently described in the moment of coherence between principles and judgments in a reflective equilibrium. This entails a constant revision of the intuitive judgments, even though they are considered judgments, made under favorable conditions and not subject to the most serious distortions. This leads to an analogy – which later became famous – with Chomskyan grammars. According to this analogy, strictly from the methodological viewpoint, moral philosophy would look more like grammar than, for instance, physics. We are less willing to correct our intuitive judgments in the name of theoretical principles in ethics (and in our natural language) than we would be in physics (TJ 49). According to Norman Daniels, this analogy is partially misleading since practical philosophy with respect to the judgments would have more normative strength than grammars with respect to language.[10] However, we probably need to take Rawls' analogy in a less stringent manner.

The notion of reflective equilibrium becomes complicated if we consider the possibility of two different ways of figuring it out. In its first consideration, we are to take into account a single suitable description of the class of considered judgments with respect to merely a set of principles. In the second one, instead, we are to take into account a number of descriptions and a number of principles by no means immediate. According to Rawls, as becomes increasingly clear with the passing of time, the second alternative is the correct one.

Another problem is connected with the uniqueness of reflective equilibrium. In abstract terms, there is the possibility that each person might reach a reflective equilibrium that is incompatible with that of the others. In this case, there would be no possibility whatsoever of a public dialogue on justice. Rawls confines himself to claiming that, usually, this does not happen, assuming a certain affinity of doctrines and judgments among persons of the same historical society. However that may be, any attentive reader must first of all confront the opinions of the author and, in the end, what counts is merely the opinions held by the author and the reader who face each other on reflective equilibrium being reached.

6.3 Narrow and Wide Equilibrium

It is by now standard practice to draw a distinction, within the theory of reflective equilibrium, between narrow and wide reflective equilibrium. Narrow equilibrium concerns only the class of considered judgments and of moral principles.[11] When dealing with wide reflective equilibrium, we do not confine ourselves to evaluating concrete cases, going back and forth between principles and judgments. Instead we put the full complexity of the theoretical convictions at stake. Thus, wide equilibrium is formed by a triple ordinate that adds to the two preceding groups the set of moral theories most suitable for formulating interesting principles that are subsequently to be compared with considered judgments. Rawls presents the concept of wide reflective equilibrium in an article of 1975 devoted to "The Independence of Moral Theory." To quote him on this point:

> because our inquiry is philosophically motivated, we are interested in what conceptions people would affirm when they have achieved wide and not just narrow reflective equilibrium, an equilibrium that satisfies certain conditions of rationality. That is, adopting the role of observing moral theorists, we investigate what principles people would acknowledge and accept the consequences of when they have an opportunity to consider other plausible conceptions and to assess their supporting grounds. (IMT, in CP 289)

In this case, the back-and-forth movement proposed by the method obviously becomes more complex, because we are required to mutually correct not only the principles and judgments, but also the background theories. While the narrow equilibrium takes into consideration the projects for the adjustment of theory and principles that relate to a person at a given time, the wide reflective equilibrium takes also into consideration the conceptions of others. Considering the two types of reflective equilibrium, the latter is viewed as being more profitable by Rawls.[12] In fact, the process of wide reflective equilibrium also includes philosophical arguments that are for or against the different systems of principles integral to our society. Actually, it is only within the context of wide equilibrium that we may think that our judgments are subject to serious revision and hope to extend the method to intellectual and cultural traditions different from our own. This impression is strengthened by the fact that – as we know – moral disagreements are often caused not only by strictly ethical reasons but also by independent general convictions that only wide reflective equilibrium may involve.

The purpose of the article on "Independence" is to separate moral philosophy from the theory of meaning, epistemology, and the most complex considerations of the philosophy of mind. Within this framework, there is also the more specific independence of reflective equilibrium from epistemology. As Rawls says:

> The independence of moral theory from epistemology arises from the fact that the procedure of reflective equilibrium does not assume that there is one correct moral conception. It is, if you wish, a kind of psychology and does not presuppose the existence of objective moral truths. Even should everyone attain wide reflective equilibrium, many moral conceptions may still be held. One conception may unanimously win over all the rest and even suffice to limit quite narrowly

our more concrete judgments. On the other hand, anyone may affirm opposing conceptions. (IMT, in CP 289–90)

Ultimately, the inter-theoretical comparison furthered by wide reflective equilibrium allows both a greater critical activity and a more vigorous pluralism. Once equilibrium has been reached, it allows a more radical normative correction of the considered judgments. It is not clear whether wide reflective equilibrium should be viewed as a set, or as a sort of weighed average of a variety, of different narrow equilibriums. In this case, the outcome of wide reflective equilibrium could be conceived as the outcome of the comparison of a number of narrow equilibriums reached within different theoretical frameworks. For instance, in a contemporary philosophical-political context, a Kantian equilibrium would face a Rawlsian equilibrium, and both of them would face a utilitarian or Nozickian equilibrium.[13] Supposing that this might be possible – and Rawls' text does not help us much on this point – it remains unclear whether the ultimate wide reflective equilibrium might succeed in working out a comparative classification of the various narrow equilibriums being considered. As far as I know, Rawls hinted just once at this possibility (JFR 31), referring to an eventual general reflective equilibrium capable of such a synthesis.

Daniels seems to be optimistic on this point. In fact, taking the aforementioned analogy with grammar in earnest, he affirms that this analogy is meaningful in the case of the narrow reflective equilibrium, while it would not be so in case of the wide reflective equilibrium.[14] In the former case, one would take the current moral competence of the person more seriously, while in the latter one would lay emphasis on the ideal competence. Ultimately, wide reflective equilibrium would have a normative strength that would be missing in the narrow reflective equilibrium. Such a distinction proves extremely valuable since, should it be accepted, it would afford an argument to dispute with those who criticize the theory of reflective equilibrium for its normative deficit. Following this interpretation of the philosophical role of reflective equilibrium, the Rawlsian method automatically distances itself from any form of pure descriptivism or mere moral anthropology.

However, remaining within the context of just the Rawlsian view in TJ, if we take the idea of a justification method based on wide reflective equilibrium in earnest, then the entire interpretation of the theory of justice as fairness may somehow be inscribed within it. As for the three stages referred to above, it is necessary for the third one – that is, the stage of the theoretical pluralism – to provide, within the context of wide reflective equilibrium, a further and independent control with respect to the coherence test between judgments and principles (corresponding to narrow reflective equilibrium). This means that the background theories of the third stage must not be mere generalizations of considered judgments that strive for coherence with the principles. It is indeed in this perspective that we may conceive the Rawlsian social contract as an aspect of a more extensive theoretical movement.[15]

Hence, we can imagine a final level for the appeal to narrow reflective equilibrium, the actual test of the coherence between principles of justice and considered moral judgments. In any event, this outcome is preceded by the level where the background theories – which, in Rawls' case, are a theory of procedural justice, a theory of the person and a theory of a well-ordered society – are set against one another. The outputs of these background theories account in their turn for the structure of the original position. For instance, the substantial constraints on motivation and knowledge, connected with the "veil of ignorance," depend in the first place on a theory of procedural justice. However, they stem also from a peculiar political conception of the person.[16] On the other hand, the formal constraints on the concept of right depend, in addition to the theory of procedural justice, on a vision of the institutions within the context of a well-ordered society.

We are not dealing with a mere rewriting of the theory of justice as fairness in a vocabulary that takes into greater account the processes of adjustment in reflective equilibrium. This might seem to be the case since the theory is the comprehensive outcome of this complex apparatus being tested in the wide reflective equilibrium. However, it is not so, because the normative outcomes would be different from those that would result had we failed to use such a modified procedure. In particular, a similar interpretation shows that the theory of justice as fairness does not derive merely from a hypothesis of procedural justice. There are substantive theses in the background that justify the Rawlsian contract. Therefore, not only do the principles chosen in the original position need to pass the test of coherence with considered judgments, but also the way in which the original position is constructed presupposes an independent set of background convictions.

It goes without saying that this further step does not come for free. In fact, while providing new argumentative and normative strength to Rawlsian contractualism, at the same time it introduces further background theoretical hypotheses that need to be checked and evaluated. This means a move away from the Kantian ideal of the contract. The latter is no longer the contract that would be accepted *sic et simpliciter* by any rational being capable of serene thinking. The proposed acceptance becomes more charged with theoretical premises since one needs to accept a background of theories that are not immediately accepted by everyone. The last section in TJ seems to support such a broad interpretation of wide reflective equilibrium. I refer to the idea of the permanent circularity of justification in ethics that Rawls seems to appreciate and endorse. From this holistic and coherentist perspective, there are no fixed points that justify a moral theorem. Our considered intuitive judgments are unquestionably important, but they may always be reviewed. The same applies to the principles of justice, but even the profound theories that formulate the principles of justice are not immutable and need to be subjected to a test to show their coherence with considered judgments. All this is a partly unstable permanent equilibrium that is, nonetheless, indispensable for gaining an insight into the fundamental relation between theoretical construction and a natural sense of morality.

6.3.1 A note on the justification method

A broad interpretation of wide reflective equilibrium provides an image of the entire apparatus justifying the theory of justice as fairness that differs from the standard reading. We are used to conceiving the original position as the main theoretical instrument of this justification. As shown by the intuitive moral argument in favor of the second principle of justice, this is already called into question in the second chapter of TJ.

Let us try to imagine this justificatory device in the form of two concentric circles. We can assume that the original position is the demonstrative core of the inner circle. However, if we are to understand in full the role and meaning of the principles, we need to realize instead that the original position itself does not depend merely on a deductive argument based on the idea of procedural justice; it presupposes quite a few substantial assumptions. As far as Rawls is concerned, procedure and substance can never be fully separated. However, bringing the profound theoretical background of the main theses into play and testing it against considered judgments, we have a method of justification at the same level as the theoretical task we have undertaken.

This method-related conclusion applies in particular if we accept the idea of wide reflective equilibrium. In this case, our control over considered judgments does not come about because of a single ethical-political theory but in the light of a family of theoretical considerations that result from a variety of theories. It should be noted that, towards the end of TJ, Rawls stresses the distinction between proof and justification (TJ 580–3; rev. edn. 508–11), claiming to be interested in the latter rather than the former. The main difference lies in the fact that the justification initially presupposes a relative consensus. Should we assume this thesis, then we may understand how a coherentist control, like the one that occurs through reflective equilibrium, may have convergent results. Obviously, nothing excludes there being doubts as to the possibility that such a consensus exists.[17]

6.4 Three Critiques

The theory of reflective equilibrium has not escaped theoretical critiques. Rawls' intention to formulate a general critique of utilitarianism may help to explain the nature of such criticisms. As previously pointed out, utilitarianism often proves to be counterintuitive. It leads to theoretical solutions that do not adequately take into account prerogatives – such as, for instance, freedom, sincerity, and solidarity – that we cherish in our natural vision of ethics. Indeed, quite a few authors have stressed these counterintuitive aspects of utilitarianism, basing their objections on moral intuitions. However, when dealing with utilitarianism, these intuitionist objections were viewed more as partial limits of the utilitarian theory as a whole than as structural alternatives to it. Instead, Rawls intends to start with the criticism of utilitarianism in order to construct a systematic alternative. For Rawls, from this point of view, the claims of any appeal to moral intuitions are too modest. However, were we to discover that even the theory of justice as fairness has a background that is substantially similar to that of intuitionism, then even his theoretical claims would end up being reassessed. This commitment to reassessing the general value of Rawls' criticism of utilitarianism is probably the main reason behind the criticisms concerning reflective equilibrium. I am going to consider three of them that may in part mutually overlap:

(i)   it reproduces a sophisticated form of moral intuitionism;
(ii) it is a theoretically conservative expedient;
(iii) it has relativistic outcomes.

Let us take each of these in turn.

6.4.1 Does the theory of reflective equilibrium reproduce a sophisticated form of moral intuitionism?

As pointed out by Richard Hare in a critical note on TJ,[18] Rawls seems to find a nearly empirical referent which is to be used to check the theory of justice – namely, a set of morally relevant "facts." In the tradition of ethical intuitionism, these moral facts are drawn from moral intuitions on which persons have thoroughly meditated. However, according to Hare, this strategy entails a form of basic subjectivism, since it causes the validity of the theory to depend on agreement with the moral intuitions of some individual.[19] Such a thesis is questionable if one bears in mind the more complex concept of wide reflective equilibrium that brings into play other theoretical visions. Indeed, in this case, the potential for revision is given not only by considered judgments but also by comparative evaluation of the theories.[20]

Based on this reading, the set of shared starting points that Rawls thinks should limit the context of initial disagreement in political philosophy would merely end up moving the level of disagreement itself. If there is a close connection between intuitionism and subjectivism, Rawls would be an intuitionist even though he says quite the reverse. Hence, the fault of the method would be clear. In order to work, the theory of justice as fairness requires a prior consent. However, given that this consent depends on Rawls' intuitions themselves, the principles will ultimately be coherent with the basic consent. Given the aforementioned premises, this ends up being predictably circular.

Worse still, Hare charges, recourse to intuitions alters the model of choice in the original position based on a theory of rational choice. After all, for Hare, the author's moral intuitions enter the model to determine its starting conditions and the nature of the decision-maker. In so doing, a rational choice now depends on such basic intuitions. Should they be missing, the mechanism of the choice would instead dictate a traditional utilitarian-type solution. Hence, Rawls' theory fails in its most ambitious project of finding an original alternative to utilitarianism. In fact, his alternative amounts to intuitionism or is non-existent (as it would coincide with utilitarianism).

A Rawlsian can respond to Hare by pointing out that Rawls may hardly be taken for an intuitionist, for both epistemic reasons and metaphysical reasons.[21] Standard forms of ethical intuitionism must have a realist metaphysical base, so that there are unalterable primitive moral facts. Additionally, from an epistemic point of view, intuitionism assumes that intuition provides the most prevalent, if not the only, way to become acquainted with moral facts.[22] Now, it seems that, however we consider the theory of justice, it proves substantially extraneous to a theoretical picture of this type. Indeed, for Rawls, moral knowledge is not prevailingly intuitive and realism is not the favored metaphysical option. Rather, Rawls is a constructivist who takes important moral facts to depend on construction procedures. He is also a Kantian in the sense that moral truths that come from outside us would essentially be heteronomous.

Luckily for the interpreter, this incompatibility (already present in Ph.D.) has been debated at length by Rawls, after the article by Hare referred to above: for instance in PL, Lecture III, where he explains the meaning of what he calls "political constructivism," and, even earlier, in the Dewey Lectures of 1980 on "Kantian Constructivism." The vision of the theory of justice as fairness is constructivist (PL, Lecture III, section 3) and we are dealing with an explicitly Kantian constructivism. In PL (91ff.), Rawls explicitly criticizes the intuitionist view for the following reasons:

(i)   intuitionism, and not the theory of justice as fairness, features an independent order of moral values;
(ii) in intuitionism, and not in the theory of justice as fairness, one may get to know the moral values in a purely theoretical manner;
(iii) intuitionism has a different and poorer (just) epistemic conception of the person;
(iv) intuitionism claims the correspondence between moral judgments and an outside moral value.

Rawls counters these four characteristics with the need for a procedure of construction at the center of the theory, the priority of practical reason, and a more complex notion of person.

6.4.2 Is the theory of reflective equilibrium a theoretically conservative expedient?

The second criticism concerns the role of moral and political philosophy and, in particular, the role of the theory of justice as fairness. According to a few, this should have a more plainly revisionist outcome. As a result, this theory should succeed in reviewing previous judgments more than would be allowed by assuming the centrality of reflective equilibrium (which, as previously pointed out, requires coherence with pre-theoretical intuitions). From this point of view, the doctrine of reflective equilibrium would condemn the theory of justice as fairness to play a conservative theoretical-methodological role.

This sort of objection is typically raised by utilitarians who, to remain in the Rawlsian metaphor referred to above, claim that the ethical theory looks more like physics than linguistics. According to a few interpreters,[23] the very coherentist justification method chosen by Rawls would end up being disastrous. The ability to justify a coherentist argument in ethics would be fully questionable. In this case, it is said that comparing principles with data would be useful were data fully independent, but this cannot be so if the assumed data are, as in the case of reflective equilibrium, dependent on the author and his intuitions. The outcome may only be a conservation strategy with respect to the primitive intuitions of whoever writes and reads.

This objection may be met by saying that it misinterprets Rawls when it assumes that he starts from any intuition, descriptively presented in the theory of justice. Instead, these intuitions are already judgments, and, to boot, considered judgments, that have been submitted to a prior emendation process. Furthermore, it is not clear how a substantive theory of justice can do without such judgments. Moreover, the theory of reflective equilibrium upholds first of all that such judgments can, and indeed need to, be reviewed whenever the theory gives them a hard time. Therefore, it is not conservative in this sense. Indeed, it might be affirmed that, in such a way, the conservation and reform requirements are effectively reconciled. Rawls explicitly defends a similar thesis in the article of 1975 referred to above devoted to "The Independence of Moral Theory." Here, Rawls claims that the strategy of reflective equilibrium cannot really be considered conservative solely on account of the fact that, in its ambit, "there are no judgments on any level of generality that are in principle immune to revision" (IMT 8).

The conservatism-related objection is not successful. Actually, and this is the source of some ambiguity, Rawls insists on the descriptive nature of reflective equilibrium. From this point of view, it must account for the convictions on justice of a group of persons. The fact that political philosophy needs to start from the shared ideas of a few within liberal-democratic society may be disarmingly naive and give grounds for the suspicion that it relies on a form of ingenuous relativism. At any rate, we need to consider the following remarks. First, it is hard to see where else one should start from, given the nature of the problem. Second, the appeal to the convictions of the citizens of a democratic society, including us, is nothing else but the beginning of a long theoretical work. Frankly, whoever has read Rawls must be aware of how much and which theory he adds to this (indispensable) starting point. Third, the initial considered judgments are clearly intended to be reviewed in the course of a complex theoretical process. Bringing different theoretical visions into play, the thesis of wide reflective equilibrium makes this aspect especially clear.[24]

The theory of justice as fairness and, actually, any political theory worthy of its name, is not designed to sanctify the starting convictions but to amend them and correct them for good reasons. Rather than talking about conservatism, I would like to linger on the likely difficulties of such a revisionist operation. Is it really possible, we may wonder, to change cultural traditions and beliefs held for time immemorial in the light of an abstract theoretical reasoning? The thing becomes even more complicated if we introduce a substantial basic pluralism in the model of wide reflective equilibrium.

It is not clear if and how the charge of being conservative may be brought against the thesis of reflective equilibrium from a political point of view. On the one hand, such a charge may be considered misleading, since reflective equilibrium relates to the method rather than to the political substance of the theory. On the other hand, however, it may be affirmed that considered judgments are affected by education and the latter by tradition. Hence, the charge of political conservatism could be meaningful if it was taken as an objection to the fact that the dogmas of the tradition revive in the present. At any rate, I believe that even in this case, even in the light of what has been said in the preceding subsection, any politically radical alternative could not be fully incompatible with considered judgments. Hence, the method would be out of trouble in any event. That is, the charge of conservatism fails because the method allows for the possibility of radical revision.

6.4.3 Does the theory of reflective equilibrium have relativistic outcomes?

Finally, it may be objected that the theory of reflective equilibrium would necessarily have relativistic outcomes.[25] This critique takes up the two preceding ones and counsels wariness as to the possibility of attaining that harmonization project between judgments and principles that Rawls desires.[26] The trouble arises from two facts. First, the theoretical principles must be fitted to the considered judgments of each individual independently. Second, everyone may have different moral intuitions, at least in abstract terms. If this is the case, then the method could lead to infinite equilibria. Obviously, when Rawls deals with the question of the uniqueness of reflective equilibrium in TJ (TJ 50; rev. edn. 43–4), he fails to give a precise answer and suggests that at least a restriction on the possibilities is required. Ultimately, he assumes a partial convergence.

More generally, this same problem of implicit relativism in the theory of reflective equilibrium may be raised in a different way by claiming that Rawls moves with this thesis from a normative philosophy of public ethics to a kind of descriptive moral anthropology. In support of this charge, it has been noted that the method of reflective equilibrium has a family resemblance with the idea of the hermeneutic circle – a proposal involving an entirely different philosophical context.[27] In any event, the circularity must be rejected for reflective equilibrium since it presupposes an independent control in which every proposition confronts the totality of the beliefs. Above all, the theoretical revision of the basic convictions, in the form provided for by reflective equilibrium, would find no space at all within a traditional hermeneutical position.

From the hermeneutical point of view, it may be objected that a descriptive moral anthropology has no normative meaning and, therefore, does not give rise to any interesting result for the core of a substantive moral theory. From a similar perspective, Joseph Raz claims that the theory of reflective equilibrium can at the most be considered an empiric method to improve one's own judgments and try to cause them to converge to the greatest degree possible with those of others.[28] All this, however, has nothing to do with the capacity of the theory from the perspective of the justification. In short, as Raz claims, the phenomenology of the moral intuitions is one thing and the structure of the moral theory is another. For these critics, the theory of reflective equilibrium falls fully within the former without ever reaching the level of the latter. Reflective equilibrium would be a mere description of our moral sense.[29] Besides, from this point of view, it seems strange that if the purpose of reflective equilibrium is to present a description of the moral sense, it might be possible for non-considered judgments to be excluded from among those relevant for the theory.

This final point seems interesting. Provided that we accept Rawls' idea that it is important to reconstruct the inner constitution of our moral capacity, then it is at least controversial to exclude moral judgments based on rather vague criteria, such as the following: be aware of the important facts; be able to concentrate on the merit of the matter; do not have pre-constituted interests.

The nature of the control we exert on judgments, the one that causes them to shift from non-considered to considered ones, is after all scarcely clear. Is it a philosophical or a merely empiric and psychological control? Quite naturally, in the latter case it would not directly concern the moral theory and would have no normative ethical strength. The problem becomes even more serious if we consider the matter diachronically. While in Ph.D., ODPE, and TJ Rawls lays down quite a few control conditions that ensure the reliability of considered judgments, this caution seems to disappear when starting from the shared convictions on which the political conception of PL is based.[30] However, this distinction is too complicated to succeed in probing into it before getting to the heart of the main PL theses. Furthermore, if we accept the idea of wide reflective equilibrium, the control of the theory is provided not only by considered judgments, but also by a much more complex apparatus of theories and cultural traditions.

A further way to answer an objection about the normative importance of reflective equilibrium, in my opinion, is to refer to the holistic and coherentist aspects of Rawls' theory. The other side of coherentism is a normative commitment that originates from the very operation of revising judgments in the light of the theory and vice versa. Obviously, this presupposes that the line between what has moral relevance and what does not is fainter than is usually believed. Therefore, one can legitimately question whether a procedure – such as reflective equilibrium, which is at the same time ethical, logical, empirical and psychological – might have not only a descriptive but also a substantially prescriptive outcome. In any event, it is unquestionable that this is Rawls' intent, supported by plausible arguments.

6.5 A Reconciliation between Ethics and Politics

The theory of reflective equilibrium, particularly in its wide version, has two interesting theoretical consequences. I am referring, on the one hand, to a possibility of reconciling the Rawls of TJ with the Rawls of his subsequent works, and, on the other, to the use of the method in an attempt to bridge the gap between applied ethics and political philosophy.

In the first case, the theory of wide reflective equilibrium could be useful in shifting the normative strength of the theory of justice from the procedural argument of the original position to the theory of justice taken as a whole. I have tried to highlight – in chapter 4 – how Rawls' interpreters have lately tended to reduce the specific weight of the argument of the original position in the context of the justification of justice as fairness. This may depend on a variety of factors such as: (i) the critiques of the apparatus of the decision theory that underlies the theory; (ii) the implausibility that the mere maximization of the share of primary goods might be sufficient to account for our sense of justice; and (iii) a more careful consideration of Rawls' reasoning in TJ, according to which what counts is not only procedural justice but also additional substantive moral arguments. In any event, this reading finds an authoritative confirmation in Rawls' self-interpretation after TJ.

On these grounds, the theory of wide reflective equilibrium[31] can help in the attempt to extend the central argument of the theory of justice. For instance, the theory of reflective equilibrium potentially reconciles the argument of the original position with the people's assumptions from a political point of view, assumptions that Rawls increasingly moves towards the center of the theory. In so doing, procedural fairness – through the original position – would recompose with the ideas of equality and freedom of the person from the point of view of justification. This interpretation supports my initial thesis on the relevance of legitimation as complementary to justification in Rawls' work.

In the second case, the theory of reflective equilibrium can help to reduce the ambit of lasting moral disagreements. This would occur when the theory of reflective equilibrium is integrated into a procedure of deliberation that affects the way in which political institutions make the most important decisions. Deliberative processes of this type force individuals to choose one solution or another, more or less as happens in the case of a jury when it is required to choose between "innocent" and "guilty." The dialogue among the parties is binding in the deliberative procedure. Likewise, the procedure of equilibrium between considered judgments and principles may be especially profitable for the convergence of persons. However motivated, they might be able to find a solution starting from different moral assumptions.

The very idea of reflective equilibrium helps us to gain an insight into the relation between general theory and concrete cases. It is not a question of applying the general ethical-political theory to concrete cases but rather of finding a fair balance between the requirements of moral theory and those that originate from the reality of actual situations. Engineering applications of the general theories are not particularly useful. Instead, the thesis of reflective equilibrium may contribute to finding innovative solutions.

Here, if we move on to the level of gradual modifications of the concept of reflective equilibrium introduced by Rawls over time, two further questions critically crop up. The first again concerns the normative capacity of reflective equilibrium. A method of justification should help to make a distinction between the theoretical options that are congruent with it and others that are not. Now, it would seem that Rawls, by making the concept of reflective equilibrium increasingly inclusive and permissive over time, ends up not excluding anything. In other words, the selective function of the method of justification, according to this hypothesis, would gradually lessen, particularly on account of the fact that, in the initial phase, Rawls seems to present the method of reflective equilibrium in a more explicitly non-foundationalist way. In so doing, reflective equilibrium would directly exclude several types of moral theories, such as ethical intuitionism and ethical naturalism. However, in PL, Rawls seems to offer a more moderate version of the method. In this second version, although our considered convictions still need to "fit together" in reflective equilibrium, taking for granted a wider pluralism, it would seem that any well-formed moral theory could be allowed to come into play. I am not sure of the plausibility of this interpretation, but it does not make Rawls' "constructivist" battle against foundationalist ethics any less fierce.

This is not the most serious problem raised by the most inclusive conception of reflective equilibrium in PL. Once the question of the relation between stability and pluralism comes into play, a new difficulty crops up related to the way in which we may rely on the convictions of different persons. I have already said that, with the passage from TJ to PL, control over primitive intuitions seems less necessary to Rawls, but, then, such convictions will be substantially affected by the comprehensive doctrines on which the persons rely. Consider the convictions of an average Catholic on the matter of abortion. Such convictions are not necessarily excluded by the method of reflective equilibrium, which, as previously pointed out, has been made more permissive.

However, if we refer to the parallel method of justification based on the theory of stability, an evident difficulty emerges. Public reason, which is an essential element within the theory, does not allow citizens openly to disclose ideas that appeal directly to their background comprehensive doctrines (see chapter 11). The so-called "duty of civility" does not allow appeals to every reason in the name of the respect that is due to all those who fail to share such comprehensive doctrines. At this point, if the method of wide reflective equilibrium allows anyone to confirm their own convictions, which prove to be coherent with any reliable moral theory, we would evidently be in the presence of a dilemma. On the one hand, reflective equilibrium would allow a strategy that, on the other, public reason would forbid.[32]

I believe that there are two ways to cope with such a problem. The first relies on the fact that comprehensive doctrines have little to do with the convictions of justice that refer to the fundamental public ideas of a liberal-democratic society. However, it is highly questionable that such a process of self-emendation might take place, for instance, in predominantly Catholic countries such as Italy, and it is even less likely that it might do so within different cultures, e.g. Islamic, to which – hopefully – no one would deny the possibility of accessing political liberalism.

Second, we might suppose that a point of convergence between the various options of the wide reflective equilibrium being offered coincides with the legitimation of the liberal democracy. Actually, as we are going to see later on, the huge variety of ethical, metaphysical, and religious doctrines that may be a part of the shared wide reflective equilibrium is a required premise to cause the convergence, given a regime of pluralism, of different forms of justification within the context of a legitimation structure.

7

MAIN CRITICISMS OF RAWLS

Chapter 7 examines some of the main objections to Rawls. Three critical approaches are discussed: (i) the communitarian (7.1); (ii) the libertarian by Nozick (7.2); and (iii) the deliberative democratic by Habermas (7.3). My ambition in this chapter is modest, and I have no intention of adjudicating the case between the rival doctrines. Some preliminary comments are necessary. First, the criticisms of Rawls discussed in this chapter are not the only ones. There are others in the standard literature, such as Marxist, republican, religious, postmodern, Schmittian (they are mentioned throughout in this volume). Nobody could, however, deny that the criticisms explicitly treated here are among the most significant. Second, while communitarian and libertarian criticisms are prevalently directed at TJ, Habermas' concerns also target arguments and questions taken up in PL. This very fact might generate some confusion, in particular because I will discuss PL only in chapters 9–11 of this book. The choice to present these criticisms here rests, however, on the fact that, in their light, PL can be better understood. Finally, the three criticisms outlined above probably provoked the hottest debate among scholars concerning Rawls, so it seems appropriate to consider them together in a single chapter.

7.1 The Communitarian Criticism

The most well-known criticism of the theory of justice as fairness is probably the one formulated, in the first part of the 1980s, by the "communitarians."[1] One can track the origin of the philosophical theses of the communitarian thinkers to antiquity, beginning with Aristotle. The tradition of thought associated with Hegel and Marx, in particular as critics of Kant, constitutes the main modern background for the communitarian argument. This tradition can be associated also with the theoretical foundations of sociology, for example in Durkheim and Toennies, and with the Romantic attack on liberalism, as presented by Herder. From this point of view, the communitarian approach arises periodically to condemn some excesses of abstraction connected with liberalism. If we take liberal individualism as one of these abstractions, while in the first part of the twentieth century the majority of criticisms came from Marxists, in the case of contemporary communitarians they come prevalently from a Hegelian matrix.[2] For this reason, and because communitarianism often appeals to the values of tradition, one could note a sort of conservative attitude in it, albeit more in a cultural than in a political sense. The novelty behind the arguments of the scholars discussed in this section consists mainly in transforming old communitarian criticisms of liberalism into new objections against Rawls and his theory of justice.

It is not at all easy to properly define the boundaries of communitarianism, even when we are more interested in arguments that are not only anti-liberal but also anti-Rawlsian. In this regard, the most relevant communitarians are Sandel,[3] MacIntyre,[4] and Taylor.[5] Walzer[6] serves as a borderline case and other critics such as Bellah,[7] Unger,[8] Rorty,[9] and Williams[10] fall outside the communitarian paradigm (even if their arguments have something in common with communitarian arguments). For the rest of this section, I will discuss a few arguments by these first scholars, emphasizing Sandel, who formulates the communitarian criticism most explicitly directed against TJ (in 1982).

From a substantive point of view, communitarians believe that liberals neglect the basic value of community. However, the main communitarian arguments against Rawlsian liberalism are more philosophical and foundational, concerning the metaphysical and ethical basis of liberalism. Three typical communitarian criticisms are the following:

(i) the individualistic and abstract nature of the Rawlsian self;
(ii) the controversial nature of the priority of the right over the good;
(iii) the liberal under-evaluation of tradition and social roots.

These arguments are differently tailored by different communitarian critics (as we shall see). All of them coincide, however, in maintaining that liberalism is both a risk for the community and a misinterpretation of its actual life.[11] From this point of view, communitarian criticisms are often jointly directed against the liberal institutional system and liberal thought (including Rawls'). This conjunction may engender confusion.[12]

In fact, it can be hard to distinguish communitarian objections to liberalism as a descriptive thesis from the objections to liberalism as normative political theory. The result consists in an overlap between the descriptive and normative sides of some communitarian arguments. These two kinds of argumentation can trigger different outcomes. In the descriptive version, a communitarian argument maintains that liberalism simply describes the sense of the actual life of contemporary liberal regimes. For the communitarians, the actual life of liberal regimes is perverse in the light of the sharp divide between self and community which characterizes them, and liberalism merely describes this trend. In other words, liberalism is an asocial doctrine which corresponds to the asocial world it represents.[13] In the normative version, instead, the attack concerns liberalism as normative political theory. From this point of view, normative liberalism, seen from the communitarian perspective, misrepresents the actual praxis of contemporary liberal-democratic societies. These societies could not even exist without a strong communal background. But liberals – including Rawls – would either deny this necessary premise or smuggle it underneath the surface of their arguments. In the first option, isolated and severed individuals – as they are imagined by liberal thinkers – cannot create a working society, and normative political liberalism is, from this standpoint, simply a misrepresentation of reality.[14] There is no society – not even a liberal society – without a community behind it. In the second option and for the same reason, liberal arguments are systematically supposed to recur to hidden communitarian premises. And just at the cost of this contradictory device, they succeed in giving a plausible representation of a working society.

These two versions of communitarian criticism seem in tension: in the first version, liberalism is accused of a proper representation of a perverse reality, whereas, in the second, liberalism is under attack for misrepresenting reality or for using hidden premises in contrast with the main paradigm.

7.1.1 The liberal political subject

A first kind of communitarian criticism targets the way in which Rawlsian liberalism conceives the moral and political subject. It often concerns also the concept of "agency" within liberalism. That is, the criticism targets the motivational structure of the individual and its relationship to the identity of the person. The thesis here is that the standard moral and political subject of liberalism – as presented in Rawls' theory of justice – is substantially empty, because liberals base their theories on a wrong vision of the constitution of the self. According to this vision, there is a pre-social self who is formed before society exists. For the communitarians, this liberal conception of the self is not only impossible, but also unappealing from a normative point of view. Within the communitarian horizon, one perceives the liberal conception of the subject as skeptical and shallow because people can only have deep goals if such goals are rooted in the life of the community. The same criticism can be presented in a different way, by saying that liberals have a parochial view of the subject (it is a view only liberals can believe in). The final outcome of these two different versions, however, does not amount to divergent results.

Such a criticism has been formulated by both Sandel and MacIntyre. Each concerns the nature of personal identity (the self) as the basis for ethics and political theory. According to both Sandel and MacIntyre, Rawls presents a highly abstract and artificial account of personal identity. The noumenal self *à la* Rawls amounts to an empty box, which Sandel calls "unencumbered self." Rawls is supposed to think that this kind of subject could rationally select his goals, independently from any previous link with the community. But this vision of the self is simply false. The self is always "embedded" (Sandel) in a network of actual practices including social roles and interpersonal relations. As Sandel, rephrasing Rawls (TJ 506; rev. edn. 443), says with some efficacy, the self is not "prior to its ends." Rather, it consists in them. It would be impossible – for Sandel and MacIntyre – to claim that there exists an identity defined by what we choose. On the contrary, our identity is defined by a set of goals and constraints that we do not choose. Rather, we always find or discover these within the concrete contexts of life. Even assuming that it makes sense to say that someone decides upon their existence, this decision cannot consist in a pure selection of objectives. It consists rather in fully understanding that we are members of a specific community. In this regard, the basic question cannot be the one posed by normative liberalism *à la* Rawls – that is: "What life plan am I supposed to select in agreement with principles of justice?" Rather it should be: "Who am I in my own community?"

The standard liberal objection to this kind of argument has a normative premise: nobody can guarantee that our concrete context of life and our community are acceptable from an ethical-political point of view. Moreover, within this liberal argument, the metaphysical foundations of the self do not have anything to do with the real nature of political liberalism, as Rawls himself claims in his IMT (1975). Problems of liberalism, instead, arise when already-given selves have access to institutional associations, and consist in controlling from the normative point of view the voluntariness of the eventual participation in them. For liberals, communitarians – particularly radical communitarians – do not take this seriously enough. It is sufficient to think of the German and Soviet communities during the 1930s to understand that the acceptance of a community tradition per se is not always good. Moreover, a liberal would say that there is a sort of obscure intersection between normative and positive levels within the communitarian thesis. Even accepting that our goals are not independent from the community we share, this does not imply that the community is coherent with a normative conception of justice. To go back to the nature of the subject, to say that our nature depends on the discovery of a self in a dense network of relations – as Sandel and MacIntyre often maintain – seems to be only part of the ethical-political significance of the subject itself. Sometimes, to act morally, one has to disentangle oneself from the context of one's community.

There is, I believe, another strategy that makes this kind of communitarian argument more plausible. From this point of view, one can interpret both communitarianism and liberalism as two projects intended to mediate between (individual) choices and (communal) constraints. To be born somewhere, to be a member of a given community, and to be part of a sexual gender are things one cannot choose. Normative political liberalism, however, sometimes devaluates this kind of background and risks becoming exceedingly voluntaristic in understanding many contextual elements only in terms of options and alternatives. Rawls' contractualism, in particular, with devices such as the original position and the veil of ignorance, at least if taken in isolation from the rest of TJ, is taken to exemplify the voluntarism implicit in the ethical-political obligation within a Kantian framework. To take the communitarian criticism at its best, one can simply emphasize the implausibility of the voluntaristic vision of the self. Freud, among others, emphasized the falsity of the omnipotence presupposed by this allegedly liberal vision of the self in his work.

I do not think, however, that Rawls himself accepts such a kind of voluntarism. The status of Rawls' attitude towards voluntarism and individualism can be traced back to his early work published as BIMSF (see, in particular, chapters 1 and 2 of this volume). In this work, Rawls identifies sin with the "repudiation of community" and says that the appropriate sense of community can only emerge if egotism is brought under control.

When communitarians emphasize the dependency of the self on the context, liberals usually insist on responding at the normative level (more or less as I myself did before).[15] Such an answer, however, runs the risk of trivializing the communitarian argument. To be fair, the communitarian argument can be seen as a limit to the liberal argument. Any liberal argument, albeit normative, cannot be too unrealistic. More interestingly, the political-theoretical question does not look well formulated if we put purely free choices on the one hand (liberalism) and merely context-dependent attitudes on the other (communitarians). The real nature of political behavior seems to be in equilibrium between these two options. If we adopt the assumption of the equilibrium between the given and the chosen, every political theory has to mediate between them. Political theory cannot rely on a mere acceptance of the given, but its critical subject cannot be detached from associative links. Considered in this way, the communitarian critique points to the need for an intermediate option.

We find, in Sandel, two different communitarian criticisms of the liberal self, the first moderate and the second radical. According to the moderate criticism, one can opt for a mediation between a "disembodied" subject and a "situated" subject. It is possible to revise one's plan of life in the light of chosen values. According to the radical criticism, abstract context-independent choices simply do not make sense. The subject cannot make choices until it discovers itself within a network of specific roles and relations. The moderate option is not too different from Rawls' position. The radical one, by contrast, is far removed from it but at the cost of being implausible if one intends to keep some normative sense of the theory. In this version, it would be impossible for the subject critically to form and revise her opinions.

A similar comment can be made about MacIntyre. He also levels both criticisms. On the one hand, he is ready to accept the idea of a purely community-determined subject. On the other, he is inclined, not always convincingly, to defend the reflective nature of such a subject.[16] Radical communitarianism assumes that deep commitments, coming from the embeddedness of the subject, and life-plan choices, being independent from the context, are incompatible. Moderate communitarianism and Rawls' liberalism instead defend their compatibility. If we accept the idea that this kind of compatibility is necessary, then the communitarian criticism of the liberal self oscillates between implausibility (if radical) and irrelevance (if moderate).

Charles Taylor's position is substantially similar to Sandel's and MacIntyre's. It reveals an analogous difficulty in opting for a moderate version of communitarianism. Taylor, exploring the notion of "human agent," identifies an agent's main characteristic with responsibility. Responsibility, in turn, implies a capacity to have second-order desires,[17] evaluative desires concerning other desires. From this point of view, each person's second-order desires are defined by her capacity for strong evaluation. Strong evaluation thus serves as the core of responsibility since this notion is fundamental for both ethics and political theory. The deep structure of the self – for Taylor – has been neglected by contemporary culture's dominant received views: utilitarianism and existentialism. In fact, both views appear to him "atomistic," as he says with Hegel's expression in the *Philosophy of Right*. Within utilitarianism, quality is reduced to quantity. Consequently, desires count for what they are and not for what they could be if modified according to evaluative reasons. Up to this point, Taylor is largely compatible with the normative version of the subject usually taken up by liberal political theories. For liberal political theories, too, emphasize the critical capacities of the subject in assuming that they start with its "highest-order interests" (Rawls).

Taylor is less compatible with liberal political theory when he discusses the way in which a capacity for strong evaluations takes its form. In fact, he refuses a normative vision of this capacity, explicitly stating: "Our evaluations are not chosen. On the contrary they are articulations of our sense of what is worthy or higher, or more integrated, or more fulfilling and so on."[18] This thesis does not imply that he agrees with the radical communitarian critique of the liberal subject, because he also writes:

> Much of our motivation – our desires, aspirations, evaluations – is not sharply given. We give it a formulation in words or images . . . Thus we are not simply moved by psychic forces comparable to such forces as gravity or electromagnetism, which we can see as given in a straightforward way, but rather by psychic "forces" which are articulated or interpreted in a certain way.[19]

Taylor maintains that these psychical forces do not amount to mere descriptions. They are rather intellectual constructions. Here, Taylor is in trouble since he needs to show how contextually shaped desires are not simply given in order to keep the significance of his own idea of evaluative responsibility. In other words, he cannot consistently claim that the idea of evaluative responsibility depends on a normative thesis: even a creative "articulation" of contextually shaped desires does not justify a responsible decision. His thesis is here twofold and cannot overcome a structural ambiguity. On the one hand, when it relies on second-order desires, it is compatible with normative liberalism *à la* Rawls. On the other hand, when Taylor claims that our desires strictly depend on the context, he faces the same criticism leveled against Sandel and MacIntyre concerning their vision of the self.

For Sandel's more explicit criticism of Rawls, the Rawlsian vision of a disembodied subject, which one can derive for him from the original position, is simply wrong. According to Sandel, Rawls would not be able to locate this notion within the limits of a precious conceptual equilibrium between complete autonomy on the one hand and radical contextualization on the other. His original position would be too abstract and formal to permit such an equilibrium.[20] Rawls (PL 27 – text and footnote) coldly replies that the communitarian criticism, according to which the Rawlsian self is prior to its choices, is off-track. It is based – Rawls claims – on a deep confusion between the political meaning of the self and its epistemological-metaphysical meaning. Sandel takes into consideration the second notion whereas Rawls, by his own admission, is only interested in a political vision of the subject.[21]

The debate, so formulated, fails to clarify the sense of the communitarian critique. This conclusion depends on two misinterpretations, the first being Sandel's and the second that of a Rawlsian liberal. First, Sandel – and more generally communitarians – wildly exaggerate the formalistic nature of the Rawlsian subject.[22] Such a misinterpretation can be detected in two parallel ways. One can carefully read TJ, as we tried to do in the previous chapters of this book. Alternatively, one can take into account Rawls' self-revision and self-interpretation as expressed in KCMT (see section 8.3).

Carefully reading TJ, one can note immediately what follows: if chapters 1–3 can give the impression that the Rawlsian subject is an "unencumbered self" (Sandel), it becomes clear that this is not Rawls' position in chapters 6–9.[23] The theory of the good, the Aristotelian Principle, the thesis on stability, the idea of a sense of justice, and the conception of society as "social union of social unions" all together widely counterbalance any abstract rationalism in the first part of TJ, assuming it is there at all. Moreover, even if the (partial) contextualization of the self in the third part of TJ is more evident, the view already appears in the first part. The relevance of reflective equilibrium and the roots of the subject in the basic structure, show a less purely Kantian framing of TJ by Rawls, and perhaps some Hegelian influence.[24] To sum up, the Rawlsian conception of the person in TJ relies on a critical notion in which reflective self-knowledge plays a fundamental role connecting person and society in a specific manner. In such a way, one could say that the Rawlsian persons presuppose an idea of social justice and share ends which are discovered more than chosen. One reader[25] has, for this very reason, also spoken – with evident but understandable over-statement – of a kind of Rawlsian "liberal communitarianism."

On the other hand, looking at KCMT (1980), we see how Sandel's attack on the nature of the Rawlsian self becomes evidently misplaced. In KCMT, the primacy of rationality is under-evaluated in the light of the relevance of the "reasonable" (see chapter 9 in this volume). Moreover, the embeddedness of the Rawlsian subject becomes crystal clear, as the self is situated within a specific political tradition. Here, Rawls conceives politics as starting not with an asocial self but rather with a network of contingent social relations among situated individuals and groups. With the intention of defending the communitarian critique, one could argue that this Rawlsian self-revision comes later than TJ, is completely evident just in PL, and anyway is not transparent at all before 1980. The communitarian argument, on the contrary, is mainly formulated in the shadow of TJ. As noted before, however, the abstract nature of the subject even in TJ is intrinsically controversial. And there is a further consideration. Sandel's *Liberalism and the Limits of Justice*, probably the most influential communitarian text on this topic, was published after KCMT (1980), meaning that Sandel was fully conscious of the directions Rawls was exploring. In his book, Sandel never mentions them.[26]

The second reason for which the debate on the nature of the self has been less fruitful than one could have hoped depends on the liberals. I have already mentioned Rawls' insufficient response, in which he substantially denies the metaphysical background of his position. According to this view, the conception of the person in TJ has a purely "political" meaning, as distinct from "comprehensive" (see chapter 9), and cannot be criticized on other grounds. Even if this notion, in fact, were to have been forced out by Rawls simply for reflecting about justice, it could be taken as too narrow or inappropriate. A similarly restrictive reaction has been widely shared by liberals (with some exceptions, such as Kymlicka). I believe this reaction has been unproductive. It may be true that the communitarian criticism of the Rawlsian subject is philosophically misplaced. It contributed, however, to highlighting some controversial aspects of normative liberalism and of Rawls' view. At stake here is a fundamental difference between philosophical attitudes. Communitarians believe that to have authentic critical choices one must assume the presence of "authoritative horizons" (Taylor). For liberals, authentic critical choices require some detachment between self and context. The communitarian criticism of the self helped at least to emphasize this significant difference, and to inspire feminist and radical critics of liberalism, and may also have provoked some significant Rawlsian self-revisions since 1980.[27]

To conclude, I think it is fair to say that the Rawlsian theory of the person (starting with the third part of TJ and, more evidently, since 1980 onwards) is not the one envisaged by the communitarians. No doubt, the Rawlsian person must be conceived as separated from her natural endowments, to be seen in the light of her "highest-order interest" to form, to revise, and to rationally pursue a conception of the good. This is indeed the core of the "political" conception of the person – that is, a conception of a person *qua* citizen. This conception, however, is not at all severed by its communal background. On the contrary, for Rawls it is latent in the public culture of liberal democracies. In such a way, Rawls' conception of the person does not correspond to the unencumbered noumenical self attacked by the communitarians. Instead, it derives from a substantive moral doctrine and presupposes commitment to some communal values. As we will see (chapter 11), if there is some problem with this Rawlsian conception of the person, this problem does not consist in its *deracinementi* but rather in the neat separation between "the personal and the political" that it assumes.

7.1.2 The priority of right criticized

The communitarian critique of the priority of right overlaps with the previous one. For the communitarians, Kantian deontological liberalism as the ideal of social justice is weak because, also due to the impoverished conception of the person we discussed in the last section, it undermines identity, common attachments, and the possibility of significant self-understanding. According to this criticism, Kantian deontological liberalism, which bases itself on the priority of right, is substantially empty from the ethical point of view. The connection with the argument about the self is clear. For the communitarians, a self separated by its traditions and isolated from its own community is unable to nourish profound and durable values. For the communitarians, Rawls' aim to defend the priority of right deprives people of their authentic values. By defending the priority of right in a way that prevents humans from developing authentic values, Rawls ultimately defends a sophisticated form of skepticism while claiming to defend pluralism.

A communitarian critique formulates two arguments along these lines. The first problem with the priority of right is meta-theoretical and – as Sandel says – consists above all in distinguishing "a standard of assessment from the thing being assessed."[28] The second problem is more general. It concerns liberal neutrality and its intrinsic impossibility: to avoid conceptions of the good in politics presupposes a liberal conception of the good.

The distinction between standard of assessment and thing to be assessed appears – for Sandel – in TJ as devaluing one's fundamental values and basic aims by transforming them into elementary needs and immediate wants. Compared with these, the Rawlsian concept of right takes the form of an Archimedean point able to override the residual "pure preferential choices."

The Rawlsian moral world looks like a world devoid of objective value.[29] Only in this world without soul and sense could a thin deontological subject reign. The cost of this operation is very high: by supposing an empty moral world and a noumenal subject, particular commitments, including the commitment to defend the Rawlsian principles of justice, become impossible.[30] Sandel argues that such a defense would require a communitarian embedding of the subject and a more robust theory of good than the one permitted by the Rawlsian deontological model and the priority of right. Liberals, by distancing the subject from its goals, render it a slave of deontology devoid of all meaning.

To maintain this thesis, Sandel repeatedly returns to an argument stemming from the libertarian criticism of Rawls. According to this argument, the second principle of justice unfairly treats individual talents as "common assets" (see 7.2). For Sandel, this vision is always connected to the Rawlsian conception of the self. The Rawlsian conception separates the self from its background and would have the result that nobody deserves anything because eventually nobody owns anything including themselves. But such a separation cannot be sufficient to justify the egalitarian difference principle. Consequently, Rawls, in order to defend the difference principle, would be obliged to buy into a strong vision of the community. But this strong vision would be incompatible with the priority of right and the Kantian conception of the self. Thus, the difference principle itself would come out as improperly justified by Rawls in TJ.

To this objection one can respond in two ways. First, Rawls is not so anti-meritocratic and he does not separate individuals and talents (see chapter 2). Second, the reasoning for the difference principle is not in conflict with the Kantian conception or the priority of right. Especially since 1980 (KCMT), the argument for the difference principle was not purely formal, but included substantive egalitarian elements as parts of self-respect. Within Rawls' vision, Kantian individuals, being rational and reasonable, have a right to a social minimum in order to exercise their own "highest-order interests."

The second attack on the priority of right regards the communitarian identification between a neutral conception of the good and a liberal vision. According to this criticism, the Rawlsian assignment of priority to the right over the good begs the question, in the sense that in such a way Rawls simply restates a liberal dogma in another terminology. Only liberals, if we follow this line, would believe that one can have a substantive political conception without presupposing a particular theory of the good. The evident problem with this criticism is that Rawls does not want to exclude the theory of the good from his vision. On the contrary, in his writing after TJ in particular – from PRIG to PL – Rawls frankly admits that the theory of justice as fairness in TJ uses four ideas of the good: goodness as rationality, primary goods, political virtues, and the good of a well-ordered political community. Of course, for Rawls, the neutrality of the theory of justice as fairness depends on its capacity to adopt these ideas of the good without being a comprehensive (religious or moral) doctrine.

But also limiting this reconstruction to the view proposed in TJ, for Rawls, there exists a twofold theory of the good: the thin theory and the thick theory. The priority of right is part of the thick theory of the good, and presupposes parties already informed of the principles of justice that they themselves had selected in the light of the sole thin theory of the good. The thin theory, however, is not so evanescent as to preclude rational and reasonable decisions oriented to the "highest-order interests" of the parties.[31] Here, Sandel makes an error of interpretation. The thin theory of the good is not so formal after all, containing elements not only of the "Rational" but also of the "Reasonable" (see chapter 10 of this volume). That is why the parties in the original position can, in the light of the thin theory, opt for the principles of justice. The priority of right here only says that the parties, once they are informed about the nature of the principles, would avoid desires that contrast with them (TJ 560).

In this regard, Rawls' liberalism does not deny that the choice of the principles of justice includes elements from a theory of the good.[32] Rawls just emphasizes the fact that public institutions have to take into consideration the fact that persons and groups have different conceptions of the good. He wants a pluralistic, not empty, conception of justice. The final goal of the liberal outlook *à la* Rawls is always that the individuals can enjoy a good life. It is simply stated that a good life is either difficult or impossible without criteria that ensure mutual respect and the capacity to critically revise one's own opinions. This depends on the reasons in favor of pluralism and neutrality that we mentioned. Communitarians present a contrasting vision by arguing that a society, characterized by different traditions, cannot be reunited by abstract principles of justice.

At this point, one could say that the four ideas of the good that Rawls admits as implicit in his vision do not coincide with the thin theory of the good. Notions such as the idea of political virtues and the good of a well-ordered society frankly exceed the thin theory (TJ, Sect. 60).[35] With these further ideas of the good, Rawls seems to state that a political society is an intrinsic good. And no doubt the line between this conclusion and a comprehensive view is subtle. In other words, Rawls seems here to go beyond the limits of his own political liberalism. Moreover, it's not easy to defend such an option against someone arguing that a perfectionist doctrine can perform better in some circumstances. Here again, Rawls seems to resist the communitarian attack by going towards some communitarian claims, but in such a way that he opens the door to other possible objections.

The communitarian alternative consists in a society characterized by a unique vision of the common good. For Sandel, as for all communitarians, the community is not the product of the free associations of individuals, but rather a pre-existing entity. For this very reason, justice cannot be the sole virtue that binds an institutional system. Liberalism seems to ask for the impossible by asking individuals to sacrifice for the sake of abstract principles alone.[33] The same sacrifices could instead be asked of persons united by strong traditional bonds.

The communitarian criticism of the priority of right takes for granted that liberal theories *à la* Rawls do not have a substantive theory of the good. This interpretation, however, goes against both the letter and the spirit of Rawls' text in TJ. Rawls' conception of justice is neither empty nor formal. Maybe – as one can note in analyzing PL – there is in Rawls' liberalism a prejudice in favor of critical attitudes. The delicate relationship between the right and the good in TJ is elaborated in the light of individuals who have a specific conception of the good which presupposes the possibility of critically revising it. Normative elements are surely hidden in this vision. It is difficult, though, to condemn these normative elements from a normative point of view. The experience of totalitarianism and fundamentalism makes us think that the values of toleration and pluralism that liberalism embodies are not easy to put aside in the name of some form of communitarian integrity.

7.1.3 Detachment from the community

Both communitarian criticisms we have discussed only attack part of Rawls' liberal theory. On the one hand, the communitarian idea of a (liberal) self prior to and independent from its goals is an evident exaggeration. This exaggeration makes the criticisms, if taken literally, highly implausible. After all, the notion of person in political philosophy cannot solely be a matter of pure self-discovery, excluding any normative appeal. On the other hand, even if we accept the communitarian critique, there is still meaning in looking for principles of justice.

Communitarians, however, present another kind of criticism that we can take seriously in the light of a general attention to the critical attitudes towards liberal theories *à la* Rawls. The criticism charges that Kantian liberals do not give due consideration to the sense of community. From this point of view, communitarians believe that liberals overlook two important truths: (i) there is no valuable conception of the good without a proper social and communal basis; and (ii) the value of the political community is a fundamental good. This kind of criticism has been put forward by practically all communitarians and in particular by Michael Walzer.[34] Here, the philosopher as philosopher is too neatly detached from their own community. All communitarians take this idea of the philosopher as a detached outsider, who recognizes what is just only in the cold light of reason, to be misleading.

One can take this criticism in two different ways. First, the criticism can be interpreted as a claim for a philosophical liberalism that is more inclined to take community in consideration. So understood, this criticism is both very reasonable and compatible with liberalism (in particular with Rawls' liberalism). Second, the criticism can be interpreted as saying that the idea of distributive justice itself is intrinsically implausible, because the nature and significance of the goods depend on the shared meanings that distributive justice is supposed to overlook. So taken, the criticism is less compatible with liberalism and substantially more difficult to accept.

This second version of the criticism has been proposed, with great elegance, by Michael Walzer in *Spheres of Justice* and in other essays. For Walzer, a theory of justice must be pluralistic, aiming at complex equality rather than the simple equality typical of traditional liberalism. Complex equality takes as its primary consideration the shared meanings of a given community, treating social goods in relation to them. Distributive justice then assigns opportunities and obligations in accordance with the social meanings of the goods, which we can group in several "spheres." In this way, goods concerning health are distributed according to need, those concerning education and culture according to talents and capacity, punishment according to previous responsibilities, and citizenship according to constitutional traditions. The division into spheres, coherent with a communitarian premise, depends on specific traditions and cultures. The thesis is polemical concerning Rawlsian liberalism, which is supposed to overlook any distribution of goods in relation to their shared meanings.

The problem with the approach based on shared meanings is evident. A theory of justice cannot be based only on shared meanings. Such meanings in fact could reproduce a totally unjust social order, such as a caste society. Problems of justice usually arise just when shared meanings either fail to be reproduced or are normatively unacceptable. In this event, we need a normative version of the priorities connected with the question at stake in a way independent from the shared meanings. Proposals like Walzer's appear *prima facie* reasonable exactly because we live in liberal societies in which some form of substantive legitimation holds. From this point of view, Rawls makes clear that his conception of justice embodies a fair understanding of social justice only because this is part of the culture of a liberal-democratic society.

7.2 The Libertarian Criticism

Rawlsian liberalism conjoins two fundamental principles. The first of these rests on liberty. The second defends equality and democracy. Many criticisms of Rawlsian liberalism come from the left. According to them, a strong protection of individual liberty threatens equality and democracy. There are, however, also criticisms against Rawls from the right. They are symmetrical to the leftist ones. Critics from the right often maintain that the tendency to equality and democratic control – in Rawlsian liberalism – jeopardizes individual freedoms. Among such rightist criticisms, Nozick's libertarian critique, from chapter 7 of his *Anarchy, State and Utopia*,[35] is the most well known.

Nozick's criticism of Rawls can be considered as a critique of the welfare state in the name of a minimal state. Similar criticisms are often based on one of several pragmatic arguments against the welfare state.[36] For instance, all government tends to overspend regardless of its good intentions. Additionally, libertarians claim that production and distribution cannot be separated, as many liberals and social-democrats – who treat the first coherently with the market and the second in a "constructionist" mood – would have it.[37] Rawls, however, is not particularly touched by these pragmatical arguments. His theory is mainly an ideal theory. This is why Nozick's approach is particularly to the point. Nozick presents mainly ethical-political objections to Rawls. For him, as similarly for Hayek, a theory of justice such as Rawls' would end in unjustly limiting individual rights.[38] In doing so, the theory would not take seriously just this "separateness of the persons," reproducing the chief problem that Rawls attributes to the utilitarian tradition. The first, now famous, sentence of ASU says: "Individuals have rights, and there are things no person or group may do to them (without violating their rights)" (p. ix). In such a way, the attack is not directed at the institutional and pragmatic consequences of the theory, but rather to its ideal core.

Redistributive theories of justice *à la* Rawls violate, for Nozick, some fundamental individual rights such as personal autonomy and private property. According to Nozick, these rights should instead be protected by absolute "side constraints" of a Kantian nature. These constraints are absolute because no "maximization," of whatever social goal, can violate them. As Nozick writes:

> The moral side constraints upon what we may do, I claim, reflect the fact of our separate existences. They reflect the fact that no moral balancing can take place among us; there is no moral outweighing of one of our lives by others so as to lead to a greater overall social good. There is no justified sacrifice of us for others. (ASU 33)

If Nozick is right here, Rawls would be in trouble. He could not defend the theory of justice as fairness solely from the liberal point of view based on the protection of individual rights he himself proposed. Nozick's argument can be divided into two parts: a *pars construens* in which he presents an alternative (to Rawls') vision of social justice and a *pars destruens* in which he formulates a criticism of Rawls' theory of justice in TJ.

7.2.1 The entitlement theory

Nozick's theory of justice in ASU is based on the idea of "entitlement." An entitlement theory *à la* Nozick presupposes a vision in which individual rights, the justification of a minimal state and a libertarian account of utopia play a major role. As matter of fact, it is the inviolability of some individual rights, like life and property, that determines the moral justification of a "night-watchman" minimal state and of a libertarian project of utopia. Within this framework, Nozick provides his theory of justice together with his criticism to Rawls in chapter 7 of ASU. These two aspects are reciprocally connected. It is difficult to understand his objections to Rawls without going through his theory of entitlement.

Nozick's approach can be divided into two parts, one positive and one critical. The positive part is based on the centrality of "historical principles," according to which the justice of a distribution depends on how it came about.[39] The critical part initially defines an "end-result principle" as the negation of a historical principle. Then, it attacks all theories of justice whose principles are "patterned," that is principles following which "distribution is to vary along with some natural dimension, weighted sum of natural dimensions, or lexicographic ordering of natural dimensions" (ASU 156).

Patterned theories typically fill up the gap in sentences like "to each according to his . . ." where we can complete the sentence by words like "merit," "need" or "IQ": "the justice of a distribution is determined by how things are distributed (who has what) as judged by some principle(s) of distribution" (ASU 153).

For Nozick, end-state theories of distribution are implausible. Principles of justice must instead be unpatterned and historical. They must be sensitive to the historical feature that generates an eventual pattern of distribution and not vice versa. From this point of view, Nozick's thesis is crystal clear. It is sufficient to think about grading students after a course: would it be just for a professor to grade them according to an a-priori pattern of distribution independently from the way the students behaved during the course and performed at the exams? The answer here is evidently "no!" Analogously, Nozick argues that a just distribution is impossible without relying on the way in which individuals behaved and performed during the production process. Nozick writes in another celebrated ASU passage:

> If things fell from heaven like manna, and no one had any special entitlement to any portion of it, and no manna would fall unless all agreed to a particular distribution, and somehow the quantity varied depending on the distribution, then it is plausible to claim that persons placed so that they couldn't make threats or hold out for specially large shares would agree to the difference principle rule of distribution. But is this the appropriate model for thinking about how the things people produce are to be distributed? (ASU 198)

Again, we are confronted with a rhetorical question, and again the answer is clearly "no!" According to Nozick, only the history of how a good is produced can justify its distribution.

To avoid the implausibility of patterned and end-state distributive theories, Nozick presents an option for an unpatterned and historical distribution: his entitlement theory. It is characterized by three features: (i) a principle of

initial acquisition; (ii) a principle of transfer; and (iii) a principle of rectifica-
tion. Every socio-economic distribution generated by the recursive use of
these three principles, via legitimated passages, is considered. The entitlement theory is also absolute: there are no other principles of justice that
supplement it.[40]

The entitlement theory so conceived does not violate fundamental individual rights like theories based on end-state and patterned principles.[41] From
this theory, one can derive a theory of the state. This theory – in ASU – aims to
distinguish Nozick's entitlement theory from anarchical positions, which do
not justify any form of state, including the minimal one. Nozick formulates
a Lockean hypothesis where the progressive formation of a justifiable state
is based on the construction of protective agencies. This process is followed
by the progressive dominance of one among them, until this one achieves a
monopoly on legitimate force.

7.2.2 The critique

For Nozick, no distributive justice theories, aside from entitlement theory, can
be morally acceptable. In fact, these theories are supposed to interfere systematically with individual rights. This particularly applies to utilitarianism and
Rawls' theory of justice as fairness. Within the framework of ASU, liberty
usually removes the patterns. This generates a permanent conflict between all
patterned principles and the possibility of free, voluntary exchanges among
consenting adults.

According to Nozick, a patterned theory of justice cannot be implemented
without "continuous interference with people's lives." Independently from
the vision of distributive justice, which is inherent to the specific pattern, any
patterned theory looks like a Procuste's cage constraining the free will of the
people. Nozick defends the thesis with the example of Wilt Chamberlain,
the famous basketball player. Basketball fans are disposed to contribute to
Chamberlain's wealth via voluntary contributions, for example paying for
their tickets or watching TV. But if the government tries to use – via taxation
– their money for other goals (even the noblest ones), it does not seriously
respect their own intentions. The example is supposed to highlight the conflict between patterned principles and individual rights from which Nozick's
political-theoretical position originates.

Nozick's criticism of Rawls presupposes both the *pars destruens* and the
pars construens of the aforementioned thesis. Nozick considers Rawls' principles of justice as both patterned and end-state. Devices such as Rawls' veil
of ignorance exclude a priori the possibility of any historical distribution like
the one based on the entitlement theory. Nozick's minimal state would be
based only on a historical conception of justice, which could not result in the
same errors as Rawls' conception. Here Nozick points out an immanent conflict within the Rawlsian argument between the procedural side of the theory

of justice as fairness and its roots in an end-state pattern of argumentation. It is the second which condemns Rawls' theory to a deep anti-historical foundation. Frankly, Nozick never succeeds in showing where this anti-historical foundation is located in Rawls' theory.[42] On the contrary, the idea itself of basic structure, so central in Rawls, emphasizes the historical nature of any distribution coherent with the theory of justice as fairness. In fact, if we accept that the basic structure is the primary subject of justice then there is no justice independently from a given social context (see chapter 12).

Nozick, in particular, criticizes the egalitarian conviction on which Rawls' moral intuitive argument depends. This conviction rests upon two basic Rawlsian assumptions: first, any account of just distribution must rely on the priority of cooperation; second, social and natural characteristics of the persons are not only individual but also collective goods, their effective worth determined by the institutional framework.

Nozick is vigorously opposed to both these Rawlsian assumptions. First, he thinks that not all the social product is caused by an increase in cooperation, which could be the outcome of an egalitarian strategy. Only part of the social product depends on an increase of cooperation. Consequently, not all the social pie should be distributed as if it were celestial manna; that is, without considering individual contributions. Instead, only the part of it for which one can demonstrate a connection with some increase of cooperation should be socially distributed. Second, Nozick is convinced that – through the difference principle – the worst-off citizens do not offer fair terms of cooperation to the best-off. The difference principle is too severe.

The second point introduces a significant argument. This argument criticizes Rawls' intuitive moral thesis according to which both social and natural lotteries would give to the most advantaged prizes that are "arbitrary from a moral point of view." Nozick, being possibly the first to understand the importance of the intuitive moral thesis within Rawls' theory of justice as fairness, claims that Rawls overlooks the real meaning of natural liberty. To have talent – notwithstanding Rawls' interpretation – does not entail the ability to use it. To use it, one needs "unnatural" effort and sacrifice. Moreover, to intervene by appropriating such talents in favor of the community – as may be required by the difference principle – implies a potentially strong and durable violation of individual rights. Finally, the argument against the talented is substantially an argument against the same incentives that, on the other hand, the difference principle itself is supposed to encourage.

In this regard, the theoretical problem consists in deciding whether the second principle of justice – and the difference principle in particular – could be the basis for fair terms of cooperation. Within the difference principle, inequalities can be admitted when they favor the worst-off group. Of course, the worst-off group is not in a position to protest against the difference principle. But what if one puts oneself in the shoes of the better-off group? Shouldn't we think that the difference principle mistreats the better-offs? The difference principle, in other words, could be biased in favor of the worst-offs. Rawls would reply that the better-offs are advantaged by being given more social assets (like class or family) and natural assets (like intelligence or strength) that cannot be thought of as deserved. That is why to have them is "arbitrary from a moral point of view." This is the reason why Rawls himself tends to see these assets as common goods, which do not belong only to single individuals but rather belong to the community as a whole. The difference principle is simply a consequence of this.

Now, many liberals would agree that social advantages are often undeserved. But in what sense can we say the same thing concerning natural talents? Clearly, Rawls' thesis here is far more controversial. After all, it is true that to have talent is not enough to use it properly. One must also be willing and able to put it to work. A possible Rawlsian way to meet this objection consists in saying that to put talents to work is not independent from moral arbitrary factors, such as social status and natural goodwill.

Here, Nozick raises three objections to the Rawlsian thesis. First, Rawls' thesis could imply a de-responsibilization of the person "attributing everything to certain sorts of external factors" (ASU 214). Following a critical path that will be taken up by Sandel, this kind of de-responsibilization would be the consequence of a too abstract conception of the self. For Nozick and Sandel, instead, the self is not separable from its qualities. Sandel will later note that a criminal could use the same kind of Rawlsian argument, in this de-responsibilizing sense, to avoid punishment for her acts.

Second, Nozick maintains that – taking seriously his own theory of justice – persons are entitled to exploit their own talents even if they do not morally deserve them. Receiving the benefits is just if their own entitlement is opportunely connected with the way in which some goods are produced.

Third, Nozick levels against Rawls roughly the same criticism that Rawls himself raises against utilitarianism. Utilitarians, according to this criticism, do not take seriously the separateness of persons. Nozick maintains that Rawls commits the same error with the difference principle (attributing the fruit of individual talents to the community as a whole).

A Rawlsian reply to these three criticisms can be imagined in the following terms. To the first criticism, one could object that the intention underlying the difference principle does not consist in expropriating individual talents, but rather in limiting the consequences of such diversity of talents in terms of primary goods. As a result, there is not any Rawlsian attempt to separate the persons from their qualities, but rather a much more modest redistributional aim of the theory. The seriousness of the second criticism depends on the correctness of the entitlement theory. And, as we shall see, there are serious doubts on that theory's validity. To the third criticism, one can object that Rawls' emphasis on distribution, with the priority of the worst-off, is an antidote to the utilitarian disregard for the diversity of the persons. This disregard is in fact the other face of the aggregative utilitarian point of view, in which just the sum of the utilities counts without considering the way in which these utilities are distributed among people.

Nozick's position itself faces objections. Nozick does not sufficiently consider the relational side of wealth: the same objective individual qualities can have completely different outcomes within two different social structures. Take two people with similar commercial capacities during the 1950s. One of them lives in San Francisco and the other in Beijing. Clearly their economic destiny would be different.

These relational aspects also have meaning from the social point of view.[43] Failing to take this side of the argument into account potentially jeopardizes social cohesion. In any historical society, excessive differences in terms of primary goods are relevant from the point of view of stability. Moreover, Nozick's individualistic model overlooks the role of social context. The product of the individual talents is not easily separated from the social setting.[44] Finally, the symbolic value of equality is not given enough weight by Nozick, as he himself was to admit in one of the very rare occasions he went back to the issues of ASU.[45]

There are also more general objections both to the entitlement theory of justice and to Nozick's criticism of Rawls. First, Nozick's theoretical absolutism is troublesome. Maybe – as he asserts – any attempt to realize an ideal, especially an egalitarian ideal, originates in violations of individual rights. Nozick, however, seems to have in mind a continuum of these violations, so that he cannot properly distinguish legitimated taxation from forced labor. Behind this extreme radicalization we can detect an enormous exaggeration. One must understand why an individual claim is not allowed and how relevant an eventual violation of individual claims is. For example, more taxation to defend national territory from foreign assault and to protect public health from contagious diseases would seem justified to the majority of us.

Similar objections can be raised against Nozick's rights fundamentalism. Liberals allow that the protection of some basic individual rights is a relevant part of any acceptable political conception. It is difficult to believe, however, that respecting rights requires such a robust barrier. Nozick, in fact, never justifies his preferred list of fundamental rights.[46] One could have in mind a different and reduced list of rights. For example, Nozick is notoriously keen to defend individual rights to voluntary exchange within a capitalistic market, the premise of the argument being that market relations do permit purely voluntary exchanges. The socialist and cooperative movements, however, are born from the idea that in a capitalistic market the exchanges – beginning from those between workers and capitalists – are not voluntary in a full sense. This points to an important distinction between Rawls and Nozick.[47] Both of them think that consent is basic in a liberal outlook. However, Nozick wants effective consent to count, where Rawls relies on ideal choice. But the normativity of any political model seems much more connected with the ideal consent. If true, this distinction would deprive Nozick's thesis of part of its normative significance.

The distinction between actual and hypothetical consent hides a profound difference between the two visions of fundamental rights. Nozick sees rights as absolute and intractable. For Rawls, instead, they cannot be considered independently from a whole conception of justice for the basic structure. This is one of the reasons why Nozick's thesis does not require a theoretical justification of the fundamental rights. As maintained by Nagel, Nozick's individual rights – on which also his criticism of Rawls is based – are taken for granted. Nozick's rights are, to use Nagel's expression, "without foundations."[48] That is why nobody would be convinced by them unless they were previously already in agreement. Nozick himself is inclined to accept something similar when he says that ASU is not presented as a "precise theory of the moral basis of individual rights" (ASU xiv).

Furthermore, Nozick never explains why considerations concerning individual rights cannot be overridden by considerations of justice. He simply enunciates general moral principles, such as the following: "No person can be sacrificed for the benefit of any other person" (ASU 33). "Each person must be treated as an end and never merely as a means" (ASU 31–2). "Each person is individually responsible for choosing his life plan" (ASU 34). However, Nozick never tries to show how these principles lead to the derivation of specific rights or what limits may exist to such rights.

We could claim, for example, that, during their periods in office, both Hitler and Roosevelt violated certain individual rights. It would be perverse to say that those violations had similar significance and value. One can also maintain that a reasonably just society could not exist without overriding various property rights for justifiable reasons.

Finally, two considerations are needed, keeping in mind an evaluation of Rawls' work. First, Nozick does not sufficiently consider the meaning of the rule of law and the first principle in Rawls' work. Second, Rawls does not treat the distribution of resources as manna. The difference principle, on the contrary, is supposed to be a way of reconciling incentives with fair terms of cooperation: this reconciliation takes the history of production seriously.

7.3 The Habermas–Rawls Exchange

The Habermas–Rawls[49] exchange (HRE) – first published in the *Journal of Philosophy* in 1995 – constitutes a peak within social and political philosophy of the twentieth century.[50] This depends both on the prestige and the cultural relevance of the authors and on the nature of the issues they discuss. To be honest, Habermas and Rawls do not always understand each other in the exchange.[51] Habermas makes the more remarkable effort to understand Rawls, even if he accentuates their differences. Rawls is less prone to understanding Habermas even if he takes his criticism very seriously, also by underscoring their similarities.

Habermas tends to see Rawls' thought as if it were one of the moments of his own thought, in terms of a proceduralization and a "social" vision of Kant's categorical imperative. Habermas shares the aims, but does not seem in agreement with the way in which Rawls moves in this direction. That is why one can speak of an immanent criticism on his side (JPh 110). Rawls too shares some substantial aims with the Habermasian project. From this point of view, in the exchange he distinguishes three levels of analysis: (i) direct confutation of some of Habermas' theses; (ii) criticism of Habermas' general vision; and (iii) a reformulation of some of his own theses in order to avoid Habermas' objections. It must be noted that, with regard to point (iii), at least on two main points – that is, the nature of justification in PL and the "four-stage sequence" in TJ – Rawls is clearer than elsewhere. But, to understand this, we need to start from Habermas' criticism.

In the 1995 exchange, Rawls publicly discusses Habermas for the first and last time. Habermas instead had already discussed Rawls at length at least twice, and would continue in his critical argument later on. I have here in mind chapters 2 and 3 of *Between Facts and Norms* and pages 25–8 of "Remarks on Discourse Ethics," written before the exchange, "Reasonable versus True, or the Morality of Worldviews" (written before HRE and published afterwards in *The Inclusion of the Other*), and "Religion in the Public Sphere," written afterwards[52] (and several other passages in different papers).

These other writings considerably help in understanding Habermas' intentions as an interpreter of Rawls. Habermas agrees with Rawls in conceiving a pluralist but normative social philosophy ("Reasonable" 79) and in opting for Kant rather than Hobbes from a foundational point of view. In particular, Habermas is in favor of Rawls' intention to let a Kantian scheme merge into the "social world" ("Remarks" 26). At the same time, he condemns Rawls' contractualism for its voluntaristic background. This very voluntarism would make the notion of truth unreachable for Rawls in PL, condemning him exaggeratedly to rely on a not sufficiently investigated, in terms of philosophical anthropology, notion of the person.

These criticisms start from the assumption that Rawls' political theory is not able to capture the (Habermasian) distinction between morality and ethics. Morality, for Habermas, moves from a Kantian, universalistic and normative background, whereas ethics is concerned with the self-understanding of a group within a "post-metaphysical," that is roughly speaking "pluralist," society. In this regard, Habermas – in *Between* (62–5) – had already attributed to Rawls the merit of giving this distinction a realistic background and had refuted any contextualist interpretation of Rawls *à la* Rorty. In the exchange, Habermas accepts this framework but rejects what he sees as an aprioristic Rawlsian method, the so-called "methods of avoidance," and critically emphasizes the role of the "overlapping consensus" within PL.

After the exchange, Habermas generally insists on the same issues. He stresses the political–metaphysical distinction and attacks Rawls' public reason for transforming the necessary state–religion separation into an excessive mental and psychological burden for religious people.[53] The core of Habermas' critical argument here rests on an attack on Rawls' conception of "freestanding" neutrality. This Rawlsian conception would isolate politics from morals, epistemology, and metaphysics – and from philosophy altogether – in an unacceptable way. Such a problem would not be overcome by Rawls' answer to Habermas in the exchange. Rawls presupposes in his public justification an already existing social consensus, which for Habermas, in contrast, must not be taken for granted. According to Habermas, Rawls should not pretend to transform a "social fact," like the overlapping consensus, into a normative theoretical concept.

In "Reasonable" – published after the exchange – Habermas, substantially repeating his previous view, focuses on the nature of the "political" in Rawls as opposed to the "metaphysical." Rawls' use of the metaphysical–political distinction would correspond, first, to a peculiar view of neutrality, separated from any profound doctrine; and second, to a special epistemic status that would permit the coexistence of different comprehensive doctrines. Habermas maintains that, through this, Rawls isolates political theory from ethics, religion, and metaphysics in an improper (read "arbitrary") way. Substantially, Habermas thinks that the metaphysical–political distinction is intrinsically flawed, at least as it is conceived in Rawls' terms.[54]

The cash value of Habermas' criticism consists in saying that Rawls confuses the descriptive and normative level of his own analysis. This confused overlapping would create a lack of distinction between ideology and philosophical argument within Rawls' liberalism. From this point of view, Habermas is convinced that his own idea of democratic legitimation works much better than Rawls' vision of liberal justice.

The core of Habermas' arguments against Rawls is already substantially present in the 1995 exchange. In this, Habermas says that – notwithstanding efforts in the direction of more realism (appreciated by Habermas, see HRE 109–10) – Rawls is unable to make the "reasonable" less aprioristic and monological. At the same time, Habermas repeatedly maintains that the overlapping consensus machinery exhibits a structural confusion between the positive and normative levels. This confusion allows liberal pluralism to trump the categorical force of the normative argument. Such a thesis explains Rawls' first reaction to Habermas: the Habermasian discourse ethics expresses a comprehensive view, whereas the Rawlsian position in PL expresses just a political one. The political view presupposes a freestanding vision of liberalism:

> I think of political liberalism as a doctrine that falls under the category of the political. It works entirely within that domain and does not rely on anything

outside it . . . Habermas' position, on the other hand, is a comprehensive doctrine that covers many things far beyond political philosophy. Indeed, the aim of his theory of communicative action is to give a general account of meaning, reference, and truth or validity both for theoretical reason and for the several forms of practical reason. (PL 374–6)

The main characteristics of Rawlsian political liberalism are substantially reaffirmed in HRE: (i) it concerns just the "basic structure" of society; (ii) it can be formulated independently of any comprehensive doctrine; and (iii) all its main ideas come from the category of the political, we ourselves being familiar with them because they are part of a liberal-democratic culture.

7.3.1 Habermas' three critical arguments

In HRE, Habermas presents a threefold criticism of Rawls: (i) the original position is unable to guarantee the level of impartiality it aims at (111–19); (ii) Rawls cannot properly distinguish – especially when he discusses the overlapping consensus – between abstract acceptability, that is justification, and concrete acceptability, and thus loses a substantial part of the cognitive and normative value of his argument (119–26); and (iii) Rawls is not in a position neatly to separate the liberty of the ancients from that of the moderns, and in his vision liberalism obscures democracy (126ff.). These criticisms, if joined, permit Habermas to state that Rawls' liberal vision should be modest from a normative point of view, but not modest "in the wrong way" (110–11).

On the original position, Habermas repeats – in a personal way – a traditional critique of Rawls. He maintains that Rawls cannot attain the level of "full autonomy" by joining the rationality of the parties and the veil of ignorance (HRE 111). Neither the "sense of justice" of the parties nor their capacity to have a conception of the good depend on these Rawlsian assumptions. Rawls' mere procedural rationality cannot guarantee the existence of a political subject with similar characteristics. Habermas splits into three this general argument. First, the passage from self-interest to highest-order interests cannot be reached within the Rawlsian framework. Second, Rawls' basic rights cannot be assimilated to primary goods. Finally, the claim that the veil of ignorance does not imply neutrality.

The first sub-argument simply states that one cannot reach a full autonomy of the citizens if the parties, which are supposed to represent citizens, are considered purely rational in the traditional social sciences' sense. Habermas thinks that it is not possible even to suppose that rational agents would be able to decide in a morally significant way (HRE 113). The Rawlsian parties in their original position decide as if they were autonomously respecting deontological principles. But actually – in the Rawlsian framework as interpreted by Habermas – they cannot do so, and they accept just external constraints.

This objection seems indeed to be overcome by Rawls' KCMT (1980) and later writings, with the introduction of the "reasonable" as a primary characteristic of citizens, the derivation of primary goods from highest-order interests, the suppression of rational choice theory, and the centrality of the person. One could maintain, however, that an objection like Habermas' cannot stand up in the face of a careful reading of TJ. TJ, at least if we take in account Part III, presents a more complex derivation of the principles of justice. Independently from this last point, Habermas' argument seems much weaker if considered after 1980.

The second sub-argument about the original position concerns the overlapping between a theory of the good and a theory of rights behind the notion of primary goods in TJ. In Habermas' words: "Rawls thereby adopts a concept of justice which is proper to an ethics of the good" (HRE 114).

According to Habermas, there is a substantial confusion in the Rawls of TJ between deontology and teleology. This criticism, too, is somewhat misleading, because the option for some primary goods follows after certain constraints, incorporating values, have been selected. Perhaps it would have been easier for Habermas to say that the priority of right incorporates an intrinsically difficult position insofar as it presupposes a detachment between rights and good, which is difficult to understand.

The third critical sub-argument, about the original position, casts doubts upon the moral efficacy of the veil of ignorance. Habermas does not believe that a conjunction of self-interest and ignorance could constitute the basis for a substantive morality. He sees, on the contrary, the veil of ignorance as a neutralizing device, in place of which he would prefer an appeal to proceduralism.

As Habermas maintains: "Rawls could avoid the difficulties associated with the design of the original position if he operationalised the moral point of view in a different way, namely, if he kept the procedural conception of practical reason free of substantive connotations by developing it in a strictly procedural manner" (116).

This criticism reveals some incomprehension about the procedure–substance relation in Rawls. Procedure and substance are never reciprocally separated in Rawls, giving rise to a significant meta-ethical novelty in his work. In practice, where Rawls prefers a relation between noumenical individuals and substantive principles, Habermas would have preferred a relation between procedural principles and real individuals. This difference would lead Rawls – invariably, in Habermas' view – to unduly privilege the observer's position over the participant's. And for Habermas, such an "idealized consensus" could never be sufficient for a public justification (HRE 129). Of course, it is difficult to say in the abstract who is right on sophisticated philosophical matters such as these. Nevertheless, Habermas here proposes – more than an internal criticism – a position external to Rawls. In consequence, he does not fully hit his target.

Considering the whole Habermas argument about the original position, Rawls seems to be right in saying that it depends on the fact that Habermas – contrary to himself – defends a comprehensive doctrine. From this point of view, Rawls maintains that Habermas' "doctrine [is one] of logic in the broad Hegelian sense: a philosophical analysis of the presuppositions of rational discourse which includes within itself all the apparent substantial elements of religious and metaphysical doctrines" (PL 382).

And this Habermas argument, rooted in his discourse ethics, would not be – contrary to what Rawls is looking for – limited to a political conception. This difference between the nature of Habermas' and Rawls' arguments would be made evident by the distinction between public sphere (Habermas) and public reason (Rawls), where the first has a much wider scope than the second (see here chapter 11 in this volume, and PL 382, n. 13).

Habermas' most successful criticism is probably the one based on the overlapping between normative and descriptive, or between ideal acceptability and de facto acceptance, which would occur in PL in general and in Rawls' treatment of the overlapping consensus in particular (see chapter 11). Habermas thinks that Rawls here meets too timidly the challenge of the communitarian arguments, and that in so doing he almost hides some basic normative arguments within his own theory of justice as fairness. From this underlying weakness results the controversial Rawlsian distinction between politics and metaphysics. For Habermas, this distinction, made explicit by the "methods of avoidance," would in the long run be a simplistic way to avoid some philosophical difficulties.

This conclusion is considered particularly evident if we approach Rawls' construction of an overlapping consensus: Habermas is convinced – and frankly so am I – that the overlapping consensus plays a central role within Rawls' theory in PL. He is worried though, because – without opportunely distinguishing the normative from the positive – the whole Rawlsian model could lose its cognitive and normative value. The risk here is of Rawls confusing overlapping consensus as a normative device able to support moral stability, with overlapping consensus as an empirical fact able to support just social stability. In these terms, the overlapping consensus would oscillate between a "cognitive role" and a mere "instrumental role."

This criticism is deep, but I do not think it is altogether fair to Rawls. Acceptability criteria, on which moral stability depends, are partially internal to the theory in TJ. It is not so in PL, where the obligation to respect pluralism makes a straightforward congruence between the right and the good impossible (see chapters 2, 9, 10, and 11). In the PL model, the theory of justice as fairness itself requires an extra external control by the citizens, the final outcome of which is not foreseeable in terms of the theory itself. The main consequence of this shift is that if in TJ the philosopher could nourish a reasonable expectation to anticipate theoretically the process of stabilization, this could never happen in PL, where the self-stabilization of the theory of justice rests outside the theory itself. Habermas' problem is here crystal clear: either the overlapping consensus has an independent normative force or it cannot solve this problem. This is so because, in the second option, the overlapping consensus would not be a way to establish the acceptability of the theory but rather an instrument to control its already realized acceptance. Of course, Habermas believes that Rawls is much nearer to this second version of the overlapping consensus.

In other words, if Habermas is right there could not be any new normative contribution coming from the overlapping consensus. But is he right here? In fact, Rawls' construction of the overlapping consensus in PL aims to reach an intersubjective consensus stemming from contrasting individual and group positions, positions that are reflected in the comprehensive doctrines of the citizens. In this regard, it is partially true that to reach an overlapping consensus on such a basis represents, if not exactly a miracle, then at least a lucky outcome. There are no a-priori guarantees that it will arrive. "It just happens . . ." – as Habermas observes of the overlapping consensus. This conclusion does not convince Habermas. He would prefer that – also admitting an un-eliminable pluralism within a post-metaphysical milieu – it could exist at another level in which the real discourses of democratic citizens could converge. Of course, the problem with this view is that it concedes too little to pluralism, because the equilibrium it is supposed to reach is simply another and higher form of Kantian impartiality. Rawls' thesis instead – assuming we are justified in hoping for a lucky outcome (Rawls himself accepts the idea that public justification "just happens . . .") – opts for another level of pluralism. At this further level we can get a possible, and surely not guaranteed, convergence among citizens believing in different comprehensive doctrines but accepting a consensus on some fundamental institutional matters. These matters correspond, for example, to some prerogatives in the American constitutional regime and to human rights as a premise for decent global interaction (see chapter 12). From this point of view, Rawls' claim that Habermas' theory of communicative action is a comprehensive view makes sense. For Habermas claims – in contrast to Rawls – that there is an independent and superior level of truth with respect to single religious, metaphysical and moral doctrines (PL 378–9).

Rawls tries to meet Habermas' objection to the overlapping consensus with an argument of special interest in which he formulates his threefold thesis on justification (see here chapter 11). He also separates here two different kinds of consensus and links the whole to the notion of "liberal legitimacy." Within Rawls' thesis we have three kinds of justification. The first justification is only political and its value is merely "pro tanto," because it rests only on political value and can be overridden by a justification rooted in citizen-comprehensive doctrines. The second type of justification is called by Rawls "full," and it concerns the whole person of the citizen, beginning from her deep comprehensive doctrines. This justification trumps the political one. The core of the overlapping consensus consists, however, in the third "public" justification. Solely within the public justification a fusion of horizons between different comprehensive doctrines happens, and consequently their equilibrium within a political society can be realized (PL 386–7). Within public justification, reasonable members of a political society accept the political conception, even if they start from and keep their comprehensive doctrines. In such a way, we see how, in the overlapping consensus, acceptability and acceptance cannot be neatly separated. There exists no third fixed point from which we can look at them from a distance so as to observe the comprehensive doctrines as mere aspects of our past. The comprehensive doctrines instead survive within a generally shared political conception, in a permanent dialectic between two ethical stances, one of them being more profound and less shareable and the other, in contrast, being more superficial but more shareable.

Such a justification process is completed by the progressive formation within a liberal-democratic society of a "general and wide" reflective equilibrium, through which citizens endorse the basic principles underlying their institutional setting. This reflective equilibrium cannot be anticipated a priori, but eventually it is the only equilibrium that can offer a proper justification in a pluralistic regime. The success of this strategy already presupposes, however, the existence of an overlapping consensus. Habermas seems to think that this concedes too much to contextualism (HRE 121–3). Rawls distinguishes here between two kinds of consensus: the first is more empirical and only the second expresses a "reasonable overlapping consensus." Thus political sociology overlaps with normative theory and social stability becomes part of moral stability. The progressive formation of the overlapping consensus permits the parallel formation of a widespread "stability for the right reasons," which in turn constitutes a premise of "liberal legitimacy" (see chapter 11).

This Rawlsian solution does not make Habermas happy. He still maintains that the public justification based on overlapping consensus is a fortuitous event ("Reasonable" 91). Habermas' thesis rests on his criticism of Rawls' idea of the reasonable in PL. Habermas maintains that this idea appears to be dangerously in equilibrium between, on the one side, normative claims and, on the other, empirical claims. This difficult coexistence is revealed by Rawls' failure to present the "true" in tandem with the reasonable, where the true would – according to Habermas – correspond to cognitive validity and the reasonable to ethical-political validity. For Habermas, this parallelism is always impossible within Rawls' framework, because the logical space of truth is occupied by comprehensive doctrines. As a consequence, Rawls' idea of the reasonable cannot support epistemically significant claims in ethics and politics. Rawls' political theory, in other words, cannot pretend to ground itself on a true doctrine. It rather takes its significance from a successful compromise among different comprehensive doctrines, each of them having its own truth-claims. Substantially, this objection is not different from the previous and more general one: in a pluralistic regime Rawls' equilibrium

– for Habermas – cannot advance normative claims which present themselves as stronger than those advanced by different comprehensive doctrines. Habermas, on the contrary, opts for his discourse ethics in which one is supposed to reach a superior impartial point of view with all its truth-claims. For him, the moral point of view is partially implicit in the practice of socio-ontological public (democratic) argumentation. Habermas explicitly maintains: "The question is whether the citizens can grasp something as reasonable if it is not open to them to adopt a third standpoint besides that of an observer and the participant" ("Reasonable" 87).

For Rawls, on the contrary, reasonableness in politics is based on two premises: (i) every citizen respects other citizens; (ii) everyone is ready to accept the burdens of the judgment. From this point of view, the notion of truth is not useful for a political conception, and the reasonable does not express a *sui generis* truth-claim but rather a generic "reflective attitude to toleration." In other words, the notion of truth has nothing to do with political liberalism and in this regard the notion of the reasonable is more than enough (PL 394–5). It is of course controversial to decide whether the reasonable can properly be interpreted – as Habermas does – in terms of "abstinence" from truth (see chapter 11). Perhaps, the level of the reasonable presents a more profound epistemic vision, coherent with liberalism, a vision according to which you are supposed to accept many worldviews in ethics and politics.

A third Habermasian argument appeals to the relation between liberty of the ancients and liberty of the moderns. The liberty of the moderns covers classical civic liberties, whereas the liberty of the ancients concerns participation and communication. In the background, there is the distinction between public and private autonomy. Explicitly, Habermas says: "Rawls could satisfy more elegantly the burdens of proof he incurs with his strong and presumptively neutral concept of the moral person if he developed his substantive concepts and assumptions out of the procedure of the public use of reason" ("Reconciliation through the Public Use of Reason," 127).

For Habermas, the way in which the principles of justice are derived from the original position makes the citizens in "flesh and blood" subject to norms that have been already anticipated from a theoretical point of view (HRE 128). Thus: "they cannot reignite the radical democratic embers of the original position in the civic life of their society, for from their perspective all of the essential discourses of legitimation have already taken place" ("Reconciliation" 128).

In this regard, they can contribute to (what Rawls calls) political stability, but at the cost of being deprived of their political autonomy. The individual rights, so conceived, remain for Habermas implausibly pre-political. In the Rawlsian framework, a boundary separating the private from the public would arise, ignoring Habermas' postulate according to which human rights and popular sovereignty are supposed to be co-generated.[55] Only by assuming their co-originality, instead, could one make private and public autonomy correspond. Habermas' idea is that, in Rawls' political liberalism, individual rights would trump democratic practice. Rawls' theory of justice would expropriate citizens of their own democratic powers. The Habermasian alternative consists in taking seriously the democratic law-formation process. In this way, the discursive procedural approach would be confirmed. For Habermas, the meaning and force of the law cannot depend on philosophical reasoning. They rather presuppose the actual commitment of public reason in discursive democratic practices.

Habermas' point of view is here curiously both more modest and more ambitious than Rawls'. It is more modest as far as within its ambit the public use of reason is exclusively procedural: philosophers are not entitled to decide on substantive matters of justice, these being left to dialogue among citizens. It is more ambitious as far as Habermas does not accept a method of avoidance, which would permit – in Rawlsian optics – the bypassing of some fundamental controversies within the public use of reason. Rawls insists on this point by saying that his own position is philosophically much more prudent, avoiding matters concerning truth and rationality and confining itself within the political realm (PL 380). Furthermore, Rawls maintains that his theory leaves all decisions to the citizens, by returning to what is not only a dialogue but a veritable "omnilogue." For Rawls, this is already evident in the way in which the four-stage sequence is formulated in TJ. From this point of view, Habermas' thesis becomes necessarily metaphysical, at least in the traditional Hegelian sense, because it derives substantive elements of collective morality from the rational discourse presuppositions (HRE 378–9). Again, Habermas' criticism is based – for Rawls – on a comprehensive view that, as such, is unable to pass the test of pluralism.

It is here that Rawls turns again to his four-stage sequence argument. Habermas – according to Rawls – would not go beyond the first stage, that of the original position, and on this basis alone he imagines that the principles of justice are decided there "once and for all" (PL 399). For Rawls, instead, it is opportune to consider that passage from the first stage (original position) to the second (constitutional convention), to go then to the third in which there are "legislators enacting laws," and to end up with the fourth stage (application of the norms) (PL 397). A different level of information is available to each of these stages, in which citizens progressively confront each other and themselves with the main institutions. They do not derive their authority from the wisdom of a philosopher but rather from the "work of past generations" (PL 399).

In such a way, the political autonomy of citizens is guaranteed within political liberalism. Liberty and equality are not regulated by an instantaneous decision but rather by a continuous intergenerational process. In any case, the "non public values," as Rawls prefers to call them, cannot be derived by the ontological contents determined by a comprehensive doctrine. They are derived instead from the "will of the people" (PL 405). In this regard, Habermas would be wrong in assimilating Rawls' vision to a sort of natural law project, imposing on the citizens an external will (PL 406). Rawls' argument does not imply there are no injustices in the actual realization of the four-stage sequence. But these injustices depend more on the passage from an ideal theory to the real world than on a philosophical vision.

From this perspective, Rawls does not accept Habermas' main thesis in *Between Facts and Norms*. If one embraces that thesis, liberalism *à la* Rawls cannot show how "public and private autonomy are co-original and of equal weight" (PL 412). For Rawls, instead, the relation between the original position and the other three stages of the sequence ensure an opportune equilibrium between public and private autonomy. In this regard, Rawls is keen to deny that his liberalism "leaves political and private autonomy in unresolved competition" (PL 416). Political liberalism – without exception, for Rawls – faces instead a structural and inevitable dilemma of democracy: moral laws cannot be imposed on people's sovereignty, and people's sovereignty should not violate some basic rights. Substantially, says Rawls, within political liberalism there is no "unresolved competition" between public and private autonomy.

The last argument invites Rawls to criticize the procedure–substance distinction, which in some way Habermas would impose on his own view. Rawls' thesis here is twofold. On the one hand, procedure and substance are not easily separable, and the idea of an agreement based exclusively on procedures is illusory. On the other hand, procedural justice depends on substantive justice, as Rawls says with Joshua Cohen. The idea that one can reach an agreement on procedures, bypassing substance, is for Rawls utopian in the bad sense. On the other hand, Rawls maintains that even Habermas' discourse ethics is not fully procedural (as Habermas would claim), because discourse ethics itself presupposes a background substantive theory (PL 424ff.). The idea that there exists a kind of purely procedural legitimation works if and only if this legitimation assumes some fundamental criteria of justice. Habermas himself – so Rawls says – should accept such an account if he is to be loyal to the discourse ethics project.

7.3.2 A final evaluation

A balanced evaluation of the HRE is difficult. There are many reasons for this. One of them consists in the twofold level at which Habermas develops his criticism. On the one hand, his objections work within Rawls' paradigm; on the other hand, they work from outside it. From this second point of view, Habermas is probably more effective. This implies that to make sense of what he says we must take into consideration certain basic philosophical distinctions between Habermas and Rawls. First, Habermas finds implausible what he sees as Rawls' reduction of the political to the public. Rawls would sacrifice – according to this vision – the political significance of a substantial part of the public sphere.

For Habermas, the distinction itself between background culture and public reason is intrinsically flawed. Rawls insists in the HRE that he does not subscribe to this reductionist view. In this regard, notwithstanding Rawls' denial, the difference at stake here is clear. For Habermas, the limits of the political cannot, a priori, be decided either constitutionally or philosophically. They must instead be decided via an actual debate among real individuals. This debate presupposes the generalization coming from a non-distorted public discussion. Rawls' thesis is more philosophically and constitutionally oriented on this point.

The same difference is confirmed by the way in which Habermas reads Rawls on the participant–observer distinction. According to Habermas, Rawls would make the observer disappear in the most relevant social dynamics, starting from the overlapping consensus. Rawls, again, denies occupying such a position, but he does not convince Habermas.

This fundamental difference between Habermas and Rawls is more evident when one reflects upon the priority of right. Such a priority cannot be determined – for Habermas – via philosophical or constitutional arguments. Just citizens, animated by different conceptions of the good, can specify what one must mean by "right" and its limits.

For Habermas, analogous argumentation can be applied to the "monological" nature of Rawls' reasonableness. Habermas believes that Rawls tends to pre-decide on what the reasonable is and what its limits are, imposing this decision as a constraint upon the political debate. Of course, Habermas is convinced that things should go the other way round: it is the political debate that should decide what is reasonable, and not vice versa.[56] The aprioristic way would make Rawls' view fundamentally monological, with the consequence that it fails in the attempt to transform Kantism into a more social vision. The omnilogue, mentioned by Rawls, would not take place.

The fundamental intellectual cleavage is here between Habermas' theory of communicative action and Rawls' liberal pluralism. The reader – to settle the dispute – is so obliged to take a position on general philosophical positions, concerning which it is far too difficult to make a stand. Perhaps, to make sense of Habermas' criticism one should remember his Marxist origins. In this regard, the very idea of distributive justice is an abstraction in the light of the structural relations of power and class. To speak purely of distributive justice would mean overlooking the fact of *dominium*. Habermas bets, from this point of view, on reproducing in the realm of a critical theory of communication some basic constraints that are supposed to make sense of the *dominium*. The suppression in the dialogue of relevant and generalizable interests must be considered a signal of a more general socio-economic problem. The aim is basically to eliminate the actual *dominium* via the overcoming of communicative constraints.

8

From *A Theory of Justice* to *Political Liberalism*

Chapter 8 is divided into three parts, respectively dedicated to: (i) the revisions Rawls made to the original text in the second edition of TJ; (ii) JFR; and (iii) KCMT.

These parts are preceded by an overview of Rawls' major works (8.1). In 8.2, I discuss the revisions to the first edition of TJ. These revisions are mainly directed at avoiding misunderstandings. Nevertheless, there are significant changes. The most important ones coincide with the reformulation of the first principle of justice and with the new derivation of the list of primary goods. In both cases, Rawls tracks the bases for the second version in the "highest-order interests" of the citizens of a liberal-democratic society, anticipating a motif that will become foundational within PL. There are also other relevant revisions, like the substantial refutation of the analogy between the difference principle and the maximin rule of decision, the downsizing of the "general conception," and the introduction of the notion of "property-owning democracy."

In 8.3, I discuss JFR. This book came out in 2001, after PL (1993, 1996), but it substantially precedes PL in terms of content, being a collection of lectures given by Rawls during earlier years. JFR is a significant effort at self-explanation and self-criticism. In the book Rawls has two explicit principal aims. One is to rectify some serious faults in TJ that have obscured – according to the author – some basic ideas of justice as fairness. The other is to connect the conception of justice presented in TJ with the main ideas found in the essays from 1984 onwards. From this second point of view, there are two important innovations: a new proposition of Kantian constructivism (different from the one presented in KCMT) and an original formulation of the political conception. More generally, in JFR, we can say that Rawls states in a kind of abridged form some of the basic concepts we will see discussed in PL.

In 8.4, I examine KCMT. This article gathers the so-called "Dewey Lectures," given by Rawls at Columbia University in 1980. A long article, divided into three parts, KCMT is particularly significant in affording a passage between Rawls1 and Rawls2. Janus-like, it closes some paths suggested in TJ and opens other ones that we will find analytically reformulated in PL. Probably the most significant innovation of the article consists in presenting a Kantian view, within which the conditions for justifying a conception of justice hold only when a basis is established for political reasoning and understanding within a public culture. This social role of a conception of justice is formulated in order to allow all members of society to make their shared institutions and basic arrangements mutually acceptable.

In addressing the public culture of a liberal-democratic society, Rawls appeals to Kantian constructivism to formulate a conception of the person implicitly affirmed in that culture. This conception of the person, presented in the first Dewey Lecture, implies the distinction and the compatibility between the "Rational" and the "Reasonable." The Reasonable, without a conception of the good, does not provide any reason to care about notions of right and justice. On the other hand, the Reasonable subordinates the Rational because the principles of right limit the ends that can be pursued.[1] The Rawlsian conception of the person is political, and it corresponds to the idea of free and equal citizen, examined in the second Dewey lecture. In the third Dewey lecture, Rawls – starting from Kantian constructivism – formulates a notion of objectivity in terms of a suitably constructed social point of view.

8.1 From *A Theory of Justice* to *Political Liberalism*

There is continuity between the period of Rawls' work based on TJ, or "Rawls1," and the period based on PL, or "Rawls2." Abiding by the hermeneutic principle not only to read the whole in terms of its parts but also to read the parts in terms of the whole, I suggest that TJ ought to be read in the light not only of the secondary literature regarding it, but also of PL and the essays leading up to it. More specifically, I will argue that the theory of justice as fairness, which constitutes the heart of TJ, develops into a comprehensive reasonable theory. It thus becomes a specific conception of justice and not a universal account of the concept of justice, albeit a specific conception that is basic for the model of pluralism set out in PL.

This reading extends beyond the first edition of TJ and PL, and concerns the following texts in particular:

(i) the numerous revisions made to the first edition of TJ, which first appear in the second German edition of 1975;

(ii) the publication of JFR, in which the passage from Rawls1 to Rawls2 is presented most clearly;

(iii) the publication, in 1980, of KCMT, a text which, given its importance for the passage between the two periods, I consider to represent the dividing line between them;

(iv) the articles of the late 1970s and 1980s, in which various aspects of TJ are critically reconsidered, and the way prepared for the publication of PL.

It is not easy to identify and date these different texts precisely. The revisions to TJ were made over a lengthy period of time, from 1971 onwards. Although JFR was published in 2001, a very similar draft circulated among students and scholars for many years before, in the form of lectures entitled "Guided Tour" (mainly concerned with Rawls' own interpretations and critical revisions of TJ). KCMT can be dated to 1980 with precision, but it encompasses the content of certain articles of the 1970s. Finally, the articles of the late 1970s and 1980s constitute a kind of continuum, in which Rawls moves progressively from his earlier to his later paradigm. Most of the novel elements introduced in these articles can be found in KCMT, PL, and JFR. For this reason, in this chapter I will concentrate only on the main revisions made to TJ, on JFR, and on KCMT.

I will follow Kukathas and Pettit in dividing Rawls' revisions of TJ into two periods. However, while Kukathas and Pettit distinguish the revisions of 1981–2 from those of 1982–9, I see no reason not to consider 1980, rather than 1982, as the dividing line between the two periods, particularly given that 1980's KCMT appears to mark the passage from Rawls1 to Rawls2, as Kukathas and Pettit also recognize.[2]

More significant than their dating of the two periods are the grounds upon which Kukathas and Pettit distinguish them. They hold that the first period concerns a substantial revision of the Kantianism involved in the theory of justice as fairness that Rawls had presented in the first edition of TJ, while the second develops the piecemeal formulation of the political conception that would later be central to PL. This distinction makes for persuasive readings of some significant articles of the 1970s, such as "Fairness to Goodness" and "A Kantian Conception of Equality," both of 1975, and "The Basic Structure as Subject" of 1977, and rightly implies that the Rawls1 period ends with KCMT of 1980.[3] The second period begins with KCMT, proceeds. with the Tanner Lectures of 1982 on "The Basic Liberties and Their Priority" and ends with the articles of the second half of the 1980s. Articles such as "Social Unity and Primary Goods" of 1982, and particularly "Justice as Fairness: Political not Metaphysical" of 1985 and "The Idea of Overlapping Consensus" and "The Priority of Right and Ideas of the Good" of 1988 employ the political conception which is later central to PL. This thematic–temporal distinction should not be pushed too far – for instance, "The Independence of Moral Theory" of 1975 is rather awkwardly included in the first period. But the distinction generally holds and is confirmed by Rawls' inclusion in PL of the above-mentioned articles of the 1980s, from KCMT onwards.

The textual revisions made to TJ in 1974–5 anticipate some of the theoretical developments that are present in the above-mentioned articles of the second half of the 1980s. These revisions also reveal that the political conception cannot be fully understood without also understanding Rawls' rejection of the "congruence" between the right and the good as a ground for stability. A reading of JFR is essential in this regard, although the full implications of the rejection of such "congruence" are made clear only in PL.

8.2 Revision of *A Theory of Justice*

The standard edition of TJ is now the second English edition, published in 1999. As mentioned above, this edition presents the modifications which Rawls made to the first, 1971 edition, for the most part between 1974 and February–March 1975. He first published these modifications in the German edition of 1975, and then in editions in other languages, including French, Portuguese, and eventually English. However, the task of tracing the critical debates surrounding the book is complicated by the fact that these debates have generally continued to focus on the first edition (until 1999). Still, the second English edition includes a conversion table which allows one to move more easily between the two editions.

The comparison between the two editions is significant for the understanding of Rawls' theory. He made modifications, often substantial ones, to 130 of the approximately 600 pages of the first edition. At least a quarter of these modifications are modifications of content, regarding theoretical points with which Rawls had become dissatisfied either in the light of others' criticisms or for reasons of his own. Many of the other modifications, although primarily stylistic, are often also intended to correct errors or obscurities of content.

The meaning of these revisions is difficult to grasp adequately, even when one reads the two editions in parallel, as I did in editing the second Italian edition. However, Rawls himself provides some guidance in his preface to the second editions in French, Portuguese, and English, when he writes that he was primarily concerned with revising his treatment of two main aspects of the theory of justice as fairness.[4] Firstly, regarding the first principle of justice and the conception of liberty that is central to it, he responds to a criticism made by H. L. A. Hart in an article of 1973, according to which it is impossible to derive this principle and its priorities from the rationality of the parties in the original position (see chapter 3).[5] Although he provides a more lengthy and detailed presentation of his response in an article of 1983, "The Basic Liberties and their Priority," later included as the eighth lecture in PL, as far as the revisions to TJ are concerned the most relevant passages are sections 11 and 82 of TJ. Here Rawls now claims that the basic liberties – from now on referred to exclusively in the plural – and their relative priorities are necessary in order to guarantee the social conditions essential for all citizens to realize their two moral powers – namely, the capacity to have a sense of justice and the capacity to have a conception of the good.[6]

Rawls articulates this claim in terms of two basic cases, the first of which concerns the conception of the good and the second the sense of justice. His additions to the text are dedicated primarily to the first case, and, in particular, to a partial revision of his "thin" conception of the good. He does not also revise his understanding of the sense of justice, probably because characterizing the contracting parties in the original position as having a sense of justice *ab initio* would contravene the assumption of their reciprocal disinterest.[7] Still, in attributing to the contracting parties a "common higher interest" in developing their moral powers, Rawls makes an important change to his theory, one that opens the way to Kantian constructivism. (TJ; rev edn. xii)

The second main aspect of the theory of justice as fairness that Rawls aimed to revise regards the nature of primary goods. In presenting his theory of goodness in chapter 8 of the first edition, Rawls describes primary goods simply as those goods which all rational persons want, independently of their goals. Recognizing that this description obscured the moral conception of the person that underlies the list of primary goods, in the second edition Rawls appeals to the two moral powers – that is, to the capacities to have a conception of the good and a sense of justice – in order to argue that persons who have highest-order interests require primary goods in order to exercise and develop their moral powers. From then on, Rawls justifies primary goods as those goods which free and equal persons require in order to maintain relationships of reciprocity and cooperation. The relevant revisions begin at section 15 of TJ, although, again, they are treated more completely elsewhere – in this case, in the articles "Social Unity and Primary Goods" and "The Priority of Right and Ideas of the Good," the latter also later included as the fifth lecture in PL.[8]

In these articles, Rawls reconsiders five senses of the "good" used in his work from TJ onwards, namely: (i) goodness as rationality, (ii) primary goods, (iii) permitted conceptions of the good, (iv) political virtues, and (v) the goodness of a well-ordered society. This reconsideration is made necessary by the lack of a distinction between a comprehensive theory and a political conception in TJ (PL, Introduction to the paperback edition).

Beyond the revisions made to these two aspects of the theory, Rawls also makes less general ones that are nonetheless of theoretical importance. These include his deletion of the majority of references to the "general conception" of justice as fairness in sections 26, 46, and 82 of the first edition. These deletions might be thought to imply that Rawls now attributes less importance to the difference principle, since the "general conception" of justice had established a basic egalitarian presupposition on the basis of which the difference principle could be generalized. But this implication finds no support in Rawls' defense of the difference principle against his opponents, in which he retains the theoretical argument against utilitarianism and re-emphasizes the distinction between his position and Nozick's libertarian claims. These points are treated more systematically in JFR, the publication of which after PL tells against some commentators' claims that Rawls abandons the difference principle in PL. On this point, in the revised edition of TJ the claim as to the social nature of individuals' talents is retained and the injustice of rewarding those bestowed with more talents is re-emphasized.

The section on "The Tendency to Equality" itself is revised to make more modest claims. In particular, while in the first edition Rawls writes that "the difference principle represents, in effect, an agreement to regard the distribution of natural talents as a common asset and to share in the benefits of this distribution whatever it turns out to be," in the second edition he states merely that the principle represents "an agreement to regard the distribution of natural talents as in some respects a common asset and to share in the greater social and economic benefits made possible by the complementarities of this distribution." (TJ 104; rev. edn. 87) Relatedly, he modifies the following passage, which in the first edition reads, "No one deserves his greater natural capacity nor merits a more favorable starting place in society. But it does not follow that one should eliminate these distinctions. There is another way to deal with them." (TJ 102; rev. edn. 87) In the second edition, this passage is modified to make the following, more cautious claim: "But of coursem, this is no reason to ignore, much less to eliminate, these distinctions."(TJ; rev. edn. 87)

The removal of the reference to "another way" of treating this problem would appear to be a response to Nozick's criticism.[9] Still, it must be admitted that in these particular instances, although it may be somewhat clearer, the revised edition is probably slightly less effective.[10] Rawls also seems to modify the nature of the original position itself, for one of the most revised chapters of the text is the third chapter. In the revised version of this chapter, Rawls tends to present the original position less as a deductive argument, capable of identifying principles of justice independently, and more as a simple "device of representation." For instance, he no longer presents the original position as an interpretation that takes the perspective of noumenal selves, but rather claims only that it resembles such an interpretation. He also adds to his account of the original position more contextual features specifying the nature of a liberal-democratic system, in an attempt to defend the Kantian foundation of the theory against the criticisms of communitarians and Hegelians.[11] The price that he is willing to pay for this is an empiricist reading of Kant, which is undertaken primarily in articles of the second half of the 1970s, and most clearly in "A Well-Ordered Society" of 1979 (previously published, in 1975, under the title "A Kantian Conception of Equality").[12] But this reading is also present in the second edition of TJ, and particularly in section 40, which presents the Kantian interpretation of the theory of justice as fairness and to which Rawls adds an insistence on "abandoning" Kantian dualism. (TJ; rev. edn. 226–7).

Besides these revisions to the third chapter, Rawls paid particular attention to revising the second and fourth chapters, and made very few modifications to the rest of the book – among the latter modifications, the most notable are the substantial rewritings of part of section 44 on "just savings," which involves a radical reworking of the first edition's treatment of intergenerational justice, and section 82 on the priorities among liberties, which reflects the revision of the treatment of the first principle of justice and the related idea of liberty that I discussed above.

In his preface to the second English edition, dated November 1990, and then later in JFR, Rawls also claims that, had he been able, he would have made two more radical changes to the theory of justice as fairness, one of which is of particular theoretical significance.[13] This regards the way in which the two principles of justice are derived from the original position. In particular, Rawls claims that each of the two principles ought to have been compared with utilitarianism separately, since, while the first is more readily acceptable, the distinction between the difference principle and the principle of average utility is more subtle and can be a plausible subject of reasonable disagreement. Again, however, this claim should not be taken to imply that Rawls now considers the difference principle to be less important – indeed, in this regard he adds a new claim to section 28 in the revised edition: namely, that his theory is preferable to the principle of average utility also because it concerns an agreement between real people and not mere receptacles of utility.

Of all of Rawls' revisions to TJ, there is a further one that implies a broader rethinking of his theory. This concerns the relation between the theory of justice as fairness and the theory of rational choice.[14] While in the first edition Rawls presents TJ as part of a theory of rational choice, he gradually distances it from this. It is not clear how much this revision derives from internal developments in his thinking and how much it owes to the criticisms made of the formal and deductive aspects of the theory by scholars such as Arrow, Harsanyi, and Sen. Whatever its origins, this revision opens a huge gap between the difference principle, which Rawls continues to defend, and the maximin rule of rational choice, which he now generally discards. With reference to the analogy between the difference principle and the maximin rule, Rawls adds the following, unequivocal statement to section 13: "Economics may wish to refer to the difference principle as the maximin criterion, but I have carefully avoided this name for several reasons. The maximin criterion is generally understood as a rule for choice under great uncertainty (sect. 26), whereas the difference principle is a principle of justice." (TJ; rev. edn. 72–3)

An analogous claim is also made in JFR.[15] It is also notable that in the revised edition of the text Rawls removes the word "choice," and the verb "to choose," when used in relation to the principle of justice and the original position, and generally replaces them with the word "agreement," or the verb "to agree." Thus, while the theory of justice as fairness had an undeniable relation to rational choice in the first edition of TJ, now the distinction between the two is explicit. A concrete indication of this change is given by the distinction between the "Reasonable" and the "Rational" that Rawls introduces in the revised edition, and the systematic subordination of the latter to the former.

As he puts it in KCMT, "the Reasonable presupposes and subordinates the Rational" (notably, a claim that he had already made in his Ph.D. thesis).[16] In chapter 10 below, I will show how significant this distinction is for Rawls' development of a new theory of stability.

In order to understand Rawls' theory of justice as fairness, including the revisions that he made to it, it is generally necessary also to read: (i) the articles that he published in the 1980s; (ii) JFR, published in 2001 but circulated among scholars for many years before; and (iii) Rawls' second major work, PL, published in a first edition in 1993 and in a second in 1996. These readings allow one to understand the specific modifications that Rawls made to his theory in preparing the second edition of TJ, modifications that would otherwise remain obscure. They allow the revision of the liberty principle, the revision of the concept of primary goods, the reconsideration of the argumentative status of the original position, the distinction of justice as fairness from the theory of rational choice, and the greater emphasis placed on the institutional tradition and the history of liberal democracies to be incorporated in a coherent, innovative reading. On this reading, the stability of the system is clearly given priority over its normative desirability, and realism is generally given a more explicit role than is often supposed. In other words, one cannot read TJ today without also giving sufficient attention to what Rawls wrote later, beginning with the revisions that he made to TJ itself.

In the terms used by Rawls himself in his later works, a contemporary reader – that is, one who has read not only TJ, but also at least PL – can no longer treat his TJ as a comprehensive moral conception, but must rather consider it as a political conception. Generally, this means that TJ must now be read more as political theory than as applied ethics.[17] This has profound implications. To arrive at principles of justice one must begin from the moral nature of citizens as free and equal, as Rawls has written in an addition to section 26.(TJ; rev. edn. 131–2)

This change of emphasis reduces the significance given to distributive justice, and reinforces the aspect of the theory concerned with the moral powers of having a conception of the good and a sense of justice. Of course, a revisionary reading such as this reduces the universal and deductive character of the argument from the original position. But, in exchange, it offers a hermeneutics of liberal democracy and of the kind of moral personality that best corresponds to it. Furthermore, this reading raises the issue of the relationship between reasonable pluralism and stability, which constitutes the core of PL.

8.3 The Restatement

In interpreting PL as continuous with TJ, as I have proposed doing, it is helpful to begin with JFR. This book derives from part of the course in political philosophy which Rawls held regularly at Harvard. Rawls made only minor changes to the content of the lectures as they were in 1989 – such as the addition of section 50 on the family, the removal of the sections on global justice (the treatment of which had been superseded by *The Law of Peoples*), and some reorganization of sections within the text.[18] Nor are there significant differences between the published version and the manuscript of the lectures that circulated during the 1980s under the title, "Guided Tour." This is due partly to Rawls' illness, which prevented him from revising the text before publication (notable particularly in parts 4 and 5 of the book), and his editor's unwillingness to make significant changes herself.

JFR is of particular interest for the development of an interpretation of PL as continuous with TJ because it treats many themes discussed in the texts that Rawls wrote in the period between the publication of these two major works – basically, between 1984 and 1989. It does so in a way that, in the light also of the implications of his revisions of TJ, allows for a revisionary reading of TJ as consistent with PL. Indeed, Rawls begins his preface to JFR by stating that:

> In this work I have two aims. One is to rectify the more serious faults in TJ that have obscured the main ideas of justice as fairness, as I called the conception of justice presented in that book . . . The other aim is to connect into one unified statement the conception of justice presented in Theory and the main ideas found in my essays beginning in 1974.[19]

Reading JFR may therefore help support a reading of Rawls1 as continuous with Rawls2, and may even offer more in this regard than PL itself despite the fact that the latter is a more carefully prepared text and has a more significant place among Rawls' works. Indeed, I will attempt to show that in JFR Rawls neither rejects the main claims made in TJ nor modifies substantially the view of justice that he presented there. Rather, he aims to reformulate the argumentative structure of the theory. This is indicated in the text primarily by the attention that Rawls gives to re-emphasizing the egalitarianism which informs his whole intellectual project, as well as by the emphasis that he gives to the second principle of justice and its defense. Both these moves demonstrate that the passage from Rawls1 to Rawls2 is not a passage from a defense of both liberty and equality, and the relevant principles of justice, to a defense only of liberty and the first principle of justice.[20] Indeed, the first principle is revised and corrected in JFR no less than the second principle.

Two elements of Rawls' revision of the theory presented in TJ can be identified in JFR: a broadly Kantian reading of the priority of right and a more political, rather than metaphysical or ethical, conception of the theory of justice. The Kantian element is present primarily in KCMT of 1980 and also in the articles published in 1985. In JFR, this element plays a role in: (i) Rawls' opposition to utilitarianism, as in TJ; (ii) the inclusion of the theory of justice within the theory of rational choice, unlike in the first edition of TJ; and (iii) the fundamental parts played by the notion of the person and by constructivism. The political conception of the theory of justice, on the other hand, comes to the fore in the works of the 1990s. The political conception emphasizes the notions of stability and publicity – the former understood in non-Hobbesian terms – each of which is derived explicitly from Kant.

Admittedly, if it holds, this distinction between a renewed Kantianism and an increasingly political conception of the theory is more conceptual than textual and often involves merely subtle differences. The two elements are often interrelated and Rawls' revisions to the theory often concern both of them. Kukathas and Pettit's distinction of a Kantian and liberal revision of the theory in 1981–2 from the formulation of the political conception in 1982–9 therefore presents Rawls' development as rather more linear than it actually was. It is more accurate to identify both Kantian liberal and political elements in the writings of the period between 1974 and 1989, and to see KCMT of 1980 as marking the beginning of his extended attempt to revise his theory.

These two elements are both found in the more mature and coherent view presented in PL. For this reason, it is again worth recalling that JFR was written before PL, although it was published after it. The two main theoretical themes of JFR – first presented in KCMT, albeit without the emphasis that they would later be given – are those of reasonableness and public reason, both fundamental constitutive elements of PL.

Beyond developing self-criticism, Rawls reveals an attempt to reply to various kinds of critiques by bringing together elements introduced in several earlier works. In this regard, Rawls re-emphasizes and defends the Kantian nature of the theory, primarily against communitarian and Hegelian criticisms, by reintroducing claims made in articles like "Themes in Kant's Moral Philosophy" (1989) and 1980's KCMT. Rawls does not reply to these critics by distancing himself from their positions, but rather by moving closer to them. That is, he becomes more Hegelian, although Hegel on his rather idiosyncratic reading is a Kantian liberal. Most clearly, in his LHMP, he presents Hegel as almost his predecessor, considering himself to be an institutional thinker like Hegel. Rawls thus presents a liberal and Kantian "Hegel" in terms of the notion of *Versöhnung* or "reconciliation," between reason and history, individualism and sense of community. In the first part of JFR Rawls states explicitly that such reconciliation constitutes one of the four fundamental goals of political philosophy.

This allows Rawls to re-emphasize two aspects of TJ that his critics had not fully appreciated. Firstly, he insists that the individualism of the theory is compensated for by the highly social and collective nature of the cooperative project that underlies it as a whole.[21] Rawls' conception of the person – a term that he prefers to "individual" – is based on an idealized view of citizenship, and, being thus of a political nature, ultimately bears little or no relation to the "disembodied self" to which communitarians object.[22] Secondly, the transcendental Kantianism of the theory is qualified by a strong institutional, social, and historical grounding. As Rawls puts it in KCMT:

> We are not trying to find a conception of justice suitable for all societies regardless of their particular social or historical circumstances. We want to settle a fundamental disagreement over the just form of basic institutions within a democratic society under modern conditions. We look to ourselves and to our future, and reflect our disputes since, let's say, the Declaration of Independence.[23]

Rawls makes clear that he does not aim to provide a transcendental conception of justice valid for all times and places. Rather, he presents a view of a well-ordered society capable of providing a public conception of justice in contemporary liberal-democratic societies such as the United States. If this is still Kantianism, then it is a broadly contextualized and historicized one.

Rawls also responds in JFR to the standard libertarian criticisms. Specifically, in sections 15–16 of JFR he distinguishes his view of the basic structure from the more historical one of Nozick and Locke. He had always held that the central role of the basic structure in his theory did not preclude its having a historical character, if only in the sense that the theory is not presented as "absolute" but as holding in a determinate context and the principles of justice are supposed to act on the primary institutions over time.[24] In JFR, however, his concern is with Nozick's neo-Lockean claim that distributive outcomes are justified better by historical processes than by any theoretical argument based on end-state principles. Against this "historical process view," Rawls proposes a "social process view," which insists on the arbitrariness of the initial distribution of talents and skills and of distributive differences among persons based on them. Basically, he holds that the priority of the basic structure requires that importance be given to the initial conditions in which we enter into society. Libertarians such as Nozick treat the starting points as negligible when compared with the importance of individual merit.

In sections 20–3 of JFR Rawls re-emphasizes his criticism of any non-egalitarian distribution based on merit. In this regard, he has in mind Nozick's well-known criticisms.[25] Here, as in the earlier sections, he expresses himself cautiously. His basic reply is that individuals do not have merit independently of institutions, and that it is only in an institutional system that behavior can be defined as deserving of reward. For Rawls, common assets are not constituted by talents – which he too considers to be "attached" to the person – but by the distribution of goods which, for reasons of reciprocity, can be treated only in collective terms.[26]

The third object of Rawls' replies consists of the criticisms made of the maximin principle as a criterion of social choice by scholars of welfare economics such as Harsanyi and Arrow.[27] In this regard, repeating claims made in earlier works, he reduces the formal aspect of the theory, and presents the difference principle, not as the conclusion of a rational choice argument, but rather as a political element of the theory.

The fourth kind of criticism to which Rawls replies in JFR concerns the criticisms made of the first principle of justice by Herbert Hart, among others. In reply, Rawls emphasizes the idea of a system of liberty and tends to give more emphasis to the value of liberty in the theory overall.[28]

The fifth kind of criticism consists of those made by Sen on the grounds of his capabilities approach, regarding the lack of flexibility of primary goods. Here Rawls' replies are based on claims made in "The Priority of Right and Ideas of the Good" (1988) and "The Idea of Overlapping Consensus" (1987), and, besides perhaps indicating the seriousness and rigor with which he treats his critics' objections, they add little to the points already made in revising these aspects in TJ. The general idea is still that of a political Kantianism, which, on the one hand, gives meaning to the fundamental liberties and, on the other, reduces the importance given to the formal aspect of the theory. Rawls himself, however, considers his primary aim in JFR to be the defense of the two principles of justice. He divides the numerous criticisms made of these principles into two kinds – namely, those concerning the formulation and content of the principles and those concerned with the deduction of the principles from the original position. He dedicates much space in JFR to the second kind of criticism, presenting the original position as a "heuristic device" and thus as a "model conception" intended to mediate between those of the moral person and the well-ordered society.[29] Rather than providing a purely deductive derivation of the principles of justice, then, the original position is increasingly presented as a heuristic device with the function of organizing the various elements of the theory, from the general moral argument to reflective equilibrium. Indeed, on the last page of KCMT, Rawls writes explicitly that: "So understood, the original position is not an axiomatic (or deductive) basis from which principles are derived but a procedure for singling out principles most fitting to the conception of the person most likely to be held, at least implicitly, in a modern democratic society."[30]

Such an interpretation of the original position might be considered controversial. But it is Rawls himself who reinterprets the original position in this way. If this interpretation is to be rejected, then, it must be on the basis of a careful consideration of the claims and arguments that he makes regarding it and not merely out of nostalgia for a supposed purity of the original theory.

Furthermore, Rawls relates this reinterpretation of TJ to the positive part of JFR in which he formulates a political conception of justice and claims that TJ can be understood only in terms of this conception. It might be thought that the revisions to the first edition in response to critics are more Kantian than I am suggesting. That is, the revisions may go beyond the particular sense of "Kantian" mentioned above and the political conception itself may be more independent of this basic Kantianism. Even the fact that the basic elements of the political conception are presented in an article dedicated to "Kantian Constructivism in Moral Theory" indicates this. The "public" aspect of the political conception ultimately depends on an extended inter-pretation of the Kantian requirement of publicity. In several articles of the 1980s, and in KCMT, Rawls claims that the conception of justice as fairness is political rather than metaphysical. Rawls employs certain key ideas, which include the following:

- the distinction between the comprehensive and the reasonable;
- the emphasis on the moral person, characterized in terms of the two main moral capacities;
- the importance of publicity;
- the importance of stability;
- the understanding of society as a fair system of cooperation based on reciprocity;
- the notion of a basic structure.

The primary difference between JFR and TJ has to do with presentation, not content. Even the fact that Rawls begins with the "fundamental ideas" constitutes a significant shift in argumentative strategy. The original posi-tion and the principles of justice are justified not on the basis of a few simple premises, but on the grounds of the rich fabric of a liberal-democratic society. Liberal-democratic society provides the most significant premises – such as those of the person and the well-ordered society. Of these premises, it is that of the person which reveals itself to be the most significant innovation in Rawls' reinterpretation of the theory.

8.4 Kantian Constructivism

KCMT provides a Kantian reformulation of certain parts of TJ and an inno-vative treatment of questions that are later central to PL.[31] In addition to reformulating TJ and anticipating PL, KCMT systematically reformulates the notion of publicity. The invention of "constructivism" provides one way for Rawls to bring together his different justificatory strategies, such as the original position and reflective equilibrium.[32]

Rawls begins with his own particular understanding of the term "Kantian."[33] Besides his obvious intention to indicate an analogy between Kant's work and his own, Rawls' reinterpretation of his own Kantian reading of TJ – pre-sented particularly in section 40 of the book, "The Kantian Interpretation" – is interesting for its explicit goal of eliminating the dualisms of Kant's thought. Rawls attributes a similar goal to Dewey (to whom the "Kantian Constructivism in Moral Theory" lectures were dedicated) in pursuing a Hegelian criticism of Kant.[34] In particular, for Rawls it is necessary to relate the Kantian interpretation of TJ to the political ideas implicit in a political culture. As he writes at the beginning of KCMT:

> On the Kantian view that I shall present, conditions for justifying a conception of justice hold only when a basis is established for political reasoning and understanding within a public culture. The social role of a conception of justice is to enable all members of society to make mutually acceptable to one another their shared institutions and basic arrangements.[35]

More generally, on the following page he writes:

> The aim of political philosophy, when it presents itself in the public culture of a democratic society, is to articulate and to make explicit those shared notions and principles thought to be already present in common sense . . . In addressing the public culture of a democratic society, Kantian constructivism hopes to invoke a conception of the person implicitly affirmed in that culture.[36]

There is, of course, a sense in which Rawls' constructivism is undoubtedly Kantian. It offers an ethical justification that is intended to be ontologically anti-realist without thereby sacrificing objectivity. But it is difficult to treat his insistence on a shared democratic political culture as Kantian.[37] The grounding of the theory in such a public culture is important for Rawls because it connects moral objectivity to a social perspective and, more generally, involves a kind of justification in political philosophy that is practical, rather than epistemological. (Notably, his rejection of Kantian dualisms does not extend to that between theory and practice.) It is in JFR that he states explicitly that a conception of justice can have a meaning only as part of a tradition and a culture. This is an important point both for the revision of TJ and for the view later presented in PL, which begins with the shared convictions of free and equal citizens regarding a well-ordered society. For Rawls, beginning with societal values does not imply a collapse into relativism because he reformulates moral objectivity in Kantian terms.[38]

Rawls begins the first lecture, entitled "Rational and Full Autonomy," by presenting the theory of justice in terms of the relations between three "model conceptions": the original position, the well-ordered society and the moral person. Surprisingly given its role in TJ, the original position is presented as the least important of the three since it depends on and links the other two. The presentation of the model conception of the well-ordered society provides few novelties in setting out a public conception of justice, a notion of the members of a well-ordered society as free and equal persons, and certain more "residual" requirements, such as stability. This conception of the well-ordered society is highly idealized and depends on the basic structure, which Rawls generally identifies with the nation-state. In referring to free and equal persons, it also relates clearly to the model conception of the moral person. Indeed, the latter is the most novel of the three model conceptions and provides the basis for Rawls' substantial reinterpretation of the theory of justice as fairness.[39]

Although Rawls is extremely cautious in his presentation of the model conception of the moral person, almost as if he wished to hide its novelty, this conception redefines Kantian constructivism as a constructivism that adequately incorporates a Kantian conception of the person. More precisely, it incorporates an ideal of the person taking "ideal" in an ethical-political sense and "person" in a largely psychological one.[40] Rawlsian "persons" possess the moral powers of having a sense of justice and a conception of the good. These powers are expressed in the formulation of highest-order interests, being the heart of the ideal of the person. Moreover, they ground the identification of primary goods, which Rawls had justified differently in TJ.

The notion of a moral power as that to which responsibility and rights are attributed is less innocuous than it might seem. Rawls' caution is probably due partly to the awareness that to require such a "normal" capacity excludes those who do not possess it, such as the mentally disabled. This is significant, because the reciprocity central to Rawls' view of justice is applicable only to persons who cooperate normally in the economic and social life of the basic structure. This does not preclude providing assistance to those with disabilities, but it implies that such assistance must be of a humanitarian nature and not a matter of justice. Much of Rawls' treatment of international justice is also informed by this particular idea, although many commentators have failed to appreciate it. The same can be said for Rawls' criticisms of so-called "luck egalitarianism," which I discussed in chapter 4.

However, the most noteworthy element introduced in this part of the first lecture of KCMT is the deconstruction of the concept of the autonomy of the person. Here Rawls distinguishes rational autonomy from full autonomy. The discussion of rational autonomy offers little of note, beyond simply making explicit the role of such autonomy in the theory. Rawls' main aim in this regard is to translate the highest-order interests into inputs for the parties to the original position. Full autonomy, on the other hand, provides a kind of procedural version of the categorical imperative and of Kantian autonomy. While rational autonomy is based on the "Rational," full autonomy is based on the "Reasonable," terms which here are introduced for the first time and become crucial to the theory overall. As Rawls writes in a passage that has since become particularly well known: "The Reasonable presupposes and subordinates the Rational . . . The Reasonable presupposes the Rational, because without conceptions of the good, there is no point to social cooperation nor to notions of right and justice . . . The Reasonable subordinates the Rational because its principles limit, and in a Kantian doctrine limit absolutely, the final ends that can be pursued." This passage makes clear the complementary nature of the Rational and the Reasonable and the fact that each corresponds to a moral power – the Reasonable to the capacity to have a sense of justice and the Rational to the capacity to have a conception of the good. The Reasonable and the Rational thus together express the unity of practical reason and a deep sense of the priority of the right over the good. It might perhaps be added that the Reasonable represents an element of the priority of right, and is intended to have a specific function. The presentation of the Rational and the Reasonable certainly resolves certain problems raised by TJ (see chapter 10).[41]

Most interesting, however, is Rawls' inversion of the model conception of the person and that of the original position. In KCMT, the function of the original position is to translate the characteristics of the person into a procedure that supports them. This function of the original position has two significant implications. First, it avoids communitarian criticisms such as those of Michael Sandel since it does not conceive of the person as entirely "unencumbered." Second, it opens the way to the position that Rawls adopts in PL. Indeed, it is for this reason that I have insisted on the centrality of this text in Rawls' work overall. Of course, the priority later given to the conception of the person also problematizes the neutrality of the decision procedure by which the principles of justice are derived. It is no coincidence that this becomes the central concern of PL.

The Reasonable shares with the original position the conditions and limits that restrict the choices available to the parties. The result is that the principles of justice depend, not on the original position as such, but on how the original position represents both the dialectics between the Reasonable and the Rational and the ideal of the person implicit in it. Social cooperation itself is possible only if there is a harmonious relation between the Rational and the Reasonable. All of the main features of the original position, including the veil of ignorance, thus tend to proceduralize the characteristics of the Rawlsian person. This is why the original position represents a model of pure procedural justice. Only in this sense is the decision of the parties in the original position just. The notion of pure procedural justice now serves to stress the autonomy of the person. Indeed, if the decision made in the original position were not made in terms of procedural justice, then the parties to it would be guided by something beyond themselves and their motives, and would therefore be heteronomous, rather than autonomous, subjects.

The model conception of the original position acts as a background against which the other two model conceptions can be presented. This further indicates the reduced argumentative role given to the original position, a reduction that is later confirmed in PL. In TJ, Rawls considered the argument from the original position, with the test of reflective equilibrium, to be capable of demonstrating to a universal reader the rightness of choosing the two principles of justice. In PL he limits both his ambitions regarding this argument and the kind of subjects that he thinks can be persuaded by it. This limitation concerns the sharing of a liberal-democratic regime and its basic culture. KCMT can thus be seen as an intermediate stage between the universalism of TJ and the contextualization of the argument in PL.

8.4.1 Person, liberty, and equality

The reformulation of the original position in KCMT is marked by the central role given to the full publicity condition in the second lecture, entitled "Representation of Freedom and Equality." Publicity had such a role in TJ without its being made explicit, and its role is later extended in PL, in notions such as that of public reason. Publicity is primarily a matter of methodology, which must always correspond to commonsense and the progress of scientific research. It also requires that, under the conditions set by the veil of ignorance, all of the parties to the original position must be aware of certain aspects of social theory and moral psychology. Certain beliefs are thus excluded from the original position, in particular religious and metaphysical ones. This exclusion has been subject to continued, and sometimes bitter, debate. The novelty of KCMT consists in Rawls' justification of such exclusions in terms of publicity – that is, on the grounds that in the case of religious and metaphysical beliefs not all citizens could be adequately informed of others' beliefs.

Rawls' analysis of the person proceeds in the second lecture with an examination of the concepts of liberty and equality in the theory of justice as fairness. The citizens of a well-ordered society consider each other as free and equal persons. The underlying notion of the person here is still conceived in terms of the two moral powers. Rawls holds that citizens consider each other as free in the following three senses:

(i)   Persons are "self-originating sources of valid claims." That is, persons are capable of shaping the structure of the well-ordered society on the grounds of their highest-order interests, and within the limits set by justice.
(ii) Persons are capable of having a conception of the good which they may change as they wish. The capacity to change a conception of the good means that there is no independent conception of the good which everyone must recognize.
(iii) Persons are responsible for the ends that they pursue, and are therefore capable of limiting themselves.[42]

The citizens of a well-ordered society are equal in the sense of being "equal moral persons."[43] They are also capable of understanding and dealing with a public conception of justice, considering everyone to be capable of contributing to the construction of a well-ordered society on the basis of their highest-order interests. These elements of citizens' equality are expressed in the requirements of symmetry that characterize the original position.

These characteristics of freedom and equality must be formally represented in the model conception of the original position. For instance, the sense of justice of the parties in the original position is initially empty for the simple reason that a complete conception of justice does not yet exist. The same holds for the capacity to formulate and revise a conception of the good, since the parties are unaware of their ultimate aims. The capacity to be a self-originating source of valid claims also lacks specific content and is thus reduced to the capacity to deliberate appropriately in the original position. This formal representation of the characteristics of freedom and equality in the original position is expressed in Rawls' thick understanding of the veil of ignorance. The Kantian excludes information that a Humean would admit, in order to guarantee the autonomy of the parties.

8.4.2 Constructivism and objectivity

The third lecture of KCMT, entitled "Construction and Objectivity," concerns two related problems raised by Rawls' Kantian constructivist method. This method links a conception of the person as free and equal to the principles of justice that govern a well-ordered society. Moreover, the method does so by means of an appropriate definition of the constructive procedure. In defining the procedure, Rawls is obliged to defend it against two opposed positions. The first is metaphysical realism, which he considers in the form of moral intuitionism. Regarding this, his constructivist reply is to claim that: "a Kantian doctrine interprets the notion of objectivity in terms of a suitable constructed social point of view . . . This rendering of objectivity implies that, rather than think of the principles of justice as true, it is better to say that they are the principles most reasonable for us."[44] Due to the social understanding of objectivity, Rawls needs to reply to the challenge that this view leads to relativism. In other words, critics could charge that Rawls endorses a non-cognitive ethical methodology similar to that of an emotivist theory. Clearly, Rawls should resist this. He replies by elaborating his own notion of moral objectivity consistent with his Kantian constructivism.

Rawls first distinguishes Kantian constructivism from moral intuitionism. He considers the latter a position that dominated moral philosophy from Plato onwards. More recently the view was adopted in the English-language tradition by Clark, Price, Sidgwick, Moore, and Ross in a more refined form and in the German tradition by Leibniz and Wolff. He considers the position to rest on two postulates – namely, that the fundamental concepts of the right, the good, and the moral worth of persons are not analyzable in terms of non-moral concepts and that moral principles are self-evident truths.[45] On these grounds, moral intuitionism holds that "an effective conception of justice is founded on the recognition of self-evident truths about good reasons."[46] For a Kantian constructivist, this claim is heteronomous, just as Humean psychological naturalism was for Kant.[47] This heteronomy consists in the positing of a given order of moral objects that is independent of the decisions that persons make regarding them. Basically, both attempts to derive morality from nature, such as psychological naturalism, and claims to understand the moral order by means of a series of primitive intuitions are heteronomous. Rawls further draws this parallel to Kant in his earlier article, "Themes in Kant's Moral Philosophy," in which he denies that "first principles as statements about good reasons are regarded as true or false in virtue of a moral order of values that is prior to and independent of our conceptions of person and society."[48]

In contrast, as I have said, an ideal of the person plays a central role in Kantian constructivism. For moral intuitionism, the idea of the moral person is largely empty. She is limited to absorbing a truth that comes from outside her, and moral activity becomes a merely epistemological enterprise. It is precisely this reduction that Rawls wishes to avoid.

Having thus distinguished Kantian constructivism from moral intuitionism, Rawls turns to the limits of constructivism itself. Despite using terms similar to those of mathematical and logical constructivism, he does not compare Kantian constructivism with either of these in KCMT. In PL he makes only the following, brief remark: "In both cases the idea is to formulate a procedural representation in which . . . all relevant criteria of correct reasoning – mathematical, moral, political – are incorporated . . . Judgments are reasonable and sound if they result in following the correct procedure correctly (PL 102)." Rawls' refusal to relate Kantian constructivism to mathematical and logical constructivism presumably derives from his desire, expressed particularly in IMT, to separate ethical and political issues from epistemological and metaphysical ones. In KCMT he explicitly denies any relation between his constructivism and constructivist logics and theories of the truth.[49]

From the point of view of moral objectivity, constructivism, unlike intuitionism and realism more generally, must ensure that its reasoning is influenced by the human capacities of reflection and judgment. These capacities, Rawls claims, "are not fixed once and for all, but are developed by a shared public culture and hence shaped by that culture."[50] It follows that the moral conception derived from constructivism must have a primarily social function, as part of public culture. Consequently, for reasons of publicity, the principles of justice and the methods used to arrive at them must be relatively simple and comprehensible. What Rawls calls "schematic and practical distinctions" must therefore be adopted in order to create a conception of justice that is feasible and appropriate to the basic structure to which it refers. This is why, unlike utilitarianism, constructivism does not assume that all moral questions can be answered. So conceived, constructivism implies a relation between its method and its ethical sphere of competence – namely, public judgments – that is clearly different from that characteristic of communitarianism.[51]

It follows that, for Kantian constructivism, moral objectivity consists in the contractualist construction procedure as exemplified by the theory of justice as fairness. According to Kantian constructivism, there are no reasons of justice other than those produced by the combination of the arguments from the original position and reflective equilibrium. It is thus up to the parties to the original position, and then citizens in the test phase, to decide which are the salient moral facts and how they should be treated. In doing so, they realize an ideal of pure procedural justice that is consistent with moral experience. Objectivity consists in the capacity to map the moral conceptions of the person and the well-ordered society in the original position such that the principles that result are confirmed by reflective equilibrium. Were someone to object that such a procedure is no guarantee of objectivity on the basis of a moral realism or intuitionism, the constructivist will simply reply that this is no argument since it denies a priori the possibility of constructivism.

Ultimately, the two positions make similar, yet opposed, claims: while for the realist (or intuitionist) objectivity depends on moral truths that exist independently, the constructivist holds precisely the opposite view. The results of the constructivist procedure then find confirmation in reflective equilibrium, and one would expect them to be more consistent with considered judgments than the results of alternative theories. Rawls' Kantian constructivism is thus epistemologically coherentist and metaphysically anti-realist. This might seem to be threatened by the conception of the person employed by the theory, since this conception might appear to manifest a hidden moral realism.[52]

As matter of fact, not everything can be constructed in Rawls' paradigm. Something must serve as premises for the procedure of construction. These assumptions, however, are not Platonic reproductions of prior moral facts.[53] Rather, they are convictions of justice privileging a public, rather than private, conception of the person.[54] Indeed, this is why constructivist objectivity ultimately consists in what he calls "the publicly shared point of view of citizens in a well-ordered society," and not in a correspondence with some mythical perspective of the universe.[55] Constructivist objectivity ultimately rests on the consent of the parties. In this version, contractualism considers moral truth to depend on the adequate correspondence between the decisions produced by the decision method and the ideal of the person.

It is only in this sense, I would suggest, that Rawls can be considered a realist. Although he does not consider meta-ethical issues extensively here, it is clear that objectivity depends on our preference for a social order rather than an independently existing natural one.[56] Intersubjectivity is the grounds of objectivity, and thus the grounds of any agreement. He considers agreement to depend on convictions shared in the public culture of a well-ordered society. This is perhaps a non-Kantian element of Rawls' constructivism, and it is odd that in KCMT there is no trace of his systematic reading of Kant. In particular, Rawls does not present his understanding of the objectivity of Kantian morality in terms of the complex notion of the "fact of reason" – a notion that, however controversial, would have offered him more solid grounds for moral objectivity than those presented in KCMT.

It may be that this is one of the reasons Rawls replaces moral constructivism with political constructivism in PL. As we will see, political constructivism presupposes the political conception, and underlying this conception is the legitimization provided by liberal-democratic institutions. The pure justification in terms of the original position appears less defensible were it not for this further, political legitimization. Rawls thus revises the demonstrative pretensions of the central argument of the theory of justice as fairness in the manner discussed above. For the Rawls of PL, without political legitimization the principles of justice cannot be affirmed. Justification depends on public reason, and "[t]hose who reject constitutional democracy . . . will of course reject the very idea of public reason."[57]

9

INTRODUCING *POLITICAL LIBERALISM*

Chapters 9, 10, and 11 can be read as a unique critical introduction to PL.[1] In chapter 9 the structure of PL is presented (9.1.1, 9.3); in chapter 10 the main problem of the book – given this structure – is analyzed; and finally in chapter 11 the Rawlsian solution is examined.

Chapter 9 begins with an attempt to explain why PL is a particularly difficult book. The first reason for such a special difficulty probably depends on the fact that PL is a highly abstract book, much more so than TJ. In TJ, the author had a clear foundational goal and a clear critical target, namely to present an original liberal theory of justice and to undermine some theoretical bases of utilitarianism. In PL, both these objectives are absent. No doubt, a central topic in PL is the relation between toleration and stability in the light of liberal legitimacy (9.2). There are two standard philosophical grounds for liberal toleration. The first is skeptical, and the second is based on the value of pluralism. Rawls selects the second version, and is obliged to face the problem that pluralism itself, if taken as a moral thesis, is controversial. Starting from here, Rawls goes back to TJ, and one of the main aims of PL becomes to try to show that the idea of the well-ordered society in TJ may be reformulated so as to take account of the fact of reasonable pluralism. To do this, Rawls modifies the doctrine of justice as fairness into a political conception of justice that applies to the basic structure of society. Rawls now sees TJ as presenting an "unrealistic idea of a well-ordered society." This is so because it appears impossible that in a liberal-democratic society all people would be united in affirming one and the same comprehensive doctrine, even if this doctrine is Rawls' theory of justice as fairness (9.2). The chapter ends by presenting in some detail the concept of legitimation – here introduced within the theoretical hypothesis (chapter 1) – that will eventually permit the solution of the dilemma posed by the coexistence of pluralism and stability.

9.1 Introduction

In October 1995, the University of Santa Clara in California held a conference, attended by Rawls himself, to celebrate the twenty-fifth anniversary of
the publication of TJ.[2] Rawls was asked, among other things, what it felt like
to have written a book that was so widely read and cited. He replied, with
something between irony and modesty, that the main reason for the book's
being so widely read and cited was that in his life he had had only one idea
and written only one book. Many of those present at the conference believed
that Rawls was right to suggest that he would not write anything of similar
importance in the future, and that his other works were merely glosses on
the theory of justice presented in TJ. But this was to prove not to be the case.
Indeed, Rawls had already published the first edition of PL in 1993, and
while the main elements of the book are admittedly comprehensible only in
the context of the debates following the publication of TJ, it is not concerned
only with responding to criticisms made of TJ or with presenting the revisions made to it between 1973 and 1991. Rather, it discusses important new
issues, which, I will argue, illuminate all of his work, from the first writings
onwards.[3]

The aim of the following discussion of PL is to identify and resolve the
main theoretical problems raised by it. In my view, there are basically two
such problems. The first regards the vexed question of the relation between
PL and TJ, and its implications for Rawls' realism and his treatment of stability. The second concerns the distinction that grounds the novel theory of
political legitimacy presented in PL, namely that between normative force
and democratic acceptability.

In the next part of this chapter, I will reconstruct the overall structure of
the book, before proceeding in the third and fourth parts to formulate an
interpretative approach, on which I will base my treatment of the two main
theoretical problems in the following two chapters.

In chapter 10, I will identify the central problem of the book, which derives
from Rawls' attempt to reconcile stability and pluralism by means of the
"political conception," which separates the realm of the political from that
of ethics and metaphysics.[4] The notions of being "freestanding," of a "comprehensive doctrine," and of "reasonableness" give substance to the political
conception. In order to give space to pluralism by means of toleration, this
conception is also separated from the deep moral and religious convictions of
citizens' "comprehensive views," and this creates a systematic problem of stability. In PL Rawls adopts a moral view of politics and the stability which he
aims to ensure is a moral one – that is, a stability "for the right reasons." Yet
by proposing to resolve this problem by means of the political conception he
risks separating citizens' political behavior from their right reasons. He thus
appears to be faced with a dilemma: establishing moral stability, a stability
for the right reasons, would seem to threaten pluralism, and vice versa.

In chapter 11, the third and final chapter on PL, I will examine Rawls' proposed solution to this dilemma. In presenting his theory of political tolerance, he introduces two fundamental concepts, those of an "overlapping consensus" and of "public reason." Rawls claims that only a consensus among different comprehensive reasonable doctrines, or, rather, between citizens who believe in such different doctrines, will ensure the possibility of a public justification based on liberal legitimation. But such a fragile equilibrium has certain costs for the community, the most important of which is that of respecting the obligations of public reason regarding certain fundamental constitutional issues and matters of basic justice. It follows that, in the most important, circumscribed realms of politics, citizens must express themselves not in terms of their ultimate convictions, but rather in terms that are appropriate to the feelings and ideas of all other citizens in a regime of reciprocal respect.

9.1.1 The structure of Political Liberalism

The main theoretical novelty introduced in PL is probably the conception of legitimacy as an element that is capable of determining not only the possibility of enforcing justice but also the content of justice itself.[5] This new conception is part of a liberal theory of justice that nonetheless also remains fundamentally moral, rather than skeptical or realist. This theory of justice involves a revised view of autonomy and of the primacy of politics that also shed light on all of Rawls' work, before and after PL. In PL, commitments in politics are conceived as relatively independent of deep views of life, whether ethical or metaphysical, and as based on a certain interpretation of the practices of liberal-democratic regimes. Consequently, the egalitarian view of social justice characteristic of TJ, although not absent, becomes more of a background element in PL, as one of the premises of its argument.[6]

The text of PL has a long and complex history, as can be seen by a glance at the chapters, or "lectures," of which it is composed. The first three lectures reformulate the claims made in KCMT, in a way that is clearer and more consistent with the rest of the book. The seventh and eighth lectures are revised versions of two articles, "The Basic Liberties and Their Priority" of 1982 and "The Basic Structure as Subject" of 1978, which constitute the more explicitly institutional part of the book.[7] Of the same period is the article "Social Unity and Primary Goods," of 1982. Rawls had already felt the need to revise TJ at that time, but (in the preface to PL) he also notes the lack of a basic unity between the various parts that will later make up the text of PL (xiv). After 1980, he wrote other articles that were intended to complete the presentation of PL – namely, "Justice as Fairness: Political not Metaphysical" in 1985 (part of which is included in the first lecture of PL), "The Idea of Overlapping Consensus" in 1987, "The Priority of Right and Ideas of the Good" in 1988, and "The Domain of the Political and Overlapping Consensus" in 1989. The latter two essays, together with the only original article in the book, "The

Idea of Public Reason," constitute lectures 4, 5, and 6 of PL, respectively. The last lecture, lecture 9, "Reply to Habermas" of 1995, was included in the paperback edition of PL, published in 1996.[8] The text should also be read in the light of the introduction to this edition, and the article of 1997, "The Idea of Public Reason Revisited."[9]

The structure of PL can be outlined by following the order of the lectures, by Rawls' posing of the problem of the relation between stability and pluralism in the introduction and the first three lectures, and by his ensuing attempt to resolve it in lectures 4–8 of the first edition, or 4–9 of the second.

(i)   The first lecture, "Fundamental Ideas," begins with the formulation of the so-called "basic questions," which raise precisely the problem of the relation between stability and pluralism. The novel notions of the "political conception" and the "freestanding view" are then presented, indicating the differences between the approach adopted in PL and that of TJ. Rawls then examines the "fundamental ideas" of persons as free and equal citizens, each with the two moral powers: of society as a "fair system of cooperation", and of a well-ordered society. These ideas hold together a well-ordered society in which diversity is moderated by a common public culture.

(ii) In the second lecture, "Powers of the Citizens and Their Representation," Rawls clarifies the crucial distinction between the Rational and the Reasonable, and reveals the essential role of the reasonable in the formulation of his main claim. In specifying the notion of the reasonable, he also introduces the idea of "burdens of judgment," which make ethical-political disagreement normal.

(iii) The third lecture, "Political Constructivism," clarifies the nature and scope of political constructivism by contrasting it with two alternative views, moral constructivism, which was endorsed by Kant and by Rawls himself (before PL), and which I discussed in chapter 8 above, and rational intuitionism. Here Rawls also discusses the notion of objectivity.

(iv) In lecture 4, the "overlapping consensus" is presented, giving substance to the idea of the ultimate limits of reasonable disagreement, and a solution is proposed to the problem of stability. According to my interpretation, this chapter formulates the core of Rawls' central thesis in the book.

(v)   In lecture 5, "The Priority of Right and Ideas of the Good," Rawls provides a reformulation of the priority of right in terms of the five ways of understanding the good employed in the theory of justice as fairness. Here Rawls also discusses certain criticisms of TJ, such as those made by Arrow and Sen, and the issue of the neutrality of the theory of justice as fairness, which Rawls claims does not consist in treating all theories in the same way.

(vi)   The sixth lecture, "The Idea of Public Reason," presents the eponymous idea, along with the related notion of "duty of civility," on which political communication is to be based in a regime that keeps the standards of "liberal legitimacy."

(vii)   Lecture 7, "The Basic Structure as Subject," provides a general view of the institutions to which the theory of justice as fairness is to be applied, and which are also central to PL. The important complementary role of "background justice," which regards principles of taxation (among other issues), is also clarified, and there is an interesting discussion of the Hegelian criticism of contractualism.[10] The basic structure is distinguished from the fields of local and global justice, a point to which I will return when discussing *The Law of Peoples* in chapter 12.

(viii) In lecture 8, "The Basic Liberties and Their Priority," the basic liberties are presented in the context of the basic structure.

(ix)   In the second edition, published in 1996, PL concludes with "Reply to Habermas," which I have discussed in chapter 7 and which, while not being integral to the book, helps in understanding certain important points, including that of liberal legitimacy. This edition also includes a significant new introduction, which undertakes to remove certain misunderstandings of the book.

9.2 A Difficult Book . . .

PL is a difficult book. Indeed, it is probably more demanding on the reader than TJ. In the introduction to the second edition, Rawls admits that it presents a real difficulty in "its failing to identify explicitly the philosophical question it addresses," something that the defense of a particular view of social justice in TJ had avoided (PL xxxvi–xxxvii). There are at least two main reasons for this. The first concerns the abstract character of the book, while the second regards its aim to both revise the theory of justice presented in TJ and formulate a new political version.[11] As I have mentioned, the book is further complicated by its being in between a unitary text and a collection of revised versions of earlier articles on related themes.

The first difficulty is that of the abstract character of PL. In this, it differs substantially from TJ, which had a concrete and explicitly identified goal: namely, to develop an ethical-political theory of social justice based on an egalitarian liberalism, and which explicitly criticized, methodologically and theoretically, the two dominant approaches to practical philosophy of the time, i.e. utilitarianism and formal, semantic approaches. In contrast, PL provides no substantive theory of social justice, and has no particular critical target.

The basic theme of PL is liberal legitimacy. Such legitimacy concerns consensus among citizens regarding fundamental political issues, which is a necessary condition of the use of coercive powers in a liberal-democratic regime.[12] This is, of course, a familiar theme of classical political philosophy, which owes much to the thought of Locke and Kant.[13] It is precisely this theme that Rawls treats in an abstract and meta-theoretical manner in PL, beginning with the idea of tolerance. Roughly speaking, there are two ways of understanding political tolerance from a liberal perspective, one being skeptical, the other being based on the value of pluralism. In understanding tolerance in the second way, Rawls faces the problem of supporting such an evidently controversial moral claim as the value of pluralism.[14] Thus the complex task of PL becomes that of demonstrating the consistency between pluralist liberalism and a particular, non-skeptical moral view of politics.

As I have mentioned, unlike TJ, PL also lacks clearly defined methodological and theoretical opponents. Perhaps communitarianism might be considered to have such a role, given that Rawls returns repeatedly to the question of the priority of the right over the good. But he did not consider communitarian claims to be particularly important, and certainly did not cultivate the same interest in them as he had done in utilitarianism. As he writes: "The changes in the later essays are sometimes said to be replies to criticisms raised by communitarians and others. I don't believe there is a basis for saying this" (PL xvii, n. 6).

Basically, in PL, Rawls presents a kind of meta-theory of political legitimation, based on liberal tolerance. This can be confusing for the reader, who finds admitted into the theory of PL certain non-liberal – comprehensively reasonable – doctrines, such as religious social doctrines and utilitarianism. Indeed, the book can appear paradoxical for precisely this reason, insofar as in it Rawls might appear to present a theory of justice without being entirely convinced of it. This is not the case. Rawls rather does something analogous to Russell's opting for a theory of types in logic and semantics. In other words, he defends not a single theory of justice, but a liberal meta-theory that is capable of containing other theories, under certain principles. This is done on the grounds not of merely procedural or epistemological commitments, but rather of a substantive ethical one.[15] In other words, the meta-theory that Rawls proposes is not morally neutral, but rather presupposes consensus regarding certain basic liberal principles, like the affirmation of a list of basic liberties and related priorities, the possibility to have access to these liberties and to enjoy a fair equality of opportunity, and the possibility of a social minimum for the worst-off.

To understand PL, it is necessary to appreciate the dual role that liberalism plays in it. Using the analogy with the painting and its frame, one could say that in PL the meta-theoretical liberalism of the "frame" coexists with the ethical-political liberalism of the "painting," which is based on the theory of justice as fairness. The former is overarching, while the latter can be based on different comprehensive reasonable doctrines, with justice as fairness being one of them.

The second difficulty that arises in interpreting PL is that regarding its dual aims: (i) to revise certain aspects of TJ in the light of the debates that it had given rise to and the doubts that Rawls himself had developed; and (ii) to present an original philosophical–political view of liberalism that would have its own theoretical coherence, independently of Rawls' previous works.

Rawls' critical revision of TJ is thus of fundamental importance for understanding the overall meaning of PL. It is also significant that in PL, as in most of the articles of the 1980s which were later incorporated in the book, Rawls does not provide a systematic discussion of all of the criticisms made of TJ. Indeed, he never engaged directly with the debates that arose around the book. These debates concern certain central points of the work, such as: (i) the meaning and implications of Rawls' criticisms of utilitarianism; (ii) the formal nature of the deduction of the principles of justice from the original position; (iii) the libertarian criticisms, such as those made by Nozick; (iv) the possibility of giving a convincing argument for the priority of the right over the good; and (v) the idea of Rawls' theory of justice and whether, as expressed by Habermas and others, it is unrealistic and partly renders democratic debate irrelevant. I have discussed these points earlier in the book.[16] My concern here will rather be to show how in revising his theory of justice in PL Rawls treats only the last two of these points, namely that regarding the priority of the right over the good and that regarding TJ's supposed lack of realism.[17]

The need to understand these two aspects is made more urgent by my claim about the continuity of Rawls' thought. That is, if, as I am arguing, Rawls1 (before 1980) and Rawls2 (after 1980) have a common aim, despite the change in the main object of Rawls' thought, then (i) the revisions made in PL to the theory of justice presented in TJ do not involve a radical shift in the structure of his thought, and (ii) PL can be read in terms of the theme that links it to TJ, namely, the priority of the right over the good, and in terms of an understanding of the relation between the right and the good that he employs from some of his earliest works onwards. In this regard, it is worth recalling that by "the priority of the right" Rawls means the moral limits that principles of justice place on permissible ways of living and the necessity that ideas of the good used in politics be political ones (PL 209).

The first of the two points – that regarding whether the revisions made to the theory in PL distort the project of TJ – presents an immediate difficulty. It concerns the possibility of accounting for Rawls' theory of justice as fairness in terms of the themes of PL, namely, legitimation and tolerance. In other words, *prima facie* it is not clear how much of the egalitarian paradigm of TJ, and of the theory of justice as fairness itself, survives in PL.[18] This point has relevant implications, since, were the political liberalism presented in PL to be entirely lacking in the distributive elements characteristic of TJ, then this would tell against my interpretative claim regarding the continuity of Rawls' thought.[19] This difficulty arises from the fact that in PL Rawls treats his own theory of justice in TJ as itself a particular brand of liberalism and removes the second principle of justice from what he calls the "constitutional essentials." In short, to return to my analogy with the "frame" and the "painting," parts of the liberalism of the "painting," which is based on the theory of justice as fairness, should remain within the meta-theoretical liberalism of the "frame" if the continuity of Rawls' thought is to be upheld.

The evidence for a substantial continuity between PL and the egalitarian liberalism of TJ is to be found primarily in the introduction to the second edition of PL and in lectures 5 and 6 of the book.

In the introduction to the second edition, Rawls insists on the minimal features that characterize the liberalism of what I have called the meta-theoretical "frame." These features serve to exclude, for instance, the libertarian position, which fails to satisfy the requirements of equality. They are not merely formal features, but rather include such things as the public financing of elections; a fair equality of opportunity, especially in education; a decent distribution of income and wealth; government policies to promote employment; and basic public health care for all (PL lvi–lvii).

In lecture 5, Rawls provides a more "technical" treatment, in the form of a reply to Arrow and Sen regarding the need to better specify the index of primary goods in the view of justice as fairness. The main issue here is how "variations among persons in their capacities" are to be treated in interpersonal comparisons of utility (PL 182–3). Regarding this, Rawls distinguishes differences according to which some individuals are below the minimal level of ability to be normal – in the sense that illness or disability makes them unable to compete with others over primary goods – from other differences. While the latter differences are to be the responsibility of standard liberal-democratic institutions, one would expect a system of free public health care for all to provide the basis for that fair equality of opportunity that is one of the fundamental elements of the theory of justice as fairness. Thus Rawls rejects, among other things, Sen's paradigm based on "capabilities" – that is, on the structural relation between resources and persons' capacities. He defends his "resourcist" approach, based on primary goods, but allows exceptions to be made to it in cases in which the distribution of social goods does not adequately respond to serious incapacities due to illness or disability (PL, levture v, section 3).

In lecture 6, Rawls distinguishes the defense of social equality from the defense of the basic liberties, the first being considered more controversial than the second. The appropriate structure of the basic liberties presented in lecture 8 re-emphasizes that these liberties are far from formal in nature, since they involve significant egalitarian elements such as those mentioned in the introduction to the second edition. All this implies a relative continuity between TJ and PL in this regard.[20]

It would seem more straightforward to give a positive answer to the second question: that regarding whether in PL Rawls maintains the priority of right which he insisted upon in TJ. Perhaps Rawls' main motivation in writing PL was that of replying to the common criticism that in TJ he had unsuccessfully attempted to present a political theory of justice in terms of the priority of right, and thus independently of any specific view of the good. In fact, the liberal and individualist elements of Rawls' own view of the good were not fully excluded from his theory of justice as fairness.[21] The entire dialectic between stability and pluralism that is central to PL constitutes a reaffirmation of the priority of right at a more sophisticated level. In this respect, TJ and PL both treat the same problem, albeit in different ways.

One can nonetheless accept Rawls' claim in the essay of 1997, "The Idea of Public Reason Revisited," that TJ and PL are "asymmetrical works," if this is understood to mean that the two works use different means to reach a similar end, as Rawls himself claims in his interview to the journal *Commonweal*.[22] He clarifies this point in the third section of his introduction to the second edition of PL, in which he writes,

> Thus, a main aim of PL is to show that the idea of the well-ordered society in TJ may be reformulated so as to take account of the fact of reasonable pluralism. To do this it transforms the doctrine of justice as fairness as presented in TJ into a political conception of justice that applies to the basic structure of society. (PL lxi)

Indeed, in "The Idea of Public Reason Revisited," Rawls also notes that the theory of justice as fairness is not the exclusive basis of PL, which is rather based primarily on the ideas of "public reason" and the "reasonable."[23]

Thus the relation between TJ and PL can appear rather vague. The vagueness can be avoided by noting that, although the theory of justice as fairness remains important in PL, it cannot be the only basis on which PL is constructed. The philosophical justification of the theory of justice as fairness in TJ is not sufficient to resolve the problem of political legitimacy posed in PL.[24] To simplify, one might say that even the best philosophical justification of a theory of justice, which Rawls still claims to have provided in TJ, cannot succeed in winning the approval of all, or nearly all, of the citizens in a modern democratic society.

The well-known name given to the theoretical heart of TJ, "justice as fairness," thus becomes merely a "proper name," in the sense that the theory of "justice as fairness" cannot be one that holds for all.[25] Rawls writes in the introduction to the second edition of PL, "I put this phrase, i.e., justice as fairness, in italics because it is the proper name of a particular account of justice and it is always to be so understood (PLxxxv, n.2)."

In PL the theory of justice as fairness becomes only one liberal political theory – even if a special one – in a broader family of political conceptions compatible with liberalism.[26] PL is intended to provide a moral interpretation of public culture, according to which a coexistence among different citizens is possible – an aim which my previous analogy of the frame and the painting was intended to capture.

These complex conceptual difficulties provide a partial explanation for the rather less enthusiastic reception that PL first received, when compared to that given to TJ, especially among those who had most appreciated the earlier book. The differences between the content and aims of the two books probably disappointed those moral and political philosophers who had considered TJ to mark a return to substantive ethics in social and political theory, and considered PL to be a step backwards in that regard.[27] However, although it is true that Rawls gives less space to moral philosophy in PL, it would be wrong to treat the book this way. Indeed, over time the suspicions with which it was first greeted have generally been replaced by a widely held belief in the book's importance, at least insofar as the issue of liberal tolerance is concerned.

9.3 From the Ideal Theory of *A Theory of Justice* to the Non-ideal Theory of *Political Liberalism*

Rawls' changed aims in PL, and particularly his combining of justification, considered primary in TJ, with legitimation, also involve a change in his philosophical premises. Hegel, Hume, and the American pragmatist tradition exert a greater influence on PL than on TJ. Of course, Rawls does not surrender himself to historicist or hermeneutical wanderings, or give up the traditionally Kantian structure of his thought. But these new influences make the Kantianism more sophisticated, beginning with its meta-ethical model of acceptability. In TJ, the acceptability of the principles of justice depends directly on the degree to which the arguments supporting them – from the argument from the original position to that regarding reflective equilibrium – are rationally convincing, such that over time the senses of justice and the views of the good of the citizens of a well-ordered society are to coincide. In PL Rawls no longer understands acceptability in this way.

The reasons for this change are significant. There are substantial differences between the problems posed in TJ and those treated in PL, differences that lead Rawls to employ forms of arguments in the latter that are less concerned with philosophical justification in the strict sense. Perhaps the most important of these differences concerns TJ's ideal, even utopian account of the well-ordered society in a regime of "strict compliance."[28] Rawls gradually became dissatisfied with this approach, and in PL he employs certain novel ideas to provide a non-ideal, more realistic theory, an account of a society in a regime of what might be called "partial compliance."[29] For this reason the deductive, Kantian form of argument is replaced by one in which the historical experience of liberal democracy plays a more significant role.

In PL the sphere of justification is extended not only to new subjects – that is, to those who, while being convinced liberal democrats, may not be convinced of the intellectual superiority of the theory of justice as fairness – but also to the preliminary conditions that determine the structure of the original position. In PL citizens are to accept a liberal-democratic view of politics only in part on the grounds of there being a convincing theory that justifies it. This does not upset Rawls' basic paradigm too much. For, even in TJ, when the veil of ignorance is raised and the parts enter the field of non-ideal theory, citizens may realize that the principles of justice that they decided upon in the original position do not correspond to their actual profound ethical and religious views, and yet, if the liberal-democratic regime in which they live seems legitimized in liberal-democratic terms, they may still give some support to it – this is what has been called "partial compliance." This possibility makes it necessary to revise the criteria of acceptability presented in TJ, and to connect this new element to a different motivational force. Thus the priority given to pure moral justification in TJ is replaced by a combination of justification and political legitimation in PL. This is evident even in the two immediate critical aims regarding TJ that Rawls has in PL: those regarding, respectively, realism and stability.

In very general terms, it can be said that in PL Rawls attempts to remedy the lack of realism from which his view in TJ had previously suffered, and thus, as he himself puts it in the introduction to the second edition of PL, to revise the "unrealistic idea of a well-ordered society as it appears in TJ (PL xvi)." In PL Rawls is clearly more sensitive than he was in TJ to the ideals of positive liberty and political participation that are characteristic of philosophical republicanism.[30] The supposed lack of realism of TJ is in any case closely related to the issue of pluralism. Rawls gradually became convinced that, contrary to what he had claimed in TJ, the citizens of a liberal-democratic regime are unlikely to be able to agree on a single theory of justice. The lack of realism consists precisely in failing to appreciate this unlikelihood. And precisely this unlikelihood raises the issue of stability.

Rawls' concern with realism also implies a view of "jurisprudence" that differs from that of TJ, in that he presents the citizen more explicitly as a "lawmaker."[31] This is suggested by Rawls' including his "Reply to Habermas."[32] Whether or not this is due to the influence of republican readings, the juridical-institutional argument is clearly given more importance in PL.[33] For instance, constitutionalism is more significant in PL than in TJ, and the juridical aspect takes precedence over socio-economic ones in the work's overall philosophical structure. Indeed, if there is one clear difference between PL and TJ, it consists precisely in the fact that in PL the analysis of socio-economic goods given, for instance, in the second principle of justice of TJ is progressively replaced by an analysis of juridical-institutional mechanisms.[34] In PL, Rawls aims to reveal the political content, indirect and profound, of documents such as the United States Declaration of Independence, the Preamble to the United States Constitution, the Declaration of Human

Rights, and some of Lincoln's speeches.[35] Re-reading TJ in the light of PL, one can say that Rawls effectively intends to explain to us how the consensualist mechanism involved in the social contract ultimately becomes more important than the socio-economic object of the contract.[36]

The second revision of TJ that Rawls makes in PL is undoubtedly the more important one. It concerns stability, an issue which I will consider in more detail in the following chapter (but see also the final part of chapter 2). As I have mentioned, Rawls claims that the issue arises from the unrealistic assumption made in TJ that in a well-ordered society all of the citizens will agree on the same theory of justice. This assumption, Rawls now holds, derives from his having presented the theory of justice as fairness (in part) as a comprehensive doctrine. In defining a comprehensive doctrine, he writes that "[a] doctrine is fully comprehensive if it covers all recognized values and virtues within one precisely articulated scheme of thought; whereas a doctrine is only partially comprehensive when it comprises certain (but not all) non-political values and virtues and is rather loosely articulated (PL 175)." Rawls therefore attempts to resolve the problem of stability by means of a critical treatment of comprehensive doctrines. The criticisms made of TJ by communitarians in the 1970s and 1980s are not particularly significant in relation to this.[37] The critical revision of the theory of stability in TJ, leading to the formulation of the concept of a comprehensive doctrine in PL, instead derives from an attempt to partially separate the political acceptability of an institutional arrangement from the particular ethical or religious doctrine on which it is usually based, even in the case of the theory of justice as fairness that Rawls himself presented in TJ.

This attempt is, in turn, based on the central distinction that Rawls introduces in PL between "comprehensive doctrine" and "political conception."[38] Rawls writes that, "[i]f we think of a political society as a community united in affirming one and the same comprehensive doctrine, then the oppressive use of state power is necessary for political community (PL 37)." In the public sphere, then, "the fact of the oppression" is linked to the prevalence of a single comprehensive doctrine, while "reasonable pluralism" is linked to the political conception. To summarize, the idea is that, in a regime of PL, it cannot be assumed that reasonable persons can all agree on the justification of the (political) authority, even if this is based on the best conceivable comprehensive doctrine. Clearly, the problem of stability arises from this, since pluralism could lead to chaos rather than order. Thus the problem of stability basically coincides with that of the limits of pluralism.

9.4 How to Read *Political Liberalism*

In this final section of the chapter, I will present a way of reading PL that moves progressively away from the text itself, by introducing a distinction between justification and legitimation that Rawls himself does not draw. My aim is functional – that is, I think that this way of reading the text will assist in understanding certain concepts essential to the theory presented in it, whilst hopefully also having a theoretical value of its own.

The main difficulties involved in reading PL concern two theoretical issues which, although analytically distinct, are closely related and the meaning of which can, I believe, be best understood by means of the reading that I am proposing. Above I have already mentioned the first of the two issues, which regards the relation between the descriptive and the normative part in the conceptual structure that Rawls proposes. For all of the most significant concepts in PL – from "political conception" to "pluralism" and from "overlapping consensus" to "public reason" – oscillate between the descriptive and the normative, such that one wonders whether they are intended to refer to collective practices in liberal-democratic regimes or to prescriptions based on the ethical-political theory presented in PL. Clearly, to consider these concepts as simultaneously descriptive and normative is of little help. It is more fruitful to examine how in PL Rawls presents the descriptive and the normative as corresponding and hierarchically arranged levels, and why he does so. This will help not only to resolve a significant theoretical difficulty with Rawls' position in PL, but also to clear up corresponding misunderstandings among commentators, who equally tend to oscillate between the contextual and the prescriptive in their readings, without paying adequate attention to the relation between the two.

The second issue is, as I mentioned, closely related to the first. In PL, Rawls attempts to present liberalism in a double form – that is, partly as the result of a theory of social justice such as that proposed in TJ and partly as the result of a broader political conception that makes greater concessions to realism and to pluralism.[39] This raises a difficulty analogous to that regarding the relation between the descriptive and the normative, namely that of explaining the relation between the two approaches, and once again the difficulty cannot be resolved simply by insisting on both sides of it.

Here I will examine the meaning and implications of these two issues. I will do so, as indicated earlier, by interpreting the text in terms of a distinction which is not Rawls' own, but which I believe helps in understanding the two issues and Rawls' solution to the main problems posed in the text. Rawls' point of departure is the central role of justification in his general theoretical scheme – for him, justice basically means the capacity of citizens reciprocally to justify fundamental social structures, those that constitute the framework of the basic structure. I will therefore begin with Rawls' notion of justification, which is complicated notably in PL with respect to his earlier work, and then proceed to introduce a notion of legitimation which supplements that of justification and which is relatively original, and differs in particular from Rawls' own notion of "legitimacy."

In TJ, the concept of justification plays a central role that goes beyond the significant one attributed to it in two important sections of the book, respectively at its beginning and its end. In section 4, "The Original Position and Justification," Rawls presents the original position in terms of justification, by explaining why an agreement made in an appropriately defined status quo should be considered "fair." This means that the theory of justice as fairness can be justified on certain conditions. For Rawls, a correct justification occurs both deductively, from the original position, and inductively, by means of a reflective equilibrium. It requires the equality of the parties in the original position, which represents human beings as moral persons with the two fundamental (moral) powers: those of having a conception of the good and a sense of justice. Rawls writes that these elements imply that "[a] conception of justice cannot be deduced from self-evident premises or conditions on principles; instead, its justification is a matter of mutual support of many considerations, of everything fitting together into one coherent view (TJ 21; rev. edn. 19)."

In the last section of TJ, "Remarks on Justification," on the other hand, Rawls explains how his constructivist concept of justification differs from that implicit in two traditional models of moral philosophy. The first model is the intuitionist one, which Rawls calls "Cartesian" and which appeals to self-evident premises, while the second introduces non-moral concepts as primitive and Rawls claims it "is called naturalism for an abuse of language (TJ 578; rev. edn. 506)." Rawls considers both models to be unsatisfactory, and defends his alternative, constructivist model of justification, based on the "mutual support of many considerations (TJ 579; rev. edn. 507)." In the complex process of constructivist justification, he admits that it remains the case that "justification is an argument addressed to those who disagree with us, or to ourselves when we are of two minds." Yet at the same time, to arrive at a justification, rather than a mere logical demonstration, Rawls holds that one cannot avoid appealing to "what all the parties to the discussion hold in common (TJ 580; rev. edn. 508)." Thus understood, the public nature of justification is a significant constitutive element of it, because it allows each party to justify his or her behavior to everyone else and thus to realize Rawls' idea of society as a "social union of social unions (TJ 520–9; rev. edn. 456–64)."

This general notion of justification is still used in PL, but it is complicated, for there are three distinct, competing notions of justification in the text. These can be understood as three moments in a Hegelian dialectic, in that the third, that of "public justification," synthesizes, by encompassing and superseding, the first two, opposed notions, those of "*pro tanto* justification" and "full justification."[40]

Pro tanto justification is characteristic of the political conception and its most direct expression. Its main feature is that it considers only political values, and therefore excludes any reference to those other – ethical, religious, and metaphysical – values that are significant in the lives of all of us (even the skeptic believes at least in skepticism). Rawls presupposes that political values have a distinctive independence, such that it is possible to balance them reciprocally and resolve conflicts between them. Thus a (purely) political conception may be capable of finding reasonable solutions to many political problems. But Rawls calls this kind of justification *"pro tanto"* precisely because it does not exhaust the justificatory process. For citizens' comprehensive doctrines, which involve the values excluded by *pro tanto* justification, complicate matters and make the decisions taken in the process of *pro tanto* justification appear inadequate.

The justificatory process therefore reflects a person's complexity. A political theory treats people primarily as citizens, and as such they are to behave according to the political conception. But in civil society they live complex lives and cultivate their comprehensive doctrines in a network of multiple, public and private relationships, or "social unions," as Rawls calls them in TJ. They nonetheless remain the same persons as when considered as citizens, and therefore draw from comprehensive conceptions the moral and intellectual energies that act as a background to the justification of political conceptions. For Rawls, comprehensive doctrines can be either reasonable or unreasonable. In the former case – that treated in PL – one moves from a claim involved in a comprehensive doctrine to a justification of the political conception by means of a serious consideration of what other citizens believe. In the latter case, the process of political justification is independent of what others believe: a basically totalitarian or fundamentalist approach that it would clearly be preferable to avoid. But it remains up to citizens to decide how they will balance background comprehensive doctrines with political conceptions. At the extreme, each citizen might have his own way of balancing values of justice with purely political ones. The political conception would therefore be of no assistance – it would remain opaque to the values involved in the comprehensive doctrines, and the balance would therefore be in favor of these doctrines. But the independence of political conceptions, their being what Rawls call "freestanding," does not exclude their also being involved in comprehensive doctrines.

At this point one arrives at a certain impasse. This would remain were it not for the third kind of justification, "public justification." This kind of justification constitutes an original element that Rawls introduces in PL, and is presented as fundamental to political society, just as comprehensive doctrines are fundamental to civil society (here echoes of Hegel are undeniable). A balance can be maintained between the political conception and comprehensive doctrines only if "reasonable" citizens endorse the same political conception, on the basis of their different comprehensive doctrines. As I will show in chapter 11, only in this way can the challenge posed to stability by pluralism, the central problem posed by Rawls in PL, be resolved. Thus the realization of an overlapping consensus and public reason, and therefore pluralism's compatibility with a stability for right reasons, depend strictly on the possibility of a public justification. In the sphere of public justification, citizens reciprocally clarify the origins and the meanings of their different comprehensive doctrines and, in the light of these, decide to share the [same] political conception. They are able to arrive at this decision primarily because, while they make explicit to each other their respective comprehensive doctrines, they are concerned not with evaluating the doctrines themselves, but only with whether an overlapping consensus among these doctrines can be achieved to ensure the required stability. Nothing more can be asked for, if one wishes to achieve a stability for right reasons – that is, a stability that is moral, and not merely social or Hobbesian. Thus, for Rawls, social unity depends on public justification.

The main perplexity that this solution raises is clear, even to Rawls himself. That is, one wonders how the limits of the political conception, which is justified in a merely *pro tanto* manner, can be overcome in order to arrive at a public justification. Rawls' response to this, which further raises the level of sophistication of his solution, is to claim that the overlapping consensus in itself is not enough, since citizens must also be aware and convinced of it. For Rawls, only this will ensure that reasonable citizens consider political values to be overriding, such that they can accept the sacrifice of some of the demands of their comprehensive doctrines, ultimately on the grounds precisely of these doctrines themselves.

This way out is not entirely satisfactory. Admittedly, this is not so much because it suffers from an intrinsic weakness – that might suggest a better solution – but because there is something "unsaid" in it, an aspect that is not made entirely explicit. This regards the idea of "legitimacy," to which Rawls himself appeals in support of his solution. For in PL, he ought first to show that disagreement in contemporary society is reasonable, so as to be able to then show that this disagreement exists only within certain limits, beyond which there is "reasonable agreement."[41] But, in my view, the notion of legitimacy that Rawls presents in the book is inadequate to fulfil this function, and it is for precisely this reason that I think it is necessary to introduce the stronger, more substantial, and more flexible notion of legitimation.[42] But first it is necessary to explain what Rawls means by "legitimacy" in PL.

In my view, Rawls' concept of legitimacy in PL oscillates ambiguously between two notions. On the one hand, there is a formal and procedural notion, fitting into the Weberian tradition. According to this notion, while, say, the law(s) and the constitution may be legitimized, Rawls' two principles of justice may not, even if they might be fully justified. This notion holds for any kind of political power, assuming, among other things, that it is impossible to compare value frameworks. On the other hand, however, Rawls insists on a liberal legitimacy. This is intended to relate legitimate authority to consensus necessarily in a specific way, and it is therefore, unlike the first notion, not purely formal.

This ambiguity regarding legitimacy is present in certain important pages of Rawls' "Reply to Habermas" – specifically, on a series of pages from page 427 onwards. Rawls' aim in this article is to reply to Habermas' claim that in PL he ought to have used the term "legitimacy," rather than "justice" (see chapter 7 in this volume). In his "Reply," Rawls denies this on the grounds that "legitimacy is a weaker idea than justice," but nonetheless admits that legitimacy is an "idea having its own interests (PL 427)." He then proceeds to clarify what it would mean to put the emphasis of the argument on legitimacy. I quote the following, lengthy passage because it is particularly significant for appreciating the ambiguity in Rawls' understanding of the term.

> To focus on legitimacy rather than justice may seem like a minor point, as we may think "legitimate" and "just" the same. A little reflection shows they are not. A legitimate king or queen may rule by just and effective government, but then they may not; and certainly not necessarily justly even though legitimately. Their being legitimate says something about their pedigree: how they came to their office . . . The same holds under a democratic regime. It may be legitimate and in line with long tradition originating when its constitution was first endorsed by the electorate (the people) . . . Yet it may not be very just . . . Laws passed by solid majorities are counted as legitimate, even though many protest and correctly judge them unjust or otherwise wrong. Thus legitimacy is a weaker idea than justice and imposes weaker constraints on what can be done. It is also institutional, though there is of course an essential connection with justice. Note first that democratic decisions and laws are legitimate, not because they are just but because they are enacted in accordance with an accepted legitimate democratic procedure (PL 427–8).

A little further on, Rawls writes that, "[while] the idea of legitimacy is clearly related to justice, it is noteworthy that its special role in democratic institutions . . . is to authorize an appropriate procedure for making decisions (PL 428)."

In these passages, Rawls employs legitimacy in a formal, Weberian sense.[43] He proceeds. then to claim that, even if it is true that such legitimacy does not necessarily imply justice, in a well-ordered society legitimacy cannot easily be kept separate from justice. For Rawls, what ultimately matters are our substantive judgments of justice, which can cause legitimacy to be withdrawn when it does not correspond with such judgments (PL 429). According to Rawls, this holds as much for Habermas' ideal of discursive communication as for his own view.

When in the chapter on overlapping consensus Rawls discusses "liberal legitimacy," however, his concept of legitimacy seems less formal and more substantive. In lecture 4 of PL, he writes the following words: "our exercise of political power is fully proper only when it is exercised in accordance with a constitution the essentials of which all citizens as free and equal may reasonably be expected to endorse in the light of principles and ideals acceptable to their common human reason. This is the liberal principle of liberal legitimacy (PL 137)." Admittedly, Rawls is here discussing liberal legitimacy, and not legitimacy in general. Yet he refers here, not to the "pedigree" lying behind a law or policy, but to its substantive content. Indeed, he appeals to nothing less than human reason. It is precisely this second, richer notion of legitimacy, and not the first, formal one, which allows him to arrive at the overlapping consensus, and thus to resolve the central problem of PL. I propose, then, to set aside the first notion of legitimacy, as adequate only for more limited uses, and to enhance the second notion, which in its strengthened version I will call "legitimation" to distinguish it from Rawls' version. In other words, I propose that we distinguish more carefully than Rawls does between a descriptive kind and a normative kind of legitimacy, and that we do so by strengthening the normative kind, without going so far as to identify it with justification.[44]

My claim, then, is that, in order to resolve the fundamental impasse that Rawls treats in PL, without abandoning the framework within which he proposes to resolve it, a version of the second notion of legitimation is required that is more grounded and distinct from alternative possibilities. To clarify this version, it will be helpful to first distinguish it from other foundational concepts of law. Legitimation in my sense is a legitimacy that is almost general in scope and that is recognized widely in the social group to which it refers. It also has a distinctive moral content, the meaning of which is best explained by distinguishing legitimation from such similar concepts as effectiveness, legality, and validity. The mere fact that a law works, its effectiveness, implies little regarding its legitimation, since legitimation requires not only compliance with the law, but also a moral commitment to it, albeit perhaps only a partial one. Similarly, if more subtly, the formal acceptability of a law's pedigree involved in legality does not guarantee that the reason for such a consensus is consistent with reasons of justice – there is no such consistency in the case of the king and queen mentioned by Rawls, for instance. Finally, if the validity of a law rests on a combination of legality and effectiveness, then this is still insufficient to guarantee legitimation as I understand it, for legitimation requires that the acceptance of the law be for the right reasons.

Distinctions such as these serve to emphasize the public, moral aspect of legitimation. This moves legitimation closer to justification as I have presented it above, and there is a partial overlap between the two concepts. In this regard, I think that A. J. Simmons is mistaken to claim that it is possible that what the state may do, and what justifies it, is entirely separable from the consensus of its citizens, which merely legitimates it.[45] Legitimation is a different matter from justification, because legitimation constitutes a right to exercise coercion, a right that in a democracy derives from the consensus of the governed, while justification provides reasons for their being an institution that is subject to the test of legitimation. Yet there is another difference between the two concepts that makes it fruitful not only to distinguish between them, but also to stress their complementariness. This concerns the fact that, by its very nature, justification cannot have the generality or diffusion of legitimation, if one assumes Rawls' "reasonable disagreement" – in a pluralistic legal-moral regime, different justifications will coexist, but there will be a single legitimation. As I have mentioned above, this means that there is a sphere in which disagreement is permitted and encouraged, and another in which it is not, due to the general priority of right. This problem arises more clearly in PL than in TJ, given the emphasis in the former on pluralism in the sense that the rightness of justifications in a pluralistic regime will be based on different cultural, metaphysical, and ethical horizons. If one thinks of what Rawls calls "burdens of judgment," which I will discuss in the next chapter, it seems clear that a systematic convergence of different deep, ethical, and metaphysical justifications is not conceivable even in principle.

This idea of legitimation, on the other hand, is based on notions of convergence and widespread acceptance. In my view, this convergence rests on the broad moral acceptance of a legal and political system, which alone gives a plausible reply to the Hobbesian question of order – namely, that lasting stability presupposes a combination of a social-political perspective with an ethical-legal one.[46] This is due to the fact that we are not entirely convinced that certain fundamental legal norms need to necessarily be accepted by all, or by almost all, citizens in order to give meaning to the legal and moral order. Such norms concern, albeit naturally in different ways, the rules of a state, its "constitutional essentials" in Rawls' terminology, and also international rules, which I will discuss in the final chapter. In both cases, legitimation appeals to certain basic aspects of the rules of moral significance. This kind of legitimation, if complemented by justification, works at the level of these rules by means of the formation of an overlapping consensus. As I will show, this in turn is the basis of the consistency between stability and pluralism in PL.

Of course, there remains the question of how different interpretations of such rules could be distinguished in terms of such a general kind of consensus. For while opposed interpretations such as Nazism are clearly excluded, I will show below that substantial difficulties arise in distinguishing between interpretations that are all at least minimally liberal-democratic.

10

THE STATE OF THE PROBLEM

Chapter 9 asks the question: how can we have a credible theory of liberal toleration? Chapter 11 lays out Rawls' answer based on the idea of overlapping consensus. The aim of chapter 10 is to show some philosophical complexities one can find in answering the question. The main difficulty, for Rawls, consists in showing how equal citizens deeply divided by their moral, religious and philosophical doctrines can coexist within the same basic structure (10.1). Is consent on justice possible in the presence of different comprehensive views?

Rawls begins by presenting some "fundamental ideas" such as the fair terms of cooperation, a political conception of the person, and a well-ordered society (10.1, 10.1.1). Having in mind the question about toleration, Rawls treats these ideas under the umbrella of "reasonable pluralism" (10.2). Reasonable pluralism derives from two main sources, one epistemic and the other ethical-political (some criticisms of both sources are discussed in 10.2.1). The first depends on what Rawls calls the "burdens of judgment." Making judgments about ethics and politics is intrinsically controversial, because many variables impede a plausible convergence of opinions. The second comes instead from the fact that people are profoundly influenced by their comprehensive doctrines that include metaphysical, religious, and ethical elements. Rawls undermines the epistemic motivation behind toleration, taking for granted the "fact of pluralism," and emphasizes the ethical one. Under this presupposition, he formulates the conception of a "reasonable comprehensive doctrine." Such doctrines – or, better, the people who endorse them – respect the priority of right in the sense that they tailor their conceptions of the good to the limits of the political conception. In so doing, they behave like reasonable persons tolerating other people who endorse different reasonable doctrines. This conception eventually transforms Rawls' moral constructivism into political constructivism – a view presupposing the structure and the content of a political conception (10.3).

10.1 Fundamental Ideas in *Political Liberalism* and the Political Conception

The major problem posed by PL consists in finding a form of moral stability for a well-ordered society in the light of pluralism. PL requires an argument that might make the different comprehensive doctrines of individuals and groups compatible with the fundamental principles of justice that govern the basic structure. Rawls rejects the solution to the moral stability problem he provided in Part III of TJ because it ignores the fact of pluralism. It is hardly plausible for all members of a well-ordered society to find their comprehensive visions converge on the same theory of justice, even Rawls' theory of justice as fairness.

In PL, having assumed pluralism as normal in our contemporary societies, Rawls formulates a "freestanding" political conception distinct from any comprehensive doctrine. A comprehensive doctrine covers not only political questions but also religious-metaphysical and moral ones. The political conception is instead limited to the political ambit and, as previously pointed out (see section 7.3), corresponds to a *pro tanto* justification. Then, how is it possible that individuals accept the political conception in the light of their comprehensive views? Rawls upholds that, in order to do so, they need to be "reasonable" persons.[1] Reasonableness, as Rawls sees it, has both an epistemological and an ethical-political aspect, and the latter prevails over the former. Being reasonable means that the agreement on a political conception takes into account what other people think. The reasonable acceptance of pluralism solves the problem of stability.

Rawls begins with an attempt to answer three fundamental questions (see the beginning of Lecture I in PL). The first question is: "What is the most appropriate conception of justice for specifying the fair terms of social cooperation between citizens regarded as free and equal and as fully cooperating members of society over a complete life, from one generation to the next?" (PL 3). The second question is: "What are the grounds of toleration . . . given the fact of reasonable pluralism as the inevitable outcome of free institutions?" (PL 4). Rawls combines the first two questions to formulate a third one, which succeeds in summarizing them: "How is it possible for there to exist a just and stable society of free and equal citizens who remain profoundly divided by reasonable religious, philosophical and moral doctrines?" (PL 4).

The first chapter in PL is entitled "fundamental ideas." These are the ideas that Rawls deems essential for addressing the problem posed by this third question. In TJ, Rawls answered the first one of these three questions by appealing to the original position, separating the parties from their personal choices. However, the final part of TJ tries to reconcile the choices of parties in the original position with those of citizens in a well-ordered society to secure stability. PL calls into question this type of reconciliation, giving rise to the centrality of tolerance and reasonable disagreement as shown by the second question. In its turn, this implies the problem of stability posed by the third question.

The principles of justice in TJ are not formulated to answer the questions in PL. The sense of these questions is re-proposed by Rawls as laid down below: "How might political philosophy find a shared basis for settling such a fundamental question as that of the most appropriate family of institutions to secure democratic freedom and equality?" (PL 8).

The first step is an attempt to confine, through the recourse to a shared basis that supposedly characterizes the convictions of liberal-democratic citizens, the scope and nature of disagreement. Rawls' strategy in PL is to assume a collective interest in the agreement on a liberal democracy, which I have previously linked to the idea of legitimation. This assumption permits the achievement of a progressive reduction of the scope of disagreement, connected in this case with the idea of justification. We are dealing, once again, with the same stance adopted in the last section of TJ, which tells us that justification is bound to overcome a diversity of convictions but starts from partially shared premises (TJ, rev. edn. 508). What is new in PL is that the starting point is a reference to public culture and, ultimately, reasonable disagreement does not affect the core of liberal democracy. It must be recognized that this reasoning opens itself to criticism from both those who deny the plausibility or truthfulness of a priority interest in such a type of agreement and those who insist on the differences among various disagreements, even when reasonable. For example, the disagreement voiced by a libertarian or a communitarian is one thing and the disagreement voiced by a Marxist is definitely something else.

Adopting this point of view, the first step towards making sense of Rawls' solution for stability can be made by recalling how unanimous consensus has been reached on moral issues that once were dramatically divisive, such as slavery and religious tolerance. The same approach can be applied to the political core of liberal democracy. If we are to accept a convergence of various ideals around the core of a liberal democracy, then we can count on that shared basis. Otherwise, the problem of stability would defy any solution. Ultimately, we may hold that the reasonable pluralism of justifications is confronted here with the nearly unanimous consensus on the liberal-democratic legitimation.

As suggested by Rawls, to move further in this direction we need to look first at the liberal-democratic "public culture" that is in itself a "shared fund of implicitly recognized basic ideas and principles" (PL 10). Rawls already did something similar in TJ. Appealing to the method of "reflective equilibrium" and to stability, Rawls attempted to solve the problem of "acceptability" in a manner that was not purely deductive. Actually, the theory of justice as fairness presents itself in TJ as: "a conception of justice that may be shared by citizens as a basis of a reasoned, informed and willing political agreement.

It expresses their shared and public political reason" (PL 10). However, this may not provide a solution to the initial problem in PL. In order to answer it, we need a political conception,[3] "independent of the opposing and conflicting philosophical and religious doctrines that the citizens affirm (PL 9)."

It is only by having this that political liberalism potentially succeeds in applying "the principle of toleration to philosophy itself" (PL 10). It remains to be seen whether doing so is conceptually possible. Indeed, the reference to a freestanding doctrine could conceal an attempt to appeal to a comprehensive liberal doctrine, perhaps backed by a metaphysical view of the person and society.[4] Rawls decidedly denies any such possibility, affirming that he "offers no specific metaphysical or epistemological doctrine beyond what is implied by the political conception itself" (PL 10).

Rawls works out these fundamental ideas in an ambiguous way. On the one hand, he starts from a shared basis found in democratic public culture, a descriptive perspective. On the other hand, he moves from a freestanding view that presupposes a normative ground. The intersection between the descriptive and the normative level in PL often proves, as in this case, rather obscure and presents a clear problem throughout the book.

The political conception (see PL, Lecture 1, section 2) has three characteristic features: (i) the presupposition that it is a moral conception – "but a moral conception worked out for a specific kind of subject" (PL 11): namely, the basic structure of a democratic society; (ii) it is presented as a freestanding view (PL 12); and (iii) it "is expressed in terms of certain fundamental ideas seen as implicit in the public political culture of a democratic society" (PL 13).

The first of these three features – the constraint caused by the basic structure – includes an important assumption regarding the scope of the political conception. It includes in it the individuals' starting institutional conditions (family, education, etc.), considering them as elements of citizenship. It is not at all a pacific assumption. A libertarian, for instance, would not agree. The political conception, starting with a shared basic structure, presupposes a membership condition.[5]

The second requirement regards reciprocal respect among citizens. It says that the political conception has to be freestanding, that is, different and distinct from any comprehensive view applied to the basic structure. A doctrine is comprehensive when it "includes conceptions of what is of value in human life, and ideals of personal character, as well as ideals of friendship and familial and associational relationships" (PL 13). The comprehensive doctrines differ from each other and belong to the "background culture" (PL 14) which is and remains social rather than political. The background culture includes the typical culture of churches, universities, scientific associations, and clubs. While it is indeed possible for each citizen to derive his interpretation of the political conception from his comprehensive doctrine, he is not going to formulate it in terms of a comprehensive doctrine.

The third feature relates to the content of the political conception, which is limited to some basic ideas shared within the liberal-democratic culture. The public culture relates to the constitutional interpretation and the historical tradition of a political community. This is the only way to attain a considerable convergence on the political conception, which is limited to only the ideas shared within the public liberal-democratic ambit.

We can say that if the second feature prevails over the third, and we insist on the freestanding nature of the theory, we get a (more) normative view. If instead the third feature prevails over the second, and we insist on the shared basis, we have a (more) hermeneutical view. All three conditions emphasize that the political conception is distinct from a moral one.

By bringing these three features together, we may derive Hegel's classical distinction between the pluralism of the civil society and the unity of the state.[6] In practice, this distinction between political culture and background culture is rather rough. Indeed, it is quite hard to say where one starts and the other ends. However, one way to distinguish them is based on the difference of scope. While an association or a church usually tends to promote an end that is predetermined and formulated within the context of the background culture, the political conception has no specific ends other than those of its citizens.

This final distinction may help us to differentiate the "conception of the good" and the "comprehensive view." The main difference is that the former is individual and limited while the second is social and far-reaching. The political conception limits the comprehensive doctrines in the name of reasonableness, but it does not address directly conceptions of the good. The latter remain mostly individual forms of reflection and self-examination rather than turning into public ideals. Conceptions of the good in fact are compatible with the political conception because (PL 176): (i) they can be shared by all the citizens as free and equal persons; (ii) they do not presuppose a fully comprehensive doctrine. Hence, the political conception poses limits that correspond to those posed in TJ by the priority of right. In so doing, Rawls preserves the "neutrality of aims," whereby the state must not favor any comprehensive doctrines. In turn, the neutrality of aims is not equivalent to pure procedural neutrality since it actually supports just liberal-democratic institutions. Nor is it equivalent to neutrality of the effects or results (which Rawls deems impossible), which would entail that, given the simultaneous presence of various comprehensive conceptions in a well-ordered society, none of them takes advantage of the others (PL 191–4).[8] All this should be enough to differentiate political liberalism, linked to the political conception, from any form of comprehensive liberalism that promotes a complete lifestyle.[9]

The political conception comprises three fundamental ideas (which specify in an improved manner its third feature): (i) the idea of society as a "fair system of cooperation"; (ii) the idea of citizens as free and equal persons; (iii) the idea of a well-ordered society. They are subsequently associated with three concepts having a more definite theoretical nature that counterbalance the three fundamental ideas: the concept of basic structure, the concept of the original position, and the concept of public justification.

10.1.1 Reciprocity and well-ordered society

The first fundamental idea implicit in the political conception is the idea of society as a fair system of cooperation. Such cooperation lasts in time from one generation to the next and results from the democratic public culture. In this sense, cooperation is distinct: "from the merely socially coordinated activity, for example, from an activity coordinated by orders issued by some central authority. [On the contrary], cooperation is guided by publicly recognized rules and procedures that those cooperating accept and regard as properly regulating their conduct" (PL 16). This type of cooperation presupposes "fair terms": "these are terms that each participant may reasonably accept, provided that everyone else likewise accepts them" (PL 16). The fair terms of cooperation assume a substantial reciprocity. Such reciprocity is halfway between impartiality and mutual advantage.[10] One may also say that reciprocity is "a relation between citizens in a well-ordered society as expressed by its public political conception of justice" (PL 17). There is a link between primacy of the basic structure and reciprocity viewed in these terms. The basic structure limits the scope of the political conception based on membership, but it does not do so by chance. Reciprocity between citizens provides a structural reason to conceive of a common membership.

In Rawls, two interpretations of reciprocity coexist. The first one aims more directly at interests and is exemplified by the fair terms of cooperation as they result from the distribution of the primary goods. The second one starts from the citizens' ability mutually to justify their comprehensive doctrines in terms of public reason. The latter ends up being the prevailing interpretation in PL.

The second fundamental idea is laid down in paragraph 5 of Lecture I in PL, devoted to the "political conception of the person." Here, answering the communitarians, Rawls says that TJ does not presuppose any special metaphysical view of the person: "To understand what is meant by describing a conception of the person as political, consider how citizens are represented in that (I am adding "original") position as free persons" (PL 29).

According to Rawls, persons can be conceived as free persons in the following ways:

(i)   first, "they conceive of themselves and of one another as having the moral power to have a conception of the good" (PL 30);
(ii) "[a] second respect in which the citizens view themselves as free is that they regard themselves as self-authenticating sources of valid claims" (PL 32);

(iii) third, they view themselves as responsible citizens, capable of reconciling their claims with available goods (PL 33–4).

These aspects describe an idea of citizenship consistent with the political conception of society, viewed as a fair system of cooperation, and therefore: "we say that a person is someone who can be a citizen, that is, a normal and fully cooperating member of society over a complete life" (PL 20).

Citizens are conceived as free and equal persons, endowed with two moral powers: the sense of justice and a conception of the good. From this point of view, the political conception of the person may be interpreted as a revised version – suitable for the purposes of PL – of the conception of the person presented earlier by Rawls in KCMT. There is a connection between being endowed with moral powers and being a citizen capable of respecting the fair terms of cooperation.

A society governed by a public conception of justice is also characterized by the ideal of a well-ordered society (PL, Lecture I, paragraph 6). To say that a society is well ordered is tantamount to saying that: (i) it has a public conception of justice, in which each person acts on the basis of the same principles of justice and knows that the others do the same; (ii) each person is aware of the working of the main institutions (the basic structure); (iii) each person is endowed with a sense of justice that ensures that she complies with the fundamental institutions (PL 35).

This third fundamental idea is a corollary of the first two combined. The political conception of the person allows a fair cooperation based on reciprocity. Both characterize a well-ordered society. Ultimately, the latter points to a case of successful cooperation between free and equal citizens. We already know that, given the "fact of reasonable pluralism," we may no longer find in PL that identification between well-ordered society and the theory of justice as fairness that had characterized TJ. The well-ordered society in PL is instead characterized by structural pluralism.

The outcome of a well-ordered society viewed as specified above – as we are going to see better in the next chapter – is the formation of an overlapping consensus. A public conception of justice can fail because it cannot gain the support of "reasonable citizens who affirm comprehensive doctrines" (PL 36). The reason for this is that the political culture of a democratic society is characterized by three "general facts": (i) the variety of reasonable comprehensive doctrines present in the public space, which is not an "unfortunate condition of human life" but a virtue of democratic societies; (ii) the risk of coercion, which emerges when a single comprehensive doctrine is endorsed by the state (producing for Rawls "the fact of oppression"); and (iii) the need to acquire the political support of a majority of the population, something that would be impossible to obtain without a political conception moving beyond the various religious and ethical-political comprehensive doctrines. Such a conception must be limited to the "domain of the political"

(PL 38). Hence, citizens have a dual view of society and politics: one that coincides with their comprehensive doctrine and the other with the political conception.

The fundamental intuitive ideas are connected with a theoretical counterpart in three ways. The first of them is the original position, a concept that Rawls takes up in PL in section 4 of Lecture I. The idea of the original position is formulated with a view to finding principles of justice suitable for implementing conditions of equality and freedom once society is governed by fair terms of cooperation (PL 22). In TJ, this analytical tool is re-purposed to provide a version of the social contract that avoids traditional faults with this model, such as clarifying the purely hypothetical and virtual character of the contract. The original position becomes in PL essentially a "device of representation." In the original position, the agreement reached differs from that of a standard contract because the latter takes place within background conditions while the agreement in the original position must also regard the "background institutions."

A society based on a political conception is neither a community nor an association (PL, Lecture I, paragraph 7), since it is a political structure and does not have predetermined purposes. However, the ambit of the political conception in PL does not coincide with that of the (lack of) coercion by the state; the latter leads to something such as "think whatever you want about the meaning of life and its ultimate values, provided that you do not insist that the state forces others who hold an opinion that differs from yours to behave according to the dictates of your comprehensive doctrine." The issue is more complicated – as we are going to see when debating the concept of "public reason" – since it is the very linguistic exchange and, in general, the interaction among democratic citizens that must respect otherness when it affects essential aspects of the constitutional life and problems of "basic justice." The scope of pluralism is deeper, based more on respect for the other than is the pure and simple lack of coercion.

A significant problem associated with this idea of political conception is connected with a dual way of conceiving the agreement between citizens in a regime of pluralism. As argued by Fred D'Agostino, there are two main forms of agreement among differently motivated persons: one works by consent and the other by convergence.[11] In the former case, there is a neutral and a-priori argument that succeeds in convincing the parties to reach an agreement. In the latter case, the parties – although sticking to their different opinions – decide to meet on a common ground. The problem with the political conception of Rawls in PL is that it seems to include both the agreement and the convergence models. The former is more closely connected with the freestanding nature of the political conception, while the latter makes greater appeal to the shared basis. Should we accept the reading in terms of justification and legitimation that I have given in the last section of the preceding chapter, then we may appreciate that the merger of the two models is by no means due to chance. It results from the complementarity of the two main elements of the Rawlsian model.

10.2 The Centrality of the Reasonable

In the second Lecture of PL, entitled "Powers of Citizens and Their Representation," Rawls proposes the idea that the "diversity of reasonable comprehensive doctrines" (PL 36) can find common ground within a liberal-democratic regime. In Lecture I, Rawls presented the main problem posed in PL, the problem of the stable and just coexistence of free and equal citizens who affirm different reasonable religious, moral, and philosophical comprehensive doctrines. In Lecture II, he focuses on the concepts of "reasonable" and "reasonableness."[12] Their analysis leads to a distinction between "rational" and "reasonable," the notion of reasonable comprehensive doctrine, the difference between rational or complete autonomy, and the exposition of a moral psychology consistent with reasonableness. They are fundamental premises if we are to understand how a lasting overlapping consensus may subsequently occur.

Before getting to the heart of these points, I would like to summarize the central argument Rawls presents:

(i) various reasonable comprehensive doctrines coexist in a liberal-democratic regime;

(ii) a citizen "A" who believes in a reasonable comprehensive doctrine "X" may not be requested to abjure it in order to accept freely a state where constitutional essentials and basic matters of justice are based on a reasonable comprehensive doctrine "Y" affirmed by citizen "B" (where "X" and "Y" are somehow incompatible);

(iii) what is needed, instead, in order to avoid what is laid down in (ii) is a principle of liberal legitimation according to which the agreement on the constitutional essentials and the basic matters of justice can be potentially reached by all the reasonable citizens (who affirm the analogous comprehensive doctrines);

(iv) given what has been said in (ii) and (iii), it may be affirmed that there is no traditional political view that may succeed in meeting the liberal legitimation requirement playing on a single reasonable comprehensive doctrine;

(v) only a purely political conception may obtain the agreement of all the reasonable comprehensive doctrines;

(vi) thus, the agreement on a political conception provides the only way to avoid violating the principle of liberal legitimation.

Given what has been affirmed in (ii) with respect to reasonable disagreement, the problem posed by this argument is that it presumes the possibility of being able to affirm (v) and (vi). That is, the solution meets the principle of liberal legitimation through a political conception that claims to be freestanding with respect to every reasonable comprehensive doctrine. Two problems arise from the appeal to a freestanding political conception. On the one hand, the political conception may not be truly independent; on the other, the political conception could merely be the fruit of an expedient compromise.

The reasonable is different from the rational. This difference between the reasonable and the rational can be seen, first of all, in ordinary language (for instance, when we say, "Tom could also make this move, given his greater bargaining strength, but it would be absurd and unreasonable for him to do it").[13] However, in PL the distinction has a definite ethical-political significance. Reasonable persons are willing to adjust their behavior based on principles that take into account consequences that may affect not only themselves but also other persons. In so doing, reasonable persons cooperate on fair terms, provided that the other people behave likewise. This allows a mutual justification of the rules of conduct.[14] From this point of view, reasonableness presupposes reciprocity (and vice versa), and does not necessarily entail an altruistic motivation based on the will to assert the common good.

Being reasonable is a standard feature of the agents in the political life of a democracy. But the concept of reasonableness includes a pretension of a normative validity. The semantic oscillation between these two meanings – the descriptive and the normative – is a constant feature in PL. There are properties of the reasonable persons and properties of the comprehensive doctrines. The two versions may be reconciled: reasonable citizens, even when they have political power, would not repress "comprehensive views that are not unreasonable, though different from their own" (PL 60). Hence, it may be affirmed that the reasonable properties depend on the behavior of citizens who are reasonable persons, and, as such, prepared for tolerance.

The semantic oscillations of the term "reasonable" are also related to its "history" within Rawls' work. Indeed, the term dates back to Ph.D., and is already present in ODPE of 1951. In both cases, reasonableness is a specific quality of impartial judges. According to a Kantian version of this term, the difference between reasonable and rational corresponds to the difference existing between the categorical and hypothetical imperative.[15] Rawls explains the distinction for the first time in KCMT. He translates "vernünftig," the term used by Kant, both as "rational" and as "reasonable," as may be seen in his lectures on Kant.[16] The meaning of reasonable may be found by looking at Rawls' particular use of the categorical imperative. He shifts it from the domain of practical reason to that of liberal-democratic politics[17] where it turns into a sort of normative counterpart of citizenship. Another recognized source of the term is an article by Sibley in 1953, a position that is halfway between the first two domains and stresses the difference from rational.[18] Rawls' reasonableness is related to what in TJ is the "sense of justice," one of the fundamental moral powers of Rawlsian individuals.

Conversely, rationality differs from reasonableness. The rational applies to individuals or associations in the pursuit of their ends and interests. The latter are not necessarily egoistic (one can rationally desire the good of others), and rationality is not limited to the means–ends reasoning. What is missing in particular in the agents as rational beings is the sensitivity that allows entrance into a fair cooperation. Indeed, Rawls says that a purely rational agent would look like a psychopath (PL 51). From this point of view, reasonableness helps to justify the notion of reciprocity.

In both TJ and PL, the reasonable and the rational are distinct though complementary, "and neither the reasonable nor the rational can stand without the other" (PL 52). There is no attempt in TJ (according to Rawls himself) to derive the reasonable from the rational. The complementarity is a requirement: merely reasonable persons (PL 52) would be empty, having no ends of their own, while merely rational persons would be unable to cooperate properly. Reasonableness lays down the terms of a basic political agreement on which persons come to an understanding, while the rational represents the possibility of end-oriented individual and collective actions. The rational–reasonable dichotomy reproduces the dichotomy between a conception of the good and a sense of justice, and we also say that "the right and the good are complementary" (PL 173).

The reasonable is eminently public, while the rational is not. The reasonable is connected with reciprocity (between impartiality and mutual advantage), in the sense that free and equal persons are aware of the diversity of their claims and agree on fair terms of cooperation. Through the reasonable, we take part in the life of the collective world; we realize that the purpose of politics is not only the attainment of results but also the ability to establish suitable relations among persons.[19]

The idea of the reasonable is a presupposition of liberal tolerance. It allows and furthers the reasonable pluralism of the comprehensive doctrines. If the first motive in favor of tolerance is the ethical-political ability to exchange reasons with others in a regime of reciprocity, the second motive lies halfway between epistemology and politics. It is represented by the presence of what Rawls call the "burdens of judgment." The burdens of judgment are at the base of our use of public reason in directing the legitimate exercise of political power in a constitutional regime (PL 54–8). The burdens of judgment explain why reasonable disagreement in ethics and politics is long-lasting, unlike what happens in the field of scientific research, and why the only way to avoid reasonable disagreement in politics is the recourse to coercive power. This does not depend on the fact that we act based on narrow interests but, indeed, on the fact that certain limits of intersubjective agreement are intrinsic in the problems posed by ethics and politics.

The idea of reasonable disagreement as based on the presence of the burdens of judgment presupposes the existence of sources or causes (PL 55), as outlined below:

(i)   proofs are hard to find;
(ii) even when in agreement on important considerations, there is the possibility of disagreement with respect to the weight to be attributed to each one of them;
(iii) our concepts in this context are often vague;
(iv) the way in which we think morally and politically depends to a considerable extent on the experience gained by each one of us;
(v)   cases are often controversial because normative considerations having similar significance weight on both sides;
(vi) in a confined social space, at times it is impossible to give priority to different values.

All this causes a reasonable agent to make room for reasonable disagreement. Rawls assumes that reasonable persons only endorse "reasonable comprehensive doctrines." From the point of view of reasonableness, comprehensive doctrines may be defined based on three characteristics:

(i)   they cover fundamental religious, philosophical, and moral aspects of human life in an altogether consistent manner;
(ii) each differs from the other ones in respect of the choice of a few values as being fundamental and of overriding importance;
(iii) they usually belong to more or less univocal traditions of thought.

If what has been specified in the matter of reasonable disagreement is connected with the characteristics of the comprehensive doctrines, we see that, in a democratic society, the same reasonable comprehensive doctrine cannot be shared by all.

Reasonable persons accept the pluralism of reasonable comprehensive doctrines and do not aim to force others – by resorting to coercive power – to believe in their comprehensive doctrine. Those willing to do something like that would seem ready to insist on what they take as true based more on strength than on the possibility of an adequate justification (PL 61). Reasonable persons, acknowledging the burdens of judgment, favor freedom of thought and conscience. From this point of view, reasonableness is not so much an epistemological virtue, even though in its origins there are cognitive motivations, as it is ethical-political and an aspect of citizenship (PL 62). One may be unreasonable from an epistemological and metaphysical point of view while remaining reasonable from the political point of view.[20]

Rawls adds two comments on this subject. The first concerns the difference between skepticism and recognition of the political meaning of the burdens of judgment. The difficulty of agreeing on major political themes is not the product of philosophical skepticism so much as the outcome of concrete historical experience. As previously pointed out, even if there is an epistemic sense of the reasonable, resting on the burdens of judgment, it is clear that

Rawls takes the term to have a prevailing moral meaning. This is why Rawls does not need to take a skeptical stance towards epistemology and metaphysics. Nonetheless, the question of skepticism cannot be solved in such a simple manner. Rawls insists that his theory of the burdens of judgment has nothing to do with an epistemological and metaphysical view, though there is still a suspicion that there is a sort of "abstinence" (the term has been used by Joseph Raz) from the truth.[21] Political ideas, in this case, could not aspire to be true but only reasonable.

The second comment concerns the distinction between the "fact of pluralism" and the "fact of reasonable pluralism." Unlike simple pluralism, reasonable pluralism rules out the possibility that a difference in opinion might be due to mistakes and prejudices or pure unreasonableness. Rawls introduces an interesting retrospective distinction that concerns the theory of justice as fairness (PL 64). He differentiates two stages of the theory. At the first stage, the very theory of justice as fairness appears as being "freestanding" and articulates the values of political justice and public reason. It is only at the second stage that the question of stability arises, when the theory of justice as fairness gets to grips with actual people. At the first stage, the question about the nature of pluralism – for instance, whether it is reasonable or not – is not particularly important. At the second stage, when the overlapping consensus comes into play and the question of stability becomes central, the principles of justice have already been chosen and one ought to see whether the persons trust the institutions after having made their choice. What becomes relevant in this second case is the reasonableness of pluralism. This remark stresses once again how the reasonableness of pluralism is somehow connected with the revision of the third part of TJ. It concerns the prospect of stability after the choice of the principles in the original position has already taken place and how this part of PL improves upon the preceding work. Moreover, this bears out the hypothesis of continuity in Rawls' interpretation (see chapter 1).

A well-ordered society is governed by a public conception of justice (PL 66ff., Lecture II). The public nature (publicity) of this process in the theory of justice as fairness features three aspects:

(i) a first level, reached when a society is really governed by a public conception of justice;
(ii) a second level, where the citizens of a well-ordered society use publicly shared forms of reasoning and methods of investigation;
(iii) a third level, connected with the "full justification" that, if not always present in the public culture, must be at least available.

If all of the three aspects exist, then the "full publicity condition" is met. The democratic political power belongs to the public and, in a condition of a fully attained publicity, the citizens can trust each other to a greater extent.

The intrinsically public nature of the liberal-democratic power brings out the importance of the need to justify political actions that concern the fundamental aspects of collective life. From the point of view of the reasonable, it is not enough for the citizens to account for the reasonableness of their position to themselves. They must be ready to account to others. The citizens will mutually endeavor to clarify their claims in a regime of publicity. In this sense, we may join Scanlon[22] in saying that an argument is reasonable if it is possible to hope that there are no reasons for others to refuse it. The reasonable has something to do not only with the burdens of judgment and epistemic uncertainty, but also with the founding ideas of reciprocity and cooperation. Within the context of a cooperative project of society, the liberal-democratic citizens – assuming reasonableness – consider the others as free and equal citizens. Against the background of this concept, there is also the principle – underlying liberal legitimation – according to which in a liberal democracy public coercion may be exercised based only on reasons that, as a rule, may be shared by all the citizens. Persons – to say it as Rawls does – "are entitled to equal respect and consideration in the design of their common institutions" (CP 270).

All this underlies the distinction between rational autonomy and complete autonomy, where the former is "artificial and non-political" and the latter is "political and non-ethical." Rational autonomy is based on intellectual and moral powers. It is what makes the original position a form of pure procedural justice. In its context, the citizens pursue – within fair limits – their conceptions of the good and find the motivations to attain their highest-order interests. Such rational autonomy is artificial in that it is that of the parties in the original position rather than that of actual persons. On the other hand, the complete autonomy does not depend on how the parties deliberate in the original position, but on the constraints and the structure of the original position. It is not the parties who are endowed with full autonomy but, indeed, the citizens who attain it when they act in conformity with the principles of justice and establish among themselves fair terms of cooperation. It is a complete political and non-ethical autonomy because it is fulfilled in public life by applying the principles of justice.

10.2.1 Problems of reasonableness

Reasonableness provides the basis to attain what Rawls calls the "liberal principle of legitimacy." In this regard, citizens do not necessarily agree on a specific type of political judgment because it can be justified. They nonetheless agree on the fact that, in justifying it, they must take themselves mutually in earnest, considering themselves reasonable. In so doing, they really belong to the same political society. We may find the theses of the others inconsistent or simply mistaken but, in a climate of reasonableness, we accept their public nature. In short, reasonable citizens acknowledge one another as "fully cooperating members of society" (PL 55). If citizens put reasonableness aside and insist on asserting their theses as such, they break off this circle of mutual recognition and respect.[23]

A problem becomes at this point quite evident. This prospect may lead to several cases of stand-off in which this method fails to be efficacious: one can find it hard to choose among various alternatives consistent with its principles.[24] The problem becomes more serious when we consider a non-ideal situation – that is, a situation not characterized by strict compliance. If, for instance, we consider international cultural conflicts, but also some of the most sensitive domestic conflicts, it can hardly be affirmed that the confrontation on such matters always takes place based on the recognition of someone else's reasonableness.[25] In all these cases, the way out appears quite tricky: either one chooses a certain continuity between the favorite comprehensive doctrine and the political conception, thereby betraying political liberalism, or one abides by political liberalism, waiving a theoretically acceptable decision.

The first option – the choice of a relative continuity between comprehensive doctrine and political conception – is demanding since it potentially excludes people from citizenship in the name of liberal reasonableness.[26] Is it reasonable to marginalize those who do not appear "reasonable" based on these criteria? By what right can one do it, and with what consequences? Besides, is it not an "expedient" to disavow a priori those who are not sufficiently convinced of the fundamental assumptions of liberal democracy, in this case judging them and/or their arguments as non-reasonable?[27] In other words, is this not a form of comprehensive liberalism – which, as such, is less tolerant than how Rawls instead claims it to be – concealed beneath the doctrine of the reasonable?[28]

Let us consider the question also from the point of view of those who could suffer such marginalization. For instance, several ethnic and cultural minorities are often not considered reasonable yet reside, sometimes with citizenship rights, in states characterized by a liberal-democratic system. These groups include the Amish and the Quakers in the United States or gypsies and Islamic minorities in many Western countries.[29] In what sense are they required to respect criteria of liberal reasonableness, as desired by Rawls, if their profound preferences prevent them from doing so? Let us imagine that these persons respect the legal and constitutional rules of the polity under consideration in a purely formal manner. As we are going to see, the overlapping consensus on which Rawls' liberal reconciliation is based is a moral instrument and may not be satisfied with a merely ostensible and fictitious support.[30] Even my interpretation in terms of legitimation presupposes a certain degree of institutional loyalty. But how can we impose it, from a liberal perspective, on those who – from the point of view of their comprehensive doctrine – have excellent reasons to question the liberal legal and constitutional principles? Muslims with respect to women, gypsies with respect to regular work, the Amish with respect to the will to review traditional conceptions of the good, and Quakers with respect to war are all groups facing similar problems. To impose the liberal solution, viewing them as being a priori unreasonable, seems a serious solution fraught with risky consequences from the very point of view of stability.

There are apparently two opposite points where the Rawlsian thesis on reasonableness may be most successfully attacked: the claim that reasonableness is not a neutral virtue and the claim that reasonableness is somehow not separable from the lack of a specific commitment to truth, which in its turn can be considered philosophically indispensable.[31] Furthermore, the two critiques can be presented together, claiming that the alleged lack of a pretension of truth, in the name of the reasonable, makes the liberal exclusion in the name of unreasonableness purely arbitrary.[32] I refer to the advocates of the criticism based on the arbitrariness of the exclusion as "political" and to the ones based on the lack of truth as "epistemic," and present the third intermediate option as a passage from the political to the epistemic criticism.

The political critiques highlight the potential arbitrariness of the liberal exclusion based on non-reasonableness.[33] Those who are not in favor of liberalism may view the charge of unreasonableness by liberals as a devious and preliminary way to condemn someone else's theses without adequately considering them. This critique charges that since the concept of reasonableness directly relates to the initial fundamental ideas of PL, those who fail to concur with these premises would not be reasonable.[34] Moreover, the concept of reasonableness is not only a consequence of the fundamental ideas, but also the pivot of a normative doctrine of political liberalism. To this it may be objected that to assume the plausibility of the liberal-democratic paradigm without taking into account, for instance, the opinions of its radical critics (for instance Marx, Nietzsche, or the Muslim Brothers), is itself an illiberal intellectual operation.[35] From this point of view, the very concept of reasonableness may prove to be controversial.

This type of criticism may take a more radical political turn if one argues – as Chantal Mouffe does – that the request for reasonableness conceals a form of repression of diversity.[36] If one reflects upon those Carl Schmitt-type decisionist premises endorsed by Mouffe, then the point may be understood in the following way. Political action is always somehow arbitrary and refers to the basic pre-theoretical distinction between friend and foe. The liberals, charging their opponents with unreasonableness, would do nothing else but apply the same method as non-liberals without having the courage to admit it explicitly.[37] Mouffe's thesis starts from the presuppositions that politics may not actually escape the aggressive exclusion of the other and that the liberal claim of avoiding something like that is simply deceptive.[38] If what counts in politics is power rather than reasons, there are no exceptions – however sophisticated they might be – that such a thesis may hold up. The rest is pure "academic mystification."[39]

It is hard to consider these types of political objections, as I have defined them, given their fully general nature connected with the concept of the political. In any event, insofar as Rawls' notion of reasonableness is concerned, it should be recalled that the exclusion it entails is quite limited. Above all, as it has been pointed out,[40] this exclusion does not impinge on the "background culture" and, therefore, a full range of themes having definite political relevance is not affected. Second, the exclusion ultimately relates to very few aspects of public life. We are dealing with those aspects, on which – in a liberal-democratic perspective – it would seem inadvisable to insist. The fact that Rawls gives the example of slavery as something that should be excluded from public debate speaks volumes for how prudent and limited the Rawlsian liberal exclusion is. In short, there is no substantial content of controversial public themes removed from the democratic political agenda in the name of reasonableness.

However, at this point I want to defend Rawls' thesis against these political critiques in a different way. Such a complex theory as that of reasonableness in PL cannot start from no assumptions and must offer some political premises. Considering Rawls' premises, the major one is, in my opinion, connected with the idea of legitimation: liberal democracy as such has a normative value. This means that it is worth defending and worth trying to show how the friend–foe fight may move to another level that is more symbolic and respectful of others. Rawls has no arguments against those who stand outside these limits. From this point of view, to claim that the concept of reasonableness is vague means very little. Moreover, one may insist on the fact that it is meaningful to exchange sensible arguments on political themes, instead of resorting to pure violence. In my opinion, this kind of argument allows us, *prima facie*, to accept the sense of the Rawlsian distinction on the reasonable even if we may have doubts about the specific way Rawls defends it.

The other critical argument on reasonableness – which I call the epistemic argument – is based on an alleged epistemological and theoretical disengagement that should be implicit in the concept of the reasonable. In our case, it may be expedient to refer to Gaus' objection. Gaus upholds that the political justification in PL lacks an authentic normative value.[41] In his opinion, Rawls in PL would appeal to the factual consensus of the citizens rather than to the theory where reasonableness needs to be justified.[42] This is the reason why the objection being made is that of "justificatory populism." In so doing, no doubt Gaus exaggerates, even though he seizes upon a likely problem within Rawls' thesis on this matter.[43] Indeed, the distinction between ideal consensus of the persons, which presupposes the soundness of the theory, and empirical consensus of the citizens, which presupposes a factual acceptance, is often fleeting in Rawls' text.[44]

Gaus' critical argument may act as a connection between the epistemological argument and the political argument, for this reason: if the theoretical argument on reasonableness were really based only on the factual consensus of the citizens, rather than on philosophical-normative presuppositions, then any exclusion of persons or arguments from the political debate in the name of reasonableness would be arbitrary (as supported by Rawls' political critics). I do not believe that Gaus is totally wrong on this point (his argument should be examined more thoroughly than I can do here). Rawls actually superimposes two subjects on reasonableness, one that appeals to normative principles and one that refers to the shared basis. In so doing, he may be hazy at times, but that does not mean he is philosophically "populist" (suffice it to read PL, *inter alia*, to see how little Rawls' approach is populist). One way out of the impasse is to confirm the dual function played by liberalism in Rawls: what I have called the picture-frame. Rawls is very keen on differentiating "political values" from "moral doctrines." For he maintains that values are not moral doctrines. The latter are on a level with religion and first philosophy. By contrast, liberal principles and values, although intrinsically moral values, are specified by liberal political conceptions of justice and fall under the category of the political".

Now, the distinction between a political and a philosophical or moral sphere, as endorsed by Rawls, is not easy to maintain since what should be considered political as such is intrinsically controversial (Gaus says "essentially contested"). In this sense, Rawls assumes something that should be proved – namely, that there is something political as such that may be distinguished from the rest of our views of the world. In this case, Gaus has his reasons. But, once again, I would go back to the responses countering the political objections to Rawls: if we fail to assume an exemplary and normative value of the liberal democracy – the one I have associated with the idea of legitimation – the entire concept of the reasonable will be empty. But can we fail to assume it? In the end, I am more inclined to think that Gaus' critical argument causes us to consider Rawls' normative standard in PL as being too weak with respect to what is needed, something upheld by epistemological critics of reasonableness. If, as previously pointed out, the very practice of democracy as such is for Rawls a political value and this underlies his central idea of political legitimacy, then we can always refuse to accept such a premise.

If we go back to Rawls' epistemic critics, the first point seems to be connected with Gaus-type theses: there are topical times in public life where the standards that determine the reasonableness of a disagreement are controversial. These standards are complex, being on the one hand epistemological (as regards this subject, Rawls distinguishes: matters of fact, methods of inquiry, and test criteria), and on the other political. Is it possible, in the major public discussions, to keep them separate and distinct? Is it plausible to affirm something like, "I put the former aside and keep the latter"? It is not at all easy to answer in the affirmative. The issue of abortion shows how that separation is both difficult and necessary. It is difficult because the unsolved crux of the problem depends on a metaphysical, ethical, and scientific question, such as: when does life originate? It is necessary, because there is no way to move ahead without sidestepping this type of question.

However, the theory presents us with another misgiving, that is, can this type of distinction in the matter of reasonableness be maintained without providing philosophical foundations and attributing them to a sort of evidence that comes from the domain of the political? Without a doubt, deep epistemic disagreements pose problems that are indeed connected with the definition of the ambit of what is political, and this creates trouble for the theory of the reasonable. Can this type of difficulty with political liberalism be overcome, and how?[45]

Joseph Raz – probably Rawls' most authoritative epistemic critic – argues that such a difficulty should be overcome through a greater epistemological commitment, thereby avoiding that "epistemic abstinence" that supposedly represents the authentic weakness of Rawls' theory of the reasonable.[46] According to Raz, the epistemic abstinence lies in the fact that Rawls avoids claiming that his doctrine of justice is true.[47] Raz says that the main philosophical commitment is always that of favoring truth and that a philosopher cannot abstain from claiming that his theses have a pretension of truth. This critique ultimately relates to the entire political justification presented in PL, but applies in particular to the idea of the reasonable. Rawls explicitly affirms in PL that the political conception is founded on the reasonable rather than being founded on the true. In fact, he leaves the concept of truth entirely to the comprehensive doctrines.

If we ask ourselves why Rawls seeks reasonableness rather than aspiring to truth, a first defense of the Rawlsian position consists in suitably delimiting the ambit of his interests in the matter. By this, I mean to say that, while the truth concerns the ambit of knowledge in general, in PL Rawls debates in the political conception just a few values that relate to the basic structure. He does not address the values as a whole that relate to the person in its entirety. Second, Rawls' approach has always assumed a constructivist rather than a realist ontological perspective. Rather than talking about the truth of his theses, one should perhaps talk about objectivity as general acceptability. Third, Rawls' controversial "methods of avoidance" may be understood by assuming, as Rawls does, that the philosophical disputation on truth is too "intractable" to be included in a political-theoretical argument. Regardless of these attempts to defend Rawls' stance against an objection such as that of Raz's, we may endeavor to find a solution that might explain the difference between the two positions. Raz argues that truth, at least for a philosopher, is much more important than the "stability" about which Rawls is so concerned.

Raz's alternative, however, may perhaps be wrong-footed. Given a background of doctrinal pluralism such as that present in PL, and given the need for a common space of reasons on which the idea of stability is based, the concept of truth becomes problematic. However, it is perhaps possible to distinguish the truth of a few specific policies and the philosophical disputations on the nature of truth from the concept of truth itself, saving the latter although rejecting the former. From this point of view, it is not wrong to believe that Rawls' overall view might aspire to a sort of peculiar truth, meant as a political conception of truth.[48] Such an argument may be applied against those who argue that the truth of a comprehensive doctrine is of no use to Rawls in PL. What is needed is a version of truth that is likely to prevent the claims of individual groups that consider themselves "reasonable" being imposed on others.[49] This would be a minimal truth that allows differentiation between various claims of reasonableness. I believe that my justification–legitimation thesis somehow answers this type of need.

Nonetheless, what is more interesting in a Rawls-type thesis is the inevitability that seems to be connected with the type of argument that he presents on this point. We have already mentioned that, according to Rawls, tolerance takes priority over philosophy because it is a political virtue of the liberal-democratic systems that may not be set aside. From this point of view, practice may not be turned into theory; on the contrary, it has an irredeemable specificity of its own. Indeed, in a way that is not always clear, it would seem that participation in the game of democratic politics represents for Rawls the base of reasonableness. A person becomes reasonable by catching the spirit of democracy, which, for Rawls, consists in the constant exchange of reasons among citizens aware of the burdens of judgment and endowed with a solid respect for others. In so doing, epistemology and politics are connected and Aristotle meets Kant.

Let us assume the possibility of a separation, putting liberalism – as a doctrine of principles – on one side and democracy – as an exercise of consensus – on the other. If we have a preference for the contractualist jargon, we can also talk about an ideal liberal consensus and a factual democratic consensus. The problem is to see how these two levels of consensus can intersect to create a mixed theory of justification and legitimation. Liberal perfectionists, such as Raz, drawn to the epistemic criticism of reasonableness, tend to think that what counts is merely the ideal consensus on principles. For them, the factual consensus is, from a normative point of view, a necessary consequence of the ideal consensus. In such a way, we witness the working of what could be defined, from a meta-ethical point of view, as a strong internalism. According to strong internalism, the acceptability in the abstract of the doctrine of the principles automatically determines the motivation of the political behavior. If correct, liberalism incorporates democracy. In my jargon, on this view what counts is not the legitimation but merely the justification. In stark contrast, the political critiques tend to consider irrelevant, if not thoroughly hypocritical, the level of the principles. Hence, they seriously evaluate only the level of the factual consensus. So, for instance, Rorty – interpreting Rawls in his own way – argues that what counts in politics is democracy and not philosophy.[50] In this case, the justifications are only hypocritical supports for political legitimations obtained otherwise. Now, in my opinion, the point on which Rawls is adamant – the one that I perceive as being a fundamental intellectual conquest in PL – is that he argues that there must be a structural connection between the two types of consensus – between liberalism and democracy and between justification and legitimation.

This argument may perhaps allow for affirming that the epistemic critiques as such are mistaken because they fail to catch the profound normative level of Rawls' proposal. In PL, Rawls formulates a normative proposal that concerns the morality of politics from a liberal perspective. There is a space for Rawlsian normative reasons that takes its place between the individual justifications, which refer to comprehensive theories, and the consensus based on the liberal-democratic legitimation. Although this space is limited, merely including the constitutional essentials and the matters of basic justice, it is crucial as a foundational presupposition of the liberal-democratic public life. The chief purpose of this moral space is to create conditions of mutual respect and trust among citizens. The reasonable coincides with the boundaries of this space.

10.3 Political Constructivism

Reasonableness presupposes ideal consensus in the background, but it is won in the practice of democracy. The latter is redeemed by Rawls by its facticity and endowed with an autonomous normative meaning. The inner rules of the democratic game are an element of legitimation. Democracy as a practice is "normativized" in PL in a manner that is original from a formal point of view but that, in substance, is not too different from what the theorists of the deliberative democracy and the republican theorists actually do. In such a way, we get to what is perhaps the central thesis in PL: people who maintain a basic distinction in the matter of principles can nonetheless participate with equal dignity and similar results in the democratic game. The resulting stability becomes evident in the progressive attainment of an "overlapping consensus."

In such a way, political liberalism shapes the horizon within which various theoretic-political families and democratic practices meet. Hence, liberalism becomes less ethical and more political while at the same time democracy becomes less procedural and more normative. Here is also where the difference between TJ and PL lies: in TJ, acceptability in principle is the basis for the factual acceptance of the liberal theory; in PL, instead, it is the factual acceptance that partly rises up to the level of the principles. In other words, with my own jargon, in PL justification gives way to legitimation.

The political conception of justice is formulated by Rawls through a methodological option that he calls "political constructivism"[51] (Lecture III). In this way, Rawls closes the first three lectures in PL, those that draw more directly on the themes and problems proposed for the first time in KCMT in 1980, while explaining at the same time what is the point of greatest separation between 1980 and PL. In fact, the philosophical purpose remains quite similar, being a question of joining an ideal of practical reason with role-related conceptions that are connected with the person and society. And the difference mainly concerns the method: "Political constructivism is a view about the structure and content of a political conception. It says that once, if ever, reflective equilibrium is attained, the principle of political justice (content) may be represented as the outcome of a certain procedure of construction" (PL 89–90). Political constructivism is presented by drawing a specific distinction from Kant's moral constructivism and moral intuitionism, viewed as a specific form of realism in ethics. The main difference from moral constructivism lies in the fact that the latter is ultimately a thesis on the objectivity of morals and, therefore, cannot help but be a definitely controversial thesis. However, in stating what it does, it contradicts those requirements of uniformity and pluralism clearly shown by the political conception. Hence, if moral constructivism corresponds somehow to the Kantian idea of moral autonomy, then political constructivism will have to work for a Rawlsian notion of political autonomy.[52]

According to political constructivism, the principles that govern a well-ordered society depend on a construction procedure. The latter is based on practical reason rather than on theoretical reason. Political constructivism starts from the model conceptions of person and society referred to above and applies the idea of the reasonable. The difference from a Kantian position depends on the fact that political constructivism is not a comprehensive doctrine, does not share a constitutive idea of autonomy, does not assume conceptions of person and society that derive from the transcendental idealism, and has no parallel purposes. Instead, political constructivism starts from an original agreement and endeavors to provide the ways in which citizens mutually justify their claims on the matter of basic justice. In so doing, Rawls aims to get to the objectivity of his particular political conception.

The thesis of political constructivism is another controversial passage within the context of PL. In fact, political constructivism implies the idea that the construction of political conceptions of citizen and society that are somehow philosophically neutral is actually feasible. This requirement corresponds to the attempt to create a freestanding political conception based on what Rawls calls "doctrinal autonomy" (PL 99ff.). Hence, political autonomy is attained by separating the construction procedure from the individual comprehensive doctrines in the background. Quite a few readers of Rawls seem to rule out the possibility that something like that might occur. However, this is a critical argument that looks very much like the one we have debated at length on the subject of reasonableness and is the origin of the Rawlsian view of the political legitimation of a liberal democracy.

10.4 The Question of Stability

The profound motivations of PL certainly include the fact that Rawls had been dissatisfied for quite a time with the third part of TJ. This part deals with stability, and Rawls, since the very Introduction to PL (xix), clearly says: "the problem of stability is fundamental to political philosophy." We are dealing with the development of the "sense of justice" and the congruence between the good and the right as the basis of stability in a "well-ordered" society.[53] In PL, we clearly detect the reason for Rawls' dissatisfaction. Through the formulation of the thesis in favor of stability, the theory of justice as fairness proves to be a "comprehensive philosophical doctrine" and we all know too well that PL argues that such a doctrine may not be the bedrock of a modern liberal-democratic society. Instead, liberal-democratic society is characterized "by a pluralism of incompatible yet reasonable comprehensive doctrines. Not one of these doctrines is affirmed by citizens generally. Nor should one expect that in the foreseeable future one of them, or some other reasonable doctrine, will ever be affirmed by all, or nearly all, citizens" (PL xvi).

Stability, when based on "right reasons" – as is the stability that Rawls has in mind – presupposes a convergence between the moral interests of the persons and the theory of justice that is theoretically considered the best. Quite obviously for Rawls, the latter is the theory of justice as fairness presented in TJ. The "highest moral sentiments" Rawls refers to are the capacity to have a conception of the good and the capacity to have a sense of justice. The consistency between these moral sentiments and the theory of justice is the basis of the stability of a well-ordered society in TJ because, in a relatively just society, the parties find a correspondence between their view of the good and the theory of justice as fairness on which the society they live and work in is constructed. Hence, stability imposes on the rational agent a sort of motivational priority centered on the sense of justice.

The question of stability has considerable relevance in TJ. After all – though in an intermittent manner and with a few digressions – Rawls devoted nearly 200 pages in Part III to the subject of stability. It is quite surprising that Rawls' clear interest in this subject has not been met by similar heated critical debate prior to the publication of PL. From the very beginning, Rawls fails to show any special interest in a Hobbesian type of stability, that is, the aspiration to social peace as such. Instead, he is interested in a moral stability founded on "right reasons" within a society that may be recognized as being just or nearly just. Originally, the Rawlsian argument on stability had drawn on an idea developed by Kant. Kant focused on the problem of how it is possible for humanity to have a just constitution. He stressed that it was not enough to have an adequate view of the just constitution in order to obtain it. Kant added that goodwill was also required. Citizens need to be ready to accept the very type of constitution that had been envisaged.[54]

Indeed, the preference for Kant's model rather than that of Hobbes allows us to note at once a peculiar aspect in Rawls' formulation of the concept of stability. Rawls transforms a typically psychological, sociological, and institutional notion of stability into a fundamentally moral notion.This is the reason why Rawls may affirm – as in the Introduction to PL – that the concept of stability "has played very little role in the history of moral philosophy" (PL xvii) even if it "is fundamental to political philosophy" (PL xvii). It is also strange that Rawls subsequently believes the topic is neglected, given that the problem of order – a synonym of stability – often featured prominently.[55] This shows, however indirectly, the originality of his moral view of stability. Rawlsian stability is not a structural feature of the political systems since it is a consequence of a psychological and moral attitude. In other words, Rawls' stability does not relate to the order of society in general, but to that of the ethical relation between citizens and just societies. Such a view of stability seems to link the theory of justice tightly to a given psychological–moral view that is reminiscent of Kantian autonomy.

In any event, the model of the Kantian argument is taken up by Rawls in TJ when he suggests that a just constitution – as Kant calls it – is not possible without the free support of rational and reasonable citizens. Assuming that we have an adequate idea of the theory of justice – says Rawls in Part III of TJ, entitled "Ends" – how can we know that our theoretical construction corresponds to the real motivations of the persons? The answer to this question should actually be provided by the argument on stability (end of chapter 7, and chapters 8 and 9 of TJ). However, notwithstanding the relevance attached to this subject in TJ, it cannot be denied that the problem becomes truly central only in PL. Rawls himself, with a view to stressing the central distinction between TJ and PL on the point at issue, writes: "To understand the nature and extent of the differences one must see them as arising from trying to resolve a serious internal problem to justice as fairness, namely from the fact that the account of stability in Part III of *Theory* is not consistent with the view as a whole" (PL xv–xvi).

Taking a step backwards, it may be noted that the question of stability actually goes back to the way in which the doctrine of the social contract is formulated. In short, the Rawlsian contract aims at two things. First, it aims at acceptance based on a deductive argument given by the agreement of the parties in the original position. But second, the argument resorts to fairly factual elements that may be traced back to the stability of the system and to the notion of "well-ordered society," which includes the "strains of commitment" and reflective equilibrium. In PL, stability is more clearly placed at the center of the reasoning. Rawls recognizes that his thesis on stability in TJ has a problem that becomes clearer as the years go by. Rawls' theory is based on an unrealistic assumption since it presupposes that all the citizens share the substance of the theory of justice as fairness. As Rawls says in TJ, in a well-ordered society "everyone has a similar sense of justice and in this respect a well-ordered society is homogeneous. Political argument appeals to this moral consensus" (TJ 263; red. edn. 232).

Since the early 1970s,[56] the most acute critiques of TJ have stressed that – despite the attempts to gain relative neutrality – Rawls' position includes a substantial part of a liberal view of the good within the theory of justice as fairness. In other words, the consistency between good and right referred to above and, therefore, the stability according to TJ, depends on the fact that the Rawlsian parties are already convinced of the plausibility of a liberal moral view. This is the only way they would find the theory of justice as fairness acceptable from the point of view of consistency with their conception of the good. In essence, in the version of stability provided in Part III of TJ, Rawls assumes that all citizens in a well-ordered society "hold the same comprehensive doctrine, and this includes aspects of Kant comprehensive liberalism, to which the principles of justice as fairness might belong. But given the fact of reasonable pluralism, this comprehensive view is not held by citizens generally, any more than a religious doctrine, or some form of utilitarianism" (PL xlii).

10.4.1 Two arguments on stability

In point of fact, Rawls presents two arguments for stability in TJ in separate parts of the book. In his opinion, the first – linked to the "publicity condition" – escapes criticism better than the second. In the course of the first argument (TJ, Part I, chapter 3, section 29, 175 ff.; rev edn. 153ff.), Rawls argues in favor of the theory of justice as fairness as opposed to utilitarianism and perfectionism. He uses the "publicity condition" as an aspect of stability that only his doctrine of justice would be comparatively able to safeguard. Justice as fairness better captures the publicity condition for two reasons. First, protecting the most disadvantaged, once publicly known, allows a greater stability of the social system since those more entitled to complain about the existing state of things would feel protected on this view more than they would be within the context of alternative political views. Second (TJ 179–92; rev. edn. 156–62), the principles of justice, once publicly known, would strengthen the sense of reciprocity among the citizens and would allow the practice of self-respect better than likely alternatives. This first argument on stability has not been revised in a significant manner in PL. The second argument on stability, presented in Part III of TJ, is the one that Rawls revises more thoroughly in PL.[57] Even this argument may be broken down into two sub-parts. The former, presented in chapter 8 of TJ, concerns more explicitly evolutionary moral psychology and starts from the presupposition that the principles of justice in a well-ordered society promote among the citizens the development of a sense of justice consistent with respect for the institutions. This sense of justice develops somehow in parallel with the institutions and, ultimately, makes it possible to get over the mere pursuit of one's personal interest and, therefore, allows support for reciprocity among citizens.[58] As Rawls states:

> When institutions are just (as defined by this conception), those taking part in these arrangements acquire the corresponding sense of justice and desire to do their part in maintaining them. One conception of justice is more stable than another if the sense of justice that it tends to generate is stronger and more likely to override disruptive inclinations and if the institutions it allows foster weaker impulses and temptations to act unjustly. The stability of a conception depends on a balance of motives: the sense of justice that it cultivates and the aims it encourages must normally win toward injustice. (TJ 454; rev edn. 398.)

This argument is not immune from criticism. The development of the sense of justice, which not at all haphazardly originates and forms from a primitive, authoritarian morality, always remains halfway between a descriptive process in terms of evolutionary psychology and a normative ethical-political thesis. Perhaps, this is a fault present in every psychological-moral view linked to institutional questions. Rawls attaches no relevance to this fault other than, perhaps, indirectly. This may be observed from two different points of view. On the one hand, the last two paragraphs of Lecture II in PL insist on a strictly political interpretation of psychology, moving away from the more descriptive psychological argument in TJ. In so doing, Rawls strays also from the evolutionary moral psychology in TJ, to come to a different view based on desires dependent on the (political) conception.[59] On the other hand, it may be observed that, had he been fully satisfied with his argument on the sense of justice, he would have had no need to have recourse to the second part of the argument on stability, which is unquestionably more complex and controversial.

The second part of the argument in chapter 8 of TJ presupposes that citizens have a sense of justice and attempts to prove that this sense of justice promotes the good of citizens in the long run. We are dealing here with the so-called "congruence argument." The congruence being considered is between the point of view of goodness and the point of view of justice. Rawls tries to argue that the sense of justice should prevail over the set of people's rational motivations. In TJ, Rawls argues on this point that "whether these two points of view are congruent is likely to be a crucial fact in determining stability. But congruence is not a foregone conclusion in a well-ordered society" (TJ 567; rev. edn. 497).

The good of the citizens is traced back to the notion of rationality developed within a plan of life. This means, first, that the presence of just institutions supports the formation of better plans of life and, second, that it is rational for every citizen to support the model of institutions, as laid down in the scheme of the theory of justice as fairness in TJ. These institutions will give rise to and strengthen that sense of justice that, in turn, is "congruent" with the rationality of the citizens. According to Rawls, the moral psychology implicit in the argument is subsequently strengthened through the appeal to the so-called "Aristotelian Principle" (TJ section 79), which calls upon us to pursue the higher and more sophisticated aspects of our personality. The moral psychology is further consolidated by the Kantian interpretation of the theory of justice as fairness (TJ section 40). From the point of view of the Aristotelian Principle, participating in the life of a well-ordered society, conceived as a social union of social unions, is in itself a rare and precious good that allows us to realize in full human flourishing. From the point of view of the Kantian interpretation, the choice of the principles of justice favors the autonomy (in the Kantian sense) of the individuals. To act fairly is something we want as free and equal rational beings.

Now, the problem that such a position gives rise to is quite clear. There are no guarantees – even assuming that every citizen in a well-ordered society has a sense of justice – that the same principles of justice will be rational for all citizens to follow. Indeed, this is the problem that should be answered by the argument on congruence. Individuals' rational life plans are formed, according to Rawls, based on the "thin theory of the good"[60] and individuals choose in full deliberative rationality. However, the same thin theory is also assumed by the original position. The difference is that the theory of the good carries out a different function when we talk about deliberative rationality rather than the original position. In the former case, it addresses the individuals and their interests while, in the latter, it attains a result that has pretensions of universality. The argument on congruence tries to prove that following the principles of justice, which result from the original position, is in the individual interest of every person from the point of view of deliberative rationality.

How can one make sure that this congruence actually occurs? Rawls uses various arguments on this point. First, he starts from the very Kantian presupposition that rational agents self-conceive themselves as moral persons (TJ 563; rev. edn. 493). Indeed, this is the reason why they will strive to cause their plans of life to comply with this fundamental characteristic. But if the reasoning that leads from the original position to the principles of justice is accepted, the latter are those that express the institutional morality of the basic structure. It ensures, assuming the sense of justice, that the principles of justice have priority when deliberating about life plans. It is not at all hard to understand that at least two points in this type of reasoning are highly controversial: the Kantian presupposition and the fact that only the principles of justice represent the institutional morality of the basic structure.

The two objections are linked together. Rawls must show that, in the first case, every person, whatever his conception of the good, wishes to be a just person and, in the second case, that being a just person entails abiding by the principles of the theory of justice as fairness. Only when both of these are true can the argument on stability in TJ work. But, even if we were to succeed in showing the pre-eminence of justice and the correspondence between this pre-eminence and the theory of justice as fairness, Rawls warns us in PL, insurmountable problems would arise, beginning with the lack of realism of the construction as a whole. As we know, the biggest abstraction relates to pluralism. The citizens of a well-ordered society will be able to agree on a few general principles of democratic coexistence, but it is quite unlikely that all of them will agree on the same justification. Besides, there is practically no question about the fact that, from the point of view of the justification, each one of them will have recourse to his favorite comprehensive doctrine. The same thing applies to the Kantian premise.

10.4.2 The separation between morals and politics

From this point of view, the required mechanisms of separation between profound moral convictions and structure of the right – present in TJ – do not work adequately, as Rawls himself says in PL. Rawls claims that the central point lies in the fact that "no distinction is drawn between moral and political philosophy" (PL xv). In substance, the congruence argument in TJ presupposes that the moral background of the theory is too widely shared to be suitable for the pluralist liberal political view that Rawls defends in his writings of the 1980s and then formulates in a more accomplished manner in PL. The level splitting of the theory of the good – differentiated into "thin" and "thick" – in TJ may be a warning of this type of uneasiness prior to PL. As it has been observed, the entire mechanism of the original position in TJ, beginning with the famous "veil of ignorance," may perhaps succeed in effectively separating the persons from their material interests but it does not succeed in the same way when ideals come into play.

After TJ, Rawls becomes aware of the problem. Indeed, many of his writings in the subsequent years aim at an improved separation of the ambit of the good, conceived in this case also under the aegis of the "reasonable" rather than merely the "rational." He moves towards a perspective of ideals rather than interests.[62] This work is carried out in PL by the notion of "comprehensive" doctrine – a term used by Rawls to show the profound moral and religious visions that derive from a tradition and have, all in all, a comprehensive view of life – and by the concept of "reasonable pluralism." The starting point is the assumption that, in a liberal-democratic society, there is a pluralism of reasonable, religious or non-religious, liberal and non-liberal comprehensive doctrines, and that an adequate political conception must take this fact into account. Now, leaving aside Rawls' detailed arguments in PL on this point, it is easy to understand that, once pluralism is forcibly introduced, it is quite hard to ground a moral view of stability on the "congruence argument." Not all citizens who, at any rate, contribute to the stability of a liberal democracy can recognize themselves in the congruence argument. Ultimately, the claim in TJ that "acting justly is something we want to do as free and equal rational beings" (TJ 572; rev. edn. 501) is no longer acceptable, at least if one does not come out of the confined ambit of the theory of justice as fairness.

Perhaps there is also another argument that explains Rawls' different attitude with respect to stability in TJ and in PL. In the preceding section, we have recalled the distinction between a conception of the good and a comprehensive doctrine. The former is typically individual and formal, based on the thin theory of the good. Substantially, in its perspective, it makes sense to say that it is rational for individuals to back the sense of justice and, therefore, decide their plans of life in harmony with just institutions. Instead, a comprehensive doctrine is collective and substantial. Perhaps this is the reason why it is an obstacle and a permanent source of alternatives with respect to any formulation of a political conception that has moral significance. The relation with the theory of justice as fairness changes if, instead of considering a conception of the good, we evaluate it from a comprehensive doctrine. In the first case we are talking about morals and in the second we are talking about politics. In PL, Rawls means to attain a more general end-purpose, including in the view of stability even the citizens who, strictly speaking, are not liberal but, nonetheless, agree on the fundamental core of a liberal democracy. In this case, any moral theory must be set apart from the political theory, even though the latter keeps on being defined in ethical terms. Ultimately, we move in this case from a purely moral stability1, typical of TJ, to a sort of stability2, which is and still remains moral although founded on a political ground. It is also clear – in my opinion – that stability1 merely presupposes a sufficient justification; that is, an adequate moral argument. Stability2, however, must look for that complementarity between justification and legitimation on which we have insisted from the beginning in presenting our third hermeneutical hypothesis – the one we have defined as theoretical (see chapters 1 and 9).

In TJ, Rawls argued, by his own account mistakenly, that "a moral doctrine of justice is not distinguished from a political conception of justice" (PL xv). In PL, instead, given the fundamental pluralism, it is not possible for society to be held firmly together by a political view conceived as a specific form of ethics applied to the institutional domain. Failing to see this distinction between the political and the ethical in TJ is tantamount to not taking sufficiently into account the moral sentiments of a few citizens. In particular, the theory ignores those who, although failing to share a liberal comprehensive doctrine such as the theory of justice as fairness, respect liberal-democratic society. Take note that the thesis on stability2 in PL has nothing to do with abandonment of the moral supremacy in the name of a Hobbesian view. Stability2 is always for the right reasons, but it presupposes a restriction of its ambit with respect to the agreement on the political conception. Put differently, it assumes that all those who support stability2 agree on the pre-eminence of the liberal democracy. This is what the legitimation we had referred to at the beginning is all about.

Neither do I believe that the congruence argument in TJ might be a disguised form of a perfectionist and teleological argument. All in all, section 86 in TJ, entitled "The Good of the Sense of Justice," where Rawls summarizes this argument, follows two sections devoted to the themes of the dominant end and hedonism (represented here as a sort of rationalization of the thesis of the dominant end). Rawls is critical with respect to both themes.

The theory of justice as fairness vehemently opposes the idea that, first, an objective needs to be established and, subsequently, that the right consists in realizing it. Whatever the case, the main subject matter of the theory of justice as fairness is the agreement between the social parties and the political subjects and, therefore, the exact opposite of a perfectionist and teleological thesis. All things considered, even the congruence argument fits into Rawls' extensive controversy with utilitarianism in TJ.

Instead, during the long period of working on PL, Rawls appeared to be particularly worried about a certain type of consequence of the argument on stability1 in TJ that, in his opinion, coincided with the exclusion of those liberal democrats that were not strictly liberal in the Kantian and Rawlsian sense. In particular, he believed that quite a few good liberal-democratic political ideas had a deep connection with religious feelings, which have nothing to do directly with the liberal Kantian view supported in TJ. Talking about this theme, he often used to quote the examples he cherished of Lincoln and Martin Luther King. A good case of what may be meant by stability2, for Italians like me, may be represented by the conduct of Communists and Catholics at the time of the Constituent Assembly in our country after the Second World War: the ethical views of those persons had definitely no liberal inspiration but, at the same time, they succeeded in formulating an unquestionably liberal-democratic constitution from a political point of view and, afterwards, in respecting its principles. Were we to posit, in order to ensure stability and full participation in the democratic life, a complete correspondence between deep moral sentiments and the structure of justice, as presented in TJ, we would run the risk of excluding those who behave, like them, from the heart of the democratic life, with a great loss for all. Then, as suggested by Rawls in PL, what is needed is a non-comprehensive political conception: that is, a wider conception that, while remaining an essentially moral view, could draw an improved distinction between being in agreement with an ethical political doctrine and participating in the democratic life. This type of criticism of the TJ model paves the way for the new model of politics presented in PL. Were we to summarize this idea, we could say that, in PL, political stability, although being an ethically oriented politics, replaces the moral stability of TJ. Politics, in this sense, works like a sort of subset of morals, since: "While a political conception is, of course, a moral conception, it is a moral conception worked from a specific kind of subject, namely for political, social, and economic institutions" (PL 11).

As a consequence of this change, we need to believe in the fact that various persons – although starting from different cultural, religious, and moral perspectives – tend to converge, from the point of view of stability, when they adopt a fair behavior towards the liberal-democratic institutions. This fact is revealed – as we are going to see in the next chapter – by the existence of an "overlapping consensus" that rests on moral sentiments, intensifies over time in liberal-democratic societies, and shows at the same time both the existence of ideal conflicts and the possibility of overcoming them when persons have faith in a liberal-democratic system. It is nonetheless clear that this fortunate eventuality is by no means a certainty, and that there is a sort of political threshold (Rawls, for instance, points to the case of Northern Ireland in its most tragic periods) beneath which overlapping consensus and stability may hardly be assumed. It should be noted that this political threshold brings to mind the economic threshold (in TJ) beneath which the theory of justice proves unfeasible.

11

OVERLAPPING CONSENSUS AND PUBLIC REASON

The first part of chapter 11 concerns Rawls' idea of "overlapping consensus." The overlapping consensus explains how collective support for institutions is possible, without coercion, in a pluralistic society. It is realized when citizens, endorsing different reasonable comprehensive doctrines, accept the same liberal-democratic vision (11.1).

For Rawls, the model is to be found in the history of liberalism, being a kind of reinterpretation of it (11.1). Historical liberalism has been either skeptical, basing its appeal on the absence of faith, or comprehensive, basing its appeal on a sort of secular faith. Rawls' political liberalism, through the idea of an overlapping consensus, refuses these two alternatives. The majority of the objections to the idea of overlapping consensus argue that this Rawlsian third way is impossible (11.1.1).

The resistance towards the idea of overlapping consensus comes from the widespread impression that Rawls is using a double standard when discussing disagreements about the good and disagreements about the right (11.1.3). Disagreements about the good would be widely tolerated whereas disagreements about the right have to be limited. In such a way, Rawls is accused of intending to immunize liberal democracy from conflicts about justice. Here my distinction between justification and legitimation can be usefully reintroduced. For the Rawlsian idea of overlapping consensus can be defended only if we accept that justifications are intrinsically plural, whereas there is convergence on legitimation (11.1.3).

PL's peculiar meta-theoretical intention becomes evident when we analyze – in the second part of this chapter – the notion of "public reason" (11.2.1). Public reason does not concern a specific object, but rather the limits of public debate in a liberal-democratic society (11.2.1). From the objective point of view, public reason can be required only if we are engaged in debates about "constitutional essentials" and "basic matters of justice." The great majority of political debates exceed these, being part of the "background culture." From the subjective point of view, the main problem of public reason derives from the fact that, in using it, one should rely not on the whole truth – or in any case not on our comprehensive doctrines – but only on a part of it compatible with the restrictions that public reason imposes (11.2.5).

Public reason meets the "criterion of reciprocity." Respect for the "duty of civility" and for the criterion of reciprocity fits the requirements of liberal legitimacy. To meet these requirements, it is crucial that public reason is not specified by any one political conception of justice, not even by Rawls' justice as fairness. Rather, its content derives from a family of reasonable political conceptions (11.2.4). In summary, the argument for public reason exemplifies one of the main aims of Rawlsian contractualism (11.2.8).

11.1 From the Political Conception to an Overlapping Consensus

In PL, Rawls tries to make stability compatible with pluralism. In the first three lectures, he presents the fundamentals of a "freestanding" conception – that is, a political conception disentangled from its own metaphysical, moral, and religious background. The goal of this political conception consists in reformulating the notion of stability in a well-ordered society, because the way in which this notion was conceived in TJ appears now unrealistic (see end of chapter 2 and chapter 10 in this volume). Reasonable pluralism does not permit us even to imagine that all citizens will agree on the same theory of justice. The underlying idea consists here in separating citizens from their comprehensive doctrines. This idea is not so different from the one implicit in the concept of veil of ignorance in TJ. In PL, however, the strategy is more radical. In the name of pluralism, citizens must separate themselves also from Rawls' theory of justice as fairness. This more radical strategy implies a more sophisticated process of reconciliation.

The core of the argument for reconciliation relies on the idea of "overlapping consensus." The attack on the notion of stability in TJ and the "freestanding" political conception presented in PL can be considered as a premise for reaching an overlapping consensus. A freestanding political conception – as we know – requires two conditions: (i) it must be developed for the basic structure; and (ii) the political power must be coercive (PL 135–6).

The fact that power is imposed, within a basic structure in which citizens believe in different comprehensive doctrines, generates what Rawls calls the problem of "liberal legitimacy." Liberal legitimacy implies that in liberal democracy power cannot be justified on the basis of only one comprehensive doctrine. It can be justified only if all reasonable people can reasonably accept the use of that power. One can also say that liberal legitimacy makes more specific – without changing it – the initial problem of reconciling stability and pluralism.[1] Liberal legitimacy makes this reconciliation dependent on the gradual assertion of an "overlapping consensus." In this way, the realization of political liberalism itself stands or falls with the possibility of realizing this overlapping consensus. That is why Lecture IV of PL (on the idea of overlapping consensus) begins with a section entitled "How is Political Liberalism Possible?"

In Rawls' vision, an overlapping consensus consists in a situation in which citizens who adhere to different comprehensive doctrines progressively accept (the fundamentals of) the same liberal-democratic political outlook in a well-ordered society. This process does not assert itself from the outside, but rather takes place for all citizens "from within their own comprehensive view," taking advantage of "the religious, philosophical and moral grounds it provides" (PL 147). Each citizen, regardless of whether her basic comprehensive doctrine is Muslim or Catholic, secular or Buddhist, utilitarian or Kantian, skeptical or pluralist, should find she agrees on the liberal and egalitarian essentials of political justice. The reasons for this agreement are different, since they are to be found in different comprehensive doctrines. Note that, according to Rawls, the resulting consensus is not superficial or prudential, but is of a strictly moral nature. We are not dealing with a compromise, with what Rawls calls a mere "modus vivendi." The overlapping consensus does not depend, in other words, on any balance of power that might be achieved at any time between rival worldviews. Following Rawls:

> That an overlapping consensus is different from a modus vivendi is clear . . . it is affirmed on moral grounds, that is, it includes conceptions of society and of citizens as persons, as well as principles of justice, and an account of the political virtues through which these principles are embodied in human character and expressed in public life. An overlapping consensus is not merely a consensus on accepting certain authorities, or on complying with certain institutional arrangements, founded on a convergence of self and group interests. All those who affirm the political conception start from within their own comprehensive view. (PL 147–8)

The overlapping consensus has its own moral grounds. It presupposes a psychological background not so different from the support given to stability by the "sense of justice" in the third part of TJ: "given certain assumptions specifying a reasonable human psychology and the normal conditions of human life, those who grow up under just basic institutions acquire a sense of justice and a reasoned allegiance to those institutions sufficient to render them stable" (PL 142).

The theory of justice as fairness in TJ cannot be the only basis for such a consensus, even if it happens to be a significant premise of it. Rather, one can find some continuity the other way round: it is this argument on consensus in PL that can solve the problems created by the third part of TJ on stability. In this sense, PL reformulates the theory of justice as fairness. From PL's point of view, we see justice as fairness as twofold: (i) if we take it as the conjunction of the original position and the principles of justice, then justice as fairness is the basis for a political conception; and (ii) if we include in it the third part of TJ on stability, then justice as fairness can be seen as a comprehensive doctrine.[2] As a consequence, consensus moves from the substantive elements of the theory of justice as fairness to a wider form of political liberalism, given also that it "goes down to the fundamental ideas within which justice as fairness is worked out" (PL 149).

The core idea is here a recurrent one in Rawls' view, consisting in splitting individuals' morality into two parts. On the one hand, there is the full integral morality of the persons, rooted in their comprehensive doctrines. On the other hand, there exists a more austere institutional morality, concerning the persons as citizens. This kind of political morality is more directly based on the loyalty towards the liberal-democratic system (PL xiv). Only the institutional morality can adequately take into account reasonable pluralism, which is a virtue of an open society, achieving at the same time stability. This is the main outcome of an overlapping consensus between citizens who, while keeping faith in their own comprehensive doctrines, are nevertheless able to put that faith to one side in (part of) political life. In this domain, they accept the common institutional morality characterized by the overlapping consensus (PL xlvii). This acceptance implies reciprocal reasonableness and mutual respect.

Rawls exploits here the potentialities of the priority of right. In a well-ordered society, pluralism reigns. This is not just a matter of fact. It is normatively right that different aesthetic, ethical and religious views may meet and confront each other as a result of the operation of reason under free institutions. This pluralism, however, cannot concern – for Rawls – the entire institutional order and the fundamental structures of liberal democracy. Here, on the contrary, we need a certain degree of consensus. This unity cannot be founded on a single ethical and political conception. That is why we need a consensus that is perhaps less deep but surely broader, whose primary subject is the political conception.

The model for such a consensus is inspired by the birth of classical liberalism. Classical liberalism arises out of the existence of profound religious conflict and the attempt to find some remedy for it. In the Introduction to PL, Rawls insists on the fact that his own political liberalism theoretically recapitulates that glorious history. It expands the laborious conquest of religious tolerance during the period of reform to the contemporary political realm. After the many clashes of the previous centuries, European civilization discovered with the rise of liberalism "a new social possibility: the possibility of a reasonable harmonious and stable pluralist society" (PL xxv). Before that time it was possible to believe that "social unity and concord require agreement on a general and comprehensive religious, philosophical or moral doctrine" (PL xxv). After that time, however, Europeans became more Rawlsian and convinced themselves that "it is difficult, if not impossible, to believe in the damnation of those with whom we have, with trust and confidence, long and fruitfully cooperated in maintaining a just society" (PL xxv).

This is the prehistory of political tolerance, the contemporary formulation of which concept Rawls himself aims to interpret. The thesis – examined in the previous chapter – according to which in politics the reasonable prevails over the true, is simply a consequence of this narrative. According to this view, one cannot separate liberalism from tolerance, nor tolerance, in turn, from the loss of the certainty that there is only one truth. If liberalism of the European tradition, which is the tradition Rawls has in mind, appears as a result of loss of orthodoxy, then even today any liberal theory should be characterized by a certain loss of absolute faith. It is not surprising that this separation between liberalism and certainty has been traumatic from a historical point of view. One needs a lengthy process, with various intermediate stages, before achieving the maturity that Rawls considers proper for contemporary political liberalism. Therefore, it was in part natural that the first type of liberalism was grounded in the pure loss of faith and, like Voltaire's, was skeptical. Likewise, a second type of liberalism reacted in the opposite way, operating with the conviction that it was searching for foundations that could work as alternatives to religions, albeit equally deeply, as in the cases of Kant and Mill. Rawls' political liberalism rejects these two options, and takes an intermediate view based on the idea of an overlapping consensus. To quote Rawls:

> Political liberalism does not question that many political and moral judgments of certain specific kinds are correct and it views many of them as reasonable. Nor does it question the possible truth of affirmations of faith. Above all, it does not argue that we should be hesitant and uncertain, much less skeptical, about our own beliefs. Rather, we have to recognize the practical impossibility of reaching reasonable and workable political agreement in judgment on the truth of comprehensive doctrines, especially an agreement that might serve political purposes, say, of achieving peace and concord in a society characterized by religious and philosophical differences. (PL 63)

In some ways, the situation in which classical liberalism was born is repeated today. As was once the case for religion, today politics is divided by bitter conflicts, sometimes not so different from the religious ones of the past. These conflicts generate the need for a point of view capable of enabling individuals and groups with different convictions to live together in peace and harmony. This is a key task for political philosophy, given that we turn to it primarily "when our shared political understandings . . . break down" (PL 44). The overlapping consensus is, in PL, the climax of this process of reconciliation.

Rawlsian overlapping consensus is characterized by three main features. The first of them presents two general presuppositions:

(i)   the existence of reasonable pluralism (different from the simple fact of pluralism);

(ii) the existence of a freestanding political conception.

Rawls introduces the second feature by presenting four objections to it (I will discuss them in 11.1.3.). The third feature is instead treated within what Rawls calls a "model case." This model case is in turn formulated by connecting the overlapping consensus to three different doctrinal positions:

(i)   a tolerant religious doctrine (often referred to as "free faith");

(ii) a comprehensive liberal doctrine like Kant's and Mill's;

(iii) a pluralist view, which joins the political conception and some non-political values.

Only the first two cases exemplify pure comprehensive doctrines, whereas the third presents a sort of compromise. Rawls maintains that people adhering to these comprehensive doctrines can reach the level of overlapping consensus from within these doctrines. (In the second part of Lecture IV, utilitarianism is also considered as a comprehensive doctrine compatible with the overlapping consensus.)

11.1.1 Some criticisms

Rawls' idea of overlapping consensus is open to three immediate criticisms. First, it is not clear whether and how he succeeds – to use TJ vocabulary – in presenting justice as relatively independent of any conception of the good.[3] There is, in fact, a widespread suspicion that such a thesis, in neatly separating the private person from the public person, starts from an assumption that only a liberal mentality is ready to accept. In other words, are we sure that Rawls is not proposing here another version of comprehensive liberal doctrine?

A second possible criticism says roughly the opposite of the first. According to this second criticism, an overlapping consensus can have only pragmatic features, and cannot reach the desired theoretical level. It is plausible to claim that, in order to avoid wild conflicts, people often accept a sort of moral ceasefire, detaching themselves from the deepest moral and metaphysical convictions. But they would do so – according to this criticism – simply in order to achieve some kind of compromise, or, to use Rawls' expression, in order to adopt a "modus vivendi."

A third possible criticism is of a comparative nature. Take, for example, the different comprehensive doctrines included in the so-called "model case." The support of a Kantian outlook does not appear particularly difficult to obtain, given the similarity between that outlook and the Rawlsian approach. But, can we express the same opinion on the basis of religious doctrines, for example on the basis of the theses maintained by a convinced Roman Catholic?[4] Rawls is optimistic here in maintaining that all historical religions have a path towards what he calls "free faith" (PL 170). It seems, however, that any attempt to converge with Rawls turns out here to be controversial. Utilitarianism could be considered to lie, roughly speaking, in between the first two classes of comprehensive doctrines. Moreover, there are some problems with the limits of the overlapping consensus. What about certain other comprehensive doctrines which, being reasonable but not being included in the model case, lie at the limits of the overlapping consensus? How are we supposed to treat them? And are they all at the same level or is there some index, on the basis of which we can distinguish between comprehensive doctrines that are nearer and farther from inclusion within the overlapping consensus?

Rawls is not particularly keen to meet these possible criticisms directly. In practice, we do not find in PL a great answer to the questions they raise. Rawls offers two arguments, the first focused on the centrality of the political and the second insisting on the general limits of every comprehensive doctrine. Neither of them seems conclusive. According to the first: "values of the political are very great values and hence not easily overridden: these values govern the basic framework of social life – the very groundwork of our existence – and specify the fundamental terms of political and social cooperation" (PL 139).

The second argument, by contrast, emphasizes the relative "looseness" of comprehensive doctrines. These doctrines are often partial, if not ambiguous, and the political conception is needed as an instrument to complete them in case of political disagreement. Moreover, in the case of overlapping consensus we are speaking of "reasonable" comprehensive doctrines (168ff.), which already include some elements of a liberal vision.

The problem with these two arguments – beyond some structural vagueness – consists in their failing to answer the three standard criticisms we just mentioned. Neither of Rawls' arguments can rule out, in other words, that the overlapping consensus is based on another kind of liberal comprehensive doctrine, or is rooted in a *modus vivendi*, or is difficult for a religious person to accept.

11.1.2 Four self-objections

Rawls seems conscious of these limits. He himself presents in PL four typical objections to the idea of overlapping consensus, which are discussed at length during Lecture IV. In some ways, these four objections correspond – albeit indirectly – to the first two criticisms we have just presented (overlapping consensus might be based on a liberal comprehensive doctrine, or depend on a pragmatic agreement).

The first of these objections is probably the most significant, in examining the distinction itself between overlapping consensus and _modus vivendi_ (PL 147ff.). With this distinction in mind, many commentators have argued that via overlapping consensus we lose the possibility of a true political community (PL 146). Rawls notes that, instead, what we can lose in this way is just an illiberal political community, because many of the goals in any society, however important they might be, are pursued outside politics (PL 146 and footnote). This is a relevant argument: political liberalism believes in the profound values of a community. It is just that it sees them flourishing both in the realm of political society as "social union of social unions" and within voluntary associations and movements outside the political domain.

The distinction between overlapping consensus and _modus vivendi_ appears plain to Rawls from the start, because the political conception is itself a moral conception. It presupposes a moral object and a moral ground, as the process described in the model case would show. Accepting the overlapping consensus is different from accepting a compromise. The stability of liberal democracy is itself dependent on this moral vision: the structure of a liberal-democratic society must be immune from changes that merely result from shifts in power relations. This is the opposite of what would happen within a _modus vivendi_, seen by Rawls as a sort of truce due to prudential reasons.

In order to maintain the distance from any form of _modus vivendi_, overlapping consensus must have depth and breadth. The question of depth concerns how far the overlapping consensus has to penetrate the different comprehensive doctrines. The question of breadth regards the institutional scope to which it applies. The depth of the overlapping consensus reaches the shared fundamental ideas on which the agreement on fair terms of cooperation between free and equal citizens is based. Its breadth coincides with the limits of the political conception, and is addressed to the basic structure (PL 149).

In section 4 (Lecture IV), Rawls discusses his second objection, which sees as a necessary condition of an overlapping consensus some skeptical background. This skeptical background would depend on the attempt to bypass the deepest parts of any comprehensive doctrine. In this way, a strategy based on overlapping consensus would run the risk of "bracketing" (Sandel)[5] – through a kind of systematic ethical abstinence – the most sensitive problems of politics.[6] More generally, overlapping consensus can give the impression that truth is irrelevant in politics. From this impression comes the link between overlapping consensus on the one hand and skepticism or indifferentism on the other. Rawls' reply is simple: each citizen can take the political conception as true, starting from within her own comprehensive doctrine. This suggestion implies that every conception of the truth compatible with public reason must be a political conception. By a political conception one can mean a conception suited for the purposes of political reflection in a regime of pluralism.

Nevertheless, the overlapping consensus could seem to represent a premise for a general strategy of avoidance, according to which divisive issues are systematically excluded from the political agenda. Rawls neither concedes nor rejects the objection by answering that: "We appeal instead to a political conception of justice to distinguish between those questions that can be reasonably removed from the political agenda and those that cannot" (PL 151). In other words, a strategy of avoidance is not necessarily wrong. We have learned from the wars of religion, for example, that liberty of conscience must be kept independent from the democratic game. A similar argument can be used for slavery. As explained in footnote 16 (Lecture IV), the strategy of avoidance applies to all questions that we are not ready to decide through a majority vote. This thesis can appear vague, and Rawls indeed does not offer objective criteria by means of which one could distinguish what political issue should (or should never) be normally excluded from the democratic game. We just know that sometimes philosophical and religious issues must be avoided.

Rawls' thesis does not imply that we are not allowed to use our deepest convictions – rooted in reasonable comprehensive doctrines – in the construction of the political conception. It merely implies that we may do so only within certain limits, being those limits based on what people could reasonably accept (consistently with the principle of liberal legitimacy). The example of the "rational believers" helps us to understand the nature of these limits. Rational believers – such as, for example, some Thomists – believe that the truths of faith are provable, and for this same reason do not fully accept reasonable pluralism. In criticizing them from a liberal Rawlsian standpoint, however, one is not maintaining that their beliefs are false. One simply states that they cannot be directly used in politics (PL 153). The indirect way in which one can use them has to do – as we shall see in the second part of this chapter – with the idea of public reason.

The third objection says that – even if we can distinguish an overlapping consensus from a *modus vivendi* – "some may say that a workable political conception must be general and comprehensive" (PL 154). Without a similar view, it would be impossible to order the plurality of conflicts of justice that arise in public life. As some may say, the deeper and more divisive these conflicts are, the more comprehensive and general a political conception must be. Rawls replies by introducing the notion of a "partially comprehensive view" (PL 155ff.). A political conception depends on some comprehensive view, for Rawls, but does not depend on the non-political aspects of it. Political consensus is plausible only if we exclude a lot of difficult questions from the political agenda. This solution allows us to avoid intractable conflicts in politics.

How is it possible – Rawls asks – that a political conception may express values able to outweigh other values in cases of conflict? The answer is: the values of the political conception must be political values. They not only protect basic rights, but also "insure that all citizens have sufficient material means to make effective use of those basic rights" (PL 157). This is a meaningful step, because Rawls here includes distributive matters within a broadly speaking liberal political conception. A merit of this liberal political vision consists in its shaping of virtues such as tolerance, fairness and reciprocal respect.

The fourth and last objection to overlapping consensus insists on its utopian nature (PL, Lecture IV, section 6): either overlapping consensus is impossible to obtain or stability cannot depend on it, because there are not enough psychological, political, and social forces to maintain it. Rawls here does not answer the objection directly. Rather, he prefers to discuss two progressive stages of political consensus. The first ends with constitutional consensus, and only the second ends with overlapping consensus.

Constitutional consensus presupposes consensus on "political procedures of democratic government" and some fundamental rights (PL 159). Within it, for example, one accepts the value of electoral procedures for reducing the political impact of rival comprehensive doctrines. Constitutional consensus is however, for Rawls, unsatisfying, because it depends more on convenience and tradition, beyond some looseness of the comprehensive doctrines, than on a sincere ethical conviction. This difficulty can be summed up by saying that: "[t]he constitutional consensus is not deep and also not wide: it is narrow in scope, not including the basic structure but only the political procedures of democratic government" (PL 159).

Constitutional consensus is not deep, because it concerns just rules and procedures and not a political conception of justice, like the one based on justice as fairness; it is not wide or broad, because it does not enter into substantive matters concerning distributive justice or basic liberties. Historically speaking, constitutional consensus is based on a stable pragmatic incorporation in public culture of liberal-democratic rules and procedures. It looks like the acceptance of the tolerance principle, as a durable *modus vivendi*, in order to avoid destructive civil strife. This kind of progressive acceptance of constitutional traditions implies, nevertheless, a weakening of the comprehensive doctrines previously held by citizens. That is why constitutional consensus, albeit insufficient, plays a preparatory role towards the forming of a real overlapping consensus. The principles of a political conception achieve stability across time just through the political functioning of the constitutional consensus (PL 161).

Liberal principles, which at the first stage of a constitutional consensus were only accepted reluctantly, as a kind of *modus vivendi*, reinforce themselves progressively and guarantee some basic liberties and democratic procedures (PL 163). Nevertheless, constitutional consensus remains insufficient. Liberal principles are not deeply shared and "rights and liberties and procedures included in a constitutional consensus cover but a limited part of the fundamental political questions that will be debated" (PL 166). With time, however, the liberal principles implicit in the constitutional consensus become the bases for an overlapping consensus. The depth of the overlapping consensus requires that its political principles use the ideas of person and society founded on a political conception of justice like the one we find in justice as fairness. Its breadth requires political principles able to cover the whole basic structure (PL 164).

Confronted with different liberal conceptions, the one based on the over-lapping consensus must have two particular characteristics:

(i)   it must be based on the truly fundamental ideas of a liberal-democratic culture;
(ii) it must be stable in view of the different interests that support it (PL 168).

Rawls insists on the thesis according to which an overlapping consensus does not consist in a compromise between different reasonable doctrines. Rather, an overlapping consensus can be independently derived from several com-prehensive doctrines. Rawls mentions: liberal religion, Kantian autonomy, utilitarianism, and pluralism (with a slight difference from its model case). Nozick's libertarianism is excluded.[7]

There is an evident difficulty with the overlapping consensus so conceived. One can never fully understand how Rawls can present his normative account of overlapping consensus while also providing a descriptive interpretation of the life of a liberal political system.

11.1.3 A double standard?

Many scholars have been puzzled by the solution of an overlapping con-sensus as proposed by Rawls. The main reason for their distrust of Rawls' solution lies in the double standard with which Rawls seems to view politi-cal and cultural disagreements. In any society there are apparently two types of political and cultural disagreements:[8] those concerning the conception of the good and those concerning the conception of the right. The former include, first and foremost, religious disagreements, but also disagreements between secular concepts of the good. The latter include the different ways of viewing social justice, such as, for example, the conflict between liberals and socialists, which for many of us marked political debates during our youthful years.

It is obviously interesting to see what type of relationship we can imagine between these two types of cultural and political disagreements. There are two main alternatives in this respect. According to the first, there is continu-ity between the disagreements about the good and those about the right. The issue of abortion in Italy, a country in which the Catholic Church plays a significant political role, is a good example of the first alternative. In this case, political conflict substantially depends on the fact that the opposing parts have two different conceptions of the good: for example, one based on the sacred nature of human life and the other on the Kantian autonomy of the individual. The same occurs with respect to the way in which the public sphere is traditionally viewed in Muslim countries, regarding relations between religion and politics. Of course, the continuity between the two models of disagreement may also concern comprehensive secular concepts. By contrast, the second alternative assumes discontinuity between the two types of cultural and political disagreements. In this case, the conceptions of the right are separate from those of the good. Conceptions of the right are somehow asymmetrically located, in the sense that their principal institutional function is to regulate conflicts that inevitably arise – given the existence of pluralism – between the conceptions of the good.

If we ask ourselves which of the two models of relations between disagreement on the good and disagreement on the right Rawls adopts in PL, we can reply that his position is closer to the discontinuity model. According to Rawls – in both TJ and PL – the conflicts relating to the good are distinct and different from those relating to the right. This distinction confirms the priority of right. In TJ (section 68, entitled "Several Contrasts between the Right and the Good"), Rawls explicitly says: "A second contrast between the right and the good is that it is, in general, a good thing that individuals' conceptions of their good should differ in significant ways, whereas this is not so for conceptions of right. In a well-ordered society citizens hold the same principles of right" (TJ 447–8; rev. edn. 393). In PL, Rawls reformulates the problem in a more sophisticated way, introducing new concepts such as those of "political conception" and "comprehensive doctrine." The concept of political conception in PL does not coincide with the idea of right in TJ; nor is it the case that the concept of comprehensive doctrine in PL coincides with the idea of good in TJ. According to many readers of PL, however, these distinctions do not succeed in eliminating the "contrast" between right and good; they just reproduce it in a different way.

It is precisely this strong distinction between disagreements about justice and about goodness that poses the most obvious problem. The reason lies in the fact that by doing so Rawls seems to immunize the notion of justice from conflict. The praise of pluralism, even his insistence on the burden of judgments that we find in PL, seems limited to the disagreements on the good. But then the "shared convictions," the "fundamental ideas," the "political conception," and, even more so, the "overlapping consensus" seem to confirm the impression that, faced with deep disagreements on the good, there is a certain unity of outlook on at least several general characteristics of justice.[9] Hence, the reaction of the critics: is it possible to conceive a world, such as the one we live in, without thinking of it in the light of robust conflicts of a political and moral nature on justice?

A negative answer to this type of question is the reason why promoters of the typical objections to Rawls propound two principal critical alternatives: either the immunization of politics occurs through a de facto compromise, a *modus vivendi*; or Rawls reintroduces in PL the conception of stability taken from TJ, and thus formulates another version of a liberal "comprehensive doctrine."

We have already discussed at some length how neat the distinction between an overlapping consensus and a *modus vivendi* may be. It is also difficult to believe that Rawls merely repeated in PL a doctrine of stability roughly analogous to the one in TJ that he himself so vigorously criticized. There is in fact a clear distinction between stability in TJ and stability in PL. In TJ, stability depends on accepting for purely normative reasons the congruence between the theory of justice as fairness and the theory of the good. This argument in PL is considered highly unrealistic. That is why we need a more sophisticated strategy, such as the one based on overlapping consensus.

Jeremy Waldron – like, in some respects, Sunstein and Habermas[10] – believes that the Rawlsian immunization of justice is so robust as to render political democracy almost meaningless. A promising solution to the problem for these authors could be found through a rehabilitation of deliberative democracy.[11] My own reading of Rawls is different. I believe that to respond to these objections it is necessary to begin by assuming that Rawls uses two interpretations of liberalism simultaneously. In the first, liberalism is viewed as a (partially) comprehensive doctrine, and we can positively identify it with the theory of justice as fairness, but also with a Kantian conception based on autonomy, or yet something else again. This, however, concerns mainly the level of what I have called "justification," which is grounded on the comprehensive doctrine of each person. This is a profound level, but it is also certainly a level exposed to attacks based on the "fact of pluralism." If we were to move only on this level, it would be impossible to find convergence between conceptions of justice. From this awareness, there arises Rawls' idea of using a second interpretation of liberalism, which has to do less with justification and more with what I have called "legitimation." In short, this second interpretation of liberalism suggests that there are basic liberal-democratic institutions and practices that no "reasonable" person would want to do without. These are few and fundamental and concern the essential elements of a liberal constitution and some questions of basic justice, including several social bases of equality. My thesis is that the overlapping consensus – and consequently Rawlsian liberalism – can exist only insofar as it reunites these two interpretations of liberalism, the one based on justification and the other on legitimation.

There are also critics who put forward objections that differ from the standard ones. In other words, they do not accuse overlapping consensus of being too similar either to a *modus vivendi* or to a renewed comprehensive doctrine. These are usually radical critics – like postmodernists, Schmittians, Marxists, etc. – who usually do not recognize the principle of liberal legitimacy according to which one cannot rightly impose a view without reasonable acceptance. If my interpretation of the overlapping consensus in terms of justification and legitimation is sound, then there is not too much to say to these critics. Either they believe in liberal legitimacy – because they think they can impose their values, these values being superior – or not. In the first case, after all they believe also in a liberal-democratic culture, within which theory can look around for a source of ideas that others in society can also accept.

In case they do not believe in liberal legitimacy, simply PL does not address their problems, given that legitimation implies the previous acceptance of liberal democracy. Consequently, these critics cannot be convinced by Rawls' thesis of overlapping consensus.

A more controversial case rests on a distinction between tractable conflicts and "deep" conflicts.[12] The American people, for example, have numerous conflicts concerning fiscal policies and the best strategies to achieve a fair rate of taxation. This kind of conflict, however, does not exceed the liberal-democratic background and the institutional setting of the American republic. There are instead deeper conflicts of principle, beginning with religious ones, in which such a basic consensus cannot be presupposed. In these cases, the possibility of an overlapping consensus *à la* Rawls seems to depend on the dynamic capacity of the society to react to the challenges in a plausible way. In other words, I see the solution to this type of dilemma as more empirical than theoretical.

My interpretation, based on the convergence of justification and legitimation, looks also like a plausible answer to the question concerning the continuous oscillation between normative and descriptive to which Rawls' theory of overlapping consensus is exposed. This oscillation, in fact, becomes more a necessity then a problem. Justification is typically normative whereas legitimation is prevalently descriptive (even if there are normative elements within it), and they are supposed to go together. In a well-known review of PL, Stuart Hampshire[13] wrote that the Rawlsian type of consensus is impossible. For Hampshire, liberal-democratic pluralism would permit consensus just on procedures and never on substance. Joshua Cohen, taking his lead from Hampshire's review of PL, explained that in Rawls procedure and substance are always inseparable.[14] The same principles of justice are substantive principles but derived by a fair procedure, and, vice versa, a procedure like democracy always rests on a substantive content. In a way, my reconstruction of overlapping consensus theoretically restates, in the domain of the overlapping consensus, Cohen's general position.

To conclude: the very idea of legitimation takes into account the fact that Rawls always tries to include in his theory elements of historical experience capable, so to speak, of qualifying consensus with the support of external factors that are independent of the favored theoretical approach. According to this perspective, the way out can only be inspired by actual experience, which, in the public domain, is constituted by the way in which the basic structure functions in the ambit of a liberal-democratic system. And this, on closer examination, is the vantage point from which Rawls views the theory of tolerance in PL, compared to his modern forerunners, such as Locke and

Bayle, who, after all and unlike him, could not rely on an exemplary practice for reference.

11.2 Public Reason

In PL Lecture VI, entitled "The Idea of Public Reason," Rawls proposes the only topic of this book never treated in previous writings, taken from his 1990 Melden Lectures. Later he would further explore the same topic in the second paperback edition of PL (1996) and in another article entitled "The Idea of Public Reason Revisited" (1997). We know that the argument from "publicity" played an important role in Rawls' theory from TJ onwards. It carried weight in the comparison with utilitarianism, and was part of the argument for stability – the part, by the way, that Rawls decided to save (unlike the part on congruence). Moreover, it is an important feature of TJ that the principles of justice must be public, because justice consists in more than a fair distribution of primary goods. The argument from publicity later carried even greater weight within Rawls' theory in his Dewey Lectures (1980). Eventually, however, it took its proper role within the discussion on pluralism in PL. Here, Rawls rediscovers the Kantian thesis on public reason,[15] public reason through which a liberal-democratic society formulates its collective plans. Principles of justice are the principles that citizens affirm on the basis of a shared political basis.

Rawls' public reason does not concern a determinate object, but rather the limits of the public debate when fundamental questions are at stake within a liberal-democratic society.[16] From this point of view, public reason is the reason of the citizens, being public in three ways: (i) as reason of the citizens, it is also the reason of the public; (ii) its subject is the good of the public when constitutional essentials and matters of fundamental justice are concerned; (iii) its nature and content are public insofar as they are provided by the political conception (PL 213).

The first constraint imposed on public reason is an institutional one. There are many political topics that are not included in this domain. Public reason does not apply *prima facie* to the cultural debates that, albeit politically significant, take place outside these institutional constraints, such as those that take place in churches, families, universities, and other associations. All these non-public debates are part of what Rawls calls "background culture." The criteria of public reason do apply, on the other hand, when we have political deliberations in "public forums" and, more controversially, when citizens discuss voting and, more generally, constitutional essentials and matters of public justice (PL 215).[17]

Grasping the basic distinction between "background culture" and "public culture" is certainly not a simple matter, especially if we take into consideration the role played by legal coercion in the definition of the limits of public reason. Rawls' doctrine of public reason mainly addresses public officials[18] whose decisions are binding, in particular, judges (even if Rawls says also voters among should be within the limits of public reason). What kinds of argument are permissible for them? And on what basis?

To answer these questions, we have to realize that there are two – partially overlapping – kinds of grounds for the requirements of public reason. The first kind is objective: it depends on the content. Rawls confines the requirements of public reason to the arguments that discuss "constitutional essentials" and "matters of basic justice." The second kind is subjective: it depends on the persons and the roles involved, including most obviously public officials (judges in particular).

Rawls often appears obscure when this distinction is in focus. It is not altogether clear whether public reason constraints apply only when constitutional essentials and matters of fundamental justice are at stake (objective), or also when state coercion is implied through the binding decisions of public officials (subjective). I think that objective constraints required by content, the "what" of public reason, appear more important than subjective constraints depending on the nature of the person involved, the "who" of public reason.[19] We can set this out as follows, imagining the "what" in relation to the "who" of public reason in different possible situations concerning its requirements:

(i)   in appropriate forums;
(ii) in private discussions;
(iii) in the legislature;
(iv) elsewhere

Public reason requirements hold in full just in (i). They hold mildly in (ii). They probably do not hold in (iii) and (iv). Rawls contrasts public reason with both non-public and comprehensive reasons.

11.2.1 From public reason to liberal legitimacy

The idea of public reason re-proposes the general priority of justification, central to the whole of Rawls' work and basic for the central notion of the social contract. Public reason is a method of justification.[20] If we take pluralism seriously, then there is a straightforward consequence: justifications citizens should offer each other cannot be derived by a specific comprehensive doctrine. On the contrary, all citizens have a right to be respected through being given reasons they could reasonably understand and eventually accept. That is why in a pluralist democratic society justification and public reason are parallel notions.

One can better understand the nature of public reason by confronting it with non-public reasons (PL, Lecture VI, section 3). Non-public reasons are part of the background culture, and their standards of rightness and justificatory criteria derive from the subject they treat and from the kind of association involved.[21] By contrast, the content of public reason depends on the political conception and presupposes the institutional authority. As has been noted, one should not confuse public reason with the public sphere. The public sphere – but not public reason – includes the background culture. And public reason constraints cannot be applied within the domain of the background culture.[22] Rawls states in IPRR that: "The idea of public research does not apply to all political discussions of fundamental question, but only to discussions of those questions in what I refer to as the 'public political forum'" (CP 575).

There are two different grounds for public reason. The first consists in reciprocity. Reciprocity implies that in liberal democracy only justifications that all citizens can reasonably present each other and presumably accept are permissible.[23] The second derives from legitimacy: public institutions are required to offer arguments based on the political values of the whole community and not on the political values of a subset of it.[24] Joining these two grounds, public reason requires us to avoid arguments depending on controversial comprehensive doctrines.

The term "reciprocity" is a complicated one for Rawls' interpreters, because it is used in different ways over time. In TJ Part III, "reciprocity" is the basis for the psychological laws regulating moral development. In both TJ and PL, "reciprocity" is connected with "fair terms of cooperation." However, the notion of reciprocity also concerns the mutuality of justificatory criteria. The language of cooperation and political exchange must be so conceived that potentially all citizens should be able to understand it. It is in this third sense that "reciprocity" is connected with liberal legitimacy and public reason.[25]

In IPRR, Rawls insists on the criterion of reciprocity, which appears central in the light both of the principle of liberal legitimacy and of the idea of public reason (CP 579). He maintains that public reason and public justification meet the 'criterion of reciprocity'; they proceed from reasons and premises we reasonably think others could reasonably accept, to conclusions they also could reasonably accept (CP 578–9).

The fundamental ground for public reason is, however, the second one, based on political legitimacy. Rawls connects political legitimacy to the principle of "liberal legitimacy" (PL 216ff.). According to the principle of liberal legitimacy: "our exercise of political power is proper and hence justifiable only when it is exercised in accordance with a constitution the essentials of which all citizens may reasonably be expected to accept in the light of principles and ideals acceptable to them as reasonable and rational" (PL 217). From this principle, Rawls derives a moral obligation called the "duty of civility." The basis of this duty of civility consists in the duty all citizens have to reciprocally justify the political principles they adopt in the light of public reason. It is liberal democracy itself that imposes a special link, based on reciprocal respect, among citizens. To respect each other, the citizens have to adopt a common language. This presupposition does not imply that any widely shared political thesis passes the test of public reason. One needs a background liberal vision. For example, the Pope in Italy represents a popular authority, often much more popular than that of professional politicians. However, a political campaign based on the Pope's religious principles is not included within the domain of public reason.

Liberal legitimacy represents a necessary condition for the legitimacy of any system of government: all the laws, and the system itself, can be legitimated on condition that some basic components of the system are universally accepted. From this perspective, even Rawls' principles of justice – also assuming their rightness – cannot claim to be formally legitimated. Liberal legitimacy depends on consensus through a democratic procedure, and it is difficult to imagine citizens believing in the same comprehensive doctrine (including Rawls'): "Democratic decision and laws are legitimate, not because they are just but because they are legitimately enacted with an accepted legitimate democratic procedure" (PL 428).

When in public forums we discuss constitutional essentials and matters of fundamental justice, public reason does not permit any direct appeal to philosophical or religious (comprehensive) doctrines. It is possible, on the other hand, to rely on the most relevant scientific theories, when they are generally approved by the community of scholars. In this sense, public reason has in such a way its own epistemological side. Popularity is not enough to pass the test of public reason. Darwinism, one can suppose, is compatible with public reason, whereas creationism is not, even if in some regions of the USA the latter is more popular than the former.[26] Needless to say, such a thesis is not easily accepted by the supporters of creationism.

Rawls introduces the idea of public reason, starting from his theory of justice as fairness, from which he takes two kinds of constituent values of public reason. These are: first, the values of political justice, which support the principles of justice; second, values coming from "guidelines of public inquiry, which makes this inquiry free and public" (PL 224). In the realm of TJ, the guidelines of inquiry derive their basis from the substantive principles of justice. Within the domain of PL, on the contrary, they are relatively independent: different liberal-democratic conceptions do not necessarily have the same substantive principles of justice (PL 226). Accepting the principle of liberal legitimacy and the idea of public reason does not mean sharing the same political comprehensive doctrine. It merely implies participating in a general liberal and egalitarian position. As a result, also, Rawls' theory of justice as fairness in TJ must be considered as just one of the possible liberal-democratic alternatives compatible with public reason: "It is crucial that public reason is not specified by any one political conception of justice, certainly not by justice as fairness alone. Rather, its content – the principles, ideals, and standards that may be appealed to – are those of a family of reasonable political conceptions" (PL l–li). This "family" unites a set of liberal-democratic positions. This idea has significant implications: every political hypothesis we select – in the domain of PL – must be compatible with a shared liberal-democratic view. Thus, one does not consider all other political theories. Public reason, however, accepts pluralism within the liberal-democratic domain, albeit with the limits on comprehensive doctrines we mentioned. Within these limits, citizens are supposed to choose their favored option by the methods of deliberative democracy.[27] From this twofold "strategy of avoidance" – concerning non-liberal-democratic and comprehensive theories – comes a typical difficulty implicit in the notion of public reason. In the most relevant political debates, public reason suggests avoiding the appeal to the whole truth and more generally to comprehensive doctrines. One should instead take seriously just that part of such doctrines which is coherent with the constraints of public reason (PL, Lecture VI, section 3).[28] So understood, public reason often has the appearance of seeming too vague or thin a concept to be useful.[29] In other words, it is difficult to see what the doctrine of public reason can exclude. Or perhaps it is better to say that ordinary political discourse in western democracies already follows the limits of public reason. So although public reason is exclusive, its restraints are not controversial in real politics.[30]

11.2.2 A constitutional device

Public reason does not concern the whole domain of the political, but rather only a part of it, beginning from the constitutional essentials. The constitutional essentials presuppose a general agreement by the citizens and are of two kinds:

(i) principles that specify the general structure of the government and the political process (for example: legislative, executive, and judicial powers);
(ii) equal rights of the citizens that majorities are to respect, such as liberty of conscience, freedom of thought and association, and the protections connected with the rule of law (PL 227).

There is a clear difference between constitutional essentials under (i) and under (ii). Those under (i) can vary, whereas those under (ii) cannot (PL 228). There is also a strong difference between the basic rights and liberties that are part of the constitutional essentials under (ii) and the principles of political justice (PL 228). Both in the Preface to the revised edition of TJ, and in JFR, Rawls emphasized that, had he had a second opportunity to write TJ, he would have imposed a clearer separation between the first and the second principle of justice. He said this having grown convinced over the years that basic liberties could be more widely accepted than other parts of his own theory, including the difference principle. Basic liberties are, in other words, more essential to the development of those moral powers that characterize a liberal-democratic citizen. That is why in PL some elements of distributive justice that are central to the structure of TJ cannot be constitutionally protected in the same way as are basic liberties. Rawls says:

> Whether the constitutional essentials covering the basic freedoms are satisfied is more or less visible on the face of constitutional arrangements and how these can be seen to work in practice. But whether the aims of the principles covering social and economic inequalities are realized is far more difficult to ascertain. These matters are nearly always open to wide differences of reasonable opinions. (PL 229)

On this epistemological basis, which has consequences for the justifiability of principles, the difference principle, in particular, is not a part of the constitutional essentials (PL 229). This exclusion does not imply that, within the horizon of PL, one can be liberal-democratic without being egalitarian and without taking seriously the difference principle. In JFR, published after PL, Rawls convincingly defends the difference principle. One can therefore reasonably suppose that the justification of the difference principle also remains valid for the Rawls of PL. Using my previous distinction, one could nevertheless say that in PL the legitimation of the difference principle is questionable. There could be a reasonable disagreement about it.

Regardless of the status of the difference principle, liberal-democratic constitutionalism includes some strong egalitarian requirements in PL, such as free public education, health care for all, and public financing of electoral campaigns. It is not immediately clear why these elements should be presuppositions of public reason, unless one considers them as an essential part of a free and equal citizenship in a regime of reciprocity. One of the reasons behind the distinction between basic liberties and socio-economic guarantees consists in the fact that violations of the basic liberties can be more easily detected. This implies, for Rawls, more possibilities of general agreement (PL 230).

The Supreme Court constitutes – in PL – the exemplar of public reason at work, in a regime of judicial review. "Public reason is the reason of [the] Supreme Court," says Rawls quite explicitly (PL 231). He makes here a distinction between five general principles of constitutionalism:

(i) there is a difference between people's constituent power and ordinary political power;
(ii) one must consider the distinction between ordinary and constitutional law;
(iii) the constitution is the expression of a liberal-democratic ideal based on self-government, and public reason tries to articulate it;
(iv) certain constitutional essentials are fixed once and for all;
(v) ultimate power cannot be left in the hand of the legislature, but it is

held by the constitutional balance of the three main powers (legislature, executive, judiciary).

In this sense, every liberal-democratic constitution is structurally dualist, because the democratic power of the people is balanced by the power of the Court and the judiciary.[31] The power of the Supreme Court, so conceived, is anti-majoritarian.[32] The Court is supposed to apply the criteria of public reason to constitutional interpretation (PL 234). That is why the Court can work as an "exemplar" of public reason, putting it into practice.

Section 7 (PL, Lecture VI) treats the apparent difficulties that can derive from such a conception of public reason. The first of these is that public reason can offer more than one answer to any particular question. The typical solution, when disagreement in balancing values is persistent, consists in voting, and citizens are required to vote with "sincere opinion." The second difficulty depends on the fact that citizens interpret public reason in the light of their comprehensive doctrines. This appeal to the whole truth could shake their confidence in the political conception, and render their "sincere opinion" less sincere when political values are at stake. Rawls says that this need not necessarily be so (PL 241–2). We can always hope that we reconcile ourselves with divisive axioms when the theorems we deduce from these axioms are convincing (see PL, footnotes 31 and 32).[33] The third apparent difficulty parallels the first one: if, appealing to public reason, we can have different answers to the same question, it is also possible that we get no answer at all. Yet we would like the political conception to be complete. Such an option looks extremely difficult to realize in the face of urgent and complicated problems[34] – such as, for example, our problems concerning future generations, or problems with nature and non-human animals. Public reason can here only provide one among several reasonable solutions. We can then only hope for a realization of some form of overlapping consensus, and nobody can guarantee that each comprehensive doctrine will find the conclusions of public reason "within its leeway" (PL 246). To argue for a universal and necessary consensus is beyond the limits of public reason.[35]

Rather than listing "apparent difficulties," it is important to disentangle public reason from too strict a link with the role of the Supreme Court.[36] This link would, in fact, make public reason too institutional,[37] and could lead us to miss what is, to my mind, the true richness of public reason, namely its capability to open a dialogue on controversial matters among citizens of a liberal-democratic polity. I see public reason, in other words, as the anti-chamber of a process of collective deliberation.[38] This interpretation is favored by a reading of IPRR. In conclusion, the practice of public reason encourages reciprocity among citizens. In so doing, it contributes to realizing mutual respect, to separating ethics from politics, to confirming the centrality of the basic structure, to fixing once and for all the discursive and pluralist attitude of the whole approach in PL.

11.2.3 The paradox of public reason

According to public reason, citizens need to consider what kind of reasons they can give each other when fundamental political questions are debated. Given the basic pluralism that characterizes liberal democracy, they cannot reach agreement or even approach mutual understanding on the basis of their irreconcilable comprehensive doctrines. If we follow the most direct interpretation of this thesis, comprehensive doctrines should never be introduced into public reason (PL 247). This reading corresponds to the so-called "exclusive view" of public reason (PL 247ff.). This view, however, appears too severe, which explains why there is another view – which Rawls himself came to favor – based on a rival reading, labeled the "inclusive view." The inclusive view permits the use, in certain circumstances, of what citizens regard as the basis of the deepest political values rooted in their comprehensive doctrines. In general, the more stable the background consensus in a society is, the more we can rely on the political conception without running into any appeal to the comprehensive doctrines. By contrast, in the presence of strong social and political divisions, with constitutional consequences, the appeal to comprehensive doctrines sometimes can be justified. Recalling some cases in which this kind of appeal was necessary, Rawls mentions the religious arguments behind the abolitionists and Martin Luther King.[39] Later, he would introduce a "wide view of public reason" with a special "proviso" (see 11.2.6), admitting this kind of argument when certain precautions are adopted.

It comes as no surprise that some of the most well-known criticisms of the idea of public reason derive from some of the ambiguities emphasized in the previous pages. These criticisms can be roughly divided into two broad families: (i) on the one hand, there are "continuist" critics, who consider Rawls' moral claims, connected with public reason, to be too limited insofar as they sacrifice too much information about the good life – they want more continuity between ethics and politics; (ii) on the other hand, there are "discontinuist" critics, who consider Rawls' moral claims to be too rich, notwithstanding the limiting role of public reason[40] – they claim that basic disagreements concern not only comprehensive doctrines but also the political conception. They want less continuity between (liberal) ethics and politics.

Similar distinctions depend on the basic complexity of notions like public reason. Continuist critics state that the model of public reason is too permissive. It concedes so much to tolerance and neutrality that it cannot exclude any doctrine.[41] Discontinuist critics, in contrast, think that the model of public reason incorporates too much of institutional morality, thus becoming extremely austere and excluding too many doctrines.

For the first family of critics, Rawls' public reason imposes too few constraints, whereas for the second these constraints are too many. Continuist critics see Rawls' position as too timid, whereas discontinuist critics see it as too exacting. Continuist critics want to avoid the separation of the citizen from the moral remainder of us, whereas the latter group, by contrast, maintains that Rawls puts too much morality into his political conception. Among the continuists, we find the thesis that public reason implies a "bracketing" of the real problems (Sandel), or that it is based on moral and epistemological abstinence (Raz),[42] or that it requires a strategy of avoidance (Habermas).[43] Among the discontinuists, we can consider postmodernist and relativist critics (Rorty, Fish),[44] or republican and realist critics (Sunstein).[45]

These contrasting objections evidently cannot all be correct at the same time. Nevertheless, they emphasize the same problem of public reason. This problem has something to do with what Rawls himself calls the "paradox of public reason," even if he claims this paradox is only an apparent one. This paradox consists in the limits of public reason in terms of justification. What remains unclear is the way in which the citizen is supposed to act when the duties connected with public reason are in conflict with the duties deriving from the preferred comprehensive doctrine. The way in which the paradox of public reason intersects the two families of critics mentioned before, the families of the continuists and the discontinuists, is not difficult to understand. Both criticisms invite Rawls to adopt a stronger position: either emphasizing the normative side of political liberalism, or forcing its dependency on the context. Either way, the paradox of public reason would be bypassed. Rawls, however, avoids any move towards one or the other of these two directions. Public reason looks for a kind of moral normativity which is not independent from institutional history. A similar position characterizes the whole of PL. In the previous section of this chapter, discussing the nature of the overlapping consensus, I maintained that this equilibrium depends on the desire to make legitimation and justification converge. Probably the same thesis can be applied to public reason.

11.2.4 Excluding religion?

Among the classic questions concerning public reason are the following: how does public reason constrain our arguments? Is it acceptable for such constraints to exist, and, consequently, that some kinds of arguments must be avoided in political debates? In particular, is the way in which Rawls formulates these constraints the right one? These questions can concern the relation between public reason, (possible) constraints and different views on race, ethnicity, or gender. However, they have been more frequently raised and hotly debated during a prolonged series of religious criticisms of the idea of public reason. For many religious people, the liberal aspiration to think about politics in a way independent from religion is intrinsically non-neutral. And Rawls' public reason is no exception.[46]

To put the discussion on the right track, we need two premises: it is fair to begin by disentangling the idea of public reason from the notion of secular reason;[47] it is opportune to separate and distinguish a traditional liberal view of religion from Rawls' more mature view.[48]

First, secular reason aims to exclude religious arguments from the political debate, whereas public reason does not. According to the standards of public reason, the appeal to religious values is admitted, even though it must be presented in a specific form under certain constraints, the goal of which is that of respect for other citizens. Moreover, while secular reason is usually supposed to be sufficient to express people's motivations in political debates, Rawls' public reason requires a sort of complementarity between the religious background and the political discourse. Public reason might require a sacrifice of religious sentiments and values, but this sacrifice is surely much smaller than that required by secular reason. The Rawlsian believer is not seen as a fundamentalist. On the contrary, it is possible that his or her religious background can help to solve political dilemmas. Rawls simply thinks that a religious citizen cannot be certain that the other citizens will immediately understand his or her motivations based on faith. But this does not imply any negation of these motivations. Rather, in some specific and limited cases, the religious citizen is obliged to make his or her creed compatible, at least from a communicational point of view, with the political opinions of the other citizens. To speak, in the case of Rawls, of "secular fundamentalism" is simply misleading.[49]

Second, Rawls' view of the relation between politics and religion is different from traditional liberal views. Traditional liberal philosophers see the relation between politics and religion in terms of potential conflict. For historical reasons, they feel that religion threatens stability and think that liberalism is the standard antidote to this risk. From this hermeneutics of suspicion comes the idea of putting certain restraints on religion. That is why religion – for a traditional liberal – is and must be private. Such an ethics of restraint is essentially different from an ethics of (reciprocal) respect, of the kind endorsed by Rawls. For the ethics of respect, the problem is not that religion threatens stability, but rather that we need a cement of society based on a universal consensus. For this kind of Kantian legacy to be universal and to preserve pluralism, it must be based on shared institutional premises. Rawlsian public reason embodies in such a way the institutional morality of an ideal meta-community. It is the most significant "part of society's political capital" (PL 157). Moreover, we know that its exclusionary capacity, albeit relevant, is absolutely modest.

Rawls was certainly a religious person, even though his relation with religion became more controversial across the years.[50] This background religious attitude became generally transparent with the posthumous publication of Rawls' senior thesis under the title "A Brief Inquiry into the Meaning of Sin and Faith" (BIMSF). This work makes explicit how important the religious dimension of life is for Rawls. Probably one of the deepest motivations behind PL consists precisely in conceding to religious people the maximal space compatible with a liberal-democratic polity. Thus, in PL, the nexus between public reason and comprehensive religious doctrines is never denied and is generally considered with appreciation.

Nevertheless, there have been numerous religious objections to Rawls' idea of public reason.[51] One can group them in several classes, variously claiming that: (i) while Rawlsian public reason may have some advantages, the costs it carries are too high;[52] (ii) liberals place an excessive epistemological and ethical burden on religion, a burden which liberalism itself is not able to support;[53] (iii) religious arguments alone can adequately support public claims.

(i)   According to some religious critics, the supposed exclusion of religious arguments from politics via public reason is a consequence of an "over-simplification." This oversimplification is said to depend on a reductionist view of politics. Politics, in this reductionist view, is identified with political decisions that have coercion as an outcome. Politics, however – these religious critics maintain – is much more than this, since it has a social dimension that cannot be ignored. Within this social dimension, the role of religion is significant and un-eliminable. There is no need to deny this role, however, if we have in mind the importance given by Rawls to the background culture, which is independent of public reason. As I have already said, public reason is only a subset of the public sphere. And of course we can also do politics within the public sphere, where political arguments based on religion have – for Rawls – all the room they deserve. In conclusion, Rawls does not seem to be in substantial disagreement with his critics on this point.

Within this debate,[54] one can also maintain – as Paul J. Weithman[55] has – that the supposed exclusion of religious arguments via public reason implies a tremendous loss for the community, in terms of civic and political energy. This thesis, however, does not seem to conflict with Rawls' thought. Rawls' thesis, in particular his inclusive view, does not in fact exclude religious arguments from politics. On the contrary, religious arguments, such as Lincoln's and King's, are held in great consideration.

(ii) The second criticism can be split into three parts.

First, Rawls intends to limit the public usage of religious arguments, in a very restricted domain, via a "proviso": one can rely on religious arguments in politics, provided that one is able to reformulate them in a form consistent with public reason. Religious critics might object to this proviso.[56] They might maintain that it creates an asymmetry between lay and religious people.[57] The former must not have recourse to religious arguments, whereas the latter may. This thesis, however, is not fully defensible, if we read Rawls carefully. The proviso does not apply only to religious doctrines, but also to all comprehensive ones. In other words, the problem is not only a religious one.[58] It is applicable also to lay people, such as Kantians, utilitarians, and – why not? – even to Rawlsians. Public reason, so interpreted, does not imply any unfair asymmetry between lay and religious people. Rawlsian public reason is opposed to all forms of sectarian interpretation of the political life of liberal democracy. The sectarian interpretations rely on comprehensive doctrines, regardless of whether such doctrines are secular or religious.

Second, religious critics can maintain that even liberals are not able to live up to the exacting standards of public reason. Liberalism – according to this thesis – would not be able to create its own support. In a true regime of pluralism, liberals could not suppose that there are "shared" views, creating allegiance to public authority, independently of particular virtues, like those that religious people cultivate.[59] Civic virtues come from traditions, and traditions include religions. The ideal institutional meta-community that the liberals have in mind simply does not exist if founded on a voluntaristic basic (like contractualism). To put it more radically, liberalism, in these terms, is another form of "political theology."

Third, there is another possible way to conceive a possible asymmetry of the burden of proof against religious people. One could recognize the necessity of an honest justificatory effort of the sort Rawls has in mind in PL, while at the same time denying the necessity to locate religious arguments within the range of the arguments unable to perform this justificatory task. To impute unreasonableness to everyone who opts for a solution that is different from a broadly speaking contractualist one would be in some way to beg the question in favor of a liberal thesis. Moreover, it would be offensive to oblige religious people to restrain themselves from engaging in discussions by taking as their starting point premises that come directly from their faith. In this way, Rawls would underestimate persons religious "collateral commitments"[60] in the name of the liberal-democratic community's right to protect itself. This Rawlsian proposal – according to Stout – would imply too much "group thinking," given that single individuals could be ready to discuss policy arguments critically, based on religious premises.[61] This criticism can be disputed in two ways. First, it is controversial that Rawls simply wants to put some restraints on people relying on comprehensive doctrines. Perhaps he is offering them an extra opportunity: to believe in their own faith while they bet on a kind of institutional morality when discussing certain topics in the public domain.[62] Second, if we follow my initial theoretical hypothesis (see chapter 1) we have the possibility of recognizing the justificatory effort of religious people while at the same time accepting an ideal of public reason according to which some uniformity is necessary in terms of legitimation.

(iii) The third criticism maintains that a religious rationale alone is often sufficient to support a basic public claim. There is a sense in which this can be taken as a straight consequence of the previous argument. If, in other words, the epistemic and ethical substance of the liberal and religious arguments are not so different, then one is supposed to have the option of relying on the religious argument too. Moreover, virtues like personal autonomy or institutional loyalty can have a religious origin and background. Sometimes, this argument is reinforced by an "exceptionalist" thesis. This kind of thesis maintains that liberal philosophers, even in the mature form of the respect-based view, accept some exceptions to the strategy of public reason. Standard exceptions – accepted by Rawls among others – are support for public reason based on the anti-abolitionist argument and civic rights argument *à la* Martin Luther King. But, one could put on the table other useful arguments in terms of liberal public reason, in favor of religion, such as, for example, pro-family and anti-polygamy arguments, or arguments against the legalization of dueling.[63] Needless to say, this thesis makes sense. One could simply object that the problem posed by public reason is a normative rather than descriptive one.[64] This implies that even if one accepts the positive role of religion in civil society, one is not obliged to accept that, in principle, religion has a role comparable to that of public reason's.

11.2.5 An inclusive view

The distinction between public and secular reason, presented in the previous section, also helps us to understand what kind of arguments are generally acceptable within public reason. In the case of religion, I have tried to show why the interpretation (of public reason) according to which citizens are supposed to keep a significant part of their non-public reasons outside the political domain is misleading. While there is a temptation to interpret public reason in terms of mere exclusion, another, more fruitful, line of reasoning is that of inclusion.[65] Over the years (from 1990 to 1997), Rawls himself opted for this inclusive option. But what is meant by this strategy of inclusion? I would answer in the following way: while arguments based on a comprehensive doctrine are not directly apt for a political justification regarding certain fundamental issues, at the same time they cannot be seen as superfluous or non-admissible in the public arena. From this point of view, it is simply false to say that Rawls tries – via the idea of public reason – to avoid radical conflicts a priori.

The distinction between an "inclusive view" and an "exclusive view" is presented by Rawls in PL (247ff.). Through an inclusive view, one indicates the forms in which non-public reasons can also be used in political debates on fundamental questions. In PL, two classes of cases in particular are indicated in which the contribution of comprehensive doctrines appears justifiable:

(i)   the case of a well-ordered society, when an appeal to deepest convictions can help to create an atmosphere of reciprocal confidence among citizens;

(ii) the case of an evidently unjust society, when an appeal to deepest convictions can help to put certain fundamental matters of justice on the political agenda.

Lawrence Solum has made an effort to render more precise the conditions that recommend the inclusive view of public reason.[66] Within his interpretation, the role of non-public reasons consists mainly in giving supplementary justifications, when this seems necessary after the presentation of an argument in terms of public reason. In such cases, non-public reasons can guide us to a reciprocal clarification and may favor an appeasement between opposed parties. This is not necessarily the case, however. If one thinks of a case like abortion, it might well happen that the appeal to non-public reasons increases conflict among citizens. Notwithstanding this risk – for Solum – the inclusive view is significant, because the presentation of the deepest motivations could contribute to reciprocal respect among citizens.

In the second edition of PL and in IPRR, Rawls seems to be in agreement with this larger interpretation of the inclusive view (PL lii). From it, we get what Rawls calls a "wide view" of public reason and the formulation of the "proviso," which regulates the relation between comprehensive doctrines and public discourse in the most general way: "I now believe, and hereby revise VI 8 – PL first edition – that such doctrines may be introduced in public reason at any time, provided that in due course public reasons, given by a reasonable political conception, are presented sufficient to support whatever the comprehensive doctrines are introduced to support" (PL li–lii). The exclusive view is thus rejected. Still, the proviso itself is not devoid of ambiguity, given that we are not told how non-public reasons must be presented in order to be acceptable. It is not even clear whether public reasons must necessarily be joined to non-public reasons, or whether they need only to be available if requested. This last interpretive option is perhaps more convincing, offering a simplification of the political debate.

Swayed by these considerations, one might be tempted to say that public reason, far from being too restrictive, is too vague to be practically useful in political debates. In other words, it seems that there are many political dilemmas that public reason cannot solve. Rawls himself states, however, that this is not the aim of public reason: "Public reason is not a view about specific institutions or policies, but a view about how they are to be argued for and justified to the citizen body that must decide the question" (PL lii, n. 28).

The question that now naturally arises is: why does one need such a sophisticated strategy if it is not able in principle to solve divisive political problems?[67] Often, critics have mentioned the case of abortion as an example of the vagueness and decisional poverty of public reason. For the strategy of public reason seems unable to decide between a pro-life and pro-choice thesis in relation to abortion.[68] Perhaps we could object to this kind of argument that there is something intrinsically un-decidable about the morality of abortion. We might also suggest that the appeal to public reason, even if it is not able to solve the profound dilemma posed by abortion, could at least favor mutual respect under the duty of civility. In sum, while public reason may not be able to lay down necessary and sufficient conditions to solve a case, it can contribute to a better atmosphere between citizens of a liberal-democratic polity. And with this better atmosphere, one can suppose also that political deliberation becomes less difficult.

It has also been noted that only rarely does a typical citizen abandon his or her spontaneous comprehensive views in the name of something so abstract and impersonal as public reason.[69] In everyday life people are used to deliberating via the support of non-public reasons.[70] Is it plausible to see them as departing from their standards in rare and delicate cases? I do not see any direct answer to this question. Perhaps it might be suggested that our life incorporates a division of labor between the private and public domain, and such a division does not necessarily imply a dramatic split of the self. Finally, the "wide view of public reason" permits a reconciliation between these two parts of the social world and of the self. Within this wide view, Rawls extends inclusiveness and admits the "vital social roots" of political arguments, including those dependent on religion.

11.2.6 Public justification

Public reason implies that sometimes, in order to be politically relevant, one needs self-restraint and to bracket off part of one's deepest convictions. This trade-off is a consequence of the detachment from comprehensive doctrines that public reason requires. One could say with Rousseau, that, to get to the level of public reason, you must separate *l'homme et le citoyen*. It seems natural to raise doubts about the auspiciousness of such a strategy. Perhaps people need – partly in order to favor what Rawls calls a "duty of civility" – to pursue more integrity than public reason permits. Several objections have taken this view as their starting point. Some are listed here, grouped around five points:

(i) *Dissimulation.* The very idea that to be included in the world of politics you must be different from what your conscience naturally dictates seems to imply that you need to be ready to cheat or at least to be unfaithful to yourself. Many criticisms are based on the supposition that public reason implies insincerity, false consciousness, and lack of authenticity and honesty. The Machiavellian word (invented by Balthasar Gracian) "dissimulation" indicates a capacity to disguise, perhaps in the name of the *ragion di stato* (reason of the state). The accusation here consists in saying that from public reason one can derive an excess of political realism.

(ii) *Repression.* We move here from Machiavelli to Freud. Public reason is considered as the origin of a repression of true personality. Of course, this criticism is similar to the previous one. But, it is not identical, because here it is not a trade-off in the name of political realism that one has in mind. Rather it is the internalization of political norms, with a consequent loss of critical capacity.

(iii) *Robustness (lack of).* The idea of public reason is judged to be too thin. To accept public reason would imply – according to this criticism – the impossibility of using the whole force of our philosophical and religious convictions for political purposes.

(iv) *Smuggling.* This is the opposite of the previous criticism. We are told that the separation between public reason and comprehensive doctrines is simply impossible. Public reason merely (secretly) presupposes a comprehensive liberal doctrine.

(v) *Avoidance.* Rawls is accused of the a-priori exclusion of fundamental topics from the political debate via the filter of public reason. Democratic participation and deliberation are in this way pre-empted and made innocuous.

All these criticisms attack in some way the same Rawlsian argument, namely the argument based on the possibility of distinguishing between "full justification" and "public justification" within public reason. Public justification, in other words, is said to stand and fall with the full justification. The price we are supposed to pay for public reason is considered too high: to play the liberal-democratic game, we need to separate deep interiority and political exteriority. And this separation would force us to disown either a sensible understanding of the situation or our ethical roots.

An objection that can be raised against this critical strategy consists in emphasizing that the argument for public reason is still a moral and philosophical argument, albeit *sui generis*. It rests upon the idea of liberal-democratic legitimation and its relation to justification. The normativity of this argument is once again troublesome. Public reason implies that we can separate in principle a particular political topic from the argument we use to discuss it. To see how this is so we have to go back to Rawls' general justificatory strategy in PL.

Rawls – as his position is described in his "Reply to Habermas" – has in mind three kinds of justification, labeled "*pro tanto* justification," "full justification," and "public justification." *Pro tanto* justification works within the limits of the political conception (PL 386). Full justification rests on the links every citizen keeps with her comprehensive views, and overrides *pro tanto* justification (PL 386). Finally, public justification moves from the presupposition that every citizen knows that fellow citizens follow a common path (*pro tanto* and full justification). Citizens thus appeal to their capacity to achieve a wide reflective equilibrium and to accept at least some aspects of the same political conception starting from different deep reasons. As a consequence, if at the stage of full justification one avoids epistemic abstinence, at the public justification stage one does not rely on truth-claims. The appeal to truth or rightness is acceptable in the intermediate phase of full justification but not in the final one of public justification. In this way, public justification realizes a liberal-democratic ideal. Liberal-democratic power depends on symmetric communication between citizens ready to avoid publicly appealing to part of their deepest convictions in the name of respect for their fellow citizens. Public reason is a basic device through which this process takes place.

To understand Rawls' idea of public justification, it is useful to see it at work. Consider public debates about sexual behavior.[71] Let us take the case of an individual right of constitutional nature connected with sexual behavior, say a case such as homosexuality in public. There are two ways to defend such a right. The first is substantive. It maintains that there is nothing wrong with homosexual behavior, and therefore that there is no reason to constrain it. The second way is less direct. It says that there is no need to interrogate our comprehensive views about homosexuality, for we are confronted here with a political prerogative of a constitutional nature, the aim of which is to protect individual liberty. Society has no right to intervene on the basis of moral substantive convictions. Rawlsian public reason favors this second, less substantive and thinner, defense. Now, I suppose that without any doubt many people who are de facto inclined to accept this second way of defending homosexual behavior are also ready to accept the first (they think there is nothing wrong with homosexuality). Still, if I have correctly understood Rawls' idea of public reason, that idea invites us to select the second kind of argument. What Rawls has in mind is a kind of justificatory neutrality. This neutrality cannot be based on comprehensive views, which are – so to speak, by definition – intrinsically open to reasonable disagreement.

11.2.9 Public reason and contractualism

The conclusion of the previous section leaves room for a more general consideration concerning the nature of contractualism. I have already stressed that the idea of public reason seems to bring about modest results after huge efforts. This fact, of course, can appear as a fundamental problem. In my mind, however, this is so only if we assume a *lato sensu* consequentialist view, in which the core of political theory coincides with the results we are able to bring about. It is not so, on the other hand, if we assume a relational and deontological view of political theory. In this second view, the outcomes of public reason become much more significant, because they reinforce mutual respect and reciprocity among citizens. If, by contractualism, one means a political theory the main element of which is interpersonal, then public reason is certainly not a trivial device, and we can understand all the effort that Rawls devotes to it.

Different types of justification work together in PL. If Rawls makes an appeal to moral and metaphysical principles within full justification, he avoids the same appeal in public justification. One cannot deny, however, a normative claim in both kinds of justification – one might say a more traditional one in full justification and a less traditional one in public justification. True, public justification does not aim directly at truth and rightness. Still, it is not based on pure empirical consensus either. Public justification offers a mediation between these two options. Ultimately, public justification oscillates between two levels, presupposing legitimation on the one hand and looking for justification on the other.

We must never forget that, for Rawls, in liberal democracy and within a pluralist society legal power cannot derive from just one view of truth and rightness. Assuming this, Rawls makes use of the idea of public reason in an attempt to give an alternative account of politics, based on the communicative symmetry among free and equal citizens in a regime of reciprocal respect. Liberal-democratic power is intrinsically collective and depends on the way in which its citizens agree with each other. The idea of public reason and the consequent division between citizen and citizen derive from taking seriously the nature of liberal democracy within a contractualist outlook.

Of course one can resist this kind of argument, for instance by saying that it departs from the canon of normative Kantian justification that Rawls is supposed to accept. Such a thesis might leave some room for a more contextualist interpretation of PL. Contextualists would insist on the centrality within Rawls' framework of the "shared basis" of public culture connected with liberal-democratic citizenship. The real argument in PL – for contextualists – does not rely on any particular normative force but rather on the successful comparative experience of liberal democracy. The language of the reasonable and of public reason would be designed to capture this widespread awareness. David Rasmussen has brilliantly formulated a similar interpretation, emphasizing the continuity between the core concepts of PL and the institutional history of the USA.

The main problem of the contextualist interpretation, read by Rorty in terms of a priority of democracy over philosophy, consists in a relativistic misunderstanding of the normative claims in PL. Rawls does not insist on truth in politics, but he firmly believes in objectivity. Normative categories like public reason embody this claim to objectivity. From it, we can detect at least three different perspectives within which we may better grasp the normative meaning of PL:

(i) Rawls holds a particular Kantian view of objectivity. This view can be defined as a form of intersubjectivity based on reciprocal respect.

Concepts like the reasonable and public reason make this view central within the horizon of PL.

(ii) Since the beginning of his philosophical activity (since ODPE, published in 1951, but even since his senior and Ph.D. theses), Rawls has worked on a dual level of justification. This dual level consists in the normative core of the theory on one hand and in some external test on the other, such as reflective equilibrium and stability. It follows that, for Rawls, justification is never purely internal to the theory. It is always partially external to it. The dual level is represented by the dialectics of normativity and shared basis, person and citizen, legitimation and justification.

(iii) This last interpretive step, based on the coexistence of two levels in the justificatory structure of PL, is made particularly evident in Lectures IV and VI of PL, concerning, respectively, overlapping consensus and public reason. Ethical justification and political legitimation do converge, in these central lectures, so as to realize an ideal of tolerance and pluralism within liberal democracy.

12

THE LAW OF PEOPLES

TJ and PL try to show how a well-ordered liberal-democratic polity is possible. LoP hopes to show how a world society of liberal and decent peoples might be possible. Methodologically speaking, the model of political justice in LoP is roughly the same as that discussed in PL (12.1). The very fact that this book expands a model, created for the nation-state, to the global scenery creates several problems. The realm of international relations has often been seen in the past as a state of anarchy in which one can find neither the proper sense of an ethical justification nor the general consent implicit in a legitimation that apply to liberal democracies. This state of anarchy makes it difficult to expand the central notion of basic structure beyond its traditional state–national limits. These methodological flaws provoke what critics see as the two most important failures of Rawls' book. On one hand, Rawls seems to look for international stability by favoring a restricted interpretation of human rights at the cost of stability "for right reasons" (12.2.2). On the other hand, in LoP Rawls weakens his egalitarian apparatus by accepting socio-economic inequalities at the international level that he would never admit at the national one.

LoP is divided into two main parts. The first deals with ideal theory and the second concerns non-ideal theory. Within the ideal theory, liberal and decent peoples would join together via an international social contract to form a society of people (12.1.1, 12.1.2). Surely, peoples are nearer to states, the notion preferred by political realists, than to individuals, the notion preferred by cosmopolitans. However, Rawls insists on distinguishing peoples from states. States are often seen as merely rational, concerned with their power and guided by their basic interests. For peoples, instead, rationality does not exclude the reasonable. Peoples, but not states, respect the priority of right.

Liberal peoples have three basic features: a reasonably just constitutional democratic government; citizens united by "common sympathies"; and a

moral nature (12.1.2). Decent peoples are not properly liberal, but are pacifist, respect basic human rights, and use procedures of consultation. Together,
liberal and decent peoples would accept eight principles of international
justice. These principles are traditional, and include self-determination, *pacta
sunt servanda*, equality among peoples, non-intervention, self-defense, respect
for human rights, restriction in the conduct of war, and duty of assistance
(12.2).

The most controversial principles in this list are those concerning respect
for human rights and the duty of assistance. Rawls' list of human rights
seems extremely austere. And his conception of the duty of assistance
towards what he calls "burdened societies" appears to many less egalitarian
than it should be. The presence itself of decent peoples within the society
of peoples creates an element of perplexity (12.2.1). For example, decent
peoples are considered culturally homogeneous, which is highly controversial, and it is not clear how we could safeguard their minorities against
majoritarian domination.

Outside ideal theory, there are outlaw states, burdened societies, and hierarchical non-decent peoples (12.4.1). Rawls says practically nothing about
hierarchical non-decent peoples. He is also very parsimonious in treating
the case of war and, more generally, the destiny of outlaw states. There is,
however, an interesting argument about burdened societies and the duty of
assistance which liberal peoples have towards them (12.4).

12.1 From National Justice to International Justice

Global justice is considered sporadically in Rawls' main works from 1950
to 1993. These works are limited to justice within a "basic structure," the
borders of which largely coincide with those of the nation-state. Many commentators considered this to be a serious limitation, particularly in a time
in which globalization had become a central issue. Yet even in TJ there are
references to the possibility of extending the basic model of justice to the
international realm by means of what Rawls called "the law of nations."[1] In
the spring term of 1969 at Harvard, Rawls held a course on "Problems of the
War" – "the war" being, of course, that then being fought in Vietnam. In later
years, Rawls dedicated two essays to issues of international justice – "The
Law of Peoples," given as an Oxford Amnesty Lecture in 1993, and, in 1995,
"Fifty Years after Hiroshima," a brief article on the immorality of the nuclear
bombing of Japan (notable also for the fact that Rawls himself served on the
Japanese front towards the end of the war).

Unsatisfied with the treatment given in the Oxford Amnesty Lecture, Rawls
devoted much time to the same topic in subsequent years, giving a series of
three seminars at Princeton in April 1995. Out of these he developed his most
systematic treatment of global justice in the book LoP, which he completed

during the academic year 1997–8. The manuscript itself was, however, never subjected to a full revision due to the stroke that disabled Rawls in 1998.

Two kinds of questions arise when studying LoP. First, the work raises questions regarding its relation to Rawls' earlier thought. Second, it raises questions regarding the inherent difficulties of developing an ethical-political theory of international relations such as that offered in the book.

Regarding questions of the first kind, Rawls himself insists on the continuity of his thought in the introduction to LoP, when he writes, "Both TJ and PL try to say how a liberal society might be possible. LoP hopes to say how a world Society of liberal and decent Peoples might be possible" (LoP 6).

Rawls also emphasizes that the conception of justice employed in LoP is the political conception first presented in PL rather than the one employed in TJ.[2] This continuity raises a problem of its own. For the theoretical model that Rawls employs – both in TJ and in PL – was first developed in his treatment of domestic politics in a pluralistic society, before being transferred to issues that extend beyond the national context. This difficulty has two, related aspects – to put it in Rawlsian terms – an institutional aspect, related to the first principle of justice, and a socio-economic aspect, related to the second principle of justice. This substantive discontinuity is compensated through all the three books by a methodological unifying commitment, namely that the construction of justice cannot be independent from the institutional practices they refer to.[3]

From an institutional perspective, the coexistence of individuals with differing, albeit reasonable, conceptions of the good within a national, political society presupposes a unitary basic structure that the global political society just does not have. In particular, the nation-state is traditionally characterized by a central authority, capable of enforcing the law and of guaranteeing a certain degree of liberty and autonomy to minorities. The same cannot be said of the international community, which has no central authority capable of enforcing the law and of protecting minorities and the oppressed. Moreover, one must admit that some egalitarian ideals in which Rawls' principles are grounded are not embedded in the global public culture.[4]

From a socio-economic perspective, the main issue raised by extending the national model to the international context concerns the possibility of defending a normative requirement of relative socio-economic equality between peoples. In LoP, Rawls removes the three pillars of the egalitarianism of TJ: the fair value of the basic liberties, the fair equality of opportunity and the difference principle.[5] Clearly, he does this because there is no world basic structure comparable to the national one.[6] It is not surprising that many critics, including many sympathetic to Rawls' theory at the national level, have been perplexed by this lack of egalitarian liberalism at the international level.

As regards the second question, it must be said that the issues treated in LoP are intrinsically controversial and that they present difficulties for any view of international relations.[7] Even political realism, the dominant theory of international relations in the twentieth century from Morgenthau to Kissinger, faced its fair share of problems in recent decades. In particular, it had to adapt to a new world in which two of its basic theoretical pillars had been much weakened – namely, national sovereignty and the traditional identification between people and state. At the same time, the traditional opponent of realism, the natural law tradition originating in Christian philosophers such as Vitoria, Suarez, Grotius, and Pufendorf that extends to contemporary liberal cosmopolitanism, has significant problems in applying its conception of universal justice to the concrete problems of the world.[8] Rawls himself thinks that cosmopolitanism's ultimate concern is for the wellbeing of individuals and not – as he thinks it should be – for the justice of societies (LoP 119). Rawls, when elaborating his central notion of a "realistic utopia" in LoP, is concerned to avoid the most obvious weaknesses of both political realism and the abstract utopianism involved in certain cosmopolitan views.

12.1.1 A "Realistic Utopia"

LoP concerns a particular political conception of justice, to be applied to the relations between peoples. The use of the term "peoples" is itself significant. As was mentioned above, Rawls prefers it to alternatives such as "states" or "individuals." For a continental European, this terminology brings to mind the *jus gentium* of Roman law.[9] Rawls defines the "law of peoples" as "a particular political conception of right and justice that applies to the principles and norms of international law and practice" (LoP 3). The fundamental idea is that there is a "Society of Peoples" constituted by those peoples that respect some principles of justice in their relations with each other. The notion of justice implicit in the behavior of these peoples is based on the social contract. It must nonetheless be sensitive to a particularity of the international context, namely that each people has its own autonomous government and cultural tradition. It is for this reason that the theory bases international relations on a kind of "realistic utopia."[10]

Rawls' realistic utopian theory distinguishes five kinds of national societies, each of which is subject to the law of peoples in a different way. The first two kinds, liberal and "decent" peoples, are both called "well-ordered," a term Rawls adopts from Jean Bodin. These two kinds are distinguished from each other by the fact that, unlike liberal peoples, decent peoples are usually organized hierarchically, even if they respect human rights and allow citizens some participation in political decision-making. Liberal and decent peoples constitute the Society of Peoples, the ideal part of Rawls' theory. The non-ideal part is constituted by the relations between this Society of Peoples and the other three kinds of national societies, generally referred to as "states" or "societies," rather than as "peoples." These latter kinds include "outlaw states," "burdened societies," and "benevolent absolutisms," which, while they respect human rights, have decision-making structures that lack the popular participation of liberal and decent peoples.

Rawls considers the basis of justice for peoples to lie in an extension of the idea of the social contract. In this particular context, though, the original position and the contract have two levels. First, there is the level of the ideal theory, concerned with liberal and decent peoples. This "Society of Peoples" is subject to the principles of justice for peoples. Second, at the level of the other three kinds of societies or states, each incapable of participating in the Society of Peoples, there is the non-ideal theory, which Rawls discusses in the second part of LoP. A second original position operates at this level and takes into account the historical and institutional conditions that prevent these societies or states from participating in the Society of Peoples.

The most distinctive element of LoP is the conviction, consistent with the priority of right, that political injustice is the cause of the greatest human tragedies and that the development of international institutions provides the best way of preventing such injustices. In this regard, it is important to note that, unlike TJ, LoP does not present the parties in the original position as symmetrical. Thus Rawls is not concerned to identify the best form of international relations from the perspective of all peoples, societies, and states, but rather to provide an abstract model of foreign policy for liberal (and decent) peoples. One could summarize Rawls' realistic utopian position as consisting of the following three levels of justice:

(i)   the substantive level, identified in the national basic structure;
(ii)   the level regarding relations between well-ordered societies;
(iii) the general international level, at which all peoples should maintain reciprocal relations, irrespective of the kind of society which they constitute.

Rawls himself mentions three kinds of cases in which progress in justice, in terms of the gradual realization of liberal-democratic ideals, provides for concrete improvements – namely, just war, immigration, and use of nuclear weapons.

12.1.2 The centrality of peoples

In identifying peoples as the main subjects of international relations, the model presented in LoP assumes a particular social ontology.[11] As we have seen, the content of LoP is to be determined by extending the original position. In this case, however, the contracting parties are not representatives of individual citizens, but representatives of entire peoples.[12] This appears problematic, since the political theory of international relations generally takes either states or individuals to be the main subjects of international relations. Generally speaking, the realist model focuses on the state while the cosmopolitan model focuses on the individual. Rawls' choice of peoples as the basic subjects of international relations thus corresponds to an intermediate model.

Rawls probably excludes the possibility of taking individuals as the subjects of international relations because this would contradict his initial view of global politics as a meeting place of politically autonomous governments and relatively independent cultures. He focuses mainly on liberal and decent peoples to emphasize the shared culture, history, and language that characterize a people and to underline its moral nature. Thus he writes: "Liberal peoples have three basic features: a reasonably just constitutional democratic government that serves their fundamental interests; citizens united by what Mill called "common sympathies"; and finally a moral nature. The first is institutional, the second is cultural, and the third requires a firm attachment to a political (moral) conception of right and justice" (LoP 23–4).

However, here too a problem arises. For even if a people has a liberal-democratic government and some shared cultural traditions, in what sense does it have a moral nature? The most plausible answer is that, for Rawls, political theory within a state has an interpersonal basis while global political theory has an inter-people basis.[13] Rawls thus stresses the influence that political institutions and the culture that they produce can exert on the formation of the collective moral character of a people. Identifying peoples rather than states as the basic subjects of international relations is therefore a way of emphasizing these ethical-political aspects over issues of mere sovereignty, which are more closely related to the idea of the state.[14] This distinction emerges clearly in the following passage:

> [States] are often seen as rational, anxiously concerned with their power . . . and always guided by their basic interests . . . If rationality excludes the reasonable . . . if the state's concern with power is predominant . . . then the difference between states and peoples is enormous . . . A difference between liberal peoples and states is that just liberal peoples limit their basic interests as required by the reasonable. (LoP 28–9)[15]

Essentially, Rawls employs an analogy between the characteristics of individuals and those of peoples. Just as he considers individuals as rational and reasonable – where being rational means acting in one's own self-interest and being reasonable means having a concern for other individuals – so he considers peoples as capable of having ethical-political concerns, albeit to varying degrees.

While it is easy to understand such claims when speaking of individuals, their meaning is ambiguous when applied to peoples. Is Rawls speaking of real peoples in broadly descriptive terms, or is he, rather surreptitiously, introducing a normative model? If he is indeed speaking descriptively, then cases such as Belgium or Indonesia, not to mention the ex-Yugoslavia or any state that undergoes a large-scale migration, suggest that the kind of cultural and ethical unity hypothesized by Rawls does not in fact exist. In general, as can be seen in the cases of the Palestinians and Kurds, peoples and political borders do not correspond precisely in today's world.

It is more probable, however, that Rawls takes peoples to be a normative idea. But then two questions arise. First, Rawls fails to provide an argument for this normative position beyond distinguishing peoples from states. Second, many critics insist that normatively it would seem preferable to base the theory on the morality of individuals rather than on the more mysterious one of peoples. This criticism accompanies the belief that fairness towards peoples, understood as separate units, will generally be followed by unfairness towards individual members of those peoples.[6] Rawls says little on this matter, but I expect that he would reply by claiming that it is highly unrealistic to conceive of the world only in terms of relations between individuals. Such a pragmatic reply is rather unconvincing, however, if we are supposed to be adopting a strictly normative point of view. Nonetheless, it may be possible to reconcile Rawls' position with that of his critics by means of the idea of a realistic utopia, which is, after all, a way of binding our normative assumptions to factual reality. Such a reply, however, may undermine Rawls' distinction between peoples and states. Indeed, as Allen Buchanan has pointed out, if one were to accept Rawls' reasoning in LoP, then it would be impossible to imagine a case in which a people could not be identified with a state.[17] If this is so, then the idea of peoples amounts to a sort of weakened state. Alternatively, peoples could be considered as idealized states, in opposition to political realist conceptions of states.[18]

While this latter possibility is certainly open to interpretation, it nevertheless suggests a possible defense of the notion of peoples. That is, it may be that the Society of Peoples as a whole is not strictly speaking a political structure at all, but rather only one generic form of cooperation. This would make peoples, rather than states, plausible subjects of international relations, just as churches or universities are the subjects of religious or scientific cooperation. Such an interpretation would at least make the intended distinction between peoples and states clearer.

12.2 Principles of International Justice

In LoP liberal and decent peoples – or more precisely their representatives, as the subjects of the original position – are conceived as "free and equal," analogously to individuals in the original position in the national context. The Society of Peoples, in this ideal phase, is conceived as pluralist and not based on any particular conception of the good. Under these conditions, a principle of reciprocity between peoples holds, such that peoples are obliged to accept the interests of each of the others in remaining independent over time and in enjoying self-respect (thus extending to states an optimistic understanding of Rousseauian *amour propre*).[19] In this modified original position, Rawls argues, subjects would choose eight principles of justice. While in TJ the principles of justice are determined in preference to an alternative, utilitarian conception, in LoP the principles of justice are merely stated. They concern the following issues:

(i)   the freedom and independence of peoples;
(ii) respect for treaties;
(iii) equality between peoples;
(iv) the duty of non-intervention;
(v)   the right of self-defense;
(vi) respect for human rights;
(vii) restrictions on how war may be waged;
(viii) the duty of assistance to peoples excluded from the Society of Peoples.

This list provides some guidelines for a sort of international moral constitution. The first five principles and the seventh principle basically restate ideas already present in TJ. However, the sixth and eighth principles are new for Rawls. They deal with fundamental aspects of LoP that are also the most controversial ones. Indeed, as I will show below, both Rawls' conception of human rights and his treatment of the duty of assistance have been subject to vigorous debate. Furthermore, all of the principles are subject to interpretation and to mutual qualification. For example, the duty of non-intervention holds only insofar as there are no overt violations of rights by other states.

It is interesting to identify the most obvious ways in which the model of the original position that Rawls applies to peoples in international relations in LoP differs from the model applied to individuals in the national context in TJ. Rawls himself notes the following three differences:

(i)   while individuals in the original position have a conception of the good, peoples do not;
(ii) while the main interests of individuals concern the realization of their moral powers, those of peoples are political, in the sense identified in PL;
(iii) while individuals in the standard original position decide upon determinate principles of justice, peoples in the international original position decide between different interpretations of principles.

A consequence of these differences is that, unlike in the original position considered in TJ, in LoP utilitarianism is not presented as an alternative theoretical candidate. No people would accept a loss of utility in exchange for a gain in utility for another people, and peoples are not generally willing to surrender their basic equality. This helps to explain why the decision regarding the principles of LoP is not presented as a decision between competing alternatives.

In this ideal model of the Society of Peoples, the intended outcome is stability. Unlike the political realist model of international relations, however, this model bases stability not on a balance of power or *modus vivendi*, but rather on respect for principles. The type of stability sought is therefore stability for right reasons, although this is a rather problematic aim.

Nonetheless, Rawls suggests that the progressive establishment of LoP over time will lead to the formation within peoples of characteristics that promote stability for right reasons, such as moral education, reciprocal trust, and an appropriate form of patriotism. A liberal-democratic peace thus appears intrinsically different from a realist one. The peace enjoyed by a liberal-democratic society is distinguished by a discursive attitude and by the acceptance of pluralism, which both favor peaceful means of conflict resolution. Thus an ideal of public reason is to develop over time, in parallel with the diffusion of the Law of Peoples. For Rawls, this can also be demonstrated historically, although he admits that liberal democracies have not always been equal to their normative task.

The eight principles of international justice thus express the pacifist tendency of liberal democracy. In this, Rawls again gives an original twist to a Kantian theme, and also revisits Doyle's and Russett's argument regarding "democratic peace." Doyle and Russett argue that liberal-democratic states generally do not wage war against each other.[20] Rather than affirming this as a descriptive claim, Rawls formulates it as a normative one concerning what liberal-democratic states ought to do and how far we would condemn any departure from this normative standard. Rawls also follows Kant in considering a federation of free states to be preferable to a single world state. A world state might impose its own will, according to its own particular conception of the good, and thus not sufficiently respect local cultures and aspirations.

12.2.1 Decent peoples

The most novel aspect of Rawls' ideal theory of international relations involves extending the principles of justice to relations between liberal-democratic peoples and what he calls "decent hierarchical" peoples. To be part of the Society of Peoples a decent hierarchical people must fulfil the following two criteria:

(i)   in international relations, it must renounce any aggressiveness and expansionist ambitions;
(ii) in internal politics, it must respect human rights and impose certain moral duties on all individuals through a system that, being governed according to a broadly shared conception of the good, administers justice in a reasonably egalitarian way.

These two criteria express a notion of "decency" that is a kind of weakened version of Rawls' "reasonableness" in PL.[21] For any liberal, I would suggest, the very concept of "decency" represents a concern as important as it is problematic: that of balancing tolerance for cultural diversity against certain limits.[22] I showed in my analysis of PL how Rawls expresses this concern at the national level, but it is even more important at the international level, given the greater differences between cultures and traditions. From this point of view, decency represents a sort of ideal boundary, an equilibrium at which peoples who do not respect all of the rules of liberal democracy can nonetheless be tolerated by liberal peoples.

Decent peoples are not liberal, for they do not enforce all of the rights distinctive of liberal societies, such as the freedom of conscience for all and equality in the eyes of the law. Even the freedoms of association, speech, and participation are limited for these peoples. But, for Rawls, members of liberal-democratic peoples must nonetheless tolerate their inclusion within the Society of Peoples.[23] Rawls' understanding of tolerance is demanding. It requires liberal-democratic peoples "to recognize these nonliberal societies as equal participating members in good standing of the Society of Peoples" (LoP 59).

This tolerance underscores the idea that a liberal-democratic attitude concerns decent peoples as groups or classes (in Hegel's sense) and not as single individuals. Rawls considers an imaginary state, "Kazanistan," which bases public life upon religious and, specifically, Islamic principles and nonetheless satisfies the two criteria mentioned above. Kazanistan should therefore be included in the Society of Peoples. Of course, the inclusion of decent hierarchical peoples in the Society of Peoples depends on the possibility of extending the argument from the original position to this kind of situation. Indeed, the associationist approach, according to which reasonableness belongs to groups rather than individuals, makes it plausible to consider the representatives of decent hierarchical peoples as capable of understanding and accepting the eight principles of LoP. It thus seems crucial that in such hierarchical societies there is respect for human rights and a functioning consultative regime. A hierarchical basic structure, however, may not be capable of ensuring respect for human rights since these rights are clearly linked to a liberal vision of institutions and an individualistic conception of persons. If this is the case, then Rawls' Society of Peoples fails to satisfy his own liberal requirements. Yet Rawls maintains that a decent society, even if hierarchical, may respect human rights sufficiently to defend an acceptable degree of internal pluralism and deny other states the right to intervene in the event of violations. Nonetheless, it is certainly not clear when a hierarchical society crosses the line such that its behavior is no longer consistent with the idea of a decent people.

Beyond these practical difficulties regarding the extent to which a hierarchical society can be tolerated, Rawls' model faces a theoretical question: how can we balance individuals' freedoms with tolerance for differences of tradition and history?[24] According to many critics, particularly cosmo-politans, Rawls' solution is not compatible with the principles of liberalism. On this view, liberal peoples are not under an obligation to tolerate decent ones, which means decent societies ought not to be included in the Society of Peoples.

The extension of tolerance to hierarchically organized decent peoples presents serious problems. First, a liberal-democratic state's toleration of illiberal groups, within the limits that guarantee the protection of the groups' members and of the state's other citizens, differs substantially from the pro-tection offered by illiberal regimes, which do not guarantee fair treatment of individual citizens. Second, Rawls argues that in decent hierarchical socie-ties all citizens tend to share the same conception of the good. This fact is supposed to explain our acceptance of them within the Society of Peoples. But is such a claim really plausible or does it express an overly optimistic view? The elites that govern decent hierarchical peoples have an interest in making it appear that citizens share a conception of the good. In reality these peoples may be reasonably divided on political and moral grounds. After all, Kazanistan does not really exist. If we try to imagine a real country of this kind – Iran, say – it seems more plausible to suppose that the theocratic regime in power tries to project an image of its citizens as living according to the same conception of the good even if this is far from the truth.

In my view, Rawls' theory is thus unable to avoid an unattractive implica-tion regarding the treatment of liberal-democratic minorities within a decent state. It is not clear how agreements between decent states and liberal peoples could be justified to the liberal-democratic minorities in decent states who, quite rightly, contest the legitimacy of that state from within. Could we Westerners really say to liberal Tunisians that we support their "benevolent" dictator because to us he seems "decent" in Rawls' sense, while they are being repressed by him?[25] Practically, how could we not support these abused and enlightened minorities? Suppose, for example, that a decent people aspiring to belong to the Society of Peoples, such as Rawls' hypothetical Kazanistan or the current regime in Saudi Arabia, systematically violates women's rights, perhaps for traditional or religious reasons. How can liberal peoples have relationships with these peoples based on principles of justice and claim to justify them both to liberal-democratic public opinion and to those women who rightly consider themselves mistreated by the institutions of a decent people?

These problems arise due to both the institutional model of justice that Rawls employs and his transfer of it from the national to the international context. The change in the subject of the model, from individuals to peoples, raises the question of whether the use of the term "peoples" obscures impor-tant differences between the individuals and groups that might constitute this subject. Rawls complicates this ontological question by expanding the Society of Peoples to include decent peoples. As I have shown, the necessary conditions of the realization of Rawls' Society of Peoples are essentially those of the realization of the just national society presented in PL, transferred to the international level. Stability for right reasons which, according to PL, binds a well-ordered society in a pluralistic national regime is also a necessary condition of the realization of a just international society. Yet it is not clear that stability at the international level could really be a stability for "right reasons," rather than the consequence of a mere equilibrium produced by a *modus vivendi*. The litmus test for such a hypothesis lies in the extent to which individuals and minorities in decent hierarchical states are protected from non-liberal elites' abuse of power.

In PL, the possibility of stability for right reasons was ensured within the liberal-democratic state by the fact that such a state itself guarantees political neutrality with respect to ethical and metaphysical claims. In moving from the national to the global level, however, such political neutrality cannot be guaranteed. At the international level, these metaphysical–moral differences are not analogous to the ones within a liberal state. These differences influence political structures.[26]

Although one of the defining characteristics of a decent people is that it does not wage aggressive wars against other peoples, it does not follow that a decent people necessarily also respects its internal minorities. Here, the consideration of peoples, and not individuals, as the subjects represents an additional risk. For there may be hegemonic elites that ensure a relative internal and international tranquility, but do not offer any guarantees towards those that do not belong to them. In this case, the stability ensured by such groups would not be for the "right reasons," as in the national context considered in PL. Instead, stability would derive from a contingent equilibrium produced by the persistence of a *modus vivendi*. This account runs a risk of mistaking social stability for moral stability, of mistaking a Hobbesian order for a Rawlsian or Kantian order.

Rawls is aware of this risk and there is a thoroughgoing coherence to his theory. His choice of peoples as the primary subjects of international relations, his inclusion of decent peoples within the Society of Peoples and, as we will see, his minimalist notion of human rights are all coherent aspects of a single, unified model of international relations. Fundamentally, this coherence reflects a general unwillingness to make moral evaluations of peoples and the relations between them.

12.2.2 Human rights

The topic of the second part of the ideal theory in LoP is human rights. The number of human rights and the degree of respect for them that Rawls proposes are limited. He is led to these limitations by two broad considerations. First, Rawls' eight principles of international justice place much emphasis on state sovereignty, and therefore prevent him from endorsing an extensive theory of human rights that would limit this sovereignty. Second, as a liberal, Rawls is particularly concerned to defend cultural pluralism. For this reason he is obliged to privilege a narrow conception of human rights.

In the section on human rights, Rawls only acknowledges as fundamental those generally recognized human rights which he calls "special urgent rights." These rights include "freedom from slavery and serfdom, liberty (but not equal liberty) of conscience and security of ethnic groups from mass murder and genocide" (LoP 79). However, in the chapter on decent peoples he presents the following, less parsimonious list:

> the right to life (to the means of subsistence and security); to liberty (to freedom from slavery, serfdom, and forced occupation, and to a sufficient measure of liberty of conscience to ensure freedom of religion and thought); to property (personal property); and to formal equality as expressed by the rules of natural justice (that is, that similar cases be treated similarly). (LoP 65)

Although it is surprising that Rawls presents two different lists of human rights, and that the more comprehensive of the two is presented in the chapter on decent peoples rather than the one on human rights, the two lists may be combined.[27] Even when combined, however, the resulting list excludes many of the most generally recognized human rights, including some of the most important of those included in the United Nations Declaration of 1948 and in related covenants. I have already discussed one reason for this – Rawls' treatment of respect for human rights as a necessary condition of entrance into the Society of Peoples. The condition of respecting human rights particularly regards decent peoples. This presumably explains why Rawls' list excludes such fundamental civil and political rights as the rights of free speech, association, and democratic participation.[28]

Yet, even admitting such a motivation, Rawls' list may still appear too austere, and one wonders why he was not more demanding in identifying necessary conditions of entrance into the Society of Peoples. Charles Beitz has suggested that Rawls' list privileges stability over the possible victims of human rights violations due to the belief that requiring respect for a few fundamental human rights may prevent some peoples from becoming outlaw states. In such a way, one could preserve international peace. Requiring respect for a more comprehensive list of human rights may lead to conflicts.[29] One can respond to this suggestion in two ways. On the one hand, if Rawls privileges the pursuit of stability, is this stability for right reasons? On the other hand, nothing excludes the possibility of externally peaceful states being internally aggressive. Thus, if Rawls does indeed privilege international peace, this suggests that he was not sufficiently concerned with preventing human rights violations within states. In general, and especially from a liberal point of view, human rights ought not to be conceived merely as a standard

306 Rawls: An Introduction

for international politics, but also as a guarantee for inhabitants of non-liberal-democratic states.

According to a view of justice such as that adopted by Rawls, a violation of human rights should have a stronger meaning. But this is undermined by Rawls' substitution of an individualist approach to justice with one based upon the rights of peoples.[30] Suppose, for instance, that an individual's rights are violated by a hierarchical regime. Is it really acceptable to attempt to justify this in terms of international stability, assuming that the people in question is generally considered decent? Only pragmatic reasons would lead one to think so, but, as I have mentioned, the model itself excludes appeals to such reasons. One can certainly reply that, at least in theory, a people should not violate the rights of its citizens if it is to be classified as "decent." But then one need only imagine the violation of rights not included in Rawls' list, such as non-violent gender discrimination, to realize that with regard to human rights the shift from individuals to an evaluation of the moral qualities of a people allows some rather serious injustices towards individuals. This contrasts with the spirit of a liberal ethics of international relations. Moreover, it is rather paradoxical that the same philosopher who famously criticized utilitarianism in the name of the "separateness of persons" argues that a people may be evaluated without considering sufficiently how it treats individuals and their rights.

One can provide a conceptual reply to some of these objections by emphasizing that Rawls' treatment of LoP always remains within the realm of his ideal theory.[31] This theory presupposes the Society of Peoples composed of liberal and decent peoples, which, despite their differences in social organization, are nonetheless well ordered. This alone provides an a-priori guarantee against certain violent human rights violations. But it is not sufficient necessarily to exclude other violations, such as the exclusion of girls from basic education on religious grounds or the collective denial of gay rights. All of the ambiguities associated with the notion of a decent people would thus seem to arise again.

In response to the apparent arbitrariness and parsimony of Rawls' list of human rights, Samuel Freeman attempts to identify a more general justification by appeal to the following passage:[32] "What have come to be called human rights are recognized as necessary conditions of any system of social cooperation. When they are regularly violated, we have command by force, a slave system, and no cooperation of any kind" (LoP 68).

On the basis of this passage, Freeman develops an interpretation of Rawls' view of human rights as conditions of cooperation, and argues that Rawls intends the human rights on his list to constitute a minimum without which cooperation among peoples would be impossible. This provides a persuasive response to the accusation of arbitrariness. However, it does not seem to provide a response to the accusation of parsimony, since one wonders why the minimum necessary for cooperation among peoples should not be more substantial – requiring, say, religious freedom.[33] Of course, here Rawls is concerned not to base his list on any comprehensive conception of justice, including liberal ones, but this concern alone is not sufficient to justify any particular minimum for human rights.

Until now I have discussed the limits of Rawls' list of human rights only with regard to civil and political rights. I have neglected socio-economic rights. While Rawls recognizes a general right to subsistence, he again appears extremely cautious. Admittedly, he dedicates ample space elsewhere in LoP to defending the obligation of the Society of Peoples to assist burdened societies, and here he maintains that fulfilling basic needs is more demanding than defending human rights (LoP 38). But, as I will show below, the appeal to the duty of assistance in fact creates new and more significant problems.

12.3 The Non-ideal Theory: War

Thus far, I have discussed Rawls' ideal theory. In the third part of the book, he develops a non-ideal political theory, which treats relationships between, on the one hand, liberal-democratic peoples and decent peoples, and, on the other hand, societies and states that are not well ordered and therefore not members of the Society of Peoples. The fact that such peoples fail to meet the minimum requirements for participation in the Society of Peoples does not mean that the Society of Peoples has no relations with them, or that no moral questions arise in these non-ideal contexts. In particular, "outlaw" and "burdened" states deserve special attention, if only because, according to Rawls, liberal peoples should assist these states to satisfy the conditions necessary for joining the Society of Peoples.

In this part of the book, Rawls discusses the two principal questions that regulate the relationships between the two types of states: armed intervention (war) and assistance to less fortunate nations.

Rawls' discussion of war is not particularly original and it relies substantially on Michael Walzer's theory.[34] With slight modifications, Rawls makes claims regarding the "just cause" for war, the defense of human rights, the respect for civilians and the moral status of soldiers that are similar to Walzer's. For both, civilian immunity may be violated only in cases of "supreme emergency," although, unlike Walzer, Rawls limits this exception to liberal peoples in cases of self-defense.[35]

A moral consideration of the principles of a just war naturally brings to mind the natural law tradition and the relevant Christian doctrines. But Rawls' theory differs from these in its "political" character. Well-ordered peoples – that is, liberal and decent ones – have a right to go to war only in cases of self-defense or serious and persistent violations of human rights or so-called "humanitarian law." Yet even in war, well-ordered peoples are subject to principles of justice, including those regarding how the war itself is conducted. Among such principles are the following:

(i) the ultimate goal of the war must be a more stable peace;
(ii) a well-ordered people can engage in war only against a people that is not well ordered;
(iii) in a people that is not well ordered, it is necessary to distinguish between the members of the regime and the common people, so that, for instance, leaders and army officials are distinguished from mere civilians;
(iv) it is necessary to respect the enemy's human rights as much as possible;
(v) well-ordered peoples must exhibit in both their public discourses and their behavior the kind of peace that they intend to achieve by means of the war;
(vi) the means of destruction employed must be commensurate with the goals of the war.

These principles are to be interpreted in the light of specific contexts. In cases of extreme wartime crisis *jus in bello* exemptions are permissible. That is, occasionally extremely cruel and destructive measures may be adopted if the goal of the war renders them necessary. This would apply in a case such as the Allied bombing of Germany at the beginning of the Second World War, but not in a case such as the American use of the atomic bomb in Japan at the end of the war. Rawls takes up the analysis of the latter case again here, and by appeal to the general principles argues that bombing Hiroshima and the destruction of other Japanese cities was a great moral error, manifesting a serious failure of the American leadership.

12.3.1 The non-ideal theory: the duty of assistance

A particularly significant issue treated by the non-ideal theory regards the relationships between peoples that are members of the Society of Peoples and burdened societies. By burdened societies, Rawls means societies lacking in "the political and cultural traditions, the human capital and know-how, and, often, the material and technical resources needed to be well-ordered" (LoP 106). Such societies, while not participating in the Society of Peoples, differ from outlaw states such as Nazi Germany insofar as they are economically underdeveloped and do not necessarily have expansionist aspirations. With regard to these burdened societies, well-ordered societies have a general duty to assist them to satisfy the conditions necessary for entrance into the Society of Peoples. This duty is expressed by Article 8 of the international contract that binds members of the Society of Peoples, which reads as follows: "Peoples have a duty to assist other peoples living under unfavorable conditions that prevent their having a just or decent political and social regime" (LoP 37).

How exactly a people is to respect this principle is not specified in LoP. Rawls does not think that it is a matter of applying principles of distributive justice to burdened societies. Instead, he thinks this duty includes applying a principle analogous to that which, with respect to national politics, Rawls calls the principle of "just savings." The principle of just savings is presented in TJ as a kind of saving that present generations undertake in the interests of future generations, although Rawls states explicitly that it is not possible "to define precise limits on what the rate of savings should be (TJ 286; rev. edn. 253). This claim has provoked controversy because the principle of just savings requires less than the second principle of justice.

The lack of the difference principle in LoP has been amply discussed by critical Rawlsians such as Pogge and Beitz and is seen as a problem in Rawls' position.[36] Indeed, the theory presented in LoP – for many interpreters of Rawls – lacks not only a principle analogous to the difference principle, but any theory of distributive justice whatsoever. The most common criticism – made by Pogge, for instance – is that the ethical double standard regarding the national and global levels that Rawls' theory involves cannot be philosophically justified.[37] In other words, Rawls' theory would tolerate socio-economic injustices at the global level that would not be tolerated within a single nation. Pogge claims there is a kind of inconsistency between the Rawls' position in TJ and that presented in LoP.

Let us try to understand why Rawls limits the responsibility of assistance in a way that might appear inconsistent with his general view of distributive justice. First, from TJ onwards, Rawls assumes that distributive justice concerns a basic structure, treated as corresponding approximately to the fundamental institutions of the nation-state (see next section).[38] In this limited sphere, one may presume that global interdependence is negligible. Second, Rawls makes a claim regarding international economics, according to which the causes of a nation's poverty are substantially endogenous. They consist of the limited capacities of local elites, and particularly of a society's political culture. Rawls thus tends to exclude both the direct responsibility of first-world citizens for economic conditions in burdened societies and the possibility of improving these conditions by the investment of economic resources. Third, Rawls invokes comparative fairness. If, of two peoples that begin from approximately the same socio-economic level, such as Korea and Sudan in the early 1970s, only one works to improve its situation, it would not be fair to redistribute the benefits that it obtains. On the basis of these claims, Rawls attributes responsibility for the unfavorable economic situation of a burdened society to the inhabitants of those societies. It is precisely for this reason that, on the broadly Kantian assumption that duties cannot exist without corresponding responsibilities, Rawls limits the duty of assistance.

Critics such as Pogge and Beitz reply by emphasizing how, in today's world, global socio-economic interdependence has increased considerably. This is particularly true for burdened societies, the objects of the duty of assistance, which are frequently obliged to accept the normative authority of international economic institutions such as the World Trade Organization, the World Bank, and the International Monetary Fund. For these critics, such fundamental changes in the global economy require Rawls to expand the basic structure to the international level.

Pogge also attempts to show how unconvincing it is to claim that first-world states have no political or economic responsibility for the underdevelopment of many parts of the world. The way in which global commerce is organized, for example, favors wealthy states over poor ones. Indeed, for Pogge, wealthy states are favored by most international institutions. Consequently, the harm principle alone entails that wealthy states have duties towards poor ones, basically because the former violate the negative rights of the latter. Admittedly, it is difficult to show that wealthy states have contravened the harm principle with respect to poor states, since this would require complex empirical studies which, without undertaking them, I would suggest present a kind of *probatio diabolica*: that is, an impossible evidence.[39] It is impossible to say, for example, that international organizations provoked a kind of general harm to Korea and Singapore in the past thirty years. But, also avoiding appeal to the harm principle, Pogge's criticism of an unjustified double standard at the national and global levels nonetheless could hold.

Charles Beitz criticizes LoP by means of a distinction between two general approaches to the question of global justice. He calls the first approach "social liberalism," and attributes it to Rawls, while he calls the second "cosmopolitan liberalism," and attributes it to himself and other critics of Rawls.[40] For Beitz' "social liberals," international society serves only to ensure the basic conditions under which individual nations can cultivate, internally, the wellbeing of their citizens. For "cosmopolitan liberals," on the other hand, the social world is comprised not of nations but of persons. On these grounds, Beitz criticizes Rawls' social liberal claims in various ways. Here, I will concentrate on Beitz' criticisms of Rawls' claims regarding distributive justice and the related duty of assistance. Unlike the principles of justice presented in TJ, the duty of assistance has a clear limit beyond which it does not hold. On Beitz' reading of Rawls, duties of justice are limited to the point at which the burdened society "can support just institutions and a decent life for its people." Beyond this point, Rawls expresses no further concern for distributive justice.[41] Beitz considers such a limit to be arbitrary and unsatisfactory, for three reasons. First, Beitz maintains that Rawls could not justify his claim that the economic situation of burdened societies is caused exclusively by endogenous conditions. Second, Beitz doubts that Rawls could justify his claim regarding comparative fairness: that it is wrong to redistribute economic wealth irrespective of states' different behavior. Third, and most importantly, Beitz maintains that the true reason for Rawls' failure to discuss global distributive justice lies in his treatment of the national and international realms as two distinct things, as if the economic differences between nations were irrelevant to the dignity of people and the stability of the international system.

While Pogge's and Beitz' criticisms are not mistaken in themselves, perhaps they misunderstand the general framework of distributive justice that Rawls adopts. Nagel and Freeman have offered interesting replies to this effect.[42] For Nagel, Rawls is right to follow Hobbes in holding that the full standards of justice do not apply beyond the state, because only in a liberal-democratic state are there genuine citizens who serve as both creators and subjects of the laws.[43] According to Freeman, Rawls' aim in LoP is not to provide a theory of global distributive justice, but instead to furnish the basic theoretical principles of foreign policy for a liberal state.[44] If we accept this premise, then Rawls holds that the current lack of a basic structure at the international level means that the legal grounds for cooperation, which would justify a theory of distributive justice, are lacking. In short, for Freeman, Rawls does not consider the Society of Peoples to be a genuine political society. Since a global political authority is also lacking, both Nagel and Freeman emphasize that a state's external behavior is the result of voluntary decisions. This brief summary of Nagel's and Freeman's arguments does not do justice to them, but my concern here is simply to emphasize a view which they both share and which I consider important for understanding Rawls' position in LoP. Distributive justice, including the difference principle, rests upon an institutional order that has established itself over time and not merely upon economic interdependence.[45]

12.4 A Critical Reconstruction of Rawls' Argument Regarding Global Distributive Justice

The criticism made of Rawls' treatment of the duty of assistance, and, more generally, of the (supposed) lack of a theory of distributive justice in LoP, maintains that – by not allowing justice beyond the realm of the nation-state – Rawls adopts a position that is inconsistent with his own general individualist and egalitarian commitments.

Rawls' position here seems to rely on a symmetry between the nation-state, on the one hand, and the basic structure, on the other. In TJ Rawls writes, "I shall be satisfied if it is possible to formulate a reasonable conception of justice for the basic structure of society conceived for the time being as a closed system isolated from other societies" (TJ 8; rev. edn. 7). By means of a conception of social justice, then, Rawls intends to provide a normative standard for the evaluation of the distributive aspects of the basic structure only of a national or state society. It must be admitted that it is unclear whether Rawls considers this limitation to be a permanent one or merely provisional (as his use of the phrase "for the time being" suggests). He may only view this as a means of simplifying the problem (as he implies after emphasizing the limitation, when he states, rather elusively, "With suitable modifications such a theory should provide the key for some of these other questions"). Regardless, the limitation of the theory of justice to the realm of the nation or state is undeniable, particularly in TJ.

This way of reasoning depends on Rawls' basic structure argument (or BSA; see this volume, chapters 2 and 5). A straightforward application of the BSA to global justice runs roughly like this:

(i)   justice requires the existence of the basic structure;
(ii) the basic structure applies only to national societies;
(iii) there is, then, no justice beyond national societies.

There are, however, two different possible readings of BSA (see chapter 2). On the first strict reading (BSA1), the existence itself of the basic structure already includes significant normative elements. It is in some way moralized, for the basic structure exists to favor social cooperation; but social cooperation is here meant to be a "fair" social cooperation. On this strict reading, the existential condition of the basic structure coincides with its own moralized version. The conclusion is that where there are not yet fair terms of cooperation – like in the global setting – justice does not apply. In the second more tolerant reading (BSA2), one can distinguish between the existence of the basic structure and the relevance of some demands of justice independent from its full moral version. Demands of justice can exist even if there is no prior presence of "fair" terms of cooperation. The mere fact that there is social cooperation – like in the global setting – might create sensible demands of justice. As said before, I find BSA2 more plausible, if for no other reason than that it does not show a bias in favor of the status quo.

Going back to the limitation of justice to the nation-state, we can ask if it is really acceptable in the light of all that has changed on the global level. There are two main reasons why we tend to resist such a limitation today. These reasons are mixed, but we can say that the first is of a more positive or descriptive character and the second of a more normative or prescriptive one.

(i)   The first reason is empirical. Global interdependence, both in socio-economic terms and in terms of the creation of international institutions, is now so great that states can no longer be considered to be the only subjects of international relations.[46] As a consequence. our rights and duties, our opportunities and life chances, no longer depend on the state alone, but also on the international community. To use David Held's fine expression, we are now all members of the same "overlapping community of fate."[47]

(ii) The second reason is normative. Many ethical and legal ideas, starting from human rights, are now implicit in the shared bases of global politics. In political philosophy, this can be expressed by saying that there is a kind of overlapping consensus on such rights.

Here, two crucial related questions arise. The first concerns how the first of these reasons informs the second, or in other words whether and how the empirical side of the question determines the manner in which the normative side is treated. The second concerns the relevance of membership in explaining the nature of the normative relations between subjects. This second question can be reframed in terms of the relation between recognition and distribution: what relation is there between being members of the same community (recognition) and the manner in which distributive conclusions are drawn (distribution)?[48]

In order to answer this second question, I propose to introduce a distinction which I consider particularly illuminating in this regard. This distinction concerns the relation between an associative and an allocative conception of distributive justice.[49] The associative conception requires that one first determine whether the global subjects are members of a single community. The tie of belonging thus precedes the substance of the distribution, and there are no reasons to distribute goods outside the relationship of membership. The manner in which subjects are treated is, at least partly, dependent on the answer to this prior question. In the terms of a traditional distinction, recognition implies distribution. The allocative conception, on the other hand, allows for certain forms of ethical-political relations between subjects who do not belong to the same community. Thus, here, the substance of the distribution precedes the tie of belonging, and distribution is in some way recognition-independent. Rawls' argument in LoP is clearly associative and I suggest that it is precisely for this reason that he limits the duty of assistance and does not provide a theory of distributive justice analogous to the one he provides for the nation-state at the global level.[50] As I will say later, however, the allocative argument can have less restrictive normative consequences.

I am suggesting that Rawls fails here to coordinate recognition and distribution clearly. If we introduce here the BSA, this point becomes more transparent. The kind of closed society that he considers in BSA1 does not exist in the current global world. Here, the interdependence of nations is the rule rather than the exception, flows of people and capital between nations are commonplace, and international institutions play a continually increasing role in the lives of individual nations. Indeed, Rawls himself considers the hypothesis of a closed society to be an abstraction, and in TJ he admits that the political conception must at some point treat international relations in these terms. It seems clear that considering a "basic structure" to be linked to a closed society excludes the possibility of stronger moral obligations between peoples.[51] Yet there is no need to abandon the associative position, which is clearly linked to the relational nature of contractualism, to grasp a better option. Even if one adopts an associative, rather than allocative, conception, the borders of political society need not coincide with the traditional borders of the nation-state.[52] The associative conception itself might thus be complicated.[53] If, for example, we assume BSA2, then we can say that global interdependence creates a system of cooperation which implies demands of justice that we have to confront.

This does not mean that parallel problems are not raised by the positions taken by Rawls' cosmopolitan critics when they insist on the impossibility of basing obligations and rights on subjects other than individuals and consider all individuals to occupy the globalized world in the same way. Indeed, criticisms that proceed from this global individualism must appear unrealistically utopian to anyone who takes Rawls seriously. Is it really plausible that, in a world such as the one in which we now live, a citizen of Illinois treats a citizen of Wisconsin and a citizen of Uganda in the same way economically? Or that she treats a Western European just as she does a citizen of certain areas of Eastern Asia? The pure cosmopolitan replies in the affirmative, and in this, I believe, she is mistaken. For, in my view, it is much more plausible to think that there are composite duties of justice, ranging from full intra-state reciprocity to minimal kinds of natural duties towards foreigners. In this respect, then, cosmopolitanism too fails to coordinate the levels of belonging and treatment, recognition and distribution. In assuming pure individualism and universalism, it also assumes that the institutional or associative question is irrelevant, and thus applies egalitarianism to a community that is not defined clearly.

I suggest, then, that the primary weakness of Rawls' theory is that of considering the allocative structure as normatively secondary to the associative one in an unspecified way. Thus, one might say, the theory risks becoming overly legalistic – in particular by limiting the sphere of the associative structure to the nation-state, without adequately defending this limitation. Ethics is thus marginalized by politics, or, in the terms of Rawls' utopian realism, the utopia is subordinated to realism. The weakness of his cosmopolitan critics is precisely the opposite; namely, they consider the allocative structure as independent of the associative one – or, one might say, that they are not legalistic enough. Thus cosmopolitans sacrifice politics to ethics, or, in Rawls' terms, they lose sight of realism in their pursuit of a utopia.

12.4.1 A modest proposal

In light of the preceding discussion of Rawls' position and the criticisms that have been made of it, I did not say how a plausible interpretation in terms of BSA2 can be formulated. My proposal is to consider a modified "basic structure" as the subject of global politics. This modified basic structure provides a broader legitimization of duties of assistance and generally permits sensible demands for justice at the global level. This will show how one may affirm a stronger duty of assistance while accepting an associative conception such as that of Rawls.

In order to formulate this proposal more clearly, I will here introduce two further distinctions. The first is the distinction between gradualism and discontinuity. On Rawls' view of the basic structure, the associative conception would appear to face a radical discontinuity. It must consider the basic structure to be like the state or non-existent.[54] It must be either one or the other, and *tertium non datur*. But such a strong opposition seems odd, even rather perverse. Indeed, it would seem much more reasonable to think not in binary terms but, rather, in gradualist terms.[55] That is, it is possible that a global basic structure is not to be identified with that of the state, but could rather be part of a "work in progress" that justifies this structure over time. Basically, one could opt for greater continuity and gradualism.

At this point, there arises the problem of gradualism's consequences. Here the second distinction, that between an egalitarian position and a sufficientarian one, is relevant.[56] For the egalitarian, the relations of equality between subjects are absolute, being considered independent of the prior assumption of either an allocative or an associative conception. Thus the normative aspect of the question is rendered independent of the empirical aspect, since the consequences for egalitarian distribution between persons will always be the same regardless of their institutional relationship. For the sufficientarian, the intersubjective validity of egalitarian ethical–political claims is controversial. Sufficientarianism limits itself to guaranteeing everyone a minimum necessary for their survival and fundamental freedoms. It considers everyone having a basic minimum as more important than a general tendency towards equality.[57] Sufficientarianism might thus be considered as the application of a moderate form of the maximin principle. Any brand of sufficientarianism must certainly determine a plausible minimum threshold, and probably must also be supplemented with a theory of welfare to apply once this threshold has been reached by everyone. But these are issues internal to sufficientarianism and I will not discuss them here. My concern here is simply to note the plausibility of this approach as a model of solidarity between "strangers."

An interesting working hypothesis can be developed if one bears in mind that, as I argued above, the distance between the basic structure of a state and the global community is better understood in terms of degree. The answer to the question of whether we belong to a global basic structure is neither "yes" nor "no," but rather "it depends on what degree." One can then take the empirical aspects to determine the normative ones in a progressive manner. We can consider the relational element that regards how closely subjects are reciprocally related within a specific basic structure to influence the normative element regarding the nature and limits of the treatments proposed. These treatments will differ across different cases. The closer a relationship is, the more normative egalitarianism should predominate. Meanwhile sufficientarianism should predominate in more distant relationships.

Assuming BSA2, the basic structure might grow in a gradual and progressive manner. It follows that a position regarding relationships between "strangers" should initially be sufficientarian. The relationship should evolve beyond this minimal requirement over time. One of the problems raised by cosmopolitanism is precisely the lack of such a gradual and progressive approach – it is too idealistically egalitarian *ab initio*. This can be appreciated clearly if one thinks of the relationship between legitimate individual claims, on the one hand, and collective duties of a universalistic kind, on the other. If one admits that it is reasonable for most people to aim to satisfy their personal desires and to achieve a certain self-realization, then introducing gradualism and sufficientarianism would seem to make this aim more acceptable with respect to the duty of assistance. Were this not so, we would be required to sacrifice too much of ourselves for an ideal of equality which is not currently perceived as "normal" at the global level. The more modest claims of sufficientarianism thus serve to bridge the gap between a normal self-development and a concern for the less fortunate.[58]

In my view, a normative conception of global justice based on socio-economic human rights is that which best mitigates associative presuppositions, considering every person also independently of her ties of belonging, while also being consistent with the sufficientarian approach. This is a notable theoretical advantage. Essentially, an approach based on socio-economic human rights serves to undermine the idea that state sovereignty is absolute and impermeable, an idea which allows of no distinction between people and the state to which they belong. A human rights-based paradigm entails that the subjects of global politics are not limited to states.[59] At the same time, sufficientarianism also allows it to avoid being overly demanding since, beyond the state, sufficientarianism requires that a minimum level of survival be guaranteed to all. This does not require that equality be achieved among all.[60] Furthermore, my approach need not presuppose what Allen Buchanan has called a "subject-centered" perspective. I am not proposing in other words a non-associative duty that is supposed to hold independently of the political and institutional priorities that are characteristic of Rawls' view (based as it is on the notion of the basic structure as Freeman and Nagel, among others, interpret it). On the contrary, human rights are institutional devices which correspond to an internationally accepted practice. In this way, they fit the requirements of Rawls' normative institutionalism (see chapter 1).

Further support is given to this proposal by the distinction between justification and legitimation, which I discussed particularly in chapters 1, 9, and 11. Rawls himself implicitly employs this distinction in PL in order to account for the dilemma of stability and pluralism. He is forced to admit that the mere philosophical justification of liberal democracy through a theory of justice as fairness – of the kind he himself presents in TJ – is insufficient for achieving the desired equilibrium between pluralistic normative claims and institutional stability. It is for precisely this reason that he too appeals to a social mechanism attributed with a more general normative validity – the overlapping consensus. The later Rawls maintains that in a well-ordered society citizens with comprehensive yet reasonable visions of the world will coexist peacefully with other such citizens. However, this balance depends on a successful constitutional history, such as that which has characterized public life in the United States since the founding fathers. Only this loyalty to the past allows for the cooperative coexistence of doctrines and people expressing profoundly different ethical and metaphysical *Weltanschauungen*. The history of an empirical success, such as the American constitution, is thus rendered consistent with the normative ethical-political premises of Rawls' argument. In my terms, a factual legitimacy based on the history of the American public sphere is added to the philosophical justification provided by the principles of justice.

If this argument regarding how justification can be complemented by legitimization is applied to the philosophical question of the grounds of distributive justice at the global level, then the model of socio-economic human rights provides the necessary legitimization while philosophical political liberalism provides the justification. My basic claim is that a global basic structure depends not only on a theoretical justification, but also on a successful model of interaction over time. Since human rights are at once a legal–political entity and an ethical project, a human rights-based approach ensures that ethics does not take excessive priority over politics. This avoids the negative consequences of cosmopolitanism.[61] Socio-economic human rights are now recognized as an essential element of international relations even if their full realization still remains far off.

It is precisely this hybrid legal and moral nature that allows human rights to combine justification and legitimization. The justification derives from the ethical argument advocating respect for the basic rights of all human beings. The legitimization derives from the fact that human rights constitute a (fairly) successful practice in the context of international relations. Cosmopolitanism lacks the ability to combine justification and legitimization because it adopts a normative perspective without resolving the empirical question. Finally, the human rights-based approach is consistent with the assumption of gradualism and continuity in the basic structure's movement from the state towards the global community. In this sense, sufficientarianism appears the natural starting point for the development of human rights-based policies.

In the last part of this chapter, I moved considerably away from the text of LoP. To conclude the section, it is perhaps worth emphasizing certain differences between my proposal and Rawls' theory. In LoP some egalitarian implications of liberalism are excluded, being part neither of Rawls' parsimonious notion of human rights nor of the minimal duty of assistance towards burdened societies. This means that – even without adopting the difference principle, as some liberal cosmopolitans would perhaps have preferred him to do – Rawls could in theory have adopted a more egalitarian position. In my proposal, I have attempted to show how a more egalitarian perspective can be adopted, within the paradigm of LoP, that respects the priority of the basic structure without appealing to the utopian perspective of liberal cosmopolitanism. It is possible to do this, I have claimed, by enriching the conception of human rights with an extended interpretation of socio-economic rights and by adopting a gradualist and progressive understanding of the current expansion of the basic structure.

12.5 Pluralism and Liberalism

Both military action and the fulfilment of duties of assistance towards disadvantaged nations highlight the role of statesmen and distinguish it from that of the mere politician. Rawls claims that, while the politician thinks only of the next election, the statesman is primarily concerned with coming generations (LoP 97). He has in mind here figures such as Washington and Lincoln. In both cases the statesman embodies a typical feature of liberal societies: namely, the desire for a world in which all peoples live in well-ordered political regimes. As I have shown, however, Rawls makes no direct substantial proposals regarding distributive justice. He argues that the differences between peoples may be maintained and that the mere redistribution of goods and economic resources would not help disadvantaged societies to become well ordered. Redistribution alone will not help because political and cultural elements are also crucial to economic development.

In the above, I emphasized some cosmopolitan and liberal criticisms that can be raised against Rawls' theory. His theory may also be unsatisfactory to those with different points of view, such as moderate cultural relativists.[62] The construction of Rawls' model of the Society of Peoples is based on a form of pluralism according to which each society must be considered, and perhaps even promoted, in terms of its own principles. In Rawls' view, this ensures that the model is not ethnocentric. However, this seems rather debatable given that liberalism predominates in the model as a whole. Certainly, the reciprocity principle characteristic of Rawls' understanding of liberalism ensures that dominant and subordinate positions are not created and that non-liberal societies can be included in the "club" of decent societies without having to embrace liberalism or renounce their own traditions. Yet some critics nonetheless claim there to be universalistic aspects to Rawls' emphasis on human rights and on imperatives of justice; aspects which can, of course, be considered expressions of a particular, Western liberal, culture. Perhaps what is certain in this regard is just that Rawls attempts to develop a Western and liberal position which is the least culturally imperialistic possible.

Of course, there is something at least partially utopian about all of Rawls' theory, yet it also presupposes the possibility that the utopia could be realized. Philosophical reason and the actual history of peoples must therefore find some kind of long-term reconciliation. The hope for such reconciliation rests on a historic understanding consisting of four basic points:

(i)   the fact of a reasonable pluralism;
(ii)   the fact that it is possible to create some kind of unity within this diversity;
(iii) the fact of public reason;
(iv)   the fact of a democratic peace.

On these grounds LoP is a realistic utopia. Of course, the formidable obstacles that face this reconciliation are not difficult to appreciate, particularly if one thinks of the various opposing fundamentalisms and the great material and spiritual miseries that exist in the world. Perhaps the best response to the skepticism that understandably faces Rawls' utopia can be found with his own words from the very end of LoP:

> If a reasonably just Society of Peoples whose members subordinate their power to reasonable aims is not possible, and human beings are largely amoral, if not incurably cynical and self-centered, one might ask, with Kant, whether it is worthwhile for human beings to live on the earth (LoP 128).

NOTES

1 INTRODUCTION

1 TJ has been translated into nearly 30 languages. It is an unexpectedly popular book even in China, notwithstanding the presence of an institutional system and cultural traditions that are obviously different. As for the German reception of this idea and its centrality, see the debate between S. Critchley and A. Honneth, "Philosophy in Germany," *Radical Philosophy* 89 (May/June 1998).

2 P. Laslett, "Introduction" to the first series of *Philosophy, Politics and Society* (Oxford: Blackwell, 1956), pp. vi–vii, says: "for the moment, anyway, political philosophy is dead."

3 No one has described this trend better than H. L. H. Hart: from "the old faith that some form of utilitarianism must capture some form of political morality" to the new one, according to which "the truth must lie within a doctrine of basic human rights . . ."; see "Between Utility and Rights," in A. Ryan (ed.), *The Idea of Freedom* (Oxford: Oxford University Press, 1979), p. 77.

4 Like Robert Nozick and Michael Walzer, on whom see ch. 7.

5 Monographs in English dedicated to Rawls' thought are: R. P. Wolff, *Understanding Rawls* (Princeton, NJ: Princeton University Press, 1977); R. Alejandro, *The Limits of Rawlsian Justice* (Baltimore and London: Johns Hopkins University Press, 1998); R. B. Talisse, *On Rawls* (Belmont, CA: Wadsworth, 2001); S. Freeman, *Rawls* (London: Routledge, 2007); T. Pogge, *John Rawls: His Life and Theory of Justice* (New York: Oxford University Press, 2007; originally published in German, 1994); C. Audard, *John Rawls* (Montreal: McGill-Queen's University Press, 2007); P. Graham, *Rawls* (Oxford: Oneworld, 2007).

6 I have relied, beyond personal knowledge, upon the following: Pogge's *John Rawls*, ch. 1, possibly the best biographical sketch of Rawls; R. Dworkin and C. Korsgaard, both in *The Harvard Review of Philosophy* 11 (Spring 2003); T. Nagel, "The Rigorous Compassion of John Rawls: Justice, Justice Shalt Thou Pursue," *New Republic* 221 (15) (October 25, 1999); S. Freeman, *Rawls*, ch. 1; T. Scanlon, C. Korsgaard, Amartya Sen, and Dennis Thompson, "Memorial

Minute," Harvard University, April 12, 2005; and M. Nussbaum, "The Enduring Significance of John Rawls," *The Chronicle of Higher Education* (20 July 2001).

7 One of the best ways to approach Rawls' attitude towards the classics can be found in A. Reath, B. Herman, and C. M. Korsgaard (eds.), *Reclaiming the History of Ethics: Essays for John Rawls* (Cambridge, UK: Cambridge University Press, 1997).

8 This thesis was upheld in 1961 in a famous article by Isaiah Berlin entitled "Does Political Theory Still Exist?" in the second series of *Philosophy, Politics and Society*, ed. P. Laslett and W. G. Runciman (Oxford: Blackwell, 1964), which dealt with the widespread conviction that the death of political philosophy could be attributed to the meta-theoretical and formalist nature of the political philosophy of their time. The same thesis was suggested by *The Times Literary Supplement* (May 5, 1972), p. 1505, and was taken up in the Introduction to *Reading Rawls* – the first significant anthology on Rawls (New York: Basic Books, 1975; 2nd edn., Stanford, CA: Stanford University Press, 1989, pp. xi–xii) – by its editor N. Daniels, and by M. Cohen in "The Social Contract Explained and Defended," *New York Times Book Review* (July 16, 1972), p. 1, where Cohen traces Rawls, in contrast to his predecessors, back to the tradition of British substantive philosophy from Hume to John Stuart Mill.

9 On this point, see S. Fleischacker, *A Short History of Distributive Justice* (Cambridge, MA: Harvard University Press, 2000).

10 See E. Rapaport, "Classical Liberalism and Rawlsian Revisionism," in Kai Nielsen and Roger A. Shiner (eds.), *New Essays on Contract Theory* (Guelph, Ontario: Canadian Association for Publishing in Philosophy, 1977), pp. 95–119.

11 This can be taken as Rawls' most general "preunderstanding," to use P. Ricoeur's expression in his *The Just* (Chicago: University of Chicago Press, 2000).

12 "Remarks on Political Philosophy," LHPP, p. 1.

13 The derivation of constructivism in Rawls is clearly Kantian. See his chapters on Kant in LHMP. Kant's political philosophy is presented systematically in his *Metaphysics of Morals* ([1797] Cambridge, UK: Cambridge University Press, 1992), in particular in the "Doctrine of the Right," and in several essays, including "What is the Enlightenment?" (1784) and "Perpetual Peace" (1795), both in L. W. Beck (ed.), *Kant Selections* (London: Macmillan, 1988). See also P. Riley, *Will and Political Legitimacy: A Critical Exposition of Social Contract Theory in Hobbes, Locke, Rousseau, Kant and Hegel* (Cambridge, MA: Harvard University Press, 1982) and "On Kant as the Most Adequate of the Social Contract Theorists," *Political Theory* 1 (1973): 450–71. See also L. Krasnoff, "How Kantian is Constructivism?" *Kant Studien* 90 (1999): 385–409.

14 On the social contract, see (among others): D. Ritchie, "Contributions to the History of Social Contract Theory" in his *Darwin and Hegel and Other Philosophical Studies* (London: Swan Sonnenschein, 1893), pp. 196–226; J. W. Gough, *The Social Contract* ([1936] Oxford: Oxford University Press, 1957); M. Lessnoff, *Social Contract* (London: Macmillan, 1986); D. Boucher and P. Kelly (eds.), *The Social Contract from Hobbes to Rawls* (London: Routledge, 1994); S. Darwall (ed.), *Contractarianism/Contractualism* (Oxford: Blackwell, 2003). For a critical appraisal, see J. Gray, "Social Contract, Community and Ideology," in his *Liberalism and the Limits of Philosophy* (London: Routledge, 1989), and, of

course, D. Hume, "Of the Original Contract" (1752) in his *Essays Moral, Political and Literary*, but also William Godwin, *Enquiry Concerning Political Justice* ([1793] Harmondsworth: Penguin, 1976), in particular pp. 212–16; and Hegel, *Philosophy of Right* (Oxford: Oxford University Press, 1952) but also *Lectures on the History of Philosophy* (London: Kegan Paul, 1892–6), vol. III.

15 J. Rawls, "Some Remarks about My Teaching," written in 1993 and published as "Burton Dreben: A Reminiscence," in Juliet Floyd and Sanford Shieh (eds.), *Future Pasts: Perspectives on the Place of the Analytic Tradition in Twentieth-Century Philosophy* (New York: Oxford University Press, 2000).

16 I take for granted that the different adjectives I used here are not particularly significant, given that in some way all these hypotheses are jointly interpretive, methodological, and theoretical. The distinction between these three terms thus has a mainly pragmatic sense.

17 As far as I understand him, I am in substantial agreement on this point with L. Weinar, "The Unity of Rawls' Work," *Journal of Moral Philosophy* 1 (2004): 265–75. A sophisticated intermediate (between continuity and discontinuity) interpretation is A. S. Laden's, in "The House That Jack Built: Thirty Years of Reading Rawls," *Ethics* 113 (2003): 367–90.

18 Also the origin of the priority of right is, for Rawls, Kantian. See his LHMP, pp. 230ff.

19 I rely here on Rawls' "Remarks on Political Philosophy" – the Introduction to his LHPP – a brief and somewhat vague text by Rawls that every student of his work should – in my opinion – read to understand his most general political philosophical intentions.

20 See R. Dworkin, "Foundations of Liberal Equality," in G. B. Peterson (ed.), *The Tanner Lectures on Human Values*, vol. XI (Salt Lake City: University of Utah Press, 1990), pp. 3–119, now reprinted in R. Dworkin, *Sovereign Virtue: The Theory and Practice of Equality* (Cambridge, MA: Harvard University Press, 2002).

21 See B. Barry, "John Rawls and the Search for Stability," *Ethics* 105 (1995): 874–913; P. Kelly, "Justifying Justice: Contractarianism, Communitarianism and the Formulation of Contemporary Liberalism," in Boucher and Kelly (eds.), *The Social Contract from Hobbes to Rawls*, pp. 226–44.

22 Beyond Barry and Dworkin quoted before, see also B. A. O. Williams, "A Fair State," *London Review of Books* (May 13, 1993), pp. 7–8; P. Anderson, "On John Rawls," *Dissent* (Winter 1994): 139–44; S. Holmes, "John Rawls and the Limits of Tolerance," *The New Republic* (October 11, 1983), pp. 39–47; S. M. Okin, "Review of *Political Liberalism*," *American Political Science Review* 87 (1993): 1010–11; B. Ackerman, "Political Liberalism," *Journal of Philosophy* 91 (1994): 364–86.

23 This notion has – for Rawls – a Kantian origin; see LHMP, pp. 237ff.

24 In this and the next paragraph I draw on Freeman's account of the priority of right in his "Utilitarianism, Deontology and the Priority of Right," now in his book *Justice and the Social Contract* (Oxford: Oxford University Press, 2006). I do not take a position however on Freeman's critique of Kymlicka concerning the relation between deontology and the priority of right.

25 An exception is A. J. Simmons, *Justification and Legitimacy: Essays on Rights and*

Obligations (Cambridge, UK: Cambridge University Press, 2001). My distinction between justification and legitimation is different from Simmons' (mine is not Lockean). A. Buchanan, "Political Legitimacy and Democracy," *Ethics* 112 (2002): 689–719, speaks of legitimacy from a normative point of view but in terms of monopoly of political power and in the light of political authority.

26 J. Habermas, *Between Facts and Norms: Contributions to a Discourse Theory of Law and Democracy* (Cambridge, MA: MIT Press, 1996).

27 Rawls derives it from the proceduralization of the categorical imperative in Kant (see LHMP). The same attempt is explicitly recognized by Rawls in TJ section 40 and in KCMT.

28 From now on, I will use the words "contractualism" and "contractualist" to characterize Rawls' approach, instead of the alternatives "contractarianism" and "contractarian." Even if – so far as I know – Rawls does not use the first terms, it seems to me better to use them, leaving "contractarianism"/"contractarian" for Hobbes' and similar approaches to the social contract. The most evident distinction is that in contractarianism equality is *de facto*, whereas in contractualism it is *de jure*.

29 Again here, the complementarity of reasonable and rational is taken by Rawls from his interpretation of Kant in LHMP.

2 THE THEORY

1 Paul Ricoeur held to a similar reading when debating with Rawls in Naples during the mid-1980s. See P. Ricoeur, "Is a Purely Procedural Theory of Justice Possible? John Rawls's Theory of Justice," now in his *The Just* (Chicago: University of Chicago Press, 2000), pp. 36–56.

2 The point is quite effectively explained by E. Phelps, *Rewarding Work* (Cambridge, MA: Harvard University Press, 1997), particularly in ch. 9.

3 The primacy of the basic structure in TJ was subjected from the very beginning to interesting criticism by H. A. Bedau, "Social Justice and Social Institutions," *Midwest Studies in Philosophy* 3 (1978): 159–75; rptd. in H. S. Richardson and P. Weithman (eds.), *The Philosophy of Rawls: A Collection of Essays* (New York: Garland, 1999), vol. I, pp. 91–107.

4 See JFR, sections 15 and 16. In this volume, we will discuss the concept of basic structure more specifically three times: twice in ch. 4 (in relation to luck egalitarianism and anti-monism) and in ch. 12 (concerning the limits of global justice).

5 This specificity contrasts with utilitarianism which is a general theory (whereas Rawls' principles of justice are not suitable for a general theory).

6 While "procedural justice" is a classical expression in TJ, the term "background" was added in JFR.

7 For Nozick's criticism of this stance, see ch. 7 in this volume. In ch. 7 of *Anarchy, State and Utopia* (New York: Basic Books, 1974), *inter alia*, Nozick criticizes the idea of a central position of the basic structure, noting that moving the problems to a macro level – as Rawls would do – does not help to solve them any better (see in particular pp. 204–13).

8 John Rawls, "The Basic Structure as Subject," in PL 268–9; Thomas Nagel, *Equality and Partiality* (New York: Oxford University Press, 1991), pp. 53–4, 60–2.

9 See A. J. Julius, "Basic Structure and the Value of Equality," *Philosophy & Public Affairs* 31 (2003): 321–55.

10 See A. James, "Constructing Justice for Existing Practice: Rawls and the Status Quo," *Philosophy & Public Affairs* 33 (2005): 1–36. For the idea of constructive interpretation, see R. Dworkin, *Law's Empire* (Cambridge, MA: Harvard University Press, 1986), pp. 65–6.

11 These debates concern: the Rawlsian interpretation of utilitarianism and libertarianism, the role of individual responsibility in Cohen's argument for deep egalitarianism, and the debate on the boundaries of "the political." Pietro Maffettone is currently systematically developing the idea of basic structure in his Ph.D. dissertation (LSE).

12 For a criticism of Rawls on disabilities, see M. C. Nussbaum, *Frontiers of Justice: Disabilities, Nationality, Species Membership* (Cambridge, MA: Harvard University Press, 1996), and for a defense of Rawls, see Samuel Freeman's review of Nussbaum in "Contractarianism vs. the Capability Approach," *Texas Law Review* 85 (2006): 385–430. For the treatment of foreigners, see ch. 12 in this book.

13 I draw here on A. Abizadeh, "Cooperation, Pervasive Impact, and Coercion: On the Scope (not the Site) of Distributive Justice," *Philosophy & Public Affairs* 35 (4): 318–58.

14 S. M. Okin, "Reason and Feeling in Thinking about Justice," *Ethics* 99 (1989), pp. 229–49, and A. R. Baehr, "Toward a New Feminist Liberalism: Okin, Rawls and Habermas," *Hypathia* 11 (1996): 49–66, both reprinted in H. S. Richardson and P. Weithman (eds.), *The Philosophy of Rawls: A Collection of Essays* (New York: Garland Publishing, 1999), vol. III.

15 See C. Gilligan, *In a Different Voice*, rev. edn. (Cambridge, MA: Harvard University Press, 1993); A. M. Jaggar, *Feminist Politics and Human Nature* (Totowa, NJ: Rowman and Allanheld, 1983), C. Pateman, *The Sexual Contract* (Stanford, CA: Stanford University Press, 1988).

16 For these criticisms see W. J. Friedman *et al.*, "Beyond Caring, The De-Moralization of Gender," *Canadian Journal of Philosophy* (1987).

17 As regards this subject, see S. M. Okin, "Justice and Gender," *Philosophy & Public Affairs* 16 (1987): 89–109.

18 In the mid-sixties, the concept of social contract from a regulatory point of view was also being used by W. G. Runciman, *Relative Deprivation and Social Justice* (London: Routledge & Kegan Paul, 1966), part 4.

19 I call the Hobbesian tradition "contractarian" and the Rawlsian "contractualist" (see ch. 1). See D. Boucher and P. Kelly (eds.), *The Social Contract from Hobbes to Rawls* (London: Routledge, 1994). It is also worth noting that in his thesis (BIMSF 126–7), Rawls presents a significant point against traditional contract theory criticized in the name of community. His argument here is directed not only against Hobbes but also against Locke (ibid. 126) and, to an extent, Rousseau (127).

20 In his review of PL, J. Gray – "Can We Agree or Disagree?" *The New York Times*

Book Review, 16 May 1993, p. 35 – upholds the view that Rawls' new thesis is not new as it draws on Hobbes. Such a thesis has been taken up by R. Rhodes, "Reading Rawls and Hearing Hobbes," *The Philosophical Forum* 33 (2002): 393–412. The thesis has been effectively criticized by S. Freeman, *Justice and the Social Contract* (New York: Oxford University Press, 2007), pp. 18ff.

21 As regards this subject, see D. Gauthier, "The Social Contract as Ideology," *Philosophy & Public Affairs* 6 (1977): 130–65.

22 See Rawls on Hume in LHPP.

23 J. Feinberg, "Rawls and Intuitionism," in N. Daniels (ed.), *Reading Rawls*, 2nd edn. (Stanford, CA: Stanford University Press, 1989), pp. 108–24, finds that Rawls' argument against utilitarianism is quite valuable but does not need the contract to assert itself.

24 See S. Maffettone, *Utilitarismo e teoria della giustizia* (Naples: Bibliopolis, 1983).

25 Against Rawls' apparent rule-utilitarianism, see Joseph Margolis, "Rule-Utilitarianism," in Richardson and Weithman (eds.), *The Philosophy of Rawls*, vol. I, pp. 24ff.

26 Rawls, "Two Concepts of Rule," *Philosophical Review* 64 (1955): 3–32. The concept of utilitarianism supported in this article upholds – starting from such phenomena as the keeping of promises – the thesis that the rules that define a practice are logically higher than the practice itself. As a consequence, utilitarianism-based exceptions within a practice that would seem to authorize a violation of the rules that define it are unable to do so. For a criticism of this conception, see H. J. McCloskey, "Two Concepts of a Rule – A Note," in Richardson and Weithman (eds.), *The Philosophy of Rawls*, vol. I, pp. 30ff.

27 W. D. Ross, *The Right and the Good* (Oxford: Oxford University Press, 1930).

28 See TJ, ch. IX, section 83.

29 B. Barry, *Political Argument* (London: Routledge & Kegan Paul, 1965).

30 N. Rescher, *Distributive Justice* (Indianapolis: Bobbs-Merrill, 1967).

31 See Feinberg, "Rawls and Intuitionism."

32 The initial idea is deemed to date back to 1950 – Rawls was in Oxford in 1952–3, see letter quoted in J. P. Sterba, "Toulmin to Rawls," in R. J. Cavalier, J. Gouinlock and J. P. Sterba (eds.), *Ethics in the History of Western Philosophy* (Basingstoke: Macmillan and New York: St. Martin's Press, 1989), p. 410 – and may be found in embryo in an essay by Rawls that is not included in CP: "Review of Stephen Toulmin, *An Examination of the Place of Reason in Ethics*," *Philosophical Review* 60 (1951): 572–80. In the letter quoted by Sterba, Rawls says that the idea of the original position came by reading Frank Knight and reflecting upon game theory. See also D. A. J. Richards, *A Theory of Reasons for Action* (Oxford: Oxford University Press, 1971). See S. Darwall, *Impartial Reasons* (Ithaca: Cornell University Press, 1983). From this point of view, the grounds of Rawls' moral theory may be traced in the writings of scholars such as Toulmin, Hart, Austin, and Baier.

33 S. Scheffler (ed.), *Consequentialism and its Critics* (Oxford: Oxford University Press, 1988).

34 In this case, I am following Freeman, *Justice and Social Contract*, pp. 46ff.

35 See B. A. O. Williams, "A Critique of Utilitarianism," in J. C. C. Smart and B. A. O.

326 Notes to pp. 38–50

Williams, *Utilitarianism: For and Against* (Cambridge, UK: Cambridge University Press, 1973).

36 W. Kymlicka, *Liberalism, Community and Culture* (Oxford: Oxford University Press, 1989), ch. 2.

37 A criticism of Rawls' conception of intuitionism is found in M. B. E. Smith, "Rawls and Intuitionism," *Canadian Journal of Philosophy*, supp. vol. 3 (1977): 163–78. Smith upholds that intuitionism merely reasserts that one cannot go into moral philosophy without taking as its starting point a few shared points that require a systematic reflection.

38 See his discussion of Mill in LHPP.

39 The notion of a property-owning democracy is already present in ch. 5 of TJ but, according to Rawls himself, it is not presented in this context in a suitable manner and, in particular, TJ fails to explain the difference from welfare state capitalism. This is the reason why he returns to it in detail in the fourth part of JFR.

40 For instance, the contribution to the total product depends on the law of supply and demand.

41 Such a thesis may be attributed to J. Feinberg, *Doing and Deserving* (Princeton, NJ: Princeton University Press, 1970), pp. 64ff.

42 A similar criticism is elegantly formulated by D. Miller in ch. 7, "The Concept of Desert," of his *Principles of Social Justice* (Cambridge, MA: Harvard University Press, 1999). For a morally neutral evaluation of desert, see also J. Lamont, "The Concept of Desert in Distributive Justice," *Philosophical Quarterly* 44 (1994): 45–64.

43 S. Scheffler, "Justice and Desert in Liberal Theory," *California Law Review* 88 (2000): 965–90.

44 See G. Doppelt, "Beyond Liberalism and Communitarianism: Toward a Critical Theory of Social Justice," in D. Rasmussen (ed.), *Universalism vs. Communitarianism* (Cambridge, MA: MIT Press, 1990), pp. 39–60.

45 See J. Feinberg, "Duty and Obligation in the Non-Ideal World," *Journal of Philosophy* 70 (1973): 263–75.

46 The absurdity of which is highlighted by Hugo Bedau, review of Carl Cohen, *Civil Disobedience: Conscience, Taxes, and the Law*, *Yale Law Journal* 59 (1972): 179–86, 185.

47 The criticism of a standard relation between nature and morality is already present in Rawls' senior thesis BIMSF under the edge of a frank anti-naturalism (see BIMSF chs. 1 and 2).

48 Personal communication.

49 It is controversial to state which part of this argument fails, according to Rawls himself. See S. Freeman, *Justice and the Social Contract: Essays on Rawlsian Political Philosophy* (New York: Oxford University Press, 2007), in particular pp. 143–72, and the critical assessment of this book by P. Weithman, *Notre Dame Philosophical Reviews* (http://ndpr.n.d.edu/review.cfm?id=10405, accessed 13 March 2007). Freeman says that the main failure of Rawls' argument on congruence lies in the impossibility that all people will have the desire to act fairly. Weithman suggests that this is not the main argument against congruence in TJ. The main argument, for Weithman, is instead one based on the impossibility of

imagining a universal will to promote the relational attitudes that characterize a well-ordered society.

3 The First Principle of Justice

1 LHMP 366. The distinction is proposed by Rawls debating Hegel's position.
2 I. Berlin, *Four Essays on Liberty* (Oxford: Oxford University Press,1969).
3 See D. Lyons, "Rawls vs Utilitarianism," *Journal of Philosophy* 69 (1972): 535–45.
4 The general conception had already been introduced by Rawls in "Justice as Fairness" (1958).
5 Like B. Barry, "John Rawls and the Priority of Liberty," *Philosophy & Public Affairs* 2 (1973): 274–90, 276.
6 Like H. L. A. Hart, "John Rawls on Liberty and its Priority," in N. Daniels (ed.), *Reading Rawls: Critical Studies on Rawls's* A Theory of Justice (New York: Basic Books, 1975).
7 K. Arrow, "Some Ordinalist–Utilitarian Notes on Rawls' Theory of Justice," *Journal of Philosophy* 70 (1973): 245–63; H. Shue, "Liberty and Self-Respect," *Ethics* 85 (1975): 195–203; J. De Marco and S. Richardson, "A Note on the Priority of Liberty," *Ethics* 87 (1977): 3–31.
8 As advocated by R. S. Taylor, "Rawls' Defense of the Priority of Liberty: A Kantian Reconstruction," *Philosophy & Public Affairs* 31 (3) (2003): 246–71.
9 As regards this subject, see Shue, "Liberty and Self-Respect."
10 Hart, "John Rawls on Liberty and its Priority," *Reading Rawls*, pp. 230–52.
11 See N. Bowie, "Equal Basic Liberty for All," in H. G. Blocker and E. H. Smith (eds.), *John Rawls's Theory of Social Justice* (Athens: Ohio University Press, 1980), pp. 110–31.
12 T. Scanlon, "Rawls' Theory of Justice," in Daniels (ed.), *Reading Rawls*, pp. 169–205.
13 See Hart, "John Rawls on Liberty and its Priority," *Reading Rawls*, pp. 234–7.
14 T. Scanlon, "Adjusting Rights and Balancing Values," *Fordham Law Review* 72 (2004): 1477–86, correctly argues that one must stress the distinction between values and rights. Here, Rawls is supposed to speak of rights.
15 As stressed by Pogge in his *John Rawls* (Oxford: Oxford University Press, 2007), pp. 82ff.
16 As Samuel Freeman has done in his *Rawls* (London: Routledge, 2007), ch. 2.
17 As Barry argues in "John Rawls and the Priority of Liberty," p. 277.
18 Hart, "John Rawls on Liberty and its Priority," *Reading Rawls*, pp. 239–40.
19 His request is taken up by other critics, who, like Feinberg, find the system of Rawlsian liberties formalistic, or, like Scheffler, find it vague.
20 See Thomas Scanlon, "Adjusting Rights and Balancing Values."
21 As pointed out by Norman Daniels in "Equal Liberty and Unequal Worth of Liberty," *Reading Rawls*, pp. 253–81; rptd. in H. S. Richardson and P. Weithman (eds.), *The Philosophy of Rawls: A Collection of Essays* (New York: Garland, 1999), vol. II.
22 See Scanlon "Adjusting Rights and Balancing Values," p. 1480.

23 See J. Waldron, "Disagreements about Justice," *Pacific Philosophical Quarterly* 75 (1994): 372–87.
24 See also the debate with Habermas in ch. 7 below.
25 See Bowie, "Equal Basic Liberty for All."
26 I owe this way out to a discussion with Doug Paletta.
27 See the debate on Rawls and religion (here in ch. 11).

4 THE SECOND PRINCIPLE OF JUSTICE

1 The first time Rawls used the expression "difference principle" was in "Distributive Justice," in P. Laslett and W. G. Runciman (eds.), *Philosophy, Politics, and Society*, 3rd series (Oxford: Basil Blackwell, 1967), pp. 58–82; rptd. in CP 130–53. The expression was repeated in a form that more closely resembled the final one in "Distributive Justice: Some Addenda," in CP 154–75.
2 See Adina Schwartz, "Moral Neutrality and Primary Goods," *Ethics* 83 (1972): 294–307. Allen Buchanan defends Rawls' list against the thesis upheld by Schwartz in "Revisability and Rational Choice," *Canadian Journal of Philosophy* 5 (1975): 395–408. Such a defense is based on the idea that Rawls' primary goods presuppose the capacity to review one's ethical-political opinions.
3 It does not seem that this is solved by the celebrated Harsanyi's theorem (1955), which shows that social welfare is a linear combination of individuals' welfare. This is due to the fact that Harsanyi's "strong independence axiom," derived by von Neumann–Morgenstern, is known for being controversial, just as is the assumption that any individual may be equiprobably any other one (an assumption that differs from Rawls' veil of ignorance). The latter assumption brings into play the axiom of insufficient reason that, as we are going to see in the next chapter, is justly criticized by Rawls.
4 A similar thesis is somehow formally, though indirectly, reasoned by A. Sen's "Welfare Inequalities and Rawlsian Axiomatics," *Theory and Decision* 7 (1976): 243–62, an article addressing more directly an analysis of the maximin, in its form called leximin, by Sen.
5 See R. A. Musgrave, "Maximin, Uncertainty and the Leisure Trade-Off," *The Quarterly Journal of Economics* 88 (1974): 625–32.
6 See T. Pogge, *John Rawls: His Life and Theory of Justice* (New York: Oxford University Press, 2007), p. 107.
7 K. J. Arrow, "Some Ordinalist–Utilitarian Notes on Rawls' Theory of Justice," *Journal of Philosophy* 70 (1973): 245–63, in particular, pp. 253ff.
8 Amartya Sen, more explicitly in his criticism of Rawls in "Justice: Means versus Freedom," *Philosophy & Public Affairs* 19 (1990): 111–21; more generally in "Equality of What?," in M. S. McMurrin (ed.), *Tanner Lectures on Human Values*, vol. I (Cambridge, UK: Cambridge University Press, 1980); rptd. in Sen, *Choice, Welfare and Measurement* (Cambridge, MA: MIT Press, 1982); Sen, *Inequality Re-examined* (Cambridge, MA: Harvard University Press, 1992). Rawls answers Sen in PL 182–7. See also M. C. Nussbaum, *Frontiers of Justice: Disability, Nationality, Species Membership* (Cambridge, MA: Belknap Press of Harvard University Press, 2006).

9 Norman Daniels, in "Democratic Equality: Rawls's Complex Egalitarianism" – in S. Freeman (ed.), *The Cambridge Companion to Rawls* (Cambridge, UK: Cambridge University Press, 2003), pp. 241–77 – suggested the inclusion of health among the primary goods in order to solve the problem and mediate between Rawls' and Sen's approach. His suggestion follows the thesis expounded in his book, *Just Health Care* (Cambridge, UK: Cambridge University Press, 1985).

10 See S. Freeman, "Contractarianism vs. the Capability Approach," review of Martha Nussbaum's *Frontiers of Justice*, *Texas Law Review* 85 (2) (December 2006): 385–430.

11 J. Waldron's proposal in "John Rawls and the Social Minimum," ch. 11, of his *Liberal Rights* (Cambridge, UK: Cambridge University Press, 1993), is an alternative and – in my opinion – interesting way to consider the social minimum. According to Waldron, the social minimum could be evaluated in terms of needs rather than in terms of distributive egalitarianism. A similar proposal would seem definitely productive in terms of global justice, and I am going to deal with this matter in chapter 12 below, when talking about so-called "sufficientarianism."

12 This is noted quite clearly by P. van Parijs, "Difference Principle," in S. Freeman (ed.), *The Cambridge Companion to John Rawls*, p. 203.

13 I do not consider here a critique of the incentives argument, according to which there could be a distribution D3 where disadvantaged people could be better off than in D1 but without recompensing the most talented individuals. Such an argument can be found in G. A. Cohen, *Rescuing Justice and Equality* (Cambridge, MA: Harvard University Press, 2008), in particular ch. 2.

14 Pogge, *John Rawls*, p. 118.

15 R. Dworkin, *A Matter of Principle* (Cambridge, MA: Harvard University Press, 1985).

16 See B. Barry, *Theories of Justice* (London, Sydney, and Tokyo: Harvester-Wheatsheaf, 1989), ch. 6; T. Nagel, *Equality and Partiality* (Oxford: Oxford University Press, 1991), in particular ch. 7; W. Kymlicka, "Liberal Equality," in *Contemporary Political Philosophy: An Introduction*, 2nd edn. (Oxford: Oxford University Press, 2002). Barry intends to show that Rawls favors (the Kantian) impartiality with respect to mutual advantage (in terms of rational choice) as the dominant reason of his argument, while Nagel suggests that the Rawlsian assumptions in favor of equality, but with a few limits, are a confirmation of an eternal and general tension between impersonal (egalitarian) aspirations and (non-egalitarian) personal attachments. On the other hand, Kymlicka upholds the deficiency of the second principle with respect to the task of reducing the natural differences among individuals.

17 For a general presentation of the topic, see S. Olsaretti, *Liberty, Desert and the Market* (Cambridge, UK: Cambridge University Press, 2004).

18 See J. Feinberg, "Justice and Personal Desert," in his *Doing and Deserving* (Princeton, NJ: Princeton University Press, 1970) and D. Miller, *Social Justice* (Oxford: Clarendon Press, 1976).

19 See W. Kymlicka, *Contemporary Political Philosophy* (Oxford: Oxford University Press, 1990), p. 70, which attributes to Rawls the original idea on which luck egalitarianism depends – that is, the distinction between choices and circumstances, and the fault of not having pursued it.

330 Notes to pp. 85–93

20 On luck, see T. Nagel, "Moral Luck," in his *Mortal Questions* (Cambridge, UK: Cambridge University Press, 1979), and B. Williams, "Moral Luck," in his *Moral Luck* (Cambridge, UK: Cambridge University Press, 1981).

21 See W. Kymlicka, *Liberalism, Community and Culture* (Oxford: Oxford University Press, 1989), p. 72.

22 See S. Freeman, *Justice and the Social Contract: Essays on Rawlsian Political Philosophy* (New York: Oxford University Press, 2006), ch. 4.

23 "What is Egalitarianism?" *Philosophy & Public Affairs* 31 (1) (2002): 17.

24 Scheffler, "What is Egalitarianism?" p. 5.

25 See E. Anderson, "What is the Point of Equality?" *Ethics* 109 (January 1999): 287–337.

26 From this point of view, the composition of the basic structure governs the legitimate expectations of the individuals. However, given the continuous nature (in a mathematical sense) of Rawls' argument, a basic structure can become instantaneously unjust and engender problems for the persons in their capacity to plan the future based on legitimate expectations. A similar thesis is advocated by A. Buchanan in "Distributive Justice and Legitimate Expectations," *Philosophical Studies* 28 (1975): 419–25.

27 As Scheffler happens to say, "What is Egalitarianism?" p. 21.

28 Nagel, *Equality and Partiality*, ch. 7.

29 See Salvatore Veca, *Della lealtà civile* (Milan: Feltrinelli, 1998).

30 According to D. Gauthier, "Justice and Natural Endowment: Toward a Critique of Rawls's Ideological Framework," *Social Theory and Practice* 3 (1974): 3–26, this type of inference would be incompatible with Rawls' standard assumption of rationality.

31 R. Dworkin, "Equality of Resources," in his *Sovereign Virtue* (Cambridge, MA: Harvard University Press, 2000).

32 J. Roemer, *Equality of Opportunity* (Cambridge, MA: Harvard University Press, 1998).

33 Rawls was also criticized with respect to the relation between personality and talents by Michael Sandel, who attributes a curious split to Rawls, so that:

the various natural assets with which I am born may be said to belong to me in a weak, contingent sense that they reside accidentally within me, but this sense of ownership or possession cannot establish that I have any special rights with respect to these assets or any privileged claim to the fruits of their exercises. In this attenuated sense of possession, I am not really the owner but merely the guardian or repository of these assorted assets and attributes located "here." (Sandel, *Liberalism and the Limits of Justice* [Cambridge, UK: Cambridge University Press, 1982], p. 82)

In any event, this objection by Sandel may be argued against by saying that either it corresponds to the one by Nozick, and then it can be similarly countered, or – as it seems – it is inspired by a metaphysical disputation on the nature of the person, and then it has little to do with the distributive question being debated.

34 R. Nozick, *Anarchy, State and Utopia* (New York: Basic Books, 1974), p. 192.

35 J. P. Dupuis, *Le sacrifice et l'envie: le liberalisme aux prises avec la justice sociale* (Paris: Calmann-Lévy, 1992).

36 See Paul Voice, "Rawls' Difference Principle and a Problem of Sacrifice," *South African Journal of Philosophy* 10 (1991): 28–31; rptd. in H. S. Richardson and P. Weithman (eds.), *The Philosophy of Rawls*, vol. II: *The Two Principles and their Justification* (New York: Garland, 1999), pp. 114–17, for this thesis expressed in a formal manner.

37 Such an argument is upheld by S. W. Ball, "Maximin Justice, Sacrifice, and the Reciprocity Argument: A Pragmatic Reassessment of the Rawls/Nozick Debate," *Utilitas* 5 (1993): 153–84; rptd. in Richardson and Weithman (eds.), *The Philosophy of Rawls*, vol. III: *Opponents and Implications of* A Theory of Justice (New York: Garland, 1999), pp. 73–100.

38 G. A. Cohen, "Incentives, Equality and Community," in G. B. Peterson (ed.), *The Tanner Lectures on Human Values*, vol. XIII (Salt Lake City: University of Utah Press, 1992), pp. 261–329; "Where the Action Is: On the Site of Distributive Justice," *Philosophy & Public Affairs* 26 (1997): 3–30; and *If You're an Egalitarian, How Come that You Are So Rich?* (Cambridge, MA: Harvard University Press, 2000). See also J. Narveson, "A Puzzle about Economic Justice in Rawls' Theory," *Social Theory and Practice* 4 (1976): 1–28; J. Carens, "Rights and Duties in an Egalitarian Society," *Political Theory* 14 (1986): 31–49; D. Estlund, "Liberalism, Equality and Fraternity in Cohen's Critique of Rawls," *Journal of Political Philosophy* 6 (March 1998): 99–112; L. Murphy, "Institutions and the Demands of Justice," *Philosophy & Public Affairs* 27 (1998): 251–91; A. Williams, "Incentives, Inequality, and Publicity," *Philosophy & Public Affairs* 27 (1998): 225–47; M. G. Titelbaum, "What would a Rawlsian Ethos of Justice Look Like?" *Philosophy & Public Affairs* 36 (2008): 289–322; van Parijs, "Difference Principle."

39 An equal critique is addressed to Rawls from the right by J. Narveson, "A Puzzle about Economic Justice in Rawls' Theory."

40 See also Murphy, "Institutions and the Demands of Justice."

41 As he does recognize in the very first page of his "Where the Action Is: On the Site of Distributive Justice."

42 Cohen's argument is presented in its best form in his recent *Rescuing Justice and Equality*, which came out after this chapter was written. See also B. Felthan (ed.), "Justice, Equality and Constructivism: Essays on G. A. Cohen's *Rescuing Justice and Equality*," *Ratio*, special issue (2008).

43 See *Rescuing Justice and Equality*, pp. 253–4.

44 In any event, in the attempt to confute Cohen, P. van Parijs in "Social Justice and Individual Ethics," *Ratio Juris* 8 (1995): 40–63, affirms that the persons in Cohen's model would not choose the "socially optimal occupation." The article is rptd. in Richardson and Weithman (eds.), *The Philosophy of Rawls*, vol. II, pp. 118–42.

5 The Original Position

1 The main difference relates to the so-called "veil of ignorance." In the article of 1958, the contracting parties know all that there is to know about the present but they commit, under conditions of ignorance, even subsequent generations. As we are going to see in a little while, in TJ (and the subsequent works) the

veil of ignorance is constructed differently. As regards this difference, see Rawls, "Remarks on Political Philosophy," in LHPP 19.

2 Even if there is a clear-cut difference with respect to Hobbes' contractualism. See S. Freeman, "Reason and Agreement in Social Contract Views," in his *Justice and Social Contract: Essays on Rawlsian Political Philosophy* (New York: Oxford University Press, 2007), pp. 18–25, where the difference between the Kantian–Rawlsian model and Hobbes' model lies in the fact that the former presupposes unshakeable moral bases, while the latter does not. For a Hobbesian criticism of Rawls, see D. Gauthier, "The Social Contract as Ideology," *Philosophy & Public Affairs* 6 (1977): 130–64.

3 On this point, see LHPP 16ff.

4 This element is present throughout Rawls' lessons on the history of political thought and contractualism. Rawls believes that even Hobbes and Locke had demonstrative rather than prevailingly descriptive claims in their formulation of a theory of the contract, although he recognizes Kant's merit for having expressed this requirement so clearly. See LHPP 14. For Kant's more explicit view on the matter, see "On the Common Saying: This May Be True in Theory but it Does Not Apply in Practice" (1793), in H. Reiss (ed.), *Kant's Political Writings*, trans. H. B. Nisbet (Cambridge, UK: Cambridge University Press, 1970).

5 Kant, "On the Common Saying," *I. Kant, Political Writings*, ed. H. S. Reiss, Cambridge: Cambridge Univesity Press (1991) p. 79.

6 Obviously, whether Rawls succeeds in such intent without violating the fundamental Kantian axiom of autonomy is quite controversial. As we are going to see later on in this chapter, the "fair" choice of the parties in the original position depends on the veil of ignorance, so that no one knows who will benefit from the decisions being taken. The fact remains that the parties are "motivated" by the promotion of their own interests, the pursuit of which is only blocked by the fact that they are in the dark at the time of their choice. Such motivation could be considered "heteronymous" in Kantian terms, as upheld for instance by O. A. Johnson, "The Kantian Interpretation," *Ethics* 85 (1974): 58–66. Rawls explicitly denies this in KCMT, claiming that Kant's autonomy should not be linked to the lack of self-interested motivations (which he refers to as "desires"), but rather to the way in which such motivations are rationally handled. On this point, see also S. Darwall, "A Sense of Kantian Interpretation," *Ethics* 86 (1976): 164–70.

7 For a clear presentation of the original position as a model, see KCMT, in CP 307.

8 See R. Alejandro, "Rawls' Communitarianism," *Canadian Journal of Philosophy* 23 (1993): 75–99 (rptd. in H. S. Richardson and P. Weithman, *The Philosophy of Rawls*, vol. IV: *Moral Psychology and Community*, New York: Garland, 1999, pp. 295–320), who even talks about a creeping communitarianism of Rawls.

9 M. Sandel, "The Procedural Republic and the Unencumbered Self," *Political Theory* 12 (1984): 81–96 (rptd. in Richardson and Weithman (eds.), *The Philosophy of Rawls*, vol. IV, pp. 217–32), considers the Rawlsian movement insufficient since it would shift the axis from a no-longer-credible Kantian-type transcendental person to a just as improbable unencumbered self. We will return to this point in detail in ch. 7.

10 The centrality of the concept of the person as endowed with moral powers and

11 Rawls' definition in KCMT 304.

12 C. W. Morris, "A Contractarian Account of Moral Justification," in W. Sinnott-Armstrong and M. Timmons (eds.), *Moral Knowledge? New Readings in Moral Epistemology* (New York: Oxford University Press, 1996); Thomas Scanlon, "Utilitarianism and Contractualism," in A. Sen and B. Williams (eds.), *Utilitarianism and Beyond* (Cambridge, UK: Cambridge University Press, 1982).

13 As regards this subject, Rawls has written an important article, "Two Concepts of Rule" (1955). See Thomas Pogge, *John Rawls: His Life and Theory of Justice*, ed. Michelle Kosch (New York: Oxford University Press, 2007), in particular section 3.1 on "Purely Recipient-Oriented Criteria of Justice," pp. 43–8.

14 These are conceived as "ideal agents" capable of endorsing "object independent desires" based on an interpretation of Kant's pure will (see LHMP 152).

15 In TJ, argument (iii) proves particularly complex, so much so as to allow it to be broken down into a series of sub-arguments, such as: (iiia) the important choice is made in the original position; (iiib) this implies an information-related constraint for all the persons; (iiic) the parties in the original position choose within moral boundaries; (iiid) some special circumstances of justice are presupposed; (iiie) a few formal constraints are implied; and (iiif) the preceding conditions allow for the possibility of a unanimous and binding agreement.

16 The distinction between two kinds of constructivism is made by B. Barry, in *Theories of Justice* (Berkeley: University of California Press, 1989), p. 269.

17 As regards this point of view, I leave out more radical positions, such as that of Jean Hampton – "Contracts and Choices: Does Rawls Have a Social Contract Theory?" *Journal of Philosophy* 77 (6) (1980): 315–38 – which views the contract as being fully superfluous in the construction of the theory of justice as fairness.

18 This thesis becomes manifest looking at the model of justice proposed by Nozick; see ch. 7 in this volume.

19 See LHPP 16ff.

20 See Barry, *Theories of Justice*, p. 174.

21 D. Hume, *Treatise of Human Nature*, ed. P. H. Nidditch (Oxford: Oxford University Press, 1978), p. 523.

22 As, according to Rawls, would be the one depending on Marx's theory of justice based on the motto "to each according to his needs."

23 D. Hume, *Enquiry Concerning the Principles of Morals*, ed. L. A. Selby-Bigge (Oxford: Oxford University Press, 1975).

24 See Rawls, "Reply to Alexander and Musgrave," CP 232–53.

25 H. Sidgwick, *The Methods of Ethics*, 7th edn. ([1874] Indianapolis: Hackett, 1981), book ii.

26 He quotes Gauthier, in PL 52, n. 4. See also Rawls on Sidgwick in LHPP 375 ff.

27 This thesis is reasserted by Samuel Freeman's personal communication.

28 This thesis is explicitly upheld by Rawls in section 40 of TJ devoted to "The Kantian Interpretation" (TJ, rev. edn. 225).

29 CP 320.

30 In any event, the concept of "public reason" in PL modifies Rawls' thought about the theme under consideration (see ch. 11 below).

31 T. Nagel, "Rawls on Justice," *Philosophical Review* 87 (1973); rptd. in N. Daniels (ed.), *Reading Rawls: Critical Studies on Rawls's* A Theory of Justice (New York: Basic Books, 1975), p. 8.

32 Ibid. p. 9.

33 A defensive argument can be found in T. Shelby, "Race and Social Justice: Rawlsian Considerations," *Fordham Law Review* 72 (2004): 1697–715. But see, *contra*, S. Moller Okin, "Justice and Gender: An Unfinished Debate," ibid.: 1537–68, regarding sex. In the same issue of the journal there is a wide debate on these topics. See also, for a criticism regarding race, C. Mills, *The Racial Contract* (Ithaca: Cornell University Press, 1997).

34 See Daniels, "Introduction," in Daniels (ed.), *Reading Rawls*, p. xix. According to Rawls, the derivation of this tool depends on a proceduralization of Kant's categorical imperative.

35 This objection is immediate if one mistakes the Rawlsian–Kantian contract for the Hobbesian contract. See the articles by Freeman and Gauthier referred to in note 2.

36 This critique is similar to Hume's criticism in his essay "Of the Original Contract" (1752); as regards the latter, see Rawls in LHPP.

37 If one has read Hume on the social contract; but see Rawls, LHMP, on this point.

38 R. Dworkin, *Taking Rights Seriously* (London: Duckworth, 1977), p. 151. A similar result through a different argument is attained by Hampton, "Contracts and Choices." A similar argument is presented by B. Barry in *Justice as Impartiality* (Oxford: Oxford University Press, 1995). Barry endeavors to replace the contractualist argument with impartiality, drawing inspiration from T. Scanlon's thesis, "Utilitarianism and Contractualism," p. 104.

39 Dworkin, *Taking Rights Seriously*, p. 151.

40 Rawls attributes to Kant a connection between the procedure of the categorical imperative and information-related constraints (see "Two Limits on Information," LHMP 175ff.).

41 See S. Maffettone, *Utilitarismo e teoria della giustizia* (Naples: Bibliopolis, 1982); Pogge, *John Rawls*.

42 Pogge, *John Rawls*.

43 From this point of view, I believe that S. Scheffler has some valid arguments in "Moral Independence and the Original Position," *Philosophical Studies* 35 (1979): 397–403 (rptd. in Richardson and Weithman (eds.), *The Philosophy of Rawls*, vol. IV, pp. 187–93). when he upholds that Rawls' position on the subject, being different from the utilitarian stance, is somehow in conflict with the agnosticism on the nature of the subject defended by Rawls in IMT.

44 On this point, see the second lecture by Rawls on Hume in LHPP and KCMT.

45 To be fair to Hampton, this interpretation is favored by reading Rawls2; that is, not only TJ but also PL. In any event, Hampton's article dates back to 1980 and, perhaps, this should have allowed her a more conscious reading of Rawls' developments.

46 Nagel, "Rawls on Justice," pp. 8–9. A similar argument is debated by Adina Schwartz, "Moral Neutrality and Primary Goods," *Ethics* 83 (1973): 294–307.

47 It is interesting to observe that Paul Ricoeur, *The Just* (Chicago: The University of Chicago Press, 2000), ch. 2, explicitly talks about circularity on this point.

However, as Ricoeur has a hermeneutical background, he considers such circularity advantageous.

48 That, after all, is going to be the heart of the communitarian attack against Rawls.

49 Schwartz's criticism ("Moral Neutrality and Primary Goods") consists in claiming that the thin definition of the good cannot lead to a choice of the primary goods without the introduction of a substantive conception of the good.

50 According to the Aristotelian Principle, rational individuals would introduce in their plans of life elements that refer to their specific abilities and, generally, the most sophisticated human capacities.

51 KCMT, in CP 330ff.

52 See Barry, *Theories of Justice*.

53 With reference to impartiality, see B. Barry, "How Not to Defend Liberal Institutions," in R. Bruce Douglas, G. M. Mara, and H. S. Richardson (eds.), *Liberalism and the Good* (New York: Routledge, 1990); see also P. Kelly, *Liberalism* (Cambridge, UK: Polity, 2005), ch. 3.

54 J. J. C. Harsanyi, "Can the Maximin Principle Serve as a Basis for Morality? A Critique of John Rawls' Theory," *American Political Science Review* 69 (1975): 594–606; Barry, *Theories of Justice*.

55 See B. Barry, *The Liberal Theory of Justice* (Oxford: Oxford University Press, 1972), and R. P. Wolff, *Understanding Rawls* (Princeton, NJ: Princeton University Press, 1977).

56 The critiques may be cumulated, as J. Fishkin does in "Justice and Rationality: Some Objections to the Central Argument in Rawls' Theory," *American Political Science Review* 69 (1975): 615–29.

57 K. Arrow, "Some Ordinalist–Utilitarian Notes on Rawls' Theory of Justice," *Journal of Philosophy* 70 (1973): 245–63; A. Sen, *Collective Choice and Social Welfare* (San Francisco: Holden-Day, 1970), and *Choice, Welfare and Measurement* (Cambridge, MA: Harvard University Press, 1987); H. Varian, "Equity, Envy, Efficiency," *Journal of Economic Theory* 9 (1974): 63–91; S. Strasnick, "Social Choice and the Derivation of Rawls' Difference Principle," *Journal of Philosophy* 73 (4) (1976): 85–9; Maffettone, *Utilitarismo e teoria della giustizia*.

58 Such an argument, which I find both profound and controversial, was not introduced in these terms by Rawls, but by T. Scanlon, "Preference and Urgency," *Journal of Philosophy* 72 (1975): 655–69.

59 A. Buchanan, "A Critical Introduction to Rawls' Theory of Justice," in H. G. Blocker and H. Smith (eds.), *John Rawls's Theory of Social Justice* (Athens: Ohio University Press, 1980), pp. 5–41.

60 In any event, in "Democratic Equality," *Ethics* 99 (1989): 727–51, Joshua Cohen claims that the maximin criterion may successfully cope with the problems posed by the mixed conceptions.

61 Arrow, "Some Ordinalist–Utilitarian Notes on Rawls' Theory of Justice."

62 Even though Rawls' vindication is not expressed in a clear manner, he seems to exclude rule-utilitarianism from the comparison – at least in certain forms, like the one proposed by R. B. Brandt, "Some Merits of One Form of Rule Utilitarianism," *University of Colorado Studies in Philosophy* (1967): 39–65, quoted in TJ (182, n. 31; TJ, rev. edn. 159, n. 32).

63 However, it may be upheld in opposition to Rawls – as G. S. Kavka does in

"Rawls on Average and Total Utility," *Philosophical Studies* 27 (1975): 237–53 – that inherent in the average principle is a bias towards existing persons rather than those not yet in existence. According to Kavka, this bias would also apply to Rawls' principles and weaken his anti-utilitarian argument.

64 It is hardly necessary to note that things do not change for Rawls if we move from the conception of utility as satisfaction of a desire to the more modern conception in terms of consumer's choices (in the way it is axiomatized by J. von Neumann and O. Morgenstern, *Theory of Games and Economic Behavior*, Princeton: Princeton University Press, 1944) (TJ, rev. edn. 143).

65 We can track this peculiar conception of the person from Rawls' senior thesis BIMSF (152–6) where he argues against the distinction between persons, taking his lead from the importance of signs within the social community. In this sense the "body is . . . an indispensable precondition of community" (ibid. 155).

66 For details of this argument, see Cohen, "Democratic Equality."

67 Even in this case, however, it should be borne in mind that risk aversion might be included in the utility function.

68 See Nagel, "Rawls on Justice," pp. 13–14.

69 See Maffettone, *Utilitarismo e teoria della giustizia*; J. Cohen, "Democratic Equality."

70 Rawls, PL xliiff; G. A. Cohen, *Rescuing Justice and Equality* (Cambridge, MA: Harvard University Press, 2008), ch. 8.

71 K. Arrow, *Social Choice and Individual Values*, 2nd edn. (New York: John Wiley, 1963).

72 A. K. Sen, *Collective Choice and Social Welfare* (San Francisco: Holden-Day, 1970); Sen, "Informational Bases of Alternative Welfare Approaches: Aggregation and Income Distribution," *Journal of Public Economics* 4 (1974); Sen, "On Weights and Measures: Informational Constraints in Social Welfare Analysis," *Econometrica* 45 (1977).

73 S. Strasnick, "Social Choice and the Derivation of the Difference Principle," *Journal of Philosophy* 73 (1976): 85–99.

74 Von Neumann and Morgenstern, *Theory of Games and Economic Behavior*.

6 Reflective Equilibrium

1 In T. Scanlon, "Rawls on Justification," in S. Freeman (ed.), *The Cambridge Companion to Rawls* (Cambridge, UK: Cambridge University Press, 2002), pp. 139–67.

2 A few doubts as to the coherentist nature of the method, for epistemological and metaphysical reasons, have been raised by D. O. Brink, "Rawlsian Constructivism in Moral Theory," *Canadian Journal of Philosophy* 17 (1987): 71–90.

3 N. Goodman, *Facts, Fictions and Forecast* (Cambridge, MA: Harvard University Press, 1955).

4 For an analysis of the concept of coherence, useful for understanding the epistemological meaning of reflexive equilibrium, see I. Scheffler, "On Justification and Commitment," *Journal of Philosophy* 51 (1954): 180–90.

5 This thesis is made explicit by Rawls in IMT.

6 For the relationship with foundationalism, see M. DePaul, "Reflective Equilibrium and Foundationalism," *American Philosophical Quarterly* 23 (1986): 59–69.

7 To probe into the problem, one might read C. F. Delaney, "Rawls on Method," in K. Nielsen and R. Shiner (eds.), *Canadian Journal of Philosophy*, supplementary volume 3: *New Essays on Contractarianism* (1977): 153–61, which insists on a change between the first (1951) and the second Rawls (1971) on reflexive equilibrium, where the first Rawls is supposedly influenced by positivism and the second Rawls is supposedly influenced by Quine.

8 Scanlon, "Rawls on Justification," p. 140.

9 N. Daniels, *Justice and Justification: Reflective Equilibrium in Theory and Practice* (Cambridge, UK: Cambridge University Press, 1996).

10 Ibid. p. 22.

11 See Daniels, *Justice and Justification*, in particular ch. 2.

12 Pogge, *John Rawls: His Life and Theory of Justice*, ed. Michelle Kosch (New York: Oxford University Press, 2007), p. 166.

13 N. Daniels, "On some Methods of Ethics and Linguistics," *Philosophical Studies* 37 (1980): 21–36; rptd. in Daniels, *Justice and Justification*, ch. 4.

14 See Daniels, *Justice and Justification*, p. 87.

15 See KCMT.

16 On this point, see K. Nielsen, "Our Considered Judgments," *Ratio* 19 (1977): 39–46.

17 N. Daniels (ed.), *Reading Rawls: Critical Studies on Rawls's* A Theory of Justice (New York: Basic Books, 1975), Introduction.

18 R. R. M. Hare, "Rawls's Theory of Justice," *Philosophical* Quarterly 23 (1973): 144–55. It would seem that P. Singer, "Sidgwick and Reflective Equilibrium," *Monist* 58 (1974): 490–517, and R. B. Brandt, *A Theory of the Good and the Right* (Oxford: Oxford University Press, 1979), are on the same wavelength as Hare.

19 N. Daniels, "Wide Reflective Equilibrium and Theory Acceptance in Ethics," *Journal of Philosophy* 76 (1979): 256–82 (rptd. in Daniels, *Justice and Justification*, ch. 2), argues that the narrow reflective equilibrium may be blamed for subjectivism, while this is not so with the wide reflective equilibrium. However, it should be noted that Hare's article had been written prior to the initiation of the debate on the wide reflective equilibrium.

20 This thesis is shared by M. R. DePaul, "Reflective Equilibrium and Foundationalism," who claims that, banally, coherentism and intuitionism are opposing ethical foundations.

21 See M. B. E. Smith, "Rawls and Intuitionism," in Nielsen and Shiner (eds.), *Canadian Journal of Philosophy*, suppl. vol. 3: 163–78. Smith says that Rawls' revisionism in wide reflective equilibrium is at odds with intuitionism.

22 See D. Lyons, "Nature and Soundness of Contract and Coherence Arguments," in Daniels (ed.), *Reading Rawls*, pp. 16–53.

23 According to M. R. DePaul, "Two Conceptions of Coherence Method in Ethics," *Mind* 96 (1987): 463–81, there are two ways to consider a coherentist method: a conservative way and a radical way (which permits changing one's opinion more easily). The wide reflective equilibrium should allow more space to the radical method.

24 This hypothesis may be countered by claiming that – unlike the decision theory

– in ethics the possibility of a coherentist argument is defendable based on a supervenience hypothesis, as S. L. Hurley does in a complex article, "Supervenience and the Possibility of Coherence," *Mind* 94 (1985): 501–25.

25 From this point of view, there is an exemplary critical argument by S. Sencerz in "Moral Intuitions and Justification in Ethics," *Philosophical Studies* 50 (1986): 77–95, where he affirms that the reflexive equilibrium does not guarantee the passage from considered moral judgments to ideal moral judgments.

26 The likelihood of disagreement rather than equilibrium is pondered by S. Lukes, "Relativism: Cognitive and Moral," *Proceedings of the Aristotelian Society*, supplementary volume 48 (1974): 184.

27 See K. Nielsen, "Searching for an Emancipatory Perspective: Wide Reflective Equilibrium and the Hermeneutical Circle," in E. Simpson (ed.), *Anti-Foundationalism and Practical Reasoning* (Edmonton, Alberta: Academic Printing and Publishing, 1987), pp. 143–64.

28 J. Raz, "The Claims of Reflective Equilibrium," *Inquiry* 25 (1982): 307–30, in particular pp. 310–12.

29 Ibid. p. 315.

30 This seems to be Weinstock's thesis in "The Justification of Political Liberalism," *Pacific Philosophical Quarterly* 75 (1994): 165–85.

31 See N. Daniels, *Justifying Justice*.

32 This aspect has been observed by Freeman, *Rawls* (London: Routledge, 2007).

7 Main Criticisms of Rawls

1 The most well-known book-length analysis of the communitarian criticism is S. Mulhall and A. Swift, *Liberals & Communitarians* (Oxford: Blackwell, 1992). The authors are probably right in maintaining that it is difficult properly to distinguish communitarian critics from feminist, radical, realist and (non-Rawlsian) liberal critics.

2 See A. Gutmann, "Communitarian Critics of Liberalism," *Philosophy & Public Affairs* 14 (3) (1985): 308–22.

3 M. Sandel, *Liberalism and the Limits of Justice* (Cambridge, UK: Cambridge University Press, 1982), and "Introduction" to M. Sandel (ed.), *Liberalism and its Critics* (New York: New York University Press, 1984).

4 A. MacIntyre, *After Virtue: A Study in Moral Theory* (London: Duckworth, 1981).

5 C. Taylor, *Hegel and Modern Society* (Cambridge, UK: Cambridge University Press, 1979), and *Philosophical Papers* (Cambridge, UK: Cambridge University Press, 1985).

6 M. Walzer, *Spheres of Justice: A Defence of Pluralism and Equality* (London: Blackwell, 1983).

7 R. Bellah et al., *Habits of the Heart* (Berkeley, CA: University of California Press, 1985).

8 R. M. Unger, *Knowledge and Politics* (New York: Macmillan, 1984).

9 R. Rorty, "Postmodernist Bourgeois Liberalism," in R. Hollinger (ed.), *Hermeneutics and Praxis* (Indianapolis: Notre Dame University Press, 1985).

10 B. Williams, *Ethics and the Limits of Philosophy* (London: Fontana Press, 1985) and his *In Principle was the Deed: Realism and Moralism in Political Argument* (Princeton, NJ: Princeton University, 2005), esp. ch. 1.

11 See A. Buchanan, "Assessing the Communitarian Critique of Liberalism," *Ethics* 99 (4) (1989): 852–82.

12 This is explicit in M. Sandel, "The Procedural Republic and the Unencumbered Self," *Political Theory* 12 (1984): 81–96. Sandel asks from his first page "What is the political philosophy implicit in our practice and institutions?," the answer being "procedural liberalism *à la* Rawls" which he is keen to criticize.

13 Here the young Marx and MacIntyre are probably the best sources for understanding this argument properly.

14 Here Hegel and the traditional sociologists (like Durkheim and Toennies) are the sources of the argument.

15 Some ambiguities of Sandel criticism – starting from the overlapping between a normative ideal and a descriptive account – are emphasized by G. Doppelt, "Is Rawls's Kantian Liberalism Coherent and Defensible?" *Ethics* 99 (4) (July 1989): 815–51.

16 A. MacIntyre, *After Virtue: A Study in Moral Theory* (London: Duckworth, 1981).

17 C. Taylor, *Philosophical Papers* (Cambridge, UK: Cambridge University Press, 1985), vol. I, p. 35.

18 Ibid.

19 Ibid. p. 36.

20 This is already evident from Rawls' communitarian reading of the person in BIMSF, even if this conception of community is different from the one we find in TJ.

21 Scheffler insists on the difference that philosophy of mind plays in the first and the third part of TJ. See S. Sheffler, "Moral Skepticism and Ideals of the Person," *Monist* 62 (1979): 288–303. This difference is noted also by K. Baynes, "The Liberal/Communitarian Controversy and Communicative Ethics," *Philosophy and Social Criticism* 14 (1988): 293–313; rptd. in David Rasmussen (ed.), *Universalism vs Communitarianism* (Cambridge, MA: MIT Press, 1990), pp. 39–60, 61–82.

22 See S. A. Schwarzenbach, "Rawls, Hegel and Communitarianism," *Political Theory* 19 (4) (1991): 539–71.

23 G. Doppelt, "Beyond Liberalism and Communitarianism," in Rasmussen (ed.), *Universalism vs Communitarianism*. See also R. Alejandro, "Rawls' Communitarianism," *Canadian Journal of Philosophy* 23 (1993): 75–99; rptd. in Richardson and Weithman (eds.), *The Philosophy of Rawls: A Collection of Essays*, 5 vols. (New York: Garland, 1999).

24 See Gutmann, "Communitarian Critics of Liberalism," and C. Kukhatas and P. Pettit, A Theory of Justice *and its Critics* (Stanford: Stanford University Press, 1990).

25 See Taylor, *Hegel and Modern Society*, pp. 157–9.

26 M. Sandel, "Justice and the Good," in Sandel (ed.), *Liberalism and the Limits of Justice*, p. 158.

27 Ibid. p. 168.

28 Ibid. ch. 2.

29 Ibid. pp. 69–95.

30 Here I follow S. Freeman, *Justice and the Social Contract: Essays on Rawlsian Political Philosophy* (Oxford: Oxford University Press, 2007), ch. 2.

31 Rawls uses – beyond the distinction between good and right – the distinction between deontology and teleology. He takes up the standard definition by W. K. Frankena, *Ethics* (Englewood Cliffs, NJ: Prentice-Hall, 1973). According to this definition, deontological theories assume the priority of right whereas teleological theories assume the priority of the good. This thesis is controversial. One can, for example, recommend a utilitarian precept of teleological nature for deontological reasons. This shows that, in part, we can use deontological/teleological independently from right/good (TJ 397, rev. edn. 349).

32 Sandel, *Liberalism and the Limits of Justice.*

33 See Mulhall and Swift, *Liberals and Communitarians*, pp. 215ff.

34 See M. Walzer, *Spheres of Justice*; "Philosophy and Democracy," *Political Theory* 9 (3) (August 1981): 379–99; "The Communitarian Critique of Liberalism," *Political Theory* 18 (February 1990): 6–23.

35 R. Nozick, *Anarchy, State and Utopia* (New York: Basic Books, 1974) (hereafter in text references, ASU).

36 In principle, a minimal state does not imply absence of redistribution, as said by J. R. Kearl, "Do Entitlements Imply that Taxation is Theft?" *Philosophy & Public Affairs* 7 (1) (1977): 74–81.

37 The only exception is the "Lockean proviso," according to which a set of transfers leaving persons underneath the state of nature would be unjust. See Nozick, *Anarchy, State, Utopia*, p. 178.

38 F. A. Hayek, *The Constitution of Liberty*, Chicago: University of Chicago Press 1967.

39 J. S. Coleman, "Rawls, Nozick and the Educational Equality," *The Public Interest* (Spring 1976): 121–8, maintains that as a consequence of this thesis "only the individual is entitled to the fruits of his labor."

40 See Rawls' answer to Nozick in JFR.

41 See J. Wolff, *Robert Nozick: Property, Justice and the Minimal State* (Stanford: Stanford University Press, 1991), in particular pp. 121ff.

42 See Sandel, *Liberalism and the Limits of Justice*, pp. 89–92.

43 See JFR 72–4 for Rawls on moral desert and legitimate expectations.

44 See T. Nagel, "Libertarianism without Foundations," *Yale Law Journal* 85 (1): 136–49; rptd. in J. Paul (ed.), *Reading Nozick: Essays on Anarchy, State and Utopia* (Oxford: Blackwell, 1981).

45 T. Scanlon, "Nozick on Rights, Liberty and Property," *Philosophy & Public Affairs* 6 (1) (Fall 1976); rptd. in Paul (ed.), *Reading Nozick.*

46 Nagel "Libertarianism without Foundations."

47 A similar thesis is maintained by J. D. Hodson, "Nozick, Libertarianism and Rights," *Arizona Law Review* 19 (1) (1978): 212–27. According to Hodson, the rights thesis and the libertarian account of justice are in contradiction.

48 See T. Nagel, "Libertarianism without Foundations."

49 J. Habermas, "Reconciliation through the Public Use of Reason: Remarks on John Rawls' *Political Liberalism*," *Journal of Philosophy* 93 (3) (March 1995):

109–31; Rawls' reply is in "Reply to Habermas," pp. 132–80 (I am quoting from the second version published in PL's expanded edition, 2005).

50 Among the works discussing Habermas/Rawls in general terms, see: K. Baynes, *The Normative Grounds of Social Criticism* (Albany: SUNY Press, 1992); S. Benhabib, *Critique, Norm and Utopia* (New York: Columbia University Press, 1986); R. Forst, *Kontexte der Gerechtigkeit* (Frankfurt: Suhrkamp, 1994). For a specific discussion of HRE see: T. McCarthy, "Kantian Constructivism and Reconstructivism: Rawls and Habermas in Dialogue," *Ethics* 105 (October 1994): 44–63; rptd. in Richardson and Weithman (eds.), *The Philosophy of John Rawls*, vol. V: *Reasonable Pluralism*, pp. 320–33. More recent are T. Hedrick, *Rawls and Habermas*, Stanford University Press, 2010, and F. Freyenhagen and S. G. Finlayson, *Habermas and Rawls*, Routledge, 2010.

51 J. Habermas, *Between Naturalism and Religion* (Cambridge, UK: Polity Press, 2008), in particular ch. 5.

52 This point has been clarified by D. Rasmussen in his lectures at LUISS University, Rome (academic year 2005–6).

53 McCarthy, "Kantian Constructivism and Reconstructivism," in Richardson and Weithman (eds.), *The Philosophy of John Rawls*, vol. V, pp. 331–2.

54 For a view according to which Habermas' theory is very close to Rawls' political liberalsim, see M. Yates, "Rawls and Habermas on Religion in the Public Sphere," *Philosophy and Social Criticism* 33 (7), 2007, pp. 88–91.

55 See J. Habermas, *The Postnational Constellation*, Cambridge, MA: MIT Press (2001), in particular ch. 5.

56 For the difference between Rawls' and Habermas' understandings of public reason, see J. D. Moon, "Rawls and Habermas on Public Reason," *Annual Review of Political Sciences* 6 (2003), pp. 257–76.

8 FROM *A THEORY OF JUSTICE* TO *POLITICAL LIBERALISM*

1 See C. Kukathas and P. Pettit, *Rawls: A Theory of Justice and its Critics* (Cambridge, UK: Polity Press, 1990). It should also be noted that, being published in 1990, Kukathas and Pettit's book could not take PL and JFR into account, although much of the content of the latter was already well known at the time.

2 Ibid.

3 "A Kantian Conception of Equality," *Cambridge Review* 96 (1975): 94–9 was later republished as "A Well-Ordered Society," in P. Laslett and J. Fishkin (eds.), *Philosophy Politics, and Society*, 5th series (Oxford: Blackwell, 1979), pp. 6–20.

4 See Rawls' preface to the second French, Portuguese, and English editions.

5 See H. L. A. Hart, "Rawls on Liberty and its Priorities," *University of Chicago Law Review* 40 (1973): 534–55; rptd. in N. Daniels (ed.), *Reading Rawls*, 2nd edn. (Stanford, CA: Stanford University Press, 1989), pp. 230–52.

6 See also TJ, rev. edn. xii – where Rawls explicitly relates "basic rights and liberties" to the development of citizens' "moral powers" – and the more complete treatment in "The Basic Liberties and Their Priority," in Sterling M. McMurrin (ed.), *The Tanner Lectures on Human Values*, vol. III (Salt Lake City: University of Utah Press, 1982), pp. 1–87, republished as Lecture VIII in PL.

7 See E. Kelly, "Rawls recente," *Filosofia e questioni pubbliche* 6 (2001): 163–72.

8 The former article was first published in A. Sen and B. Williams (eds.), *Utilitarianism and Beyond* (Cambridge, UK: Cambridge University Press, 1982), pp. 159–85.

9 See R. Nozick, *Anarchy, State and Utopia* (New York: Basic Books, 1974), p. 229.

10 T. Nagel, "The Rigorous Compassion of John Rawls," *The New Republic* (25 October 1999), pp. 36–41 also expresses a preference for the original versions of these passages.

11 On this, see Kukathas and Pettit, *Rawls: A Theory of Justice and its Critics*, especially pp. 121–33.

12 See Rawls, "A Well-Ordered Society," and KCMT.

13 The other concerns the introduction of the concept of a "property-owning democracy" in the place of that of the "welfare state" which I discussed in the second chapter. On this, I simply direct one to Rawls' own discussion of the subject in JFR.

14 On this, see "Justice as Fairness: Political not Metaphysical," *Philosophy & Public Affairs* 14 (1985), p. 237, n. 20, and "The Basic Liberties and Their Priority," p. 20.

15 JFR 43, n. 3; pp. 94–6.

16 CP 317. The distinction between the "Reasonable" and the "Rational" is central to Rawls' argument in PL.

17 Rawls perhaps most clearly insists on the separation of political theory from ethics/moral approaches in the preface that he prepared for the French edition of his writings, *Justice et Démocratie* (Paris: Editions du Seuil, 1993).

18 On the changes made to the earlier lectures in preparing JFR for publication, see Erin Kelly's editor's note. Note that the claims made in the new section on the family are developed in IPRR, and that the other part of Rawls' course on political philosophy dedicated to the history of political philosophy was published posthumously in LHPP.

19 JFR xv.

20 For Rawls' reproposition of egalitarianism, see, for instance, JFR 96ff.

21 See JFR 18–24.

22 See chapter 7 in this volume for an account of the communitarian critique.

23 CP 305–6.

24 I owe this point regarding the historicity of the basic structure to Tim Scanlon.

25 See also S. Olsaretti, *Liberty, Desert and the Market* (Cambridge, UK: Cambridge University Press, 2004). On Nozick's criticisms in particular, see chapter 7 of this volume.

26 Reciprocity is connected with the foundations of democracy by J. Cohen, "For a Democratic Society," in S. Freeman (ed.), *The Cambridge Companion to Rawls* (Cambridge, UK: Cambridge University Press, 2002), pp. 86–138.

27 See JFR 43ff. and 98ff.

28 See JFR, respectively, 49 and 148ff.

29 See KCMT [CP] 307.

30 CP 358.

31 It is notable that the term "constructivism" does not appear in TJ. Of course, this

way of understanding constructivism has nothing to do with social constructivism and its relativist implications.

32 This claim is made by Onora O'Neill, in her "Constructivism vs. Contractualism," *Ratio* 16 (2000): 319–31.

33 Oddly, here Rawls does not refer to section 40 of TJ, dedicated to the Kantian interpretation, or to his reading of Kant in terms of the "fact of reason," which he developed before 1980, although it was published only later (see LHMP).

34 As he makes explicit at the end of section 40 of TJ (rev. edn. 226–7), Rawls does not consider these dualisms to be essential to the understanding of Kant's ethics.

35 CP 305.

36 CP 306.

37 This conclusion appears to be implied by O'Neill, in her "Constructivism in Rawls and Kant," in Freeman (ed.), *The Cambridge Companion to Rawls*, pp. 347–67. Rawls' relative unfaithfulness to Kant is also noted by A. Bloom, in his "John Rawls vs. the Tradition of Political Philosophy," *American Political Science Review* 69 (1975): 648–62.

38 A telling criticism of Rawls' constructivism is that of G. A. Cohen, who argues that such a conception of constructivism mistakenly considers moral principles to be fact-sensitive. See his "Facts and Principles," *Philosophy & Public Affairs* 31 (2003): 211–45.

39 The significance of the model conception of the moral person for the understanding of Kantian constructivism presented in KCMT is emphasized by, among others, W. A. Galston, "Moral Personality and Liberal Theory: John Rawls's 'Dewey Lectures,'" *Political Theory* 10 (1982): 492–519. The development of Rawls' thought in these terms is also well understood by G. Doppelt, although he goes too far in classifying it as a liberal communitarianism. See his "Beyond Liberalism and Communitarianism," in D. Rasmussen (ed.), *Universalism vs Communitarianism* (Cambridge, MA: MIT Press, 1990), pp. 39–60.

40 Rawls makes clear in IMT that he does not consider the philosophy of mind to have a special and independent significance for his theory.

41 The difficulties resolved by the introduction of the Rational and the Reasonable include, for instance, Bernard Williams' complaint that Rawlsian persons are, like Kantian ones, deprived of their specific characters. On this, see his "Persons, Character, and Morality," in A. O. Rorty (ed.), *The Identities of Persons* (Berkeley and London: University of California Press, 1976); rptd. in B. A. O. Williams, *Moral Luck* (Cambridge, UK: Cambridge University Press, 1981).

42 CP 330–1.

43 CP 332.

44 CP 340. Here Rawls uses "Reasonable" in opposition not, as before, to "Rational," but to "true" as understood by (rational) intuitionism.

45 See CP 343.

46 CP 344.

47 This analogy holds because intuitionism and naturalism are the two forms of moral realism.

48 CP 511.

49 CP 351–2.

50 CP 347.
51 On this, see O'Neill, "Constructivism vs. Contractualism," p. 322.
52 This is, roughly speaking. D. O. Brink's claim in his "Rawlsian Constructivism in Moral Theory," *Canadian Journal of Philosophy* 17 (1987): 171–90.
53 Here I follow S. Freeman in the paper presented at the Colloquium in Ethics, Politics and Society at LUISS University, Rome, in 2007. This version seems to coincide with the realism of the reasons formulated by T. M. Scanlon in *What We Owe to Each Other* (Cambridge, MA: Belknap Press of Harvard University Press, 1998).
54 I do not think that this argument can be in favor of G. A. Cohen's mentioned criticism. There are no more primitive principles of justice from which Rawls derives all his theory.
55 CP 356.
56 See R. Milo, "Contractarian Constructivism," *Journal of Philosophy* 92 (1995): 181–204.
57 CP 574.

9 Introducing *Political Liberalism*

1 Useful readings on PL are: P. F. Campos, D. G. Carlson, M. Galston, et al., "Symposium on *Political Liberalism*," *Columbia Law Review* 94 (1994): 1751–1935; S. A. Lloyd (ed.), "John Rawls's Political Liberalism," special double issue of *Pacific Philosophical Quarterly* 75 (1994): 165–387; S. Griffin and L. Solum (eds.), "Symposium on John Rawls's *Political Liberalism*," *Chicago-Kent Law Review* 69 (1994): 549–842; "Symposium on John Rawls," *Ethics* 104 (4) (1994): 4–63; J. Fleming (ed.), "Symposium on Rawls and the Law," *Fordham Law Review* 72 (2004): 1381–2175; V. Davion and C. Wolf (eds.), *The Idea of a Political Liberalism: Essays on Rawls* (Lanham, MD: Rowman and Littlefield, 1999); H. S. Richardson and P. Weithman (eds.), *The Philosophy of Rawls*, Vol. V: *Reasonable Pluralism* (New York: Garland, 1999).
2 A manuscript of Rawls' own presentation, "TJ, PL, and Other Pieces," was distributed at the conference, but was never published and adds little to the published texts of this period.
3 The second, clothbound revised edition of PL, to which the footnotes below refer, was published in 1996 by Columbia University Press.
4 Note that I use the term "conception" when I refer to the "political conception," and reserve the term "doctrine" to refer to "comprehensive (reasonable) doctrines," as Rawls himself proposes in IPRR, in CP 573, n. 2.
5 This is claimed by, among others, A. Buchanan, in his "Justice, Legitimacy and Human Rights," in Davion and Wolf (eds.), *The Idea of a Political Liberalism: Essays on Rawls*, p. 73.
6 On this, see Barry, "John Rawls and the Search for Stability," *Ethics* 105 (4) (July 1995): 874–915, final part. This has led some commentators to claim that Rawls intends to resolve the problem of pluralism in PL by means of an unorthodox, overly social-democratic interpretation of the United States constitution.

7 I discuss Rawls' treatment of the basic liberties in chapter 3 above, and will consider the basic structure in chapter 12 below.

8 The original bibliographical details of the articles included in PL are the following: "The Basic Structure as Subject," in *American Philosophical Quarterly* 14 (2) (April 1977): 159–65; "The Basic Liberties and Their Priority," in S. McMurrin (ed.), *The Tanner Lectures on Human Values*, vol. III (Salt Lake City: University of Utah Press, 1982), pp. 3–87; "Social Unity and Primary Goods," in A. Sen and B. A. O. Williams (eds.), *Utilitarianism and Beyond* (Cambridge, UK: Cambridge University Press, 1982), pp. 159–85; "Justice as Fairness: Political not Metaphysical," *Philosophy & Public Affairs* 14 (1985): 223–51; "The Idea of Overlapping Consensus," *Oxford Journal for Legal Studies* 7 (1987): 1–25; "The Priority of Right and Ideas of the Good," *Philosophy & Public Affairs* 17 (1988): 251–76; "The Domain of the Political and Overlapping Consensus," *New York University Law Review* 64 (1989): 233–55; and "Reply to Habermas," *Journal of Philosophy* 92 (1995): 132–890.

9 See CP 608.

10 Similarities and dissimilarities between Rawls' and Hegel's projects of reconciliation are shown by J. Cohen, "A More Democratic Liberalism," pp. 1507ff.

11 Appropriately, Columbia University Press launched PL under the slogan, "Rawls Rethinks Rawls." On this topic, see ch. 1 above.

12 A. Buchanan presents a sophisticated distinction between legitimacy and authoritativeness in his "Political Legitimacy and the Morality of Political Power," *Ethics* 122 (2002): 689–732.

13 See D. Boucher and P. Kelly, *The Social Contract from Hobbes to Rawls* (London: Routledge, 1994).

14 D. Estlund has argued for the implausibility of such a claim, on the grounds that the claim itself must be affirmed as true. See his "The Insularity of the Reasonable: Why Political Liberalism Must Admit the Truth," *Ethics* 108 (2) (1998): 252–75.

15 In a well-known review, Stuart Hampshire argues that liberal pluralism can only be proceduralist, and that Rawls is therefore not sufficiently proceduralist. See Hampshire, "Liberalism: The New Twist," *New York Review of Books* (12 August 1993), pp. 4–6. Worth noting in this regard is Joshua Cohen's reply, according to which procedure and substance are never separated in Rawls. See Cohen, "Pluralism and Proceduralism," *Chicago-Kent Law Review* 69 (1994): 589–618.

16 See, in particular, ch. 7.

17 On the priority of the right over the good, see also M. Sandel's review of PL: "Political Liberalism," *Harvard Law Review* 107 (1994): 1765–94.

18 The disappointment expressed by many admirers of TJ on this score is evident in some of the first reviews of PL. See, for instance, S. Holmes, "John Rawls and the Limits of Tolerance," *The New Republic* 11 (October 1993): 39–47; S. M. Okin, "Review of *Political Liberalism*," *American Political Science Review* 87 (1993): 1010–11; B. Ackerman, "Political Liberalisms," *Journal of Philosophy* 91 (7) (1994): 364–86; N. Daniels, in his "Reflective Equilibrium and Justice as Political," in *Justice and Justification: Reflective Equilibrium in Theory and Practice* (Cambridge, UK: Cambridge University Press, 1996), even refers to a "philosophical loss" associated with the publication of PL.

19 In a well-known review of PL, "A Fair State," *London Review of Books* 13 (May

1993), Bernard Williams claims explicitly that in the new, tolerant and liberal, view presented in the book, "the Difference Principle has come to play a distinctly secondary role compared to the elements that help to define a constitutional structure within which the debates of politics can go on."

20 On this, see S. Freeman's introduction "John Rawls – an Overview," to Freeman (ed.), *The Cambridge Companion to Rawls* (Cambridge, UK: Cambridge University Press, 2002), pp. 1–60, and R. Dworkin, *Freedom's Law* (Cambridge, MA: Harvard University Press, 1996). On Rawls' view of equality, which links resourcism to self-respect, see Joshua Cohen, "Democratic Equality," *Ethics* 99 (1989): 828–51. My claim here agrees, I believe, with Norman Daniels' view, explained to me in personal communication. On the egalitarian elements of the basic liberties and the continuity of Rawls' thought in this regard, see D. Estlund, "The Survival of Egalitarian Justice in John Rawls's *Political Liberalism*," *Journal of Political Philosophy* 4 (1996): 68–88.

21 I have discussed this at various points above, and particularly in chapter 5 on the original position and Nagel's criticism (of it).

22 See CP 608 and 618, respectively.

23 CP 582, n. 28 and n. 29.

24 On the difficulties of reconciling legitimation with normative validity, see F. I. Michelman, "Constitutional Legitimation for Political Acts," *The Modern Law Review* 66 (2003): 1–15.

25 On this, see B. Dreben, "On Rawls and Political Liberalism," in Freeman (ed.), *The Cambridge Companion to Rawls*, pp. 316–46.

26 This is stated clearly in IPRR.

27 In his long critical review of PL, Brian Barry appeals to his own interpretation of TJ in terms of Kantian impartiality, presented in his *Justice as Impartiality* (Oxford: Clarendon, 1995). Against Rawls' own interpretation of TJ in PL, and, in support of his own, he cites the work of the Rawlsians Freeman and Scanlon. See Barry, "John Rawls and the Search for Stability," pp. 874–915.

28 This point is clarified in section 78 of TJ 513–20, (rev. edn. 450–6) – notably, the section which begins the chapter on the coincidence between the right and the good which is to promote stability in a well-ordered society.

29 Rawls' dissatisfaction with his approach in TJ can be seen as early as 1980's KCMT.

30 See PL 205–6 on the distinction between classical republicanism and civic humanism, according to which only the former is consistent with PL. Certain elements of the republican position are also incorporated in the political view of the person presented in PL, based on works of the 1980s and on KCMT in particular. Rawls is especially clear about his four-stage sequence (in TJ) in his "Reply to Habermas," rptd. in PL 397ff.

31 On this, see D. G. Carlson, "Jurisprudence and Personality in the Work of John Rawls," *Columbia Law Review* 94 (1994): 1828–41.

32 This assumes that Habermas' criticisms are themselves influenced by republicanism, as he himself suggests in *Faktizität und Geltung* (Frankfurt am Main: Suhrkamp, 1992); English translation by William Rehg, *Between Facts and Norms: Contributions to a Discourse Theory of Law and Democracy* (Cambridge, MA: MIT Press, 1996).

33 On this, see C. Sunstein, "Incompletely Theorized Agreements in Constitutional Law," *Social Research* 74 (2007): 1–24.

34 In this respect, PL is certainly influenced by Dworkin's position in *Law's Empire* (Cambridge, MA: Harvard University Press, 1986), and its insistence on the notion of integrity and the ethical interpretation of justice. Indeed, all of Dworkin's work on jurisprudence, from *Taking Rights Seriously* (Cambridge, MA: Harvard University Press, 1977) onwards, can be said to have been influential on PL.

35 This was indicated to me by Rawls himself in personal communication.

36 It is interesting to consider how this emphasis on the juridical argument in PL compares with the well-known problem of the relation between ethics and justice in Kant's theory of justice. On this, see Pogge, *John Rawls: His Life and Theory of Justice*, Oxford, Oxford University Press, 2007, and J. L. Cohen, "Rethinking Human Rights, Democracy and Sovereignty in the Age of Globalization," *Political Theory* 36 (4) (2008): 578–606.

37 This, in my opinion, is because Rawls' communitarian critics mistook his political theory, which considers subjects in terms of [their] liberty and equality, for a metaphysical and comprehensive doctrine of the self. W. Kymlicka makes a similar claim in his *Liberalism, Community and Culture* (Oxford: Clarendon Press, 1989), which Rawls cites approvingly in PL 28, n. 29. However, the opposing claim is made by M. Sandel, when, in his review of PL (quoted in n. 20 above), he insists that Rawls' PL is incapable of guiding decision-making, and by Kent Greenawalt, who, in his "On Public Reason," *Chicago-Kent Law Review* 69 (1994): 669–90, does not make the mistake of the communitarians, but nonetheless insists on such an incapacity with regard to religion, a criticism that Rawls took particularly seriously. Stephen Mulhall and Adam Swift provide a discussion that is compatible with what I have claimed and that absolves Rawls of the charge of anti-communitarian individualism, in their "Rawls and Communitarianism," in Freeman (ed.), *The Cambridge Companion to Rawls*, pp. 460–87.

38 The importance of this distinction is emphasized by Burton Dreben, in his "On Rawls and Political Liberalism." Dreben has a particular authority insofar as Rawls' intentions are concerned, since he worked with Rawls on the preparation of his last works.

39 However, if one reads section 79 of TJ, where Rawls presents the society at which he aims as "a social union of social unions," one find something very similar. One has the impression, here as elsewhere, that Rawls' "later" ideas are already present in TJ.

40 It is also interesting how the concept of justification is related in PL to that of "overlapping consensus," which I believe supports my view of the latter notion's priority in the general model proposed in the book.

41 I take the term "reasonable agreement" from C. Larmore's "The Moral Basis of Political Liberalism," *Journal of Philosophy* 96 (1999): 599–625.

42 A. J. Simmons makes a claim that is, at least formally, similar to mine, in his "Justification and Legitimacy," *Ethics* 109 (1999): 739–71. Simmons separates the general idea of justifying the state from that of legitimizing its sovereignty by means of a consensus. However, he considers such a separation to be possible only within a Lockean paradigm, for he considers Kantians such as Rawls to be necessarily committed to a continuist position and therefore unable to

separate justification and legitimation. I disagree with this, and in the text below I will attempt to show how a complementary relation between justification and legitimation not only has a textual basis in PL, but also helps in understanding the book.

43 Rawls' direct reference would seem to be H. L. A. Hart's *The Concept of the Law*, 2nd edn. (Oxford: Oxford University Press, 1997).

44 My proposal corresponds partly with A. Buchanan's in his "Political Legitimacy and the Morality of Political Power." However, Buchanan renders justification superfluous by over-extending the meaning of normative legitimation. I believe that the elements of legitimation that are less philosophically loaded must instead be maintained if it is to play the specific role that I am proposing for it.

45 See Simmons, "Justification and Legitimacy."

46 In this respect, Bernard Williams is mistaken in contrasting Rawls' PL, considered as an unsatisfactory moralism, with Hobbes' realism. See Williams, *In Principle Was the Deed: Realism and Moralism in Political Argument* (Princeton, NJ: Princeton University Press, 2005), especially ch. 1.

10 THE STATE OF THE PROBLEM

1 G. Doppelt, "Is Kantian Liberalism Coherent and Defensible?" *Ethics* 99 (1989): 815–51, maintains that Rawls' hypothesis presupposes a Kantian theory of value, being in this way inconsistent with the political conception. See also S. Mendus, "Tragedy, Moral Conflict, and Liberalism," in D. Archard (ed.), *Philosophy and Pluralism* (Cambridge, UK: Cambridge University Press, 1996), pp. 191–201.

2 In the previously mentioned Santa Clara conference of 1995, Rawls said that libertarianism is not liberal. This statement is of course controversial.

3 Daniels says the opposite in *Justice and Justification: Reflective Equilibrium in Theory and Practice* (Cambridge, UK: Cambridge University Press, 1996), especially ch. 8.

4 See M. Galston, "Rawlsian Dualism and the Autonomy of Political Thought," *Columbia Law Review* 94 (6) (1994): 1842–59; C. Larmore, "The Moral Basis of Political Liberalism," *Journal of Philosophy* 96 (1999): 599–625, more moderately maintains that a moral basis – which Larmore himself identifies with respect – must be presupposed.

5 From this point of view, there is not so much difference between this position and M. Walzer's in *Spheres of Justice* (New York, Basic Books, 1983), ch. 2.

6 Rawls gives, in his LHMP, a liberal interpretation of Hegel. However, one should accept that the reduction of the civil society to the state – as it is presented in Hegel's *Philosophy of Right* – can hardly be considered a model for liberal thought.

7 Doppelt, "Is Kantian Liberalism Coherent and Defensible?"

8 This argument is presented by Rawls in his "Fairness to Goodness," *Philosophical Review* 84 (1975): 536–54 (now in CP 267–85, n. 14), with a view to meeting Nagel's objection that we discussed in ch. 5.

9 Here see PL 211, n. 42. Rawls says that R. Dworkin's, "Foundations of Liberal Equality" (in Grethe B. Peterson (ed.), *The Tanner Lectures on Human Values*, vol. XI [Salt Lake City: University of Utah Press, 1990], pp. 3–119) presents a form of comprehensive liberalism. See also S. Macedo, "Liberal Civic Education and Religious Fundamentalism: The Case of God vs. John Rawls," *Ethics* 105 (1995): 468–96.

10 The reconstruction of liberalism through a normative use of reciprocity allows liberals to respond to the republican critique regarding the lack of public ethics in liberalism. I owe this insight to David Rasmussen.

11 F. D'Agostino, *Free Public Reason* (Oxford: Oxford University Press, 1996).

12 Rawls himself defines them as "vague and obscure" (PL 48). It is possible that the way in which the "reasonable" is constructed by Rawls makes it intrinsically difficult for doctrines different from justice as fairness to be considered fully reasonable. Such a worry is voiced by L.Wenar, "Political Liberalism: An Internal Critique," *Ethics* 106 (1) (1995): 32–62.

13 Rawls says: "reasonable can also mean 'judicious,'" LHMP, p. 164.

14 In this sense the reasonable corresponds to the general principle of justification proposed by T. M. Scanlon, "Contractualism and Utilitarianism," in A. Sen and B. Williams (eds.), *Utilitarianism and Beyond* (Cambridge, UK: Cambridge University Press, 1982), pp. 103–28; and then in his *What We Owe Each Other* (Cambridge, MA: Harvard University Press, 1998).

15 The relation between the reasonable–rational and categorical–hypothetical imperatives is in the Rawlsian interpretation of Kant (LHMP 165).

16 Rawls (ibid.) maintains that, in Kant, "vernünftig usually covers being both reasonable and rational" (164), giving to the first meaning a "broad sense," and to the second, a "narrower" one.

17 See ibid. 162–3. Also, for Hegel, "vernünftig" could be better translated into English as "reasonable," even if in his case the institutional side is dominant (see ibid. 332–3).

18 W. M. Sibley, "The Rational versus the Reasonable," *Philosophical Review* 62 (1953): 554–60. Sibley substantially says that from rationality we cannot derive people's ends but just their capacity to realize them.

19 The point is clarified by C. M. Korsgaard, "The Reasons We Can Share," *Social Philosophy & Policy* 10 (1993): 24–51; rptd. in Korsgaard, *Creating the Kingdom of Ends* (Cambridge, UK: Cambridge University Press, 1996), ch. 10. A similar concept is expressed by S. Freeman, "Reason and Agreement in Social Contract Views," *Philosophy & Public Affairs* 19 (1990): 141–7.

20 E. Kelly and L. McPherson, "On Tolerating the Unreasonable," *The Journal of Political Philosophy* 9 (2001): 38–55.

21 See J. Raz, "Facing Diversity: The Case of Epistemic Abstinence," *Philosophy & Public Affairs* 19 (1990): 3–46. Raz criticizes Rawls' PL also for its limited applicability, shallow foundations, and autonomy (from morals). See also J. Raz, "Liberalism, Autonomy and the Politics of Neutral Concern," *Midwest Studies in Philosophy* 7 (1982): 89–120. Both these papers are rptd. in H. S. Richardson and P. Weithman (eds.), *The Philosophy of Rawls*, vol. V: *Reasonable Pluralism* (New York: Garland, 1999), pp. 133–76, 1–32, respectively. We will come back to this in the next chapter, discussing public reason.

22 Scanlon, "Contractualism and Utilitarianism."
23 J. Cohen, "Moral Pluralism and Political Consensus," in D. Copp, J. Hampton, and J. Roemer (eds.), *The Idea of Democracy* (Cambridge, UK: Cambridge University Press, 1993), pp. 270–91.
24 Rawls himself admits this; see PL 240–1.
25 We find a similar thesis in D. Reidy, "Rawls' Wide View of Public Reason: Not Wide Enough," *Res Publica* 6 (2000): 49–72. A defense of Rawls from Reidy is in A. Williams, "The Alleged Incompleteness of Public Reason," *Res Publica* 6 (2000): 199–211.
26 Kelly and McPherson, "On Tolerating the Unreasonable," are in favor of minimal exclusion and wide toleration.
27 M. Friedman, "John Rawls and the Political Coercion of Unreasonable People," in V. Davion and C. Wolf (eds.), *The Idea of a Political Liberalism*, criticizes Rawls because his notion of reasonableness is not politically neutral, being "defined in terms of the politically liberal values he seeks to defend" (28). Friedman finds support also in S. Scheffler, "The Appeal of Political Liberalism," *Ethics* 105 (1994) 20.
28 B. Williams, personal communication.
29 The problem is discussed by A. March in relation to Islam in "Liberal Citizenship and the Search of an Overlapping Consensus: The Case of Muslim Minorities," *Philosophy & Public Affairs* 34 (2006): 373–4. For the Amish and other minorities when confronted with educational problems, see I. MacMullen, *Faith in Schools: Autonomy, Citizenship, and Education in the Liberal State* (Princeton, NJ: Princeton University Press, 2007), in particular ch. 2 entitled "Civic Education and the Autonomy Problem in Political Liberalism." See also Larry Becker and Will Kymlicka (eds.), "Symposium on Citizenship, Democracy, and Education," special issue of *Ethics* 3 (105) (1995).
30 On overlapping consensus and Islamic societies, see March, "Liberal Citizenship and the Search for an Overlapping Consensus." See also A. March, *Islam and Liberal Citizenship. The Case for Overlapping Consensus* (Oxford: Oxford University Press, 2009).
31 See D. Estlund, "The Insularity of the Reasonable: Why Political Liberalism Must Admit the Truth," *Ethics* 108 (2) (1998): 252–73. Estlund says: "My thesis is that political liberalism must assert the truth and not merely the reasonableness of its foundational doctrine" (253).
32 In this camp is Gaus, who accuses Rawls of "justificatory populism" in G. F. Gaus, *Justificatory Liberalism: An Essay on Epistemology and Political Theory* (Oxford: Oxford University Press, 1996), and in "Reasonable Pluralism and the Domain of the Political: How the Weakness of John Rawls' PL Can be Overcome by Justificatory Liberalism," *Inquiry* 42 (1999): 259–84.
33 Some of these critiques have gone farther back to Rawls' note in PL (243), where he seems to affirm that the anti-abortionist comprehensive doctrines are substantially unreasonable. In all honesty, this thesis – *inter alia* – is not presented by Rawls in this note in a theoretically sound manner; it is merely enunciated. In any event, in the subsequent "The Idea of Public Reason Revisited," Rawls has denied having any such strong pretension of exclusion, claiming that he had simply expressed an opinion in the case at issue and had not formulated an argument

(see below, section 11.2). Therefore, it seems advisable to examine this type of criticism independently.

34 See M. Friedman, "John Rawls and the Political Coercion of Unreasonable People," in Davion and Wolf (eds.), *The Idea of a Political Liberalism*, pp. 16–33.

35 This thesis is in P. F. Campos, "Secular Fundamentalism," *Columbia Law Review* 104 (1994): 1914–27.

36 C. Mouffe, "Political Liberalism: Neutrality and the Political," *Ratio Juris* 7 (1994): 314–24.

37 A similar argument is in Jacques Derrida, "Force of the Law: The Mystical Foundation of Authority," in D. Cornell and M. Rosenfeld (eds.), *Deconstruction and the Possibility of Justice* (London: Routledge, 1992), pp. 3–67.

38 This is the argument proposed by Christoph Menke at the Colloquium in Ethics, Politics and Society at LUISS University, Rome, in 2002.

39 Similar objections are raised with respect to political liberalism even by scholars who are well known in the USA, such as the leftist Sheldon Wolin and the post-modernist Stanley Fish. See S. Fish, "Mutual Respect as a Device of Exclusion," in S. Macedo (ed.), *Deliberative Politics: Essays on Democracy and Disagreement* (New York: Oxford University Press), pp. 88–102, and S. S. Wolin, "The Liberal/Democratic Divide: On Rawls's *Political Liberalism*," *Political Theory* 24 (1) (1996): 97–119.

40 James Boettcher, in his Ph.D. dissertation (Boston College), emphasizes this point.

41 See Gaus, *Justificatory Liberalism*. See also his *Contemporary Theories of Liberalism: Public Reason as a Post-Enlightenment Project* (London: Sage, 2003), in particular ch. 7 ("Rawls's Political Liberalism: Public Reason as the Domain of the Political"). See also J. Boettcher, "Rawls and Gaus on the Idea of Public Reason," in D. Shikiar (ed.), *Thinking Fundamentals* (Vienna: IWM, 2000).

42 In this way one can re-examine Rorty's argument on the priority of democracy over philosophy.

43 See S. Maffettone, "Liberalism and its Critique: Is the Therapy Worse than the Disease?" *Philosophy and Social Criticism* 26 (2000): 1–37; P. de Marneffe, "Rawls' Idea of Public Reason," *Pacific Philosophical Quarterly* 75 (1994): 232–50.

44 See an analogous argument in Habermas' criticism of Rawls (ch. 7 above).

45 See M. Sandel, "Review of *Political Liberalism*," *Harvard Law Review* 107 (1994): 1765–94.

46 See J. Raz, "Facing Diversity: The Case of Epistemic Abstinence," and J. Hampton, "Should Political Philosophy be Done without Metaphysics?" *Ethics* 99 (1989): 791–814.

47 Joshua Cohen presented a similar thesis at the Colloquium in Ethics, Politics and Society held at LUISS University, Rome, in 2006: "Truth Matters," published as "Truth and Public Reason," *Philosophy & Public Affairs* 37 (1) (2009): 2–42.

48 Estlund, "The Insularity of the Reasonable: Why Political Liberalism Must Admit the Truth."

49 R. Rorty, "The Priority of Democracy to Philosophy," in *Objectivity, Relativism, and Truth: Philosophical Papers I* (Cambridge, UK: Cambridge University Press, 1991), pp. 175–96. Also Wolin, in "The Liberal/Democratic Divide: On Rawls'

Political Liberalism," seems to misunderstand the democratic side in Rawls' PL, saying that, in Rawls, liberalism prevails over democracy.

50 R. Rorty, "The Priority of Democracy to Philosophy".
51 A recent book on this topic is P. Roberts, *Political Constructivism* (London: Routledge, 2007). On the evolution of Rawls' constructivism, see also O. O'Neill, "Constructivism in Rawls and Kant," in S. Freeman (ed.), *The Cambridge Companion to Rawls* (Cambridge, UK: Cambridge University Press, 2003), pp. 347–67. For the relation between contractualism and constructivism, see O. O'Neill, "Constructivism vs. Contractualism," *Ratio* (16) (2003): 319–31.
52 Rawls – after the Naples conference in 1988 – wrote to me that stability had to be interpreted in this way.
53 I repeat here a comment made by S. Freeman, "Congruence and the Good of Justice," chapter 5 of his *Justice and the Social Contract: Essays in Rawlsian Political Philosophy* (Oxford: Oxford University Press, 2006).
54 I. Kant, "Idea for an Universal History from a Cosmopolitan Point of View" (1784), in *Perpetual Peace and Other Essays* (Indianapolis: Hackett, 1993), pp. 33–4. This is noted by G. Klosko, "Rawls's Argument from Political Stability," *Columbia Law Review* 104 (1994): 1882–97.
55 See Rawls on Kant in his LHMP.
56 See again T. Nagel, "Rawls on Justice," *Philosophical Review* 107 (1973): 220–34; rptd. in N. Daniels (ed.) *Reading Rawls*, 2nd edn. (Stanford, CA: Stanford University Press, 1989), pp. 1–15.
57 Brian Barry maintains in his "John Rawls and the Search for Stability," *Ethics* 105 (4) (July 1995): 874–915, that – if we accept the first argument on stability – we do not need the second and more controversial argument. Barry's argument does not take into consideration the more general value of the second Rawlsian argument on stability.
58 This vision – for Rawls – would have the merit of making Kant's and Hume's ideas of moral motivation less distant; see PL 85, n. 33.
59 This is a delicate point. The thin theory is primarily used to determine the list of primary goods in the original position, which does not include the sense of justice. On this basis, it is not clear how we could go from the thin theory to the congruence argument, as observed by Po Chung Chow in his manuscript, "Rationality, Teleology and Congruence." Brian Barry – in "John Rawls and the Search for Stability" – states that after the original position agents should be fully informed and in such a way that they should leave aside the thin theory.
60 See Rawls in "Fairness to Goodness."

11 OVERLAPPING CONSENSUS AND PUBLIC REASON

1 According to D. Reidy, "Reciprocity and Reasonable Disagreement: From Liberal to Democratic Legitimacy," *Political Studies* 132 (2007): 243–91, liberal legitimacy cannot withstand a careful analysis of reasonable disagreement. He proposes an interesting version of democratic, rather than liberal, legitimacy based on LoP.
2 I owe this formulation to a discussion with Erin Kelly and Tim Scanlon.

3 This worry is expressed in a rigorous way by L. Wenar, "Political Liberalism: An Internal Critique." For Wenar, the very way in which the requisites of the political conception and the reasonable are constructed by Rawls makes it highly improbable for many theories to fit these requisites.

4 Rawls discusses the relation between PL and religious doctrines in the third Section of IPRR. He considers John Finnis and Jacques Maritain as two of the main Catholic thinkers. See J. Finnis, *Natural Law and Natural Rights* (New York: Oxford University Press, 1980), and J. Maritain, *Man and the State* (Chicago: University of Chicago Press, 1951).

5 See M. Sandel, "Review of *Political Liberalism*," *Harvard Law Review* 107 (1994): 1765–94.

6 In IPRR Rawls admits the possibility of "stand-offs" within the theory presented in PL. In particular see section 6.1(b), in which Rawls insists on the inevitability of these stand-offs. On this basis, a judge cannot come to a decision relying solely on a personal comprehensive doctrine.

7 Rawls answered in this way a question posed during the Santa Clara meeting (1995), mentioned earlier. The main reason for exclusion is that libertarians conceive inter-individual relations independently from the basic structure. See also S. Freeman, "Illiberal Libertarians: Why Libertarianism is Not a Liberal View," *Philosophy & Public Affairs* 30 (2) (Spring 2001): 105–51.

8 My argument follows Jeremy Waldron, in "Disagreements about Justice," *Pacific Philosophical Quarterly* 75 (1994): 372–87.

9 See C. Mouffe, "Political Liberalism: Neutrality and the Political," *Ratio Juris* 7 (1994): 314–24.

10 C. Sunstein, "Incompletely Theorized Agreements," *Harvard Law Review* 108 (1995): 1733–72, insists on the limits of any philosophical theory. For Habermas, see this volume, ch. 7.

11 In IPRR, Rawls moves towards deliberative democracy, quoting A. Gutmann and D. Thompson, *Democracy and Disagreement* (Cambridge, UK: Cambridge University Press, 1996), especially ch. 2, "The Sense of Reciprocity." Gutmann and Thompson maintain that "this disposition to seek mutually justifiable reasons expresses the core of the process of deliberation," which is similar to what Rawls says. Rawls, however, states that the deliberative democratic view is part of a comprehensive doctrine, being in such a way outside the framework of PL.

12 See the critical point stressed by J. Bohman, "Public Reason and Cultural Pluralism: Political Liberalism and the Problem of Moral Conflict," *Political Theory* 23 (1995): 253–79.

13 Stuart Hampshire, "Liberalism: The New Twist," *New York Review of Books* (12 August 1993).

14 See J. Cohen, "Pluralism and Proceduralism," *Chicago-Kent Law Review* 69 (1994): 589–618.

15 The sections on public reason have been discussed in particular with Alessandro Ferrara, Giancarlo Bosetti (and the "Dialogues' Foundation), Domenico Melidoro, Stephen Macedo, Claudia Mancina (see her *La laicità al tempo della bioetica*, Bologna: il Mulino, 2009), and Aakash Singh (who organized an interesting conference in Budapest on similar topics).

On the Kantian origins see O. O'Neill, "The Public Use of Reason," *Political*

Theory 14 (1986): 523–51; rptd. as ch. 2 in her *Constructions of Reason: Explorations of Kant's Practical Philosophy* (Cambridge, UK: Cambridge University Press, 1989). The themes of toleration and public reason are present in many Kantian texts: beginning with *The Critique of Pure Reason* and the section entitled "The Discipline of Pure Reason in Respect of its Polemical Employment," trans. Kemp Smith (London: Macmillan, 1929; German edn. in *Kants gesammelte Schriften*, Berlin: De Gruyter, 1902–, A739/B767–A769/B79), and going on to several essays such as "An Answer to the Question: 'What is Enlightenment?'" (1784), "What Is Orientation in Thinking?" (1786), "On the Common Saying 'This May Be True in Theory but It Does Not Apply in Practice'" (1795), and "Perpetual Peace" (1795). All these essays are in H. Reiss (ed.), *Kant's Political Writings*, trans. H. R. Nisbet (Cambridge, UK: Cambridge University Press, 1970), except for "What is Orientation in Thinking?" which is in *Immanuel Kant: Critique of Practical Reason and Other Writings in Moral Philosophy*, trans. L. W. Beck (Chicago: University of Chicago Press, 1949).

16 From this point of view, there is an affinity with Ackerman's position on "conversational constraints" as premises for a liberal dialogue – see B. Ackerman, *Social Justice in the Liberal State* (New Haven: Yale University Press, 1980), and with the idea of legitimation through discourse: see Ackerman, "What is Neutral about Neutrality?" *Ethics* 93 (1983): 372–98, 375. A similar idea is taken up by Larmore in "Political Liberalism," *Political Theory* 18 (3) (1990): 339–60.

17 Here, there is perhaps a (minor) difference between the PL and the IPRR text, because the later text lists – among people usually constrained by public reason – judges, government officers, politicians, and their campaign managers, but not citizens during election times (like in PL). Citizens' electoral discussions take into consideration public reason – also in IPRR – but only within the weaker domain of the "ideal" of public reason.

18 But Rawls also says that voters should stay within the bounds of public reason when they vote (they are treated as public officials).

19 See C. Larmore, "Public Reason," in S. Freeman (ed.), *The Cambridge Companion to Rawls* (Cambridge, UK: Cambridge University Press, 2002), pp. 368–93.

20 See T. M. Scanlon, "Rawls on Justification," in Freeman (ed.), *The Cambridge Companion to Rawls*, pp. 157ff.

21 Here Rawls follows Kant in connecting public reason with communication, and both with freedom and autonomy. See Kant's "What is Enlightenment?"

22 Larmore, "Public Reason."

23 T. M. Scanlon, "Contractualism and Utilitarianism," in A. Sen and B. Williams (eds.), *Utilitarianism and Beyond* (Cambridge, UK: Cambridge University Press, 1982), pp. 103–28; and then in his *What We Owe Each Other* (Cambridge, MA: Harvard University Press, 1998). Something similar is proposed by S. Macedo, "In Defense of Liberal Public Reason: Are Slavery and Abortion Hard Cases?" in R. P. George and C. Wolfe (eds.), *Natural Law and Public Reason* (Washington, DC: Georgetown University Press, 2000), pp. 11–49. Indeed, Macedo seems to believe that public reason is exclusive, but that its constraints are not particularly controversial within liberal democracy.

24 Dworkin, "Rawls and the Law," *Fordham Law Review* 72 (2004): 1387–405,

1397. This interpretation is endorsed by J. Stout, *Democracy and Tradition* (Princeton, NJ: Princeton University Press, 2004), in particular in ch. 3, according to whom Rawls' ideal of public reason is a peculiar form of institutional communitarianism.

25 C. Larmore says in "Public Reason," p. 368: "The conception of justice by which we live is a conception we endorse, not for different reasons we may each discover, and not for reasons we happen to share, but instead for reasons that count for us because we can affirm them together. *The spirit of reciprocity is the foundation of a democratic society*" (emphasis mine).

26 For this kind of argument, see R. Dworkin, *Is Democracy Possible Here? Principles for a New Political Debate* (Princeton, NJ: Princeton University Press, 2006), especially ch. 3.

27 The relation between reasonableness, public reason, and democracy is emphasized by A. S. Laden, "Outline of a Theory of Reasonable Deliberation," *Canadian Journal of Philosophy* 30 (2000): 551–80. In this way, always according to Laden, one could get a better agreement between feminism and liberalism, as he says in "Radical Liberals, Reasonable Feminists: Reason, Power and Objectivity in MacKinnon and Rawls," *The Journal of Political Philosophy* 11 (2003): 133–52. His point seems to be confirmed by Rawls' emphasis on the family in the last part of IPRR.

28 See the discussion of Habermas' criticisms in ch. 7 above.

29 This is roughly what is maintained by P. de Marneffe, "Rawls on Public Reason," *Pacific Philosophical Quarterly* 75 (1994): 232–50. He says that one cannot exclude controversial ideas through public reason.

30 See R. Dworkin, *Is Democracy Possible Here?* More moderately, but on the same anti-reductionist track, see S. Macedo, "Public Reason, Democracy and Political Community," paper presented at the Colloquium on Ethics, Politics, and Society at LUISS University, Rome, in 2008.

31 B. Ackerman, *We the People: Foundations* (Cambridge, MA: Harvard University Press, 1991), vol. I.

32 F. I. Michelman, "Law's Republic," *The Yale Law Journal* 97 (1988): 1493–537.

33 In footnote 32, Rawls says: "Now I believe any reasonable balance of these three values (due respect for human life, the ordered reproduction of society over time, including the family in some form, and finally the equality of women as equal citizens) will give a woman a duly qualified right to decide whether or not to end her pregnancy during the first trimester . . . Any comprehensive doctrine that leads to a balance of political values excluding that duly qualified right in the first trimester is to that extent unreasonable." Critiques of this statement are: D. J. Gifford, "Interpersonal Distrust in the Modified Rawlsian Society," *SMU Law Review* 48 (1994): 218–19; K. Greenawalt, "On Public Reason," *Chicago-Kent Law Review* 69 (1994): 669–89, and "Some Problems with Public Reason in John Rawls' Political Liberalism," *Loyola L. A. L. Review* 28 (1995): 1303–17, especially n. 54; M. Sandel, "Review of *Political Liberalism*," p. 1778, n. 40, where Sandel writes: "But if the Catholic Church is right about the moral status of the foetus, if abortion is tantamount to murder, then it is not clear why the political values of toleration and women's equality, important though they are, should prevail"; P. F. Campos, "Secular Fundamentalism," *Columbia Law Review* 104 (1994): 1826,

n. 24; L. E. Mitchell, "Trust and the Overlapping Consensus," *Columbia Law Review* 94 (1994): 1934, n. 34.

34 The relevance here of the "burdens of judgment" has been suggested to me by A. Ferrara.

35 Rawls himself emphasizes this possibility. After having signed a brief to the Supreme Court as an "amicus curiae" for assisted suicide (R. Dworkin, T. Nagel, R. Nozick, J. Rawls, T. Scanlon, and J. J. Thomson, "Assisted Suicide: The Philosopher's Brief," *The New York Review of Books*, 27 March 1997), he recognized that the decision of the Court against his own proposal was based on a "good" argument (see Rawls, "*Commonweal* Interview with John Rawls," CP 616–18).

36 On this subject, see F. I. Michelman, "On Regulating Practices with Theories Drawn from Them: A Case of Justice as Fairness," in I. Shapiro and J. Wagner DeCew (eds.), *Nomos XXXVII: Theory and Practice* (New York: New York University Press, 1995), pp. 325–36, and "Rawls on Constitutionalism and Constitutional Law," in Freeman (ed.), *The Cambridge Companion to Rawls*, pp. 396–425.

37 I owe this suggestion to Michael Walzer, who is anyway much more critical than me on this point.

38 See S. Freeman, "Deliberative Democracy. A Sympathetic Comment," *Philosophy & Public Affairs* 30 (2002): 371–418.

39 D. A. J. Richards, "Public Reason and Abolitionist Dissent," *Chicago-Kent Law Review* 69 (1994): 787–842, stressing the role of public reason maintains that religious persons were not always anti-abolitionist.

40 Of course the terms "continuist" and "discontinuist" here refer to the relation between ethics and politics, having nothing to do with the question of continuity between Rawls1 and Rawls 2 (see chapter 1 above). For the present distinction, see R. Dworkin, *Sovereign Virtue: The Theory and Practice of Equality* (Cambridge, MA: Harvard University Press, 2002).

41 In some ways, it is evident that there cannot be full tolerance, and that assimilation is in part inescapable in any kind of political regime. See S. Macedo, "Liberal Civic Education and Religious Fundamentalism: The Case of God vs. John Rawls," *Ethics* 105 (1995): 468–96.

42 See ch. 10.

43 See section 7.3.

44 R. Rorty, "The Priority of Democracy to Philosophy," in *Objectivity, Relativism, and Truth: Philosophical Papers I* (Cambridge, UK: Cambridge University Press, 1991), pp. 175–96; S. Fish, "Mutual Respect as a Device of Exclusion," in S. Macedo (ed.), *Deliberative Politics: Essays on Democracy and Disagreement* (New York: Oxford University Press, 1999), pp. 88–102.

45 C. Sunstein, "Incompletely Theorized Agreements in Constitutional Law," *Social Research* 74 (2007): 1–24.

46 See S. Macedo, "Liberal Civic Education and Religious Fundamentalism: The Case of God v. John Rawls.

47 R. Audi, "The Place of Religious Argument in a Free and Democratic Society," *San Diego Law Review* 30 (1993): 677–702, quoted in IPRR. For Rawls, secular reason risks being taken as a comprehensive doctrine.

48 This distinction is maintained by, among others, P. J. Weithman, "Introduction,"

to Weithman (ed.), *Religion and Contemporary Liberalism* (South Bend, IN: University of Notre Dame Press, 1997).

49 Campos, "Secular Fundamentalism," pp. 1814–27.

50 Rawls exposes his own relation to religion in the frank and sometimes touching paper "On My Religion," now in his BIMSF. Among other things, Rawls mentions three events, two of them linked to his own military experience and the third being the Holocaust, which made his faith more problematic.

51 A significant debate on this topic is in R. Audi and N. Wolterstorff, *Religion in the Public Sphere* (Lanham, MD: Rowman & Littlefield, 1997). An interesting defense of Rawls' position from a Catholic point of view is L. Griffin, "Good Catholics Should be Rawlsian Liberals," *Southern California Interdisciplinary Law Journal* 5 (1997): 297–373.

52 Weithman, "Introduction," p. 16.

53 See J. L. A. Garcia, "Liberal Theory, Human Freedom and the Politics of Sexual Morality," in Weithman (ed.), *Religion and Contemporary Liberalism*, pp. 218–52.

54 A brilliant introduction to this debate can be found in J. Waldron, "Religious Contributions in Public Deliberation," *San Diego Law Review* 30 (1993): 817–48. Waldron here starts from the National Conference of Catholic Bishops and its Pastoral Letter, *Economic Justice for All*, of 1986.

55 See the "Introduction" to Weithman (ed.), *Religion and Contemporary Liberalism*.

56 C. J. Eberle, *Religious Conviction in Liberal Politics* (Cambridge, UK: Cambridge University Press, 2002), argues for a direct use of religious arguments in public life.

57 A similar kind of argument is used by J. Habermas, "Religion in the Public Sphere," in his *Between Naturalism and Religion* (Cambridge, UK: Polity Press, 2008). For Habermas' criticism of Rawls, see this volume, ch. 7.

58 See Larmore, "Political Liberalism."

59 This thesis is put forward by, among others, D. A. Dombrowski, *Rawls and Religion: The Case for Political Liberalism* (New York: SUNY Press, 2001), in particular pp. 41ff.

60 The expression is Stout's in *Democracy and Tradition*, p. 70.

61 Ibid. pp. 71–2.

62 In footnote 117 of PL Rawls quotes the Catholic theologian John Courtney Murray, saying that Murray's opinions on the state and religion are compatible with his own in PL. As a matter of fact, Rawls seems right and we can observe how much Catholic thought became distanced from Murray in his later years. See J. C. Murray, *The Problem of Religious Freedom* (Westminster: The Newman Press, 1965).

63 See Eberle, *Religious Conviction in Liberal Politics*, pp. 5–7.

64 On the distinction, see ibid., and D. Hollenbach, "Active Churches: Some Empirical Prolegomena to a Normative Approach," in Weithman (ed.), *Religion and Contemporary Liberalism*, pp. 291–306.

65 The inclusive interpretation is later favored by Rawls (as one can see by reading IPRR).

66 L. B. Solum, "Inclusive Public Reason," *Pacific Philosophical Quarterly* 75 (1994): 217–31.

67 The normativity of public reason (and of the reasonable) is defended by A. Ferrara, *The Force of the Example* (New York: Columbia University Press, 2008), in particular ch. 3. According to Ferrara, however, this normativity comes from a shared ground, which seems not to be available in cases like abortion.

68 Contra the undecidability thesis, see Freeman, in his *Justice and Social Contract: Essays on Rawlsian Political Philosophy* (New York: Oxford University Press, 2007), pp. 246–8.

69 K. Greenawalt, *Private Consciences and Public Reasons* (New York: Oxford University Press, 1995).

70 A defense of public reason against the claims of comprehensive doctrines is in A. Williams, "The Alleged Incompleteness of Public Reason," *Res Publica* 6 (2000): 199–211.

71 This is a topic selected by Nagel, "Rawls and Liberalism," in Freeman (ed.), *The Cambridge Companion to Rawls*, pp. 62–85, and by M. Sandel, *Public Philosophy: Essays on Morality in Politics* (Cambridge, MA: Harvard University Press, 2005), with opposite results. Here, I am on Nagel's side.

12 THE LAW OF PEOPLES

1 For the references in TJ to the possibility of extending the basic model of justice to the international realm, see the discussion of conscientious objection in section 58 (337–9; rev. edn. 331–3). Regarding the course on "Problems of the War," in his biographical profile of Rawls, published in Richardson and Weithman (eds.), *The Philosophy of Rawls*, Vol I: *Development and Main Outlines of Rawls's Theory of Justice* (New York: Garland, 1999), pp. 1–15, Thomas Pogge tells of how the course was interrupted by a student strike, and never completed. Notably, in the preface to LoP, Rawls himself indicates that he considered developing his views on international questions from the late 1980s onwards.

2 See Rawls, PL (1993). As Rawls puts it in the introduction to LoP: "Here the idea of political justice is the same as that discussed by political liberalism, out of which the Law of Peoples is developed" (7).

3 This point has been suggested by E. Kollar.

4 As convincingly argued by L. Wenar, "Why Rawls is Not a Cosmopolitan Egalitarian," in R. Martin and D. Reidy (eds.), *Rawls' Law of Peoples: A Realistic Utopia* (New York: Wiley-Blackwell, 2006), pp. 95–114.

5 The absence of this egalitarianism in LoP is noted by, among others, Thomas Pogge, "An Egalitarian Law of Peoples," *Philosophy & Public Affairs* 23 (3) (Summer 1994): 195–224, and Leif Wenar, "Contractualism and Global Economic Justice," *Metaphilosophy* 32 (1) (2001): 79–95.

6 On this, see A. Abizadeh, "Cooperation, Pervasive Impact, and Coercion: On the Scope (not Site) of Distributive Justice," *Philosophy & Public Affairs* 35 (2007): 318–58.

7 The difficulty even of conceiving justice in international relations is stressed by H. Bull, *The Anarchical Society* (New York: Columbia University Press, 1977), in particular ch. 4.

8 For a discussion of the two opposing traditions, see D. Boucher, *Political Theories*

of International Relations from Thucydides to the Present (New York: Oxford University Press, 1998).

9 Notably, however, Charles Beitz maintains that Rawls' approach is not comparable to the *jus gentium*, because the latter is universal, while the former is not. See Beitz, "Rawls' Law of Peoples," *Ethics* 110 (July 2000): 669–96.

10 The terms "utopianism" and "realism" were made famous in the study of international relations by E. H. Carr's book, *The Twenty Years Crisis: 1919–1939 – An Introduction to International Relations* (London: Macmillan, 1939). Of course, Rawls' use of the terms differs from Carr's, whose main aim in the book was to attack internationalist liberalism.

11 The term "social ontology" is used by P. Pettit, in his "Rawls' Peoples," in Martin and Reidy (eds.), *Rawls's Law of Peoples: A Realistic Utopia?*, pp. 38–56.

12 This choice may be motivated by the idea that a normative theory ought to be directed at plausible agents, which in this case would not be individuals, but peoples. Onora O'Neill defends this idea in her *Faces of Hunger* (London: Allen & Unwin, 1986), and, more clearly, in her "Agents of Justice," *Metaphilosophy* 32 (2001): 180–95.

13 See Wenar, "Why Rawls is Not a Cosmopolitan Egalitarian."

14 Allen Buchanan has argued that peoples in Rawls' sense are states that lack the rights of full sovereignty and cannot claim a right to non-interference from other states. See his "Rawls's Law of Peoples: Rules for a Vanished Westphalian World," *Ethics* 110 (4) (July 2000): 697–721.

15 In her "Agents of Justice," O'Neill claims that Rawls here confuses the realist political conception of the state with the concept of the state in general, and that this confusion leads him to mistakenly insist on the distinction between states and peoples.

16 This belief is widely shared. See, for instance, Gary Chartier, "Peoples or Persons? Revising Rawls on Global Justice," *Boston College Law Review* 27 (2004): 1–98.

17 See Buchanan, "Rawls's Law of Peoples: Rules for a Vanished Westphalian World."

18 Kok-chor Tan makes this claim, in his "Liberal Toleration in Rawls' Law of Peoples," *Ethics* 108 (1998): 276–95.

19 See LHPP 191–248.

20 See M. Doyle, *Ways of War and Peace* (New York: Norton, 1997), and B. Russett, *Grasping the Democratic Peace* (Princeton, NJ: Princeton University Press, 1993).

21 As Kok-chor Tan claims in his "Liberal Toleration," this raises the further problem that, unlike those that coexist in a liberal democracy, the doctrines maintained by decent hierarchical regimes may be unreasonable ones.

22 On Rawls' claim that "cultural pluralism is a permanent fact of life," see Beitz, "Rawls' Law of Peoples," p. 671.

23 This aspect of Rawls' theory is applauded by Chris Brown not only for its pluralism, but also for its innovative classificatory implications for studies of international politics. See Brown, "The Construction of a Realistic Utopia: John Rawls and International Political Theory." *Review of International Studies* 28 (2003): 5–21.

24 Regarding the toleration of a hierarchical society, at a recent conference in Beijing

Daniel Bell argued that equality might be favored by the traditional hierarchy of a culture such as that of China. Regarding the theoretical and methodological question, see Kok-chor Tan, "The Problem of Decent Peoples," in Martin and Reidy (eds.), *Rawls's Law of Peoples: A Realistic Utopia?*, pp. 76–94.

25 One might perhaps claim that the only way for liberal Tunisians to deserve our full support would be for them to impose their views themselves, either by force or by becoming the majority, and that perhaps no stronger claim can be justified if, with Rawls, one takes peoples, rather than individuals, as the subjects of international relations. My thanks to Pietro Maffettone for this suggestion.

26 In *Toleration, Diversity and Global Justice* (University Park, PA: Penn State University Press, 2000), Kok-chor Tan distinguishes ethical from political tolerance, and claims that the former is compatible with liberalism, while the latter is not.

27 It may be that the two lists are intended to serve different functions, such that the second identifies the rights that a people must respect to qualify as "decent," while the first applies to Rawls' non-ideal theory regarding the relations of liberal and decent states with states that are neither liberal nor decent.

28 This aspect is emphasized by Thomas Scanlon in his "Human Rights as a Neutral Concern," in P. Brown and D. MacLean (eds.), *Human Rights and U. S. Foreign Policy* (Lexington, MA: Lexington Books, 1979), pp. 83–92, an article which Rawls cites in this regard.

29 See Beitz, "Rawls' Law of Peoples," pp. 683ff.

30 This is argued by, among others, David Fagelson, in his "Two Concepts of Sovereignty," *International Politics* 38 (2001): 499–514.

31 Samuel Freeman replies in this manner, in his "*The Law of Peoples*, Social Cooperation, Human Rights, and Distributive Justice," *Social Philosophy and Policy* 23 (2006): 29–68.

32 Ibid.

33 Doug Paletta observed that this does not criticize Freeman's account: if religious freedom is indeed necessary, it should be on the list; if it is not, then the interest of allowing as many decent societies as possible into the group seems to give *prima facie* reason to exclude it.

34 See Michael Walzer, *Just and Unjust Wars: A Moral Argument with Historical Illustrations* (New York: Basic Books, 1977; 3rd edn., 2000).

35 See the introduction to Martin and Reidy (eds.), *Rawls's Law of Peoples: A Realistic Utopia?*

36 See Beitz, "Rawls' Law of Peoples," and Thomas Pogge, *World Poverty and Human Rights* (Cambridge and Oxford: Polity Press [in association with Blackwell], 2002). Also notable is the title of Pogge's contribution in Reidy and Martin (eds.), *Rawls's Law of Peoples: A Realistic Utopia?*: namely, "Do Rawls's Two Theories of Justice Fit Together?"

37 In *World Poverty and Human Rights*, p. 95, for instance, Pogge writes: "This discrepancy in moral assessment looks arbitrary. Why should our moral duty, constraining what economic order we may impose upon one another, be so different in the two cases?"

38 Of course, there remains the problem of why the basic structure should be limited to the nation-state. This problem is discussed particularly well by A. J. Julius, in

his "Basic Structure and the Value of Equality," *Philosophy & Public Affairs* 31 (2003): 321–55.

39 It would perhaps be possible to provide such a demonstration in the case of environmental damage, in which one can demonstrate that states that leave an excessive ecological footprint damage states that consume less energy.

40 See Beitz, "Rawls' Law of Peoples," p. 677.

41 Ibid. p. 688.

42 See Thomas Nagel, "The Problem of Global Justice," *Philosophy & Public Affairs* 33 (2005): 113–47, and Samuel Freeman, "Distributive Justice and *The Law of Peoples*," in Martin and Reidy (eds.), *Rawls's Law of Peoples: A Realistic Utopia?* pp. 243–60.

43 For Andrea Sangiovanni, the reason for privileging one's fellow citizens, as well as mere residents of a territory, lies instead in reciprocity and in the provision of basic public goods. See his "Global Justice, Reciprocity and the State," *Philosophy & Public Affairs* 35 (2007): 3–39. The idea of the citizens as both subjects and creators of the law is taken by Rawls from Rousseau, see LHPP.

44 Freeman, "*The Law of Peoples*, Social Cooperation, Human Rights, and Distributive Justice," in Freeman, *Justice and the Social Contract*, pp. 259–95.

45 This view should not be confused with a communitarian denial of the existence of a super-national community, such as that expressed by David Miller, "The Ethical Significance of Nationality," *Ethics* 98 (1988): 647–62, and by Michael Walzer. For Walzer, it is a shared life that determines the requirements of justice, and not vice versa. As he writes in *Just and Unjust Wars*, p. 54: "shared experiences and cooperative activity of many different kinds shape a common life." Miller adds certain elements of political autonomy to Walzer's shared life, in his "The Ethical Significance of Nationality," p. 648.

46 For the scope of distributive justice in a constructivist account, see D. Moellendorf, "Constructing Law of Peoples," *Pacific Philosophical Quarterly* 77 (1996): 132–54; rptd. in Chandran Kukathas (ed.), *John Rawls: Critical Assessments of Leading Political Philosophers* (London: Routledge, 2002), pp. 316–37.

47 D. Held, "Cosmopolitanism and Globalization," *Logos* 1 (2002), p. 11.

48 Even leaving aside the debate over so-called "luck egalitarianism," there remains the important problem of clarifying the grounds for any "dis-analogy" between the national and the global. On this, see Simon Caney, "Cosmopolitan Justice and Equalizing Opportunities," *Metaphilosophy* 32 (2001): 113–34.

49 In my understanding of this distinction, I follow Julius, "Basic Structure and the Value of Equality."

50 This claim is also made by Freeman, in his "Distributive Justice and *The Law of Peoples*," p. 246.

51 This criticism is also made by Andrew Kuper, who further claims that the original position ought to be thoroughly globalized. See his "Rawlsian Global Justice," *Political Theory* 28 (2000): 640–74.

52 See J. Cohen and C. Sabel, "Extra Rempublicam Nulla Justitia?" *Philosophy & Public Affairs* 34 (2006): 147–75.

53 See A. J. Julius, "Nagel's Atlas," *Philosophy & Public Affairs* 34 (2006): 176–92.

54 In "The Problem of Global Justice," pp. 140–3, Nagel expresses skepticism towards the possibility of a gradualist approach.

362 Notes to pp. 315–18

55 As Pietro Maffettone has pointed out to me in conversation, the binary structure of the argument is in tension with, among other things, Rawls' recognition of five kinds of peoples, societies, and states in the international arena, as discussed above.

56 The sufficientarian position has recently become rather popular in political philosophy. The fundamental idea is that, rather than promoting equality, the morally important thing is simply that each person has enough. See Harry Frankfurt, "Equality as a Moral Ideal," in his *The Importance of What We Care about* (Cambridge, UK: Cambridge University Press, 1988). The sufficientarian position often coincides with so-called "prioritarianism." On this, see R. Arneson, "Luck Egalitarianism and Prioritarianism," *Ethics* 110 (2000): 339–49; R. Crisp, "Equality, Priority and Compassion," *Ethics* 113 (2003): 745–68; L. Temkin, *Inequality* (Oxford: Oxford University Press, 2003); and Y. Benbaji, "The Doctrine of Sufficiency: A Defense," *Utilitas* 17 (2005): 310–32. One might perhaps also include Thomas Scanlon's "Rescue Principle" within this ambit. See his *What We Owe to Each Other* (Cambridge, MA: Harvard University Press, 1998), pp. 224–5.

57 The relation between the scope of global justice and the need to take into consideration some threshold under which life becomes unbearable is discussed by T. Nagel, "Poverty and Food. Why Charity is not Enough," in P. G. Brown and H. Shue (eds.), *Food Policy: The Responsibility of the United States in Life and Death Choices* (New York: The Free Press, 1977), pp. 54–62; R. E. Goodin, "What is so Special about our Fellow Countrymen?" *Ethics* 98 (1988): 663–86; M. C. Nussbaum, *Women and Human Development: The Capability Approach* (Cambridge, UK: Cambridge University Press, 2000).

58 Wenar, "Contractualism and Global Economic Justice." See also S. Scheffler, "Relationships and Responsibilities," *Philosophy & Public Affairs* 26 (1997): 189–209.

59 My approach has only a limited overlap with J. Waldron, "Special Ties and Natural Duties," *Philosophy & Public Affairs* 22 (1993): 3–30.

60 It would seem overly demanding, for instance, to apply the principle of equality of opportunity, as Simon Caney proposes in his "Cosmopolitan Justice and Equalizing Opportunities," not to mention radical utilitarian demands such as those made by Peter Singer in his famous "Famine, Affluence and Morality," *Philosophy & Public Affairs* 1 (1972): 229–43.

61 Jonathan Glover has reminded me that one could claim that human rights are of a non-associative nature, since they refer primarily to people. However, I would suggest that their legal nature and the related functions of states and international organizations mean that they can also be treated in an associative manner.

62 According to John Gray in *Enlightenment's Wake: Politics and Culture at the Close of the Modern Age* (London: Routledge, 1995), and Barry Hindness, in "Neo-Liberal Citizenship," *Citizenship Studies* 6 (2002): 127–43, Rawls imposes a kind of liberal universalism. The difficulty in maintaining a balance between universalism and relativism in LoP is emphasized particularly well by Cecile Fabre and David Miller, in their "Justice and Culture: Rawls, Sen, Nussbaum and O'Neill," *Political Studies Review* 1 (2003): 4–17.

REFERENCES

WORKS BY RAWLS

—— Index for Walter Kaufmann, *Nietzsche: Philosopher, Psychologist and Anti-Christ*, Princeton: Princeton University Press, 1950.

—— *A Study on the Grounds of Ethical Knowledge: Considered with Reference to Judgments on the Moral Worth of Character*, Ph.D. dissertation, Princeton University, 1950, *Dissertation Abstracts* 15 (1955), pp. 608–9.

—— "Outline of a Decision Procedure for Ethics," *Philosophical Review* 60 (1951), pp. 177–97.

—— "Review of Stephen Toulmin, *An Examination of the Place of Reason in Ethics*," *Philosophical Review* 60 (1951), pp. 572–80.

—— "Review of Axel Hägerström, 'Inquiries into the Nature of Law and Morals,'" *Mind* 64 (1955), pp. 421–2.

—— "Two Concepts of Rule," *Philosophical Review* 64 (1955), pp. 3–32.

—— "Justice as Fairness," *Journal of Philosophy* 54 (1957), pp. 653–62. Expanded version in *Philosophical Review* 67 (1958), pp. 164–94.

—— "Review of Raymond Klibansky (ed.), *Philosophy in Mid-Century: A Survey*," *Philosophical Review* 70 (1961), pp. 131–2.

—— "Constitutional Liberty and the Concept of Justice," *Nomos VI: Justice*, ed. C. Freidrich and John W. Chapman, New York: Atherton, 1963, pp. 98–125.

—— "The Sense of Justice," *Philosophical Review* 72 (1963), pp. 281–305.

—— "Legal Obligation and the Duty of Fair Play," *Law and Philosophy*, ed. Sidney Hook, New York: New York University Press, 1964, pp. 3–18.

—— "Review of Richard Brandt (ed.), *Social Justice*," *Philosophical Review* 74 (1965), pp. 406–9.

—— "Distributive Justice," *Philosophy, Politics, and Society*, ed. P. Laslett and W. G. Runciman, 3rd series, Oxford: Basil Blackwell, 1967, pp. 58–82. Revised version together with *Distributive Justice: Some Addenda* in *Economic Justice*, ed. E. Phelps, London: Penguin Books, 1973, pp. 319–62.

—— "Distributive Justice: Some Addenda," *Natural Law Forum* 13 (1968), pp. 51–71.

—— "The Justification of Civil Disobedience," *Civil Disobedience*, ed. Hugo Bedau, New York: Pegasus, 1969, pp. 240–55.

—— "Justice as Reciprocity" (originally written in 1958), *Mill: Text with Critical Essays*, ed. Samuel Gorovitz, Indianapolis: Bobbs-Merrill, 1971, pp. 242–68.

—— *A Theory of Justice*, Cambridge, MA: Harvard University Press, 1971. Revised version, *A Theory of Justice*, Cambridge, MA: Harvard University Press, 1999.

—— "Reply to Lyons and Teitelman," *Journal of Philosophy* 69 (1972), pp. 556–7.

—— "Reply to Alexander and Musgrave," *Quarterly Journal of Economics* 88 (1974), pp. 633–55.

—— "Some Reasons for the Maximin Criterion," *American Economic Review* 64 (1974), pp. 141–6.

—— "The Independence of Moral Theory," *Proceedings and Addresses of the American Philosophical Association* 48 (1975), pp. 5–22.

—— "A Kantian Conception of Equality," *Cambridge Review* 96 (1975), pp. 94–9. Republished with the title "A Well-Ordered Society," in *Philosophy, Politics, and Society*, 5th series, ed. P. Laslett and J. Fishkin, Oxford: Blackwell, 1979, pp. 6–20.

—— "Fairness to Goodness," *Philosophical Review* 84 (1975), pp. 536–54.

—— "The Basic Structure as Subject," *American Philosophical Quarterly* 14 (1977), pp. 159–65. Revised version in *Values and Morals: Essays in Honor of William Frankena, Charles Stevenson, and Richard B. Brandt*, ed. A. Goldman and J. Kim Dordrecht, Holland: Reidel, 1978, pp. 47–71.

—— "Kantian Constructivism in Moral Theory: The Dewey Lectures 1980," *Journal of Philosophy* 77 (1980), pp. 515–72.

—— Preface to Henry Sidgwick, *The Methods of Ethics*, 7th edn., Indianapolis: Hackett Publishing Company, 1981.

—— "Social Unity and Primary Goods," *Utilitarianism and Beyond*, ed. Amartya Sen and Bernard Williams, Cambridge, UK: Cambridge University Press, 1982, pp. 159–85.

—— "The Basic Liberties and Their Priority," *Tanner Lectures on Human Values*, vol. III, ed. S. McMurrin, Salt Lake City: University of Utah Press, 1982, pp. 3–87.

—— "Justice as Fairness: Political not Metaphysical," *Philosophy & Public Affairs* 14 (1985), pp. 223–51.

—— "The Idea of Overlapping Consensus," *Oxford Journal for Legal Studies* 7 (1987), pp. 1–25.

—— "The Priority of Right and Ideas of the Good," *Philosophy & Public Affairs* 17 (1988), pp. 251–76.

—— "The Domain of the Political and Overlapping Consensus," *New York University Law Review* 64 (1989), pp. 233–55.

—— "Themes in Kant's Moral Philosophy," *Kant's Transcendental Deductions*, ed. E. Forster, Stanford: Stanford University Press, 1989.

—— "Roderick Firth: His Life and Work," *Philosophy and Phenomenological Research* 51 (1991), pp. 109–18.

—— *Political Liberalism*, New York: Columbia University Press, 1993. The 1996 edition has a new introduction and a "Reply to Habermas."

—— "The Law of Peoples," *On Human Rights: The Oxford Amnesty Lectures, 1993*, ed. Steven Shute and Susan Hurley, New York: Basic Books, 1993, pp. 41–82.

—— "Fifty Years after Hiroshima," *Dissent* (1995), pp. 323–7.

—— "Reply to Habermas," *Journal of Philosophy* 92 (1995), pp. 132–80.

—— "The Idea of Public Reason Revisited," *University of Chicago Law Review* 64 (1997), pp. 765–807.

—— *Collected Papers*, ed. Samuel Freeman, Cambridge, MA: Harvard University Press, 1999.

—— *The Law of Peoples*, Cambridge, MA: Harvard University Press, 1999.

—— "Afterword: A Reminiscence," *Future Pasts: Perspectives on the Place of the Analytic Tradition in Twentieth-Century Philosophy*, ed. Juliet Floyd and Sanford Shieh, New York: Oxford University Press, 2000, pp. 417–30.

—— *Lectures on the History of Moral Philosophy*, ed. Barbara Herman, Cambridge, MA: Harvard University Press, 2000.

—— *Justice as Fairness: A Restatement*, ed. Erin Kelley, Cambridge, MA: Harvard University Press, 2001.

—— *Lectures on the History of Political Philosophy*, ed. Samuel Freeman, Cambridge, MA: Harvard University Press, 2008.

—— *A Brief Inquiry into the Meaning of Sin & Faith*, ed. Thomas Nagel, Cambridge MA; Harvard University Press, 2009.

INTRODUCTION

Alejandro, R., *The Limits of Rawlsian Justice*, Baltimore and London: Johns Hopkins University Press, 1998.

Audard, C., *John Rawls*, Montreal: McGill-Queen's University Press, 2007.

Barry, B., *The Liberal Theory of Justice*, Oxford: Oxford University Press, 1972.

Bidet, J., *John Rawls et la théorie de la justice*, Paris: Presses Universitaires de France, 1995.

Blocker H. G. and E. H. Smith (eds.), *John Rawls's Theory of Social Justice*, Athens: Ohio University Press, 1980.

Daniels, N. (ed.), *Reading Rawls: Critical Studies on Rawls's A Theory of Justice*, New York: Basic Books, 1975.

—— *Justice and Justification*, Cambridge, UK: Cambridge University Press, 1996.

Freeman, S. (ed.), *The Cambridge Companion to Rawls*, Cambridge, UK: Cambridge University Press, 2003.

—— *Rawls*, London: Routledge, 2007.

Graham, P., *Rawls*, Oxford: Oneworld, 2007.

Kukathas, C. and P. Pettit, *Rawls: A Theory of Justice and its Critics*, Stanford: Stanford University Press, 1990.

Pogge, T., *John Rawls*, Munich: C. H. Beck, 1994; English trans., *John Rawls: His Life and Theory of Justice*, ed. Michelle Kosch, New York: Oxford University Press, 2007.

Richardson, H. S. and P. Weithman (eds.), *The Philosophy of Rawls: A Collection of Essays*, 5 vols., New York: Garland, 1999.

—— vol. I: *Development and Main Outlines of Rawls's Theory of Justice*

—— vol. II: *The Two Principles and Their Justification*

—— vol. III: *Opponents and Implications of A Theory of Justice*

—— vol. IV: *Moral Psychology and Community*

—— vol. V: *Reasonable Pluralism*

Talisse, R. B., *On Rawls*, Belmont, Calif.: Wadsworth, 2001.

Wellbank, J. H., S. Dennis, and D. T. Mason, *John Rawls and His Critics: An Annotated Bibliography*, New York: Garland, 1982.

Wolff, R. P., *Understanding Rawls*, Princeton: Princeton University Press, 1977.

The Theory

Arneson, R., "Primary Goods Reconsidered," *Nous* 24 (3) (1990), pp. 429–54.

Arrow, K., "Some Ordinalist–Utilitarian Notes on Rawls's Theory of Justice," *Journal of Philosophy* 70 (9) (1973), pp. 245–63.

Baier, K., "Justice and the Aims of Political Philosophy," *Ethics* 99 (4) (1989), pp. 771–90.

Barry, B., "Liberalism and Want-Satisfaction: A Critique of John Rawls," *Political Theory* 1 (1973), pp. 134–53.

Bedau, H. A., "Social Justice and Social Institutions," *Midwest Studies in Philosophy* 3 (1978), pp. 159–75.

Binmore, K., "Naturalizing Harsanyi and Rawls," *Justice, Political Liberalism, and Utilitarianism*, ed. M. Salles and J. Weymark, Cambridge, UK: Cambridge University Press, 1988.

Bowie, N., "Some Comments on Rawls's Theory of Justice," *Social Theory and Practice* 3 (1974), pp. 65–74.

Braybrooke, D., "Utilitarianism with a Difference: Rawls's Position in Ethics," *Canadian Journal of Philosophy* 3 (2) (1973), pp. 303–31.

Brock, D., "John Rawls's *Theory of Justice*," *University of Chicago Law Review* 40 (3) (1973), pp. 486–99.

Buchanan, A., "Revisability and Rational Choice," *Canadian Journal of Philosophy* 5 (1975), pp. 395–408.

—— "A Critical Introduction to Rawls's *Theory of Justice*," *John Rawls's Theory of Social Justice*, ed. H. G. Blocker and E. H. Smith, Athens: Ohio University Press, 1980, pp. 5–41.

Chapman, J., "Rawls's *Theory of Justice*," *The American Political Science Review* 69 (1975), pp. 588–93.

Cohen, J., "Democratic Equality," *Ethics* 99 (4) (1989), pp. 727–51.

Cohen, Marshall, "The Social Contract Explained and Defended," *New York Times Book Review*, July 16, 1972, p. 18.

Crocker, L., "Equality, Solidarity, and Rawls's Maximin," *Philosophy & Public Affairs* 6 (1977), pp. 262–6.

Dworkin, G., "Non-Neutral Principles," *Journal of Philosophy* 71 (1974), pp. 491–506.

Dworkin, R., "The Original Position," *University of Chicago Law Review* 40 (1973), pp. 500–33.

Feinberg, J., "Rawls and Intuitionism," *Reading Rawls: Critical Studies on Rawls's A Theory of Justice*, ed. N. Daniels, New York: Basic Books, 1975.

Fiskin, J., "Justice and Rationality: Some Objections to the Central Argument in Rawls's Theory," *The American Political Science Review* 69 (2) (1975), pp. 618– .

Fried, C., "Review of Rawls's *A Theory of Justice*," *Harvard Law Review* 85 (1971–2), pp. 169ff.

Galston, W., "Defending Liberalism," *American Political Science Review* 76 (1982), pp. 621–9.

Gauthier, D., "Justice and Natural Endowment: Toward a Critique of Rawls's Ideological Framework," *Social Theory and Practice* 3 (1974), pp. 3–26.

—— "Fairness and Cores: A Comment on Laden," *Philosophy & Public Affairs* 22 (1993), pp. 44–7.

Gibson, M., "Rationality," *Philosophy & Public Affairs* 6 (1977), pp. 193–225.

Gutmann, A., "The Central Role of Rawls's Theory," *Dissent* 36 (1989), pp. 338–42.

Haksar, Vinit, "Rawls's *Theory of Justice*," *Analysis* 32 (1972), pp. 149–53.

—— "Rawls and Gandhi on Civil Disobedience," *Inquiry* 19 (1976), pp. 151–92.

Hampshire, S., "A New Philosophy of the Just Society," *The New York Review of Books*, February 24, 1972, pp. 34–9.

Hare, R. M., "Rawls's *Theory of Justice*," *Philosophical Quarterly* 23 (1973), pp. 144–55.

Harsanyi, J., "Can the Maximin Principle Serve as a Basis for Morality? A Critique of John Rawls's Theory," *American Political Science Review* 69 (1975), pp. 594–606.

Held, V., "On Rawls and Self-Interest," *Midwest Studies in Philosophy* 1 (1976), pp. 57–60.

Hubbard, F. P., "Justice, Limits to Growth, and an Equilibrium State," *Philosophy & Public Affairs* 7 (4) (1978), pp. 326–45.

Hubin, C., "Justice and Future Generations," *Philosophy & Public Affairs* 6 (1976), pp. 70–83.

—— "Minimizing Maximin," *Philosophical Studies* 37 (1980), pp. 363–72.

Keat, R. and D. Miller, "Understanding Justice," *Political Theory* 2 (1974), pp. 3–31.

Klosko, G., "Political Obligation and the Natural Duties of Justice," *Philosophy & Public Affairs* 23 (3) (1994), pp. 251–70.

Kolm, S. C., "Equal Liberties and Maximin," *Modern Theories of Justice*, Cambridge, MA: MIT Press, 1998, pp. 169–208.

Kymlicka, W., "Rawls on Teleology and Deontology," *Philosophy & Public Affairs* 17 (1988), pp. 173–90.

—— "Liberal Equality," *Contemporary Political Philosophy: An Introduction*, New York: Oxford University Press, 1990, pp. 50–94.

Laden, A., "Games, Fairness, and Rawls's *A Theory of Justice*," *Philosophy & Public Affairs* 20 (3) (1991), pp. 189–222.

Lessnoff, M., "John Rawls's *Theory of Justice*," *Political Studies* 19 (1971), pp. 63–80.

Lyons, D., "Nature and Soundness of the Contract and Coherence Arguments," *Reading Rawls: Critical Studies on Rawls's* A Theory of Justice, ed. N. Daniels, New York: Basic Books, 1975.

—— "The Nature of the Contract Argument," *The Cornell Law Review* 59 (1973–4), pp. 1064–76.

MacCormick, N., "Justice According to Rawls," *The Law Quarterly Review* 89 (1973), pp. 393–417.

MacIntyre, A., "Justice: A New Theory and Some Old Questions," *Boston University Law Review* 52 (1972), pp. 330–4.

Mandle, J., *Rawls's* A Theory of Justice: *An Introduction*, Cambridge, UK: Cambridge University Press, 2009.

Nagel, T., "Rawls on Justice," *Philosophical Review* 87 (1973), pp. 220–34.

Nelson, W., "Special Rights, General Rights, and Social Justice," *Philosophy & Public Affairs* 3 (1974), pp. 411–30.

Nielson, K., "The Choice between Perfectionism and Rawlsian Contractarianism," *Interpretation* 6 (1977), pp. 132–9.

O'Neill, O., "The Method of *A Theory of Justice*," *John Rawls: Eine Theorie der Gerechtigkeit*, ed. Otfried Hoeffe, Berlin: Akademie Verlag, 1998.

Pettit, P., "A Theory of Justice?" *Theory and Decision* 4 (1974), pp. 311–24.

Pogge, T., *Realizing Rawls*, Ithaca: Cornell University Press, 1989.

Rae, D., "Maximin Justice and an Alternative Principle of General Advantage," *The American Political Science Review* 69 (1975), pp. 630–47.

Raphael, D. D., "Critical Notice: Rawls's *Theory of Justice*," *Mind* 83 (1974), pp. 118–27.

Ricoeur, P., "Is a Purely Procedural Theory of Justice Possible? John Rawls's *A Theory of Justice*," *International Social Science Journal* 42 (1990), pp. 553–64.

Sandel, M., *Liberalism and the Limits of Justice*, Cambridge, UK: Cambridge University Press, 1982; Italian trans., *Il liberalismo e I limiti della giustizia*, ed. Savino D'amico, Milan: Feltrinelli, 1994.

Scanlon, T. M., "Rawls's *Theory of Justice*," *University of Pennsylvania Law Review* 121 (1973), pp. 1029–69.

Schaefer, D. L., "A Critique of Rawls's Contract Doctrine," *The Review of Metaphysics* 28 (1974), pp. 89–115.

—— *Justice or Tyranny? A Critique of John Rawls's "A Theory of Justice*," Port Washington (NY): Kennikat Press, 1979.

Scharr, J., "Reflections on Rawls's *Theory of Justice*," *Social Theory and Practice* 3 (1) (1974), pp. 75–100.

—— "Equality of Opportunity and the Just Society," *John Rawls's Theory of Social Justice*, ed. H. G. Blocker and E. E. Smith, Athens: Ohio University Press, 1980, pp. 162–84.

Schwartz, A., "Moral Neutrality and Primary Goods," *Ethics* 83 (1973), pp. 294–307.

Sen, A., "Justice: Means versus Freedoms," *Philosophy & Public Affairs* 19 (1990), pp. 111–21.

Shue, H., "The Current Fashions: Trickle Downs by Arrow and Close-Knits by Rawls," *Journal of Philosophy* 71 (1974), pp. 319–27.

—— "Justice, Rationality, and Desire: On the Logical Structure of Justice as Fairness," *The Southern Journal of Philosophy* 13 (1975), pp. 89–97.

Singer, M., "Discussion Review: Justice, Theory, and a Theory of Justice," *Philosophy of Science* 44 (1977), pp. 594–618.

Sneed, J., "John Rawls and the Liberal Theory of Society," *Erkenntnis* 10 (1976), pp. 1–19.

Sterba, J., "Prescriptivism and Fairness," *Philosophical Studies* 29 (1976), pp. 1411–18.

—— "In Defense of Rawls against Arrow and Nozick," *Philosophia* 7 (1978), pp. 293–303.

Tattershall, G., "A Rawls Bibliography," *Social Theory and Practice* 3 (1974), pp. 123–7.

Teitelman, M., "The Limits of Individualism," *Journal of Philosophy* 69 (18) (October 5, 1972), pp. 545–56.

Urmson, J. O., "A Defense of Intuitionism," *Proceedings of the Aristotelian Society* 75 (1974–5), pp. 111–19.

Van Dyke, V., "Justice as Fairness: For Groups?" *The American Political Science Review* 69 (1975), pp. 607–14.

Williams, Bernard, "Rawls and Pascal's Wager," *Moral Luck*, Cambridge, UK: Cambridge University Press, 1981, pp. 94–100.

THE FIRST PRINCIPLE OF JUSTICE

Barry, B., "John Rawls and the Priority of Liberty," *Philosophy & Public Affairs* 2 (1973), pp. 274–90.

Bowie, N., "Equal Basic Liberty for All," *John Rawls's Theory of Social Justice*, ed. H. G. Blocker and E. H. Smith, Athens: Ohio University Press, 1980, pp. 110–31.

Daniels, N., "On Liberty and Inequality in Rawls," *Social Theory and Practice* 3 (1974), pp. 149–59.

—— "Equal Liberty and Unequal Worth of Liberty," *Reading Rawls: Critical Studies on Rawls's* A Theory of Justice, ed. N. Daniels, New York: Basic Books, 1975, pp. 253–81.

Hart, H. L. A., "Rawls on Liberty and Its Priority," *University of Chicago Law Review* 40 (1973), pp. 534–55.

Kymlicka, W., "Liberal Individualism and Liberal Neutrality," *Ethics* 99 (1989), pp. 883–905.

de Marneffe, P., "Liberalism, Liberty, and Neutrality," *Philosophy & Public Affairs* 19 (Summer 1990), pp. 253–74.

Parijs, P. van, "Liberté formelle et liberté réelle: la critique de Rawls par les liberteriens," *Revue Philosophique de Louvain* 86 (1988), pp. 59–86.

Pogge, T., "The Interpretation of Rawls's First Principle of Justice," *Philosophische Studien* 15 (1982), pp. 119–47.

—— "Gleiche Freiheit für alle?" *John Rawls: Eine Theorie der Gerechtigkeit*, ed. Otfried Hoeffe, Berlin: Akademie Verlag, 1998.

Raz, J., "Liberalism, Autonomy and the Politics of Neutral Concern," *Midwest Studies in Philosophy* 7 (1982), pp. 89–120.

Rodewall, R., "Does Liberalism Rest on a Mistake?" *Canadian Journal of Philosophy* 15 (1985), pp. 231–52.

Shue, H., "Liberty and Self-Respect," *Ethics* 85 (1975), pp. 195–203.

Taylor, R. S., "Rawls' Defense of the Priority of Liberty," *Philosophy & Public Affairs* (31) (3) 2003, pp. 246–71.

THE SECOND PRINCIPLE OF JUSTICE

Alexander, L., "Fair Equality of Opportunity: John Rawls's (Best) Forgotten Principle," *Philosophy Research Archives* 11 (1985), pp. 197–207.

Althan, J. E. J., "Rawls's Difference Principle," *Philosophy* 48 (1973), pp. 75–8.

Anderson, E., "What Is the Point of Equality?" *Ethics* 109 (January 1999), pp. 287–337.

Beauchamp, T., "Distributive Justice and the Difference Principle," *John Rawls's Theory of Social Justice*, ed. H. G. Blocker and E. H. Smith, Athens: Ohio University Press, 1980, pp. 132–61.

Buchanan, A., "Distributive Justice and Legitimate Expectations," *Philosophical Studies* 28 (1975), pp. 419–25.

Buchanan, J., "A Hobbesian Interpretation of the Rawlsian Difference Principle," *Kyklos* 29 (1976), pp. 5–25.

Cohen, G. A., "On the Currency of Egalitarian Justice," *Ethics* 99 (July 1989), pp. 906–44.

—— "Incentives, Inequality and Community," *The Tanner Lectures on Human Values,* Vol. XIII, ed. G. B. Peterson, Salt Lake City: University of Utah Press, 1992, pp. 261–329.

—— "Where the Action Is: On the Site of Distributive Justice," *Philosophy & Public Affairs* 26 (1997), pp. 3–30.

—— *Rescuing Justice and Equality*, Cambridge, MA: Harvard University Press, 2008.

Cohen, J., "Contractualism and Property Systems," *Nomos 31, Markets and Justice*, ed. J. W. Chapman and J. R. Pennock, New York: New York University Press, 1988, pp. 727–51.

—— "Democratic Equality," *Ethics* 99 (1989), pp. 727–51.

—— "Taking People as They Are," *Philosophy & Public Affairs* 30 (4) (2001).

Coleman, J. S., "Rawls, Nozick and the Educational Equality," *The Public Interest* 43 (1976), pp 121–8.

Copp, David, "Justice and the Difference Principle," *Canadian Journal of Philosophy* 4 (1974), pp. 229–40.

Daniels, N., "Equality of What?: Welfare, Resources, or Capabilities?" *Philosophy and Phenomenological Research* 50 (1990), Supplement: pp. 273–96.

Dworkin, R., *Freedom's Law*, Cambridge, MA: Harvard University Press, 1996.

—— *Sovereign Virtue*, Cambridge, MA: Harvard University Press, 2000.

—— "Equality, Luck and Hierarchy," *Philosophy & Public Affairs* 3 (2) (2003), pp. 190–8.

Estlund, D., "Liberalism, Equality and Fraternity in Cohen's Critique of Rawls," *Journal of Political Philosophy* 6 (March 1998), pp. 99–112.

Frohlich, N., J. A. Oppenheimer, and C. L. Eavey, "Choices of Principles of Distributive Justice in Experimental Groups," *American Journal of Political Science* 31 (3) (1987), pp. 606–36.

Gardner, M., "Rawls on the Maximin Rule and Distributive Justice," *Philosophical Studies* 27 (1975), pp. 255–70.

Goldman, A. H., "Rawls's Original Position and the Difference Principle," *Journal of Philosophy* 73 (1976), pp. 845–9.

Gordon, S., "John Rawls's Difference Principle, Utilitarianism, and the Optimum Degree of Inequality," *Journal of Philosophy* 70 (9) (1973), pp. 275–80.

Gray, J., "Contractarian Method, Private Property, and the Market Economy," *Nomos 31, Markets and Justice*, ed. J. W. Chapman and J. R. Pennock, New York: New York University Press, 1988.

Hammond, P. J., "Equity, Arrow's Condition, and Rawls's Difference Principle," *Econometrica* 44 (1976), pp. 793–804.

Kolm, S. C., "Equal Liberties and Maximin: Fairness from Ignorance," *Modern Theories of Justice*, Cambridge, MA: MIT Press, 1996, pp. 169–208.

Michelman, F., "In Pursuit of Constitutional Welfare Rights: One View of Rawls's Theory of Justice," *University of Pennsylvania Law Review* 121 (1973), pp. 962–1019.

Narveson, J. F., "A Puzzle about Economic Justice in Rawls' Theory," *Social Theory and Practice* 4 (1976), pp. 1–28.

Okin S. M., *Equality and Partiality*, Oxford: Oxford University Press, 1991.

Paden, R., "Reciprocity and Intergenerational Justice," *Public Affairs Quarterly* 10 (1996); rptd. in C. Audard et al., *Individu et justice sociale*, Paris: Seuil, 1988, pp. 249–66.

Parijs, P. van, "Rawls face aux libertariens," *Qu'est-ce qu'une société juste?* Paris: Le Seuil, 1991, pp. 193–218.

—— "Why Surfers Should Be Fed: The Liberal Case for an Unconditional Basic Income," *Philosophy & Public Affairs* 20 (1991), pp. 101–31.

—— "Rawlsians, Christians and Patriots. Maximin Justice and Individual Ethics," *European Journal of Philosophy* 1 (1993), pp. 309–42.

Scanlon, T. M., "Preference and Urgency," *Journal of Philosophy* 72 (19) (1975), pp. 655–69.

Scheffler, S., "What Is Egalitarianism?" *Philosophy & Public Affairs* 31 (1) (2002), pp. 5–39.

Smith, P., "Incentives and Justice: G. A. Cohen's Egalitarian Critique of Rawls," *Social Theory and Practice* 24 (1998), pp. 205–35.

Strasnick, S., "Social Choice Theory and the Derivation of Rawls's Difference Principle," *Journal of Philosophy* 73 (1976), pp. 85–99.

Waldron, J., "John Rawls and the Social Minimum," *Liberal Rights*, Cambridge, UK: Cambridge University Press, 1993.

Walzer, M., *Spheres of Justice: A Defence of Pluralism and Equality*, Oxford: Blackwell, 1983

Weithman, P., "Waldron on Political Legitimacy and the Social Minimum," *The Philosophical Quarterly* 45 (1995), pp. 218–24.

Williams, A., "The Revisionist Difference Principle," *Canadian Journal of Philosophy* 25 (June 1995), pp. 257–82.

—— "Incentives, Inequality, and Publicity," *Philosophy & Public Affairs* 27 (1998), pp. 225–47.

Wolff, J., "Fairness, Respect, and the Egalitarian Ethos," *Philosophy & Public Affairs* 27 (2) (1998), pp. 97–122.

Wolff, R. P., "On Strasnick's 'Derivation' of Rawls's Difference Principle," *Journal of Philosophy* 73 (1976), pp. 849–58.

THE ORIGINAL POSITION

Bagnoli, C., "Rawls on the Objectivity of Practical Reason," *Croatian Journal of Philosophy* 3 (2001), pp. 307–31.

Baynes, K., "Constructivism and Practical Reason in Rawls," *Analyse & Critique* 14 (1992), pp. 18–32

Eshete, A., "Contractarianism and the Scope of Justice," *Ethics* 85 (1974), pp. 38–49.

Freeman, S., "Reason and Agreement in Social Contract Views," *Philosophy & Public Affairs* 19 (2) (Spring 1990), pp. 122–57.

Gauthier, D., "The Social Contract as Ideology," *Philosophy & Public Affairs* 6 (1977), pp. 130–64.

Gray, J., "Social Contract, Community and Ideology," *Liberalisms*, London: Routledge, 1989.

Hampton, J., "Contracts and Choices: Does Rawls Have a Social Contract Theory?" *Journal of Philosophy* 77 (6) (1980), pp. 315–38.

Krasnoff, L., "How Kantian Is Constructivism?" *Kant-Studien* 90 (1999), pp. 385–409.

Lessnoff, M., "Justice, Social Contract, and Universal Prescription," *Philosophical Quarterly* 28 (1979), pp. 65–73.

Milo, R., "Contractarian Constructivism," *Journal of Philosophy* 122 (1995), pp. 181–204.

Nielsen, K. and R. Shiner (eds.), *New Essays in Contract Theory*, Canadian Journal of Philosophy, Supplementary Volume III, 1977.

Stark, C., "Hypothetical Consent and Justification," *Journal of Philosophy* 97 (6) (2000), pp. 313–34.

Reflective Equilibrium

Brandt, R. B., *A Theory of the Good and the Right*, Oxford: Oxford University Press, 1979.

Copp, D., "Considered Judgments and Justification: Conservatism in Moral Theory," *Morality, Reason and Truth*, ed. D. Copp and M. Zimmerman, Totowa, NJ: Rowman and Allanheld, 1985, pp. 141–69.

Daniels, N., "Wide Reflective Equilibrium and Theory Acceptance in Ethics," *Journal of Philosophy* 76 (1979), pp. 256–82.

—— "On Some Methods of Ethics and Linguistics," *Philosophical Studies* 37 (1980), pp. 21–36.

—— "Reflective Equilibrium and Archimedean Points," *Canadian Journal of Philosophy* 10 (1980), pp. 83–103.

—— "Reflective Equilibrium and Justice as Political," *Justice and Justification*, Cambridge, UK: Cambridge University Press, 1996, pp. 144–75; rev. edn. in V. Davion and C. Wolf (eds.), *The Idea of a Political Liberalism*, Lanham, MD: Rowman and Littlefield, 1999, pp. 127–54.

Delaney, C. F., "Rawls on Method," *New Essays in Contract Theory*, Canadian Journal of Philosophy, ed. K. Nielsen and R. Shiner, Supplementary Volume III, 1977, pp. 153–61.

DePaul M., "Reflective Equilibrium and Foundationalism," *American Philosophical Quarterly* 23 (1986), pp. 59–69.

O'Neill, O., "The Method of *A Theory of Justice*," in *John Rawls: Eine Theorie der Gerechtigkeit*, ed. O. Hoeffe, Berlin: Akademie Verlag, 1998.

O'Neill, R., "On Rawls's Justification Procedure," *Philosophy Research Archives* 2 (1099) (1976).
Raz, J., "The Claims of Reflective Equilibrium," *Inquiry* 25 (1982), pp. 307–30.
—— "Facing Diversity: The Case of Epistemic Abstinence," *Philosophy & Public Affairs* 19 (1990), pp. 3–46.
Sencerz, S., "Moral Intuitions and Justification in Ethics," *Philosophical Studies* 50 (1986), pp. 77–95.
Singer, P., "Sidgwick and Reflective Equilibrium," *The Monist* 58 (1974), pp. 490–517.

Main Criticisms of Rawls

Alejandro, R., "Rawls' Communitarianism," *Canadian Journal of Philosophy* 23 (1993), pp. 75–99; rptd. in H. S. Richardson and P. Weithman (eds.), *The Philosophy of Rawls: A Collection of Essays*, 5 vols., New York: Garland, 1999, pp. 295–320.
Baynes, K., *The Normative Grounds of Social Criticism*, Albany: SUNY Press, 1992.
—— "Liberal/Communitarian Controversy and Communicative Ethics," *Universalism vs Communitarianism*, ed. David Rasmussen, Cambridge, MA: MIT Press, 1990, pp. 39–60, 61–82.
Bellah, R., R. Madsen, W. M. Sullivan, A. Swidler, and S. Tipton, *Habits of the Heart*, Berkeley, CA: University of California Press, 1985.
Benhabib, S., *Critique, Norm and Utopia*. New York: Columbia University Press, 1986.
Brink, D., "Rawlsian Constructivism in Moral Theory," *Canadian Journal of Philosophy* 17 (1987), pp. 71–90
Buchanan, A., "Assessing the Communitarian Critique of Liberalism," *Ethics* 99 (4) (1989), pp. 852–82
Coleman, J. S., "Rawls, Nozick and the Educational Equality," *The Public Interest* (Spring 1976), pp. 121–8.
Cohen, G. A., "Facts and Principles," *Philosophy & Public Affairs* 31 (2003), pp. 211–45.
—— *Rescuing Justice and Equality*, Cambridge, MA: Harvard University Press, 2008.
Doppelt, G., "Is Rawls's Kantian Liberalism Coherent and Defensible?" *Ethics* 99 (4) (July 1989), pp. 815–51.
Forst, R., *Kontexte der Gerechtigkeit*. Frankfurt am Main: Suhrkamp, 1994.
Gutmann, A., "Communitarian Critics of Liberalism," *Philosophy & Public Affairs* 14 (3) (1985), pp. 308–22.
Habermas, J., *Justification and Application: Remarks on Discourse Ethics*, Cambridge, MA: MIT, 1993.
—— "Reconciliation through the Public Use of Reason: Remarks on John Rawls' Political Liberalism," *Journal of Philosophy* 92 (3) (March 1995), pp. 109–31.
—— *The Inclusion of the Other*, Cambridge, MA: MIT, 2000.
—— "Religion in the Public Sphere," *European Journal of Philosophy* 14 (2006), pp. 1–25.
Hodson, J. D., "Nozick, Libertarianism and Rights," *Arizona Law Review* 19 (1) (1978), pp. 212–27.
Larmore, C., "The Moral Basis of Political Liberalism," *Journal of Philosophy* 96 (12) (1999), pp. 599–625.

MacIntyre, A., *After Virtue: A Study in Moral Theory*. London, Duckworth, 1981.

McCarthy, T., "Kantian Constructivism and Reconstructivism: Rawls and Habermas in Dialogue," *Ethics* 105 (October 1994), pp. 44–63; rptd. in H. S. Richardson and P. Weithman (eds.), *The Philosophy of Rawls: A Collection of Essays*, vol. V: *Reasonable Pluralism*, New York: Garland, 1999, pp. 320–33.

Mulhall. S. and A. Swift, *Liberals & Communitarians*. Oxford: Blackwell, 1992.

Nagel. T., "Libertarianism without Foundations," *The Yale Law Journal* 85 (1), pp. 136–49; rptd. in J. Paul (ed.), *Reading Nozick: Essays on Anarchy, State and Utopia*, Oxford: Blackwell, 1981.

Nozick, R., *Anarchy, State and Utopia*, New York: Basic Books, 1974.

Okun, V., *Equality and Efficiency*, Washington: The Brookings Institution, 1975.

Rabinowitz, J. T., "Emergent Problems and Optional Solutions," *Arizona Law Review* 19 (1) (1978), pp. 62–157.

Rorty, R., "Postmodernist Bourgeois Liberalism," *Hermeneutics and Praxis*, ed. R. Hollinger, Indianapolis: Notre Dame University Press, 1985.

Sandel, M. (ed.), *Liberalism and its Critics*. New York: New York University Press, 1984.

—— "The Procedural Republic and the Unencumbered Self," *Political Theory* 12 (1984), pp. 81–96.

Scanlon, T., "Nozick on Rights, Liberty and Property," *Philosophy & Public Affairs* 6 (1) (Fall 1976); rptd. in J. Paul (ed.), *Reading Nozick: Essays on Anarchy, State and Utopia*, Oxford: Blackwell, 1981.

Schwarzenbach, S. A., "Rawls, Hegel and Communitarianism," *Political Theory* 19 (4) (1991), pp. 539–71.

Sheffler, S. "Moral Skepticism and Ideals of the Person," *Monist* 62 (1979): 288–303.

Taylor, C., *Hegel and Modern Society*, Cambridge, UK: Cambridge University Press, 1979.

Taylor, C., *Philosophical Papers*, Cambridge, UK: Cambridge University Press, 1985.

Unger, R. M., *Knowledge and Politics*, New York: Macmillan, 1984.

Varian, H. R., "Distributive Justice, Welfare Economics and the Theory of Fairness," *Philosophy & Public Affairs* 4 (3) (Spring 1975), pp. 223–47.

Walzer, M., *Spheres of Justice*, London: Blackwell, 1983.

—— "The Communitarian Critique of Liberalism," *Political Theory* 18 (February 1990), pp. 6–23.

Williams, B. A. O., *In Principle was the Deed: Realism and Moralism in Political Argument*, Princeton, NJ: Princeton University, 2005.

Introducing Political Liberalism

Ackerman, B., "Political Liberalisms," *Journal of Philosophy* 91 (7) (1994), pp. 364–86.

Arneson, R., "Introduction (Symposium on Rawlsian Theory of Justice: Recent Developments)," *Ethics* 99 (1989), pp. 695–710.

Barry, B., "In Defense of Political Liberalism," *Ratio Juris* 7 (1994), pp. 325–30.

—— "John Rawls and the Search for Stability," *Ethics* 105 (4) (July 1995), pp. 874–915.

Brighouse, Harry, "Civic Education and Liberal Legitimacy," *Ethics* 108 (1998), pp. 719–45.

—— "Is There Any Such Thing as Political Liberalism?" *Pacific Philosophical Quarterly* 75 (1994), pp. 318–32.

Charney, E., "Political Liberalism, Deliberative Democracy, and the Public Sphere," *American Political Science Review* 92 (1) (1998), pp. 97–110.

Cohen, J., "Moral Pluralism and Political Consensus," *The Idea of Democracy*, ed. D. Copp, J. Hampton, and J. Roemer, Cambridge, UK: Cambridge University Press, 1993.

—— "A More Democratic Liberalism," *Michigan Law Review* 92 (6) (1994), pp. 1503–46.

—— "Pluralism and Proceduralism," *Chicago-Kent Law Review* 69 (1994), pp. 589–618.

Daniels, N., "Reflective Equilibrium and Justice as Political," *Justice and Justification*, Cambridge, UK: Cambridge University Press, 1996, pp. 144–75.

Dworkin, G., "Contracting Justice," *Philosophical Books* 36 (1995), pp. 19–26.

Estlund, D., "The Survival of Egalitarian Justice in John Rawls's *Political Liberalism*," *Journal of Political Philosophy* 4 (1996), pp. 68–78.

—— "The Insularity of the Reasonable: Why Political Liberalism Must Admit the Truth," *Ethics* 108 (2) (1998), pp. 252–75.

Freeman, S., "Political Liberalism and the Possibility of a Just Democratic Constitution," *Chicago-Kent Law Review* 69 (1994), pp. 619–68.

Galston, M., "Rawlsian Dualism and the Autonomy of Political Thought," *Columbia Law Review* 94 (6) (1994), pp. 1842–59.

Galston, W., "Pluralism and Social Unity," *Ethics* 99 (1989), pp. 711–26.

Gaus, G. F., "Reasonable Pluralism and the Domain of the Political: How the Weaknesses of John Rawls's Political Liberalism Can be Overcome by a Justificatory Liberalism," *Inquiry* 42 (1999), pp. 259–84.

Griffen, S. M., "Political Philosophy versus Political Theory: The Case of Rawls," *Chicago-Kent Law Review* 69 (1994), pp. 691–708.

Habermas, J., "Reconciliation through the Public Use of Reason: Remarks on John Rawls's Political Liberalism," *Journal of Philosophy* 92 (1995), pp. 109–31.

Hampshire, S., "Liberalism: The New Twist," *New York Review of Books* (August 12, 1993), pp. 43–6.

Hampton, J., "Should Political Philosophy be Done without Metaphysics?" *Ethics* 99 (1989), pp. 791–814.

Hollenbach, D., "Contexts of the Political Role of Religion: Civil Society and Culture," *San Diego Law Review* 30 (1993), pp. 877–901.

Holmes, S., "John Rawls and The Limits of Tolerance," *The New Republic* 11 (October 1993), pp. 39–47.

Klosko, G., "Political Constructivism in Rawls's *Political Liberalism*," *American Political Science Review* 91 (3) (1997), pp. 635–46.

Larmore, C., "Political Liberalism," *Political Theory* 18 (3) (1990), pp. 339–60.

—— "Pluralism and Reasonable Disagreement," *The Morals of Modernity*, Cambridge, UK: Cambridge University Press, 1996.

Maffettone, S., "The Moral Basis of Political Liberalism," *Journal of Philosophy* 96 (1999), pp. 599–625.

—— "Political Liberalism: Reasonableness and Democratic Practice," *Philosophy and Social Criticism* 30 (5–6) (2004), pp. 541–77 .

—— Mandle, J., "The Reasonable in Justice as Fairness," *Canadian Journal of Philosophy* 29 (1999), pp. 75–107.

de Marneffe, P., "Liberalism and Perfectionism," *The American Journal of Jurisprudence* 43 (1998), pp. 99–116.

Martin, R., "Rawls's New Theory of Justice," *Chicago-Kent Law Review* 69 (1994), pp. 737–62.

Mendus, S., "Tragedy, Moral Conflict and Liberalism," *Philosophy and Pluralism* ed. D. Archard, Cambridge, UK: Cambridge University Press, 1996, pp. 191–201.

Michelman, F., "The Subject of Liberalism," *Stanford Law Review* 46 (6) (July 1994), pp. 1807–33.

Mouffe, C., "Political Liberalism: Neutrality and the Political," *Ratio Juris* 7 (1994), pp. 314–24.

Mulhall, S., "Promising, Consent, and Citizenship," *Political Theory* 25 (1997), pp. 171–92.

Murphy, L., "Institutions and the Demands of Justice," *Philosophy & Public Affairs* 27 (1998), pp. 151–91.

Okin, S. M., "Review of *Political Liberalism*," *American Political Science Review* 87 (1993), pp. 1010–11.

O'Neill, O., "Political Liberalism and Public Reason: A Critical Notice of John Rawls' Political Liberalism," *Philosophical Review* 106 (1998), pp. 411–28.

Nickel, J. W., "Rethinking Rawls's Theory of Liberty and Rights," *Chicago-Kent Law Review* 69 (1994), pp. 763–86.

Raz, J., "Disagreement in Politics," *The American Journal of Jurisprudence* 43 (1998), pp. 25–52.

Rorty, R., "The Priority of Democracy to Philosophy," *Objectivity, Relativism and Truth: Philosophical Papers 1*, Cambridge, UK: Cambridge University Press, 1991, pp. 175–96.

Salvatore, I., "Liberalism, Pluralism, Justice. An Unresolved Strain in the Thought of John Rawls," *Philosophy and Social Criticism.* 30 (5–6) (2004), pp. 623–41.

Sandel, M., "Review of *Political Liberalism*," *Harvard Law Review* 107 (1994), pp. 1765–94.

Scheffler, S., "The Appeal of Political Liberalism," *Ethics* 105 (1994), pp. 4–22.

Simmons, A. J., "Justification and Legitimacy," *Ethics* 109 (1999), pp. 739– 71.

Solum, L., "Introduction: Situating *Political Liberalism*," *Chicago-Kent Law Review* 69 (1994), pp. 549–88.

Waldron, J., "Disagreements about Justice," *Pacific Philosophical Quarterly* 75 (1994), pp. 372–87.

Weithman, P., "Liberalism and the Political Character of Political Philosophy," *Liberalism and Community Values*, ed. C. F. Delaney, Lanham, MD: Rowman and Littlefield, 1994, pp. 189–211.

Williams, B., "A Fair State," *London Review of Books*, May 13, 1993.

Wolin, S. S., "The Liberal/Democratic Divide: On Rawls's *Political Liberalism*," *Political Theory* 24 (1) (1996), pp. 97–119.

Young, I. M., "Rawls's *Political Liberalism*," *Journal of Political Philosophy* 3 (2) (1995), pp. 181–90.

OVERLAPPING CONSENSUS AND PUBLIC REASON

Brower, B., "The Limits of Public Reason," *Journal of Philosophy* 91 (1994), pp. 5–26.

Finnis, J., "Abortion, Natural Law, and Public Reason," *Natural Law and Public Reason*, ed. R. P. George and C. Wolfe, Washington, DC: Georgetown University Press, 2000, pp. 75–106.

George, R. P. and C. Wolfe, "Natural Law and Public Reason," *Natural Law and Public Reason*, ed. R. P. George and C. Wolfe, Washington, DC: Georgetown University Press, 2000, pp. 51–74.

Greenawalt, K., "On Public Reason," *Chicago-Kent Law Review* 69 (1994), pp. 669–89.

Kelly E. and L. McPherson, "On Tolerating the Unreasonable," *The Journal of Political Philosophy* 9 (2001), pp. 38–55.

Korsgaard, C. M., "The Reasons We Can Share," *Social Philosophy & Policy* 10 (1) (1993), pp. 24–51.

Kraus, J. S., "Political Liberalism and Truth," *Legal Theory* 5 (1999), pp. 45–73.

Macedo, S., "Liberal Civic Education and Religious Fundamentalism: The Case of God v. John Rawls," *Ethics* 105 (April 1995), pp. 468–96.

—— "In Defense of Liberal Public Reason: Are Slavery and Abortion Hard Cases?" *Natural Law and Public Reason*, ed. R. P. George and C. Wolfe, Washington, DC: Georgetown University Press, 2000, pp. 11–49.

Mandle, J., "Having It Both Ways; Justification and Application in *Justice as Fairness*," *Pacific Philosophical Quarterly* 75 (1994), pp. 295–317.

de Marneffe, P., "Rawls on Public Reason," *Pacific Philosophical Quarterly* 75 (1994), pp. 232–50.

Nielsen, K., "Our Considered Judgments," *Ratio* 19 (1977), pp. 39–46.

O'Neill, O., "The Public Use of Reason," *Constructions of Reason: Explorations of Kant's Practical Philosophy*, Cambridge, UK: Cambridge University Press, 1989.

Raz, J., "Disagreement in Politics," *American Journal of Jurisprudence* (1998), pp. 25–52.

Richards, D. A. J., "Public Reason and Abolitionist Dissent," *Chicago-Kent Law Review* 69 (1994), pp. 787–842.

Solum, L., "Inclusive Public Reason," *Pacific Philosophical Quarterly* 75 (1994), pp. 217–31.

Wall, S., "Public Justification and the Transparency Argument," *The Philosophical Quarterly* 46 (1996), pp. 501–7.

Weithman, P., "Citizenship and Public Reason," in *Natural Law and Public Reason*, ed. R. P. George and C. Wolfe, Washington, DC: Georgetown University Press, 2000, pp. 125–70.

Westmoreland, R., "The Truth about Public Reason," *Law and Philosophy* 18 (1999), pp. 271–96.

THE LAW OF PEOPLES

Amdur, R., "Rawls's Theory of Justice: Domestic and International Perspectives," *World Politics* 29 (3) (1977), pp. 438–61.

Beitz, Charles, "Justice and International Relations," *Philosophy & Public Affairs* 4 (4) (Summer 1975), pp. 360–89.

—— *Political Theory and International Relations*, Princeton, NJ: Princeton University Press, 1979, pp. 127–69.

—— "Rawls' *Law of the Peoples*," *Ethics* 110 (July 2000), pp. 669–96.

Brown, C., "The Construction of a Realistic Utopia: John Rawls and International Political Theory," *Review of International Studies* 28 (2003), pp. 5–21.

Buchanan, A., "Rawls's *Law of Peoples*: Rules for a Vanished Westphalian World," *Ethics* 110 (4) (July 2000), pp. 697–721.

—— "Justice, Legitimacy, and Human Rights," *The Idea of a Political Liberalism*, ed. V. Davion and C. Wolf, , Lanham, MD: Rowman and Littlefield, 2000, pp. 73–89.

—— "Political Legitimacy and The Morality of Political Power," *Ethics* 112 (2002), pp. 689–719.

Crisp, R., and D. Jamieson, "Egalitarianism and a Global Resources Tax: Pogge on Rawls," *Ways of War and Peace*, ed. V. Davion and M. Doyle, New York: Norton, 1997.

Follesdal, A., "The Standing of Illiberal States: Stability and Toleration in John Rawls' *Law of Peoples*," *Acta Analytica* (1997), pp. 149–60.

Julius, A. J., "Basic Structure and the Value of Equality," *Philosophy & Public Affairs* 31 (4) (2003), pp. 321–54 .

Moellendorf, D., "Constructing a Law of Peoples," *Pacific Philosophical Quarterly* 77 (2) (June 1996), pp. 132–54.

Okin, S. M., "The Problem of Global Justice," *Philosophy & Public Affairs* 33 (2005), pp. 113–47.

Pogge, T., "An Egalitarian Law of Peoples," *Philosophy & Public Affairs* 23 (3) (Summer 1994), pp. 195–224.

—— "Human Flourishing and Universal Justice," *Social Philosophy* 16 (1) (1999), pp. 333–61.

—— *World Poverty and Human Rights*, Cambridge, UK: Polity Press, 2002.

Russett, B., *Grasping the Democratic Peace*, Princeton, NJ: Princeton University Press, 1993.

Sangiovanni, A., "Global Justice, Reciprocity and the State," *Philosophy & Public Affairs* 35 (1) (2007), pp. 3–39.

Tan, K. C., "Liberal Toleration in Rawls's *Law of Peoples*," *Ethics* 108 (1998), pp. 276–95.

Wenar, L., "Contractualism and Global Economic Justice," *Metaphilosophy* 32 (1) (2001), pp. 79–95.

INDEX

382   *Index*

Harvard University 5–6, 7, 8, 15, 197, 294
health 74
    see also disabilities; natural primary goods
Hegel, G. W. F. 198
hermeneutical hypotheses 16–24
hierarchical decent peoples 301–4
Hiroshima 4, 294, 308
history of philosophy 5–6, 8, 15, 198
Hobbes, T. 34
Holocaust 3–4
human rights 294, 300, 302, 304–7, 316, 317
Hume, D. 34, 105
hypothetical contracts 112–13

"The Idea of Public Reason Revisited" (IPRR;
    Rawls) 7, 31, 32, 213, 218, 274, 276,
    287
ideal theory 40, 44, 45, 219–21
    The Law of Peoples 293, 296–9
impersonality 113–14, 125–6
incentives
    Cohen's criticism 95–6, 98–9
    difference principle 76, 81
inclusion strategy, public reason 286–8
"The Independence of Moral Theory" (IMT;
    Rawls) 146–7, 152, 207
index of social primary goods 73–4, 217
individual, the *see* person, conception of
individuals, principles for 45–6
    see also *The Law of Peoples*
inductive argument, reflective equilibrium
    142–5
inequalities *see* equality
institutions 10–11, 12, 16
    collective support for *see* overlapping
        consensus
    Habermas–Rawls Exchange 186
    international justice 295, 298, 309–10,
        316–17
    justification–legitimation complementarity
        21–4
    political conception of justice 230–1, 232
    Political Liberalism – A Theory of Justice
        relation 199, 214, 220–1, 253–5
    public reason 274–92
    stability 253–5
    theory of justice 25, 40–6
        anti-monism 94–9
        basic structure 27–33, 93–8
        definition 94
        four-stage sequence 41–2, 65–9, 186
        luck egalitarianism 85, 86–7
        origins of inequality 89, 92–3
        principles for individuals 45–6
        principles of justice 41–5, 65–9, 74, 85,
            86–7, 89, 94–9

social contract 33
social primary goods 74
utilitarianism 37
insufficient reason principle 122–3, 124,
    125–6
intergenerational justice 44–5
international justice 8, 293, 294–307
    distributive 309–18
interpersonality 113, 114, 125–6
interpretive hypothesis 16–19
intuitionism 35, 36, 39–40
    from *A Theory of Justice* to *Political
        Liberalism* 206–8
    institutionalization of the principles of
        justice 42–3
    justification 223
    original position 104–5, 107
    principles for individuals 45–6
    Rawls' Harvard courses 6
    reflective equilibrium 149–51

Japan 4, 294, 308
judicial-administrative stage, principles of
    justice 41, 42, 66
just savings principle 44–5, 71, 195, 309
justice
    as fairness 11, 26–7, 38–40, 218–19
        see also *Justice as Fairness: A
            Restatement*; *A Theory of Justice*
    political conception *see* political conception
        of justice
    sense of *see* sense of justice
Justice as Fairness: A Restatement (JFR;
    Rawls) 8, 15, 189
    feminist criticism 31, 32
    first principle of justice 53
    from *A Theory of Justice* to *Political
        Liberalism* 189, 191, 192, 195–201,
        202
    property-owning democracy 42
    second principle of justice 71
    social contract 34
justification 16
    global distributive justice 316–17
    Habermas–Rawls Exchange 183–4
    legitimation and 16, 21–4, 209, 219,
        222–8, 231, 248–9, 272–4
    overlapping consensus 183–4, 272–4
    pro tanto 223–4, 225, 289–90
    public 11–12, 223, 224–5, 288–90,
        291
    public reason 275, 276–7, 285, 288–90,
        291–2
    Rawls' strategies 139, 140–2, 149, 209
        see also original position; reflective
            equilibrium; stability theory